Enterprise Resource Planning for Global Economies:
Managerial Issues and Challenges

Carlos Ferran
The Pennsylvania State University, USA

Ricardo Salim
*Universidad Autónoma de Barcelona, Spain
and Cautus Networks Corp., Venezuela*

INFORMATION SCIENCE REFERENCE

Hershey · New York

Acquisitions Editor:	Kristin Klinger
Development Editor:	Kristin Roth
Senior Managing Editor:	Jennifer Neidig
Managing Editor:	Jamie Snavely
Assistant Managing Editor:	Carole Coulson
Copy Editor:	Maria Boyer
Typesetter:	Jeff Ash
Cover Design:	Lisa Tosheff
Printed at:	Yurchak Printing Inc.

Published in the United States of America by
     Information Science Reference (an imprint of IGI Global)
     701 E. Chocolate Avenue, Suite 200
     Hershey PA 17033
     Tel: 717-533-8845
     Fax: 717-533-8661
     E-mail: cust@igi-global.com
     Web site: http://www.igi-global.com

and in the United Kingdom by
     Information Science Reference (an imprint of IGI Global)
     3 Henrietta Street
     Covent Garden
     London WC2E 8LU
     Tel: 44 20 7240 0856
     Fax: 44 20 7379 0609
     Web site: http:///www.eurospanbookstore.com

Library of Congress Cataloging-in-Publication Data

Enterprise resource planning for global economics : managerial issues and challanges / Carlos Ferran and Ricardo Salim Kuossa, editors.

     p. cm.

   Summary: "This book provides authoritative research on the theoretical frameworks and pragmatic discussions on global implementations of information systems, particularly ERP systems. This book offers professionals, managers, and researchers who want to improve their understanding of the issues and challenges that arise when information systems cross national boundaries with an authoritative, essential research resource"--Provided by publisher.

   Includes bibliographical references and index.

   ISBN-13: 978-1-59904-531-3 (hbk.)

   ISBN-13: 978-1-59904-533-7 (e-book)

   1. Management information systems. 2. Database management. 3. Information technology--Management. I. Ferran, Carlos. II. Kuossa, Ricardo Salim.

   HD30.213.E59 2008

   658.4'038--dc22

                              2007038033

British Cataloguing in Publication Data
A Cataloguing in Publication record for this book is available from the British Library.

Table of Contents

Section III
Organizational Aspects

Section IV
Cultural Aspects

Detailed Table of Contents

Section I
Rise and Globalization of ERPs

The chapter narrates the history of the accounting needs of individuals and organizations and explains their successive technological solutions, up to today's ERPs. The ledger, double-entry accounting, cost accounting, departmental accounting, material requisitions systems for production, human resources systems, and finally the enterprise-wide resource planning or management systems are analyzed in terms of how IT has—and has not—been able to "computerize" and integrate them. The main functionalities of ERPs are explained: the enterprise resource functionality and the planning functionality, as well as to what extent organizations need these functionalities and should pay its high prices. The expectations that have not yet been sufficiently satisfied by current systems, such as the ERP for SMEs, the transfer of "best practices," the interconnection of supply chains via ERP, and the ERP for global organizations, are discussed.

Chapter II

Companies around the world are placing increasing emphasis on strategy development and implementation. Some argue that this increased emphasis is in response to market forces of increased competition and globalization, and the need to be flexible and adaptive to the business environment. Strategy development and implementation is a multifaceted task reliant on a number of interdependent factors. One of these is the role of information technology which in recent times has become an integral part of most companies' strategies. This chapter discusses the role of strategy development and the importance of the alignment of business and IT strategies in a global environment. It discusses the role of enterprise resource planning systems on strategy development and how these systems underpin many strategic objectives companies strive for in a global environment.

Section II
Investment Aspects

The chapter develops generic strategies for the specification and implementation of an enterprise resource planning (ERP) system in a multinational company. After the presentation of a framework for categorizing companies by their global business orientation, ERP strategies corresponding to each category are derived. Subsequently, various implementation strategies are developed for each type of ERP strategy; they provide decision makers with a high degree of freedom in specifying an implementation strategy in accordance with a company's strategic goals. The results are summarized in a phase model; the overall approach is illustrated by two polar cases.

Chapter IV

Open source software is becoming more prevalent in businesses today, and while still a relatively immature offering, open source enterprise resource planning (OS-ERP) systems are becoming more common. However, whether or not an OS-ERP package is the right software for a given organization is a little researched question. Building on the current real options thinking about platform acquisitions, this chapter proposes the five most critical factors to consider when evaluating an OS-ERP package. To adequately do this, a great deal of detail about the current offerings in OS-ERP software is presented, followed by a review of the real options theory thinking behind using these factors to evaluate OS-ERP options. The international implications of OS-ERP are presented in the "Future Trends" section.

Enterprise resource planning (ERP) systems are becoming popular in medium and large-scale organizations all over the world. As companies have to collaborate across borders, languages, cultures, and integrate business processes, ERPs will need to take globalization into account, be based on a global architecture, and support the features required to bring all the worldwide players and processes together. Due to the high cost of implementation for these systems, organizations all over the world are interested in evaluating their benefits in the short and long terms. This chapter discusses various kinds of business benefits in a comprehensive way in order to justify the acquisition and implementation of ERP systems in organizations in the present global context.

The role of a global ERP champion is to guide a business through process transformation and ERP system implementation. A "change curve" model that depicts the "Valley of Despair" illustrates what a champion can expect and do to initiate new business processes, to address resistance to change, and to promote the advantages of a globally integrated system. The model, which anticipates a drop in business performance during the transition period, encourages change leaders to minimize time spent in the valley, to minimize the depth of the valley, and to maximize the slope of the value realization path out of the valley. A new perspective, drawn from experience, redefines a successful global ERP implementation in terms of a seamless transition to a new, integrated, efficient global system.

This chapter suggests that reengineering is an analysis of existing processes you wish to change to achieve dramatic improvements in critical, contemporary measures of performance, such as cost, quality, service, and speed. There are two distinct methods of reengineering, technology-enabled and clean-slate, with most global companies choosing somewhere in between. There are also a number of principles any reengineering project team should understand before embarking on a reengineering effort, and these are discussed from a global perspective. The chapter concludes with how to select processes to reengineer, lessons learned from global reengineering, benefits of global reengineering, and future implications.

This chapter studies the deployment of the SAP B2B (business-to-business) procurement application in Ericsson between 1999 and 2003, and argues that it enabled complex organizational change in a three-phase process: the implementation of said application in Spain; the evolution of the application into a regional B2B procurement platform; and its final transformation into a global, pan-European B2B procurement unit. As described in the chapter, the enterprise system allowed the company to flexibly support the majority of changes that took place during a period of explosive growth of mobile phone sales followed by an unexpected market downturn. In light of the above, this investigation studies how and why enterprise systems are able to support fast-paced changes on a global scale. In other words, this chapter presents enterprise systems as flexible and responsive infrastructures that enable organizational change.

Chapter IX

In this chapter we look at the factors that influence the successful implementation of a global enterprise resource planning (ERP) system. We identify 12 issues that need to be considered when implementing such systems. Each one of these issues is expanded upon with relevant literature and examples. In this chapter we also look at factors that lead to the development of information systems by employees in addition to or outside the implemented ERP. We introduce the concept of feral systems to explain this phenomenon. Other factors such as employee mistrust of the system are also discussed. Finally we look at future directions with respect to ERP implementations.

Section IV
Cultural Aspects

Chapter X

The chapter considers the complexities of cultural differences for global enterprise resource planning (ERP) implementation. An extensive review of the literature related to societal and organizational culture is followed by a delineation of the stages of ERP implementation and the actors involved in each stage, reflecting the basic assumption that global ERP systems are not universally acceptable or effective, and that testing the cross-cultural generalizability of ERP systems in organizations will produce a managerial agenda that facilitates the implementation process. The recognition and discussion of these differences can provide a stimulus for identifying and modifying the limitations of technological implementation and use policies to improve the benefits generated by the technology. Topics of explicit concern to ERP implementation in global organizational economies related to organizational and societal culture are discussed, and suggestions for managerial mechanisms for overcoming major obstacles in this process are proposed.

This research has investigated the implementation of ERP as mediation process—that is, as an interactive process developed between the organization's members and external consultants. The adoption of a mediation lens helps identify how global and local skills have been combined in ERP projects, and how these different arrangements have affected the project results. Underlying our analysis were two main questions: (1) How do patterns of mediation emerge, and what kinds of elements influence their emergence? and (2) What kind of association can be established between patterns of mediation and project results? Our conclusions point towards certain drivers. The local firm's position regarding the head office and the meaning attached to each project have directly influenced the way external consultants are perceived by the local firm's members, and these perceptions influence team members' and consultants' roles. Team members' and consultants' roles, in turn, contribute to reinforcement or transformation of established mediation patterns.

Section V
Auditing Aspects

The effort to comply with the Sarbanes-Oxley Act (SOX) has focused management attention in companies all over the world on the importance of assessing, developing, and maintaining an effective and efficient internal control system. Enterprise resource planning (ERP) systems are a crucial factor in developing such a system. Despite the attention this has attracted in practice, little academic research has focused on this area. This chapter addresses the question: How are ERP systems implicated in Sarbanes-Oxley compliance? It aims to show how SOX requirements regarding assessment and improvement of internal controls are related to the functionalities of an ERP system both in local and global implementations. It examines a solution (mySAP ERP) offered by one specific vendor (SAP) and what functionalities are relevant to global SOX compliance. Based on this, the chapter discusses likely developments regarding compliance functionalities in future releases of ERP systems.

This chapter examines the effectiveness of ERP systems in implementing internal controls in global organizations, particularly controls required by the Sarbanes-Oxley Act (U.S. Congress, 2002), or SOX. It aims to understand the extent to which ERP systems are able to meet these requirements and challenges organizations face in enhancing their ERP systems for this purpose. The chapter reports the results of interviews with ERP systems managers and directors in four organizations with significant global operations. It reveals a substantial degree of completion of SOX requirements by these organizations, often facilitated by consultants, and often accomplished as part of broader systems, processes, and strategic management improvement initiatives. It also highlights some significant technical and cultural implementation challenges, such as systems inflexibility and diversity, systems security weaknesses, and resistance to change, as well as some benefits upon completion, such as improved process efficiency and systems security, and potential intangible long-term benefits.

Section VI
Success Evaluation Aspects

Chapter XIV

In this chapter we present the factors for the success of ERP implementation projects. In the first section, we present the outcome of three surveys on the process and success factors for ERP projects. The first survey was undertaken in 2003 in Germany, the second in 2004 in the United States, and the third in 2006 in Turkey. The results are discussed in light of Hofstede's model of cultural factors. In the second section we evaluate common ERP lifecycle models. In spite of the great variety of potential advantages, it is also necessary to illuminate the real effects of standard ERP software in practice. Recent studies have revealed that 81% of German companies interviewed using SAP do not fully exploit the software's ability to optimize business processes, though 61% stated that SAP offers very good process optimization opportunities (Ploenzke, 2000). Therefore we evaluated popular lifecycle models with respect to their suitability to implement standard software in a process-driven way (Kuehl & Knoell, 2002). In the third section we present a semi-process-oriented approach lifecycle model for the implementation and release changeover of ERP systems. This lifecycle model was developed from the authors' experience in practice, and its practical relevance was evaluated in real-world projects. This approach is also assessed in light of the criteria presented in the second section.

Deanna House, University of Nebraska at Omaha, USA
Gert-Jan de Vreede, University of Nebraska at Omaha, USA
Peter Wolcott, University of Nebraska at Omaha, USA
Kenneth Dick, University of Nebraska at Omaha, USA

This research observes a global implementation of enterprise resource planning (ERP)/human resources management system (HRMS) software at an international company. The software was implemented in 16 countries. Variables such as cultural differences, communication-distance, management support, trust, and resistance to change were evaluated in the literature review. These variables have an impact on implementation success during global HRMS implementation. Further analyses on specific success factors faced with global implementations were evaluated using semi-structured interviews. The authors prepared a questionnaire to further explore the data. Respondents rated questions related to management support the highest overall. An interesting find was that the semi-structured interview results indicated that the software chosen was not a perfect fit for the global community. The mean for questions related to global HRMS success was higher for respondents located in the United States than those located in other locations.

Section VII
Trends

This chapter highlights the key trends in the ERP market, with a focus on the challenges related to the implementation of these systems in the Middle Eastern Gulf region. The key trends discussed here include consolidation of the ERP market, diversification of the ERP product, new modes for ERP application delivery, ERP and new technologies, changing ERP pricing structures, ERP support operations, growing demands for ERP vertical solutions, demanding ERP customers, inter-organizational ERP solutions, and regional adaptations for ERP products. The chapter further provides insight into emerging and future trends in the region. Awareness of these issues plus knowledge of the local environment gives us a richer understanding of key ERP issues and how they apply within the unique limitations and opportunities of this region.

Chapter XVII

Enterprise resource planning (ERP) systems integrate into one single system the control and accounting of all the enterprise resources. Just like the previous systems (material requirements planning and accounting information systems among others) became ERPs, it is highly probable that ERPs will keep evolving towards a different and more comprehensive system. Logically, this evolution will be driven by the unsatisfied expectations of the current markets. One of these expectations is to lower the emphasis on the mid- and long-term planning functionality in favor of some kind of short-term, more dynamic planning functionality. In this sense, the chapter glimpses at a system that could be called ERM, where the "M" stands for management instead of the "P" for planning. The chapter also discusses the potential effects of the Open Source Initiative on ERPs. Other outstanding expectations examined are: (1) lower cost and duration of the implementation process, (2) less dependency on external consultants for the implementation, and (3) improved and standardized interaction functionality—or middleware—between different ERPs.

Preface

Enterprise resource planning systems (ERP) are currently one of the most, if not the most complex information systems for businesses. Consequently, they are also the most expensive piece of the organizational IT/IS puzzle. Their complexity derives from the myriad of requirements that they must satisfy at the same time. And the number of requirements increases considerably when the systems have a global coverage. The costs of these systems are the licensing fees (which are not always high and in some cases are even null) plus all the implementation costs (which go from training to changing standard operating procedures). The chapters in this book look into the costs and benefits (not only from a financial point of view) derived from successfully implementing a global ERP. Each chapter looks at a different and very relevant aspect of the ERP adoption and implementation process.

In today's global village, adequate information systems are a business requirement. They are very clearly needed by large organizations that manufacture, process, distribute, and deliver items worldwide. But they are also critical for small and medium-sized companies that are inevitably part of a larger global supply chain. Both transaction and internal costs are reduced by the use of effective information systems. But individual information systems that only satisfy the needs of a given department or function easily become islands that impede the necessary flow of information. Nonetheless, each of these individual systems have by themselves a very extensive set of demands that becomes quite complex when we try to integrate them together into a single system that satisfies not only the needs of the individual departments but of the entire organization or the entire supply chain. Never before had we developed such complex and large systems. Even the most critical systems developed to fly a rocket ship or to simulate the behavior of a nuclear reactor are much smaller and do not have as many interrelated parts; therefore they have less complexity than today's global ERPs.

Furthermore, implementing these systems is not only a technical matter. Even if we had a perfect, bug-less piece of software, the implementation of an ERP requires extensive training and organizational change to be successful. Each organization is different and it has its own peculiarities that will affect not only the process but the final outcome. A successful ERP is more than a machine running a piece of software; it is the sum of the technology, its people, and the organizational procedures.

ERPs have been around for more than a decade. They not only have already developed their history but have also inherited the history of the systems that came before them. The first chapter of this book "From Ledgers to Global ERP" recalls this history and with it, it describes not only its evolution but also the functionality included in them. It describes how ERPs have integrated the functionality of its predecessors, like material requirement planning (MRP) and accounting information systems (AISs), and also added novel functionality that satisfies new organizational needs like supply chain management (SCM) and customer relationship management (CRM). And these new needs keep on growing, particularly when we consider that many organizations have a global scope. The chapter titled "Enterprise Resource Planning Systems in a Global Environment" adopts a case study research approach to discuss how a company used an ERP system to support its global transformation, the issues associated with corporate strategy, and how information systems can underpin the achievement of corporate goals. The decision to implement a global ERP is part of a strategy, and the ERP itself becomes part of the organizational structure. In the chapter titled "A Conceptual Framework for Developing and Evaluating ERP Implementation Strategies in Multinational Organizations," the authors show that while an extensive literature exists in regard to the management of multinational organizations, the aspect of ERP implementations in such a multinational context has not yet been sufficiently addressed, and thus a framework for multi-site ERP implementations contingent on the general business strategy of a company is developed.

Contrary to what is generally said, the elimination of licensing costs through an open source license does not reduce substantially the total cost of successfully implementing an ERP. The savings in licensing generally come at the expense of higher implementation costs. The chapter titled "Enterprise Resource Planning Under Open Source Software" provides a review of real options theory literature in examining factors that go into determining whether an open source enterprise resource planning (OS-ERP) package is a valuable option for a corporation. The high consulting and service costs associated with an ERP, particularly those with a global scope, are partly due to the complexity in the software, but are also due to the large variety of aspects that are involved in accomplishing a successful implementation. In "Achieving Business Benefits from ERP Systems," the author shows how organizations around the world are very interested in evaluating the short- and long-term benefits of investing in the implementation of these increasingly expensive systems.

Organizational resistance to adopt new technologies, procedures, and systems is ever present in the implementation of ERPs. To cope with this resistance, there is a discipline called "change management" that is now included in the curriculum of most MBA programs. The chapter titled "The Secret Success of a Global ERP Champion: Everything Changed and Nothing Happened" explains the role of a global ERP champion in guiding a business through process transformation and ERP system implementation. This chapter also has a very interesting and surprising discussion on what can be expected when we pass the switch in a new implementation.

Process reengineering is a discipline that helps determine and plan the changes needed in an organization. Some consultants recommend the obliteration of all existing processes and the development of completely new ones; others are more conservative and suggest making small but successive changes. As mentioned earlier, change is always difficult; and the more dramatic the change, the more difficult it is, particularly when there is nothing on which to mold the new organization. Therefore many organizations rely on the implementation of an ERP to succeed in their reengineering process. The chapter titled "Business Process Reengineering and ERP: Weapons for the Global Organization" provides a current perspective on business process reengineering as it relates to ERP, while critically discussing past research in the field.

ERPs are frequently presented as very rigid systems that have little or no flexibility at all. Many times it is argued that it is the organization, not the ERP, that needs to change for the implementation to be successful. The chapter titled "Enterprise Systems as an Enabler of Fast-Paced Change: The Case of Global B2B Procurement in Ericsson" questions this assertion by using a case study. The chapter shows that ERPs can also be flexible tools in terms of being able to reconfigure and adapt themselves correctly to organizational changes. A de facto answer to the alleged rigidity of ERP has been the development of information systems by employees in addition to or outside the implemented ERP. To explain this phenomenon, the concept of "feral systems" is introduced in "Feral Systems and Other Factors Influencing the Success of Global ERP Implementations."

Cultural aspects among global ERP users have become a major issue in the successful implementation of these systems. The chapter titled "Experiences of Cultures in Global ERP Implementation" considers the complexities of cultural differences for global enterprise resource planning implementation, and the chapter titled "The Implementation of ERP Packages as a Mediation Process: The Case of Five Brazilian Projects" investigates the implementation of ERP as a mediation process—that is, an interactive process developed between the organization's members and external consultants. However, the set of cultural differences between ERP users are just one of many challenges faced by managers of multinational or global projects.

Two chapters discuss the changes needed to adapt ERPs to the new regional and international audit standards (i.e., the well-known Sarbanes-Oxley Act (SOX) in the United States) that have risen since the fraudulent demise of several well-known enterprises a few years ago. The chapter titled "Sarbanes-Oxley Compliance, Internal Control, and ERP Systems: The Case of mySAP ERP" tackles some of the managerial issues inherent in addressing SOX compliance in ERP systems. "ERP Systems Effectiveness in Implementing Internal Controls in Global Organizations" reports the results of interviews with ERP systems managers and directors in four organizations with significant global operations regarding the implementation of new internal controls through the use of ERP.

We are still far from understanding what makes a global implementation successful. There are many factors involved and too few studies that allow a better understanding of these factors. The chapter titled "Implementing ERP Systems in Multinational Projects: Implications for Cultural Aspects and the Implementation Process" presents—with a detailed analysis of the validity—three surveys performed in Germany, the United States, and Turkey on the success factors of ERP implementation projects. It also includes an evaluation of common lifecycle models for implementing ERP software systems and a new lifecycle model based on the author's findings. The new and until-not-long-ago unsuspected dimensions of global ERP implementation projects have forced managers to rethink how to measure success and which are the factors that cause it. After showing that there are few field studies on global enterprise resource planning implementations, the chapter titled "Success Factors for the Global Implementation of ERP/HRMS Software" presents a field study for a global implementation of enterprise resource planning software. It focuses on the experience of one company in a global implementation, with particular focus on cultural differences, management support, resistance to change, trust, and communication-distance. It finds, among other results, that while the software implementation overall was considered successful, the non-U.S.-based locations perceived that their existing processes did not improve with the ERP implementation.

Cultural differences tend to show their strongest expression in the laws and regulations of each market. The chapter titled "ERP Trends, Opportunities, and Challenges: A Focus on the Gulf Region in the Middle East" highlights the key trends in the ERP market, with a special focus on the challenges related to the implementation of these systems in the Middle Eastern Gulf region. It identifies key opportunities, challenges, and issues pertaining to ERP implementation in the region.

ERPs have gone further than their predecessors (material resource planning systems and accounting information systems, among others) and integrate into a single system the control and balance of almost all the organizational resources. This was one of the main challenges that ERPs were meant to solve from their beginnings. However, ERPs are still far from being accessible by many companies worldwide, particularly small and medium-sized companies. For these companies, the cost of an ERP—particularly the implementation cost—is too high, their implementation times too long, and their dependency on outside consultants too difficult to manage. In addition, the planning capability, inherent to ERPs and critical for large enterprises—which are still the main market for ERPs—is of very little use to them and in fact is in many cases an obstacle. Furthermore, current ERPs lack standards for interaction and exchange of information, making most systems incompatible. When the entire supply chain uses the same ERP, the interaction is viable, but when each company uses a different ERP then each company is isolated from the rest. However, while large organizations may purchase or develop middleware that facilitates this communication, SMEs cannot afford them and become islands inside this critical river of information. The chapter titled "The Future of ERP and Enterprise Resource Management Systems" discusses these challenges and foresees some avenues to confront them by proposing enterprise resource management (ERM) systems as a potential solution. This last chapter also raises questions on the future of the ERP market and on the role that Microsoft (today's 800-pound gorilla) could play in it.

The set of chapters that constitute this book provides an important and critical overview of the complex world of global ERPs. The reader will be able to truly understand what is meant by a global ERP, how to value it, what benefits can and cannot be expected from them, how long it takes to implement them, and what many of the risks involved are. The reader will also learn about the main internal and external factors that negatively and positively affect their implementation, which are the previous relevant experiences and how can they be managed. Finally, the reader will have acquired an idea of what can be expected of these systems and this industry in the near future.

Each chapter included in this book has been rigorously selected and improved through at least two rounds of a double-blind peer review process. Part of the selection criteria used was the extent to which the global aspect was discussed, its novelty, and its usefulness to both practitioners and academics. The arguments presented are supported by prior literature, analytical reasoning, and data (whenever applicable). Each chapter also offers a selection of additional readings that allows the reader to delve further into each topic.

The book is divided into seven parts that classify the chapters into different aspects that are relevant to global ERPs. The following sections present the academic and managerial relevance statements developed by the individual authors for each chapter.

SECTION I: RISE AND GLOBALIZATION OF ERPS

Chapter I. From Ledgers to ERP

Academic Relevance Statement

The history of the accounting needs and their successive technological solutions—which today is the ERP system—are examined using as many references to the relevant literature as possible. The ledger, double-entry accounting, cost accounting, departmental accounting, material requisitions systems for production, human resources systems, and finally the enterprise-wide resource planning or management systems are analyzed in terms of how IT has—and has not—been able to "computerize" and integrate them effectively, particularly throughout the last two decades. The main functionalities of ERPs are studied: the enterprise resource functionality and the planning functionality. Then, the expectations that have not yet been satisfactorily fulfilled by current systems are also analyzed: the ERP for the global organizations and the ERP for SMEs. The high implementation costs, the problem of interconnecting the ERPs, and the problems or transferring the "best practices" are discussed from a conceptual point of view.

Management Relevance Statement

After reading this chapter the manager will know—well beyond commercially biased arguments—what ERPs are and what organizations can expect from the current systems. Is ERP just a fashionable accounting system? Is it more than a MRP II system? The chapter shows how ERPs integrate these and other business-oriented systems. It also explains in detail the resource and the planning functionalities of an ERP, and discusses the extent to which organizations really need these functionalities and the "best practices" incorporated in them. It analyzes the current cost factors of an ERP and their tight relation with the intrinsic complexity and therefore intrinsic cost of developing an implementing and ERP. What is a global ERP? Are they meant for global organizations or for every organization of the globe? This theme is discussed from different points of view, assessing that even if global ERPs were meant for global organizations, they will need to interact with other, eventually local ERPs, which implies the globalization of at least the interaction subsystems.

Chapter II. Enterprise Resource Planning Systems in a Global Environment

Academic Relevance Statement

Extensive research has been documented in regards to the implementation and use of ERP systems. However, much of this research focuses on a single implementation in one country. The research that has been carried out on global implementations has been limited. This chapter adopts a case study research approach to discuss how a company used an ERP system to support its global transformation. The case study provides a foundation for researchers to further investigate global implementations and the role ERP systems play.

Management Relevance Statement

ERP systems are an essential information technological infrastructure for many of the world's leading companies. They are now considered a mechanism to assist with corporate transformation, especially for companies operating in a global environment. This chapter discusses the issues associated with corporate strategy and how information systems can underpin the achievement of corporate goals. It discusses how one company used an ERP system to assist in its transformation of its global operations.

Chapter III. A Conceptual Framework for Developing and Evaluating ERP Implementation Strategies in Multinational Organizations

Academic Relevance Statement

This chapter adds an important perspective on the implementation process of ERP systems in a multinational context to the literature. While an extensive literature exists with regard to management in multinational organizations, the aspect of ERP implementations in a multinational context has not yet been sufficiently addressed. The critical success factor literature rarely deals with the existence of a global ERP and implementation strategy, and its influence on the implementation process. In order to address this shortcoming, the chapter develops the concept of a global ERP strategy and derives generic implementation approaches.

Management Relevance Statement

In this chapter the authors develop a framework for multi-site ERP implementations contingent on the general business strategy of a company. The critical success factor literature demonstrates that the reasons for failures and delays in implementation processes often lie in a disregard for the strategy component and the alignment between business and information technology. This chapter will help to develop an ERP implementation strategy and to identify the appropriate implementation approach for multi-site ERP implementation projects based on the company's overall business strategy.

SECTION II: INVESTMENT ASPECTS

Chapter IV. Enterprise Resource Planning Under Open Source Software

Academic Relevance Statement

This chapter provides a review of real options theory literature in examining factors that go into determining whether an open source enterprise resource planning package is a valuable option for a corporation. Building upon current real options valuation criteria, three new criteria are discussed as particularly relevant in the OS-ERP context: customization, quality of the source code, and business model of the open source software vendor. These factors—in addition to current factors relevant to platform decisions, like susceptibility to network externalities and prospects for network dominance—provide a solid basis for valuing OS-ERP options. Academics interested in real options theory, valuing IT platforms, ERP systems, and open source applications will find this chapter useful.

Management Relevance Statement

This chapter starts with an overview of open source technologies and quickly builds to provide an assessment of the current enterprise resource planning offerings available as open source software. Then, it provides criteria for managers or executives to use to determine whether an open source ERP package is right for their organization. These criteria will prove valuable to managers assessing any open source application, and in particular OS-ERP applications. Although OS-ERP offerings are relatively immature as compared to other ERP offerings, there is a definite global focus, as is discussed in this chapter. The chapter will prove useful as a primer in OS-ERP applications and useful to key stakeholders familiar with these applications looking to make the right decision for their organization.

Chapter V. Achieving Business Benefits from ERP Systems

Academic Relevance Statement

This chapter discusses the tangible and intangible benefits of enterprise systems implementation in organizations globally. The chapter will motivate students and academics to assess the benefits in different organizations all over the world and compare the results. It will also be interesting to know why organizations should adopt enterprise systems globally to accomplish maximum benefits in terms of efficient operations and productivity. With the growing proliferation of ERP systems, including midsize companies, it becomes critical to address why and under what circumstances one can realize the benefits of an ERP system. ERP systems can provide the organization with competitive advantage through improved business performance by, among other things, integrating supply-chain management, receiving, inventory management, customer orders management, production planning and managing, shipping, accounting, human resource management, and all other activities that take place in a modern business.

Management Relevance Statement

This chapter discusses the benefits that organizations may accomplish from their investment in implementing enterprise systems. ERP system investments are strategic in nature, with the key goal often being to help a company grow in sales, reduce production lead time, and improve customer service benefits (tangible and intangible). It is important for managers to understand business benefits comprehensively in order to justify the acquisition and implementation of ERP systems in organizations globally. In the present context of globalization, mergers, and acquisitions, it is more significant to know this so that it can be applied in an optimized way to get the return from enterprise system implementation. These benefits have reportedly been acquired through enterprise implementation. This may also be helpful in constructing enterprise system roadmaps in organizations.

SECTION III: ORGANIZATIONAL ASPECTS

Chapter VI. The Secret Success of a Global ERP Champion: Everything Changed and Nothing Happened

Academic Relevance Statement

The role of the champion in a global ERP implementation and business process change effort is framed within a conceptual model borrowed from a classic work on how people cope with traumatic life changes. This approach to change management seems to resonate with practitioners, as some similar frameworks have appeared in various consultant and trade publications. The application of this framework in the present case analysis offers interdisciplinary insight for theory development and applied research. In particular, the model described here anticipates a decline in business process performance when a large-scale change is rolled out in a global organization. The model includes three specific efforts that a champion can initiate to move a business out of the anticipated period of decline. With regard to global ERP implementation, this chapter also encourages applied research that considers some alternative definitions of success and "value realization" associated with globally integrated information technology change. For example, rather than expect outcomes such as return on investment when a new ERP system "goes live," framing the introduction of new technology in a larger change context suggests alternative outcomes that underscore a successful implementation and integrated business processes. Finally, the present chapter emphasizes the importance of the "people component" when a new system is introduced in a multi-cultural organization and offers some suggestions for studying the role and behaviors of effective change champions.

Management Relevance Statement

The successful implementation of an enterprise resource planning system on a global scale depends upon champions who must be prepared to guide everyone involved in the project through this change. But how does a champion of change prepare to lead an effort that uproots legacy systems and established regional business processes in favor of a globally integrated system and a new set of procedures? Global ERP champions need to develop a sense of what to expect—and what not to expect—regarding the implementation of a global ERP system and the business process changes required, and they need to be able to communicate these expectations to business leaders and managers involved in and ultimately affected by the project. In an effort to prepare managers and change leaders as they embark on a global systems integration and change effort, the following chapter provides a guiding framework developed from the first-hand experience of a successful global ERP champion.

Chapter VII. Business Process Reengineering and ERP: Weapons for the Global Organization

Academic Relevance Statement

This chapter provides a current perspective on business process reengineering as it relates to ERP, while critically discussing past research in the field. Research on reengineering has, for the most part, disappeared over the last few years. This chapter renews interest in the subject from a research perspective, by stating that reengineering in organizations has not stopped. Many organizations are still reengineering, clean-slate or with ERP, and the lessons learned are invaluable. While large-scale studies of reengineering still have not taken place, this chapter seeks to renew interest in the subject matter while enlightening readers of the possibilities of future research endeavors.

Management Relevance Statement

Alexander Graham Bell said, "Knowledge is a process of piling up facts. Wisdom lies in their simplification." This chapter aims to increase your knowledge of business process re-engineering and how it can go hand in hand with enterprise resource planning systems. By simplifying the drivers of these disciplines and adding real-world insights, we aim to share our wisdom so that the reader may adopt, adapt, and implement successful change in a timely manner. The ideas, advice, and lessons learned will be invaluable for any manager, director, or project leader tasked with improving profitability, reliability, and customer satisfaction. This is not the "painting by numbers" or "reengineering for dummies" approach. It is a collection of insights learned in the battlefield that ultimately impact success. Many will seem like "common sense"; others will stretch your imagination and test your understanding of what really causes outcomes. Whatever you attempt to reengineer, our experience suggests you could achieve upwards of a 30% reduction in cost. Marry that with the change in philosophy you will bring to your organization, and you have a powerful approach that enables you to embrace the future with confidence.

Chapter VIII. Enterprise Systems as an Enabler of Fast-Paced Change: The Case of B2B Procurement in Ericsson

Academic Relevance Statement

Enterprise systems (ESs) flexibility is considered a key priority in business environments. Some have argued that ESs are too inflexible. There are criticisms of two specific issues. The deployment cycle for an ES is too long. It could take several years. On the other hand, an ES does not permit full customization to meet specific business needs, and mutual adaptation between the organization and the system is required. However, as has been argued, in response to this inflexibility claim, we would ask managers and scholars, "As compared to what?" The answer to this question leads us to the conclusion that an ES is one of the more flexible information tools for companies. Of course, there is room for improvement as evidenced by new advances. For example, service-oriented architecture emerges as an evolution of ES that allows companies to have more enterprise system flexibility to respond more quickly to changes driven by the business environment.

This debate has also been relevant in information system literature, which includes development of a flexibility construct for IT architectures. In particular, this study of Ericsson has borrowed that flexibility construct to illustrate how SAP can be considered a flexible information tool for companies. The result is a chapter that makes a contribution to this debate and brings interesting knowledge to the field. The study adopts a stance similar to that of past researchers and presents ES as a flexible infrastructure to enable change. In particular, this study shows how SAP can support fast-paced change in a global context. The system was able to adapt to different business models going through different levels of change over time: from a local context (i.e., the Spanish solution) to a regional context (i.e., the European solution) to a global environment (i.e., the centralized solution for the global company). Having only one system worldwide was critical when it came to responding effectively to business changes. But it was not just any kind of system: SAP offered the three critical components of a flexible platform (i.e. integration, modularity, and personnel).

Management Relevance Statement

The findings of this investigation have important implications for practitioners. The study shows that enterprise systems (e.g., SAP) can be flexible tools in terms of being able to reconfigure and adapt themselves correctly to organizational changes. In this specific case, Ericsson developed three major transformations in its procurement processes, and the system was able to adapt and align itself to three different business models over a transformation period of four years. First, the system followed a local and decentralized procurement process; then the system was reconfigured to support a regional "shared service" for procurement; and finally the system was adapted to enable a global and centralized procurement process led by the head office in Sweden. When talking about these findings with dozens of managers in different executive education programs, they all acknowledge that in this kind of fast-paced change, a packaged system like SAP is the best technological option with which to tackle organizational change. Compared to custom-made software, packaged systems are better able to respond quickly and flexibly to changes in business strategies and models. Two questions remain, however: Will it be possible to reconfigure and adapt the system faster? And what further organizational and technological capabilities are needed?

A second implication for managers is that they learn that implementing a single system vendor for all functions and processes in a company can bring positive net benefits. In this case, Ericsson decided to implement the B2B procurement functionality of the ERP system already in place. The decision to keep the same vendor allowed the company to take advantage of the integrated and modular characteristics of a single system, and hence adapt it quickly to the required organizational changes. Moreover, selecting the same leading ES vendor afforded companywide previous knowledge of the system, and worldwide support from external consultant IBM. In other words, when a company selects a software vendor, it should take into account if the knowledge it has of the system is localized or companywide. Another key factor is the ability of the vendor to supply external technical resources worldwide. This case shows that the selection of a single, leading vendor is a good decision for a global company immersed in a dynamic business environment.

Chapter IX. Feral Systems and Other Factors Influencing the Success of Global ERP Implementations

Academic Relevance Statement

This chapter is relevant to academic research and teaching because it provides summary information on research undertaken in the 12 enterprise resource planning systems implementation problem areas as identified by ERP consultants (Rockford Consulting). These problem areas have the potential to provide a useful division of the ERP implementation problem domain in terms of areas that could be studied by researchers around the world. The chapter provides an initial literature review of some of the background research and a summary of research findings in the 12 research areas that an academic may wish to pursue. The chapter also introduces the concept of feral systems, which are described as information systems that are developed by individuals or groups to help them with their work, but are not condoned by management or are not part of the accepted information systems for the corporation. Continued research into the positive and/or negative aspects of these feral systems is vital for a clearer understanding of their role in organizations, and academics are encouraged to continue research in this area. The author's current research indicates that there is a dichotomy of opinion in the study corporation he was involved with. This dichotomy is highlighted with employees at the operations level of the corporation indicating positive aspects to feral systems—these include more comprehensive reporting and easier data entry into the ERP—while others, notably senior managers and information professionals, express concern over information technology integration and maintenance issues.

Management Relevance Statement

This chapter provides practical solutions to global enterprise resource planning systems implementation problems for managers. It gives the reader a checklist of 12 factors that influence the effective implementation and subsequent adaptation of global ERPs. It also provides practical examples of common implementation problems and a brief history of ERP failures. The chapter provides a generic step–by-step guide to implementation success, as well as the suggested approach as outlined by a major ERP vendor, namely, SAP. The chapter covers both the well-documented practical problems of a lack of top management support, lack of staff training, poor communications, inadequate allocation of resources, and poor project management approaches, as well as the not-so-well-reported problems of employee resistance to change. The chapter introduces a new concept of feral systems, which are described as information systems that are developed by individuals or groups to help them with their work, but are not condoned by management or are not part of the accepted information systems for the corporation. The development of these systems appears to stem from a mistrust of the system and poor employee training, as well as the desire for employees to stick with their own legacy systems. The author cannot conclude whether feral systems are a negative or positive within an organization, because research in this area indicates that some employees consider that these systems inform the ERP and provide useful summary reports, while others consider them to be a problem with respect to information systems integration and maintenance.

SECTION IV: CULTURAL ASPECTS

Chapter X. Experiences of Cultures in Global ERP Implementation

Academic Relevance Statement

Despite agreement among IT investigators on viewing cultural sensitivity as a key issue in global IT implementation, global research on the impact of societal and cultural differences on IT implementation is difficult and scarce. As a result, it is proposed to integrate two bodies of research findings: the findings related to differences in various aspects of societal cultures, and the findings related to typical stages and processes of enterprise resource planning implementation. Instead of Hofstede's study, the most frequently used work in current research efforts on cultural differences in global ERP implementation, use is suggested of the GLOBE findings which extend Hofstede's work and overcome most of its methodological deficiencies. Applying these recent research findings to global ERP implementation stages and actors will contribute to our understanding of the social construction of technology in different parts of the world. Additional research on proposed mechanisms that promote fit between local societal culture and cultural aspects embedded in ERP systems is suggested.

Management Relevance Statement

The routine operation and exploitation of a global enterprise resource planning system in a particular organization is the last stop in a long journey that typically begins in a different country or region. Designers and engineers that plan and manufacture technological systems imprint their values and practices onto these systems, without fully realizing that inconsistencies in cultural dimensions between developers and users may result in poor implementation of the new system due to resistance to change, among other causes. Therefore, managers' awareness of cultural differences is a necessary condition in formulating ERP policies for implementation in different organizational settings across countries. The chapter offers detailed examples of cultural differences between countries and their relations to the different stages of technology implementation, which may serve as a guideline for engineers, vendors, consultants, and managers of global ERP systems interventions in formulating mechanisms for global implementation. Implementation managers are advised to adapt ERP systems to their own set of beliefs through the establishment of joint global and local teams that represent all parties in the process. In this manner, rather than a cultural conflict, ERP implementation becomes a cultural exchange that reduces resistance to change.

Chapter XI. The Implementation of ERP Packages as a Mediation Process: The Case of Five Brazilian Projects

Academic Relevance Statement

This research has investigated the implementation of ERP projects as a mediation process—that is, an interactive process developed between the organization-client's members and the external consultants. The adoption of a mediation lens sharpens perception of ways in which global and local knowledge and skills have been combined in different ERP projects, and how these different arrangements have affected the project results. Brazilian subsidiaries of global (transnational) firms were investigated with a view to analyzing the process of ERP implementation, its interdependence with national and organizational contexts, and the dynamics of interaction among groups during implementation. Underlying our analysis were two main questions: (1) How do patterns of mediation emerge, and what kinds of elements influence their emergence? (2) What kind of association can be established between patterns of mediation and project results? Our conclusions point to certain drivers for patterns of mediation. The local firm's position (status and relationship) regarding the head office (global firm) and the meaning attached to each project directly influence the way external consultants are perceived by the local firm's members, and these perceptions influence team members' and consultants' roles. In turn, the way these roles are performed contribute to reinforcement or transformation of established mediation patterns.

Management Relevance Statement

The elements discussed in this chapter hold lessons for managers in both global and local firms. Our research addresses the critical choices managers and executives are likely to be faced with when implementing ERP projects within the framework of global or transnational companies. Certain recognizable patterns are identified based on the recurrent nature of problems and solutions associated with the same technology. Our investigation focuses on patterns in the relationship between clients and consultants, in the context of a global firm's decision to implement ERP packages in its subsidiaries. These patterns are then related to the project results. Important note is taken of the fact that patterns of mediation are dynamic processes that can change over time. Thus, understanding how patterns of mediation work and evolve lays the groundwork for developing better policies and methods of ERP implementation. What is provided here is not a fixed recipe, but an assemblage of insightful concepts that provide a basis for better decision making.

SECTION V: AUDITING ASPECTS

Chapter XII. Sarbanes–Oxley Compliance, Internal Control, and ERP Systems: The Case of mySAP ERP

Academic Relevance Statement

Compliance management is becoming a management function in national and international companies. Academics need to understand the tasks involved, the processes employed, and the effects on performance and organization, for example. This chapter addresses how compliance with a specific legislation is supported by an ERP system by examining the functionalities of this system. It also raises some further research issues in this area.

Management Relevance Statement

Compliance with laws and regulations demands more management attention today than ever before. Understanding how ERP systems can support and improve compliance performance on a local, regional, and global level is therefore a relevant managerial issue. This chapter addresses some of the managerial issues inherent in addressing SOX compliance in ERP systems.

Chapter XIII. ERP Systems Effectiveness in Implementing Internal Controls in Global Organizations

Academic Relevance Statement

The internal control requirements imposed by the Sarbanes-Oxley Act, commonly referred to as SOX, over financial reporting can result in significant design challenges for ERP systems in most public organizations. However, little theoretical guidance or models exist to help researchers understand control implementation challenges and enhance ERP systems for control purposes in competitive global organizations. This chapter reports the results of interviews with ERP systems managers and directors in four organizations with significant global operations. It provides some exploratory evidence on the extent to which ERP systems meet, or can be enhanced to meet, SOX requirements. It reveals some significant technical and cultural challenges, such as systems inflexibility and diversity, systems security weaknesses, and resistance to change, as well as some benefits, such as improved process efficiency and systems security, and potential intangible long-term benefits. These findings enhance researchers' understanding of critical systems design features and processes, as well as common implementation challenges and benefits in global organizations. As such, they can serve as a basis for developing a comprehensive model of ERP systems effectiveness for implementing and operating effective controls in future research.

Management Relevance Statement

In response to prominent financial scandals, the Sarbanes-Oxley Act imposed stringent internal control requirements over financial reporting for public organizations. This chapter examines the extent to which ERP systems are able to meet these requirements and challenges global organizations face in enhancing their ERP systems for this purpose. The four organizations studied have substantially completed their SOX implementations, although some work is still necessary. SOX requirements have often been implemented as part of other process and strategic improvement initiatives. The organizations have had to overcome some technical and cultural challenges, such as systems inflexibility and diversity, systems security weaknesses, and resistance to change. On the positive side, they also reported some benefits of SOX implementation, such as improved process efficiency and systems security, and potential intangible long-term benefits. These findings provide systems managers some insight into challenges and opportunities in enhancing ERP systems for SOX compliance, which can ultimately contribute to identifying best practices and enhancing long-term organizational effectiveness. Although controls cannot guarantee the prevention of future financial scandals, they can reveal significant errors, omissions, and questionable practices, and thus allow timely corrective actions. Such threats exert pressure on global organizations to continuously enhance controls and ERP systems, resulting in continuous cycles of control and systems adjustments.

SECTION VI: SUCCESS EVALUATION ASPECTS

Chapter XIV. Implementing ERP Systems in Multinational Projects: Implications for Cultural Aspects and the Implementation Process

Academic Relevance Statement

In this chapter, after a literature review on ERP implementation, three surveys on the success factors of ERP projects, performed in Germany, the United States, and Turkey, are presented with a detailed analysis of the validity of the results. Twenty-three hypotheses postulated in advance of the surveys are tested. Despite the very different outcome of the surveys, it proved all the hypotheses to be true. In the second section, three common lifecycle models for the implementation of ERP projects are evaluated in light of their capability of business process improvement. Finally, in the third section, the authors present a new semi-process-oriented lifecycle model, which avoids the shortcomings of the previously assessed ones and takes into account the findings from the surveys.

Management Relevance Statement

In this chapter the authors present factors for the success of ERP implementation projects, an evaluation of common lifecycle models for implementing ERP software systems, and finally a new lifecycle model, which is based on the authors' findings. They performed surveys in Germany, the United States, and Turkey on the process and success factors for ERP projects. The results are discussed in light of Hofstede's model of cultural factors. In spite of the great variety of potential advantages, it is also necessary to illuminate the real effects of standard ERP software in practice. Recent studies have revealed that 81% of German companies interviewed using SAP do not fully exploit the software's ability to optimize business processes, though 61% stated that SAP offers very good process optimization opportunities. Therefore the authors evaluated popular lifecycle models with respect to their suitability to implement standard software in a process-driven way. Finally, the authors present a semi-process-oriented approach lifecycle model for the implementation and release changeover of ERP systems. This lifecycle model was developed from the authors' experience in practice, and its practical relevance was evaluated in real-world projects. This approach is also assessed in light of the criteria presented in the second section.

Chapter XV. Success Factors for the Global Implementation of ERP/HRMS Software

Academic Relevance Statement

There are few field studies on global enterprise resource planning implementations. This chapter focuses on one specific company's experiences with a global implementation, with particular focus on cultural differences, management support, resistance to change, trust, and communication-distance. All of these success factors, identified using existing literature, are evaluated against a global enterprise resource planning software implementation experienced by a real company, Global Software, Inc. Data were collected using semi-structured interviews and a questionnaire. The information within the chapter is useful for academicians conducting research on global ERP implementations, global information system implementations, and for those with an interest in learning more about success factors related to ERP implementations. Additional information is included regarding human resource management systems (HRMSs), a particular module within ERP software. HRMS is the focus of the field study due to company implementation time constraints.

Management Relevance Statement

This chapter describes a field study for a global implementation of ERP software. Due to implementation time constraints put forth by the company, particular emphasis is placed on the human resources management system software module, which was implemented on a global basis. The HRMS stores employee data and supports payroll, benefits, and compensation processes. The information in this chapter will benefit companies, managers, and individuals interested in learning about issues a company experienced while implementing a global system. There are many factors that should be considered when implementing a global system. Five success factors, identified using existing literature, are evaluated against the implementation. Cultural differences, communication-distance, trust, management support, and resistance to change are discussed in-depth. While the software implementation overall is considered successful, the non-U.S.-based locations did not have a perceived improvement to existing processes. Data were collected using semi-structured interviews and a questionnaire.

SECTION VII: TRENDS

Chapter XVI. ERP Trends, Opportunities, and Challenges: A Focus on the Gulf Region in the Middle East

Academic Relevance Statement

This chapter identifies key opportunities and challenges pertaining to ERP implementation in the Gulf region of the Middle East. While many issues identified here have global applications, some are very particular to this region. For example, the adaptation of the ERP product to support the practices governing business operations in some industries, such as banking, is key to a successful ERP adoption. How an ERP system could support the development of financial institutions in this region with consideration to Islamic banking rules and regulations is both a challenge and an opportunity. Much of the academic literature on ERP is focused on western countries, with the exception of a few articles on South East Asian countries such as India and China. This chapter hence serves the academic community through providing an insight into: (1) the local context for this region, (2) ERP implementation issues that are relevant in this region, and (3) ERP implementation research opportunities in this area.

Management Relevance Statement

What are the important issues pertaining to ERP implementation in the Gulf region of the Middle East? With rising oil revenues, continuous positive growth, and relative political stability, there are extensive business prospects in the region, for both local and global investors. This chapter provides an overview of the opportunities available for ERP-related businesses in the region. It also highlights challenges, particularly those related to the local environment which vendors, consultants, and clients need to be aware of. Through exploring currents and future trends, this chapter not only helps ERP-related businesses focus their operational and strategic plans to capture business opportunities in this region, but also aids managers in client organizations in identifying ERP and ERP-related solutions that are likely to contribute to creating or maintaining a competitive position in the markets in which they operate.

Chapter XVII. The Future of ERP and Enterprise Resource Management Systems

Academic Relevance Statement

The chapter begins with a theoretical analysis of the low adaptability of current ERPs to the needs of the organizations that should constitute their largest market in the near future: the small and medium-sized enterprises, as well as other organizations whose priority is not the mid- and long-term resource planning but the short-term and dynamic management of resources. It shows that the resource functionality must be structurally strengthened—and suggests a data structure for that goal—to allow ERPs to evolve into enterprise resource management systems. Then, the chapter discusses the main issues that future global or local ERPs will have to address to be able to satisfy some of the main expectations that current ERPs have not fulfilled: lower costs of licensing and implementation, including the Open Source Initiative licensing option; more standardization; higher inter-system compatibility; and less need for consulting.

Management Relevance Statement

The chapter addresses some of the questions that managers, consultants, and other practitioners are asking about the future of ERPs:

1. What is the future of ERPs?
2. How can ERPs satisfy the needs of SME and other organization—even big ones—whose priority is not the mid- and long-term resource planning but the short-term, dynamic management of resources?
3. Will licensing and implementation costs become accessible for SMEs?
4. Will ERPs reach a global standard comparable to, say, the Microsoft Office suite or an open source propagation model like that of Linux?
5. Is there an intrinsic impediment for the standardization of ERPs or at least of the middleware aimed to make different ERPs compatible, communicable, and really able to transfer the best practices?

The chapter discusses the effects of a negative or positive answer to these questions and introduces some potential improvements that would facilitate the evolution towards the more dynamic short-term management of resources.

Carlos Ferran
The Pennsylvania State University, USA

Ricardo Salim
Cautus Networks Corp
Caracas, Venezuela

Section I
Rise and Globalization of ERPs

Chapter I
From Ledgers to ERP

Ricardo Salim
Universidad Autónoma de Barcelona, Spain
Cautus Networks Corp., Venezuela

Carlos Ferran
The Pennsylvania State University, USA

ABSTRACT

The chapter narrates the history of the accounting needs of individuals and organizations and explains their successive technological solutions, up to today's ERPs. The ledger, double-entry accounting, cost accounting, departmental accounting, material requisitions systems for production, human resources systems, and finally the enterprise-wide resource planning or management systems are analyzed in terms of how IT has—and has not—been able to "computerize" and integrate them. The main functionalities of ERPs are explained: the enterprise resource functionality and the planning functionality, as well as to what extent organizations need these functionalities and should pay its high prices. The expectations that have not yet been sufficiently satisfied by current systems, such as the ERP for SMEs, the transfer of "best practices," the interconnection of supply chains via ERP, and the ERP for global organizations, are discussed.

INTRODUCTION

The ledger records all the commercial and tributary transactions of an entity. Its use started thousands of years ago. Since antiquity, the records of all commercial and tributary transactions of an entity have been filed in ledgers. The recorded monetary value of the items transacted provides very useful summary information: the difference between all that came in minus all that went out for a given entity. This difference represents the wealth or patrimony of that entity and is also known as the fundamental accounting equation. However, frequent errors, omissions, and inconsistencies were generated between ledgers and reality. In the fourteenth century the double-entry method was developed to minimize them. This method requires that each transaction includes at least two entries: one representing where the money comes from and the other where it goes. The list of transactions of the accounts was called the "general ledger." In the mid-twentieth century, computers started to be used to record and summarize these transactions; nonetheless, for several decades technical limitations impeded the immediate detailed recording of both entries for individual operations. Therefore, individual operations were managed and recorded by independent and often isolated systems that took care of a specific business function—like production, invoicing, or human resources—and the general ledger gathered the daily summarization that came from those systems. In the early 1990s new technologies allowed the development of systems capable of integrating the general ledger with individual subsystems; thus providing immediate online information regarding the movements and status of all the resources that affected the patrimony. These systems are currently called enterprise resource planning (ERP) systems.

This chapter begins by narrating the history of ledgers from the ancient times when they were recorded on clay tablets to the early twentieth century, when they were recorded on cardboard cards and processed with a mechanical clock technology artifact called the tabulating machine. It continues by relating the rise and evolution of computers with the improvements of ledger recording and accounting, up to the completely computerized accounting information systems of the 1980s and then to the mid-1990's ERPs. Later it explains the main functionalities of ERPs—that is, the enterprise resource functionality and the planning functionality. Finally, that is followed by a discussion on the extent to which these functionalities—and the current costs—satisfy the expectations that ERPs have aroused to present.

ACCOUNTING: FROM CLAY TABLETS TO THE TABULATING MACHINE

The representation of exchange transactions using some type of symbols is a very old practice that is still in place, although the physical support in which they are written has changed: clay tablets, papyrus, parchments, holes in cardboard cards (punch cards), electromagnetic tapes and disks, micro-circuits, and semi-conductors. However, the purpose has not changed: to keep the account between what comes in and out of a given patrimony. The difference is in itself what we define in accounting terms as the patrimony: What I have (my patrimony) is equal to what I get or what I own as a creditor (my assets) minus what I hand over or what I owe as a debtor (my liabilities). This is known as the fundamental accounting equation:

Patrimony = Assets – Liabilities

The following is a brief account of the practices used to keep this equation balanced and updated before the computer era.

From the Clay Tablets to the Double-Entry

The representation of exchange transactions using symbols is a very old practice. In Mesopotamia there are traces of this practice as early as 3500 B.C. Later, the Hammurabi's Code (circa 1760 B.C.) ordered the recording of certain commercial records. Hammurabi's Code ordered the recording of certain commercial records. In "They Wrote on Clay" (Chiera, 1938), it is said that the Mesopotamian scribes recorded dates, the object of transaction, and the stamps of the parties involved in commercial transactions on clay tablets. In other ancient cultures different supports like parchment or paper were used to register tax collection and commercial transactions as a receipt or proof that the transaction took place (see Alexander, 2002; Ezzamel, 1994).

A set of transaction records constituted an account book, also called a ledger. With the appearance of currency (cf. "A History of Money from Ancient Times to the Present Day" (Davies 2002)), records began to be quantitative. To the qualitative data an amount of currency was added to recognize the value of the object transacted by the parties. This allowed the summation of the values contained on the records. Thus, the daily sales records provided a total of the income registered during that day. The total sum of the purchases and acceptance of services made the total daily expenses. The difference between these two totals was the profit—or loss—of the day. This allowed the calculation of summary information during a commercial or tax period. Intuitively, the most useful summary information was (and still is) the difference between the income and the expenditures of a specific patrimony.

Nonetheless, too often government employees and businessmen found that the detailed information in the ledgers and the total sum did not always correspond with the real content of the treasury. Furthermore, the information was not enough or it was too dispersed to be useful for a timely test.

The merchants of Renaissance Venice were the first to adopt a method specially designed to diminish this problem. According to this method, developed by the monk Luca Pacioli, each income or expense record required an additional piece of data: the cashbox used to either obtain or place the cash transacted. This way there were no surprises regarding the amount contained in each box at the end of the day. The sum of the daily incomes and expenditures of the day had to match with the initial amounts plus the total deposits and withdrawals on those boxes for that same day. And the initial amounts were in fact the surplus or

patrimony accumulated until the day before. But money was not the only thing coming in and going out; there were also items that came in and out of warehouses (generally in exchange for money) and financial documents that represented payment promises (debts or credits). Thus, the sum of all income and expenditures had to be compared, not only with the cashbox but with the inventories of goods, debts, and credits. This represented the widely accepted method known as "double-entry." The double-entry method is still in use and there is no substitute in sight. The second entry (counter-debit or counter-credit) indicates the cashbox or bank where the money is deposited or withdrawn, the box where the debt or credit document generated in the transaction is stored, or the warehouse where the item transacted is placed or taken from. At the end of each operation, the algebraic sum of the variations in the patrimony and the value contained in the warehouses, cashbox, and other boxes must be equal to zero (see Crosby, 1997; Macve, 1996).

The Industrial Revolution and Cost Accounting

The early industrial revolution meant a strong increase in volume and complexity of doing business. Accountants and administrators had to handle increasingly complex transactions. The sale of manufactured items could not be accounted for in a simple two-line document, but in a longer one that listed the value and origin of each individual raw material as well as all the labor used in the manufacturing process; however, all this information was generally dispersed across many different documents and ledgers. If this information was not collected appropriately and in a timely manner, then the transaction could occur based on erroneous information and cause a loss instead of the expected revenue. If the cost of a manufactured item is not correctly calculated on a timely basis, then the price at which it is sold could be by error and not by need below cost, and therefore cause an unnecessary loss to the enterprise (see Lee, Bishop, & Parker, 1996).

Cost information became as useful as patrimony information. And just like it, appropriate accounting methods had to be followed in order to obtain it timely and accurately. Cost information required a more complex double-entry registry. Cost accounting reflects not only the origin or destination of a product, but it must reflect the individual items used or consumed in its manufacturing; the accountant must track not only the finished product and its sale, but also the raw materials used, their purchases, and their usage.

In essence, the double-entry method for tracking both costs and patrimony consists of not waiting until the totals are calculated to test the fundamental accounting equation, but to do it in each individual transaction. The idea is to not wait until the totals do not match to start, with a forensic attitude—in which an autopsy or post-mortem audit may explain the problem—but to verify the equation in each individual and simple step and therefore assure, live, that the records are correct. This way accounting information represents live information that can be used to make appropriate decisions. Thus, accounting becomes useful for planning, for looking into the future, and not just to have a story of the past (see Kleiner, 2004).

Tabulating Machines and the Mechanization of the Accounting Books

The industrial revolution is identified with mechanization. All repetitive tasks began to be susceptible to mechanization. The daily ordering of accounting records is a repetitive task. For example, all documents for day one are placed in box number one, all documents for day two are placed in box number two, and so on.

It took a long time before the industrial revolution developed the electronic machines that could identify numbers by its (graphical) form (Aspray, 1990). It developed first clock-like machines that could mechanically react to the presence or absence of a hole in a specific position of a punch card. Then, another machine separated, classified, and grouped punch cards that contained accounting information written in the form of holes instead of graphical symbols. Therefore, towards the end of the nineteenth century, we exchanged the chisels on clay tablets and the pens on paper for machines that perforated and classified cardboards. The first of these machines was developed and manufactured by Hollerith to process the data from the 1890 census in the United States (see Austrian, 1982; Martin, 1891). And early in the twentieth century, we started using tabulating machines to represent and classify economic transactions.

ACCOUNTING: FROM THE FIRST COMPUTERS TO THE GENERAL LEDGER

In 1928 the IBM 301 (better known as the Type IV) accounting machine was marketed as "the first card-controlled machine to incorporate class selection, automatic subtraction and printing of a net positive or negative balance...This machine exemplifies the transition from tabulating to accounting machines. The Type IV could list 100 cards per minute" (see http://www-03.ibm.com/ibm/history/reference/faq_0000000011.html; Bashe, Johnson, H., & Pugh, 1985).

In the 1930s the first electromagnetic media came out to replace the cardboards. With these systems the ancient history of accounting was repeated. Very large ledgers were implemented on the first systems and their summarization (in terms of currency) could be calculated quite quickly. However, they did not include the information necessary to verify the fundamental accounting equation on their totals—and much less on each individual transaction. Partially, this problem arose due to the fact that the first electronic storage systems mimicked the paper-and-pencil storage system and therefore they were unable to establish the appropriate relationships between separate files. These systems are known as file-based systems. Solutions to this problem started to appear in the mid-1960s with the development of storage systems based on hierarchies and networks, and with the development of the first "high-level" programming languages. High-level languages were those that had a grammar that was easier to understand by human beings than the early machine languages. Examples of such languages are ALGOL, FORTRAN, and COBOL. This last one, common business oriented language (COBOL), was specifically oriented to businesses (see Wexelblat, 1981).

It was in the late 1960s when the first computer systems, oriented to support accounting records and capable of establishing and maintaining the relationships between a debit and its compensating credit (or viceversa) based on the double-entry method, came out. They were known as general ledger (GL) systems. However, the technical capabilities (of the computer hardware and software) were still not sophisticated enough to allow for the test of the fundamental accounting equation at the document level, but only at the aggregate level using totals from the different functional areas of the business—production, point of sale, warehouse, accounts receivable, accounts payable, payroll. At the same time many different systems that managed individual functional areas without any connection between them or with the GL were developed and implemented in organizations across the world. Material requirements planning (MRP) systems allowed the entry, process, and analysis (basically group by production line and summarize) of the transactions of raw materials needed and used in production. Human resource (HR) systems similarly worked on transactions that went from hiring and keeping personnel records to taking care of the payroll. Invoicing systems processed sales transactions. This pro-

liferation of independent systems brought about many islands of information inside the organization, islands of information that solved punctual problems but not the more systemic problem of managing the organization as a whole.

FROM GENERAL LEDGERS SYSTEMS TO ACCOUNTING INFORMATION SYSTEMS

From the mid-1970s and during the 1980s, a new breed of systems was oriented to provide some integration between the functional systems (manufacturing, sales, inventory, payroll, treasury, etc.) and the general ledger. These systems were developed using programming languages that provided instructions to develop improved user interfaces and better database management. They were generically called accounting information systems (AISs). However, the integration accomplished by these AISs was only partial and indirect. It was partial because not all the functional systems were included, and it was indirect because these systems did not share the same dataset and therefore only "messages" and summary data were copied and moved across them.

Figure 1 shows an ideal and general connection scheme for an accounting information system with the auxiliary functional modules. In the figure, the double arrows reflect a level of integration and interaction between modules that is more an ideal than what the systems from that generation really accomplished. Most of the time, these modules were not initially designed as part of a single system, but were integrated into one. There were two integration modalities: the first occurred when the modular systems came from different manufacturers and an integrator developed the integration; the second modality occurred when all the modules came from the same developer and the developer itself programmed the integration.

Integrating modules from different manufactures was less than ideal. Each module tended to have a different user interface, type of database, operating system, and even hardware and tele-communication requirements. Furthermore, most manufacturers tended to frown upon and not help in the development of interfaces that integrated their module with that of a potential competitor. Integrating modules developed by different software houses usually became a project similar to building the tower of Babel. On the other hand, this option seemed to provide a cheaper solution since it used the modules that had already been purchased and deployed in the organization; however, the reality usually was that the development of the integration tended to be as expensive as the repurchase of the systems and the end results of lower quality.

Some developers got very close to the integration depicted in Figure 1 by developing modules that were thought from the start to be part of the whole. The individual modules had the same user interface and shared the same hardware and software requirements. In some cases they even attempted to develop a single database design that would encompass all the modules. However, the single database design was not accomplished very well, if at all. This database problem was due to three basic factors: (1) the technology at the time was not powerful enough to appropriately manage such an ambitious integration; (2) it was a seller's market where customers were hungry for modules that at least worked, although they may still have problems and were not integrated; and (3) a fully integrated database model implied certain changes in the way that accountants worked, and they were strongly against them.

Figure 1. General diagram of an AIS with auxiliary functional modules

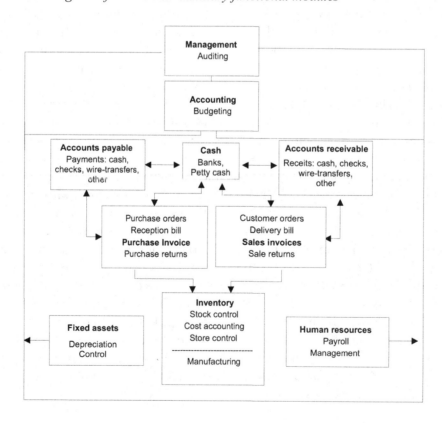

This last of factors is still present today and is partially justified. Most information systems have been shown to fail at one time or another, and accountants do not trust them enough to allow for the changes that a comprehensive integration requires. Therefore, there was very little financial incentive to work on the development of a comprehensive integration. In fact, the larger and more successful software houses of those days were those that developed modules and not integrated systems (see Bagranoff, Simkin, & Strand, 2005; Hollander, Denna, & Cherrington, 1999).

The first versions of every system that today is considered an ERP were many years ago an integrated AIS with different departmental modules, even though some of them never were known as something different than an ERP. Examples of AISs integrated with departmental modules include: Oracle applications, J.D. Edwards, Platinum, Solomon, EasyMax, Real World, FlexLine, PeachTree, QuickBooks, among others.

FROM AIS TO ERP

New technology (hardware and software) that allowed the development of highly integrated systems was developed during the 1990s. As the market became more demanding, developers started to redesign their modules to take advantage of this new technology. Just integrating the modules was gradually not enough; there was a need for a single integrated system that would manage all the different functional areas of the organization. Therefore, since the mid-1990s there has been an accelerated development of software that managed the enterprise as a whole. That breed of enterprise-wide system was—and is—currently referred to as enterprise resource planning systems. These systems unified three main types of systems: accounting information systems, human resource management systems, and manufacturing resource planning systems (see Brady, Monk, & Wagner, 2001; Mabert, 2007; Wight, 1982).

Nonetheless, even though these were new developments, they were not developed new from the ground up. Developers reused existing code in order to lower development costs, accelerate delivery times, and improve backward compatibility. Proof of this reuse was very clear with the so-called Y2K bug; had these systems been developed new, the Y2K bug would not have been a concern. Furthermore, in order to reuse the code and maintain that backward compatibility, many of the database structures were kept untouched from the original designs and continued to have ample redundancy. The systems continued to do more "messaging" than data sharing. While to the user the new systems seemed to be a single system with multiple functions, the layers below the interface still used separate although related files to store the information for each functional unit.

MRP, MRP II, and on

Material requirements planning systems were centered on the flow of physical resources (like raw materials, consumables, and spare parts) for manufacturing. Figure 2 shows the essential information flow of an MRP.

As shown in Figure 2, the plan or set of orders is broken up into production bills which are then broken up into the list of materials needed to manufacture all the products included in that bill. Then the system generates a material requisition and verifies if the items are currently available in the warehouses. If available, the system reserves or puts them aside. If not available, it requests a purchase and verifies if the items can arrive on a timely basis. If they can arrive on time, the purchase order is confirmed and the expected items are reserved for that production bill. If they cannot arrive on a timely basis, then the orders (or production plan) must be revised to reflect what can and cannot be manufactured. The system also checks if additional materials must be ordered to replenish the stock that was reserved, and if needed, it

Figure 2.

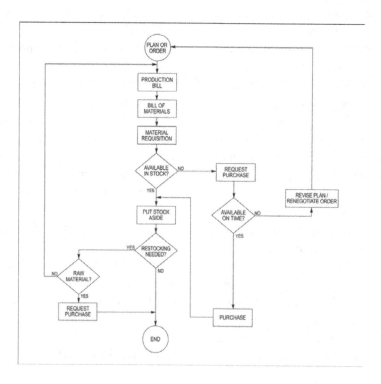

generates the corresponding purchase orders for those that are raw materials and production bills for those that are manufactured in-house.

In the procedure described above, whenever a required material is not in stock, a purchase is requested. However, this request may come back accepted or denied. If it is denied, there is no information on why. It could be because the suppliers do not have the needed items, because they cannot deliver them to the warehouse on a timely basis, or because the organization does not have the financial resources needed to pay for them. However, a denied request must launch a change in the production plan or a message to other departments (like sales or finance), indicating that either the requested products will not be available for sale or that additional resources need to be found to satisfy the material request.

In summary, an MRP is only concerned with materials and has nothing to do with the money needed to acquire them. It assumes that a separate

system takes care of that "minutiae." Manufacturing resource planning (MRP II) went forward and incorporated financial resources to the production cycle. These systems integrated budgeting and financial accounting into the manufacturing planning process. Figure 3 shows the essential flow of information in a MRP II system.

In Figure 3 we can see that MRP II includes, just like MRP, the process of material resources, but it also adds the processing of financial resources (see shadowed area). Thus, when a material is needed and is not in stock, it verifies and reserves the financial resources needed to acquire it. And it not only puts aside the needed material for a given production bill, but it also puts aside the financial resources needed.

The idea of integrated management of all the organizational resources generates the proliferation of many more possibilities and new ideas. Several experts, consultants, and developers started to use the term "MRP III" to denote new

Figure 3.

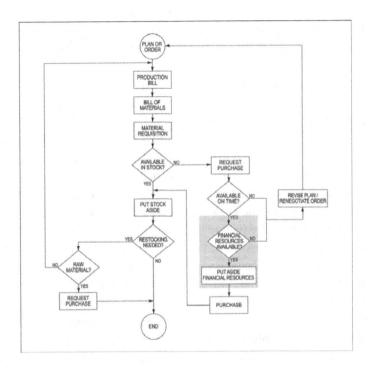

and creative evolutions of both the MRP and the MRP II schemes (cf. Graham & Freely, 1990; Louis, 1991). A quick and informal Web search reports hundreds of hits on the topic among which we can find the following:

At http://www.webpro.com/website-design-development/newsdetails.asp?nid=80, MRP III is identified with "Money Resource Planning." At http://www.abacibiz.com/products/erp/faqs.html#_MRP, MRP III is identified with an improvement from MRP II and we can read:

MRP III takes conventional MRP II to a new level with 'intelligent expediting'. With MRP III, the system looks ahead to see planned and pending orders that can fill the expedited order requirement, so it doesn't generate unnecessary orders. The problem of over-planning is eliminated, along with the 'nervousness' that accompanies it in MRP message displays.

However, this proliferation also causes comments such as the following from http://erp.ittoolbox.com/groups/vendor-selection/erp-select/is-cs3-an-erp-or-mrpii-system-62517:

Don't be confused by the name, all of them are simply (and only) evolutions from the basic MRP stuff that started back with Taylor and his associates in the early 1900s (that's another story).

These may be exaggerations, but they are not too far from being true.

Finally ERP

We could say that the ERP concept comprises all of these prior ideas and developments; however, recent articles with titles like "ERP Is Dead—Long Live ERP II" (Bond et al., 2000) seem to imply otherwise.

Ideally, an ERP operates on all the resources of the organization. It does not limit itself to physical or financial resources. It also manages human resources, and not only the internal human resources (employees) but also the external ones (customers and suppliers). An ERP manages customers using some form of a customer relationship management (CRM) module and suppliers with some form of a supply chain management module. The essential information flow of an ERP is shown in Figure 4.

It would be easy to conclude that an MRP sees the organization from a manufacturing-centered perspective (where units and neither prices nor costs are relevant), while an AIS sees the organization from an accounting perspective (where costs and prices and not units are important). Furthermore, the convergence of both becomes an ERP (where units, prices, and costs are important). However, that is not completely true. An ERP, in contrast with an AIS, has not tended to interconnect functional modules to create a single comprehensive enterprise system. In ERPs the organization is not made up of functional units that take care of specific resources (like manufacturing, finance, and human resources), but of resources that flow through the whole organization

to satisfy its needs. An ERP is not the result of interconnecting a finance-centered system (e.g., Oracle Financials) with an operationally centered system (like J.D. Edwards) with a system centered in human resources (like PeopleSoft).

At least in theory, an ERP sees (from its initial design) an organization as a single entity and not as several entities linked together. This in and by itself is a substantial step forward from the scheme of an AIS (that is made of several departmental modules). However, in practice this single-entity design did not fully crystallize. The user interface and the functionality reflected the single-entity design; however, the underlying data structures did not change much and kept most of the departmental division. We will discuss this in more detail later in this chapter.

In the early 1990s, SAP, a German software company, introduced its ERP system called SAP R/3. This system evolved from a prior manufacturing application but integrated accounting and human resource functions (Brady et al., 2001). R/3 (or SAP as it is better but incorrectly known) was the first ERP to obtain worldwide recognition and is generally considered the premier ERP, even

Figure 4.

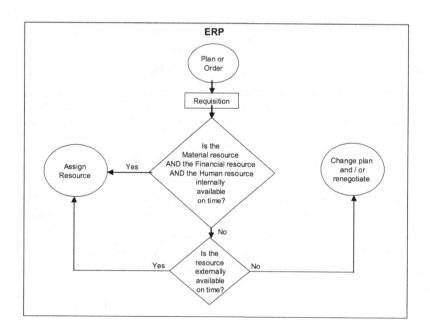

though it was neither the first one nor the only one that integrates all that functionality into a single system. Many other software houses developed systems that also incorporated a single-user interface and unified functionality that was not differentiated by departments (like Real World, Platinum, Hipermax, Great Plains Dynamics, or FlexLine), but did not have the marketing power, momentum, or even luck to push their applications around the world or the financial resources to implement them over so many platforms. Furthermore, SAP R/3 popularity forced all enterprise-wide systems to tout themselves as ERPs for marketing purposes.

Since ERPs cover the entire flow of enterprise resources, these systems integrate all the traditional functional areas of an organization. They plan, monitor, and control the acquisition or hiring, exchange, usage, consumption, transformation, and delivery or sale of financial, human, and physical resources. Thus they cover sales, purchases, payroll, inventory, fixed assets, production, payables, receivables, cash management, and bank reconciliation, all of which provide the information needed for comprehensive accounting. Furthermore, ERPs are now including extended functionality that also handles non-accounting (though partially quantitative) information like customer relationship management, supply chain management, human capital management, project management systems, logistic management systems, and a balanced scorecard.

While the main purpose of the traditional AIS is to measure and display the contribution of a given resource in the profit of an organization after the resource has been used (or "post-mortem"), the ERP tracks it from the start, when the resource is planned, requested, and/or assigned. In an AIS, all transactions are recorded after they occur, thus the system can explain what happened but not what is going to happen. ERPs allow management to make timely decisions before the lack or bad application of a resource causes a loss in the financial statements. In other words, while

AISs resemble forensic applications that perform corporate autopsies, ERPs are active applications that control and manage current operations while also keeping a picture of the past.

Since ERPs track resources throughout their entire lifecycle, their purview goes beyond the boundaries of the organization. They incorporate customers and suppliers as additional agents that affect the organizational resources. ERPs, unlike AISs, include modules that go across the entire supply chain assuring the timely reception of resources from suppliers and estimating product demand from clients. Much more about the history of ERPs can be found in Brady et al. (2001), Jacobs and Whybark (2000), Jacobs and Weston (2007), and Summer (2005).

ERP'S RESOURCE AND PLANNING FUNCTIONALITIES

It is generally considered that enterprise resource planning systems brought about two major innovations:

1. Integrate separate applications (like finance, manufacturing, and human resources) that hardly shared information into a single system with a common user interface that was able to at least partially share the data; and
2. Push the planning capability from the physical resources (present in MRP) to financial resources (present in MRP II) to even human resources. In other words, it had planning capabilities for all the enterprise resources.

The letter "E" in ERP refers to the first innovation: an ERP does not see the department as isolated units but as interconnected parts of an entire organization. The letter "P" refers to the second innovation: an ERP incorporates planning into the process and is not just about the execution. The letter "R" refers to a third, implicit innovation: an ERP sees the resource as the center of the system's functionality and manipulates all the resources of the enterprise, not just a subset of them. This third innovation is as important as or even more important than the prior ones; however, it has been conspicuously absent in most literature that discusses the advantages and disadvantages of ERPs. The next section will describe the last two innovations in detail and discuss their advantages for different types of organizations.

ERP's Planning Functionality

The planning functionality of an ERP consists on essentially: (a) check the plan in the database before making or allowing any transaction that affects a given resource (like an order from a client); (b) in the case that it is available, assign or use the required resource and immediately update its planned availability; (c) create a planning requisition if the resource is not available; (d) report on several management levels how close the plan is being followed; and (e) make the necessary changes to adjust the existing plan.

The planning functionality of an ERP is not limited, as it used to be, to a single department. This is advantageous as long as the enterprise is capable of doing that type of planning. However, the culture and the standard operating procedures of many organizations are strongly rooted on independent departmental planning, and that becomes a tremendous hurdle in the successful implementation of the ERP. It is common to find organizations where the individual plans of each department are not coordinated and the expectations or assumptions of one department regarding another may be completely offset. It is also common for departments to keep their plans a "secret" from the rest. An ERP conflicts with these philosophies. In an ERP the plans cannot be kept a secret within the organization (potentially creating political problems) and have to match,

taking the decision right from the individual departments to a global consensus.

The planning functionality typically involves high-level planning, based on actual demand and forecasts. In some cases it includes actuarial and long-term planning with the ability to create, simulate, and execute complex business scenarios, budget planning, "what-if" testing, and automated control documentation. However, for the above to be of real use and not a simple theoretical exercise, an ERP must at a minimum interact with detailed planning that has dispatching, execution, and monitoring functions. This includes automating the approval process in a common and collaborative environment, online messaging for production managers, sequential or concurrent planning, multi-site planning, order prioritization, reports on opportunity costs, routings for configured products, production schedules, close interaction with the generation of a multi-level bill of materials, and immediate update of stocking levels and production capacity.

Most major ERPs tend to offer all of the above functionality at both a high and a detailed level; however, most users recognize that they have only been able to successfully use a small fraction of it.

ERP's Resource-Centered Functionality

The subject of the functionality of an ERP lies in the resources (be they financial, material, or human resources) and not the traditional functional areas or departments (like plant, sales, procurement, human resources, or finance). The resources flow through the different areas, forcing them to interact intensively; no department has full and sole control of a given resource. For example, raw materials are requested by production, purchased by procurement, paid by finance, and consumed again by production. Human resources are no different. Any department may request a person, human resources recruits him, and finance makes the financial previsions for paying his contract. An ERP system tracks and values the resource from the time it is first required or assigned, independent of which area requested it, while the traditional systems only recorded the resource transactions after they had been processed by each department. Thus, while an ERP reports on the full lifecycle of each resource (from the time it is requested until it is consumed), the traditional departmental systems were limited to reporting what occurred in each department. Furthermore, while the ERP is able to detect in advance—"live"—if a resource will not be available when needed, the departmental system only reports the problem once it has already occurred. An ERP informs in advance and aids in solving the problem, while the departmental system only reports, post mortem, that the problem occurred.

The resource orientation implies the existence of functionality that assigns resources to requisitions originated by either a plan or an order as well as those arising from internal requirements. Therefore it needs to have the following minimum functionality: a pending requisition and available resources form, an operational breakdown of resources form, and a requested vs. served resources report.

A Pending Requisition and Available Resources Form

This form shows the needed resources to satisfy the requisition and indicates if they are available or not. It either executes an automatic assignment of resources (based on previous instructions) or offers one of the following options:

- For those resources that are available, IT either reserves the resource (changes its status from available to assigned to the specific requisition) or leaves it pending.
- For those resources that are either not available or pending, it either denies the resource

(and sends a "Resource Not Available" message to the requisition originator) or generates a requisition for the resource to procurement, HR, or finance.

An Operational Breakdown of Resources Form

The breakdown would occur based on elemental work units (like tasks or shifts), and human, physical, and financial resources would be assigned to each one. This assignment could occur automatically based on a previously specified parameter and the user would have the option of altering them.

A Requested vs. Served Resources Report

The format for this report should facilitate visualization of recurrent deficits that would aid management in taking appropriate actions.

However, in the current ERPs the resource orientation is closer to the orientation than to the resource. The orientation is reflected in the vocabulary used (starting with the "R" in ERP), in the names given to the menu options in the user interface, in some validations made when entering data into a form or to execute a procedure, and in a large set of reports oriented towards the resource. For example, in most ERPs the purchase order form cannot be completed unless information is also entered on the origin of the request for purchase and the financial authorization to make the purchase commitment. Furthermore, ERPs offer detailed reports on a given resource indicating who requested it, how the supplier was selected, the purchase order used, the expected date of arrival, potential delays, time and date it was received in the warehouse, earmark for its expected use, and so forth. However, in live implementations many of these options and data are not used and then the reports on the resource are incomplete.

These options oriented towards the resource are not often used due to two main factors: (1) neither the organization nor its managers are prepared to migrate from the departmental orientation to the resource orientation, and (2) the systems are too rigid and therefore the choice becomes either use it in its entirety or not at all. This lack of flexibility is probably the next problem that the coming wave of ERP will overcome.

CURRENT ERPS HAVE NOT SATISFIED ALL THE EXPECTATIONS

The current wave of ERPs has only satisfied a few of the many expectations that customers had when they were first launched into the market. They have fulfilled the expectation of a system that integrated the whole enterprise, removed some of the existing islands of information, and displaced the focus from the functional units to the resources. They can potentially track the resources from the original request to its final use or consumption through the various departments that use or process them. However, they have too much emphasis in a rigid plan instead of helping in the operation of a dynamic management of the resources—a fault that when added to the high costs and long implementation times makes them unattainable (or of little use) to small and medium-sized companies (SME). For many SMEs, planning is either not feasible or not a high priority, and much less if it is implied that they have to make large financial investments and divert the attention of their personnel for extended periods of time. Another unsatisfied expectation is that current ERPs have not been able to easily or even efficiently cross organizational boundaries, particularly when the organizations use ERPs developed by different manufacturers.

The following subsections will discuss in more detail some of these expectations that the current wave of ERPs have not been able to satisfy.

Cost and Length of Implementing a Large ERP

Without any doubt ERPs are the most expensive (in terms of financial and other resources) software that businesses have ever spent money on. They are the largest business applications since they include all prior applications, and they are as mission critical as any of the applications for the same reason; however, until now, all mission-critical applications were small and as simple as possible, to assure that they would not err. But ERPs are by definition complex and therefore far more prone to having bugs and inconsistencies than any of the smaller systems. In other words, the whole (the ERP) is bigger, far more complex, more sensitive, and more expensive than the sum of the parts.

The market has learned that the total cost of an ERP is not just the licensing cost but that of licensing plus that of implementing it. And implementation costs tend to be several times higher than those of the license. In addition, a higher licensing cost does not usually imply a higher total cost since the cheaper licenses are frequently more expensive to implement. It is common for inexpensive ERPs (due to the use of common open source licensing or other marketing reasons) to be very difficult and expensive to implement.

The complexity of implementing an ERP makes it very difficult to appropriately budget how much and how long it will take to successfully implement it. Due to intense competition, most ERP salespeople tend to provide initial estimates that are very optimistic and as low as possible, counting on open contracts that will allow for increases as needed. They also count on the fact that once the implementation has started, it will be much more difficult for the company to go back and start the process again with one of their competitors. It is common to find that once the implementation starts, new and unexpected costs tend to appear; however, many of these unexpected costs should have been expected.

It is also common to find some sort of complicity on the side of the client in regard to these estimation errors. The people in the client organization that really understand the need for a good ERP may not be able to justify it to their partners or those higher up, and in order to get the ERP they either ask for an under-priced proposal or look the other way when one arrives. They expect that either initial positive results or explanations like "increase in scope" and "new and emergent needs" will help justify the additional investments that were not included in the initial proposal.

On the other hand, a comprehensive proposal that clearly lists all the needs of an organization in terms of an ERP implementation is very difficult to write. It needs an in-depth analysis of the organization and that takes time and money. During the request for proposal stage, the client organization cannot allow full access to all those offering to submit a proposal because it would be too risky and too expensive (in terms of the personnel that would have to divert their attention). And the offering companies could not make such large investments on something that may or may not occur. An accepted solution to this problem is the hiring (on the part of the client) of a consulting firm that collects the relevant information, gathers the requirements, and provides the results to all the competing firms. However, this task by itself raises the initial costs, making the ERP acquisition more unlikely. Moreover, both the collection of information and the implementation take time, during which the client organization evolves and the requirements change.

Implementation costs are high because they are not simply about adapting the software to the organization but about preparing and adapting the organization to the software. They include train-ing the users on how the system works, but more importantly they include retraining the user on how to do their work. Many standard operating procedures have to be changed, the organization needs to change, and most people resist change. This process of changing the organization, its people, and the way they interact is the most expensive and lengthy part of the implementation and it is also the most difficult to predict.

Another problem regarding costs and cost perception is that a new system can rarely leverage the investment made on prior systems. Prior IS investments may have helped the organization advance or just survive, they may have changed the way it worked, but they are rarely leverageable by the next system. Managers often have trouble recognizing the concept of sunk costs regarding these past investments and insist that the new systems have to somehow leverage the prior ones. These attempts are generally costly and tend to delay the implementation of the new systems. The return on these salvaging investments tends to be negative. The only part of old systems that may be salvageable is the data and even that may result in more problems than advantages. It is often found that many of the initial bugs present in new implementation are not really due to the new system itself, but to the inconsistencies present in the salvaged data.

In summary, today a high-quality and comprehensive ERP is too expensive for most SMEs, and until a new business model appears or we have a technological jump, they will continue to be. Even if the licensing costs drop dramatically, the implementation cost will still be too high. The current ERP market has shown that an ERP that does not cost much to the organization (in terms of both time and money) is similar to a "free lunch": it hardly exists.

Interconnecting Different ERPs

ERPs have been very successful at integrating the functionality of all the different departments of an organization into a single application. This brought about the expectation that they would also be able to easily interconnect distinct organizations that used different systems, particularly if these organizations belonged to the same entity or the same industry. If ERPs can cross departmental boundaries, why can't they cross organizational boundaries? Unfortunately this expectation is far from being satisfied. In fact, ERPs are becoming an additional barrier between them.

In theory, a system that is oriented toward the resource should not be limited to boundaries that are different to the resource itself—such as departmental, organizational, and even national boundaries—and in fact as long as the different units use the same ERP, the boundaries are easily crossed. The problem comes when they use ERPs from different manufacturers or even different versions of the same ERP. The reason is quite obvious: to interconnect the departments, we implemented the same system across all of them; following the same philosophy, to interconnect the organizations we would need to implement the same system across all of them. However, the current market of ERP is quite large. There are many competitors and even with the latest corporate acquisitions, a monopoly or even an industry standard is very far in the horizon.

The barriers that ERPs are creating between enterprises are better understood with an example. Let us say that A needs a specific product that is not currently in stock in its own warehouse and therefore needs to purchase it. B and C are two companies that offer the product needed by A. A generates a request for proposal for the product to both B and C. Both A and C use the same ERP system and therefore can easily interconnect their systems. B also has an ERP, but it is a different brand and therefore it can hardly be interconnected with A's. The request to C and its response are done online and tend to be very fast. The request and response from B typically takes several phone calls and the transcription of an e-mail, all of which not only delay the process

but make it more prone to errors. Even if B is able to provide a better deal in terms of price, it is highly probable that A will buy the product from C since the process is much easier and faster. One could argue that the interconnection is one more property of the resource and therefore, overall, C's offer is a better one since it was easier and faster. However, an ERP should improve, not detract from the process. Furthermore, it is highly probable that A's management will later learn that they paid more than needed for the same product simply because their ERP was interconnected with the less favorable supplier. In such a case, it is common for management to react by disconnecting the ERP and returning to the old paper-and-pencil processes.

Another example where ERPs create barriers is when a company acquires a second company. Once acquired it is important to integrate the two in order to obtain economies of scale and reduce transaction costs. To integrate the two companies, it is then necessary to integrate or at least interconnect their information systems. Let us assume that both companies already had an ERP but each was developed by a different manufacturer. Management then has three choices: (1) interconnect both systems, (2) replace one system for the other, or (3) replace both systems for a third one. The first option would seem to be the most convenient one, but in practice is not really viable. The second option implies that one of the companies will have to make the investment for a second time. An investment from the financial point of view may be large but is probably accounted for earlier during the acquisition (if done properly); however, the problematic part is not so much the financial expense, but the repeated burden on the employees. Implementing an ERP takes a toll on the personnel, and doing it twice takes more than twice the toll. Employees tend to lose interest when they are required to do a task again, not because they did it incorrectly the first time but because the first one was lost due to management decisions. The third option is the most expensive one:

it implies twice the expense and twice the effort of the second one, but it may be necessary when the ERPs that are in place have been taken out of the market. That would be the case, for example, if one used J.D. Edwards or PeopleSoft; they would both have to move towards Oracle (since Oracle bought the other two and has announced that it does not plan to support them in the long term). This interconnection problem is currently one that complicates the analysis of mergers and acquisition, because this very large cost needs to be added to the final result or otherwise the M&A will most probably fail.

There are several well-accepted data exchange standards that help to avoid incompatibilities between systems as the one described above. The first established and commonly used one is called EDI (electronic data interchange), which precedes all of the Internet e-commerce protocols. In fact, when the Internet became popular, it started using EDI since it was assumed that the protocol is independent of the media used. However, EDI is not a single but a set of standards, some of which are more customized to the media used (or the user group) than others. There is EDI "ANSI ASC X12"; another recommended by the United Nations, UN/EDIFACT; and yet others that correspond to a specific industry or geographical region. See for example the Web site for the Data Interchange Standards Association (http://www.disa.org/), which advertises itself as "The Foremost Standards Community for E-Business Established as a not-for-profit…home for the development of cross-industry electronic business interchange standards." Moreover, the data that each ERP requires tends to be very different, not simply in naming conventions and format (which a good interface and common standards could solve) but in availability. For example, it is not simply that the identification code for an item is numeric in one system and alphanumeric in the other, but that one system may require a datum that the other does not even have. The dataset for

each form, document, or application tends to be different in each system, making their interconnections quite complex.

The enormous expansion of information networks, particularly the Internet, has produced several proposals for system interconnection which go much further than the mere adoption of simple data interchange standards. The well-known HTML and XML are oriented not only to standardize the exchange of data, but the offer and demand of IT functionality (which in this context, and particularly over the Web, is called services). Therefore we are now talking about a whole architectural platform oriented towards services or service-oriented applications (SOAs) (e.g., Erl, 2004).

Thus, while a data interchange standard establishes the data format of a purchase order, a service-oriented architecture establishes the format of the whole electronic purchase order, which can be used by a programmer to elaborate a form and publish it (on the Internet or an intranet) knowing that it could also be used by another system that shares the service-oriented platform. However, the SOA-oriented proposals are still far from solving all the practical interconnection problems faced by current ERPs. They are only prescriptions for programmers, not finished solutions for users. And there is still a heated discussion regarding the format of such services and even on the concept of SOA itself (see Jones, 2005; also the OASIS Web site at http://www.oasis-open.org/home/index.php).

In summary, the existence of data interchange standards and of service architectures is still not enough to solve the interconnection problem faced by today's ERPs, and in and by itself it is yet another problem—that of standards and architecture compatibility. Also, for practical purposes, for company A of our previous example, it is of little interest if the problem is one of ERP incompatibility, of data exchange standards compatibility, or of architectures oriented or not to services.

Transferring Best Practices

Another common expectation is that an established ERP contains best practices. Therefore, it is assumed that implementing that ERP will also bring about those best practices. However, are those best practices also appropriate for the new company? Many best practices are only optimal for the first one to implement them. Furthermore, the outcome is more than just the practice itself; best practices require a history that will never be present in the new place (see Peteraf, 1993; Wernerfelt, 1984, 1995). Thus, many of the expectations will never be satisfied.

To implement best practices is not simply to implement a new information system: the organization needs to change. However, most people resent change. Change is not easy and tends to be costly. Here we are then mixing two separate costs: that of implementing an ERP and that of improving the practices of the organization. However, cases abound where the ERP implementation was justified simply as a way to force the implementation of those best practices.

The implementation of best practices also assumes that the current practices are not as good. It is very viable for an organization to have great practices and still not have an ERP. However, since most ERPs already incorporate some type of practices, the organization will have to adapt its practices to those in the system. This organizational change may be detrimental to the final outcome since the organization will end up having the system it needed, but it will also have practices that are not as competitive as the ones it had before.

Another misconception regarding the transference of best practices through the implementation of ERPs is the assumption that they in fact include the best practices. Most ERPs have been developed to satisfy the needs of a given organization and are not based on a book or article written by an academic that describes the perfect practice. It is very expensive to develop an ERP, and to develop

it to the specifications and needs of someone who will not purchase it is inconceivable. It is clear that each enterprise will require modifications, so why develop it to a given standard that no one will have instead of developing it to the needs of a paying client and then modify it as needed for the next client anyway?

A Global ERP

A global ERP raises a different compatibility problem, which is not between ERPs nor of different versions of the same ERP—since the assumption is that the same version of the ERP is deployed throughout the entire organization—but of how it is implemented at each site. Let us remember that even the most standard ERP requires some degree of customization during implementation. Each site must deploy the system in a manner that is compatible with the local supply chain, the local regulations, and the local customs, while at the same time being consistent with the installations in other regions. This is a complex problem that no global organization can avoid. The problem is not simply of language: it involves issues that go from legal to cultural. For example, an organization that uses the same ERP in regions A and B may face the problem that a purchase order issued in region A must specify parameters that do not exist or have no equivalent in region B.

A global ERP is meant to help in moving data from one part of the organization to another, even if the organizations are in different countries, but this fluidity may create legal problems. Even in a normal internal data exchange or storage, a multinational organization using a single ERP may violate local privacy laws. In countries like Germany, for example, there are laws that restrict the type of information that may be exported. While a company may not be in the business of exporting data, if the server where the company stores its data is located in a country different to where the data is entered, edited, or consulted, then the company is exporting data from one country to another and therefore subject to any export limitations that either country may have.

These differences may be managed by setting operating parameters for each region; however, the term "setting parameters" is misleading since it would seem that it would be easy to simply set the regional parameters (like number and date format) and then forget about them. In reality, it is far more complex than that. Just developing a system that has comprehensive parameters is quite difficult. If those parameters include information on culture, traditions and customs, currency, and taxes for different regions, then the complexity increases. Furthermore, if the parameters need to consider the possibility of frequent changes on the values for each region (for example currency fluctuations, changes in the taxation systems and rates, and also needs to keep previous values in order to maintain historic data), then the complexity increases far more. A "foreign" system localized via parameters is generally less friendly and comprehensive than a "local" system or one custom made. The foreign (or global) system will have functions and data requirements that are not needed or applicable to the local site, and it will not have all the functions that the local site may need. It is common to find that a foreign system or one that has been "localized" is more easily rejected by its users than one that is made locally. It is never easy to convince the local users that the inconveniences presented by the global system are worthwhile for the organization as a whole, and therefore to all the sites and individuals involved.

Foreign systems also tend to generate a lot of hostility from the local IT personnel that have to provide the support to the system. To trust that support to foreign personnel is not only far more expensive, but it also tends to increase the hostility problems to sometimes critical levels, even to xenophobia.

Updating a global ERP is also more complex. It is very difficult to simultaneously update the program in all the sites, and therefore during the transition, version incompatibility problems arise. A system update is not only the process of changing the program that resides in a single or even multiple servers and to execute the necessary conversions in the data. The greatest hurdles are the organizational changes that are required for the new versions. Standard operating procedures need to be changed. Users need to be retrained on the new functionality, the new forms, and the new reports. Furthermore, the problem extends to cost assignments. New functionality generally means additional attributes, these attributes will be easily entered for the new data, but for the existing data many times will not be available and that could cause operating problems. Finally, not all regions will gain from the change, but since all of them need to update, they will resent the added costs that provide little to no benefit.

Successful implementations of global ERPs have required large investments in the development and use of methodologies, techniques, interfaces, and other tools designed for globalization. There is a tendency to solve cultural differences, not by imposing a foreign culture nor by excluding the local culture in the systems, but by understanding and including the local culture (even the local linguistic particularities) into the system. A lot has been done in this respect, but there is still much more that needs to be done.

FUTURE TRENDS

ERPs have come of age; many of them are mature systems with already more than 10 versions in their history. Nonetheless, the evolution of these systems will not stop here. However, it is highly probable that in the near future we will start seeing a new wave of systems replacing the current ERPs. We have a pretty good idea of what those systems may look like, but like all future visions, they are a possibility of what the future may be and not a certainty.

Future ERPs will have to satisfy the expectations listed above and much more. They will have to add new functionality to the existing ones and will probably alter the way that organizations interact with each other. Much like a new operating system (e.g., Windows Vista) must carry evolutionary baggage from the existing operating system (e.g., Windows XP) to leverage the existing applications, the new enterprise-wide information systems will also have to carry evolutionary baggage from the existing ERPs to leverage the data and user knowledge. However, no one can perfectly predict the future, and the new system may also become a revolutionary system that breaks away from the existing ones.

The future trends of ERPs require a whole new chapter, which is presented as the last chapter of this book.

CONCLUSION

Accounting—in its broadest sense—has come a long way since the clay tablets, the tabulating machines, and even the general ledger systems. ERPs are gigantic and complex systems that integrate many of the business information systems into a single monolithic application. They have advanced user interfaces that effectively leverage the existing technology and unify the enterprise. Nonetheless, below the hood, they still have an old database structure that does not correspond with the monolithic interface: it is fragmented and stores the information with plenty of unnecessary and inconvenient redundancies.

From an information standpoint and even from a systems point of view, the organization is no longer a group of departments working separately and independently towards a common goal, but a group of people using their specialized skills in processing and transforming resources that move freely throughout the organization. However, even though the managerial vision and understanding has realized that this process does not start nor

end inside the organization but goes across the entire supply chain, the technology has not caught up and the current wave of ERPs integrate the departments but are still islands of information that many times slow down the stream of information in the entire supply chain.

Furthermore, ERPs are so large and the problem they tackle is so complex that their implementation is very expensive and requires an army of consultants that disturb the normal operations for a very long period of time. An ERP, as its name continuously reminds users and developers, enforces extensive short, mid-, and long-term planning that while useful to some enterprises is not viable to many others and lacks many capabilities that are needed for dynamic short-term management of resources. ERPs are a need for all business enterprises, but they are still only found in an elite group of organizations that can develop the required planning and have the time and other resources needed to deploy these systems.

REFERENCES

Alexander, J.R. (2002). *History of accounting.* Retrieved from http://www.acaus.org/acc_his.html

Aspray, W. (Ed.). (1990). *Computing before computers.* Ames: Iowa State University Press.

Austrian, G. (1982). *Herman hollerith: Forgotten giant of information processing.* New York: Columbia University Press.

Bagranoff, N., Simkin, M., & Strand, C. (2005). *Core concepts of accounting information systems* (9th ed.). New York: John Wiley & Sons.

Bashe, C. J., Johnson, L. R., Palmer, J. H., & Pugh, E. W. (1985). *IBM's early computers.* Cambridge, MA: MIT Press.

Bond, B., Genovese, Y., Miklovic, D., Wood, N., Zrimsek, B., & Rayner, N. (2000). *ERP is dead—Long live ERP II.* New York: Gartner Group.

Brady, J.A., Monk, E., & Wagner, B.J. (2001). *Concepts in enterprise resource planning.* Boston: Thomson Learning.

Crosby, A.W. (1997). *The measure of reality: Quantification and western society, 1250-1600.* Cambridge: Cambridge University Press.

Davies, G. (2002). *A history of money from ancient times to the present day.* Cardiff: University of Wales Press.

Erl, T. (2004). *Service-oriented architecture: A field guide to integrating XML and Web services.* Upper Saddle River, NJ: Prentice Hall.

Ezzamel, M. (1994). The emergence of the 'accountant 'in the institutions of ancient Egypt. *Management Accounting Research (Sarasota), 5*(3-4), 221-247.

Graham, C., & Freely, M. (1990). Today, it's distributed MRP III. *Datamation, 36*(19), 117.

Hollander, A.S., Denna, E.L., & Cherrington, J.O. (1999). *Accounting, information technology, and business solutions.* Boston: Irwin/McGraw-Hill.

Jacobs, F.R., & Weston, F.C.J. (2007). Enterprise resource planning (ERP)—A brief history. *Journal of Operations Management, 25,* 357-363.

Jacobs, F.R., & Whybark, D.C. (2000). *Why ERP? A primer on SAP implementation.* Boston: Irwin/McGraw-Hill.

Jones, S. (2005). Toward an acceptable definition of service. *IEEE Software, 22*(3), 87-93.

Kleiner, A. (2004). The world's most exciting accountant. *Culture & Change, 26.*

Lee, T.A., Bishop, A.C., & Parker, R.H. (Eds.). (1996). *Accounting history from the Renaissance to the present: A remembrance of Luca Pacioli.* New York: Garland.

Louis, R.S. (1991). MRP III: Material acquisition system. *Production & Inventory Management, 11*(7), 26-48.

Mabert, V.A. (2007). The early road to material requirements. *Journal of Operations Management, 25,* 346.

Macve, R.H. (1996). Pacioli's legacy. In T.A. Lee, A.C. Bishop, & R.H. Parker (Eds.), *Accounting history from the Renaissance to the present: A remembrance of Luca Pacioli.* New York: Garland.

Martin, T.C. (1891). Counting a nation by electricity. *The Electrical Engineer, 12,* 521-530.

Peteraf, M.A. (1993). The cornerstones of competitive advantage: A Resource-based view. *Strategic Management Journal, 14,* 179-191.

Summer, M. (2005). *Enterprise resource planning.* Upper Saddle River, NJ: Pearson Prentice Hall.

Wernerfelt, B. (1984). A resource-based view of the firm. *Strategic Management Journal, 5,* 171-180.

Wernerfelt, B. (1995). The resource-based view of the firm: Ten years after. *Strategic Management Journal, 16,* 171-174.

Wexelblat, R.L. (Ed.). (1981). *History of programming languages.* New York: ACM Monograph Series.

Wight, O. (1982). *The executive's guide to successful MRP II (Oliver Wight Manufacturing).* New York: Simon & Schuster.

ADDITIONAL READING

Coomber, R. (2000). From ERP to XRP. *Telecommunications (international ed.), 34*(12), 72-73.

Møller, C. (2005). ERP II: A conceptual framework for next-generation enterprise systems? *Enterprise Information Management, 18*(4), 483.

Olsen, K. A., & Sætre, P. (2007). ERP for SMEs—Is proprietary software an alternative? *Business Process Management Journal, 13*(3), 379.

Quiescenti, M., Bruccoleri, M., La Commare, U., Noto La Diega, S., & Perrone, G. (2006). Business process-oriented design of enterprise resource planning (ERP) systems for small and medium enterprises. *International Journal of Production Research, 44*(18/19), 3797-3811.

Saran, C. (2005). Expense ahead with next-generation ERP. Retrieved November 2005 from http://www.computerweekly.com

Saran, C. (2007). Oracle extends sector specific ERP for SMEs. *Computer Weekly,* (July 31), 11.

Zhang, L., & Li, Y.C. (2006). Theory and practice of systems methodology in ERP implementation. *Systems Research and Behavioral Science, 23,* 219-235.

Chapter II
Enterprise Resource Planning Systems in a Global Environment

Paul Hawking
Victoria University, Australia

ABSTRACT

Companies around the world are placing increasing emphasis on strategy development and implementation. Some argue that this increased emphasis is in response to market forces of increased competition and globalization, and the need to be flexible and adaptive to the business environment. Strategy development and implementation is a multifaceted task reliant on a number of interdependent factors. One of these is the role of information technology which in recent times has become an integral part of most companies' strategies. This chapter discusses the role of strategy development and the importance of the alignment of business and IT strategies in a global environment. It discusses the role of enterprise resource planning systems on strategy development and how these systems underpin many strategic objectives companies strive for in a global environment.

STRATEGY DEVELOPMENT

There is a plethora of articles, books, and presentations on the importance of strategy in today's companies (Mintzberg, 1994; Porter & Miller, 1985; Kaplan & Norton, 1996). But even with this emphasis, companies struggle with their strategy development and implementation. This is reflected by a much cited reference to a *Fortune* magazine article which stated: "Less than 10% of strategies effectively formulated are effectively executed" (Kaplan & Norton, 1996). In other words more than 90% of companies that are able to create an effective strategy struggle to implement it.

A possible reason for this finding may be the diverse views of what a strategy is. The increased focus on strategy has resulted in the word "strategy" and its derivatives being concatenated with a broad range of terms in an attempt to imply a higher level of importance—for example, strategic planning, strategic learning, strategic thinking, strategic leadership, corporate strategy, business strategy, and functional strategy. This is further reinforced in Mintzberg's (1994) landmark article "The Rise and Fall of Strategic Planning," where he argues the virtues between strategic planning and strategic thinking. In terms of what a strategy actually is, Minztberg (1992) defined strategy as:

A plan—some sort of consciously intended course of action, a guideline (or set of guidelines) to deal with a situation. By this definition strategies have two essential characteristics: they are made in advance of the actions to which they apply, and they are developed consciously and purposefully.

He further attempted to define strategy from the perspectives of being a plan, a ploy, a position, a pattern, and a perspective (Ikavalko & Aaltonen, 2001). Porter's (1996) definition of strategy focuses more on the outcome: "the creation of a unique and valuable position, involving a different set of activities." He believes that a strategy is a way

an organization seeks to achieve its vision and mission, and that a successful strategy allows a company to capture and sustain a competitive advantage.

The emphasis on the effective development and implementation of strategies has resulted in a number of methodologies being developed to facilitate this process. Two of the more accepted methodologies are Porter's Value Chain (1985) and Kaplan and Norton's (1996) Balanced Scorecard. Both methodologies adopt a multifaceted approach involving a number of perspectives to strategy development and implementation. This assists in identifying the interrelationships between the various facets that impact upon strategy and facilitates the devolution of the strategy to operational terms.

The Balanced Scorecard (Kaplan & Norton, 1996) views strategy development and implementation from four interrelated perspectives:

- Financial
- Customer
- Internal
- Learning and growth

Figure 1. Scott Morton's (1991) five forces influencing strategic objectives

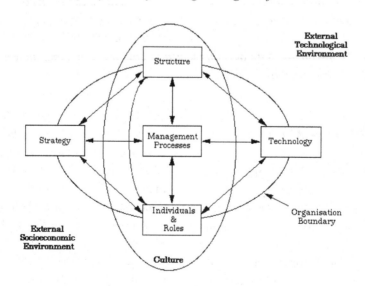

Within each of these strategic perspectives, a number of objectives are developed, and for each objective, key performance indicators (KPIs) are identified and targets determined. The methodology then encourages companies to identify initiatives whereby these targets can be obtained (BSC, 2003). For many companies this has involved the adoption of information technology solutions. Porter and Millar (1985) proposed an information intensity matrix to assist in identifying where information technology could be used strategically in the value chain. Somogyi and Galliers (1987) supported this concept by identifying how information technology could be used to assist companies in attaining competitive advantage in the various strategic focuses across the value chain.

Over the last three decades, companies have increasingly identified the importance of information technology in the achievement of strategic objectives. Scott Morton (1991) identified five interrelated factors that influence the attainment of strategic objectives. One of these factors was information technology (see Figure 1).

INFORMATION TECHNOLOGY ALIGNMENT

Even though the role of technology in strategy development and implementation has been identified, one of the major issues facing companies is the alignment of information technology (IT) strategy with their business strategy (CSC, 2000; Price Waterhouse, 1996). A recent survey of more than 300 CEOs and CIOs identified the alignment of IT and business strategy as their number one priority (Beal, 2003). The importance of this alignment has been identified as a priority for companies for the past 20 years (Brancheau, Janz, & Wetherbe, 1996). Bakos and Treacy (1986) argue that the increased attention being paid to the role IT has in the corporate strategy is mainly due to the publicity received by companies who

have gained significant advantage due to their IT utilization.

Researchers have validated the value to be gained from the alignment of IT and business strategies (Chan & Huff, 1993). Tallon and Kraemer (2003) in a survey of 63 companies found there was significant value gained from the alignment of these strategies. However lack of alignment can result in failure to gain value from IT investments (Gerstein & Reisman, 1982). Factors that have been identified and that have contributed to this lack of value realization include: lack of understanding of the potential of IT by senior management, lack of communication between IT managers and business managers, change management issues, lack of focus on opportunities for competitive advantage, and lack of availability or use of instruments to quantify possible business benefits (Gerstein & Reisman, 1982).

Broadbent and Weill (1993) define this IT-business alignment as "the extent to which business strategies were enabled, supported, and stimulated by information strategies" (p. 164). An alternative definition is: "the degree to which the information technology mission and objectives, and plans support and are supported by the business mission, objectives, and plans" (Reich & Benbasat, 2000, p. 82).

Both definitions involve a bi-directional alignment whereby other than the IS/IT strategy supporting the overall business strategy, it also can be a catalyst for the business strategy. Knoll and Jarvenpaa (1994) believe that this bi-directional reciprocal relationship is important for a company's competitive advantage—a view also supported by other researchers (Oesterle, 1991; Tallon & Kraemer, 2003).

Teo and King (1997) proposed four different scenarios or degrees of integration between the business and IT strategies. These included:

- **Administrative integration:** This is where there is littler relationship between the business and IT strategy.

- **Sequential integration:** This is where the business strategy is developed firstly in isolation to the IT strategy. The IT strategy is then developed to support the business strategy.
- **Reciprocal integration:** This is where a reciprocal and interdependent relationship exists between both strategies. The IT strategy is used to support and influence business strategy.
- **Full integration:** This occurs when both strategies are developed concurrently in an integrated manner.

This increased need for closer alignment has resulted in companies focusing on strategic information systems planning (SISP) and the development of methodologies to support this (Pant & Hsu, 1995; Hackney, Burn, & Dhillon, 2000). Hackney et al. (2000) identified the assumptions which underlie SISP and discussed their validity. They identified the main assumptions as:

- Business strategies must exist as a precursor to SISP.
- Business strategies are different from IT strategies.
- IT and business strategies can be aligned.

They argue that as business strategies evolve, it is often difficult for IT strategies to respond. They believe that IT applications often require an environment of stability and predictability to enable their development and that the maintenance or modifications to developed applications are often expensive and sometimes impossible. This requirement of stability and predictability may be at odds with the iterative approach to business strategy development. Accordingly, a business strategy may be constrained by the existing legacy IT systems which were developed and implemented in accordance with a previous business strategy. Another premise which underlies SISP

is that IT is a source of competitive advantage. For many organizations their IT systems make up a standard infrastructure to support generic information processing. Carr (2003) in his seminal article on the value of IT would argue that as IT solutions become generic and commoditized, there is no competitive advantage to be gained. He makes the analogy with the introduction and diffusion of electricity, whereby companies who initially adopted this technology gained a competitive advantage, but as other companies increasingly introduced the technology, the competitive advantage dissipated.

It can be argued that the technology in itself does not provide the competitive advantage, but how it is used to support business activities. From a different perspective Vitale (1986) proposed that rather than achieving a competitive advantage from the use of IT, IT can be used to avoid a competitive disadvantage. This is where a competitor has achieved a competitive advantage through the use of technology and a company rather than being disadvantaged by this adoption implements the same technology. Hackney et al. (2000) refer to Mintzberg's reasoning for strategic planning being an oxymoron and apply the same reasoning to SISP.

He further highlights the flaws in SISP when it is applied to the impact that enterprise resource planning (ERP) systems have had on business strategy (Hackney et al., 2000). ERP systems are widely adopted in a diverse range of organizations and define the business model on which they operate. For many companies they were relieved that an ERP system could help them define a business strategy and provide the IT infrastructure to support it (Davenport, 2000). Hackney et al. (2000) believe that ERP systems can provide a "dynamic stability" to the alignment of business and IT strategies. These systems can provide a stable predictable environment of which their usage can evolve in accordance with a company's business strategy.

ENTERPRISE RESOURCE PLANNING SYSTEMS

The term 'ERP systems' did not appear until the early 1990s. These systems evolved from material requirements planning (MRP), manufacturing resource planning (MRP II), computer integrated manufacturing (CIM), and other functional systems responsible for the automation of business transactions in the areas of accounting and human resources (Klaus, Rosemann, & Gable, 2000). The attempt to integrate all these systems coined the term 'ERP systems'.

Due to the purported benefits of ERP systems, many companies consider them as essential information systems infrastructure to be competitive in today's business world and provide a foundation for future growth. A survey of 800 top U.S. companies showed that ERP systems accounted for 43% of these companies' application budgets (Somer & Nelson, 2001). The market penetration of ERP systems varies considerably from industry to industry. A report by Computer Economics Inc. stated that 76% of manufacturers, 35% of insurance and healthcare companies, and 24% of federal government agencies already have an ERP system or are in the process of installing one (Stedman, 1999). The ARC Advisory Group (2006) estimated that the worldwide market for ERP systems was $16.67 billion in 2005 and is forecasted to surpass $21 billion in 2010. The major vendor of ERP systems is SAP with approximately 56% of the market.

Researchers believe the growth in the uptake of ERP systems is due to several factors: the need to streamline and improve business processes, and better manage information systems expenditure; competitive pressures to become a low-cost producer; increased responsiveness to customers and their needs; the need to integrate business processes, and provide a common platform and better data visibility; and as a strategic tool for the move towards electronic business (Davenport, Harris, & Cantrell, 2003; Hammer, 1999; Iggul-

den, 1999; Somer et al., 2001; Markus, Petrie, & Axline, 2001).

For many companies, underestimating the impact the system would have on their organization caused them initially to struggle with their ERP implementation. For some the barriers associated with the lack of skilled resources and inexperience with projects of this scope became insurmountable (Calegero, 2000). Davenport (2000) believes that ERP systems by their very nature impact on a company's strategy, organization, and culture. The move to become process rather than functionally focused and the resultant need for business process integration can result in a loss in competitive advantage in particular areas. However the potential benefits across the entire organization often outweigh the losses in individual areas (Holland & Light, 2001). The lack of understanding of the role ERP systems play within an organization often leads to conflict and hinders benefit realization of the ERP system implementation.

As mentioned previously, for many companies their business strategy is now being influenced by the existence of an ERP system. This is reflected in the views of researchers who believe that a bi-directional reciprocal relationship between the business strategy and the IT strategy is important for a company's competitive advantage and that the IT strategy can act as a stimulus for the overall business strategy (Oesterle, 1991; Tallon & Kraemer, 2003; Knoll & Jarvenpaa,1994; Teo & King, 1997). Companies have made a significant investment in their ERP system and realize that it has the potential to support new strategic directions. This contention is reflected in the landmark Deloitte study (1998), where 49% of the sample considered an ERP implementation to be a continuous process, as they expect to continually find value propositions from their system. This was also the finding of other researchers (Davenport et al., 2004). They surveyed 163 organizations in Europe, the United States, and Australia who had implemented an ERP system and found that no company had finished implementing the system to support all business processes. Over time the benefits companies expect to achieve from their ERP system changes in accordance with their business strategy and the improved functionality provided by the ERP vendors.

Accordingly ERP vendors added increased functionality and "bolt on" solutions to extend the reach and penetration of the ERP system, while at the same time increasing its strategic value. In 2000, the Gartner Group coined the term ERPII to describe such offerings and defined the term as a "business strategy and set of industry domain specific applications that build customer and shareholder value by enabling and optimizing enterprise and inter-enterprise collaborative operational and financial processes." They considered that ERPII would have a global focus and would extend the current ERP systems by incorporating customer relationship management (CRM), supply chain management (SCM), and other strategic solutions (Mohamed, 2002).

ERP Usage Models

Many researchers and analysts have attempted to develop models to illustrate the evolution of ERP benefits and ERP usage. Five main models have been identified from the literature: Deloitte (1998), Holland and Light (2001), Cap Gemini Ernst and Young (2002), Davenport et al. (2003), and Nolan and Norton (2000). These models are based on the premise that companies initially implement a functional component of their ERP system. After a period of time this component's usage is accepted and becomes part of normal work practices. This stabilization results in companies learning from its usage and investigating how to extend this functionality across the company and/or implement other functionality. In other words there is a significant learning curve associated with ERP usage and capabilities.

All the ERP usage models identify the evolutionary nature of how companies use these

types of systems to gain greater business value. The use of these systems moves from automating transactional processing to more strategic analytics and forecasting to assist in improved decision making. This is reflected in the two major studies that investigated the drivers and benefits of ERP usage (Deloitte, 1998; Davenport et al., 2003). The earlier study identified the key drivers/benefits of an ERP implementation as operational factors: Y2K compliancy, and disparate systems limiting information integration. Davenport et al. (2003) identified more strategic drivers/benefits in terms of improved management decision making and financial management. The different models and previous research indicate that there is a strong interdependent relationship between business and IT strategies, especially in companies that adopted ERP systems. ERP vendors accordingly have evolved their product offerings from a transactional focus to a more analytical strategic focus. This has created an extremely complex ERP environment where solutions are interdependent of each other. Many of the solutions such as customer relationship management, supplier relationship management (SRM), business intelligence (BI), and supply chain management extend the transactional focused ERP system while at the same time they are reliant on its existence. This means that the implementation of an ERP system could be considerably different from company to company due to the range of functionality and solutions available. This evolution of ERP systems has seen the increased usage of the term "enterprise wide systems."

The usage models reflect the evolutionary nature of ERP systems in supporting various strategic goals. However they do not identify specific functionality usage or solutions implemented in each stage. They indicate goals of ERP usage and organizational focus. The identification of specific functionality and solutions relevant to each phase can assist companies in developing their ERP and IT strategy. It could provide them with a roadmap while at the same time providing input into the overall business strategy. There is limited if any research in this area, and the outcomes of this type of research would greatly assist companies with decision making in relation to their ERP strategy.

These usage models tend to cover additional functionality rather than considering the penetration of functionality across the company. This becomes increasingly important when considering global and transnational companies. These companies face pressures from a number of different fronts and are becoming increasing reliant on quality information through business intelligence solutions to assist with effective decision making. However, what underpins the access to quality information is the standardization of master data definitions, business processes, and key performance indicators. Many companies struggle with this standardization in a single country operation, but the problem grows exponentially in global operations.

Many global operations are using ERP systems to support their operations in an attempt to provide this standardization. However there is the continual struggle between balancing global standardization and local customization. The concept of shared services, whereby corporate-wide activities are centralized and standardized, are becoming increasingly prevalent. The remainder of this chapter discusses how one company implemented an ERP system to support its global operations.

CASE STUDY

A case study research methodology was used for an exploratory look at how a company uses an ERP system to support its overall business strategy. The case study focused on a large company involved in the process manufacturing industry. The data collection process will include examination of existing documentation, content analysis of internal documentation, and interview of key

personnel. Yin (1994) suggests that a single, in-depth case study is an appropriate research approach under a number of conditions, one being that it is a critical case whereby it meets all the necessary conditions for testing a theory.

Initial contact was made with case study company (Fonterra) after representatives of the company presented at an ERP user group conference. They agreed to participate in the research activity. Background material about the company was collected from the company's Web site. Further contact was made with the company in February 2004, and a key staff member was identified to be interviewed. The interview was conducted at the company's head office in Auckland, New Zealand, in late February. During the interview a number of documents relating to company strategy and IT strategy were supplied. A follow-up interview was conducted with another key staff member in October 2004 via telephone conference call.

Company Background

The dairy industry is New Zealand's largest industry which accounts for in excess of 20% of the country's exports and 7% of its gross domestic product (GDP) (Fonterra, 2004a). To facilitate the export market, in the 1930s the New Zealand Government established the New Zealand Dairy Board in partnership with the numerous small dairy companies. Over the years in an attempt to achieve greater efficiencies and economies of scale, there has been numerous mergers of the smaller companies. By the end of the 1990s there existed four main dairy companies, but it was realized that extra efficiencies and maintenance of competitive advantage could not be achieved unless a major reform was undertaken. In conjunction with a consulting company, the industry identified three major focuses for its future strategy. These included:

* Maintain competitive advantage as low-cost producer of diary products

- Improve performance of existing business
- Pursue aggressive growth opportunities

A number of options were considered to how best to achieve these strategic goals, and it was concluded that "a single, integrated company that collects, manufactures and sells commodities and ingredients would create [the] most value" for the stakeholders (Fonterra, 2001, p. 5).

The proposed consolidated company, which was later to be known as Fonterra, was expected to achieve an annual savings of $310 million by the end of the third year. These savings would be achieved by a combination of: elimination of duplicated facilities and activities; an increase in productivity through the integration of manufacturing, marketing, and distribution activities; and the exploitation of new markets technology and biotechnology opportunities.

Fonterra Corporation

Fonterra is a New Zealand dairy cooperative formed in 2001 (Fonterra, 2004a). The company is responsible for the collection and processing of more than 96% of New Zealand's milk involving more than 13,000 farmers. It has an annual turnover of US$6.8 billion, which accounts for 20% of New Zealand's export receipts and 7% of its GDP; it is the largest dairy ingredients producer in the world. Its supply chain extends from New Zealand to customers in 140 countries. To support this supply chain, the company has sites in 40 countries and a workforce of more than 20,000.

The three organizations, which merged to form Fonterra, were culturally, structurally, and operationally significantly different. In an attempt to achieve its strategic goals, Fonterra developed a number of strategies to facilitate the changes that needed to occur in the company. The company identified seven strategic themes and associated metrics:

- **Lowest cost supplier of commodity dairy products:** Fonterra believed that this was its main competitive advantage and aimed to achieve an improvement across its supply chain of at least 3% per annum.
- **Leading price and inventory manager in the global commodity market:** Fonterra identified opportunities to increase its global markets through access to improved information. This will enable Fonterra to develop enhanced analytical approaches to supply chain management and product development.
- **Effective developer of dairy ingredients partnerships in selected markets:** Fonterra identified the need for improved integration and collaboration with key customers. These improved interactions will strengthen relationships with existing customers and provide opportunities to establish strong relationships with new customers.
- **Leading specialty milk components innovator and solutions provider:** Fonterra believes there are opportunities to develop new innovative products customized for particular customers and niche markets.
- **Leading consumer nutritional milks marketer:** Fonterra believes that there is an increased demand for nutritional dairy products, and accordingly strengths in branding and go-to-market capabilities need to be enhanced in existing and new markets.
- **Leading dairy marketer to food service in key markets:** Fonterra believes that opportunities exist in extending the company's presence in the food service market, and that this can occur by the development of innovative products and enhance its product and distribution coverage.
- **Develop integrated strategies for four key regional markets:** Fonterra believes that there are opportunities to be realized in the global market, but there is a need for integrated strategies across the value chain

which maximizes opportunities while at the same time manages risks (Fonterra, 2004a).

Jedi Project

Fonterra developed a number of strategic projects to facilitate change in accordance with its strategic themes. One of these projects was titled "Jedi" which commenced in November 2003. The Jedi project consisted of 40 interconnected projects with the common goal of ensuring that Fonterra would realize its strategic goals as a leader in the dairy industry. The project's underlining objectives were to provide a global business model which involved common business processes, systems, and classification of customers with a focus on simplicity. Specific goals of the project were (Fonterra, 2004b, p. 20):

- "Operations work well with all other parts of the ingredients business."
- "Managers have a better understanding of costs so they can make the right decisions."
- "All the people working in Operations have the skills and equipments they need to do their jobs to the best of their ability."
- "We have one way of doing things across the manufacturing sites."
- "People want to actively share best practice and good ideas with other sites."
- "Existing projects are completed and all projects work towards common goals."

The Jedi project consisted of four major components: sales network structure (SNS), global customer service center (GCSC), global back office (GBO), and empower.

Sales Network Structure

Before the commencement of the Jedi project, Fonterra's customers receive the same level of service independent of the revenue they gener-

ate. The sales network structure was designed to segment Fonterra's customers in an attempt to customize the level of interaction and service relevant to the customer's revenue stream. This would enable Fonterra to strengthen the collaboration and integration with key customers and thus deepen the relationship. The customers were segmented into four different categories:

- **Segment 1:** Large customers who account for more than 40% of Fonterra's revenue
- **Segment 2:** Customers who provide good business and have good growth potential
- **Segment 3:** Customers who provide a steady stream of income but have limited growth
- **Segment 4:** Intermittent customers

The customers in segments 1 and 2 would receive a highly personalized sales channel through account managers, while segment 3 and 4 customers would use self-service facilities available in the global customer service center. The sales network structure proposes how offices around the world can best service each customer segment. As part of this service, the global customer service center will be established.

Global Customer Service Center

This component is designed to be a link between sales activities and order fulfillment, and will directly service both account managers acting on behalf of customers and customers dealing with the center directly. The functions will be centralized and located in Auckland, New Zealand. Due to the organization's sales network, the GCSC needs to provide worldwide support, operate 24x7, and will have multilingual facilities with approximately 120 staff members. One of the perceived advantages of this service will be a common price list, which did not exist previously and caused the company quite a lot of embarrassment when large customers could quote different prices for the same product from different sources.

Global Back Office

This component is responsible for the handling of the majority of Fonterra's accounting and human resource transactions. It will provide a mechanism to standardize business processes in these areas while at the same time deliver efficiencies through centralization and economies of scale. The company realized finance, human resources, and the associated information systems are key areas which underpin operations across the supply chain. This realization reinforces Porter's view of the value chain (Porter, 1985). Fonterra believes that once "best practice" is adopted in these areas throughout the company, then greater attention can be paid to customer-focused operations.

Empower

This supply chain management component encompasses order management, logistics, and planning. It is envisaged to change the traditional business focus from one that was reactive to a more proactive approach whereby people would work to a plan. In other words it would allow customer orders to be matched to planned customer demand. This component is expected to drive efficiencies across the supply chain by implementing standard end-to-end processes and business rules, and integrating planning and execution.

Information Systems Strategy and Jedi

Fonterra believed that the effective selection and use of information system solutions would be essential to the project's success and thus success of the overall strategy. As the company was the result of a merger of a number of existing companies, there was already a plethora of IS solutions implemented. These included various ERP systems such as J.D. Edwards, Oracle, and PeopleSoft, which indicated a considerable investment by each corporate entity.

The first phase of the Jedi project was the implementation of Empower which had an aggressive implantation with a go-live date at the end of March 2004. It was decided to implement SAP's supply chain management solution to support these functions at an expected cost of $NZ120 million (Gifford, 2004). SAP was selected as it was considered to have incorporated "best business practice" and would ensure standardized end-to-end processes in accordance with the project's goals. One of the issues with the existing SCM solutions was that they were extensively customized, which resulted in considerable maintenance problems, and therefore it was decided that to facilitate future upgrades and the global rollout of the SCM solution, minimal customization would occur in the Empower project. To facilitate integration between its various components and across the global supply chain, Fonterra implemented the WebMethods integration solution.

The second phase of the Jedi project involves the rollout of GCSC and GBO. The sales network structure was implemented in the United States with an expected go-live date in August 2004. The rollout around the rest of the world occurred in 2005. SAP solutions were implemented to underpin this phase of the Jedi project. The financial and human resource modules were implemented to support the global back office component. This will replace in-house systems and an existing Oracle ERP system. The financial module will incorporate general ledger, accounts payable and receivable, and assets management. While the HR component will involve the implementation, the "manager's desktop," and the "employee self service" (ESS). The manager's desktop enables managers quick access to information and transactions related to employee who they are responsible for, while the ESS solutions use a Web-based interface which enables employees to view and maintain personal details, as well as quick access to transactions relating to their working environment such as applications for leave, overtime, training, and so forth. A quick win for this solution will be the savings gained by the implementation of electronic pay slips.

Although the company has implemented SAP solutions, a number of existing ERP systems will remain in some areas of distribution and financial activities in factories. This will require a number of interfaces to be developed to Jedi solutions. The non-ERP systems will remain until ROI is achieved, but eventually will be phased out for SAP solutions. Fonterra intends to adopt a "vanilla" approach to its implementation whereby minimal customization of the system occurs. This is expected to facilitate the global rollout and future upgrades, and minimize the impact of future acquisitions. There will be a single implementation of the SAP system (instance) in New Zealand, and this will be based on a global template which will have restricted localization in each of the 40 countries where it will be rolled out. This ensures standardized definitions and business processes throughout the company. This will facilitate the information flow, and thus improved reporting and decision making.

Fonterra has a number of other proposed implementations to support their strategic directions which include data warehousing, advanced planner and optimization, and customer relationship management. Eventually the company will have replaced 15 core systems with SAP solutions.

The implementation of the ERP system is considered by Fonterra as fundamental to its business transformation in a global environment. The company believes that in its global operations, it has moved from autonomous independent localized operations to standardized business processes, rules, and configurations. Fonterra has centralized its business processing and customer service center as well as centralized planning and supply chain management. It now believes that the company is in a position to quickly adjust its corporate strategy to market demands.

CONCLUSION

When companies expand their operations globally, they struggle with their information systems infrastructure to support the extended business processes. ERP systems are seen as a tool to assist in this process. However the ERP systems global model varies from company to company. This is dependent on the level of standardization of processes, master data, reporting, and user interfaces required. The greater level of standardization usually occurs at the expense of localization needs. The case study company has opted for a global template to ensure an increased level of standardization.

FUTURE TRENDS

Globalization of ERP systems is becoming a major issue for many companies. There is an increased tendency to implement a global template to ensure greater standardization and compliance. As companies' global ERP systems implementations become more mature, there may be modifications made to the global template to address localization issues. The adoption of service-oriented architecture technology will assist in this variation to the global template.

REFERENCES

ARC Advisory Group. (2006). *ERP market to exceed $21 billion, says ARC advisory.* Retrieved October 2006 from http://www.tekrati.com/research/News.asp?id=6828

Bakos, J.Y., & Treacy, M. (1986, June). Information technology and corporate strategy: A research perspective. *MIS Quarterly.*

Beal, B. (2003, October 15). *The priority that persists.* Retrieved November 8, 2003, from http://searchcio.techtarget.com/originalContent/0,289142,sid19_gci932246,00.html

Benbasat, I., Goldstein, D., & Mead, M. (1987). The case research strategy in studies of information systems. *MIS Quarterly, 11*(3).

Brancheau, J., Janz, B., & Wetherbe, J. (1996). Key issues in information management. *MIS Quarterly, 20.*

Broadbent, M., & Weill, P. (1993). Improving business and information strategy alignment: Learning from the banking industry. *IBM Systems Journal, 32*(1), 162-179.

Brown, C., & Vessey, I. (2001). Nibco's "big bang." *Communications of the AIS, 5*(1).

BSC. (2003). *Building the balanced scorecard—Practitioner's guidebook.* Sydney: Balanced Scorecard Collaborative.

Cap Gemini Ernst and Young. (2002). *Adaptive ERP.* Retrieved from http://www.capgemini.com

Calegero, B. (2000). Who is to blame for ERP failure? *Sunsaver,* (June).

Carlino, J. (1999). *AMR research unveils report on enterprise application spending and penetration.* Retrieved July 2001 from http://www.amrresearch.com/press/files/99823.asp

Carr, N. (2003). IT doesn't matter. *Harvard Business Review, 81*(5).

Carton, F., & Adam, F. (2003). Analyzing the impact of enterprise resource planning systems roll-outs in multi-national companies. *Electronic Journal of Information Systems Evaluation, 6*(2).

Cavaye, A. (1996). Case study research: a multi-faceted approach for IS. *Information Systems Journal, 63.*

Chan, Y., & Huff, S. (1993). Investigating information systems strategic alignment. In *Proceedings of the 14ᵗʰ International Conference of Information Systems,* Florida.

Chan, R., & Roseman, M. (2001). Integrating knowledge into process models—A case study. In *Proceedings of the 12ᵗʰ Australasian Conference on Information Systems,* Southern Cross University, Australia.

CSC. (2001). *Critical issues of information systems management.* Retrieved November 2002 from http://www.csc.com/aboutus/uploads/CI_Report.pdf

Davenport, T. (2000). *Mission critical—realizing the promise of enterprise systems.* Boston: Harvard Business School Press.

Davenport, T., Harris, J., & Cantrell, S. (2003). *Enterprise systems revisited: The director's cut.* Accenture.

Davenport, T., Harris, J., & Cantrell, S. (2004). Enterprise systems and ongoing change. *Business Process Management Journal, 10*(1).

Deloitte. (1998). *ERPs second wave.*

Fonterra. (2001). *Capital structure.*

Fonterra. (2004a). *About Fonterra.* Retrieved October 2004 from http://www.fonterra.com

Fonterra. (2004b). *An introduction to Jedi.*

Fonterra. (2004c). *Jedi program: Key message guidelines.*

Gable, G. (1994). Integrating case study and survey research methods: An example in information systems. *European Journal of Information Systems, 3*(2).

Gerstein, M., & Resman, H. (1982). Creating competitive advantage with computer technology. *Journal of Business Strategy, 3*(1).

Giiford, A. (2004). JEDI has kicked out the boss at Fonterra. *New Zealand Herald,* (June 29).

Hackney, R., Burn, J., & Dhillon, G. (2000). Challenging assumptions for strategic information systems planning: Theoretical perspectives.

Communications of the AIS, 3, article 9.

Hammer, M. (1999). How process enterprises really work. *Harvard Business Review,* (November/December).

Holland, C., & Light, B. (2001). A stage maturity model for enterprise resource planning systems use. *The Database for Advances in Information Systems, 32*(2).

Iggulden, T. (Ed.). (1999). Looking for payback. *MIS,* (June).

Ikavalko, H., & Aaltonen, P. (2001). Middle managers' role in strategy implementation—middle managers view. In *Proceedings of the 17ᵗʰ EGOS Colloquium,* Lyon, France.

Kaplan, R., & Norton, D. (1996). *The balanced scorecard: Translating strategy into action.* Boston: Harvard Business School Press.

Klaus, H., Rosemann, M., & Gable, G.G. (2000). What is ERP? *Information Systems Frontiers, 2*(2), 141-162.

Knoll, K., & Jarvenpaa, S.L. (1994). Information technology alignment or 'fit' in highly turbulent environments: The concept of flexibility. In *Proceedings of SIGCPR 1994,* Alexandria, VA.

Lee, A. (1989). Case studies as natural experiments. *Human Relations, 422.*

Markus, L., Petrie, D., & Axline, S. (2001). Bucking the trends, what the future may hold for ERP packages. In Shanks, Seddon, & Willcocks (Eds.), *Enterprise systems: ERP, implementation and effectiveness.* Cambridge: Cambridge University Press.

Martinsons, M. (2004). ERP in China: One package, two profiles. *Communications of the ACM, 47*(7).

Mintzberg, H. (1992). Five Ps for strategy. In H. Mintzberg & J.B. Quinn (Eds.), *The Strategy Process.* Englewood Cliffs, NJ: Prentice Hall.

Mintzberg, H. (1994). The fall and rise of strategic planning. *Harvard Business Review,* 107-114.

Mohamed, M. (2002). Points of the triangle. Retrieved May 2004 from http://www.intelligent-enterprise.com/020903/514feat2_1.jhtml?/supply_chain%7Csupply

Nolan and Norton Institute. (2000). *SAP benchmarking report 2000.* Melbourne: KPMG Melbourne.

Oesterle H. (1991). Generating business ideas based on information technology. In R. Clarke & J. Cameron (Eds.), *Managing information technology's organisational impact II.* Amsterdam: Elsevier/North-Holland.

Pant, S., & Hsu, C. (1995). Strategic information systems: A review. In *Proceedings of the 1995 IRMA Conference,* Atlanta, GA.

Porter, M. (1985). *Competitive advantage: Creating and sustaining superior performance.* New York: The Free Press.

Porter, M. (1996). What is strategy? *Harvard Business Review, (November-December).*

Porter, M., & Millar, V. (1985). How information gives you competitive advantage. *Harvard Business Review, 63*(4).

Price Waterhouse. (1996). *Information technology review 1995/96.* UK.

Reich, B., & Benbasat, I. (2000). Factors that influence the social dimension of alignment between business and information technology objectives. *MIS Quarterly, 24.*

Scott Morton, M.S. (1991). *The corporation of the 1990s: Information technology and organizational transformation.* New York: Oxford University Press.

Somer, T., & Nelson, K. (2001). The impact of critical success factors across the stages of enterprise resource planning systems implementations.

In *Proceedings of the 34th Hawaii International Conference on System Sciences,* Hawaii.

Somogyi, E., & Galliers, R. (1987). *Towards strategic information systems.* Cambridge: Abacus Press.

Stedman, C. (1999). What's next for ERP? *Computerworld, 33*(August 16).

Tallon, P., & Kraemer, K. (2003). *Investigating the relationship between strategic alignment and IT business value: The discovery of a paradox, relationship between strategic alignment and IT business value.* Hershey, PA: Idea Group.

Teo, T., & King, W. (1997) Integration between business planning and information systems planning: An evolutionary contingency perspective. *Journal of Management Information Systems, 14.*

Vitale, M. (1986). The growing risks of information systems success. *MIS Quarterly, 10.*

Walsham, G. (2000). *Globalization and IT: Agenda for research.* Boston: Kluwer Academic.

Yin, R. (1994). *Case study research, design and methods* (2nd ed.). Newbury Park, CA: Sage.

ADDITIONAL READING

Cotran, K., Buchmeiser, U. et al. (2005). HR's role in implementing JTI's global ERP system. *Strategic HR Review, 4*(5), 24-27.

Holland, C., & Light, B. (1999). Global enterprise resource planning implementation. In *Proceedings of HICSS 1999.*

Holland, C.P., & Ribbers, P. (2003). Introduction to international examples of large-scale systems: Theory and practice. *Communications of AIS,* (11), 332-333.

McAdam, R., & Galloway, A. (2005). Enterprise resource planning and organizational innovation: A management perspective. *Industrial Management & Data Systems, 105*(3).

Madapusi, A., & D'Souza, D. (2005). Aligning ERP systems with international strategies. *Information Systems Management, 22*(1), 7-17.

Sandoe, K., Corbitt, G., & Boykin, R. (2001). *Enterprise integration.* New York: John Wiley & Sons.

Sarkis, J., & Sundarraj, R.P. (2003). Managing large-scale global enterprise resource planning systems: A case study at Texas Instruments. *International Journal of Information Management, 23,* 431-442.

Shang, S. (2005). Enterprise systems in international business operations: The benefits and problems of fit in international enterprise systems implementation. In *Proceedings of the 11th Americas Conference on Information Systems,* Omaha.

Sheu, C., Yen, H.R. et al. (2003). The effect of national differences on multinational ERP implementation: An exploratory study. *Total Quality Management & Business Excellence, 14*(6).

Skok, W., & Doringer, H. (2001). Potential impact of cultural differences on enterprise resource planning (ERP) projects. *EJISDC, 7*(5), 1-8.

Utecht, K.M., Hayes, R.B. et al. (2004). Enterprise resource planning and the competitive advantage: The ease of integrating information between corporate headquarters in the United States and factories in Mexico. *Competitiveness Review, 14*(1/2), 13-17.

Yeh, C.-T., Miozzo, M. et al. (2006). The importance of being local? Learning among Taiwan's enterprise solutions providers. *Journal of Enterprise Information Management, 19*(1), 30-49.

Chapter III
A Conceptual Framework for Developing and Evaluating ERP Implementation Strategies in Multinational Organizations

Kai Kelzenberg
RWTH Aachen University, Germany

Thomas Wagner
RWTH Aachen University, Germany

Kai Reimers
RWTH Aachen University, Germany

ABSTRACT

The chapter develops generic strategies for the specification and implementation of an enterprise resource planning (ERP) system in a multinational company. After the presentation of a framework for categorizing companies by their global business orientation, ERP strategies corresponding to each category are derived. Subsequently, various implementation strategies are developed for each type of ERP strategy; they provide decision makers with a high degree of freedom in specifying an implementation strategy in accordance with a company's strategic goals. The results are summarized in a phase model; the overall approach is illustrated by two polar cases.

INTRODUCTION

Market demands are becoming more and more dynamic, forcing organizations to be flexible in order to satisfy the needs of their customers (Mabert, Soni, & Venkataramanan, 2001). At the same time, organizations face an ever increasing competition through globalization. As a result of both phenomena, business organizations tend to act in networks of tightly or loosely coupled productive units. Bartlett and Ghoshal (1998) identify four different business orientations which can be used to describe the structures of multi-national companies (MNCs). Starting from these four business orientations, this chapter presents a conceptual framework for deriving enterprise resource planning (ERP) implementation strategies in multinational organizations. This is motivated by the findings of prior research that shows the importance of aligning the IT strategy with a firm's business strategy (Ward, Griffiths, & Whithmore, 1990; Earl, 1993).

However, organizational contingencies are seldom considered in the literature on ERP implementations which focuses on critical success factors (CSFs) (Holland & Light, 1999; Akkermanns & van Helden, 2003) or critical issues and risk factors in general (Bingi, Sharma, & Godla, 1999; Sumner, 2000; Scott, 1999; Hong & Kim, 2002; Gosh & Gosh, 2003). The framework of Bartlett and Ghoshal has previously been applied in the IS field. Reimers (1997) shows how IT can be managed in the transnational organization, and Madapusi and D'Souza (2005) have used the framework to develop recommendations regarding the way ERP systems should be configured in multinational companies. While these authors also discuss the issue of appropriate implementation strategies, this discussion focuses on the issue of a 'big bang' vs. a phased implementation approach, which we deem too narrow. Rather, we propose that the configuration of an ERP system should follow an appropriate ERP implementation strategy which comprises many more issues than that of a

big bang vs. a phased implementation approach. In this chapter, we offer a framework which helps to conceptually organize the issues that should be considered in deriving an ERP implementation strategy for multinational companies and which also helps to fine-tune the implementation strategy as the implementation process unfolds.

The remainder of this chapter is organized as follows: First we will give a short review of different views on ERP before we derive ERP strategies from an organization's business orientation. Subsequently we will discuss different ERP implementation strategies. Afterwards, our framework is presented and illustrated by two examples. The chapter ends with a discussion.

BACKGROUND

The implementation of an enterprise resource planning system in a company can have different degrees of complexity which will be conditioned by the following items (this list is limited by the scope of the chapter; several more perspectives could be added in future work):

1. ERP definition
2. ERP strategy
3. Implementation strategy

Referring to O'Leary (2000), ERP systems "provide firms with transaction processing models that are integrated with other activities of the firm" (p. 7). Moreover, they can reduce information asymmetries and help to create one view on all relevant data which can be shared across the whole organization. This concept is based on a single database that contains all data of several functional and/or local areas. Bancroft, Sprengel, and Seip (1996) offer a similar definition of ERP systems focusing on SAP/R3. For them, an ERP system consists of "one database for the entire corporation without any data redundancy and with a clear definition of each [data] field" (p.

17). Firestone (2002) adds another perspective on ERP as he mentions that customers want ERP for decision-making support, although there are other (software) systems that are more specialized in this area. Markus and Tanis (2000) add the opinion of some ERP vendors who state that their software "met all the information-processing needs of the companies that adopted them" (p. 174). This includes an automatic data transfer facility between several functions within the system as well as a shared database for all applications.

These conditions could be satisfied fairly easily if one was dealing with a single-site company, but the more interesting question is what happens if a company is composed of different sites with different ranges of functionality, for example, a large producer with several distribution centers around the world or a federation of several producing and distributing companies that form one major company. Is it possible, referring to the above mentioned authors, to call the installed system across all members of such a unit one big ERP system?

Following such a scenario, what would have to be done to standardize the data of each business unit in such an organization and which benefits would result from this effort? How far should standardization go and which areas could be standardized in a useful manner? Moreover, who should be in charge of choosing and designing an ERP system fitting to a company's requirements and of keeping the system up and running? Which organizational units have to be established to lead this venture to success?

Many of these questions could not be answered in a general way but they should help to consider the different aspects of the design process of such a project. The presented framework tries to support the decision makers with a structured approach facing this task.

If the ERP system has been designed in accordance with the company's requirements, an IT strategy focusing on implementation has to be developed. Karimi and Konsynski (1991) state that an IT strategy has to be derived from the business strategy. Similarly, an ERP strategy has to be developed which shows the long-term goals to be reached by the use of an ERP system. Clemmons and Simon (2001) state that a misalignment between business and ERP strategy often causes ERP implementation delays and failures. (As will be shown later, there is a need for a centralized authority which is in charge of deciding whether a global ERP strategy is to be developed, and, if so, how to enforce it within the whole company.) In the subsequent sections the work of Bartlett and Ghoshal (1998) helps to identify four different types of business orientations for companies. These are generic views which—in reality—will be mixed in a number of ways, but for developing a general ERP strategy they will provide important insights regarding the questions of when one could speak of a global ERP strategy and how important it is to have one organizational entity for the whole company that can develop and promote the ERP strategy for all sites. In this chapter, we define an ERP strategy as containing the range of system components that have to be installed in each site, as well as the interfaces and data formats in which data transfer should be done. The chapter will go on to show different generic ways how to realize an ERP system according to the global ERP strategy (ERP implementation strategy). In this context, the problems of tailoring an ERP system fitting the company's requirements as described by Lehm, Heinzl, and Markus (2001) will be outlined. Since not all strategies require different implementation strategies, some can be discussed jointly.

This chapter focuses mainly on the first phase(s) of an ERP life-cycle (cf. Esteves & Pastor, 1999, or Markus, Axline, & Tanis, 2000). Given its academic and practical attention, the implementation phase seems to be a crucial one that motivates our focus. The consideration of all phases is beyond the scope of this chapter; for a comprehensive literature review of all phases, we refer to Esteves and Pastor (2001).

BUSINESS ORIENTATION

In 1998, Bartlett and Ghoshal published a book in which they describe a couple of companies and how their way of doing business differs. Based on an analysis of these differences, the authors conclude why one firm is more successful with its strategy than another. They develop a framework consisting of four types of multinational companies. Each type is characterized by a distinct strategy and business orientation that deals with the allocation and interconnection of the company's resources. The term "resource" is not described in detail but refers to skills, personnel, money, knowledge, and so on. Applying these insights to the topic of this chapter, ERP systems should optimize the use of such resources. The different business orientations will be explained in the subsequent sections and provide the basis for deriving appropriate global ERP strategies which are discussed in the same sections. The designer of such a system must take into account that there might be not only positive influences on the company's learning capabilities, but that side effects could cause changes in organizational values and norms (Butler & Pyke, 2003). Thus, ERP implementation goes beyond an IT project: it needs the support of top management to enable the organizational rebuilding processes.

Global Orientation

This business orientation is composed of a strong center that makes all important decisions for the whole company. The decisions made will be communicated to the single sites and have to be implemented without any adjustment to local requirements. Through this process the whole company looks—from the customers' point of view—alike all over the globe. One implication of this orientation is that the whole world is seen as one market which will be supplied with identical products. To ensure the loyalty of each site, the sites' general managers are handpicked by headquarters (HQ) to control all activities

and to implement the envisioned processes. New processes have to be developed just once and can be implemented worldwide in a short time accordingly. The global orientation is a hub-and-spoke kind of network with strong ties of the spokes to the hub, which is represented by HQ.

In this setting, HQ will make the decision to implement an ERP system and what kind of software will be used. Since the idea is that all processes should be equal in all sites, the system has to be developed just once. It can thus easily meet all the above mentioned requirements of an ERP system such as one shared database, one system, and the interconnection of all functional areas. In this context it is negligible how many functions one site will implement. That means, one site could just implement one module for sales and distribution, while another needs production and purchasing too. The integration of the functions does not differ in both cases. On the other hand, HQ has to consider all local requirements regarding the single sites such as local laws, local accounting rules, and possibly environmental stipulations (Krumbholz, Galliers, Coulianos, & Maiden, 2000). As a consequence, the 'how' seems to be less complex than the 'what'. Arguably, the planning process for such a system takes longer than in other company constellations while the implementation process could be shortened. From a strategic point of view, the MNC with a global orientation could easily add new plants to its network because it has a predefined and tested system that just has to be implemented. Besides, the MNC could realize learning curve effects from previous implementations which should ensure the success of an implementation process at a single site.

Thus, the ERP strategy implies that all sites, including HQ, get one system. In accordance with this ERP strategy, a single implementation strategy can be developed including estimated project duration, costs, and scope for the single sites (the term scope is used to mean the range of modules that should be implemented in one site). HQ determines the design of the system and the rollout sequence for all sites, and defines the pilot site where the system should be introduced and tested for the first time.

International Orientation

In this orientation HQ partly delegates control to the individual sites. Local adjustments are possible but the main decisions regarding product policies and strategies are made by HQ. Unlike the global orientation, the sites have the opportunity to reject HQ's decisions which strengthens their position. As a consequence, core competencies remain in the HQ while individual sites could develop important business competencies too.

The ERP strategy for this business orientation is similar to that of the global orientation. The major activities are initiated and coordinated by HQ. The whole company gets one system that—in contrast to the global orientation—is open to adjustments to local requirements. For this purpose the guidelines of the whole implementation have to be softened. The core system is developed by HQ but can be reconfigured by local sites. The system has one shared database which helps to collect data centrally and supports decision-making processes at the highest management level. Rollout sequence must be harmonized with regard to the interests of the individual sites, which also includes determination of a pilot site. Due to the possibility of local adjustments, the complexity of the implementation at a single site as well as of the overall process will increase. Therefore, neither the 'what' nor the 'how' seem to be that simple. If we follow the idea of Huber, Alt, and Österle (2000), the use of templates could simplify the implementation process and allow the creation of a standardized way to adjust the system locally.

Multinational Orientation

In this orientation the single subsidiaries are loosely coupled to the center. Following the explanations of Bartlett and Ghoshal (1998), every site is doing business under its own responsibility. The main strategic focus is differentiation and adjustment to local requirements. Because of the absent link between several company sites, each site creates its own data and knowledge. Regarding the definition of a global ERP strategy given above, the question whether a company has a global ERP strategy or not will have to be assessed based on the power and position of HQ.

One possibility is that HQ has no influence over the individual sites. This can mean no influence over any guidelines at all, especially regarding the IT landscape, implying that the above definition of an overall ERP strategy is not applicable in such a context. There will be no shared database, neither guidelines for one system nor for the range of modules that should be established. Regarding the whole company, there is no global resource planning at all.

Another case occurs if HQ decides to implement several modules in order to manage its business and satisfy its data needs. Following that idea, interfaces, including data formats and forms, between the individual sites and HQ have to be defined. However, this scenario will still not meet the requirements of the definition of a global ERP strategy because it focuses on HQ only and not on the entire organization.

A third scenario emerges when HQ can develop an ERP template and also has the power to implement it in the several sites. This scenario causes other problems regarding Bartlett and Ghoshal's definition of a multinational orientation. Moreover, there will be no need for one shared database or integration of all functional areas because every site manages its own operations. The production line, customers, and suppliers differ from each other. A single database has no additional benefit for the organization. The only part of an ERP system that could unite the several sites is finance, which has to be done in some way by HQ as it acts as a kind of portfolio manager.

Apparently there will be no fit between a multinational orientation and a global ERP strategy if there are no exceptions allowed regarding our definition. At that point, the decision makers in this kind of MNC have to think about the need for an ERP system. Who will benefit from a shared database? The answer to that question is fairly easy: no one, because each site acts independently and reacts to different countries' markets and customers, and deals with different products. Possibly, there is no need for some subsidiaries to implement a fully integrated software package because of their small size. A globally defined ERP system will not meet the local requirements if there are no major adjustments to the system. Thus, the ERP strategy could consist of just a minimum—that is, the data connection between the individual sites and HQ in the second scenario described above. Another ERP strategy could be that HQ is in charge of supporting implementation of ERP systems in each site that should connect with HQ. Sites will retain their independence because only the use of any system is dictated, but neither the system vendor nor the way it will be implemented is centrally prescribed. According to Markus, Tanis, & van Fenema (2000), this strategy could lead to a complete disaster for individual sites because there are no learning curve effects, while the possibility of repetition of errors that can be made within the ERP implementation is real.

The implementation strategy can be simple because only data formats and forms have to be defined which are used for data exchange with HQ.

Transnational Orientation

The transnational orientation describes an integrated network of business units. No site nor center has overall control of decisions and strategies. Moreover, each site's general manager has the opportunity to cooperate on each level or in each functional area with other sites. The initiative for such actions can come from the needs of the

firm at that moment. Bartlett and Ghoshal (1998) write about cooperation in research areas and in developing common business processes in order to illustrate the principle of the transnational orientation. Moreover, they identify different roles which a single site can play. A role depends on the site's position along two dimensions: (1) how important is the site's national or local environment to the firm's strategy, and (2) what competencies does the site have? If both dimensions indicate high levels, then the site will act as a *strategic leader* in the network of business units. Otherwise, for example when a site scores low on each dimension, the site will be a so-called *implementer*. Sites that have few local resources or capabilities (competencies) but operate in an important local market (environment) are labeled *black holes*. In contrast, a site that has strong competencies but operates in a rather unimportant market is called *contributor* (Bartlett & Ghoshal, 1998).

Because of the specific structure of a transnational organization, it is unclear who can start the initiative for an ERP strategy. People work together on a voluntary basis and the subsidiaries can implement and use business practices as they want. Regarding the roles described above, it may be argued that the strategic leader has the competencies to develop an ERP strategy and might convince other firms in the organization to take part in this venture. As soon as some sites implement a jointly developed system, a kind of domino effect could start so that ultimately every site in the network will join in the ERP project. Obviously, sites labeled black holes should have a major interest in advancing their abilities. A common and integrated database across all subsidiaries—that is the accumulated knowledge of individual sites stored in a shared database—will be a source for weaker companies to learn in an easy and inexpensive way from the experience of other network participants.

Thus, the ERP strategy includes the freedom of module choice and implementation approach in the single sites of the network. The initiative could be started by a strategic leader with core competencies in one area, while other design processes could be delegated to other sites which have competencies in a special area. However, all activities have to be coordinated within this network which is a difficult task because there is, by definition, no HQ or center within this business orientation. The strategy must contain the possibility to use individual parts of the ERP system in any way and in any combination at each site.

ERP IMPLEMENTATION STRATEGIES

An ERP implementation strategy should consist of three major parts: implementation orientation, scope of standardization, and implementation procedure.

Implementation Orientation

Referring to its business orientation, an organization may take one of the following three implementation orientations to plan the implementation of a global ERP system in its several sites: global rollout, local implementation, or mixed-mode implementation.

Global Rollout

Global rollout means the creation of a kind of global template which will be implemented in each site without any customization. This template could also be the vendor's off-the-shelf solution. The main attribute is the unchangeable configuration of the system. To ensure the success of this approach, it is necessary to collect the essential data on unique business processes in the organization. This information is the basis for the general adjustment of the kernel of the ERP system, which means a single customization of the system once before the first global rollout starts. One might argue that this single customization is

not necessary if an organization decides to change its processes according to pre-built processes in the chosen ERP system. However, we assume that, in reality, no organization will follow this kind of implementation approach, due to a wide range of problems that can occur in such an approach (Light, 2005). We propose that organizations tend to customize their system in order to increase the business performance (Holland, Light, & Gibson, 1998). In accordance with the requirements mentioned above, all sites will be assimilated and will lose any kind of procedural differentiation. On the other hand, data collection must be done just once. After a pilot implementation and the elimination of teething troubles, the implementation process will be quickly finished. The idea of the presented global rollout is closely connected to centralization within the whole IT landscape. The global rollout orientation seems to be most appropriate in an MNC with a global orientation, strong top management support which formulates clear goals and which supports sustained change management (Brown & Vessey, 2000).

Local Implementation

Local implementation is the direct opposite to global rollout orientation. Every site is enabled to customize any kind of ERP system to the company's demands. Therefore, the idea of decentralization is realized within this approach. It is assumed that some of the restrictions mentioned with regard to the global rollout have to be observed by local implementations as well because a decentralized approach, as noted in the descriptions of the multinational orientation, must have a shared base which affords management of the portfolio of sites and defines the existing organization. But the common basis could be very small and may just concern specific interfaces or number calculation metrics (Light, 1999). The responsibility for the right choice, configuration, administration, and maintenance remains in each site. If there is any grouping of site activities, the appropriate initiative comes from the sites themselves. This implementation orientation is most appropriate in MNCs with a multinational orientation; neither of the three critical success factors mentioned above (top management support, clear goals, and sustained change management) is required on a global scale.

Both implementation orientations represent the extreme points on a continuum, and in reality there will be different kinds of mixtures. The combination of these two implementation orientations might be an adequate approach for transnational organizations or international business orientations.

Mixed-Mode Implementation

Mixed-mode implementation dilutes the global rollout and local implementation orientations. On the one hand, data must be harmonized to generate global economies of scale. On the other hand, there will be a high degree of freedom to choose an ERP system according to local demands which fits the individual site. These two aspects result most likely in standardization of interfaces among sites, while hosting and administration of the systems remains the responsibility of the individual sites. Assuming the transnational organization operates in a single industry, there might be similar processes and data which could be joined within a kind of template. By generating best-practice solutions, the single sites could upgrade their position within the organization and their market. The template has to grow and evolve over the whole process and so will the degree of complexity. This includes the monitoring of new processes added to the template which might have side effects or offers new opportunities to already finished ERP implementations. This could mean the need to conduct a further project to restructure the site or its ERP system to participate in new system settings. Thereby, boundaries of a single ERP blur, implying that the allocation of costs regarding a single ERP implementation becomes more difficult for finance and cost accounting.

The mixed-mode orientation would also fit a holding company that has to cope with a network of different sites or groups of sites which constitute one or more of the above mentioned business directions.

Scope of Standardization

Davenport (1998) advised that an organization must analyze its business to find out about its unique business processes. Not until this step is done should the standardization process start. Otherwise existing business advantages could disappear because of a misalignment between standardized processes and enterprise requirements. Standardization could aim at the system/processes, the data/data formats, and/or the organizational structure of sites. The degree of standardization depends on the combination of the three items mentioned and their characteristics.

If the ERP software is specified, this also includes business processes according to the vendor's experiences with other ERP implementations. Using the same system thus means to introduce similar processes which could be customized by the purchaser. A major advantage of this approach lies in the pre-specified interfaces which interconnect the individual system modules. Data exchange should thus be easily established. On the other side, there might not be an ideal alignment between system and site in the case of heterogeneous business processes among the different sites (Mabert et al., 2001). The tailoring of an ERP system and its consequences for the implementation should be considered within the whole project plan—that is, right at the outset of the system design process. There are standardized process manuals developed by IEEE that can be used for this process (Fitzgerald, Russo, & O'Kane, 2003).

Data and data format standardization imply that there will be interface specifications that enable data flow between different systems. Besides, the prescribed data formats guarantee an integrated view on all sites on a common basis.

As mentioned before, that might be limited to data in finance and accounting departments.

If the system/processes and/or the data/data formats are standardized, some sites in an organization have to change their processes according to these specifications. Therefore, departments, mode of operations, and hierarchical power may have to be changed too. This has to be taken into consideration regarding the expected implementation duration.

Which type of standardization is most appropriate depends on the overall implementation orientation; for example, a global rollout implementation orientation will aim at standardization of site organizational structures while a local implementation orientation will focus on data standards, preferably in the financial area.

Finally, deriving an ERP strategy from the business strategy must consider costs that arise during the entire process. There will be a trade-off between the degree of system standardization which additionally includes costs for administration, maintenance, and (user) support and the created benefits of using it. For example, Light (1999) mentioned that a shared database—which is stated as a major advantage of an ERP—does not need to be installed to meet the widespread market demands of an MNC. It therefore seems to be important to invest more resources and time into defining the standardization scope to find the right fit between the degree of standardization and the costs of implementation.

Implementation Procedure

In the literature two procedures for ERP implementations are mentioned: these are big bang and phased implementation (cf. Umble, Haft, & Umble, 2003).

In a big bang approach, every site introduces the system at the same time or one site implements all modules at the same time. In the first case, the risk of failure might be at the maximum. If there is some sort of template and if this is insufficient

for the individual sites, a successful implementation ends up in a disaster for the whole organization. If there is no template, every site faces the problem of customizing its system according to the organization's specifications. There might be redundant system configurations without any learning effects from previous implementations. Depending on project management and site capabilities, the project could be successful or not.

A phased implementation can be site-by-site, department-by-department, or module-by-module. Site-by-site implementation is similar to the latter case of the big bang approach but will be discussed here. All these cases enable an organization to test single configurations of the ERP system before implementing them. Meanwhile, the old legacy system could handle market demands in its usual way. On the other hand, this procedure extends the duration of the whole implementation process which may increase costs and slow down the speed with which increased efficiency can be realized. The phased implementation approach offers the possibility to arrange a sequence for the ERP implementations which can be adjusted according to project experiences, urgency, and strategic importance of the sites. It must be pointed out, however, that HQ of an organization may not be free to arrange the sequence of implementations without obtaining support and consent of the sites affected. In multinational and transnational orientations, the individual sites have high degrees of autonomy which might put them in a position to resist the organizational change process.

Neither a big bang nor phased implementation procedure can realize learning effects if there is not a sequential implementation procedure of any kind. So the company has to install devices to collect knowledge from finished implementations to use it by project management in follow-up projects. This knowledge, for example, contains not only difficulties and solutions with system adjustments but also how the company reacted to the new system, and how people have to be trained on new functionalities or issues regarding the local legal requirements.

Another very important dimension of the implementation procedure is business process redesign (BPR). Depending on the decisions of which kind of implementation orientation and scope of standardization is chosen by the company, changes in existing business processes or the system processes are implied. For example, the implementation with a global template in a globally oriented organization demands the reconfiguration of business processes in every site in accordance with the template. For the sake of completeness, this topic is mentioned here briefly, but due to its complexity and the implied problems, for example resistance to change or maintenance of the system, the topic is beyond the chapter's scope. For a deeper insight into BPR and ERP, we refer to the literature (Ng, Ip, & Lee, 1999; Koch, 2001; Scheer & Habermann, 2000; Estevez et al., 2002; Gunson & de Blais, 2002; Luo & Strong, 2004).

CHANGING THE BUSINESS ORIENTATION

If we follow the framework of business orientations described above, companies' ERP decision makers have to bear another aspect in mind: it could be an organization's strategy to use the implementation of an ERP system in order to change the business orientation of the organization, thereby exploiting the ERP implementation process as a tool. Whether or not this use is feasible (see Future Trends and Research Directions), it complicates the task for ERP planners. New authorization procedures may have to be created and new modules may have to be established within the different sites which may result in yet another implementation. While three of the four orientations have similar implications regarding the implementation procedure, the change towards or away from a multinational orientation seems to be a special case. The reason for this

is the centralized vs. decentralized structure of data management. In the case of creating a multinational orientation, the individual sites must be enabled to do business on their own. To do so, they will need an ERP system with all functions, and the knowledge of how to handle such a system to configure, maintain, and expand the system on their own (e.g., Luo & Strong, 2004). On the other hand, if an organization is to be more integrated, for example by moving from a multinational orientation to an international one, all the separate data will have to be cleaned up and consolidated in one database. This means a long-lasting process of consensus building with regard to appearance, form, and quantity of data (cf. Oliver & Romm, 2002). Moreover, both steps presuppose a solution to the above mentioned problem regarding the need for a central authority that defines and enforces the global ERP strategy, because the possibility of initiating a change of business orientation implies a sufficiently powerful center in the organization. A change in business orientation could be necessary to stay competitive or if HQ wants to change its position itself. In the case where HQ wants to act more like a portfolio manager, a company must be reorganized if its form does not fit this intention. This could mean more decentralization of power and decoupling of sites. Because of this, the ERP implementation process could become more complicated since decision-making power and the commitment of top management is delegated one step down in the organizational hierarchy. For example, if in the original business orientation all decisions are made by HQ, they have access to all global resources of the organization. In case that one division or business unit (site) general manager is given the responsibility for an ERP implementation process for parts of the whole company, access to these resources is hampered or impossible for HQ. This will complicate the implementation of an ERP system in part of the company.

A MODEL FOR MONITORING THE ERP IMPLEMENTATION PROCESS

The discussion so far is summarized in Figure 1.

The business orientation leads to an ERP strategy based on a centralized or decentralized approach in general. Adding the required management conduct, which is a precondition for a successful realization of an ERP strategy, results in the constraints for an ERP implementation strategy. In order to evaluate the ERP implementation strategy after an implementation orientation is chosen, we distinguish three phases: intelligence phase, implementation phase, and evaluation phase. In the first phase, the scope of standardization is set by HQ which could have major effects on project duration and costs. If this phase is planned and executed well, it just has to be done once in the ERP project. In the second phase, there is the choice among a big bang or phased implementation approach. To analyze this phase in more

detail, there are other models such as those by Markus and Tanis (2000) or Somers and Nelson (2004) who divided the single implementation into several other phases. Due to the disregard of an organization's business orientation, this view seems to be too limited because the effects on the ERP strategy are not considered. The data that were collected in the implementation phase must be analyzed in the third, evaluation phase. After the experiences of prior implementations, the sequence of future implementations could be rearranged. Depending on the outcomes of this phase, the intelligence phase might have to be revised. This model should enable an organization to plan its ERP strategy and incorporate learning effects.

In the following, the three phases are—by way of example—illustrated by the two polar cases global rollout and local implementation.

Figure 1. Steps in an ERP implementation strategy

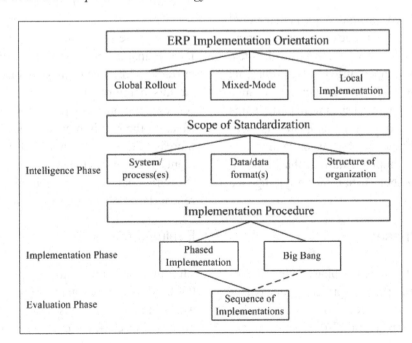

Global Rollout

Intelligence Phase

First, there is a scanning phase which comprises the collection of important information regarding established business processes, needed data/data formats, interfaces, subsystems, national regulation, and so on. Once this information is gathered, it is used by a strong moderator (most likely HQ) to generate a template. The moderator identifies core processes, adjusts these processes to unify them, and therefore defines the template's core processes. The template covers approximately 80-90% of all business processes (Umble et al., 2003). This could be a time-consuming and expensive process depending on the number and the heterogeneity of sites. Furthermore, this process becomes more complicated if the sites are located in different cultural areas (Davison, 2002; Soh, Sia, & Tay-Yap, 2000). Subject to their strategic meaning or role, not all sites have the same stake in this process.

Implementation Phase

Once the template is generated, the actual global rollout can begin. The usage of the template may cause a business process redesign within the sites, but still grants an adaptation to local requirements in the range of 10-20%. Resistance to change should be low because all sites were participants of the process producing the template. As there is only limited potential for customization, the duration of the implementation phase should be significantly shorter than of the intelligence phase.

Evaluation Phase

The subsequent evaluation phase helps the organization to improve its project management skills and therefore to reduce the time needed to introduce the template into further sites. Mean-

while, the sequence of ERP implementations is checked, for example with regard to excellent project management techniques and a well-built template, so that strategically important sites are served first.

Local Implementation

Intelligence Phase

In contrast to global rollout, only the information needs of HQ are relevant. After identifying the important data which every site has to deliver, HQ determines the data, data formats, and interfaces for interconnection within the structure. This differs from the template because it is not a finished system that could be easily implemented in each site; instead it creates constraints and demands to them for their implementation or data support. It is imaginable that HQ uses the collected data for performance comparison of each site. To reduce information asymmetries or simplify comparison, channels of data interchange may have to be standardized.

Implementation Phase

In this phase each site has to be examined by local management. The result could be a fully customized ERP system, only obeying the constraints mentioned above. Of course, every single implementation bears the same risks of failure. Meeting the requirements of the single site will increase this phase's time and money requirements. Afterwards the system is well tailored to the individual site, but each implementation will repeat the whole process over and over again.

Evaluation Phase

The outcome of the evaluation phase depends on the kind of implementation procedure. If there was a bin bang (all sites at one time) approach, no learning effects would be realized and the result of the implementation process might be unpredictable. If it was a phased implementation, learning effects can be realized through "reuse" of processes or parts which could shorten the time for the next implementation phase.

Figure 2 shows a schematic demonstration of how the allocation of time and money could differ in the two approaches. We propose these curve progressions because of the above mentioned arguments that a global rollout starts with a high budget in the intelligence phase to create a template, but could reduce implementation costs because of the repetition and learning effects from using the same process over and over again. On the other hand, the costs of the local implementation start on a low level and increase over the course of the project.

CONCLUSION

Implementation of an ERP system possibly takes years and cost millions (Mabert et al., 2001). Therefore, organizations must manage this process very carefully. Some approaches try to forecast the success of such a step (Magnusson & Nilsson, 2004) and distinguish between several dimensions. Only rarely, the implied ERP implementation strategy of such an organization method

is mentioned or examined. The exploration of the relationship between business strategy and—as recommended—the derived ERP implementation strategy can help:

a. Management to detect and identify the effects of the choice of an ERP strategy, and
b. IT departments (e.g., represented by a CIO) to explain the complexity and thus the required support by top management to lead a (successful) ERP implementation in their organization.

The framework developed in this chapter gives hints regarding important considerations and possible pitfalls in planning a global ERP implementation process. Based on these insights the presented model can help to monitor, control, and adjust the derived ERP strategy in order to meet management's expectations of the ERP system.

FUTURE TRENDS AND RESEARCH DIRECTIONS

In this chapter we implicitly assumed that the implementation of an ERP system has no effects on the structure of a corporation. The structure

Figure 2. Allocation of time/money during project phases

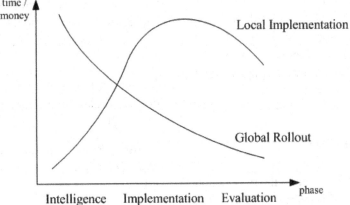

of an organization or the orientation of an MNC was considered as fixed and given. However, as we mentioned in the section 'Changing the Business Orientation', it could be one of top management's objectives to use an ERP implementation process strategically. This strategic use would imply that the implementation (process) of ERP systems has a strong effect on organizations. It would also raise the question whether ERP systems can achieve such changes in structure by themselves or whether they act as a facilitator only. In the first case, the ERP project becomes more complex and challenging for both top management and project management. In the latter one, top management must consider additional measures which enable the ERP project to reach the intended change or measures that are supported by the ERP project. Top management as well as project management must bear in mind that those additional measures can also have negative side effects on each other. What kind of measures would be appropriate, how they support ERP projects and how they are supported by such projects, and in what useful combinations they can be applied are interesting questions for future research. Furthermore, if one allows for intentional effects of ERP implementation processes on corporate structure, it becomes necessary to address the question of unintended effects. These will not only regard ERP implementation processes in corporations that are actively trying to change their structures, but also ERP projects in fixed structures which were discussed in this chapter. However, we did not discuss the implications of unintended effects on ERP implementation processes due to limitation of space and reasons of complexity. The model presented in this chapter allows for enhancement by future work and research.

ACKNOWLEDGMENT

The authors would like to thank the editors and anonymous reviewers for their useful comments and suggestions. Furthermore, the authors would like to thank Guido Schryen of RWTH Aachen University for his help in editing this chapter.

REFERENCES

Akkermanns, H., & van Helden, K. (2003). Vicious and virtuous cycles in ERP implementation. *European Journal of Information Systems,* (11), 35-46.

Bancroft, N., Sprengel, A., & Seip, H. (1996). *Implementing SAP R/3: How to introduce a large system into a large organization.* Englewood Cliffs, NJ: Prentice Hall.

Bartlett, C.A., & Ghoshal, S. (1998). *Managing across borders—The transnational solution.* Boston: Harvard Business School Press.

Bingi, P., Sharma, M.K., & Godla, J.K. (1999). Critical issues affecting an ERP implementation. *Information Systems Management, 16*(3), 7-14.

Brown, C.V., & Vessey, I. (2000). NIBCO'S "big bang." In *Proceedings of the International Conference on Information Systems.*

Butler, T., & Pyke, A. (2003). Examining the influence of ERP systems on firm-specific knowledge and core capabilities: A case study of SAP implementation and use. In *Proceedings of the 11ᵗʰ European Conference on Information Systems.*

Clemmons, S., & Simon, J.S. (2001). Control and coordination in global ERP configuration. *Business Process Management Journal, 7*(3), 205-215.

Davenport, T.H. (1998). Putting the enterprise into the enterprise system. *Harvard Business Review, 76*(4), 121-131.

Davison, R. (2002). Cultural complications of ERP. *Communications of the ACM, 45*(7), 109-111.

Earl, M.J. (1993). Experience in strategic information systems planning. *MIS Quarterly, 17*(1), 1-24.

Esteves, J., & Pastor, J. (1999). An ERP life-cycle-based research agenda. *Proceedings of the International Workshop on Enterprise Management Resource Planning Systems* (EMRPS) (pp. 359-371), Venice, Italy.

Esteves, J., & Pastor, J. (2001). Enterprise resource planning systems research: An annotated bibliography. *Communications of the AIS, 7*(8), 1-52.

Esteves, J., Pastor, J., & Casanovas, J. (2002). *Monitoring business process redesign in ERP implementation projects.* Retrieved April 13, 2007, from http://coblitz.codeen.org:3125/citeseer.ist.psu.edu/cache/papers/cs/31804/http:zSzzSzwww.lsi.upc.eszSz~jesteveszSzBPR_amcis2002.PDF/esteves02monitoring.pdf

Firestone, J.M. (2002). *Enterprise information portals and knowledge management.* Boston: Butterworth-Heinemann.

Fitzgerald, B., Russo, N.L., & O'Kane, T. (2003). Software development method tailoring at Motorola. *Communications of the ACM, 46*(4), 65-70.

Ghosh, S., & Ghosh, S. (2003). Global implementation of ERP software—Critical success factors on upgrading technical infrastructure. In *Proceedings of the International Engineering Management Conference—Managing Technologically Driven Organizations: The Human Side of Innovation and Change* (pp. 320-324).

Gunson, J., & de Blais, J.-P. (2002). *Implementing ERP in multinational companies: Their effects on the organization and individuals at work.* Retrieved April 13, 2007, from http://www.hec.unige.ch/recherches_publications/cahiers/2002/2002.07.pdf

Holland, C.P., & Light, B. (1999). A critical success factors model for ERP implementation. *IEEE Software, 16*(3), 30-36.

Holland, C.P., Light, B., & Gibson, N. (1998). Global enterprise resource planning implementation. In *Proceedings of the Americas Conference on Information Systems.*

Hong, K.-K., & Kim, Y.-G. (2002). The critical success factors for ERP implementation: An organizational fit perspective. *Information & Management, 40,* 25-40.

Huber, T., Alt, R., & Österle, H. (2000). Templates—Instruments for standardizing ERP systems. In *Proceedings of the 33rd Annual Hawaii International Conference on System Sciences.*

Karimi, J., & Konsynski, B. (1991). Globalization and information management strategies. *Journal of Management Information Systems, 7*(4), 7-26.

Koch, C. (2001). BPR and ERP: Realizing a vision of process with IT. *Business Process Management Journal, 7*(3), 258-265.

Krumbholz, M., Galliers, J., Coulianos, N., & Maiden, N.A.M. (2000). Implementing enterprise resource planning packages in different corporate and national cultures. *Journal of Information Technology, 15*(4), 267-279.

Lehm, L., Heinzl, A., & Markus, L.M. (2001). Tailoring ERP systems: A spectrum of choices and their implications. In *Proceedings of the 34th Hawaii International Conference on Systems Science.*

Light, B. (1999). Realizing the potential of ERP systems: The strategic implications of implementing an ERP strategy: The case of global petroleum. *Electronic Markets, 9*(4), 238-241.

Light, B. (2005). Potential pitfalls in packaged software adoption. *Communications of the ACM, 48*(5), 119-121.

Luo, W., & Strong, D.M. (2004). A framework for evaluating ERP implementation choices. *IEEE Transactions on Engineering Management, 51*(3), 322-333.

Magnusson, J., & Nilsson, A. (2004). A conceptual framework for forecasting ERP implementation success. In *Proceedings of the International Conference on Enterprise Information Systems* (pp. 447-453).

Mabert, V.A., Soni, A., & Venkataramanan, M.A. (2001). Enterprise resource planning: Common myths versus evolving reality. *Business Horizons, 44*(3), 69-76.

Madapusi, A., & D'Souza, D. (2005). Aligning ERP systems with international strategies. *Information Systems Management, 22*(1), 7-17.

Markus, L.M., Axline, S., Petrie, D., & Tanis, C. (2000). Learning from adopters' experiences with ERP: Problems encountered and success achieved. *Journal of Information Technology, 15*(4), 245-265.

Markus, M.L., & Tanis, C. (2000). The enterprise systems experience—From adoption to success. In R.W. Zmud (Ed.), *Framing the domains of IT research: Glimpsing the future through the past* (pp.173-207). Cincinnati, OH: Pinnaflex Educational Resources.

Markus, L.M., Tanis, C., & van Fenema, P.C. (2000). Enterprise resource planning: Multisite ERP implementations. *Communications of the ACM, 43*(4).

Ng, J.K.C., Ip, W.H., & Lee, T.C. (1999). A paradigm for ERP and BPR integration. *International Journal of Production Research, 37*(9), 2093-2108.

O'Leary, D.E. (2000). *Enterprise resource planning systems: Systems, life cycle, electronic commerce and risk.* Cambridge, UK: Cambridge University Press.

Oliver, D., & Romm, C. (2002). Justifying enterprise resource planning adoption. *Journal of Information Technology, 17*(4), 199-213.

Reimers, K. (1997). Managing information technology in the transnational organization: The potential of multifactor productivity. In *Proceedings of the 30th Annual Hawaii Conference on System Sciences.*

Scheer, A.-W., & Habermann, F. (2000). Making ERP a success. *Communications of the ACM, 43*(4), 57-61.

Scott, J.E. (1999). The FoxMeyer Drug's bankruptcy: Was it a failure of ERP? In *Proceedings of the Association for Information Systems 5th Americas Conference on Information Systems.*

Soh, C., Sia, S.K., & Tay-Yap, J. (2000). Cultural fits and misfits: Is ERP a universal solution? *Communications of the ACM, 43*(4), 47-51.

Somers, T.M., & Nelson, K.G. (2004). A taxonomy of players and activities across the ERP project life cycle. *Information & Management, 41*(3), 257-278.

Sumner, M. (2000). Risk factors in enterprise-wide/ERP projects. *Journal of Information Technology, 15,* 317-327.

Umble, E.J., Haft, R.R., & Umble, M.M. (2003). Enterprise resource planning: Implementation procedures and critical success factors. *European Journal of Operational Research, 146*(2), 241-257.

Ward, J., Griffiths, P., & Whithmore, P. (1990). *Strategic planning for information systems.* Chicester: John Wiley & Sons.

ADDITIONAL READING

Adam, F., & O'Doherty, P. (2000). Lessons from enterprise resource planning implementations in Ireland—Towards smaller and shorter ERP projects. *Journal of Information Technology, 15*(4), 305-316.

Bakos, Y. (1986). Information technology and corporate strategy: A research perspective. *MIS Quarterly, 10*(2), 106-119.

Biehl, M. (2007). Success factors for implementing global information systems. *Communications of the ACM, 50*(1), 53-58.

Chien, S.-W., Hu, C., Reimers, K., & Lin, J.-S. (2007). The influence of centrifugal and centripetal forces on ERP project success in small and medium-sized enterprises in China and Taiwan. *International Journal of Production Economics, 107*(2), 380-396.

Dowlatshahi, S. (2005). Strategic success factors in enterprise resource planning design and implementation: A case-study approach. *International Journal of Production Research, 43*(18), 3745-3771.

Fleisch, E., Österle, H., & Powell, S. (2004). Rapid implementation of enterprise resource planning systems. *Journal of Organizational Computing and Electronic Commerce, 14*(2), 107-126.

Gattiker, T., & Goodhue, D. (2005). What happens after ERP implementation: Understanding the impact of inter-dependence and differentiation on plant-levels outcome. *MIS Quarterly, 29*(3), 559-585.

Ghoshal, S., & Bartlett, C. (2001). The multinational corporation as an interorganizational network. *Academy of Management Review, 15*(4), 603-625.

Gosain, S. (2004). Enterprise information systems as objects and carriers of institutional forces: The new iron cage? *Journal of the Association for Information Systems, 5*(4), 151-182.

Grossman, T., & Walsh, J. (2004). Avoiding the pitfalls of ERP system implementation. *Information Systems Management, 21*(2), 38-42.

Hanseth, O., & Braa, K. (1998). Technology as a traitor: Emergent SAP infrastructure in a global organization. In R. Hirscheim, M. Newman, & J.I. DeGross (Eds.), *Proceedings of the 19th International Conference on Information systems* (pp. 188-197).

Henderson, J., & Venkatraman, N. (1999). Strategic alignment: Leveraging information technology for transforming organizations. *IBM Systems Journal, 38*(2&3), 472-484.

Huang, S.M., Hung, Y.C., Chen, H.G., & Ku, C.Y. (2004). Transplanting the best practice for implementation of an ERP system: A structured inductive study of an international company. *Journal of Computer Information Systems, 44*(4), 101-110.

Ioannou, G., & Papadoyiannis, C. (2004). Theory of constraints-based methodology for effective ERP implementations. *International Journal of Production Research, 42*(23), 4927-4954.

King, W. (2006). Ensuring ERP implementation success. *Information Systems Management, 22*(3), 83-84.

Krumbholz, M., & Maiden, N. (2001). The implementation of enterprise resource planning packages in different organisational and national cultures. *Information Systems, 26*(3), 185-204.

Lall, V., & Teyarachakul, S. (2006). Enterprise resource planning (ERP) system selection: A data envelopment analysis (DEA) approach. *Journal of Computer Information Systems, 47*(1), 123-127.

Luftman, J., Lewis, P., & Oldach, S. (1993). Transforming the enterprise: The alignment of business and information technology strategies. *IBM Systems Journal, 32*(1), 198-221.

Mahato, S., Jain, A., & Balasubramanian, V. (2006). Enterprise systems consolidation. *Information Systems Management, 23*(4), 7-19.

Ng, C., Gable, G., & Chan, T. (2003). An ERP maintenance model. In *Proceedings of the 36th Hawaii International Conference on System Sciences.*

Parr, A., & Shanks, G. (2000). A model of ERP project implementation. *Journal of Information Technology, 15*(4), 289-303.

Rathnam, R.G., Johnsen, J., & Wen, H.J. (2004/05). Alignment of business strategy and IT strategy: A case study of a Fortune 50 financial service company. *Journal of Computer Information Systems, 45*(2), 1-8.

Reich, B., & Benbasat, I. (1996). Measuring the linkage between business and information technology objectives. *MIS Quarterly, 20*(1), 55-81.

Reimers, K. (2003). International examples of large-scale systems—Theory and practice: Implementing ERP systems in China. *Communications of the AIS, 11,* 335-356.

Ribbers, P., & Schoo, K.-C. (2002). Program management and complexity of ERP implementations. *Engineering Management Journal, 14*(2), 45-52.

Somers, T., & Nelson, K. (2003). The impact of strategy and integration mechanisms on enterprise system value: Empirical evidence from manufacturing firms. *European Journal of Operational Research, 146*(2), 315-338.

Teltumbde, A. (2000). A framework for evaluating ERP projects. *International Journal of Production Research, 38*(17), 4507-4520.

Voordijk, H., Van Leuven, A., & Laan, A. (2003). Enterprise resource planning in a large construction firm: Implementation analysis. *Construction Management & Economics, 21*(5), 511-521.

Section II
Investment Aspects

Chapter IV
Enterprise Resource Planning Under Open Source Software

Ashley Davis
University of Georgia, USA

ABSTRACT

Open source software is becoming more prevalent in businesses today, and while still a relatively imma-ture offering, open source enterprise resource planning (OS-ERP) systems are becoming more common. However, whether or not an OS-ERP package is the right software for a given organization is a little researched question. Building on the current real options thinking about platform acquisitions, this chapter proposes the five most critical factors to consider when evaluating an OS-ERP package. To adequately do this, a great deal of detail about the current offerings in OS-ERP software is presented, followed by a review of the real options theory and thinking behind using these factors to evaluate OS-ERP options. The international implications of OS-ERP are presented in the "Future Trends" section.

INTRODUCTION

Open source software (OSS) is becoming a promi-nent part of the business infrastructure landscape. However, open source application software is still in its infancy. Success of open source enterprise resource planning (OS-ERP) systems will signify a coming of age of open source applications. There are many factors that will determine if OS-ERP systems are a valuable option for corporations, and thus whether OS-ERP systems will become as prominent as other open source offerings like Linux or JBOSS. This chapter will inform the reader of the current state of OS-ERP in the global context, and explain to potential adopters of OS-ERP the important factors to consider in evaluating an OS-ERP option.

First, a common language for defining OS-ERP systems will be developed. Second, the current state of OS-ERP software will be ex-plored. Third, the business models of OS-ERP vendors will be exposed. Fourth, the advantages and disadvantages of customization of OS-ERP software will be explained. Fifth, the factors for valuing OS-ERP options using real options theory (Fichman, 2004) are defined. Finally, the global adoption of ERP software is explored.

BACKGROUND

The first necessary requisite for understanding OS-ERP systems is to define a common language for talking about OS-ERP applications. This includes defining exactly what an OS-ERP application entails and whether the software meets the definition of open source software. There is much ambiguity in the popular press about what is and is not OSS; this is only confounded when ERP systems claim to be open source. To clarify these issues, the next section will explain historical context of OSS. Secondly, open source licensing issues are explained. Then, the issue of open source ERP functionality is addressed. Lastly some examples of OS-ERP software are provided.

History of Open Source Software

Open source software has a rich history, from an initial chaotic beginning out of a hacker culture (Raymond, 1999) to its current manifestation as a foundation for profit-seeking corporations such as JBOSS (Watson, Wynn, & Boudreau, 2005), Compiere Inc., and Red-Hat Linux. As open source has evolved, the definition of open source software has changed and the open source ecosystem has grown. Previously, open source software was defined in terms of two characteristics: (1) licenses that give programmers the ability to view, change, enhance open source code, and distribute the source code without discrimination (Feller & Fitzgerald, 2000; Open Source Initiative, 2005); and (2) the software is free of cost. While this definition was sufficient, for pure open source initiatives of the past, it does not adequately

cover all that "open source" includes today. This is in contrast to proprietary software where the license generally does not allow for distribution of the source code and is not free of cost. Evolution and commercialization of OSS have led to many products being labeled "open source" that are not free of cost. As well, proprietary software (software controlled and offered by vendors for a price) that give access to the code are termed open source, while there is no licensing to support the open source model of software development. Proprietary software that allows access to the source code still leaves the control of the source code, what is included in the source code in future versions, in the hands of the vendor, who may be less accepting of contributions of code than an open source community.

However, even under the most stringent of open source (OS) definitions, there have been many great open source successes. For example, MySQL is an open source database server that has grown phenomenally since its inception in 1995. MySQL AB is the company that supports the MySQL product. This product is free and the source code is available to everyone under the GNU General Public License (GPL). Licensing will be discussed in more detail in the next section.

MySQL is currently backed by several venture capitalists and is without debt (MySQL, 2007). There were over 12 million downloads of MySQL in 2006, and 2,500 new customers started using MySQL to power Web sites, critical applications, packaged software, and telecommunications infrastructure. MySQL is just one example of the success of OS software in the infrastructure space. Other examples in infrastructure offerings include JBOSS and Linux.

In terms of business applications, there are fewer major success stories. SugarCRM, however, is one of the most successful open source business applications. SugarCRM is a customer relationship management software package (packaged software is that which offers a "set of functionality" in a complete state that does not require programming) that is available under a "custom" open source license.[1] SugarCRM has over a million downloads and about 1,000 customers (SugarCRM, 2007). ERP systems—large packaged integrated business applications that include intensive functionality in the following areas: marketing and sales, accounting and finance, production and materials management, and human resources[2]—are relatively less prolific than these major success stories in the open source space. However, as the rest of this chapter outlines, there are several open source ERP offerings becoming available. It waits to be determined which of these applications will become widely used in businesses.

Open Source Licenses

Licensing plays a big role in definitions of OSS. As of 2006, the Open Source Initiative (OSI) recognizes nearly 60 different open source licenses (Open Source Initiative, 2006). Given this number of licenses, and that OSI is not the only organization that provides accreditation of licenses,[3] it is understandable that the definition of open source is not stable. Many companies have turned to a dual-licensing strategy, making their code available under general public license (GPL) but also offering a commercial license (Rist, 2005). Given this large number of licensing options and business models, it is understandable that there is confusion as to what software really is open source software.

Open source software still must allow access to the source code, as mentioned above. So, OS-ERP systems are defined to allow access to the code. However, under what terms this is available, including for what cost, is a question. For the purposes of understanding OS-ERP software, one must assume that the cost is not necessarily free. For the OS-ERP packages in this chapter, three general license types are utilized:

1. **Apache License Version 2.0:** "Subject to the terms and conditions of this License, each Contributor hereby grants to You a perpetual, worldwide, non-exclusive, no-charge, royalty-free, irrevocable copyright license to reproduce, prepare Derivative Works of, publicly display, publicly perform, sublicense, and distribute the Work and such Derivative Works in Source or Object form." As with all licenses, it is recommended that a full review of the license is conducted before working with any open source software (Apache, 2007).

2. **Mozilla Public License 1.1:** This license allows for access to the source code for review and modification. This is a copyleft license, meaning that all modifications involving the original source code are sent back to the originator of the software. As with all licenses, it is recommended that a full review of the license is conducted before working with any open source software (Mozilla, 2007).

3. **GNU GPL:** "GNU is a recursive acronym for 'GNU's Not Unix'; it is pronounced *guh-noo*, approximately like *canoe*...the GNU General Public License is intended to guarantee your freedom to share and change free software—to make sure the software is free for all its users." Users of software under the GNU GPL can use, modify, improve, and redistribute such software. As with all licenses, it is recommended that a full review of the license is conducted before working with any open source software (GNU, 2007a, 2007b).

However, some software companies create their own licenses with their own implications for what "open source" means to their software. In the OS-ERP space, examples include:

1. **OpenMfg:** "...the license OpenMFG uses allows companies to view and modify

source code, as well as make contributions to the source code" (Caton, 2006). However, this license does not allow for distribution of the source code. So, by definition, this is not what is generally meant by "open source" software. As with all licenses, it is recommended that a full review of the license is conducted before working with any software.

2. **avERP:** This license includes no license fees, no charge for updates, no fees charged for own programming, no obligation to pay or purchase anything at anytime, no obligation for use of services, and it is possible to alter all program modules if wished and includes source code (HK-Software, 2007). It does not appear that redistribution of the software is allowed. As with all licenses, it is recommended that a full review of the

license is conducted before working with any software.

3. **OpenPro:** This is software built on open source technologies that allows access to the source code. However, there is a license fee involved, and the right to distribute the software is not explained on the Web site (OpenPro, 2007). As with all licenses, it is recommended that a full review of the license is conducted before working with any open software.

Table 1 outlines current OS-ERP offerings, licensing, and Web sites where more can be learned about the software.

The popular press has referred to all of the software listed in Table 1 as OS-ERP, even those with cost. ERP systems are the backbone of an organization, and the cost of the initial license is

Table 1. Open source ERP licensing

Open Source Offering	License	Web Sites
Compiere	GNU GPL	http://www.compiere.org/
OpenMFG	Custom	http://www.openmfg.com/
OfBiz	Apache License Version 2.0	http://ofbiz.apache.org/
Tiny ERP	GNU GPL	http://sourceforge.net/projects/tinyerp
OpenPro	Undisclosed Cost Structure	http://www.openpro.com/
WebERP	GNU	http://www.weberp.org/
ERP5	GPL	http://www.erp5.org/
Adempiere	GNU GPL	http://www.adempiere.com/
avERP	Custom	http://www.hk-software.net/h-k.de/content/doc_138099-3-5-0.php
Fisterra	GNU GPL	http://community.igalia.com/twiki/bin/view/Fisterra
OpenBravo	Mozilla Public License 1.1	http://www.openbravo.com/
GNUe	GNU GPL	http://www.gnuenterprise.org/
Value ERP	GNU	http://www.valueerp.com/

only part of the total cost of ownership (TCO) of an ERP system or any software package. Organizations cannot rely on vendors and analysts to provide accurate TCO estimates. One practitioner notes, "...no matter how honest they try to be, neither vendor nor analyst can ever fill in all the variables of the TCO formula...The unique combination of resources, both machine and human, at work within your organization is something only you can fully understand" (McAllister, 2005). One estimate of the costs that make up TCO includes hardware and software, technical services, planning and process management, finance and administration, training, user support, peer support, and application development (Di-Maio, 2004). However, migration costs, testing, system integration, and so forth must be included in determining the total cost of switching to any software package. For a breakdown of some of the costs to consider, please see the cost comparison provided by Nolan (2005). The comparison of costs between proprietary ERP and OS-ERP systems is not readily known, as "the lack of large-scale implementations (of OS-ERP) eliminate a direct comparison with enterprise solutions, such as mySAP Business Suite or Oracle E-Business suite" (Prentice, 2006). However, even getting an accurate TCO is not adequate when deciding whether to use open source software (DiMaio, 2004, 2007). For OS-ERP software, the decision is more complex because this decision crosses the bounds of the entire organization. Decision makers involved in evaluating ERP systems are aware that even for proprietary systems, the cost estimates vary wildly (Cliff, 2003), and thus when considering OS-ERP solutions, TCO (as complex as it is) will be but one evaluative criterion. ERP evaluative criteria are often handled by complex request for proposal processes involving outside experts. Beyond this expertise, this chapter proposes factors for valuing OS-ERP options (see the "Real Options Value of OS-ERP" section) that should be considered in addition to these complex TCO estimates.

As well, the business model (see the "Open Source Vendor Models" section) behind open source offerings will explain why cost is not as much of an issue in the definition of OS-ERP systems. However, a pure definition of OS-ERP would not include AvERP, OpenPro, or OpenMFG because, although all allow access to modify and change the code, these packages either charge a license fee or do not allow for re-distribution of the software (as mentioned above).

Functionality of OS-ERP

For those interested in understanding the OS-ERP phenomena, a solid foundation of understanding the functionality of each ERP application is also important. The maturity of the proprietary ERP market has allowed convergence as to what constitutes ERP functionality. For most, an acceptable general definition of ERP systems is as follows: ERP systems are complex, modular software integrated across the company with capabilities for most functions in the organization. As mentioned in the "History of Open Source" section, ERP systems include functionality in the following areas: marketing and sales, accounting and finance, production and materials management, and human resources. Many times supply chain management and customer relationship management are also included in ERP packages. It is beyond the scope of this chapter to list and define whether each open source system that claims to be ERP actually contains ERP functionality. For practitioners looking to acquire OS-ERP software and academicians looking to do OS-ERP research, a thorough assessment of whether a particular system contains full ERP functionality is required. This is more of an issue in OS-ERP systems since most of these systems are fairly new and a consensus has not been achieved as to what is actually an OS-ERP system. In the OS-ERP market, many of the claims of what functionality constitutes an OS-ERP system is blurry:

One characteristic of open source is that different projects define their category's feature sets in different ways. This is especially true of ERP packages. Linux-Kontor, for example, defines ERP without accounting, focusing instead on customer management, order entry, invoicing, and inventory. TUTOS, on the other hand, calls itself ERP but more closely resembles a groupware suite. Clearly, some research is needed to make sure you're really getting what you expect in this category. (Rist, 2005)

Another concern with open source software is that the offerings are changing rapidly, so for up-to-date and complete information, the Web sites listed in Table 1 are the best sources for information about the offerings and the platforms on which the software is built/supports. However, just to provide a flavor of the offerings, Table 2 provides a cursory look at the functionality being offered by these software products (OS-ERP) at the time of this work. Again, since functionality is hard to pin down, (for example, if a package only lists "HR" as its offering, does this mean benefits administration is included?), those interested in this software should contact the company directly for the most accurate and up-to-date information.

OS-ERP Examples

There are many different flavors of OS-ERP packages, mostly because each package grew from a particular need (as OSS offerings often do). For example, Fisterra grew from a custom application built for an automotive glass replacement and repair company (Fisterra, 2007). Versions of the Fisterra product specifically intended for this industry are now called Fisterra Garage. This new name allows distinction from Fisterra 2—a generic ERP released in 2004. In this case, proprietary ERP definitions apply, in that the package has what most would define as full ERP functionality. However this is not always the case (as noted above).

The industry origins of the ERP package are important, as many times these are industry solutions that work best for the original industry. This is akin to SAP providing excellent manufacturing functionality because of its origins in the manufacturing industry. Another example of OS-ERP starting in a specific industry is OfBiz, which started with an emphasis on the retail industry (Adamson, 2004).

ASSESS THE OS-ERP LANDSCAPE

In the OSS arena, infrastructure products like Linux, Perl scripting language, and My SQL database management systems have been very successful and thus very prominent. Given that the developers of open source software were many times the users of open source software, this success is predictable. Less predictable is the success of open source software when used to develop applications. Most of the time, developers are developing the application for users that are very different from themselves. The users of applications are not technical, and their requirements are very different from those of technical users—thus the criticism that open source software is not "user friendly" or has a usability problem (Nichols & Twidale, 2003). This issue is important to OS-ERP, as possibly the entire organization will interface with the OS-ERP application, rather than only IT people directly working with infrastructure products.

OS-ERP is a quickly changing environment. For example, Compiere, one of the most well-known open source ERP companies, announced Andre Boisvert as chairman of the board and chief business development officer in May 2006. Jorg Janke (founder of Compiere) noted that Boisvert's success in "applying the open source business model to markets traditionally monopolized by proprietary software vendors is definitely a plus" (Compiere, 2006a). Then, in July 2006, Compiere added Larry Augustin to its board of directors. Mr. Augustin is founder of VA Linux (VA Software)

Table 2. OS-ERP platform and functionality

Software	Platform	Functionality
Compiere	Independent	Quote to Cash, Requisitions to Pay, Customer Relations, Partner Relations, Supply Chain, Performance Analysis, Web Store/Self Service
OpenMFG	Linux, Apple Mac OS X, Windows	Manufacturing, Materials Management, Supply Chain (Sales Order, Purchase Order, CRM), Accounting
OfBiz	Linux, Berkeley Software Distribution	Supply Chain Management, E-Commerce, Manufacturing Resource Planning, Customer Relationship Management, Warehouse Management, Accounting
Tiny ERP	Independent	Finance and Accounting, CRM, Production, Project Management, Purchasing, Sales Management, Human Resources
OpenPro	Linux, Windows	Financials, Supply Chain, Retail and Manufacturing, CRM and E-Commerce, Warehousing, EDI
WebERP	Independent	Order Entry, Accounts Receivable, Inventory, Purchasing, Accounts Payable, Bank, General Ledger
ERP5	Linux, Windows (coming soon)	Customer Relationship Management, Production Management, Supply Chain Management, Warehouse Management, Accounting, Human Resources, E-Commerce
Adempiere	Independent or Linux on its site	Point of Sale, Supply Chain Management, Customer Relationship Management, Financial Performance Analysis, Integrated Web Store
avERP	Linux	Sales, Manufacturing, Purchasing, Human Resource Management, Inventory Control, CAD Management, Master Data Management, Business Analyses
Fisterra	GNU/Linux	Point of Sale, Other Business Processes Specific to Automotive Glass Repair Businesses
OpenBravo	Linux, Windows	Procurement, Warehouse, Project Management, Manufacturing, Sales and Financial Processes, Customer Relationship Management, Business Intelligence
GNUe	Linux, Microsoft Windows	Human Resources, Accounting, Customer Relationship Management, Project Management, Supply Chain, E-Commerce

continued on following page

Table 2. continued

Value ERP (Project Dot ERP) http://www. valueerp. net/catalog/in-dex.php	Linux, Solaris, Berkeley Soft-ware Distribu-tion, Microsoft Windows	General Ledger, Payable and Receivable, Invoicing, Purchase and Receiving, Time Sheet Management for HR, Inventory Management and Manufacturing

and launched SourceForge.net, the largest open source development site on the Internet (Compiere, 2006b). These new additions to the board indicate an interest in growth by Compiere.

However, Compiere faces many challenges, for example a group of developers decided to "fork"[4] and created Adempiere ERP, CRM, & SCM Bazaar (commonly referred to as Adempiere). Forking (Raymond, 1999) is not unusual in the open source community. OFBiz also has a forked version called Sequoia. Sequoia in February 2006 was renamed Opentaps, meaning Open Source Enterprise Application Suite. The issue of forking is not new in open source software and thus is an issue in open source ERP applications as well. As mentioned earlier, forking usually occurs when a group of developers decides that the current direction of the project is not as they would like; take for example what happened with Compiere's fork Adempiere. Adempiere was started in September 2006 after "a long running disagreement between Compiere and the community that formed around the project" (Adempiere, 2006). The developers behind Adempiere felt that Compiere was focusing on "commercial/lock-in" aspects of the project, and decided to create a new version that could focus more on the community and the "sharing/enriching" aspects of the project. Jorg Janke refutes these allegations, nonetheless forking has occurred.

Geographic Origins, Age, and Networks of OS-ERP Projects

At this time, there is very little research (academic or practitioner) into the global status of open source ERP. It is clear that there are many vendors out there offering open source packages in multiple languages—indicating an international audience. Also, the packages analyzed for this research have geographically dispersed locations, if any location is listed at all. Many times in an open source ERP project, the Web serves as the primary location for the project, and there is no real geographic orientation associated with the project, as is indicated by "Web" in Table 3.

Most of the open source ERP companies are relatively new (see Table 3), though many have formidable numbers of partners (see Table 4). Partners are important in sustaining an open source project. Partners have some monetary interest in sustaining a viable open source offering, as they are often offering consulting services, implementation services, maintenance, or training. The number of customers is also important in assessing the maturity of the OS-ERP. As can be seen from Table 4, Compiere currently has more the three times the number of customers as any other OS-ERP application. However, it is hard to assess the number of customers because many of these open source projects have no central repository for keeping track of this information. Although

Table 3. Geographic origins of OS-ERP projects

Open Source Company	Project Founded	Where
Compiere Inc.	2001	Santa Clara, CA
OpenMFG	2001	Norfolk, VA
OfBiz	2001 (2003 migrated to java.net)	Web
Tiny ERP	2002	Belgium
OpenPro	1998 (1999 first release)	Fountain Valley, CA
WebERP	2001 (2003 first release)	Web
ERP5	2002	Web
Adempiere	2006	Web
avERP	1998 (2001 first installation)	Bayreauth, Germany
Fisterra	2002 (2003 first release)	Web
Openbravo	2001	Pamplona, Spain
GNUe	2003 (first release)	Web
Value ERP	2005	Sparta, NJ

Table 4. OS-ERP network (partners, customer, and developers)

	Customers	Partners	Developers	Data Collected From
OpenBravo	15	*	*	Serrano & Sarriegi, 2006
Compiere Inc.	240	70	50	Ferguson, 2006
ERP5	10	8	*	Serrano & Sarriegi, 2006; *www.erp5.org*
avERP	60	*	*	*http://de.wikipedia.org/wiki/AvERP*
OpenMfg	35	20	100	Ferguson, 2006; www.openmfg.com
OFBiz	59	21	*	www.ofbiz.org
TinyERP	*	34	*	http://tinyerp.com
OpenPro	*	Over 75	*	www.openpro.com
WebERP	*	9	*	www.weberp.org

* not available at time of data gathering, no information could be found for those not listed

partners that provide services for OS-ERP systems have some count of how many customers they currently have, they do not necessarily share this information. For assessing the value of OS-ERP software, the number of partners, customers, and developers provides a strong network and thus should provide greater value. More will be discussed on this topic in the "Real Options Value of OS-ERP" section.

Another important consideration in assessing the landscape of OS-ERP offerings is that most of these packages are targeted to specific audiences and may only be proven for specific sizes of organizations. Table 5 outlines the size of organization targeted by OS-ERP packages according to their Web sites.

From Table 5, it can be gleaned that most OS-ERP projects are targeting small and medium

Table 5. OS-ERP

Software	Size of Organization Targeted
Compiere	Small, Medium
OpenMFG	Small, Medium Manufacturers
OfBiz	*
Tiny ERP	*
OpenPro	Small, Medium, Large (1-1,000+ users)
WebERP	*
ERP5	Small, Medium, Large
Adempiere	Small, Medium
avERP	Small, Medium (1-300 employees)
Fisterra	Small, Medium
OpenBravo	Small, Medium
GNUe	Small, Medium, Large
Value ERP	Small, Medium, Large

* not available at time of data gathering

enterprises, with some targeting large organizations. With this target audience, the question of multinational implementation success with OS-ERP systems is raised. At this time, the limited and varying functionality (see Table 2), and lack of large-scale implementations precludes direct comparison with solutions like mySAP Business suite or Oracle E-Business suite (Prentice, 2006).

Venture Capital Funding and Project Activity in OSS and OS-ERP

The open source market is heavily funded by venture capital firms, Guth and Clark (2005) in the *Wall Street Journal* estimated that $290 million was invested in open source in 2004. However, open source ERP companies are lagging in maturity and thus their numbers for VC funding are much lower. Currently, two open source ERP companies are funded by venture capitalists: OpenBravo (Serrano & Sarriegi, 2006) and Compiere (Hoover, 2006). Both companies are funded with $6 million.

Given the importance of the community to open source project value, SourceForge.com tracks the most active projects daily. As of November 5, 2006, three OS-ERP projects fall in the top 15 most active: Openbravo ERP at #7; Adempiere ERP, CRM, & SCM Bazaar at #11; and Compiere at #14. There is clearly activity happening at the site that hosts these projects (http://sourceforge.net/top/mostactive.php?type=week). This is a sign of strength for these OS-ERP projects. Also, in trying to assess the value of OS-ERP options, VC funding and project activity would certainly positively impact the prospect for network dominance of the OS-ERP. More will be discussed on this topic in the "Real Options Value of OS-ERP" section of this chapter.

OPEN SOURCE VENDOR BUSINESS MODELS

Open source vendors have many different business models. When working with a piece of open source software, it is important to understand which type of organization/business model is in use by any

Table 6. Open source business models

Business Models	Definition	Source
FOSS	Value-added service-enabling—sell support services and complementary software products Loss-leader/market creating—goal is enlarging the market for alternative closed source products and services	Fitzgerald, 2006
OSS 2.0	Includes FOSS, adds the following: Dual product/licensing—can download for free, small percentage of downloads purchase a commercial license Cost reduction—proprietary companies offer OS as part of their solution Leveraging the open source brand—as government agencies mandate that open source be a priority option for software solutions, the open source brand becomes more valuable	Fitzgerald, 2006
Software Producer GPL Model	Entirely open source offerings	Krishnamurthy, 2005
Software Producer Non-GPL Model	Incorporate source code into a larger code base and create a new product or take an entire open source product and bundle it with existing products	Krishnamurthy, 2005
The Distributor	Derives benefits by providing it on CD, providing support services to enterprise customers, upgrade services only to open source product	Krishnamurthy, 2005
Third-Party Software Provider	Provide services for all types of products	Krishnamurthy, 2005
Pure OS Business Model	Firms that offer only OS products and OS solutions	Bonaccorsi et al., 2006
Hybrid Business Model	"They (hybrids) distribute OS products but also develop customized solutions using OS software, for which they presumably offer installation, support, and maintenance. The large majority also actively supply complementary services such as consulting, training, and to a lesser extent research and development." (p. 1090)	Bonaccorsi et al., 2006
Professional Open Source (POS)	"POS combines the benefits of open source (OS) with the development of methodologies, support, and accountability expected from enterprise software vendors." (p. 329) Three features of POS: (1) separation of product adoption and purchase, (2) seed and harvest marketing strategy, and (3) dual growth of firm and ecosystem	Watson et al., 2005
Proprietary	Inability to view and modify the source code (regardless of price)	Watson, Boudreau, York, Greiner, & Wynn, 2006

continued on following page

Table 6. continued

Open Community	Volunteers develop and support code with limited or no commercial interest	Watson et al., 2006
Corporate Distribution	Organizations create value by providing complementary services such as: interacting with the community for support, supporting the software for customers, identifying appropriate OSS for customers	Watson et al., 2006
Sponsored OSS	Corporations act as primary sponsors of OSS projects. These corporations provide funding and/or developers to the project.	Watson et al., 2006
Second-Generation OSS (OSSg2)	This is a combination of corporate distribution and sponsored OSS (the OSSg2 company provides complementary services around the products, but OSSg2 companies also provide the majority of the resources needed to create and maintain their products). These types of corporations strive to provide accountability, talented programmers, and a healthy ecosystem.	Watson et al., 2006

particular vendor. Table 4 defines the business models that have been used to describe what is happening with open source firms in general. The most simple understanding of these models can be drawn from Bonaccorsi, Giannangeli, and Rossi (2006) with Pure OS and Hybrid business models. The Pure OS model includes firms that only offer OS products or OS solutions. The Hybrid business model includes all the others that play and profit in the OS space. Hybrid business models mix products, types of licenses, and sources of revenues. As academicians and practitioners, it is important to understand what type of vendor is included in any OS project undertaken. As can be seen from the plethora of business model types, the objectives and goals of each type of business will differ and may impact the quality of service or the types of products that the vendor offers. Organizations should consider the business model of any OS vendor with whom they engage in business, as the model and the viability of the vendor will impact the value of the OS-ERP option. Proprietary vendors do not have this range of business models, so this is not an issue with proprietary ERP systems. OS-ERP option value

and its relation to business model will be discussed more in the "Real Options Value of OS-ERP" section of this chapter.

CUSTOMIZATION OF OS-ERP

Proprietary ERP system customization has been explored extensively in the ERP literature (Gattiker & Goodhue, 2004; Levin, Mateyaschuk, & Stein, 1998; Nah & Zuckweiler, 2003; Soh & Sia, 2004, 2005; Soh, Siew, & Tay-Yap, 2000). OS-ERP applications are different from proprietary ERP applications in that they are closer to custom applications than to packaged software. For example, packaged software has limitations in terms of customization because the source code is not available. The issues with packaged software, as described by Gross and Ginzberg (1984) of "uncertainty about package modification time and cost, vender viability, and the ability of the package to meet the user needs," will apply differently to open source applications. Open source software has the code available, so the user is free to change (and many times is encouraged to change) the code as needed. Therefore, the issue of uncertainty about package modification time and cost depends solely on the skill of the programmers, not on some constraint that the modification may not be allowed by the proprietary software vendor. However, the ability to change source code raises a new set of problems. The efficiencies that we reap from packaged software (standards, easy maintenance, and upgrades) will not necessarily be available with open source software. Thus customization of OS-ERP is a double-edged sword. Although it is beneficial to adopters from a flexibility of the software perspective, maintenance, upgrades, and version control become new issues with which the adopting organization must contend.

Another issue that comes with OS-ERP is that the quality of the code will not always be similar to the acceptable quality of code required by the implementing organization (Spinellis, 2006). With proprietary code this is not as much of an issue, as you do not usually have access to all that code, and maintenance is definitely the duty of the vendor. In the OSS industry, it is many times expected that the skill for maintaining the code resides in the adopter's organization. Code of questionable quality will be harder to modify and maintain.

REAL OPTIONS VALUE OF OS-ERP

Much research has been done on real options theory as a way of evaluating platform change decisions (Fichman, 2004; Fichman, Keil, & Tiwana, 2005; McGrath, 1997; McGrath & Mac-Millan, 2000). In fact, a switch from SAP R/2 to SAP R/3 was considered a platform decision and evaluated in terms of real options (Taudes, 2000). These models and methods are useful, but seem to be missing some key variables that would influence the option value of OS-ERP.

Real options theory rests on the belief that limited commitment can create future decision rights. Real options theory has a rich history borne

from the finance and economics literature, and has been applied to technology in a variety of ways. Real options theory, in terms of technology positioning projects, proposes that technologies are desirable if they provide opportunities for future rent creation. These investments require less commitment than if a full plan was created that did not allow for quitting midstream. Beyond the specific real options literature that supports the logic of committing to software with the intent of exercising some future option, the project management literature on management information systems (MIS) also supports this notion. In the case of ERP systems and large systems in general, organizations implementing technology have decided that a "staged" or incremental approach is preferable to "big bang" implementations. The staged approach allows for less radical change introduction in the organization. A logical extension of this trend in project implementation approaches to valuing technologies in the selection decision seems clear. If companies can commit to a technology, and yet have the option to proceed, as well as options for future rents, the technology is more valuable to the organization. ERP systems—and more specifically, OS-ERP systems—tend to allow for future options.

Option valuation will be performed multiple times throughout the life of a project. This is not a one-time pre-implementation exercise. This is important: as implementation techniques have changed, so have the options that are afforded by technology positioning investments. For example, a company may look at the option value of implementing specific modules of an ERP system. Future options may be to continue to implement other modules of this system, to implement an integrated best-of-breed addition, to use these modules as a stand-alone part of their system, to integrate this module back to existing legacy systems, and so forth. This approach would be in congruence with current project management practices, where the project is analyzed at different steps to ensure the project is proceeding satisfactorily. Likewise, the option value of investment should be analyzed periodically to determine how to proceed with the option[5]—the emphasis being here that option value does change with time and thus should be examined over time.

Most of the studies of real options in a technology context have used a rigorous finance-influenced quantitative methods for evaluating the value of real options (Benaroch, 2000, 2002; Benaroch & Kauffman, 1999; Clemons & Gu, 2003; Santos, 1991; Taudes, 1998, 2000). Table 7 provides important background information about these studies.

For valuing the option of OS-ERP, I propose thinking more in line with the thinking behind McGrath (1997), McGrath and MacMillian (2000), Chen and Chen (2005), and Fichman (2004). These studies apply real options thinking to a qualitative options valuation method. For example, McGrath (1997) provides factors that influence the option value of a technology positioning option. This framework was expanded with explicit items to characterize each factor in later work (McGrath & MacMillan, 2000). This theory of real options for technology positioning focuses on the factors that are necessary for specific domains: new product

development and R&D type research. Although there are many similarities in R&D investments and IT platform investments, there are also many differences (Fichman, 2004).

These differences are explained by drawing from four complementary perspectives: technology strategy, organizational learning, innovation bandwagons, and technology adaptation to develop 12 factors identified as antecedents of option value in IT platform investments (Fichman, 2004). As the focus of this book chapter is on option value of OS-ERP systems, the original factors proposed to explain option value of platform decisions (Fichman, 2004) are pared down to the most influential in this context, and the short definition is contextualized to OS-ERP option valuation. Then, several factors (see Table 8) are added based on the previous discussion of OS-ERP systems.

According to real options theory, options are valued more highly if limited commitment is required to take advantage of the option. In terms of OS-ERP options, less commitment will be required if the organization already possesses the resources to customize, maintain, and upgrade the OS-ERP software. Future rents may be cre-

Table 7. Finance-based studies of IT platform decisions as real options

Authors	Major Theme	Context	Case or Conceptual
Clemons & Gu, 2003	Strategic options in IT infrastructure	Credit card rates for Capital One (industry level)	Case
Benaroch, 2002	Manage IT investment risk that that helps to choose which options to deliberately embed in an investment	Internet sales channel	Case
Benaroch & Kauffman, 2000	Investment timing	POS debit market	Case
Taudes, 2000	Evaluates ERP platform change	SAP R/2 to SAP R/3	Case
Benaroch & Kauffman, 1999	Investment timing	POS debit market	Case
Taudes, 1998	Evaluates software growth options	EDI growth option	Case
Dos Santos, 1991	Applies real options theory to IT investments using two stages, where the first stage creates the option for the second stage	None	Conceptual

Table 8. Factors for valuing OS-ERP options

Factor	Short Definition
Susceptibility to network externalities (Fichman, 2004)	The extent to which a technology increases in value to individual adopters with the size of the adoption network. In the case of OS-ERP, this is particularly relevant as future versions of the software depend on the adoption network, the partners, and developers.
Prospects for network dominance of the technology instance (Fichman, 2004)	The extent to which the technology instance being adopted is likely to achieve a dominant position relative to competing technology instances within the same class. In the case of OS-ERP, a dominant position may be achieved by a large network of adoption, partners, and developers, as well as venture capitalists.
Customization	The extent to which an organization possesses the resources to customize, maintain, and upgrade OS-ERP software.
Quality of Source Code	The extent to which the source code associated with an OS-ERP is of high quality.
Business Model of OS Vendor	The extent to which the business model of the OS vendor is acceptable and viable to the organization.

ated by customizing and upgrading the OS-ERP software. Less resources are required if the quality of the source code is high. As well, a fit between the business model of the OS vendor and the type of services and future solutions the organization might need would require less commitment in terms of gaining acceptance of the vendor. Future rents will be created if the business model of the vendor proves to be viable and the vendor is able to survive. This phenomenon is not unlike the dot.com era where the business model was as important as the technology. As was discussed earlier, these factors cannot be ignored in evaluation of an OS-ERP software option.

FUTURE TRENDS

Global Adoption of Open Source ERP

International research on open source firms is scarce (Bonaccorsi et al., 2006). Research in the area of OS-ERP packages is scarcer. Even scarcer

still is international OS-ERP research. For that reason, some generalizations about the current state of "adoption of open source" research are attempted based on what is happening in open source software in general. As well, several open source ERP participants were asked their opinions of the international open source ERP market.

There is clearly international activity in the open source arena, as is evidenced by a study performed by Lancashire (2001) where he showed that contributors to open source software development were shifting to an international origin. However, even this study had a very small sample (two projects) and there are questions as to the generalizability of these findings. More recently, evidence of the activity internationally in open source projects comes from the samples taken for some open source research. Bonaccorsi et al. (2006) performed a survey of 175 partners and system administrators of Italian open source[6] firms. Their sample was drawn using a snowballing technique where initial contacts refer other potential participants. This sample hints at the breadth of OSS in European countries.

Currently, several open source ERP participants based in the United States see potential for international growth. One open source ERP company estimates that about 15% of their business is from outside the United States and the CEO sees "enormous growth opportunity internationally." Another participant involved with an open source ERP package based in the United States reports that in 2005 about 80% of his income came from international sources. Then there are open source vendors that are based all over the world. The small sample of ERP vendors studied for this research shows that the base country for these organizations varies greatly (see Table 3).

There are many reasons that open source ERP is being developed internationally and development services sold internationally. The requirements of ERP systems vary from country to country. For example, China has different requirements of ERP packages than the U.S. (Liu & Steenstrup, 2004) . So, where certain packages dominate the U.S. ERP market, they are less diffused in the Asian market. Similar considerations will occur with open source ERP applications internationally. There is more room for competition from open source ERP packages in countries where the requirements are not as mainstream. This observation helps explain the proliferation of open source ERP developments around the world.

As for the services of U.S. developers being sold around the world, some U.S.-based open source ERP participants feel that the international opportunity is greater because the dollar is weaker, and so development by U.S. programmers is more affordable to those outside the U.S. The economics of this assumption also work in the reverse. There are many instances of international partners to U.S.-based ERP projects that are called on to develop customizations for U.S.-based users of the software because this international labor is more affordable.

CONCLUSION

This chapter outlines the current state of several OS-ERP packages (see Table 1) along the dimensions of licensing, geographic origins, number of customers, number of partners, targeted organization size, and functionality. Then the several factors that are important to decision making about OS-ERP packages are discussed: susceptibility to network externalities, prospects for network dominance, customization, quality of the source code, and business model of the OS vendor.

These factors will be important to OS-ERP packages crossing the credibility gap. Currently, as companies scour the landscape looking for an ERP package, there are very few open source offerings that have established credibility as reliable, maintainable, and scalable. Once several OS-ERP packages cross this hurdle, more widespread use of OS-ERP can be expected. As well, since the cost of ownership of an ERP package is so complex, marketing OS-ERP packages as more affordable is probably not going to gain much traction or gain the attention of major decision makers in the ERP space. Other features of OS-ERP, like customizability (given an adequate upgrade path) and a strong OS-ERP network, most specifically customers and consulting partners, will be desirable to decision makers.

This chapter hopes to enlighten practitioners and academia about the growing field of OS-ERP systems and their role in the international ERP community. There are significant differences in the offerings of open source ERP packages, and theoretically grounded evaluation techniques of OS-ERP are little researched or published. The aforementioned topics are important for creating a clear picture of what is currently on the market and the future directions of the OS-ERP market. Given the data presented in this chapter, it is clear that while OS-ERP is entering the ERP market, OS-ERP is far from a strong player. Also, OS-ERP is currently marketed as a small and medium enterprise option, with some governmental agencies also considering its use. Future research should attempt to explore the value gained and experiences of organizations actually using OS-ERP systems.

FUTURE RESEARCH DIRECTIONS

OS-ERP is a very little researched area. Future research should be performed that rigorously interviews OS-ERP participants about motivation, as this will add to the current literature about OSS motivation (several motivation articles are listed in the Additional Reading section). Many open source software initiatives fill a gap in functionality and thus are interesting to programmers. ERP systems are mature enough to lack such gaps, and thus figuring out what interests programmers that take part in OS-ERP projects could shed more light on the issue of motivation. Also, OS-ERP in the global context is an area ripe for research. Case study research of a large multinational implementation of OS-ERP would inform academia as to how large organizations work with open source communities and whether the functionality offered by OS-ERP systems is adequate in such a setting. Survey research with global companies might shed light on the differences in companies that adopt OS-ERP solutions and those that choose proprietary solutions. Global public sector research is also needed, as the motivations and evaluation criteria for public sector organizations is noted in the popular press to be different from private companies.

To build on the ideas in this chapter, the five factors should be included in a survey of those that have adopted and not adopted open source research to determine how these factors impacted the decision, and whether there were future implications of any of these factors on the success of the OS-ERP implementation. Each factor should be further researched in terms of options evaluation in the OS-ERP domain. For example, the author has

posited that OS-ERP is closer to custom software than to packaged software. This assertion should be tested through rigorous research. This could be done by looking at how much customization is actually done to OS-ERP packages, and how upgrades and maintenance are handled on these customized systems. ERP customization literature would benefit from such research. This is a partial list of possible future research directions. All of the topics covered in this chapter: factors for evaluating options, global OS-ERP systems, and OS-ERP organizations require much more research for academia to build a complete and coherent picture of OS-ERP and its impacts.

REFERENCES

Adamson, C. (2004). *Java.net: The source for Java technology collaboration*. Retrieved November 4, 2006, from http://today.java.net/pub/a/today/2004/06/01/ofbiz.html

Adempiere. (2006). *Adempiere: It's just a community—Nothing personal*. Retrieved from http://adempiere.red1.org/

Apache. (2007). *Apache license, version 2.0*. Retrieved March 8, 2007, from http://www.apache.org/licenses/LICENSE-2.0.html

Benaroch, M. (2000). Justifying electronic banking network expansion using real options analysis. *MIS Quarterly, 24*(2), 197.

Benaroch, M. (2002). Managing information technology investment risk: A real options perspective. *Journal of Management Information Systems, 19*(2), 43-84.

Benaroch, M., & Kauffman, R. (1999). A case for using real options pricing analysis to evaluate information technology project investments. *Information Systems Research, 10*(1), 70-86.

Bonaccorsi, A., Giannangeli, S., & Rossi, C. (2006). Entry strategies under competing standards: Hybrid business models in the open source software industry. *Management Science, 52*(7), 1085-1097.

Caton, M. (2006). OpenMFG: ERP basics and more. *eWeek, 23,* 44-45.

Clemons, E.K., & Gu, B. (2003). Justifying contingent information technology investments: Balancing the need for speed of action with certainty before action. *Journal of Management Information Systems, 20*(2), 11-48.

Cliff, S. (2003, 3/6/2003). Survey finds big variation in ERP costs. *Computer Weekly, 8.*

Compiere. (2006a). *Andre Boisvert joins Compiere team.* Retrieved from http://www.compiere. org/news/0522-andreboisvert.html

Compiere. (2006b). *Compiere appoints open source thought leader to its board of directors: Larry Augustin will help drive continued growth of leading open source ERP and CRM provider.* Retrieved November 3, 2006, from http://www. compiere.org/news/0724-augustin.html

DiMaio, A. (2004). *Look beyond TCO to judge open source software in government.* Gartner (G00123983).

DiMaio, A. (2007). *When to use custom, proprietary, open-source or community source software.* Gartner (G00146202).

Feller, J., & Fitzgerald, B. (2000). A framework analysis of the open source software development paradigm. In *Proceedings of the 21ˢᵗ International Conference in Information Systems* (ICIS 2000).

Ferguson, R.B. (2006). Open-source ERP grows up. *eWeek, 23*(27), 26-27.

Fichman, R.G. (2004). Real options and IT platform adoption: Implications for theory and practice. *Information Systems Research, 15*(2), 132-154.

Fichman, R.G., Keil, M., & Tiwana, A. (2005). Beyond valuation: "Options thinking" in IT project management. *California Management Review, 47*(2), 74-96.

Fisterra (2007). *Fisterra.org: A short history.* Retrieved March 8, 2007, from http://community. igalia.com/twiki/bin/view/Fisterra/ProjectHistory

Fitzgerald, B. (2006). The transformation of open source software. *MIS Quarterly, 30*(3), 587-598.

Gattiker, T., & Goodhue, D. (2004). Understanding the local-level costs and benefits of ERP through organizational information processing theory. *Information & Management, 41,* 431-443.

GNU. (2007a). *GNU general public license, version 2, June 1991.* Retrieved March 8, 2007, from http://www.gnu.org/licenses/gpl.txt

GNU. (2007b). *GNU's not Unix! Free software, free society.* Retrieved March 8, 2007, from http://www.gnu.org/

Gross, P. H. B., & Ginzberg, M.J. (1984). Barriers to the adoption of application software packages. *SOS, 4*(4), 211-226.

Guth, R., & Clark, D. (2005). Linux feels growing pains as users demand more features. *Wall Street Journal,* (August 8), B1.

HK-Software. (2007). *HK-Software features and modules, reasons for using AvERP.* Retrieved March 8, 2007, from http://www.hk-software. net/h-k.de/content/doc_138099-3-5-1.php

Hoover, L. (2006). Compiere is on the move—again. *NewsForge The Online Newspaper for Linux and Open Source.*

Krishnamurthy, S. (2005). An analysis of open source business models. In J. Feller, B. Fitzgerald, S. Hissam, & K.R. Lakhani (Eds.), *Making sense of the bazaar: Perspectives on open source and free software.* Boston: MIT Press.

Lancashire, D. (2001). Code, culture and cash: The fading altruism of open source development. *First Monday, 6*(12).

Levin, R., Mateyaschuk, J., & Stein, T. (1998). Faster ERP rollouts. *Information Week.*

Liu, L., & Steenstrup, K. (2004). *ERP selection criteria for Chinese enterprises.* Gartner (COM-22-0114).

McAllister, N. (2005). You can't kill TCO. *Infoworld,* (August 29).

McGrath, R.G. (1997). A real options logic for initiating technology positioning investments. *Academy of Management Review, 22*(4), 974-996.

McGrath, R.G., & MacMillan, I.C. (2000). Assessing technology projects using real options reasoning. *Research-Technology Management, 43*(4), 35-49.

Mozilla. (2007). *Mozilla public license, version 1.1.* Retrieved March 8, 2007, from http://www.mozilla.org/MPL/MPL-1.1.html

MySQL. (2007). *The world's most popular open source database: About MySQL AB.* Retrieved March 8, 2007, from http://www.mysql.com/company/

Nah, F. F. H., & Zuckweiler, K. M. (2003). ERP implementations: Chief information officer's perceptions of critical success factors. *International Journal of Human-Computer Interaction, 16*(1), 5-22.

Nichols, D., & Twidale, M. (2003). The usability of open source software. *First Monday, 8*(1).

Nolan, S. (2005). Knowing when to embrace open source. *Baseline,* (48), 76.

Open Source Initiative. (2005). *Open source definition.* Retrieved from http://www.opensource.org/

Open Source Initiative. (2006). *OSI Web site.* Retrieved October 24, 2006, from http://www.opensource.org/licenses/

OpenPro. (2007). *OpenPro: The open source ERP software solutions that give you more value and more features.* Retrieved March 8, 2007, from http://www.openpro.com

Prentice, B. (2006). *The advent of open-source business applications: Demand-side dynamics.* Gartner (G001412).

Raymond, E.S. (1999). *The cathedral and the bazaar: Musings on Linux and open source by an accidental revolutionary.* Sebastopol, CA: O'Reilly and Associates.

Rist, O. (2005). Open source ERP. *InfoWorld, 27*(32), 43-47.

Santos, B.L.D. (1991). Justifying investments in new information technologies. *Journal of Management Information Systems, 7*(4), 71.

Serrano, N., & Sarriegi, J. (2006). Open source software ERPs: A new alternative for an old need. *IEEE Software, 23*(3), 94-97.

Soh, C., & Sia, S.K. (2004). An institutional perspective on sources of ERP package-organization misalignments. *Journal of Strategic Information Systems, 13*(4), 375-397.

Soh, C., & Sia, S.K. (2005). The challenges of implementing "vanilla" versions of enterprise systems. *MIS Quarterly Executive, 4*(3), 373-384.

Soh, C., Kien, S. S., & Tay-Yap, J. (2000). Cultural fits and misfits: Is ERP a universal solution? *Communications of the ACM, 43*(4), 47-51.

Spinellis, D. (2006). 10 tips for spotting low-quality open source code. *Enterprise Open Source Journal,* (September/October).

SugarCRM. (2007). *SugarCRM: Commercial open source.* Retrieved March 8, 2007, from http://www.sugarcrm.com/

Taudes, A. (1998). Software growth options. *Journal of Management Information Systems, 15*(1), 165-185.

Taudes, A. (2000). Options analysis of software platform decisions: A case study. *MIS Quarterly, 24,* 227.

Watson, R., Wynn, D., & Boudreau, M.C. (2005). JBOSS: The evolution of professional open source software. *MIS Quarterly Executive, 4*(3), 329-341.

Watson, R.T., Boudreau, M.-C., York, P., Greiner, M., & Wynn, D. (2006). The business of open source. *Communications of ACM* (forthcoming).

ADDITIONAL READING

Al Marzoug, M., Zheng, L., Rong, G., & Grover, V. (2005). Open source: Concepts, benefits, and challenges. *Communications of the AIS,* (16), 505-521.

Benkler, Y. (2002). Coase's penguin, or, Linux and the nature of the firm. *Yale Law Journal, 112*(3), 369-446.

Brown, C.V., & Vessey, I. (2003). Managing the next wave of enterprises systems: Leveraging lessons from ERP. *MIS Quarterly Executive, 2*(1), 65-77.

Crowston, K., & Howison, J. (2005). *The social structure of free and open source software development.* Retrieved from http://www.firstmonday.org/issues/issue10_2/crowston/index.html

Fitzgerald, B., & Kenny, T. (2004). Developing an information systems infrastructure with open source software. *IEEE Software, 21*(1), 50-55.

Gallivan, M.J. (2001). Striking a balance between trust and control in a virtual organization: A content analysis of open source software case studies.

Information Systems Journal, 11(4), 277-304.

Gattiker, T.F., & Goodhue, D.L. (2005). What happens after ERP implementation: Understanding the impact of inter-dependence and differentiation on plant-level outcomes. *MIS Quarterly, 29*(3).

Hars, A., & Ou, S.S. (2002). Working for free? Motivations for participating in open-source projects. *International Journal of Electronic Commerce, 6*(3), 25-39.

Hertel, G., Niedner, S., & Herrmann, S. (2003). Motivation of software developers in open source projects: An Internet-based survey of contributors to the Linux kernel. *Research Policy, 32*(7), 1159-1177.

Krishnamurthy, S. (2002). Cave or community? An empirical examination of 100 mature open source projects. *First Monday, 7*(6).

Lacy, S. (2005). Open source: Now it's an ecosystem. *Business Week,* (October 7).

Lerner, J., & Tirole, J. 2002. Some simple economics of open source. *Journal of Industrial Economics, 50*(2), 197.

Liang, H., & Xue, Y. (2004). Coping with ERP-related contextual issues in SMEs: A vendor's perspective. *Journal of Strategic Information Systems,* (13), 399-415.

Mabert, V.A., & Watts, C.A. (2005). Enterprise applications: Building best-of-breed systems. In E. Bendoly & F.R. Jacobs (Eds.), *Strategic ERP extension and use.* Stanford, CA: Stanford University Press.

Madanmohan, T.R., & Krishnamurthy, S. (2005). Can the cathedral co-exist with the bazaar? An analysis of open source software in commercial firms. *First Monday,* (Special Issue #2). Retrieved from http://firstmonday.org/issues/special10_10/madanmohan/index.html

Nelson, M., Sen, R., & Chandrasekar, S. (2006). Understanding open source software: A research classification framework. *Communications of the AIS, 17*(12), 266-287.

Niederman, F., Davis, A., Wynn, D., & York, P. (2006). A research agenda for studying open source I: A multi-level framework. *Communications of the AIS, 18.*

Niederman, F., Davis, A., Greiner, M. E., Wynn, D., & York, P. (2006). A research agenda for studying open source II: View through the lens of referent discipline theories. *Communications of the AIS, 18.*

Stewart, K., & Gosain, S. (2006). The impact of ideology on effectiveness in open source software development teams. *MIS Quarterly, 30*(2), 291-314.

Watson, R.T., Boudreau, M.-C., Greiner, M., Wynn, D., York, P., & Gul, R. (2005). Governance and global communities. *Journal of International Management, 11*(2), 125-142.

Zhao, L., & Elbaum, S. (2003). Quality assurance under the open source development model. *Journal of Systems and Software, 66,* 65-75.

ENDNOTES

[1] http://www.sugarcrm.com/crm/SPL—The SugarCRM Public License Version (SPL) consists of the Mozilla Public License Version 1.1, modified to be specific to SugarCRM. Please see the actual license to understand the terms of this license.

[2] Intensive and complete functionality for ERP vendors includes the aforementioned functional areas, though the specifics of what is included in each functional area may be termed differently by different vendors (i.e., Oracle and SAP); however, both offer much of the same functionality and this base functionality is what is intended by the author when discussing ERP systems. For details about this functionality, see SAP. com or Oracle.com.

[3] See the Free Software Foundation Web site at http://www.fsf.org/licensing/licenses/ for another source for OSS licensing resources.

[4] "Forking" is not unusual in open source communities. Forking refers to taking the code in a separate direction, usually a direction not intended by those managing the open source project. There are dissenting opinions as to whether this is cause for alarm for the original open source project.

[5] For a review of potential option outcomes, see Fichman et al. (2005).

[6] Open source is defined as firms that supply OS-based offerings, even if the offering includes proprietary solutions.

Chapter V
Achieving Business Benefits from ERP Systems

Alok Mishra
Atilim University, Turkey

ABSTRACT

Enterprise resource planning (ERP) systems are becoming popular in medium and large-scale organizations all over the world. As companies have to collaborate across borders, languages, cultures, and integrate business processes, ERPs will need to take globalization into account, be based on a global architecture, and support the features required to bring all the worldwide players and processes together. Due to the high cost of implementation for these systems, organizations all over the world are interested in evaluating their benefits in the short and long terms. This chapter discusses various kinds of business benefits in a comprehensive way in order to justify the acquisition and implementation of ERP systems in organizations in the present global context.

INTRODUCTION

Enterprise resource planning (ERP) systems have become very important in modern business operations as ERP has played a major role in changing organizational computing for the better. One study found that more than 60% of Fortune 500 companies had adopted an ERP system (Stewart, Milford, Jewels, Hunter, & Hunter 2000). These systems have been credited with reducing inven-tories, shortening cycle times, lowering costs, and improving supply chain management practices. ERP has been credited with increasing the speed with which information flows through a company (Davenport, 1998). ERP has also been credited with creating value through integrating activities across a firm, implementing best practices for each business process, standardizing processes within organizations, creating one-source data that results in less confusion and error, and providing online access to information (O'Leary, 2000). All of these features facilitate better organizational planning, communication, and collaboration (Olson, 2004). Applied Robotics increased on-time deliveries 40% after implementing ERP, and Delta Electronics reduced production control labor requirements by 65% (Weil, 1999). Therefore, in the last decade, organizations around the world have made huge investments in enterprise systems. According to a report by Advanced Manufacturing Research, the ERP software market was expected to grow from $21 billion in 2002 to $31 billion in 2006, and the entire enterprise applications market which includes customer relationships management and supply chain management software will top $70 billion (AMR Research, 2002). It was estimated that in the 1990s about $300 billion was invested in ERP systems worldwide and that this was expected to grow to $79 billion annually by 2004 (Carlino, Nelson, & Smith, 2000).

Enterprise systems include enterprise resource planning, customer relationship management (SCM), supply chain management (SCM), product lifecycle management (PLM), and e-procurement software (Shang & Seddon, 2002). ERP software integrates management information and processes, such as financial, manufacturing, distribution, and human resources, for the purpose of enabling enterprise-wide management of resources (Davenport, 1998; Deloitte Consulting, 1998; Klaus, Rosemann, & Gable, 2000).

ERP helps organizations to meet the challenges of globalization with a comprehensive, integrated application suite that includes next-generation analytics, human capital management, financials, operations, and corporate services. With support for industry-specific best practices, ERP helps organizations improve productivity, sense and respond to market changes, and implement new business strategies to develop and maintain a competitive edge. ERP is designed to help businesses succeed in the global marketplace by supporting international legal and financial compliance issues, and enabling organiza-

tions to adapt internal operations and business processes to meet country-specific needs. As a result, organizations can focus on improving productivity and serving their customers instead of struggling to ensure they are in compliance with business and legal requirements around the world. Companies that automate and streamline workflows across multiple sites (including suppliers, partners, and manufacturing sites) produced 66% more improvement in reducing total time from order to delivery, according to Aberdeen's 2007 study of the role of ERP in globalization. Those companies that coordinate and collaborate between multiple sites, operating as a vertically integrated organization, have achieved more than a 10% gain in global market share. The majority of companies studied (79%) view global markets as a growth opportunity, but of those companies, half are also feeling pressures to reduce costs (Jutras, 2007). Those companies that coordinate and collaborate between multiple sites, operating as vertically integrated organizations, have achieved more than a 10% gain in global market share (Marketwire, 2007).

BUSINESS BENEFITS FROM ERP SYSTEMS

With the growing proliferation of ERP systems, including midsize companies, it becomes critical to address why and under what circumstances one can realize the benefits of an ERP system (Gefen & Ragowsky, 2005). ERP systems can provide the organization with competitive advantage through improved business performance (Hitt, Wu, & Zhou, 2002; Kalling, 2003) by, among other things, integrating supply chain management, receiving, inventory management, customer orders management, production planning and managing, shipping, accounting, human resource management, and all other activities that take place in a modern business (Gefen & Ridings, 2002; Hong & Kim, 2002; Kalling, 2003). Thus, business benefits from

ERP systems use are multidimensional, ranging from operational improvements through decision-making enhancement to support for strategic goals (Davenport, 2000; Deloitte Consulting, 1998; Markus & Tanis, 2000; Ross & Vitale, 2000; Irani & Love, 2001; Wilderman, 1999; Cooke & Peterson, 1998; Campbell, 1998). Gartner Group (1998) also mentions enterprise systems benefits in these areas, including both tangible and intangible benefits. While some companies claim to have reduced their cycle time, improved their financial management, and obtained information faster through ERP systems, in general they still have a high initial implementation failure rate (Hong & Kim, 2002; Songini, 2004). Many prior studies examining the relationship between investing in IT and the performance level of the organization (Weil, 1999) dealt with the ratio of total IT investment (i.e., software, hardware, personnel) to the entire organization's performance (the total profit of the organization).

Many early studies found no positive relationship between the two variables. Strassmann (1985) examined service-sector firms but found no significant relationship between investment in IT and high-performing firms. Berndt and Morrison (1992) even found a negative relationship between the growth in productivity and investment in high-tech, although, as they point out, this may have been the result of measurement problems. As Brynjolfsson (1993) summarizes, positive returns from investing in IT may not have shown up in previous research because of the inadequate way it was measured. When measuring IT investment on a per-user basis, there is a positive correlation between IT investment and overall productivity (Brynjolfsson, 2003). Although there is a large variance among companies in the benefit they achieve from their IT investment (Brynjolfsson, 2003), on average there is a $10 gain in company valuation for each dollar invested in IT (Brynjolfsson et al., 2002). Showing such a positive relationship is important because it affects MIS funding.

According to Parker and Benson (1988), in order for enterprise to gain competitive advantage, the way in which IT is justified financially must change. Classical quantitative techniques (e.g., cost-benefit analysis) are not adequate for the evaluation of IT applications, except when dealing with cost-avoidance issues, which generally occur at the operational level. If these methodologies are to be enhanced, additional measures—such as perceived value to the business, increased customer satisfaction, and the utility of IT in supporting decision making—must be considered (Katz, 1993). Investment in ERP systems payoff remains a controversial question (Hitt et al., 2002; Sarkis & Sundarraj, 2003; Kalling, 2003). ERP systems are very complicated software packages that support the entire set of organizational activities. Hence, it is possible that there are many unknown factors that impact the relationship between investment in ERP and organizational productivity. This chapter observes the manager's perception of the benefits their organization gains from using ERP systems and what impacts this benefits.

ERP system investments are strategic in nature, with the key goal often being to help a company grow in sales, reduce production lead time, and improve customer service (Steadman, 1999). In IT, evaluation costs are hard to quantify in post-implementation audits and benefits are harder to identify and quantify (Hochstrasser & Griffiths, 1991; Willcocks & Lester, 1999; Irani, Sharif, & Love, 2001; Seddon, Graeser, & Willcocks, 2002). Management of organizations that adopt ERP expects many benefits from the systems. These expectations are often difficult to meet. ERP can be seen to provide more responsive information to management. There also is more interaction across the organization and more efficient financial operation (Olson, 2004). There is weaker perceived benefit from operational performance, such as improved operating efficiency, inventory management, and cash management. While more information is available at higher quality, this does not directly translate to cost efficiencies across the board.

SAP-ERP delivers business benefits where they matter most—to the bottom line—and addresses the internal and external business requirements of global enterprise. Organizations can invest in mySAP ERP with confidence that expansion or change in any country or division will be supported. The solution provides global businesses with concrete benefits that enable success, including the following (My SAP ERP, 2007):

- Improved productivity for greater efficiency and responsiveness
- Increased insight for more assured decision making
- Advanced flexibility and adaptability to cut costs and speed change
- A partner for long-term growth

In addition, businesses can reduce the costs associated with compliance and administration, in part by creating flexible processes that balance global demands with local needs and that can be adapted quickly as regulations change. Comprehensive financial and reporting features ensure that globally consolidated financial reports can be generated quickly. Support for internal controls improves financial management and reduces the risk of noncompliance. In conjunction with the Collaboration Folders (cFolders) application, employees can work in seamless virtual project teams with other departments, partners, and suppliers around the world. Analytical capabilities help organizations improve strategic insight and performance through better identification of global market opportunities and drivers (My SAP ERP, 2007).

Benefits perceived from adopting an ERP system were studied by Mabert, Soni, and Venkataraman (2000) in Midwestern U.S. manufacturing, and replicated in Sweden by Olhager and Selldin (2003). Both studies used a 1 to 5 scale, with 1 representing "not at all" and 5 representing "to a great extent." Average ratings are given in Tables 1 and 2.

Here, the results are very similar. ERP systems were credited with making information more available, at higher quality, and with integrating operations (Olson, 2004). There was neutral support for crediting ERP with providing benefits in specific materials management and financial functions. The ratings of support for customer response and personnel management were quite low (although the Swedish rating for customer

Table 1. Expected benefits of ERP systems (Mabert et al., 2000; Olhager & Selldin, 2003)

ERP Performance Outcomes	United States	Sweden
Quicker information response time	3.51	3.81
Increased interaction across the enterprise	3.49	3.55
Improved order management/order cycle	3.25	3.37
Decreased financial close cycle	3.17	3.36
Improved interaction with customers	2.92	2.87
Improved on-time delivery	2.83	2.82
Improved interaction with suppliers	2.81	2.78
Lowered inventory levels	2.70	2.60
Improved cash management	2.64	2.54
Reduced direct operating costs	2.32	2.74

Table 2. Areas benefiting from ERP systems

Area	United States	Sweden
Availability of information	3.77	3.74
Integration of business operations/process	3.61	3.42
Quality of information	3.37	3.31
Inventory management	3.18	2.99
Financial management	3.11	2.98
Supplier management/procurement	2.99	2.94
Customer responsiveness/flexibility	2.67	2.95
Decreased information technology costs	2.06	2.05
Personnel management	1.94	2.06

response was very close to neutral). Interestingly, both surveys found low support for crediting ERP systems with decreasing information technology costs. With an ERP, an organization can better negotiate with suppliers and reduce the cost of raw materials by as much as 15% (Schlack, 1992). Hence, the higher the cost of raw material, the higher the value of raw material cost reduction out of the cost of the product.

ERP BENEFITS FRAMEWORK

Shang and Seddon (2000) provided a comprehensive framework of the benefits of ERP systems. In their survey of 233 vendor success stories and 34 follow-up phone interviews from three major ERP vendor Web sites, they found that all organizations derived benefit from at least two of the five categories, and all the vendors' products had returned customer benefit in all five categories.

In the beginning of 1997 during the re-engineering process, most of the multinational organizations perceived the following benefits of implementing ERP system:

- Common processes across the globe
- Centralized operations

- Multi-language and currency capabilities
- Better tracking of inventory
- Improved utilization of raw materials
- Tighter integration of production with sales and distribution
- Tax advantages through improved asset management
- Removal of a number of existing legacy systems
- Improved development and support environment
- Real-time functional system enhancement capability

In Table 3, the first three categories are based on Anthony's (1965) much cited work on planning and control systems. Many IS benefit analyses and frameworks have been organized around Anthony's trinity of operational, managerial and strategic levels of management. One example is Shang and Seddon (2000):

- Weil (1990) evaluated the payoff from three types of IS investment—in transactional, informational, and strategic systems—in the U.S. valve industry. He found that the greatest benefits came from investment in transactional level IT.

Table 3. ERP benefits framework and extent of tangibility and quantifiability (adapted from Shang & Seddon, 2000)

Dimension/Sub-Dimensions	Tangible	Quantifiable
1. Operational		
1.1 Cost reduction	Full	Full
1.2 Cycle time deduction	Most	Full
1.3 Productivity improvement	Most	Full
1.4 Quality improvement	Some	Most
1.5 Customer services improvement	Some	Most
2. Managerial		
2.1 Better resource management	Some	Most
2.2 Improved decision making and planning	Some	Some
2.3 Performance improvement	Most	Most
3. Strategic		
3.1 Support business growth	Some	Full
3.2 Support business alliance	Low	Most
3.3 Build business innovations	Some	Some
3.4 Build cost leadership	Some	Some
3.5 Generate product differentiation	Some	Low
3.6 Build external linkages	Low	Some
4. IT infrastructure		
4.1 Build business flexibility for current and future changes	Low	Low
4.2 IT costs reduction	Full	Full
4.3 Increased IT infrastructure capability	Some	Some
5. Organizational		
5.1 Support organizational changes	Low	Low
5.2 Facilitate business learning	Low	Low
5.3 Empowerment	Low	Low
5.4 Build common visions	Low	Low

- Gorry and Scott Morton (1971) and others (Silver, 1990; Demmel & Askin, 1992) reported significant benefits from using IT for managerial decision suport.
- Porter and Miller (1985) and others (McFarlan, 1984; Rackoff, Wiseman, & Ullrich, 1985; Clemons, 1991; Venkataraman, Henderson, & Oldach 1993) noted significant benefits from the use of IT in pursuing strategic goals.

- Mirani and Lederer (1998) adapted Anthony's framework to build an instrument for assessing the organizational benefits of IS projects.
- Hicks (1997), Reynolds (1992), and Schultheis and Sumner (1989) also used Anthony's categories in classifying IT benefits as operational, tactical, and strategic. The categories were also used as frameworks for analyzing the benefits of general and enterprise-wide

information systems (Wysocki & DeMichiell, 1997; Irani & Love, 2001).

- Willcocks (1994) and Graeser, Willcocks, and Pisanias (1998) adapted Kaplan and Norton's (1996) balanced scorecard approach in assessing IS investment in financial, project, process, customer, learning, and technical aspects, and measured organizational performance along Anthony's three levels of business practice.

Therefore, there are very strong precedents in the IS literature for attempting to classify the benefits of enterprise systems in terms of organizational performance along Anthony's three levels of business practice.(Shang & Seddon, 2000).

INTANGIBLE BENEFITS IN IT AND ERP PROJECTS

Webster (1994) defines a tangible item as "something that is capable of being appraised at an actual or approximate value." But the 'value' is monetary worth, or some other measure like customer satisfaction is not certain. According to Hares and Royle (1994), "an intangible is anything that is difficult to measure," and the boundary between tangible and intangible is fuzzy at best. Determining the intangible benefits derived from information systems implementation has been an elusive goal of academics and practitioners alike (Davern & Kauffman, 2000). Remenyi and Sherwood-Smith (1999) pointed out that there are seven key ways in which information systems may deliver direct benefits to organizations. They also indicated that information systems deliver intangible benefits that are not easily assessed. Nandish and Irani (1999) discussed the difficulty of evaluating IT projects in the dynamic environment, especially when intangibles are involved in the evaluation. Tallon, Kraemer, and Gurbaxni (2000) cited a number of studies indicating that economic and financial measures fail to assess

accurately the payoff of IT projects and suggested that one means of determining value is through the perception of executives. They focused on the strategic fit and the contributions of IT projects, but indicated that researchers need somehow to capture or represent better the intangible benefits of IT. In the technology arena, as in the business areas, many projects deliver benefits that cannot be easily quantified (Murphy & Simon, 2002). Many benefits related to the information technology projects cannot be easily quantified, for example better information access, improved workflow, interdepartmental coordination, and increased customer satisfaction (Emigh, 1999). These are also the features that are listed as key attributes of ERP systems (Mullin, 1999; Davenport, 2000). ERP systems are implemented to integrate transactions along and between business processes. Common business processes include order fulfillment, materials management, production planning and execution, procurement, and human resources (Murphy & Simon, 2002). ERP systems enable efficient and error-free workflow management and accounting processes including in-depth auditing. These systems feature a single database to eliminate redundancy and multiple entry errors, and they provide in-depth reporting functionality. ERP systems provide information for effective decision making on all organizational levels (Murphy & Simon, 2002). According to Hares and Royle (1994), there are four main intangible benefits in IT investment:

1. **Internal improvement:** This includes processes, workflow, and information access.
2. **Customer service:** This ensures quality, delivery, and support.
3. **Foresight:** This is vision regarding markets, products, and acquisitions in the future.
4. **Adaptability:** This is the ability to adapt change in rapidly changing industry.

The third and fourth sets of intangibles are future oriented and include spotting market trends and the ability to adapt to change.

Hares and Royle (1994) stated that the first set of ongoing intangible benefits are those concerned with internal improvement of company operations or performance. These include changes in production processes, methods of operations management, and changes to production value and process chains with resulting benefits in increased output or lower production costs. The second group of ongoing benefits, customer-oriented intangibles, is more difficult to measure because their effectiveness is determined by external forces. The benefits of improving customer service are greater retention of customers and customer satisfaction. The third group of intangibles embodies the spotting of new market trends. If new trends can be anticipated, then technology may be able to transform or create products, processes, or services to gain new sales and market position. The final group of intangible benefits is the ability to adapt to change. As with the identification of market trends, the benefits derived include adapting products and services to market trends and the modification of production processes—a critical ability for firms in rapidly changing industries.

ERP system investments are strategic in nature, with the key goal often being to help a company grow in sales, reduce production lead time, and improve customer service (Steadman, 1999). Organizations turned up an average value of -$1.5 million when quantifiable cost savings and revenue gains were calculated against system implementation and maintenance costs. Improved customer service and related intangible benefits such as updated and streamlined technical infrastructure are important intangible benefits that organizations are often seeking when making these investments. The development and implementation of ERP systems is longer in duration and cost intensive. It is difficult to quantify in monetary terms because of the intangible nature of many of the derived benefits, for example, improved customer service (Murphy & Simon, 2002).

The literature suggests that intangibles can be converted into monetary terms through the ability to take care of the following observations:

1. Maintain and increase sales
2. Increase prices
3. Reduce costs
4. Create new business

Hares and Royle (1994) give a procedure to quantify intangible benefits. The major steps are:

1. Identify benefits to be quantified
2. Make intangible benefits measurable
3. Predict the benefits in physical terms
4. Evaluate cash flow terms

ENTERPRISE SYSTEM BENEFIT FRAMEWORK

According to Shang and Seddon (2002), the following five-dimensional framework, which is built on a large body of previous research into IT benefits, has been organized around operational efficiency and managerial and strategic effectiveness, as the outlook of strategic managers are too broad to identify casual links between enterprise system investment and benefit realization, and those of operational managers are too narrow to consider all relevant organizational goals. The most appropriate management level is business managers (middle-level management control), as they have a comprehensive understanding of both the capabilities of ES and the business plans for system use. It is not expected that all organizations will achieve benefits in all 25 sub-dimensions, or even in all five main dimensions, but it provides an excellent checklist of benefits that have been accomplished in organizations using enterprise systems.

1. Operational Benefits:

1.1 Cost reduction:
- Labor cost reduction in customer service, finance, human resources, purchasing, IT services, and training.
- Inventory cost in inventory turns, dislocation costs, and warehousing costs.
- Administrative expenses reduction in printing and other business supplies.

1.2 Cycle time reduction:
- Customer support activities in order fulfillment, billing, delivery, and customer enquiries.
- Employee support activities in month-end closing, requisition, HR and payroll, and learning.
- Supplier support activities in order processing, information exchange, and payment.

1.3 Productivity improvement:
   Production per employee, production by labor hours, production by labor costs, increased work volume with same workforce, and reduced overtime.

1.4 Quality improvement:
   Error rate, data reliability to data accuracy.

1.5 Customer service improvement:
   Ease of data access and inquiries.

2. Managerial Benefits

2.1 Better resource management:
- Better asset management for improved cost, depreciation, relocation, custody, physical inventory, and maintenance records control, both locally and worldwide.
- Better inventory management in shifting products where they were needed and responding quickly to surges or dips in demand. Managers are able to see the inventory of all locations in their region or across boundaries, making possible a leaner inventory.
- Better production management for coordinating supply and demand, and meeting production schedules at the lowest cost.
- Better workforce management for improved workforce allocation and better utilization of skills.

2.2 Improved decision making and planning:
- Improved strategic decisions for greater market responsiveness, fast profit analysis, tighter cost control, and effective strategic planning.
- Improved management decisions for flexible resource management, efficient processes, and quick response to operational changes.
- Improved customer decisions with flexible customer services, rapid response to customer demands, and prompt service adjustments.

2.3 Performance improvement in a variety of ways in all levels of the organization:
- Financial performance by lines of business, by product, by customers, by geographies, or by different combinations.
- Manufacturing performance monitoring, prediction, and quick adjustments.
- Overall operational efficiency and effectiveness management.

3. Strategic Benefits

Strategic benefits are in a wide spectrum of activities in internal and external areas in terms of general competitiveness, product strategies, strategic capabilities, and competitive position of the organization.

3.1 Support business growth:

- In transaction volume, processing capacity and capability.
- With new business units.
- In products or services, new divisions, or new functions in different regions.
- With increased employees, new policies and procedures.
- In new markets.
- With industry's rapid changes in competition, regulation, and markets.

3.2 Support business alliance by:

- Efficiently and effectively consolidating newly acquired companies into standard business practice.
- Building consistent IT architecture support in different business units.
- Changing selling models of new products developed by a merged company.
- Transiting new business units to a corporate system.
- Integrating resources with acquired companies.

3.3 Building business innovation by:

- Enabling new market strategy.
- Building new process chains.
- Creating new products or services.

3.4 Building cost leadership by:

- Building a lean structure with streamlined processes.
- Reaching business economies of scale in operation.
- Shared services.

3.5 Generating product differentiation by:

- Providing customized product or services, such as early preparation for the new EMU currency policy, customized billing, individualized project services to different customer requirements, and different levels of service appropriate for various sizes of customer organizations.
- Providing lean production with make-to-order capabilities.

3.6 Enabling worldwide expansion:

- Centralized world operation.
- Global resource management.
- Multicurrency capability.
- Global market penetration.
- Cost-effective worldwide solution deployment.

3.7 Enabling e-commerce by attracting new customers or getting closer to customers through the Web integration capability. The Web-enabled ES provides benefits in business to business and business to individual in:

- Interactive customer service.
- Improved product design through customer direct feedback.
- Expanding to new markets.
- Building virtual corporations with virtual supply and demand consortia.
- Delivering customized service.
- Providing real-time and reliable data enquiries.

3.8 Generating or sustaining competitiveness:

- Maintaining competitive efficiency.
- Building competitive advantage with quick decision making.
- Staying ahead of competitors for better internal business support.
- Using opportunities generated by enterprise systems to pull abreast of world leaders by using the same software and being compatible with customers.

4. IT Infrastructure Benefits

4.1 Building business flexibility by rapid response to internal and external changes at lower cost and providing a range of options in reacting to changing requirements.

4.2 IT cost reduction in:
- Total cost of maintaining and integrating legacy systems by eliminating separate data centers and applications, as well as their supporting costs.
- IT staff reductions.
- Mainframe or hardware replacement.
- System architecture design and development.
- System upgrade maintenance.
- System modification and future changes.
- Technology research and development.

4.3 Increase IT infrastructure capability:
Stable and flexible support for the current and future business changes in process and structure.

Stability:
- Reliable platforms.
- Global platforms with global knowledge pipeline.
- Transformed IS management and increased IS resource capability.
- Continuous improvement in process and technology.

Flexibility:
- Modern technology adaptability.
- Extendibility to external parties.
- Expandability to a range of applications.
- Customizable and configurable.

5. Organizational Benefits

Organizational benefits can be evaluated in individual attitudes, employee morale and motivation, and interpersonal interactions.

5.1 Changing work pattern with shifted focus:
- Coordination between different interdisciplinary matters.
- Harmonization of interdepartmental processes.

5.2 Facilitating business learning and broaden employee skills:
- Learned by entire workforce.
- Shortened learning time.
- Broadened employee skills.
- Employees with motivation to learn the process.

5.3 Empowerment:
- Accountability, more value-added responsibility.
- More proactive users in problem solving, transformed from doers to planners.
- Working autonomously.
- Users with ownership of the system.
- Greater employee involvement in business management.

5.4 Building common visions:
- Acting as one and working as a common unit.
- Consistent vision across different levels of organizations.

5.5 Shifting work focus:
- Concentrate on core work.
- Focus on customer and market.
- Focus on business process.
- Focus on overall performance.

5.6 Increased employee morale and satisfaction:
- Satisfied users with better decision-making tools.
- Satisfied users with increased work efficiency.
- Satisfied users in solving problems efficiently.
- Satisfied users in increased system skills and business knowledge.
- Increased morale with better business performance.
- Satisfied employees for better employee service.

DISCUSSION

The above benefits were reported by all selected cases as mentioned by Shang and Seddon (2002); also, examples of each benefit dimension were found in cases from each ES vendor. Every business achieved benefits in at least two dimensions. Operational and infrastructure benefits were the most quoted benefits: 170 cases (73% of 233) claimed to have achieved operational benefits, and 194 cases (83%) claimed IT infrastructure benefits (Shang & Seddon, 2002). Operational benefits such as cost, speed, and error rates are measurable in many cases. Managerial benefits, although less tangible, are linked directly with information used at different decision-making levels and with different resources. The most useful information on both these dimensions was provided by business managers or process owners, who had a clearer picture of the impact of the adoption of ES on the overall organization, including their own and their colleagues' decision making. Strategic benefits appear to flow from a broad range of activities in internal and external areas, and are described in terms of general competitiveness, product strategies, and other strategic capabilities. Organizational benefits are mainly reflected in individual attitudes (e.g., employee morale) and interpersonal interactions.

Operational benefits may come with increased managerial effectiveness, strategic benefits rely on operational efficiency, and organizational benefits can be realized in parallel with managerial benefits (Shang & Seddon, 2002).

Regardless of tangible or intangible benefits, it is progressively more difficult to measure managerial, organizational, and strategic benefits than infrastructure or operational benefits; this has been an issue of debate since information systems advanced beyond transaction processing systems (Murphy & Simon, 2002). With ERP systems, success has been determined based on the organization's acceptance of the changes that the system introduces. Further, Murphy and Simon (2002) observed that organizational and managerial classification benefits are not only the most difficult to obtain, but also are the hardest to quantify.

FUTURE RESEARCH DIRECTIONS

Empirical studies of ERP benefits assessments in different organizations and their comparisons might be an interesting area for further work in this direction. Furthermore, assessment of ERP benefits can be performed at two levels: first at an enterprise level, where the entire ERP system can be assessed regarding different types of benefits derived from the ERP; and second at a specific module (application) level, which offers interesting areas for future research. Future research efforts should focus on managerial, organizational, and strategic benefits, which are still unexplored in terms of intangible benefits measurement to quantify.

CONCLUSION

Assessing whether investment in enterprise systems pays off is an important issue. Organizations can achieve a number of tangible and intangible benefits due to successful implementation of ERP systems. These benefits can be derived globally, and in the context of globalization it is important to understand an organization's managerial people and shareholders as well. ERP helps organizations meet the challenges of globalization with a comprehensive, integrated application suite that includes next-generation analytics, human capital management, financials, operations, and corporate services. ERP is designed to help businesses succeed in the global marketplace by supporting international legal and financial compliance issues, and enabling organizations to adapt internal operations and business processes to meet country-specific needs. This will be helpful for decision makers (managerial people) of organizations to evaluate various available ERPs in acquisition and implementation. This will also a further aid managers in assessing the benefits of their existing ERPs in the organization in a more objective way all over the world .

REFERENCES

AMR Research. (2002). *AMR Research predicts enterprise applications market will reach $70 billion in 2006.* Retrieved from http:www.amrresearch.com

Anthony, R.N. (1965). *Planning and control systems: A framework for analysis.* Graduate School of Business Administration, Harvard University, USA.

Berndt, E.R., & Morrison, C.J. (1992). *High-tech capital formation and economic performance in U.S. manufacturing: An exploratory analysis.* Economics, Finance and Accounting Working Paper #3419, Sloan School of Management, Massachusetts Institute of Technology, USA.

Brynjolfsson, E. (1993). The productivity paradox of information technology. *Communications of the ACM, 36*(12), 67-77.

Campbell, S. (1998). Mining for profit in ERP software. *Computer Reseller News,* (October), 19.

Carlino, J., Nelson, S., & Smith, N. (2000). *AMR Research predicts enterprise applications market will reach $78 billion by 2004.* Retrieved from http://www.amrresearch.com/press/files/99518.asp

Cooke, D.P., & Peterson, W.J. (1998, July). *SAP implementation: Strategies and results.* R-1217-98-RR, The Conference Board, New York, USA.

Clemons, E.K. (1991). Evaluation of strategic investments in information technology. *Communications of the ACM, 34,* 22-36.

Davenport, T.H. (1998). Putting the enterprise into the enterprise system. *Harvard Business Review,* (July/August), 121-131.

Davenport, T.H. (2000). *Mission critical—Realizing the promise of enterprise systems.* Boston: Harvard Business School.

Davern, M.J., & Kauffman, R.J. (2000). Discovering potential and realizing value from information technology investments. *Journal of Information Management Information Systems, 16,* 121-143.

Deloitte Consulting. (1998). *ERP's second wave—Maximizing the value of ERP-enabled processes.* New York.

Demmel, J., & Askin, R. (1992). A multiple-objective decision model for the evaluation of advanced manufacturing systems technology. *Journal of Manufacturing Systems, 11,* 179-194.

Emigh, J. (1999). Net present value. *Computerworld, 33,* 52-53.

Gartner Group. (1998). *1998 ERP and FMIS study—Executive summary.* Stamford, CT.

Gefen, D., & Ragowsky, A. (2005). A multi-level approach to measuring the benefits of an ERP system in manufacturing firms. *Information System Management,* (Winter), 18-25.

Gefen, D., & Ridings, C. (2002). Implementation team responsiveness and user evaluation of CRM: A quasi-experimental design study of social exchange theory. *Journal of Management Information Systems, 19*(1), 47-63.

Gorry, A., & Scott Morton, M.S. (1971). A framework for management information systems. *Sloan Management Review, 13,* 49-61.

Graeser, V., Willcocks, L., & Pisanias, N. (1996). *Developing the IT scorecard.* London: Business Intelligence.

Hicks, J.O. (1997). *Management information systems: A user perspective.* Minneapolis/St. Paul: West.

Hitt, L.M., Wu, D.J., & Zhou, X. (2002). ERP investment: Business impact and productivity measures. *Journal of Management Information Systems, 19*(1), 71-98.

Hares, J., & Royle, D. (1994). *Measuring the value of information technology, 7,* 109-122.

Hochstrasser, B., & Griffiths, C. (1991). *Controlling IT investment: Strategy and management.* London: Chapman & Hall.

Hong, K., & Kim, Y. (2002). The critical success factors for ERP implementation: An organizational fit perspective. *Information & Management, 40*(1), 25-40.

Irani, Z., & Love, P.E.D. (2001). The propagation of technology management taxonomies for evaluating investments in information systems. *Journal of Management Information Systems, 17,* 161-178.

Irani, Z., Sharif, A.M., & Love, P.E.D. (2001). Transforming failure into success through organisational learning: An analysis of a manufacturing information system. *European Journal of Information Systems, 10,* 55-66.

Jutras, C. (2007). *The role of ERP in globalization.* Retrieved from http://www.aberdeen.com/summary/report/benchmark/RA_ERPRoleinGlobalization_CJ_3906.asp

Kalling, T. (2003). ERP systems and the strategic management processes that lead to competitive advantage. *Information Resources Management Journal, 16*(4), 46-67.

Kaplan, R., & Norton, D.P. (1996). Using the balance scorecard as a strategic management system. *Harvard Business Review,* (January/February), 75-85.

Katz, A.I. (1993). Measuring technology's business value: Organizations seek to prove IT benefits. *Information Systems Management, 10,* 33-39.

Klaus, H., Rosemann, M., & Gable, G.G. (2000). What is ERP? *Information System Frontiers, 2,* 141-162.

Mabert, V.M., Soni, A., & Venkataraman, N. (2000). Enterprise resource planning survey of U.S. manufacturing firms. *Production and Inventory Management Journal, 41*(2), 52-58.

Marketwire. (2007). *Thinking global? Don't lose sight of profitable growth.* Retrieved from http://www.marketwire.com/mw/release_html_b1?release_id=224493

Markus, L.M., & Tanis, C. (2000). The enterprise systems experience—From adoption to success. In R.W. Zmud (Ed.), *Framing the domains of IT research: Glimpsing the future through the past.* Cincinnati, OH: Pinnaflex Educational Resources.

McFarlan, F.W. (1984). Information technology changes the way you compete. *Harvard Business Review,* (May/June), 98-103.

Mirani, R., & Lederer, A.L. (1998). An instrument for assessing the organizational benefits of IS project. *Decision Sciences, 29,* 803-838.

MIT. (n.d.). *Economic performance in U.S. manufacturing: An exploratory analysis.* Economics, Finance and Accounting Working Paper #3419, Sloan School of Management, Massachusetts Institute of Technology, USA.

Mullin, R. (1999). ERP users say payback is passé. *Chemical Week, 161,* 25-26.

Murphy, K.E., & Simon, S.J. (2002). Intangible benefits valuation in ERP projects. *Information Systems Journal, 12,* 301-320.

MySAP ERP. (2007). *Globalization with localization.* Retrieved from www.sap.com/usa/solutions/grc/pdf/BWP_mySAP_ERP_Global_Local.pdf

Nandish, V.P., & Irani, Z. (1999). Evaluating information technology in dynamic environments: A focus on tailorable information. *Logistics Information Management, 12,* 32.

O'Leary, D.E. (2000). *Enterprise resource planning systems: Systems, life cycle, electronic commerce, and risk.* Cambridge: Cambridge University Press.

Olhager, J., & Selldin, E. (2003). Enterprise resource planning survey of Swedish manufacturing firms. *European Journal of Operational Research, 146,* 365-373.

Olson, D.L. (2004). *Managerial issues of enterprise resource planning systems.* McGraw-Hill International.

Parker, M., & Benson, R. (1988). *Information economics: Linking business performance to information technology.* London: Prentice Hall.

Porter, M.E., & Miller, V.E. (1985). How information gives you competitive advantage. *Harvard Business Review, 63,* 149-160.

Rackoff, N., Wiseman, C., & Ullrich, W.A. (1985). Information systems for competitive advantage: Implementation of a planning process. *MIS Quarterly, 9,* 285-294.

Remenyi, D., & Sherwood-Smith, M. (1999). Maximize information systems value by continuous participative evaluation. *Logistics Information Management, 12,* 14-25.

Reynolds, G.W. (1992). *Information systems for managers.* Minneapolis/St. Paul, MN: West.

Ross, J.W., & Vitale, M. (2000). The ERP revolution. Surviving versus thriving. *Information System Frontiers, 2*(2), 233-241.

Sarkis, J., & Sundarraj, R.P. (2003). Managing large scale global enterprise resource planning systems: A case study at Texas Instruments. *International Journal of Information Management, 23*(5), 431-442.

Schultheis, R., & Sumner, M. (1989). *Management information systems: The manager's view.* Boston: Irwin.

Seddon, P.B., Graeser, V., & Willcocks, L. (2002). Measuring organizational IS effectiveness: An overview and update of senior management perspectives. *The Database for Advances in Information Systems, 33,* 11-28.

Schlack, M. (1992). IS has a new job in manufacturing. *Datamation,* (January 15), 38-40.

Stewart, G., Milford, M., Jewels, T., Hunter, T., & Hunter, B. (2000). Organizational readiness for ERP implementation. In *Proceedings of the Americas Conference on Information Systems* (pp. 966-971).

Shang, S., & Seddon, P.B. (2002). Assessing and managing the benefits of enterprise systems: The business manager's perspective. *Information Systems Journal, 12,* 271-299.

Shang, S., & Seddon, S. (2000). A comprehensive framework for classifying the benefits of ERP systems. *Proceedings of Americas Conference on Information Systems.*

Silver, M. (1990). Decision support systems: Direct and non-directed changes. *Information Systems Research, 1,* 47-88.

Songini, M.C. (2004, August 23). *Ford abandons Oracle procurement systems, switches back to mainframe apps.* Retrieved from http://www. computerworld.com/softwaretopics/erp/story/0.10801,95404,00.html

Steadman, C. (1999). Calculating ROI. *Computerworld, 33,* 6.

Strassmann, P. (1985). *Information payoff: The transformation of work in the electronic age.* London: Collier Macmillan.

Tallon, P., Kraemer, K., & Gurbaxni, V. (2000). Executives' perception of business value of information technology: A process-oriented approach. *Journal of Management Information Systems, 16*(4), 145-173.

Venkataraman, N., Henderson, J., & Oldach, S.H. (1993). Continuous strategic alignment: Exploiting IT capabilities for competitive success. *European Management Journal, 11,* 139-149.

Weil, M. (1999). Managing to win. *Manufacturing Systems, 17*(November), 14.

Willcocks, L.P., & Lester, S. (Eds.). (1999). *Beyond the IT productivity paradox.* Chichester: John Wiley & Sons.

Willcocks, L. (Ed.). (1994). *Information management: Evaluation of information systems investments.* London: Chapman & Hall.

Wysocki, R., & DeMichiell, R.L. (1997). *Managing information across the enterprise.* New York: John Wiley & Sons.

Wilderman, B. (1999). *Enterprise resource management solutions and their value.* Stanford, CT: MetaGroup.

ADDITIONAL READING

Bingi, P., Sharma, M.K., & Godla, J.K. (1999). Critical issues affecting an ERP implementation. *Information Systems Management,* (Summer), 121-131.

Litecky, C.R. (1981). Intangibles in cost/benefit analysis. *Journal of Systems Management, 32,* 15-17.

Motwani, J., Mirchandani, D., Madan, M., & Gunasekaran, A. (2002). Successful implementation of ERP projects: Evidence from two case studies. *International Journal of Production Economics, 75.*

Olson, D.L. (2004). *Managerial issues of enterprise resource planning systems* (international ed.). Singapore: McGraw-Hill.

Simms, J. (1997). Evaluating IT: Where cost-benefit can fail. *Australian Accountant,* (May), 29-31.

van Everdingen, Y., van Hellegersberg, J., & Waarts, E. (2000). ERP adoption by European midsize companies. *Communications of the ACM, 43*(4), 27-31.

Section III
Organizational Aspects

Chapter VI
The Secret Success of a Global ERP Champion:
Everything Changed and Nothing Happened

Denise Potosky
The Pennsylvania State University, USA

Bruce Olshan
E. I. du Pont de Nemours and Co., USA

ABSTRACT

The role of a global ERP champion is to guide a business through process transformation and ERP system implementation. A "change curve" model that depicts the "Valley of Despair" illustrates what a champion can expect and do to initiate new business processes, to address resistance to change, and to promote the advantages of a globally integrated system. The model, which anticipates a drop in business performance during the transition period, encourages change leaders to minimize time spent in the valley, to minimize the depth of the valley, and to maximize the slope of the value realization path out of the valley. A new perspective, drawn from experience, redefines a successful global ERP implementation in terms of a seamless transition to a new, integrated, efficient global system.

INTRODUCTION

The adoption and implementation of an enterprise resource planning (ERP) system requires change to the information system, to the way a business is conducted, and to the people who must use the new system. Champions who lead the change effort understand that they play a key role in managing their business and their people. It is important that champions not only comprehend their role, but also that they anticipate the impact that a global ERP system will have on their people as well as on their business and processes before, during, and after implementation. The success of an implementation can be evaluated in terms of the extent to which the business and users throughout the world were prepared for the change, the time required to roll out the changes across regions, and the "seamlessness" with which the business of the company continued after the new ERP system was in place.

The description and guide provided here is based on the implementation of a global ERP system throughout a multi-billion-dollar business. The focal organization comprised manufacturing locations in the United States, Europe, Asia, and South America, and included distribution channels across 115 countries. The global ERP system implemented included sales and distribution, materials management, production planning, quality management, plant maintenance, financial accounting, controlling, fixed assets management, project management, and workflow functions. In addition, the new ERP system was designed to provide enhanced global planning capabilities such as production planning, supply chain planning, and product demand planning. A data warehouse and new reporting tools were also included in the new ERP system.

In the process of preparing for and rolling out the new ERP system, almost everything about the way business was transacted and documented across the world within this organization changed. The following description of this global ERP implementation focuses on change management and presents a model, derived from a familiar "change curve," that may help ERP change champions understand and communicate expectations throughout the implementation. Considerations regarding how to minimize negative "go-live" impact and how to speed up the value extraction from a multi-million-dollar ERP system investment are discussed. The real experience of leading a global ERP implementation revealed many key success factors that may be overlooked in smaller-scale implementation projects or that are not typically recognized in the literature on implementation projects. Finally, suggestions about ways to create and celebrate the transition to a new global system are provided.

The details about the implementation case are derived from the experience and perspective of coauthor Bruce Olshan, who served as the global process manager of the business process improvement and integration effort for the large organization described above. The description includes several quotes by this business leader from an interview between the coauthors. The information and experiences provided by this global ERP champion were researched, interpreted, and framed within the change curve model by the authors.

BACKGROUND

A champion's role is to educate other managers before, during, and after the implementation of an enterprise resource planning system. The goal is not to scare those who sponsor the effort or those who will participate in the implementation, but to help everyone develop a healthy respect for what is involved: change is involved. Further, change is not a negative consequence of implementing a global ERP system. Rather, change is a strategic decision needed for operational excellence, and a global ERP system enables the organization to achieve this excellence.

Top management needs to embrace and endorse the idea that the decision to purchase and implement a global ERP system is a strategic decision to change the business. This point is consistent with Holman's (2003, p. 513) observation that "Change is a process, not an event." The whole organization, which in a global context may seem enormous, must focus its attention on the change process and actively support new ways of doing business that will be developed during the ERP implementation effort. The global ERP champion must persuade managers to support those who are directly involved in the implementation, to appreciate new business processes that may have been developed from different cultural contexts, and to understand some unconventional definitions of success or milestones throughout and after the new system "goes live" in each region of the global business.

In a global change effort, it may be easy to overlook or discount the profound impact that implementing a global integration system will have not only on project leaders' and key users' time, but on their lives. A champion must be able to view the implementation from both "macro" global business level vantage points as well as from the "micro," individual level across a variety of cultures. Well before an implementation begins, throughout the process, and after everyone goes live with the new system, a champion must anticipate, inform, and interpret the changes involved for managers, users, and customers. It is helpful if a champion knows what to expect and can effectively communicate these expectations to others throughout the project and across cultures.

What to Expect and Communicate to Everyone Else

1. *The implementation of an ERP system is a business improvement initiative.* Describing the project as an information technology (IT) effort or focusing primarily on the technical aspects of the project may suggest to managers and end users that the changes implemented really will not affect them until the new system is in place or that their role in the implementation is less important than the technology development role. Framing the implementation project as a business improvement initiative suggests that everything, every business process, will be examined and possibly changed. Preparing global business units for this initiative

and generating acceptance for the scrutiny of each unit's business practices can be a challenge. On the other hand, reinforcing an expectation that a global ERP system is limited to an IT change and then blind-siding employees, suppliers, and customers with new requirements and changes to business practices will be a disaster.

2. *Change is essential, and resistance to change is likely.* Change means replacing multiple legacy systems with an ERP system that is potentially not as functional, as customized, or as good as the stand-alone systems that end users have been using to conduct their business. People, especially myopic (short-sighted) managers, are going to resist the process and they are going to hate the new system. They may hate it for a long time. It is important to anticipate, manage, and even accept resistance, rather than simply implement changes on a global scale and ignore the discomfort and frustration that many people will experience with the new ERP system as they recall the old, effective practices unique to their region.

3. *An unrelenting belief in integration is necessary.* There is an inherent efficiency offered by system integration. In a multi-national organization, integration has an advantage over customized, stand-alone processes developed and maintained in different regions. Implementing a global ERP system presents an organization with the opportunity to improve the efficiency of its business process transactions on a global scale. This efficiency is achieved through global integration and consistent business processes across regions. Assuming the product itself does not change, a global organization is less likely to achieve comparable efficiencies using multiple stand-alone systems, no matter how independently effective they are within their limited regions.

The above expectations may not seem surprising, and may even be generally anticipated by everyone involved with the decision to implement a global ERP system. A champion is needed, however, to translate these ideas into reality and to guide the business through the implementation. For example, although managers in any region of the world might expect that the business will be analyzed and potentially changed, they may be surprised to find out that their own business practices were not selected as "best practices" to be implemented by the new system or everyone else in other regions. A champion must negotiate support for changes that favor what is best for everyone, rather than best practices limited to a particular region or culture. And although everyone understands that change can be difficult, a champion is needed to address resistance and move the business forward. Finally, given the nature and scale of a global ERP system, a champion needs to be able to sell the belief in the advantages of integration and the underlying assumptions about efficiency. How can a champion prepare for this role? The next section describes what champions need to understand about the process of transformational change in a global project.

Understanding the Change Curve and Anticipating the Valley of Despair

The "change curve" is a model that has been adopted by many leaders in organizations as a means of moving people within a system through a period of major change. Developed in the 1960s by Elisabeth Kübler-Ross, this model was originally referred to as the "five stages of grief,"—that is, denial, anger, bargaining, depression, and then acceptance. Kübler-Ross (1969) suggested that these stages could apply to any dramatic life change. When applied in organizational development, a dip in performance is usually observed as the "depression" stage, just prior to acceptance (SKAI Associates, 2004). This dip, or impact of

dramatic change on performance, has been called the "Valley of Despair" (cf. Barr, 2003), and it is understood in Six Sigma circles as a natural or normal drop during the change process (Larson & Carnell, 2007). The people involved in a dramatic organizational change effort will each experience their own "depression," and their leaders will need to guide them through and out of the valley. This form of leadership and coaching, with a focus on morale, may fall within the role and training of a Six Sigma Black Belt (Crom, 2007).

What is less well-understood is what happens in the Valley of Despair from a more macro-level of analysis—that is, as the global business system goes through its performance depression. Ackerman (1986) categorized changes in organizations and described the most radical type of change as "transformational." The model for transformational change resembles the Kübler-Ross (1969) model, and describes a chaotic fall from a "plateau" (i.e., the status quo) that could end in "death" for the organization unless a new state emerges. The time required and the things to do when experiencing the chaotic decline from the plateau are not predictable or easy to control, and the new state is not clearly understood or known until it begins to take shape. The low, chaotic place from which an organization re-emerges is not labeled in this model, but it seems quite similar to the Valley of Despair.

Another perspective on the idea that processes decline before they get better comes from a work attributed to Jackie Fenn, an analyst at the Gartner Group (a U.S. research firm). Fenn (1995) presented a model of the expectations surrounding each new technology that enters the market for adoption by companies. This model presents "the hype cycle of new information technologies" in which organizations start off with unrealistically high expectations just after a new technology is introduced. Then, when the new technology fails to live up to hyped expectations, sentiments fall into the "trough of disillusionment." Eventually, a number of organizations persevere and experiment with the technology, developing a better understanding of its applicability and its limitations.

Phenomena that follow J-curve and S-curve patterns have been documented in a large number of studies across a wide array contexts and fields of inquiry. The models described above all use this pattern to describe a change process. Specifically, when a change is implemented, performance, productivity, and perhaps the emotional appeal of the new process or technology all tend to decline. Things seem to get worse before they get better, and whether or not the situation will improve and how long it will take before improvement occurs is not always apparent from the perspective of those who are at a low point during the transition. At the project level of analysis, a similar pattern can be used to describe a business (described in terms of its overall performance) over the time period in which a global ERP is implemented. Figure 1 depicts the Valley of Despair within the change curve of a global ERP.

A global ERP implementation is a dramatic systemic change, and the reaction of the entire business system will likely follow the change curve, and business performance will dip into the Valley of Despair. The champion's role is not only to anticipate the valley, but to shorten the time (t) spent in the valley, shorten the depth (d) of the valley, and maximize the slope of the value realization line (V) out of the valley.

Shorten the Time in the Valley

The duration of the performance "dip" anticipated as a new system is rolled out is a function of people management and development. The role of the champion in minimizing time spent in the valley is to encourage people to persevere. Bandura (1986) suggested that the level of effort and perseverance put forth by an individual is directly influenced by the belief they have in their own capabilities—that is, their self-efficacy beliefs. Self-efficacy beliefs, which represent important motivational mechanisms in social learning theory (Bandura, 1977) and social cognitive theory (Bandura, 1986, 1991), are not simply individuals' declarations of their perceptions; self-efficacy beliefs are deep convictions that are supported by experiences. These beliefs influence how much effort individuals are willing to expend and how persistent they are when facing challenges.

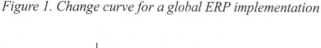

Figure 1. Change curve for a global ERP implementation

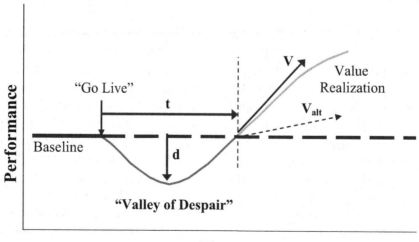

Training, practice, and examples from role models, for example, can help everyone adjust to the change. Training on the new system, practice using new businesses processes, examples of business units that have conducted their business using a particular new procedure are all likely to support the development of self-efficacy beliefs associated with the new ERP and the new business processes. These efforts need to be conducted well before the ERP system is implemented in a region, and the goal in every case is to build self-efficacy beliefs that will enable end users to persevere once the new system goes live in their region. People need to believe they are capable of making changes well before they are asked to actually do so.

Establishing self-efficacy toward a large integrated system of new business processes across global contexts presents a particular challenge. Issues associated with language, culture, and time zones seem obvious and are readily anticipated, and they should not be underestimated. Conducting real-time, global working meetings is difficult; it either involves a lot of travel or people working long hours during the evening. Managers need to support key users and free up their time so that these individuals can dedicate their attention to the implementation. This support requires more than flexible scheduling and acknowledging how many long hours these individuals spend at work, however. Support from managers here means acknowledging the importance of the role that key users play in the implementation. They are visible, credible role models who can help other users in each region persevere through the valley.

Supporting role models for best practices across cultures, training multi-cultural users on components of the system, and encouraging the practice of unfamiliar procedures in global contexts can be particularly challenging. The following quote, from the business process leader of the described global ERP implementation, illustrates the need to avoid ethnocentric assumptions regarding best practices and to identify role models in each region:

Our project was heavily staffed in the U.S., and substantial efforts were needed to overcome the perception in other countries that this was the U.S. headquarters telling them how to do their business. There was a real need to 'break through' cultural barriers, and the earlier this could be done, the better. One of our goals throughout the global implementation project was to leverage best practices, no matter where in the world they originated. Quite often, the best practice was not in the U.S., and that was hard for some to accept. Host country business experts were located in each region, and these regional business experts were responsible for implementing business practice changes.

In a global business, a few champions and key users cannot be everywhere at once. In addition to efforts to build self-efficacy prior to implementation, minimizing the time in the valley requires thoughtful deployment of key users and regional business experts. It also requires understanding that time does not stop for the rest of the business while some regions and/or project team members are in "the valley." The new system must be rolled out in a way that does not cause the rest of the business to unravel.

We made a decision not to implement or 'go live' globally, all at once [also referred to as a 'Big Bang'] because this would have required a tremendous assumption of risk and allocation of resources for training and support. Instead, we rolled out regionally. While this worked well, it did present some challenges. There was a need to build 'throw–away' interfaces so that we could continue to run our business while part of the world was using the new ERP system and part was still on legacy systems. In addition, there was a long time between the original testing and the last couple of implementations. For example, we implemented the last region more than one year after the initial global testing. During this year, people, processes, and business needs had changed.

Shorten the Depth of the Valley

If the length of time spent in the Valley of Despair is associated with people who must be engaged before, during, and after implementation, the depth (d) of the dip is more a technical concern. ERP system experts "build" the global system. When designing solutions, extra effort should go toward leveraging best practices and changing legacy processes, and the project should avoid or minimize efforts to customize the global ERP system. At the same time, technical expertise, deployed globally, is needed to ensure that the new system will meet the organization's business needs. For example, although the system should not be customized according to idiosyncratic business practices or individual business unit preferences, those who design the ERP system must anticipate and test various alternative scenarios. The "out-of-the-box" thinking needed to anticipate alternatives requires "out-of-the-culture" assumptions. Input from different cultural perspectives is needed during testing. Designing a system to meet best practices learned from a different culture requires an understanding of the business transactions as well as the goals of the various parties to the transaction.

One of the worst things that can happen is if a customer order is placed to send product from point A to point B, and the system cannot support this transaction (perhaps because the type of transaction was not set up properly or the route or the customer was not set up properly). Obviously, this is a bad thing...and imagine if the failed transaction is not isolated to one region in the world. The Valley of Despair will get deep!!

Once the system is built, the regional business experts must test all possible scenarios that are required to run the global business. There may be numerous iterations between ERP system experts and business experts to ensure that the new system meets requirements. Training is needed to expand the global network of "power users" in each region. This is to avoid the possible circumstance in which the new ERP system is designed well, but the changes required of the business process are not implemented successfully. The business processes within a region must be transformed into globally consistent processes if they are to fit well with the ERP system. Ideally, change management initiatives would be implemented prior to the ERP implementation, but the testing phase of the ERP system is an important time to determine the "fit" before business process changes arc institutionalized.

It takes a lot of foresight to start the change process early. But if the business processes don't fit the design of the system, the ERP will be blamed for the problem.

Maximize the Slope of the Path Out of the Valley

The application of the change curve to a global ERP system does not predict the level of performance observed after implementation. Performance levels observed after the change can be the same as before, lower, or higher. An incline in performance is required to at least restore performance levels to pre-implementation conditions. The steeper the slope of this incline, the greater the likelihood that the outcome of the change effort will lead to performance levels that surpass those experienced prior to the implementation. The champion needs to be able to show value realization in terms of milestones along the path out of the valley. Figure 1 depicts this value realization as the segment of the business performance line that rises above the baseline, post-implementation. Note that performance is not likely to continue indefinitely as a straight line, hence the curved performance line that levels off (hopefully above) the baseline. In order to demonstrate the desired positive slope of the line out of the valley, however, the value realization line (V) is depicted as a straight line for a period of time before performance levels off again. In order to show the need for a steep slope out of the valley, an alternative line (V_{alt}) is also shown in Figure 1. Although V_{alt} is possible, Figure 1 depicts the steeply sloped value realization line V as the goal that champions need to communicate and reinforce.

It is important to prepare the organization as well as its customers for the ascent from the valley *prior* to implementation. The marketing function needs to be involved early in the implementation process, not only to provide input regarding the relationship between products and customers, but also to help prepare the organization to communicate key business process changes with customers who are likely to be affected by the changes. The human resource planning function also needs to be engaged early on because functional positions throughout the existing business must be staffed to accommodate the draw on existing human resources allocated to the new system. Access to information within and between regions as the system rolls out in each region of the world is essential. Each region's transition to the new system must be coordinated, and everyone in each region must be prepared for the changeover. Further, the changeover must take on momentum, and key users need to be embedded within each key business process. That is, the best people to use the new system just after it is implemented in a region are those who participated in the implementation project. These individuals have already learned to adapt to change, and they are well-suited to serve their regions in leadership roles. They may be given management roles or jobs with titles such as "Process Improvement Managers" in order to acknowledge their role as leaders or experts regarding use of the new system to enact business processes.

Perhaps most of all, a steady march out of the valley hinges on the development of metrics that demonstrate the value of the new system to the business and that define success in terms of the business process improvement effort undertaken.

It may take some time, however, to realize the benefits (or "value") of the new system. Progression out of the valley may be slow, and so it is important to establish milestones that show steady movement in the desired direction. In addition, it may be discouraging to look back to the goals of the initial proposal that led the organization to embark on the change. The original reasons for implementing the global ERP may seem theoretical, unrealistic, or simply inconsistent with the organization's newly acquired experience:

We understood that the risk of not implementing the global ERP was substantial. Before we started the project, we had to prepare a business proposal that identified the benefits, estimated the funds required, and provided a clear justification for the global ERP. This information was not readily available from other companies' 'success stories'. Even after the implementation, we were still not sure if we realized all of the benefits originally proposed.

New metrics are needed to mark the path out of the Valley of Despair. For example, a proposal to implement a global ERP might attempt to rationalize the expected cost of the implementation against return on investment in new technology. Return on investment, however, may not be an appropriate metric for maximizing the slope of the path out of the valley. Benefits associated with a global ERP system are not directly derived from how much is spent on acquiring the technology or designing the tool, but how an organization uses the ERP system once new business processes are in place. Managing expectations about a new system in relation to ordinary business metrics for valuing a product or a capital investment is difficult for an ERP champion.

We expected to accomplish inventory reduction, better up-times, an improvement in the ease of doing business, and a reduction in lost customers. Initially, we spent a lot of money and it takes time to realize any savings or benefits. Everyone understood the money spent, everyone felt the pain of change, and nobody could see tangible benefits associated with the change.

If the Valley of Despair is understood and accepted, the success of an implementation can be redefined in terms of what did *not* happen. In many circumstances across the world, success means a smooth transition from a composite of legacy systems and the old, culturally-laden way of doing things to a new, integrated, standardized system. In this sense, success means nothing happens. "Nothing" is hardly a well-understood or easily recognized milestone of success.

One of the biggest frustrations was that no one knew exactly what we were doing, and this made it difficult to predict how everything would turn out or what we would have to show for our extraordinary efforts. The fear of failure was always present, and we generally knew right away if something wasn't working. But if things worked perfectly, there were no disruptions…nothing happened.

It is useful to keep in mind that the regional leaders, key users, and project team members selected to work on the global ERP implementation may be the best in the business, and these individuals are likely to have track records of accomplishments and clear indicators of past successes. These highly successful individuals will need to come to terms with the idea that implementation success is characterized by a smooth, non-disruptive transition to the new system. These talented employees will sit on a razor's edge for an extended period of time, and few managers or other people in the organization will understand what they have gone through or appreciate what it took to make everything happen seamlessly.

Certainly not my manager, me, or anyone in my business understood what it would take or how

much this project would impact everyone's lives. *In the course of two years, people quit the project, some people got very ill from stress and overwork (and many were hospitalized for illnesses brought on by these conditions), people lost/gained a lot of weight, some marriages were broken, and some more tightly-wound individuals came undone. We learned as we went. No one could tell us what we were facing or exactly what to expect next.*

Promoting a sense of accomplishment and ensuring appropriate recognition of people's efforts when a milestone out of the valley is attained is an important aspect of a global ERP implementation plan. The performance management systems that are in place in various countries or regions may not already incorporate a mechanism for acknowledging and rewarding successes defined by "seamless transitions" or by what did *not* go wrong. Note that in the following quote, rewards were not distributed for time spent in the Valley of Despair, but for steps taken out of the valley and for successful "go live" transitions to the new ERP system within each region:

When we went live in Europe, we had a champagne celebration at lunch. It was very nice. Later the Europe team was treated to a weekend in Barcelona. But there were other rewards, too. We had polo shirts, back packs, etc. to mark the occasion of a successful implementation in a region. I chose to give frequent monetary gift cards for specific milestones ($100-$200) in addition to larger sums with the final successful 'go live'. And I made sure that our top leaders, including vice presidents, general managers, and other executives, were very visible at our key events—big testing sessions, celebration lunches, etc.

What Happens After Nothing Happens?

The champion of a global ERP implementation needs to sell the advantages of global integration and its underlying assumptions about efficiency, and the advantages need to be reinforced after a successful implementation. These advantages (cf. Rodrigues, 2001) include the economy of scale benefits of pooling business activities across regions; cost reduction achieved through eliminating redundancies, errors, and over- or under-estimates of information within the system; increases in customer satisfaction and quality due to world-wide availability, serviceability, and recognition of products; and more accurate, consistent, and timely communication to enhance real-time decisions. For example, without an integrated ERP system, a global supply chain manager has little visibility of what is going on in other places in the world. This manager does not know sales in other regions and cannot optimize inventory until the end of the reporting period of the legacy system. With an integrated global ERP, decisions associated with sales expectations or inventory management can be made in real time, not after the fact.

A good example of global integration has to do with our 'Available to Promise' functionality. A customer calls to place an order for a product that is sourced from another country. Can we meet this order? Without real-time global information, we can accept the order and HOPE we can fulfill it. Maybe we will disappoint the customer. Whether we fulfill the order or not, we will need to incur costs and work on the order. We could tell the customer the truth, which is that we are not sure whether we can fulfill the order in x amount of time, and ask the customer to wait a week for a more definite answer. In that week, the customer might be able to order from a competitor, who may accept and hope or who may actually know whether they can fulfill the order. With an integrated, real-time, global ERP, we can view inventory, production schedules, and lead times online, and we can tell the customer exactly whether we can fulfill the order and what to expect.

Note that champions need not promise that employees will be much happier with the new processes or the requirements of the new, standardized system than they were with the legacy systems. In fact, users in various areas of the business who had refined and customized the local legacy system over time may never appreciate the new ERP system, which may not be as functional as any of the individual systems it replaced. Part of this lack of appreciation for the new system may be due to the personal investment that users made into learning the old system or tailoring the ways of transacting business to their local needs. The Valley of Despair, after all, was originally designed to show the grieving process that people experience when a dramatic change occurs. People may mourn the legacy systems with which they were intimately familiar. Another part of this lack of appreciation for the new system, however, may be due to real decreased functionality or flexibility of the new, global system. The power of global integration is difficult for many end users to understand, and not everyone will accept a tradeoff between customized but stand-alone functionality and more efficient global integration.

Before the global ERP, we used to be able to create invoices from a stand-alone invoice system. A sales associate could generate an invoice whenever he or she wanted one to go out. If a product were being shipped overseas, the invoice could be generated when the product was in the middle of the ocean or when it arrived in port or when the customer actually received it. An invoicing system was included in the new ERP system, but this new system required that we invoice when a product leaves a plant. Many of the sales team who were used to invoicing whenever they wanted (or whenever it made sense to the customer) still hate this requirement because in the new system the customer may receive an invoice long before the product arrives. We suggested to them that they could extend payment terms if necessary, but that the invoice must go out when the product leaves the facility as required by the new system.

Implementation of a global ERP system is part of a strategic business decision to move from a conglomeration of customized legacy systems across regions and functional areas of a business towards integration of globally consistent business processes. It represents a move from a multi-domestic business strategy in which managers in each country more or less unilaterally react to competition, to a global business strategy in which competitive moves are integrated across nations (Rodrigues, 2001). Through a global strategy, a multinational company endeavors to respond to local or regional market needs while maximizing efficiency throughout the global system (Hout, Porter, & Rudden, 1982). In sum,

global business processes must be designed to take advantage of the global ERP system, and once the tool is in place, people need to use it in order for the organization to realize the advantages of this strategic initiative.

CONCLUSION

In a global ERP implementation, the role of the champion is to prepare managers, project leaders, and the overall organization for dramatic organizational change. The focus of this work has been on how to prepare champions for this role. Champions must embark on a global ERP implementation with the understanding that change is not a result of the project, but that the implementation is synonymous with fundamental

Table 1. Checklist of practical guidelines for global ERP champions

☑ Start the change process early.

☑ Consistently use language to describe a business process improvement initiative, not simply the technical design and implementation of an ERP system.

☑ Staff the business improvement program with the best business people.

☑ Establish a commitment to examining all business processes, and seek best practices across the globe. Consider cross-cultural perceptions and cultural biases when leveraging best practices in a global context.

☑ Deploy technical expertise globally in an effort to anticipate the different ways business transactions are conducted in different cultures and contexts.

☑ Build self-efficacy by training "power users" within each region on the new system.

☑ Test the new Global processes and system thoroughly using the end users to provide final acceptance before implementation.

☑ Showcase examples of business units across the globe that have successfully conducted and continued their regional business using new procedures as the new ERP system is rolled out.

☑ Remind managers that global interaction takes more time and can be more stressful than work on other projects within a region. Involve the human resource management and staffing function early on in order to accommodate the needs of those who are directly involved in the implementation.

☑ Prepare each business unit to communicate key business process changes with customers who are likely to be affected by the changes.

☑ Establish and celebrate milestones that suggest movement toward the desired global systems integration throughout the implementation.

☑ Reward and publicly celebrate "seamless transitions."

☑ Reinforce the advantages of globally integrated business practices after the implementation is complete. Realize that users may not like each individual module since their legacy system may have been highly customized. Promote that global integration is more powerful than stand-alone systems.

change to the global business. Surprisingly, such fundamental change may be barely noticeable if the changeover to the new system goes smoothly. A global ERP implementation may be considered a great success if nothing happens when everything changes.

It is helpful if a global ERP champion cannot only anticipate the change curve, but also know what to do in the midst of it. Table 1 provides some practical guidelines in the form of a checklist for global ERP champions who may wish to keep the experiences and ideas described in this chapter in mind as they embark on a similar global business process improvement effort. In summary, a champion needs to minimize time (t) spent in the Valley of Despair by establishing mechanisms that encourage people across different cultural contexts to persevere, minimize the depth (d) of the valley by coordinating systems design and testing alongside changes that make the business globally consistent, and maximize the slope the path out of the valley in terms of metrics that show value realization (V) with each step in the right direction within each region as the system is rolled out. Finally, a champion must reinforce the advantages of integration in a global business as end users continue to use the new system in accordance with new business procedures. They may grieve the loss of local legacy systems while in the Valley of Despair, and they do not have to like the new system better than the old one. It may be important to build their self-efficacy beliefs regarding use of the new system and to provide role models who can successfully demonstrate use and advantages of the global ERP. Overall, end users do need to enact the new global business processes and use the new ERP system, and a change champion needs to continuously sell the advantages of globally integrated business processes.

The champion's guide provided here suggests that a knowledgeable champion cannot only help a business anticipate the difficult, time-consuming, and often painful changes to local practices on a multinational scale, but that a champion can also redefine everyone's post-implementation expectations and definitions of success. It may take a long time to realize conventional business indices of a worthwhile endeavor. If large-scale change is implemented, and each region goes live without dramatic localized failures or widespread disruption of the global business, there is cause for celebration. The champion of a global ERP implementation understands at the onset of the project that almost every business process will change, and if people are prepared for the change, the ERP system will go live almost without notice. Everything may change in profound ways, and if nothing dramatic happens immediately following the transition from stand-alone legacy systems to the new global ERP, the champion will have successfully fulfilled his or her important role.

FUTURE RESEARCH DIRECTIONS

The change curve model described and supported by the experience and testimony of a global ERP champion proposes that a company may expect a decline in global business process performance when the transition to the new ERP system occurs, and that the extent and duration of this decline is inversely related to what can be understood as the success of the implementation. A global ERP champion must lead the effort to minimize the extent of the decline and the time period during which business performance declines, or a slowdown is observed. This champion must also lead the business out of the Valley of Despair by celebrating the accomplishment of milestones that reflect acceptance and use of the new ERP system. Future research might focus on documenting the Valley of Despair and developing behavioral measures and business metrics associated with the three key components of the model. In particular, the leadership behaviors of global ERP champions associated with minimizing the duration and depth of the anticipated business decline and with helping organizational members and customers see the value of a globally integrated system can be documented and measured. Future applied research might inform practice relevant to the behaviors, cognitive responses, and motivational mechanisms for change leaders and end users involved in a global ERP implementation. Also, because a long time may be required to for a company to realize a return on investment associated with a global ERP system, new business metrics that redefine ERP implementation success within the broader context of organizational change can be developed and measured. These new outcome measures may be more meaningful to the end users who are directly involved in implementing the new integrated processes using the new system.

Research is needed to further examine the implied tradeoff between global integration and efficiency vs. stand-alone system functionality or effectiveness in transacting global business. Given continued technological advancements in global ERP systems, perhaps the tradeoff is more perceived (by end users resistant to change) than it is real.

Finally, the change curve model described in this chapter can be developed both conceptually as well as practically. Measures of the three variables associated with the Valley of Despair may be developed and tested, and new metrics for identifying progress out of the valley and the success of an ERP implementation are needed. If a decline in business process performance during and immediately after the transition to the new system is anticipated, an ERP system changeover that is uneventful across the globe may be considered a success. To be sure, measuring what does *not* happen in the short term may be challenging for researchers and business leaders who want to show the benefits of a new system. At a minimum, researchers are encouraged to consider new ways to show the impact of a global ERP system change and the benefits of global integration.

REFERENCES

Ackerman, L. (1986). Development, transition or transformation: The question of change in organizations. *OD Practitioner,* (December), 1-8.

Bandura, A. (1977). *Social learning theory.* Englewood Cliffs, NJ: Prentice Hall.

Bandura, A. (1986). *Social foundations of thought and action: A social cognitive theory.* Englewood Cliffs, NJ: Prentice Hall.

Bandura, A. (1991). Social cognitive theory of self-regulation. *Organizational Behavior and Human Decision Processes, 50,* 248-287.

Barr, J. (2003). *The change curve.* Retrieved February 26, 2007, from http://trends.newsforge.com/article.pl?sid=03/10/18/1342204

Crom, S. (2007). *Ways to shorten the trip through the "Valley of Despair."* Retrieved February 27, 2007, from http://europe.isixsigma.com/library.content/c040825b.asp

Fenn, J. (1995, January). *When to leap on the hype cycle.* White Paper, Gartner Group, USA. Retrieved February 27, 2007, from http://www.gartner.com

Holman, P. (2003). Unlocking the mystery of effective large-scale change. In T.D. Jick & M.A. Peiperl (Eds.), *Managing change: Cases and concepts* (pp. 509-515). New York: McGraw-Hill.

Hout, R., Porter, M.E., & Rudden, E. (1982). How global companies win out. *Harvard Business Review,* (September-October), 103.

Kübler-Ross, E. (1969). *On death and dying.* New York: MacMillan.

Larson, V., & Carnell, M. (2007). *Developing black belt change agents: "Surviving pity city and the Valley of Despair."* Retrieved February 27, 2007, from http://isixsigma.com/library/content/c020812a.asp

Rodrigues, C. (2001). *International management: A cultural approach* (2nd ed.). Cincinnati, OH: South-Western College.

SKAI Associates. (2004, September). *The change curve—A new lease on life or has it died with the source?* Retrieved February 26, 2007, from http://www.skai.co.uk/client_comm_200409.php

ADDITIONAL READING

Boudreau, M.C., & Robey, D. (2005). Enacting integrated information technology: A human agency perspective. *Organization Science, 16*(1), 3-18.

Champy, J., & Weger, J. (2005). Reengineering: The second time around. *Strategy & Leadership, 33*(5), 53-56.

Harley, B., Wright, C., Hall, R., & Dery, K. (2006). Management reactions to technological change: The example of enterprise resource planning. *Journal of Applied Behavioral Science, 42*(1), 58-75.

Lan, Y. (2005). *Global information society: Operating information systems in a dynamic global business environment.* Hershey, PA: Idea Group.

Lawler, E.E. (2006). *Built to change: How to achieve sustained organizational effectiveness.* San Francisco: Jossey-Bass.

Shore, B. (2005). Failure rates in global IS projects and the leadership challenge. *Journal of Global Information Technology Management, 8*(3), 1-5.

Swanson, C.L. (1993). *The dilemma of globalization: Emerging strategic concerns in international business.* Greenwich, CT: JAI Press.

Trompenaars, A., & Hampden-Turner, C. (2002). *21 leaders for the 21st century: How innovative leaders manage in the digital age.* New York: McGraw-Hill.

Venkatachalam, A.R. (2006). A holistic perspective on enterprise integration. *Journal of Information Technology Case and Application Research, 8*(1), 1-6.

Verdin, P., & Van Heck, N. (2001). *From local champions to global masters: A strategic perspective on managing internationalization.* New York: Palgrave.

Wei, H.L., Wang, E.T.G., & Ju, P.H. (2005). Understanding misalignment and cascading change of ERP implementation: A stage view of process analysis. *European Journal of Information Systems, 14*(4), 324-334.

Chapter VII
Business Process Reengineering and ERP:
Weapons for the Global Organization

Marianne Bradford
North Carolina State University, USA

Robert Gingras
Business Process and Technology Advisor, USA

Jonathan Hornby
SAS Institute, USA

ABSTRACT

This chapter suggests that reengineering is an analysis of existing processes you wish to change to achieve dramatic improvements in critical, contemporary measures of performance, such as cost, quality, service, and speed. There are two distinct methods of reengineering, technology-enabled and clean-slate, with most global companies choosing somewhere in between. There are also a number of principles any reengineering project team should understand before embarking on a reengineering effort, and these are discussed from a global perspective. The chapter concludes with how to select processes to reengineer, lessons learned from global reengineering, benefits of global reengineering, and future implications.

INTRODUCTION

One of the primary tasks facing global organizations today is the analysis of business processes in order to make them more efficient as well as to have a flexible process framework for continu-

ous improvement. Global competition has forced organizations to look beyond their traditional processing methods to implement major changes to their work processes. As opposed to incrementally improving processes (i.e., total quality management, or TQM), the changes global companies must make these days in order to become or remain competitive must be dramatic. Changes like this are known as business process reengineering (BPR)—the fundamental rethinking and radical redesign of business processes to achieve dramatic improvements in critical, contemporary measures of performance, such as cost, quality, speed, and service (Hammer & Champy, 1993).

Reengineering is an essential component of any enterprise resource planning (ERP) system implementation. As noted by Michael Hammer, the "father of reengineering": "[ERP] implementation equals forced reengineering" (Hammer, 1997). ERP systems make organizations consider how different functional areas interact with each other and how the process of doing business is accomplished in the firm. Understanding business processes is crucial to selecting and implementing ERP systems (O'Leary, 2000). Through requirements analysis and a study of industry best practices, organizations choose an ERP system that meets their needs, while hopefully providing them with competitive advantage. Since often the current processes of an organization are different from the process flows in the ERP system(s) the organization chooses, implementing an ERP system will most likely involve changing business processes (i.e., reengineering) to match the best practices in the software (O'Leary, 2000; Sumner, 2005). This reengineering of processes takes place during the design stage of the ERP lifecycle and generally requires strong change management skills in order to make these modifications successful (Sumner, 2005).

There are several objectives of this chapter. We first provide a background to reengineering from a practitioner and academic viewpoint. We also discuss the two distinct methods of reengineering, technology-enabled and clean-slate, as well as the principal tenets any reengineering project team should understand before embarking on a reengineering effort. These tenets are discussed from a global perspective. We continue by discussing factors to consider when selecting business processes to reengineer and the use of

process mapping to visualize "as is" and "to be" process states. Next, we discuss lessons learned from global reengineering as well as benefits that can accrue. Finally, we end with future research directions and a discussion/conclusion section.

BACKGROUND

The development of reengineering as a tool to company-wide excellence began in the 1980s when Michael Hammer began to notice that a few high-profile global companies, such as IBM and John Deere, had drastically improved their performance (Hammer, 1990). With further research it was found that these companies were not making changes to their core competencies, but were making *radical* changes to their business processes and even removing entire processes completely (Hammer & Champy, 1993). These organizations had scrutinized their employee tasks and cut out many (if not all) tasks that did not have as their primary purpose satisfying customer needs. Tasks that were put into place only to satisfy the internal demands of the organization were eliminated (Hammer & Champy, 1993).

As a result of his research, Hammer coined the term "reengineering" and has espoused his vision in numerous books over the last two decades (e.g., Hammer, 1990; Hammer & Champy, 1993; Hammer & Stanton, 1995). Business processes, which are defined as a collection of activities that take one or more kinds of input and create output that is of value to the customer, are at the heart of reengineering (Hammer & Champy, 1993). Distinguished from TQM, which focuses on continuous, incremental change, reengineering is radical and dramatic—"big bang" change with the goal of vast improvements from the status quo.

What Hammer preached was the purest form of reengineering—that of "clean-slate" reengineering. This type of reengineering involves starting from scratch, improving a process design with a blank (clean) slate. The processes are reengineered with the customer in mind foremost, and the reengineering team is allowed to design with no bounds or constraints. A free flow of ideas is encouraged in order to make the focus of the reengineering as streamlined, efficient, and effective as possible. Since the early 1990s, many organizations around the world, inspired by the legendary exploits of Ford's accounts payable department, IBM Credit Corporation, and Mutual Benefit Life, have instigated reengineering projects (Davenport & Stoddard, 1994).

Most of what we have learned about the applicability of clean-slate global BPR has been derived from case studies. In a study of 79 case studies, it was found that there is widespread geographical acceptance of reengineering (Jarrar & Aspinwall, 1999). Of the 79 cases analyzed, 59% were from the U.S., 22% from the UK, 8% from the rest of Europe, 5.5% from the Far East, and 5.5% from the rest of the world. Since the U.S. is the birthplace of the subject matter, it is not surprising that the majority of reengineering cases originated there. The data reveals, however, that although in the early 1990s when BPR was viewed mostly as an American concept, the ideas have been embraced in other parts of the world (Jarrar & Aspinwall, 1999). Indeed, it was seen that after BPR's huge successes in the U.S., "people from Europe, Latin America, and Asia began to reengineer their processes" (Hammer & Stanton, 1995). Many scholars agree that reengineering will continue to spread more and more internationally (Harmon, 1996; Hammer & Stanton, 1995). Table 1 presents examples of recent global reengineering efforts.

BPR is not applicable to only certain organizations. According to the aforementioned study, BPR has been applied in all types of organizations—manufacturing, service, non-profit, private, and public. The study revealed that manufacturing and service sectors had almost equal contributions (45.9% and 52.4%, respectively), while the public sector accounted for 1.7% (Jarrar & Aspinwall, 1999).

One of the primary concepts of reengineering (in addition to radical, dramatic, clean-slate, etc.)

is that information technology is an *enabler* of change in how work is done (Hammer, 1990). When ERP systems experienced wide-scale acceptance in the late 1990s, organizations had finally found a way in which to improve their processes without 100% "clean-slating." This was because these systems incorporate proven best practices. Thus, a new type of reengineering term was coined, that of technology-enabled (or constrained) reengineering (O'Leary, 2000). This involves the use of technology (i.e., ERP systems) to facilitate the reengineering process (i.e., the company's processes are reengineered to match the best practices in the software). In short, the ERP system *drives* the reengineering and gives companies the roadmap to get there. Advantages afforded to companies by using technology-enabled reengineering include (O'Leary, 2000):

1. The process design is bounded by the software chosen and can be implemented in a more timely manner than a clean-slate design.
2. There is evidence that the design will work since other organizations have likely adopted the software as well.
3. Process designs are likely more cost effective than clean-slate designs.
4. Processes included in the software are proven best practices.

Every organization that implements an ERP system is, in effect, reengineering. However, the *type* of reengineering is a variation from the original meaning—when implementing ERP, organizations are using technology to reengineer. However, practice has found that while many global organizations use ERP as the roadmap for reengineering, few ERP implementations will be exclusively technology-enabled or clean-slate (O'Leary, 2000). Companies should decide which approach to use based on their size, available resources, time pressure, strategic gain, and the uniqueness of the ERP solution (O'Leary, 2000). The key is having a grasp on the current processes

Table 1. Examples of recent global reengineering projects

Project	What Happened
Toray Industries, Inc. Redesign marketing and production operations	The company, whose primary business is in the apparel and textiles industries, has begun a global reengineering project to streamline its polyester film operations. In order to remain competitive in the polyester film market and to meet the growing global demand, Toray believes reengineering its production and marketing systems to be highly efficient is crucial. By reengineering these processes the company will be able to respond to changes in the marketplace more quickly and expand its market share in the magnetic recording media applications, where polyester film is used. Toray plans to restructure production systems in Japan, the United States, Europe, and South Korea.
Deutsche Bank Implement a new solution for check processing	The global investment bank, working with NetDeposit Incorporated, reengineered its payment platforms to include a remote deposit capture (RDC) solution. RDC eliminates manual check handling by converting paper-based checks into electronic transactions. The solution gives Deutsche Bank a competitive advantage opportunity by improving customer service and eliminating geographical boundaries.
Cisco Systems Integrate foreign exchange process	With the help of FXall, a currency transaction platform, Cisco reengineered its treasury operations. Due to a substantial increase in foreign currency exchange transactions, including hedging activities, the company saw a need to completely integrate its systems. Before the reengineering project, five unconnected systems in various locations completed the process. The lack of integration caused several communication issues and data to be re-entered multiple times. FXall worked with Cisco to seamlessly integrate its systems, suppliers, and partners involved in the entire foreign exchange process. With the new technology, the process is completely automated, re-keying is eliminated, and real-time information is available at any location.
Kamaz Reengineer several business processes	The heavy-duty truck manufacturer currently undertook a large reengineering project that will improve logistics, free useless production space, and fully renovate a range of products. Once the project is completed, the company expects labor productivity to increase six-fold, while a significant reduction in production facilities and the amount of power inputs is expected.
VISA Upgrade authorization system and processing center	This upgrade was the largest reengineering initiative ever undertaken by Visa. The new authorization system can handle all of Visa's debit, credit, and prepaid transactions, and will process 12,000 to 14,000 transactions a second. The old authorization systems only processed 6,400 transactions per second. The new processing center includes redundant connectivity systems that will allow Visa to bring down any processing function for maintenance and enhancements while continuing to process all transactions.

and the processes embedded in an ERP package before selecting a particular ERP system and undergoing reengineering.

BUSINESS PROCESS REENGINEERING TENETS

Reengineering uses several methods to examine processes from a holistic perspective, transcending the narrow borders of specific functions. Through case studies, interviews, and observations, certain BPR principles (or tenets) began to emerge (Hammer & Champy, 1993). As can be seen, these principles, developed without ERP in mind (Hammer, 1990), are also fundamental to best practices in ERP.

Have Those Who Use the Output of the Process Perform the Process

Many employees within a global organization do not realize the impact that changes in their jobs have on other functions in the enterprise. An example of this would be centralized product development creating product(s) to be manufactured in multiple international locations with various material substitutions, different suppliers, and costs associated with the products. It is very important that the users of the output of a process understand the integrated process from within and outside the company that drive that result. This will create a cross-functional alignment for process renewal.

Organize Around Outcomes, Not Tasks

This is incumbent in large over-arching processes that drive change across the global enterprise. Inclusion of team members, from various countries and disciplines, will begin the sharing of distinct local requirements that link together what could become a common process or function. "Order

to Cash," "Design to Sell," and "Procure to Pay" are examples of such processes that are driven by outcomes from tasks that are oftentimes embedded in functional silos (individual departments). Working with outcomes also minimizes the need for costly software code customizations that will bubble up later on in the design phase of the ERP lifecycle after the functional requirements and processes have been designed and documented.

Subsume Information Processing Work into the Real Work that Produces the Information

It is important to make the cleansing, validation, and quality assurance of data and information part of processes. The care and maintenance of the quality of data that drives decision making is the single most important task-based advantage to an organization. The lack of such discipline is a major reason why functional areas do not trust shared information and instead maintain isolated sources of information to do their work. In a global company, there are usually common customers with regional divisions and locations. The customer information will usually be required to be stored in the language of the company (e.g., English) and in the language of the country that is being serviced which requires shipping and financial documents. The matrixed global enterprise must link these like functions together in order to have a consistent process of maintaining the customer information as well as keeping the "parent/child" relationships of the customer intact for reporting purposes.

Treat Geographically Dispersed Resources as Though They Were Centralized

If all data and applications are accessible by all, then geography means less. This is especially important to global organizations, which must eliminate personal versions/isolated sources of data and make company-wide information ubiquitous. All users of the processes or systems are then virtually centralized, whether they are in Europe, Asia, or the U.S.

Link Parallel Activities Instead of Integrating Their Results

Reducing and consolidating parallel work through process streamlining will drive a new set of measurable results. A common error of global companies is not defining common measurements and measurement rules across the enterprise. This usually results in local manipulation of information. It is more important to decide on what the enterprise needs to measure and then create process flows and information to support the consistently applied performance metrics.

Put the Decision Point Where the Work Is Performed, and Build Control into the Process

From a global perspective, information visibility and transparency, resulting in both operational and strategic decision making, are the main drivers involved in BPR. Process change and information availability will push decision making to the point where the true benefits lie. The key here is the definition of where the work is being performed and what roles/level of the organization need the training to understand the impact that their decisions will have on other functions. In most global companies, the organizations are shaped differently for the same function. The common processes and controls may only be achieved if the organization is aligned either through reorganization or a common process owner at an executive level.

Capture Information Once and at its Source

Enterprises that have multiple or redundant systems have multiple sources of the truth (even multiple versions of the same software in various locations). Having an ERP system that maintains one definition of the truth drives consistent measurable results as well as feeds any data warehousing/business intelligence initiative that may follow. The capturing of this information at one point, with a common set of controls, creates an indisputable source of business value.

SELECTING A PROCESS TO REENGINEER

The key issue organizations should consider when selecting a process to reengineer is how it will influence customer-perceived value (Hammer & Champy, 1993). To determine value to the customer, global companies should compare current levels of performance to customer perceptions and expectations of the current "as is" process. For example, a manager over programmers could require that the programmers add customer satisfaction surveys to their existing applications. By gathering customer satisfaction data on all of the customers, not just the "squeaky wheel" customers, the manager can make a more informed decision on which applications or processes to redesign. It is imperative to have everyone in the organization think for the customer, rather than in terms of their own functional silo. When selecting a process to reengineer, the organization must remember the three Cs which remain indisputable: customers, competition, and change (Hammer & Champy, 1993). Further conditions that should be considered when selecting a process to reengineer are listed below.

Process as Part of a Core Competency

Core competencies vary by industry and geography, but *customer service* and *quality management* are usually targets due to their impact on customer retention and continued value. Benchmarking these processes inside and outside a company's respective industry will allow companies to make a more strategic decision on how and where to reengineer processes.

High-Cost, Low-Margin Activities

This is a symptom of operating in a highly competitive market where a company is regularly facing pricing wars. It means that there is little differentiation between suppliers, or the high cost of the process is associated with errors and rework. Typically, this activity, product, or service is seen as a "cash cow"—something that generates a lot of revenue. As such, it attracts a large investment of resources—specifically people. These activities, products, or services are perceived as "needed" because of the volume required to meet market demand. The challenge with these processes, however, is two fold:

- **Identification of "true cost":** Many companies are blinded by revenue without realizing that a product, service, or activity could actually be running at a loss.
- **Reevaluation of strategy:** If margins are low, it tends to mean that a company has many competitors. Unless companies are able to differentiate the product or service significantly, they will continually be at the mercy of pricing wars. The more resources companies add at this point, the harder it will become to invest in innovation. Existing profits get eaten up by the resources that attract "low margins." Not only does this reduce the amount of funds available for research, innovation, and new profitable,

differentiated offerings, but it locks more and more resources into a downward pricing spiral. Organizations need to recognize that all products and services have a lifecycle.

High-Defect/Rework Activities

This is the realm of Six Sigma. Each error or piece of rework consumes cost, time, and resources that could be deployed on other revenue-generating activities. The challenge is balancing the cost of reengineering or implementing controls with the value saved. Any company could potentially eliminate all errors, but the cost of doing so could far outweigh the original cost of error. As a part of a total process BPR effort, one of the more pervasive processes that are instilled across the enterprise is "quality." The impact of quality processes includes the following:

1. Reduced defects during manufacturing and packaging, and the processes to drive continuous improvements in these areas
2. Reduction of outbound shipping errors
3. Reduction of inbound material flaws and receiving

Time Intensive

Time is money! There are two focus areas here:

- **Activities that consume highly paid workers:** Companies should either reengineer to allow the same people to perform the job faster, or reengineer to allow lower paid workers to perform the activity.
- **Activities that make it harder for your customers to do business with you:** In organizations there could be unnecessary processes a customer has to follow to get or use a product or service. The classic example is a customer applying for a mortgage. Historically, approval could have taken over a week. After many reengineering attempts,

this process can now typically be done the same day, or even within minutes.

High-Complexity, Specialized-Resource Activities

Everyone has heard the adages, "keep it simple" and "less is more." In the beginning in reengineering, this is harder done than said. Inventors tend to love complexity. It is almost a way of saying, "I am very clever and can dream up solutions to the most complex challenges man has ever seen." The challenge is that inventors find it difficult to design something for people that do not have their level of intelligence. They also tend to be "perfectionists"—building in many features and components because they can (or because they feel that without them, the end result could potentially be compromised). The result is complex products or services that require highly paid specialists to implement, which in turn erodes profit margins. It also means there are a limited number of people that can help. This makes recruitment, training, and succession planning difficult and expensive. It also restricts a company's capability for growing a market. The solution is to reengineer the product or service to remove complexity, simplify deployment, and allow lesser paid employees to perform the activity.

Obsolete or Changing Technology, Especially Information Technology

Oftentimes legacy systems are built, designed, and implemented for a different and older business model. Companies need to evaluate their current business model and define where they want to be in the future. Most likely, their legacy systems will not be efficient in supporting a new business model. Companies should look to architecting a new business process model around the customer and then automating those processes onto the new service-oriented architecture through systems development or implementation. The technolo-

gies that have evolved over the past few years have been focused on process flexibility while maintaining a standard set of software features to create common integrations and security. Some of these innovations have been implemented as "business rule engines," managed by something as simple as user-friendly flowcharts that mask the underlying business process. Change the flowchart, change the process. However, this requires a governance process, as well as a change management process, in order to manage process complexity and the drive to the "common," while being mindful of the localizations needed to operate in various countries. Older technologies do not have the flexibility due to their code-based state. Change the code, use IT, test, integrate, test, deploy, and potentially lose the advantage that the change would have achieved due to the time that it takes from cradle to grave. When process change eventually becomes part of a company's culture, it will enable a quicker benefit of an acquisition or a competitive advantage that is enabled with the newer process modeling technologies pervasive in the latest ERP architectures.

VISUALIZING THE PROCESS TO REENGINEER

Recent research indicates that process modeling techniques are successfully used by leading global organizations during reengineering (Bandara, Gable, & Rosemann, 2005). One technique used to model processes is known as process mapping, a system-diagramming technique developed by General Electric in the 1980s and used by many organizations to document, analyze, streamline, and redesign their business activities (Hunt, 1996). Since General Electric's successful use of process maps, this documentation tool has gained widespread acceptance in manufacturing, systems consulting, and internal and external auditing environments (Adams, 2000).

Process maps facilitate the understanding of how processes interact in an organization's business system, help locate process flaws, evaluate which activities add value to customers, streamline and improve work flows, and identify processes that need to be reengineered (Bradford, Roberts, & Stroupe, 2001). Organizations may first choose to map out their existing "as is" business processes (see Exhibit 1 for example), which can then be used as a springboard to recommend the future "to be" state (see Exhibit 2 for example). Sometimes organizations will clean-slate this "to be" process, thinking "outside the box" on new and better ways to accomplish work in their organization. In other situations, the "as is" map will be compared to the processes in ERP systems being considered for implementation to see how business processes will need to be changed to mirror the best practices in the software "to be."

Learning to use process-mapping techniques is an invaluable skill for any person involved with analysis of business processes, criteria necessary when reengineering and/or implementing ERP systems. Poorly designed processes, redundant workflow, and inadequate controls can be eas-

ily identified in a properly documented process map, and a redesigned process can be developed and presented next to the ill-conceived process for comparison. The following are benefits of using process mapping in reengineering efforts (Damelio, 1996):

- Make work visible (the "as is") in order to improve (the "to be")
- Orient new employees and clarify roles
- Get up to speed on what your group/team provides to the rest of organization
- Evaluate, establish, or strengthen performance measures
- Determine better ways to get work done

LESSONS LEARNED IN GLOBAL REENGINEERING

Despite the sound theoretical background and striking results of reengineering, in many cases, initiatives have not always led to success. Earlier research suggests that approximately 70% of BPR projects fail (Bashein, Markus, & Riley, 1994).

Exhibit 1. As is forecasting process flow

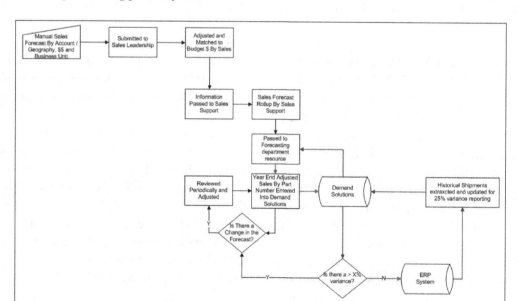

Exhibit 2. To be forecast process

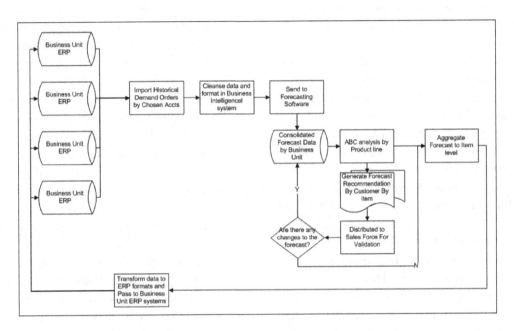

Of course in the early 1990s, BPR projects were, for the most part, clean-slate, which carries an enormous amount of risk due to the uniqueness of the solutions. Prior studies have found that these failures were due to lack of sustained management commitment and leadership, unrealistic scope and expectations, resistance to change, and non-alignment of rewards and recognition with the new business processes (Bashein et al., 1994; Klein, 1994). Not surprisingly, these factors are similar to factors leading to ERP implementation failures (Sumner, 2005).

Global companies embarking upon reengineering have learned lessons not inherent in similar projects undertaken by purely national companies. Reengineering lessons learned by both global and national companies include:

- **Labor:** It is oftentimes cheaper to put low-cost labor on a problem in lieu of implementing a system, based on where a process is being performed or sourced. As BPR outsourcing becomes more prevalent in commodity-based processes, the reliance

on an internal system to provide functionality becomes less. Another lesson learned is that scalability means both large and small; in particular, global companies need to be cognizant of processes which cannot scale to a larger organization's needs and can thus create a burden to a smaller division or geography. For instance, if a company has a small division in Thailand and is implementing a system that supports its largest division, it may indeed burden the small division with license and operational support costs that it cannot sustain. In addition, local regulatory requirements must be planned for, sometimes on a country-by-country basis. Common processes across an enterprise must be made part of the "gold" build of the software, with local process customizations only being applied as part of a regional install. Vanilla ERP does not usually apply to global companies; the challenge is prioritizing the customization emphasis on what truly makes the organization competitive, while retaining the ability to keep current on a technology investment.

- **Look outside the box:** If a company re-engineers in silos, it risks problems up or downstream. Companies must know who touches or relies on every aspect of a process, but they must also question the value of those touch points. For global companies, it is even more important to have global representation within a business function (a company never knows where its best practices are hiding) as well as having cross-functional representation between processes.

- **Look at other industries to see if they have attempted something similar:** Prior research has found that organizations do not consider benchmarking a major critical success factor in BPR programs (Jarrar & Aspinwall, 1999). However, it is our contention that while it may not be a perfect industry match, lessons learned from another company's roll out could save time and money to a company considering the same. This information can also help with setting budgets, plans, and expectations. Companies should not expect they can copy another company's process and get identical results. Many have tried to copy Dell and Toyota, but none have succeeded in getting the same results. Recognize that a process is just one aspect of success. There are many other things that influence: culture (both corporate and geographical), internal politics, incentives, people (capabilities, experience, adaptability, motivation, and values), and market perceptions.

- **Deliver sooner rather than later (for three important reasons):** *First is* **market changes.** Too many reengineering teams have attempted massive BPR implementations that have taken years to complete. Despite delivering on time and within budget, people have lost their jobs because the market had changed and made the enhancements irrelevant. Second is **internal support,** *which* speaks to a key part of change management. It is rare to get 100% support for any project. There will be fence sitters—people who wait to see how things turn out before giving their support. Then there are those who will object and will try to undermine the project's credibility and success. In order to overcome this behavior, it is important that the reengineering project plan builds in many short-term deliverables throughout the life of the project. Indeed, from 79 case studies, Jarrar and Aspinwall (1999) found that practitioners place great emphasis on the need to achieve "quick hits" and maintain a commitment to rapid results. Each deliverable should show value—be it monetary, efficiency, effectiveness, new learning, or recognition either internally or externally. Each delivery builds credibility and momentum, converting "fence sitters" and making it harder for those who oppose to undermine success. Third is **test acceptance.** Delivering segments of work early provides a great opportunity for feedback. It is confirmation that the plan works and is still on track vs. market direction, confidence that the user community can and will use/benefit from the project, and gives new ideas for refinement.

- **Think through the cascade of consequences:** The three main constituents for reengineering are: employees, interested parties, and competitors. Some **employees** fill a day no matter how much or how little they have to do. If that free time does not translate into value-added activity, then companies will still have the same "fixed" employee cost. This will reduce margins and thus profitability. Some people are "self-starters" that will invent and create new things to do. This can add value both financially and strategically. When given more time to think, some people will perform at higher levels. Others will get wrapped up in "pet projects" that add little or no value.

In fact some of these projects could detract value. *If the reengineering frees up time for employees, what will be the response?*

If the reengineering project was designed as part of a cost-cutting exercise, there is a high probability that excess human resources will be asked to leave the company. According to prior research, the area perceived to have a common deficiency in BPR implementations was the failure to pay sufficient attention to the "people" or "human factors" (Tonnessen, 2000). Many companies have done this and later have regretted it. Few BPR projects are perfect. Many reduce complexity. *If there is a flaw or error, what is the fall back position?* If staff must be let go, will there still be the experience and capacity to deal with those potential errors or flaws? If employees must be hired back, will they be available? Will they want to come back? Will they come back for the same money, or expect a pay raise? Will they be loyal and put their heart and soul into the work again, or will they do the minimum to get by? Experience can be priceless—so can loyalty. If there is excess staff, companies should do everything in their power to reallocate them to other parts of the organization. This is where understanding employee capabilities, experience, adaptability, motivation, and values becomes so important. Failure to handle this right can negatively impact morale, support, and performance across an entire organization. For instance, in Norway, BPR is very often associated with dismissals and less-than-human working conditions. This has caused much frustration, insecurity, lack of motivation, and generally affects the success of the BPR effort (Tonnessen, 2000).

All these issues are risks a company must explore and quantify at the outset. Saving $1 million per year does not look good if a consequence means losing top employees because of the way excess employee capacity was handled. This is more of an issue for companies that have not historically let go of large numbers of people before. Employees will question whether they are next and begin to explore other options to protect their finances and their families. This will reduce performance in the short term, but will also put a black mark on future BPR projects. Employees could resist change and potentially try to undermine the success of future reengineering projects.

Interested parties include partners in a company's supply chain, other divisions, or departments that either input or consume elements of work being reengineered, local communities, political lobbyists or governing bodies, and shareholders and investors. All of these could positively or negatively influence success. It is better to think through the scenarios in advance and ensure plans are established to help mitigate any negative consequences quickly and effectively. If a company does not do this, it could lose valuable time, support, and money fast, and potentially reputation—the hardest thing to win back.

Companies should ask the following questions regarding their **competitors**: Will they follow? Can they follow? How fast will they follow? Will they be able to do it better? Ideally, companies want to choose a vector that distances them so much that competitors cannot or will not follow. Achieve this, and they will achieve competitive differentiation—which means higher potential profit margins. However, as Geoffrey Moore states in *Dealing with Darwin: How Great Companies Innovate at Every Phase of Their Evolution,* there will come a time when competitors do catch up. It is not a question of "if" but "when." Companies should factor this into their project and business plans (Moore, 2005).

BENEFITS OF GLOBAL REENGINEERING

Research lacks large-scale studies on the benefits of reengineering. One study (Jarrar & Aspinwall, 1999) analyzed 79 case studies and grouped reengineering-related improvements in organizational performance into radical (69%), major (28%), and incremental (3%). The study's authors defined radical in excess of 60% improvement over the old way of working, major 30-60%, and incremental as less than 30%. Their conclusion was that "reengineering lives up to its name and if an organization successfully applies the concept, it is most likely to achieve dramatic results or at least major improvements in its set goals." Some specific benefits of BPR from our experience include:

- **Cost reductions:** Done well, reengineering should enable more to be achieved with fewer resources (e.g., people, money, equipment). This reduces the overall cost of products and services.

- **Improved customer satisfaction:** After cost reduction, improved customer satisfaction is the most common goal of BPR projects. In this respect BPR can provide very visible and therefore fast differentiation, which in turn makes it easier to protect margins and avoid pricing wars. It also provides "high gearing" as word of mouth spreads recommendations, which in turn attracts new business.

- **Improved agility:** Reengineering begins with standardizing wherever and whenever possible. Standardization makes it easier for new employees to learn and adapt to specific environments and tasks. In the case of technology, using common standards makes it easier for companies to integrate, leverage, and extend prior investments. It also reduces learning time as employees switch from one role to another and begin using different applications (based on the same standards). Standards also reduce risk of error in new activities, making it faster and easier for companies to adopt new practices. With this being said, an additional benefit for a global enterprise is that standards provide a *foundation*. This foundation is built upon common processes that are transparent to

organizations and geographies. Through the common process lens, localizations can be managed more effectively and leveraged until they become a standard themselves. The effective management of this change element provides process agility to the enterprise.

- **Increased profitability and reputation:** Handled effectively, increased profitability and reputation becomes the "net" of the other three benefits. However, there is a word of caution. Cascading consequences could mean a temporary improvement that is totally wiped away in the medium to long term. Many CEOs have been hired in to "transform" a company. The fastest way of improving profit (in the short term) is to reduce headcount. Reengineering exercises, for this sole purpose, have given the discipline a bad name and made it harder to gain acceptance and support for those projects that will truly transform an organization well into the future.

FUTURE TRENDS

As we look ahead to future reengineering projects, a few trends are already evident.

1. There will be a greater emphasis on data management, data quality, and depth of information regarding customers, suppliers, and products. As applications become more flexible, it will be the level of decision-making processes within the organization that will drive a greater understanding of the customer, as well as speed-to-market and supply chain management optimizations.

2. Organizations will change to support horizontal and diagonal processes, and implement metrics to measure the performance of the processes. Cross-functional teams will be more widely used with "cradle to grave" responsibilities. The integrated pro-

cesses will create an internal collaboration requirement to service customers and work with suppliers that will not be able to be avoided.

3. The implementation of process-based, business-rule-flexible business systems will drive enterprises to organize around global process owners of cross-functional processes like product development and supply chain management in order to support "process change management." Companies organized around process ownership will stand the best chance of reacting to market conditions and assessing the best processes to implement to maintain a leadership position.

4. One of the key questions is whether companies in the global economy are seeing more and more customization of ERP code and less reengineering. If companies focus on what the results need to be instead of dictating how tasks are completed, they can minimize the customizations of the ERP code or reduce the need for bolt-on solutions. If companies develop a "gold build" of the common requirements and deal with localizations through a governance process, they can keep the customizations to a minimum. With the newer ERP systems containing business rule engines and workflow tools, the need for customization of code will be greatly reduced as change management processes provide global governance for process and business alignment. This will also enable localization within international borders for regulatory or cultural differences without customization and maintenance costs.

5. As internal processes become more standardized and maintained, companies will negotiate these processes into their customer base as well as extend into their supply chains. This will tie customers and strategic suppliers more closely using the company as the conduit for transactions and information.

These tightly coupled processes combined with stable, predictable internal processes and systems will drive the operational efficiencies promised by both BPR and the resulting business systems that enable them.

6. The use of common bolt-ons that satisfy business requirements and are integrated into the ERP system keeps the common process reengineering in focus. With the increased use of ERP systems that contain a process modeling/business rule architecture, ERP process configuration becomes the rule of the day. Customizations are made to change the code-based business processes in the software. If the software enables process change, then configuration and maintenance of business processes becomes the work, and custom code becomes minimized. If none of the above happens, then customization requirements need to go through a governance board to prioritize only the modifications that have a financial business benefit, and take the remainder through a secondary reengineering effort to get them to fit the software model. The list of companies that have customized ERP systems and can no longer reap the benefit of commercial upgrades to commercial software will wish they had spent more time redefining their processes with future impacts in mind.

CONCLUSION

Reengineering focuses on doing the necessary and doing everything *not* to do the unnecessary. The process is rigorous, and employee direction must come from the top of the organization. Reengineering, if successful, will benefit customers through significantly reduced transaction time, flexibility in servicing, and improved value chain of service. The focus of reengineering is always the customer, and the focus on tasks is always *does this add value to the customer.*

BPR and ERP derive from a similar philosophy. Both aim to reduce costs, improve satisfaction, and deliver increased profit and reputation. Both require a change to the way people work or execute against our business goals. One of the goals of reengineering with ERP (technology-enabled) or without (clean-slate) is to take the focus out of the functional silos of an organization and place the spotlight on organizational goals and shared processes. These organizational goals must be agreed upon across the company, and the sharing of cross-functional processes must be at the forefront of management's strategy. Focusing on functional silos will only hamper efficiency, communications, customer service, and overall profitability (Hammer, 1990).

The main benefactor of an ERP system (and technology-enabled reengineering) is a company that follows (i.e., one that does not invent the game or set the rules). After all, ERP is designed to implement best practices in a technology-driven environment—processes that have been proven for accuracy, repeatability, and quality. Adopt and you become best in class almost immediately; there is no differentiation—you are the same as anyone else that buys the ERP system. In contrast, true BPR starts out with a clean slate and encourages its followers to invent or create a perfect world or future state—with no constraints. This approach will be of most benefit for those that wish to differentiate and lead the pack. The driver for this approach is increased profit potential—if no one else can match, you get to charge an increased premium.

In reality, it is not an either/or choice. ERP systems can provide a solid foundation for all. BPR activities need not start from scratch, merely where the ERP left off. This, of course, introduces another risk: you could be on your own. As ERP systems evolve, they encapsulate best practices, ironically from those who applied BPR to their ERP. If the ERP vendor adopts your insights, you are "ok." If not, you are stuck. Any upgrade could introduce major disruption and additional cost for tweaking.

Each company must assess the merits in light of its strategic direction and aspiration. Regardless of approach, we hope this chapter has opened your mind to some of the issues and challenges you need to think about—be it the change management aspect or the strategic approach of thinking through future consequences so that you are prepared.

FUTURE RESEARCH DIRECTIONS

Since Michael Hammer espoused the term "reengineering" in the 1980s, managers, CEOs, CFOs, and business process owners have seen the benefit of putting the principles to work in their companies. There are a plethora of books and articles on this subject, oftentimes telling grandiose tales of the extreme benefits of reengineering. The other side of the story, the reengineering projects that have failed, is less focused on. Using surveys or in-depth interviews with key players in reengineering initiatives that have failed would be of interest to academics as well as practitioners. The reasons for these BPR initiatives failing could point toward the scope of the project, the process being reengineered, global issues that arose because of language barriers, long-standing cultural biases, processes that were so ingrained that it was impossible to create the synergy to make a major change, and so forth.

Another research item could involve the amount of real clean-slate reengineering taking place in organizations. Are most companies just using ERP and other enterprise software to dramatically and radically move them ahead, or are they actually taking the time to design processes without constraint? Research exploring these questions using surveys or interviews could explore what types of companies are undertaking clean-slate reengineering, what differentiates these companies from other companies, what processes are likely candidates for clean-slate, and what has been the impact on companies.

Finally, customization of code is an alternative to reengineering with ERP. Most of the literature on ERP cautions against customization due to the complexity, added cost to implementation, potential for new versions to write over the customization, and lack of adhering to the built-in best practices of ERP. However, anecdotal evidence based on the authors' experiences is that many companies are still customizing ERP code. Is customization increased among organizations or has the extent stayed fairly consistent with past findings (Sumner, 2005)? What are the main process candidates for customization? Are companies satisfied with the outcomes of their customizations of ERP code vs. reengineering? How has this affected overall budgets and satisfaction of the ERP implementation process? This field is still ripe for study. Along with advances in technology and globalization, ERP theory continues to evolve. What we have learned about ERP and reengineering thus far is good theory, but the paradigm could shift. It is our duty as researchers to both study and predict the ever-evolving landscape of world-class business processes and the technology that enables them.

REFERENCES

Adams, L. (2000). Mapping yields manufacturing insights. *Quality Magazine, 39*(5), 62-66.

Bandara, W., Gable, G., & Rosemann, M. (2005). Factors and measures of business process modeling: Model building through a multiple case study. *European Journal of Information Systems, 14*(4), 347-360.

Bashein, B., Markus, M., & Riley, P. (1994). Preconditions for BPR success. *Information Systems Management, 11*(2), 7-13.

Bradford, M., Roberts, D., & Stroupe, G. (2001). Integrating process mapping into the AIS student toolset. *Review of Business Information Systems, 5*(4), 61-67.

Damelio, R. (1996). *The basics of process mapping.* New York: Quality Resources.

Davenport, T.H., & Stoddard, D.B. (1994). Reengineering: Business change of mythic proportions? *MIS Quarterly, 18*(2), 121-127.

Hammer, M. (1990). Reengineering work: Don't automate, obliterate. *Harvard Business Review, 68*(4), 104-112.

Hammer, M. (1997). Reengineering, SAP and business processes. In *Proceedings of SAPphire,* Orlando, FL.

Hammer, M., & Champy. J. (1993). *Reengineering the corporation: A manifesto for business revolution.* New York: HarperCollins.

Hammer, M., & Stanton, S. (1995). *The reengineering revolution: The handbook.* London: HarperCollins.

Harmon, R. (1996). *Reinventing the business—Preparing today's enterprise for tomorrow's technology.* New York: The Free Press.

Hunt, D.V. (1996). *Process mapping: How to reengineer your business processes.* New York: John Wiley & Sons.

Jarrar, Y.F., & Aspinwall, E.M. (1999). Business process re-engineering: Learning from organizational experience. *Total Quality Management, 10*(2), 173-186.

Klein, M. (1994). The most fatal reengineering mistakes. *Information Strategy: The Executive Journal, 10*(4), 21-26.

Moore, G.A. (2005). *Dealing with Darwin: How great companies innovate at every phase of their evolution.* London: Penguin Books.

O'Leary, D. (2000). *Enterprise resource planning systems.* New York: Cambridge University Press.

Sumner, M. (2005). *Enterprise resource planning.* Hoboken, NJ: Prentice Hall.

Tonnessen, T. (2000). Process improvement and the human factor. *Total Quality Management, 11*(4/5/6), 773-778.

ADDITIONAL READING

Bingi, P., Sharma, M., & Godla, J. (1999). Critical issues affecting an ERP implementation. *Information Systems Management, 16*(3), 7-14.

Bradford, M., & Roberts, D. (2001). Does your ERP system measure up? *Strategic Finance, 83*(3), 30-35.

Bradford, M., & Florin, J. (2003). Examining the role of innovation diffusion factors on the implementation success of enterprise resource planning systems. *International Journal of Accounting Information Systems, 4*(3), 205-225.

Bradford, M. (2004). Reengineering a process: A group project using Hammer's reengineering principles and process mapping techniques. *Compendium of Classroom Cases and Tools for AIS Applications (C3), 2*(1).

Bradford, M., Richtermeyer, S., & Roberts, D. (2007). System diagramming techniques: An analysis of methods used in accounting education and practice. *Journal of Information Systems, 21*(1), 173-212.

Bradford, M., & Richtermeyer, S. (2002). Realizing value in ERP. *Journal of Cost Management, 16*(2), 13-19.

Champy, J. (1996). *Reengineering management: Mandate for new leadership.* New York: HarperCollins.

Childress, J.R., & Senn, L.E. (2005). *In the eye of the storm: Reengineering corporate culture.* Provo, UT: Executive Excellence.

Cobb, C. G. (2005). *Enterprise process mapping: Integrating systems for compliance and business excellence.* Milwaukee, WI: Quality Press.

Collins, J. (2001). *Good to great: Why some companies make the leap...and others don't.* New York: HarperCollins.

Davenport, T.H. (2000). *Mission critical: Realizing the promise of enterprise systems.* Boston: Harvard Business School Press.

Florin, J., Bradford, M., & Pagach, D. (2005). Information technology outsourcing and organizational restructuring: An explanation of their independent and combined effects on firm value. *Journal of High Technology Management Research, 16*(2), 241-253.

Galloway, D. (1994). *Mapping work processes.* Milwaukee, WI: ASQ Quality Press.

Graham, B.B. (2004). *Detail process charting: Speaking the language of process.* Hoboken, NJ: John Wiley & Sons.

Lowenthal, J.N. (2002). *Defining and analyzing a business process: A Six Sigma pocket guide.* Milwaukee, WI: Quality Press.

Hammer, M. (1997). *Beyond reengineering: How the process-centered organization is changing our work and our lives.* New York: HarperCollins.

Harrington, H.J., Esseling, K.C., & Nimwegen, V. (1997). *Business process improvement workbook: Documentation, analysis, design, and management of business process improvement.* New York: McGraw-Hill.

Jacka, M., & Keller, P.J. (2001). *Business process mapping: Improving customer satisfaction.* Hoboken, NJ: John Wiley & Sons.

Keyte, B., & Locher, D. (2004). *The complete lean enterprise: Value stream mapping for administrative and office processes.* New York: Productivity Press.

Madison, D. (2005). *Process mapping, process improvement and process management.* Chico, CA: Paton Press.

Manganelli, R.L., & Klein, M.M. (1996). *The reengineering handbook: A step-by-step guide to business transformation.* New York: Amacom.

Monk, E., & Wagner, B. (2005). *Concepts in enterprise resource planning.* Boston: Course Technology.

Moore, G.A. (2002). *Crossing the chasm.* New York: HarperCollins.

Sharp, A., & McDermott, P. (2001). *Workflow modeling: Tools for process improvement and application development.* Norwood, MA: Artech House.

Spencer, L.M. (2001). *Reengineering human resources.* Hoboken, NJ: John Wiley & Sons.

Chapter VIII
Enterprise Systems as an Enabler of Fast-Paced Change:
The Case of Global B2B Procurement in Ericsson

Oswaldo Lorenzo
Instituto de Empresa Business School, Spain

Angel Díaz
Instituto de Empresa Business School, Spain

ABSTRACT

This chapter studies the deployment of the SAP B2B (business-to-business) procurement application in Ericsson between 1999 and 2003, and argues that it enabled complex organizational change in a three-phase process: the implementation of said application in Spain; the evolution of the application into a regional B2B procurement platform; and its final transformation into a global, pan-European B2B procurement unit. As described in the chapter, the enterprise system allowed the company to flexibly support the majority of changes that took place during a period of explosive growth of mobile phone sales followed by an unexpected market downturn. In light of the above, this investigation studies how and why enterprise systems are able to support fast-paced changes on a global scale. In other words, this chapter presents enterprise systems as flexible and responsive infrastructures that enable organizational change.

INTRODUCTION

This chapter studies the deployment of the SAP B2B (business-to-business) procurement application in Ericsson between 1999 and 2003, and argues that it enabled complex organizational change in a three-phase process. During this period the telecommunication industry in Spain went through a period of explosive growth of mobile phone sales followed by an unexpected market downturn. This triggered revolutionary changes in company processes as they prepared first for growth, then for market deceleration, and finally for the market downturn. For three years Ericsson reported heavy operating losses and the company undertook radical restructuring (e.g., offshoring, outsourcing, and downsizing). During this period the information system infrastructure, based on SAP applications, served as a key enabler of these changes. As described in the chapter, the enterprise system allowed the company to flexibly support the majority of actions throughout the growth and downturn phases. In light of the above, this investigation studies how and why enterprise systems are able to support fast-paced changes. In other words, this chapter presents enterprise systems as flexible and responsive infrastructures that enable organizational change.

The transformation process comprised three phases. Firstly, the Spanish subsidiary implemented the system as an enabler for agility and control in the MRO (materials, repairs, and operations) materials procurement process. This was a consequence of the explosive growth of mobile sales up to December 1999, when the legacy system was no longer able to support the unexpected high demand for materials and services from the sales and project areas, resulting in a lack of control over MRO materials and low service levels. The implementation of B2B procurement allowed the company to reduce the number of suppliers, the number of employees in the purchase area, and reduce maverick spending[1], as well as to develop a process that was both flexible and controlled.

In the second phase, in response to the market downturn in 2000, the system was rolled out into the Iberia Market Unit (Portugal and Spain) as an enabler of shared services for the purchase-to-pay process. This centralization allowed the company to further reduce the number of purchasing employees throughout the area, to reduce costs of the purchase-to-pay process by an average of 30%, and to build up a network of regional suppliers. In the last phase Ericsson implemented a global and centralized e-procurement model, designed to reduce costs worldwide. This entailed outsourcing services to a Nordic marketplace for the time-consuming activities of supplier activation, content management, and integration with suppliers. This phase allowed the company to develop a network of global suppliers and to obtain greater visibility throughout the whole process.

This study uses Pettigrew's (1990, 1997) framework to structure and analyze fieldwork factors from the perspective of the Spanish subsidiary. From this analysis emerges a model of evolutionary implementation of B2B procurement at different organizational stages (local, European, and global). It is based on an in-depth examination carried out from different angles, which include market and industry, local and global organization, and inter-organizational relations with suppliers and technological partners, while taking into account change processes occurring in parallel in other areas of the organization. For each period of study, the research investigated how these levels interact and how these forces influenced the B2B procurement implementation process. Furthermore, the study includes a longitudinal analysis in order to understand how the results of previous stages influenced the subsequent stages.

The relevant success factors inferred by a comparison of these experiences are: enterprise systems (ESs) and business alignment, the support of senior management, ES specialists, project management, change agents, communication strategies, organizational commitment, win-win relationship with suppliers, and information technology (IT) compatibility.

Finally, the study links its results to previous theory in order to explain the findings, and analyze said findings from the perspective of information system infrastructure and organization flexibility. Based on Anthony and Turner's (2000) dimensions of information systems flexibility (integration, modularity, and personnel), the study argues that enterprise systems like SAP can be considered flexible infrastructures for organizations. This finding contributes to the current debate on enterprise systems flexibility. In actual fact, the study supports the rejection of the myth that enterprise systems render the business model rigid, as it shows how the enterprise system chosen by Ericsson allowed the purchase organization to evolve quickly from a local-based organization, to a regional and finally a global organization in a highly dynamic environment.

This research was based on the empirical evidence and then analyzed using Pettigrew's (1990, 1997) framework and linked to IT infrastructure flexibility literature. The methodology used was that of in-depth single case study. This methodology is recommended for the study of "how" questions, and for the understanding of phenomena in early stages of research (Miles & Huberman, 1994; Yin, 1994). Data were collected using a variety of techniques: unstructured interviews, semi-structured interviews, and internal and external documentary review. This triangulation permits cross-checking. The analysis consisted of data reduction, data display, and conclusion drawing (Yin, 1998; Miles & Huberman, 1994; Eisenhardt, 1989). Even though the methodology used in this study makes it difficult to generalize the findings and conclusions, we believe these findings can be helpful to practitioners and scholars. For practitioners, the study presents ES as a flexible infrastructure to enable change. This goes against common belief and introduces learning to practitioners involved in the deployment of ES. For scholars, this study opens up debate vis-à-vis traditional research that views ES as inflexible. Further research will doubtlessly enrich the debate.

PHASE ONE: DEALING WITH GROWTH

This section describes the first stage in the transformation of Ericsson, that of accelerated growth in 1999 and 2000, from the perspective of the external drivers that generated the growth and from that of the internal processes developed by the company in response to these drivers.

External Context: Market Drivers

Between 1999 and 2000 the telecommunication sector underwent huge growth. Two causes underlie this phenomenon. First was the expansion of new telecommunication technologies and services such as mobile phones, as companies in the sector competed fiercely to gain market share for their mobile phones in different regions. As a consequence there were huge investments in the facilities and infrastructures required to support mobile networks. Second, this period coincides with the technological bubble and the "dot.com" enterprises market, a phenomenon that also affected the telecommunications sector, given that it provided many of the services demanded by the new economy.

External Context: Technology Drivers

Although ERP systems had been implemented by the majority of large companies worldwide, e-procurement functionalities were initially very limited. Hence many companies had decided at the time to develop their own custom-made applications, Ericsson's head office in Sweden among them. Later however, many Internet-based applications appeared on the market designed to give support in specific areas, including e-procurement, to companies using ERP systems. Although a world leader in ERP systems, SAP arrived late to the boom of Internet-based applications, but then moved quickly to upgrade its programs and adapt them to a Web-enabled infrastructure. When Ericsson Spain decided to purchase an effective e-procurement application rather than use that developed earlier by Ericsson's head office, SAP was searching for companies that wanted to implement the SAP e-procurement functionality as a pilot test, in order to fine-tune the first version.

Internal Context: Corporate Strategy and Business Model

Before 2000 Ericsson's corporate strategy had been one of a decentralized global company. This meant that Ericsson España (EE) could plan, execute, and control many of its activities on a stand-alone basis. For example, EE had procurement contracts negotiated locally. At that moment "each subsidiary concentrated on its own business, and it was unusual to collaborate among different countries," pointed out Rafael Berriochoa, director of IS and sourcing manager. On the other hand, the local IS department developed and bought software independently, according to its own needs, given that Ericsson's business model permitted internal capabilities in each area or business process. Thus Ericsson owned factories and R&D centers in different countries. The company had also deployed an Excellence Center (Ericsson Business Consulting), composed of 160 consultants in Spain.

Internal Context: Structure, Culture, and Processes

As a consequence of its corporate strategy, EE developed many core capabilities (e.g., manufacturing, R&D, and network installation) locally, along with support processes (e.g., purchase, administration, and systems). Creativity, independence, and an entrepreneurial spirit were all part of the company culture.

EE implemented SAP R/3 between 1997 and 1998 through its Excellence Center, having been

encouraged by the company's head office. This project meant having to embark on the standardization of processes and systems throughout the organization. After a period of time, the company had extended SAP into many areas or processes. The implementation of SAP B2B procurement formed part of this diffusion strategy.

B2B Procurement Implementation Process

The implementation process analysis was adapted from Cooper and Zmud (1990) and Lorenzo and Diaz (2005). From the analysis of data emerged an implementation process of six stages: (1) initiation, (2) process design and gap analysis, (3) implementation, (4) mutual adaptation of organization and technology, (5) supplier adaptation, and (6) establishment of a routine.

Initiation

The implementation of the B2B procurement began in 1999 when senior management identified the need for a better system for procurement of MRO materials. Explosive market growth and the internalized service culture of "always arriving first" had encouraged the need for a faster and more flexible execution of business processes. Although customers were satisfied with the high level of quality and speed of Ericsson's services, the company had sacrificed efficiency and control of its back-office processes. Procurement of MRO materials exhibited the following shortcomings:

- **Widespread maverick spending:** "Everyone was placing orders to every supplier," pointed out one of the interviewees.
- **Invoices without purchase orders.**
- **Lack of standardized processes:** "There was a different process for almost every purchase," pointed out the project manager.

In light of the above, the senior management of EE identified the need to change the MRO procurement process in order to have more control, but without sacrificing the speed and agility required to fulfill market growth. According to the sourcing and business information manager, "The only way to work at this market speed was to implement a B2B procurement application." At the end of 1999, EE began implementing SAP B2B procurement. The aim was to design an efficient, controlled, and flexible process. The company decided to choose SAP because of ensured integration between the new functionality and the ERP system. For SAP it was an exceptional opportunity to test and fine-tune its B2B procurement application.

Process Design and Gap Analysis

The purchase of MRO materials accounted for 24% of annual purchasing costs (about 100 million euros). One of the main shortcomings of the legacy process was the fact that orders were placed through "free text," which meant that the procurement department had to rewrite them one by one. At that moment the department staff comprised 22 people. "Perhaps the purchasing process was more expensive than the cost of the actual product," the project manager commented.

The process requirements were:

*   Simple and user friendly
*   Decentralization of the order process to employees
*   Use of catalogs with price and predefined supplier
*   Flexibility for managing the purchasing of non-codified materials (e.g., marketing campaigns)
*   Workflows
*   Automatic conciliation of invoice and order
*   Centralization of negotiation with suppliers

There was also an evaluation and selection of the suppliers that would continue delivering materials to the company. The key selection variables were:

*   Price and quality of the delivered materials
*   ISO 9000
*   Delivery capacity, based on an examination of processes at the supplier's plant
*   IT capacity and plans for the future, also based on examinations

Process design was performed using gap analysis of system and process requirements. Although some gaps resulted from this analysis, they were eventually conciliated (see below, Mutual Adaptation of Organization and Technology). This exercise was used to establish the to-be process.

Implementation

Implementation of the new functionality took three months, from December 1999 to March 2000. The implementation consisted of the creation of catalogs, the design of workflows, system customization, pilot testing, and training. The project team was composed of key users, Ericsson's own consultants, and the SAP consultants. For SAP it was essential to ensure the success of its first B2B implementation in Spain.

Mutual Adaptation of Organization and Technology

As a result of the gap analysis, adjustments were made to the organization and to the system, including:

*   **Change in the procurement department's role:** Purchasers were to spend more time on strategic tasks (e.g., negotiating with suppliers) than on transactional purchasing tasks.

- **Decentralization of the order process to employees.**
- **Clear definition of order approval roles.**
- **New role of cataloging in the procurement department:** This role was responsible for the joint design and management of catalogs with suppliers.

Supplier Adaptation

The new MRO materials procurement process in Ericsson brought important changes for many suppliers. First, a number of suppliers were eliminated from the Ericsson list. Ericsson España reduced the number of suppliers from 4,000 to 160 in the first year. The group of remaining suppliers (many of which were SMEs) had to introduce the use of e-mail accounts to exchange information with EE.

Establishment of a Routine

Once the implementation process was complete, the company and its suppliers began to interact through the new process and technology. The main benefits achieved were as follows.

Consequences

These changes brought a number of benefits for EE and for its suppliers:

- Personnel reduction—the number of purchasers was reduced from 22 to 4 people.
- Zero stocks of MRO materials, because suppliers delivered directly to users within two days.
- Cost reduction—the cost of an order was reduced from €140 to €14.
- Reduction of the number of suppliers from 4,000 (listed) to 160 (actives).

Figure 1. Phase one: Managing growth

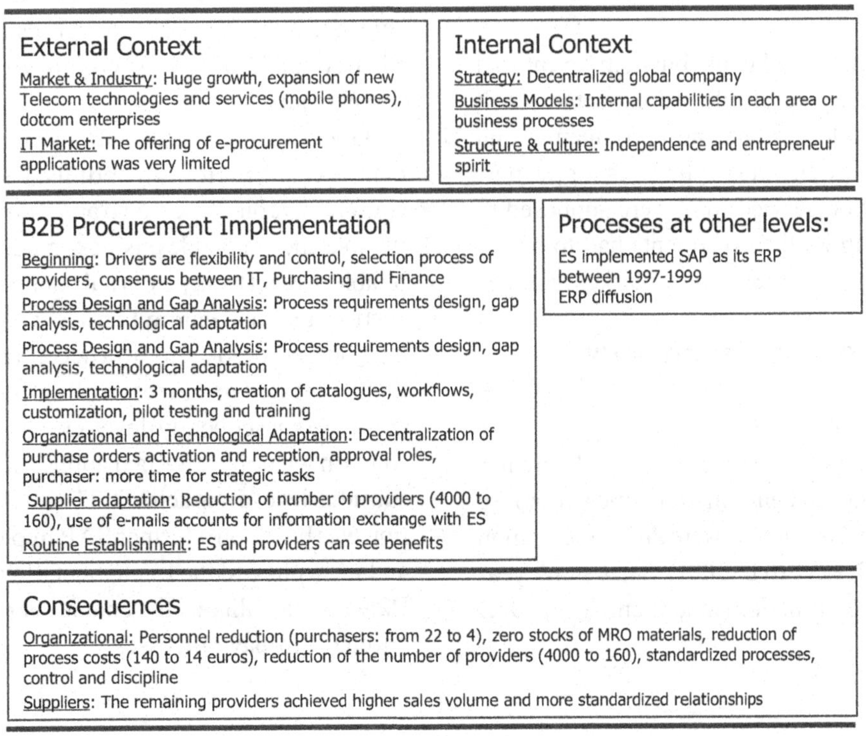

External Context

Market & Industry: Huge growth, expansion of new Telecom technologies and services (mobile phones), dotcom enterprises

IT Market: The offering of e-procurement applications was very limited

Internal Context

Strategy: Decentralized global company
Business Models: Internal capabilities in each area or business processes
Structure & culture: Independence and entrepreneur spirit

B2B Procurement Implementation

Beginning: Drivers are flexibility and control, selection process of providers, consensus between IT, Purchasing and Finance
Process Design and Gap Analysis: Process requirements design, gap analysis, technological adaptation
Process Design and Gap Analysis: Process requirements design, gap analysis, technological adaptation
Implementation: 3 months, creation of catalogues, workflows, customization, pilot testing and training
Organizational and Technological Adaptation: Decentralization of purchase orders activation and reception, approval roles, purchaser: more time for strategic tasks
Supplier adaptation: Reduction of number of providers (4000 to 160), use of e-mails accounts for information exchange with ES
Routine Establishment: ES and providers can see benefits

Processes at other levels:

ES implemented SAP as its ERP between 1997-1999
ERP diffusion

Consequences

Organizational: Personnel reduction (purchasers: from 22 to 4), zero stocks of MRO materials, reduction of process costs (140 to 14 euros), reduction of the number of providers (4000 to 160), standardized processes, control and discipline
Suppliers: The remaining providers achieved higher sales volume and more standardized relationships

- 10% reduction in the cost of MRO materials.

- Standardized control and discipline processes.

- SAP programmed new functionalities for its B2B application to improve its products and satisfy company requirements (e.g., free-text catalogs).

- The remaining suppliers achieved higher sales volumes and more standardized relationships.

PHASE TWO: PREPARING FOR MARKET DECELERATION

This section describes the second stage in the transformation process that took place in 2001, when it became apparent that the bubble was going to burst. In 2001 the company started to lose money for the first time in its history, and by the year 2003 sales were half those of 2000.

External Context: Market Drivers

In 2001, the dot.com bubble burst, an event that can be attributed to unfulfilled expectations. It also affected telecommunication companies that had invested heavily in new licenses for the new third-generation services that were supposed to be launched in 2001. Investments had to be cut dramatically in the face of new market realities.

External Context: Technology Drivers

In 2001, although ERP suppliers offered a greater range of e-procurement functionalities, in-house custom-made applications were the most common option (AMR Research, 2001). That same year SAP launched an upgraded and enhanced B2B

procurement functionality called Enterprise Buyer Professional (EBP).

Internal Context: Structure, Culture, and Processes

Although Ericsson continued to pursue a global decentralized strategy, the company began to consolidate some of the support processes in shared services. The aim was to create a more adaptable and flexible business model that permitted economies of scale and scope. Execution of the abovementioned strategy entailed creating business support centers (BSCs) for the countries in Western Europe, a decision that affected 17 subsidiaries. The BSCs used shared services for administrative, financial, and purchasing processes.

The new business model brought significant changes in EE's structure and culture. The administrative, financial, and purchasing processes were consolidated in two hubs for Western Europe. Subsidiaries defined new roles and were responsible for the internal customer relationship management. This model also meant that EE developed a service culture in back-office departments.

Given that the expectations in the telecom market changed from an optimistic scenario to a conservative one, Ericsson wanted to create a more flexible and adaptable business model that would be able to react to any external contextual change. A study by Cap Gemini Ernst & Young revealed high operating costs due to a decentralized model that duplicated resources in all subsidiaries. The company subsequently developed the market unit solution whereby it unified applications in all the subsidiaries of a market unit. The market unit solution was based on a former SAP implementation, and incorporated the implementation of the SAP B2B functionality as the enabler of consolidated purchase-to-pay processes.

The Implementation of the Electronic Purchase-to-Pay Process

Initiation

The implementation of the SAP B2B functionality into the purchase-to-pay process was a European initiative. The project was called electronic purchase-to-pay, or just ep2p, and it became a key enabler of the BSC initiative. One of the BSCs was established in Madrid to manage Portugal and Spain. The upgraded functionality (EBP) was used for this initiative.

Process Design and Gap Analysis

The modeling of the to-be purchase-to-pay process borrowed from the process already implemented in Spain. This reference process took into ac-count minor requirements from other countries like France and Holland and was redesigned to create a core model that became the standard for countries participating in BSC initiatives.

Implementation

The implementation of ep2p and the creation of the BSCs took six months in all. The ep2p project consisted mainly of the migration of the former functionality to the new version (EBP). In Spain a good communication campaign was required to explain to users the need to migrate from one version to another, even though the former version had only recently been implemented. The project was led by the local purchase area and was supported by Cap Gemini consultants, who then rolled out the system to the other European BSCs.

Figure 2. Phase two: Preparing for market deceleration

External Context	Internal Context
Market & Industry: Market deceleration, dotcom bubble burst, delays in arrival of 3G IT Market: Better offering of B2B applications, SAP launched an upgraded functionality (EBP)	Strategy: Decentralized global company Business Models: Consolidation of support processes (e.g., p2p) in shared services Structure & culture: Service culture in back-office departments

The Implementation of the e-p2p process	Processes at other levels:
Initiation: SAP B2B applications into the p2p process, European initiative, e-p2p: key enabler of the shared services concept (BSC) Process Design and Gap Analysis: Creation of a core model for all countries, the Spanish model was considered key Implementation: e-p2p and BSC implementation lasted 6 months. First upgrading to new version and latter rolling out to Europe Organizational and Technological Adaptation: Service managers were responsible for the p2p process, technological migration to a new version Supplier adaptation: No significant changes, providers took on the responsibility of cataloguing Routine Establishment: Fast adaptation to the new process	Consolidation of key processes Creation of the Market Unit Solution (MUS), based on the former SAP implementation

Consequences
Organizational: For EE this meant the loss of independence in the design and execution of local back-office processes, the corporation achieved more visibility on spending and more control over the operation; reduction of process costs by an additional 30% Suppliers: Had to catalogue all their materials into the system, capabilities for delivering in more than one country

Mutual Adaptation of Organization and Technology

This initiative focused on the transactional elements of the purchasing processes. For EE there were no significant changes in the way the company carried out the purchasing process. The main change was the introduction of a new role called 'service manager' in the subsidiaries, responsible for the service management of the purchase-to-pay process. Given that Spain was one of the places were a BSC was established, the purchasing personnel remained the same as before. From a technological perspective, this initiative consisted of merely migrating from one version to another, the second of which included a better materials classification functionality.

Supplier Adaptation

From a process and technological perspective, there were no significant changes in the way suppliers interacted with EE. However, the new initiatives did imply some major changes in organizational structure. Ericsson asked suppliers to take on the responsibility of the cataloging process. Training programs were needed to achieve this objective.

Establishment of a Routine

Once implementation was complete, the company and suppliers adapted quickly to the new processes.

Consequences

* For EE this initiative meant that it began to lose independence in the design and execution of local back-office processes. The new consolidated purchase-to-pay process allowed the corporation to have more visibility of spending and more control over the operation.

* This initiative allowed the company an additional 30% process costs reduction.
* Suppliers had to catalog all their materials into the system.
* Suppliers developed internal cataloging capabilities.
* Some local suppliers began to develop the capacity to deliver in more than one country.

PHASE THREE: COPING WITH THE MARKET DOWNTURN

This section describes the third stage in the transformation process that took place after 2001 and entailed the consolidation of back-office processes.

External Context: Market Drivers

Between 2002 and 2003, the telecom market downturn decelerated. Recovery remained slow, however, because of the terrorist attacks in New York, which extended the economic crisis to other sectors such as airlines and insurance. At that moment, telecom companies (e.g., Telefónica in Spain) began to reduce their investments and to restructure their business models.

External Context: Technology Drivers

From 2001, there was a significant increase in the offering of B2B procurement functionalities and marketplace solutions. In 2002, the diffusion of packaged software for the B2B and electronic marketplace reached 28% of the market, with SAP, Ariba, Commerce One, Oracle, and i2 (AMR Research, 2001) as main suppliers. Important electronic marketplace initiatives were adopted in different sectors by firms like Covisint (automotive), Aero Exchange International (aerospace), and ChemConnect (chemical).

Internal Context: Structure, Culture, and Processes

The telecom crisis resulted in huge losses for companies. For example, between 1999 and 2002 Ericsson's operating losses totaled €2,000 million. As a consequence the company had to make some hard decisions, for which purpose a crisis committee was set up. One of the first decisions was to develop a global company, reducing local capabilities.

In 2002, Ericsson carried out a total overhaul of its business model. The company had to adapt quickly to new market conditions. "Our new organization will put even more emphasis on serving our customers, reducing complexity, and applying our resources more efficiently," said president and CEO Kurt Hellstrom (Wireless Newsfactor, 2001). One of the main lines of action was to group subsidiaries located in 140 countries into 31 market units. Subsequently EE became part of the EMEA (Europe, Middle East, and Africa) unit. This restructuring meant downsizing employees by 24% worldwide. Further measures included offshoring (e.g., closing down the factory in Zamudio, Spain), process centralization (e.g., procurement), and outsourcing (e.g., IS global outsourcing to IBM).

The main change in the structure was the centralization of back-office processes like IS, which meant that some IS activities (e.g., programming and maintenance) were outsourced to IBM. The same occurred with IT services, which were outsourced to HP. New roles in Ericsson were created for managing service-level agreements with the outsourcing supplier. With regard to culture, the company focused on creating the concept of global employees.

In short, the company was involved simultaneously in many projects that included centralization, outsourcing, offshoring, and downsizing, and all of which were connected to one another.

The Implementation of a Global Purchasing Process

Initiation

Hence Ericsson decided to create a common global purchasing process for MRO materials. The company opted for EBP (SAP's B2B procurement tool) for this global initiative. "We work strategically to minimize the number of local, unique, homegrown solutions so that we can cut costs and groom the business support system landscape," pointed out Anders Paulsson, purchasing director (IBX Newsletter, 2003).

Process Design and Gap Analysis

The design of the new process was based on a centralized structure. Some members of this project team visited EE in order to learn from local experience in terms of both implementation and use of the system. The implementation of the new process only allowed small deviations from the established design.

Implementation

The rollout project lasted about four months in each country. The project was supported by Accenture and by the IBX specialists. The IBX specialists worked directly with suppliers to update catalogs. IBX was a marketplace created by three partners (Ericsson, SEB, and b-business) and was a key agent in the implementation of the global B2B procurement initiative. In Paulson's words:

We have two types of relations with IBX. The company is an e-procurement implementation partner. When the system goes into operation, IBX becomes a supplier that must (1) deliver operation services for application availability and for supplier and content management and (2) work continuously on improvements." (IBX Newsletter, 2003).

Mutual Adaptation of Organization and Technology

For Ericsson España this new project brought small changes in relation to the former purchasing processes. For example, one of the changes was the simplification of workflows. The centralization and standardization meant that EE lost power over local purchasing processes. Where technology was concerned, EE had to migrate to the new version of SAP's B2B procurement functionality and had to connect to the IBX marketplace.

Supplier Adaptation

This new project brought the following changes for suppliers: (1) use of the IBX marketplace to interact with Ericsson, (2) catalog management was moved to the IBX marketplace, and (3) the payment of fees for interacting with Ericsson through the IBX marketplace.

Establishment of a Routine

Once the project was completed, Ericsson España began to execute the purchasing process accordingly. Users from EE recognized that resistance to change was higher than in previous projects.

Consequences

The change initiatives that Ericsson implemented worldwide resulted in a sharp reduction in the number of employees (from 103,000 to 51,000). Although it is difficult to estimate how much each project had contributed to achieving the aim of reducing operating costs, Ericsson's management acknowledged that the B2B procurement project worldwide played a pivotal role in this change process. As a consequence of the global B2B procurement project, the company managed to build a network of global suppliers that were able to negotiate global contracts with local deliver-

Figure 3. Phase three: Coping with the market downturn

External Context	Internal Context
<u>Market & Industry:</u> Heavy operating loses, telecom companies reduce their investments drastically <u>IT Market:</u> The offering of B2B applications and marketplace solutions increased significantly. Diffusion of these solutions achieved 28% of the market. Market-place initiatives adopted in many sectors	<u>Strategy:</u> Crisis committee: global company and reduction of local capabilities <u>Business Models:</u> Consolidation of subsidiaries, ES: EMEA, reduction of employees by 24% <u>Structure & culture:</u> Centralization of back-office processes (e.g., IT and IS processes)

The Implementation of a global Purchasing Process	Process at other levels:
<u>Initiation:</u> Implementation of common global purchasing process for MRO <u>Process Design and Gap Analysis:</u> The design of the new process was undertaken in a centralized manner <u>Implementation:</u> The roll-out project took 4 months in each country. IBX as an e-procurement implementation partner, IBX delivers operation services and content management <u>Organizational and Technological Adaptation:</u> For EE this project brought small changes in the former processes: simplification of workflows, link to IBX <u>Supplier adaptation:</u> IBX marketplace, paying fees <u>Routine Establishment:</u> Change resistance was higher than for previous projects	Off-shoring and outsourcing Centralization Downsizing

Consequences
<u>Organizational:</u> Abrupt reduction of employees (103,000 to 51,000), development of global providers, global contract with local deliveries (e.g., Sun, HP, IBM, Corporate Express), EE loses control over its local processes

ies (e.g., Sun, HP, IBM, and Corporate Express). This centralization rendered the purchasing costs of MRO materials worldwide completely visible. On the other hand, EE lost control over its local purchasing process.

LESSONS LEARNED

Four key concepts emerge from the analysis: context, transformation processes, processes in other areas, and consequences of the change process. Contextual variables helped identify drivers for the transformation of relations with suppliers. A detailed description of the transformation process helped to identify key factors, in particular the process of adoption of the technological enabler. Understanding processes realized at other levels of the organization served to understand how parallel events influenced the transformation process. Finally, the analysis identified the organizational consequences of the transformation process for both the company and suppliers.

Even though this conceptual model provides an in-depth comprehension of the transformation of relations with suppliers at EE, it is important to identify key findings in the transformation process that could be applied to different enterprises. Hence an additional analysis was performed to identify the key success factors in the transformation process.

These relevant factors, as presented in Table 1, are:

1. Alignment
2. Support of senior management
3. Project management
4. Change agents
5. Communication
6. Commitment
7. Support to suppliers
8. Technological compatibility

Alignment

From the data analysis it can be inferred that the transformation process of MRO procurement at EE, at every stage, was a key business project used to support core business objectives. Hence the project was well aligned with business objectives:

- During the first phase (1999-2000), the transformation process was key for the improvement of efficiency and control of the MRO procurement process. The technology implemented therefore acted as an enabler of the change process.
- During the second stage (2001), the transformation of MRO purchases at a European level was a key business project designed to consolidate the purchases of the countries associated to each BSC. A key task for this European objective was the migration of processes and technologies in EE towards the new process and the new technology suggested for the BSC, based on existing technology.
- During the third stage (2002-2003), the transformation process of MRO purchases at a global level was key for the conversion of the company to a global centralized enterprise. A key task for this global objective was the migration of processes and technologies in EE towards the new process and the new technology suggested by head office.

Support of Senior Management

As a consequence of the alignment of transformation processes to business objectives, all three change projects were led by senior management at EE:

- During the first stage, senior purchasing management at EE was the main sponsor of the transformation process. The purchasing department assumed responsibility for the change process at all times. This role included decision making on process design and the selection of suppliers, project monitoring, and support for change management.

- During the second stage, sponsoring the transformation process was the responsibility of BSC and the local purchasing units. Subsequently, close relations were established between them. A joint monitoring group was made responsible for closely controlling migration, change management, and communications.
- Sponsoring the transformation process on a global level was the responsibility of the CEO and of the local purchasing units. A detailed control was required of head office for on-time fulfillment of each project in the rollout.

Specialists

Due to the complexities of organizational and technological change associated with each project, Ericsson's management decided to recruit the support of specialists who could bring industry-specific knowledge of business processes or of technology. These internal and external consultants brought the resources and experience required to reach the objectives in the fastest time possible:

- During the first stage, the transformation process had enjoyed the support of the internal consulting office of Ericsson. This unit was created to offer consulting services to other companies and to support Ericsson with internal implementation that required specialized personnel. This is considered a key success factor in terms of available resources. The project also had support from a team of SAP consultants who had participated in a similar project in France. For SAP the success of this first implementa-

tion of the B2B functionality in Spain was critical for its market expansion plans, and the system was customized by a SAP partner with experience in this kind of project.
- During the second stage, the transformation process was guided by consulting firm Cap Gemini Ernst & Young, which had experience in activity consolidation projects in global organizations with complex structures. According to the country manager for Portugal, this firm also played a key role in local change management and in facilitating good relations between BSC and local companies.
- During the third stage, the transformation process was supported by the consulting firm Accenture and by the implementation team of the IBX portal. Accenture guided the rollout project in all countries, and IBX guided the process of catalog updates and managing suppliers.

Project Management

Each transformation process had a project director with a clear role in planning, deployment, and monitoring. Thus projects were carefully structured. For example the first transformation process was directed by Cesar Barba, then an internal consultant experienced in IT implementations and who had previously participated in the company's ERP implementation. The second project was directed by Julio Gil, a member of the Iberian (Spain and Portugal) BSC, and highly experienced in procurement and fluent in several languages. For the last stage, a single project director for the integration of MUS-EBP-HRMS was appointed. As the head office required very fast rollouts and that a defined standard be followed to the letter, the leaders of these projects used an aggressive executive style in the fulfillment of objectives. The majority came from the sales areas of Ericsson.

Change Management

In each phase of the project, directors identified the involvement of users as a key success factor. Hence key users became change agents, supporting training and communication in the management of change:

- During the first stage, 10 key users were designated as project champions and as training facilitators. These key users were secretaries and those responsible for purchasing in the projects department.
- During the second and third stages (2001-2003), the change agents (or key users) were also designated as project champions and training facilitators. For the project leader it was very important to transmit to these champions the reasons and drivers that made EE leave a local-sourcing model for one of the back-office activities centralized first at the BSC and subsequently at the head office in Sweden.

Communication

Communication of project objectives and the reasons for embarking on the project played a pivotal role in change management throughout all three stages. This was achieved through clear intranet, e-mail, and notice board messages:

- During the first stage, the objective of the communication campaign was to explain to all employees the need for better control and efficiency in the procurement of MRO materials and services, and to expound the basic characteristics of the technological enabler.
- During the second stage of transformation, the objective of the communication campaign was to explain to all employees the need for migration and adjustment of procurement to a new model that could

consolidate purchases at a European level. It was considered very important that these changes be related to the transformations occurring in the marketplace.

- During the third stage, information was communicated in progressive fashion, given that subsequent changes were to have a profound impact on the organization. The objective was to raise awareness among employees of the economic circumstances of the organization and of the importance of moving toward centralized processes and systems in order to reduce costs. In addition to electronic means of communication (e-mail, Web sites, and intranet), there was direct communication with key users.

Commitment

The commitment of all *stakeholders* to the transformation process was obtained by demonstrating its benefits. The departments of procurement and finance participated proactively in the definition of requirements. These were subsequently negotiated with the SAP consultants, who in many cases had to customize the system to meet organizational needs. For the department of systems and IT, standardizing procurement was critical, as was compatibility with the existing ERP system. Even if final users may have perceived the project as an increase in their day-to-day responsibilities (and hence may have been prone to resist implementation), the proposed transformation promised high service levels, which resulted in commitment.

The explosion of the technological bubble, and its impact on Ericsson, was clearly understood by the employees, many of whom accepted early retirement or negotiated leaves of absence, facilitating the commitment to changes that could enable the survival of their business. Comprehending the reasons and drivers behind this change process brought commitment from key users and project participants. In addition to bonus schemes, there was an implicit psychological contract with the success of the project.

Table 1. Relevant factors affecting the transformation process

Relevant factors	Local implementation (1999 – 2000)	European implementation (2001)	Global implementation (2001 –2003)
Alignment	• Technology considered as a means for better control in purchasing of MRO materials and services	• Technology considered as a means to consolidate management of purchases of the countries in the hub	• Technology considered as a means to centralize purchases and manage of local suppliers
Support from senior management	• Direct support from purchasing management	• Direct support from BSC	• Direct support from CEO
Specialists	• Internal consulting unit provided with enough resources • Participation of an SAP specialist from France • Participation of SAP partners for system personalization	• Cap Gemini - Ernst &Young for design, launch and operation of the BSCs in western Europe	• Accenture: global agreement for rollout • IBX responsible for the implementation • After implementation systems & IT management carried out by IBM and HP.
Project Management	• Project Director: a member of the internal consulting unit in Spain	• Project Director: a member of the Iberia BSC, located in Madrid and in charge of Spain and Portugal	• Project manager for the rollout of MUS-EBP-HRMS. • Project leaders with an aggressive, executive profile (from sales)
Change agents (super-users)	• Ten key users (mainly secretaries and people responsible for project supplies) who became promoters and trainers	• Key users committed in the face of crisis	• Key for identification of problems and monitoring suppliers, particularly after *outsourcing* systems & IT and purchasing personnel reductions
Communication	• Clear and direct message from project drivers (via Intranet, boards, email)	• Clear and direct message from project drivers (via intranet, boards, email)	• Communication in stages, disclosing information in a controlled way. • Marketing and communication campaign: economic maladies + importance of centralized systems for cost reduction • Use of email, Intranet and project web page • Talks with super-users
Commitment	• Strong participation and customization • Users accepted the new model	• Project managers and key users committed to key processes, through bonuses and long term implicit commitment (psychological contract)	• The organization becomes aware of the seriousness of the crisis
Support for suppliers	• Basic training (half day) for suppliers, minimal technological requirements	• Support in the extended cataloguing process • Collaboration with language barriers	• Integration of suppliers to the IBX marketplace • Portal connection fees suspended • IBX works directly with supplier for catalogue management
Technological compatibility	• Supplier of the B2B functionality same as that of ERP	• Upgrading to new B2B functionality from supplier already used in Spain.	• Upgrading to new B2B functionality from supplier already used in Europe.

Support for Suppliers

At each stage of the transformation process, EE helped suppliers adapt to changes:

- During the first stage, the main support activity was training. This was basic and only took half a day; and as technological requirements were few (just an e-mail account), the need for support was limited.
- During the second stage, the main change for suppliers was the assignment of responsibility for the catalog, which had to include all items purchased. EE supported its suppliers at the beginning of this process through training and a support group.
- During the third stage, the main change for suppliers was their integration into the IBX marketplace. EE arranged for head office to suspend connection fee charges to the marketplace portal for a one-year period while suppliers learned to appreciate the advantages of this new means of communication. Also, to reduce language barriers, EE supported connection to Spanish suppliers through a Spanish portal called Opciona, which had alliances with IBX. Opciona and IBX worked closely with suppliers to streamline the process of updating catalogs.

Technological Compatibility

Another relevant factor for each transformation process was the selection and implementation of technologies that were compatible with or easily integrated into existing ones. Ericsson preferred to maintain a single-system platform to simplify technology management and to ease users' learning curve:

- During the first stage, the selection of SAP for the B2B functionality facilitated the integration of the new MRO procurement process into the existing ERP application.

It also eliminated the need for middleware, aided technology management, and meant that the company could use the learning curve of the previous SAP implementation as a base.

- During the second stage, the selection of the new version of SAP's B2B (EBP) to support the purchase-to-payment process at BSC simplified the new transformation process at EE, given that from a technological perspective the new project was merely a question of migrating to another version of the technology.
- During the third stage, the selection of a new version of EBP to support a centralized procurement process at the head office level facilitated the third transformation process at EE, as again, from a technological perspective, the new project was merely a question of migrating to another version of the technology.

DISCUSSION ON THE FLEXIBILITY OF ENTERPRISE SYSTEMS

This study links its results to previous theory in order to explain the findings. Hence the findings were analyzed from the perspective of information system infrastructure and organization flexibility. Anthony and Turner's (2000) study took the first step toward creating a valid IT infrastructure flexibility construct. Their findings reveal that IT infrastructure flexibility can be expressed in three factors: two related to technical issues and one to human issues. They labeled these factors as "integration," "modularity," and "IT personnel flexibility," respectively. The integration factor is a merger of the dimensions of IT connectivity and IT compatibility. Connectivity is the ability of any technology component to attach to any other component inside or outside the company. Compatibility is the ability to share any type of information with any technology component.

Figure 4. ES flexibility at Ericsson

Integration	SAP B2B functionality connects smoothly to the SAP back-office functionalities (e.g., Finance, MM).
	SAP B2B functionality shares information with other organizational departments.
Modularity	SAP B2B functionality adds easily new versions to previous implementations. Each migration was considered by users as a transparent process.
	SAP B2B functionality modifies previous configurations with no problems.
IT personnel flexibility	Ericsson personnel quickly implements and diffuses SAP B2B functionality throughout the corporation.

This factor suggests that transparent access into all platforms contributes to IT flexibility. The modularity factor is a merger of the dimensions of application functionality and database transparency. Modularity is the ability to add, modify, and remove any component of the infrastructure with ease. IT personnel flexibility is related to the depth and breadth of four types of knowledge and skills: (1) technology management knowledge and skills, (2) business functional knowledge and skills, (3) interpersonal and management skills, and (4) technical knowledge and skills. This implies that technical skills alone are not enough to implement and use IT.

If one evaluates EE's B2B implementation experience using Anthony and Turner's framework, one can argue that enterprise systems such as SAP are flexible information technologies. The three factors mentioned by Anthony and Turner are present in the case of EE. These three factors allowed SAP to evolve flexibly according to Ericsson's needs and challenges. First, the integration factor allowed the SAP B2B procurement functionality to connect smoothly to the SAP back-office functionalities, such as the financial and materials management modules. Addition-

ally, the integration factor allowed the SAP B2B procurement functionality to share information with other organizational departments.

Second, the modularity factor allowed the SAP B2B procurement functionality to add new versions to previous implementations with ease. In fact, users considered that all migrations were transparent processes. Furthermore, the modularity factor allowed the SAP B2B functionality to modify previous configurations with no problems. Finally, the IT personnel flexibility factor allowed the SAP B2B functionality to be implemented and diffused quickly throughout the corporation. Enterprise systems from leading suppliers like SAP are common tools used by many technical specialists and functional users worldwide. There is therefore a reliable supply of SAP knowledge around the world that allows companies to rollout the system quickly.

One can use Anthony and Turner's (2000) dimensions of information systems flexibility (integration, modularity, and personnel) to argue that enterprise systems like SAP are flexible infrastructures for organizations. This finding contributes to the current debate of enterprise systems flexibility. In fact, this study supports the refutation of the myth that enterprise systems make for a rigid business model. The study shows how the enterprise system chosen by Ericsson permitted the purchase organization to evolve quickly from a local-based organization to first a regional and then to a global organization in a highly dynamic environment.

CONCLUSION

This chapter provides a detailed analysis of the organizational transformation of Ericsson in Europe, from the perspective of the Spanish subsidiary. It focuses on how said organizational transformation was enabled by enterprise systems. Specifically the chapter describes this process as taking place in three stages: the implementation of a B2B procurement application in Spain; the evolution of this application into a regional B2B procurement platform; and its final transformation into a global, pan-European B2B procurement unit. We argue that this successful and rapid process, driven by drastic market changes, was partially enabled by a B2B procurement enterprise system.

This process in turn leads us to examine key success factors in ES-supported global organization transformation processes. These factors are: alignment with business objectives, support of senior management, project management, change agents, communication, commitment, support given to suppliers, and technological compatibility. Finally, this analysis suggests that enterprise systems can be considered enablers of evolutionary change, and that they are more flexible than managers realize.

Although the study generated concepts and relations shown by the transformation model for relations with suppliers (Figures 1, 2, and 3), they are not generalizable to similar processes in other companies. Further cases and cross-analysis with the current results are required to build a more robust model.

FUTURE RESEARCH DIRECTIONS

A future research agenda should include the empirical validation and elaboration of global B2B procurement adoption processes in other settings. The theoretical models were generated by analyzing only one enterprise, albeit in depth. More empirical comparisons will enrich the constructs developed here and yield more understanding of the global B2B procurement phenomenon.

In particular, further research should attempt to find more evidence that helps support the claim that enterprise systems can provide flexible information infrastructures for businesses. This could include searching for evidence in traditional enterprise system infrastructures (e.g., SAP R/3 or MySAP) coupled with a further search for evidence in new service-oriented architectures (e.g., enterprise service architecture of SAP). It could also be interesting to investigate if the customers' perceptions of enterprise systems as inflexible tools have varied between the implementation of a traditional platform and the implementation of service-oriented infrastructure.

With regard to the key factors affecting the transformation process at different levels in a global company, it may be interesting to deepen the understanding of how some of these factors work. For example, support for suppliers to implement a B2B procurement may vary depending on the internal and external contextual characteristics of the client company. For example, in the case of Ericsson, the strong position of the client company in an unfavorable business environment for all players in this supply chain seemed to help Ericsson achieve its objective of changing how it manages relations with its providers. Several questions emerge, including: What level of support should a company give to its supplier when implementing a B2B procurement system? What factors affect the decision pertaining to the level of support afforded to suppliers?

Two initial strategies for further research can therefore be proposed. The first strategy, aimed at theory building, is to compare emergent concepts and constructs with extant literature (Eisenhardt, 1989). The second strategy, designed to develop generalizable theory, is to study a reasonable number of additional cases (e.g., between 4 and 10, according to Eisenhardt, 1989). Finally, further research can be carried out to test hypotheses that can emerge from the previous qualitative studies.

ACKNOWLEDGMENT

We would like to thank Ericsson España for allowing us to carry out this study. Special thanks to Rafael Berriochoa (IS and sourcing manager) and Cesar Barba (internal consultant and project leader).

Please note: This chapter is based on a preliminary study published in the conference proceedings of the 2006 European Operations Management Association (EUROMA) conference. It differs from the original conference proceedings, however, in two aspects: (1) this chapter extends the analysis to European and global experiences, and (2) it includes an in-depth discussion of the lessons learned through these three experiences (local, European, and global).

REFERENCES

Allen, B.R., & Boynton, A. (1991). Information architecture: In search of efficient flexibility. *MIS Quarterly, 15*(4), 435-445.

Anthony, T., & Turner, D. (2000). Measuring the Flexibility of Information Technology infrastructure: Exploratory analysis of a construct. *Journal of Management Information Systems, 17*(1).

AMR Research. (2001). *Application spending and penetration report 2002-2003.*

Cooper, R., & Zmud, R. (1990). Information technology implementation research: A technological diffusion approach. *Management Science, 36*(2), 123-139.

Davenport, T. (2000). *Mission critical: Realizing the promise of enterprise systems.* Boston: Harvard Business School Press.

Duncan, N.B. (1995). Capturing flexibility of IT infrastructure: A study of resource characteristics and their measure. *Journal of Management Information Systems, 12*(2), 37-57.

Eisenhardt, K. (1989). Building theories from case study research. *Academy of Management Review, 14*(4), 532-550.

Fan, M., Stallaert, J., & Whinston, A. (2000). The adoption and design methodologies of component-based enterprise systems. *European Journal of Information Systems, 9,* 25-35.

IBX Newsletter. (2003). Global e-procurement a winner for Ericsson. *IBX Newsletter,* (3).

Lorenzo, O., & Díaz, A. (2005). Process gap analysis and modelling in enterprise systems. *International Journal of Simulation and Process Modelling, 1*(3/4).

Miles, M., & Huberman, A. (1994). *Qualitative data analysis, an extended sourcebook* (2nd ed.). Thousand Oaks, CA: Sage.

Pettigrew, A. (1990). Longitudinal field research on change: Theory and practice. *Organization Science, 1*(3), 267-292.

Pettigrew, A. (1997). What is a processual analysis? *Scandinavian Journal of Management,* 13(4), 337-348.

Wireless Newsfactor. (2001). Ericsson addresses globalization with sweeping restructuring plan. *Wireless Newsfactor.*

Yin, R. (1994). *Case study research. Design and methods.* Thousand Oaks, CA: Sage.

ADDITIONAL READING

Ash, C., & Burn, J. (2003). Assessing the benefits from e-business transformation through effective enterprise management. *European Journal of Information Systems, 12,* 297-308.

Bhattacherjee, A. (2000). Beginning SAP R/3 implementation at Geneva Pharmaceuticals. *Communications of the AIS, 4,* Article 2.

Boyler, K., & Olson, J. (2002). Drivers of Internet purchasing success. *Production and Operations Management, 11*(4).

Christopher, M. (1992). *Logistics and supply chain management: Strategies for reducing costs and improving services.* London: Pitman.

Cowan, E., & Eder, L. (2003). The transformation of AT&T's enterprise network systems group to Avaya: Enabling the virtual corporation through reengineering and enterprise resource planning. *Journal of Information System Education, 14*(3).

Diaz, A. (2000). E-business: From demand networks to techno logistics. *Supply Chain Forum—An International Journal, 1.*

Ettlie, J. (1992). Organization integration and process innovation. *Academy of Management Journal, 15*(4), 795-827.

Fraser, P., & Klassen, R. (2005). E-procurement. *MIT Sloan Management Review, 46*(2).

Frohlich, M. (2002). E-integration in the supply chain: Barriers and performance. *Decision Sciences, 33*(4).

Galliers, R. (1992). Choosing information systems research approaches. In R. Galliers (Ed.), *Information systems research.* Oxford: Blackwell.

Ives, B., Jarvenpaa, S., & Mason R. (1993). Global business drivers: Aligning information technology to business strategy. *IBM Systems Journal, 32*(1).

Johnson, M., & Whang, S. (2002). E-business and supply chain management: An overview and framework. *Production and Operations Management, 11*(4).

Kimberly, J. (1981). Managerial innovation. In P. Nystrom & W. Starbuck (Eds.), *Handbook of organizational design. Volume 1: Adapting organizations of their environments.* Oxford: Oxford University Press.

Laseter, T. (2003). *Whirlpool Corporation global procurement.* Case UVA-OM-1071, Darden Business Publishing, University of Virginia, USA.

Lee, H., & Whang, S. (2001). E-business and supply chain integration. *Proceedings of the Stanford Global Supply Chain Management Forum* (SGSCMF-W2-2001).

Leonard-Barton, D. (1988). Implementation as mutual adaptation of technology and organization. *Research Policy,* 251-267.

Lorenzo, O., Kawalek, P., & Wood-Harper, T. (2005). Embedding the enterprise systems into the enterprise: A model of corporate diffusion. *Communications of the AIS, 15,* 609-641.

Magnusson, M. (2004). Managing the knowledge landscape of an MNC: Knowledge networking at Ericsson. *Knowledge and Process Management, 11*(4).

Malone, T., & Crowston, K. (1994). The interdisciplinary study of coordination. *ACM Computing Surveys, 26*(1), 87-119.

Malone, T.W., Crowston, K., Lee, J., Pentland, B., O'Donnell, E., & Dellarocas, C. (1999). Tools for inventing organizations: Toward a handbook of organizational processes. *Management Science, 45*(3).

Markus, M. (2000). Paradigm shifts—e-business and business/systems integration. *Communications of the AIS, 1*(10).

Markus, M., Tanis, C., & Fenema, P. (2000). Multisite ERP implementations. *Communications of the ACM, 43*(4), 42-46.

Segev, A., & Gebaur, J. (2001). B2B procurement and marketplace transformation. *Information Technology and Management, 2*(3).

Smith, H.L., Dickson, K., & Smith, S.L. (1991). There are two sides to every story: Innovation and collaboration within networks of large and small firms. *Research Policy, 20*(5). 457-469.

Soh, C., Siew Kien, S., & Tay-Yap, J. (2000). Cultural fits and misfits: Is ERP a universal solution? *Communications of the ACM, 43*(4), 47-51.

Stefanou, C. (1999). Supply chain management and organizational key factors for successful implementation of ERP systems. *Proceedings of the 5th Americas Conference on Information Systems,* Milwaukee, WI.

Taylor, D. (1997). *Global cases in logistics and supply chain management.* Thomson Press.

Tyre, M., & Orlikowski, W. (1994). Windows of opportunity: Temporal patterns of technological adaptation in organizations. *Organization Science, 5*(1), 98-117.

Westerman, G., & Cotteleer, M. (1999). *Tektronix, Inc: Global ERP implementation.* Boston: Harvard Business School Publishing (Case 9-699-043).

ENDNOTE

[1] Maverick spending refers to purchases made outside established processes for ordering goods and services.

Chapter IX
Feral Systems and Other Factors Influencing the Success of Global ERP Implementations

Don Kerr
University of the Sunshine Coast, Australia

ABSTRACT

In this chapter we look at the factors that influence the successful implementation of a global enterprise resource planning (ERP) system. We identify 12 issues that need to be considered when implementing such systems. Each one of these issues is expanded upon with relevant literature and examples. In this chapter we also look at factors that lead to the development of information systems by employees in addition to or outside the implemented ERP. We introduce the concept of feral systems to explain this phenomenon. Other factors such as employee mistrust of the system are also discussed. Finally we look at future directions with respect to ERP implementations.

INTRODUCTION

With increased globalization and the accompanying need for multinational companies (MNCs) to have offices in international locations, it is not surprising that billions of dollars have been spent by MNCs over the last decade in attempts to integrate their information technology. The most common approach to this problem is the implementation of enterprise resource planning (ERP) systems. The primary object of global ERP implementation is the imperative to have totally integrated information technology resources stretching across the entire global organization. This integration will result in better alignment of IT investments against organizational goals, better accountability of IT investments and expenditure, and more timely access to data. According to Systems Applications and Products in Data Processing (SAP), the market leader in ERP sales, improved access to accurate data has a number of advantages, including "accelerating time to market of products and services, maximizing partner business results through synchronized product catalogues and improving the ability to respond and adapt to changing conditions" (SAP, 2006, p. 1).

This chapter focuses on the factors affecting the implementation and adaptation of ERPs in business. It will provide multiple perspectives to post-implementation problems for the global corporation. Much of the literature to date has concentrated on the negative aspects of ERP implementations rather than the positives that accrue from the integration of information technology resources within an enterprise. Some examples of these positive aspects include providing a means for global companies to lower costs, improve quality, increase inventory variety, and improve delivery reliability through the enabling technology of a global ERP system (Gupta & Kohli, 2006).

In summary this chapter will look at the following factors:

- Background to ERP implementations and the problems associated with them
- Examples of the positive benefits of ERP implementations
- Issues to be considered when implementing ERPs
- Factors leading to the development of systems outside the ERP
- Employee mistrust of the ERP

BACKGROUND

Global ERP implementations have had a patchy history. For example, implementations with companies such as FoxMeyer and Hershey have resulted in significant delays in work and, in the case of FoxMeyer, even bankruptcy. The lessons learned from the FoxMeyer example were that the company tried to do too many projects at once and this resulted in managerial over-commitment. Scott (2006) suggested that this over-commitment

was even more disastrous than management not being committed enough. In addition, employees knew their jobs were on the line and that a major reason for implementation was to downsize the workforce. There was a reported morale problem with many employees due to the concern of their jobs being threatened, and this even resulted in cases of employees damaging inventory and not filling orders. In addition, FoxMeyer was heavily dependent on consultants from Anderson Consulting and this made it difficult for the company to maintain proper control over the project (Scott, 2006).

The Hershey example resulted in a better outcome with the eventual successful ERP implementation, but this was not without a great deal of pain as the company had difficulty in the early stages of implementation. However these difficulties were more about the timing of the implementation during the period of very high sales, namely Halloween 1999. In reality, the problems Hershey incurred were not too dissimilar to many other enterprise systems (ES) implementations. The former CEO of Hershey, Mr. Wolfe, stated that:

Enterprise software is hard. It takes a long time [to implement]. It's hard to get people to change the way they work so that the system will function correctly. But they eventually adapt. You will have problems in your business at first because enterprise software isn't just software. It requires changing the way you do business.

Initial success can often be turned into failure. This was demonstrated in a case study conducted by Larsen and Myers (1999). Here the implementation was considered a success, but over time it turned out to be a failure. This was due to many factors including experts' delegation of duties to inexperienced junior staff and a dramatic reduction in staff immediately after implementation. This was followed by the loss of all in-house expertise. The cumulative effect of all these factors resulted in significant problems for the organization.

The Suggested Approach to Implementation

There are many textbook examples that provide a step-by-step guide to successful ERP implementations; for example Sandoe, Corbitt, and Boykin (2001, p. 140) divide the ideal implementation into six major phases:

1. **Initiation:** This is where a business case is made for the implementation, and decisions are made about scope and strategies. This phase also looks at the selection of software, vendors, consultants, and hardware.
2. **Planning:** This phase is associated with project administration, and factors such as staffing levels, goal setting, resources, and assessing measurements of success are established.
3. **Analysis and process design:** This involves the analysis of all the business processes of the organization and redesigning them if needed. It also includes process mapping of the present situation compared to what it will be after the ERP implementation.
4. **Realization:** This is when the base system is installed and customized to the organization. It also involves testing and extending the system if needed.
5. **Transition:** This is when the former system is replaced by the new ERP system.
6. **Operations:** This is the ongoing effort involved in monitoring and tuning the system, as well as the continuing job of staff training.

SAP, a major ERP vendor, advocates the ASAP or accelerated SAP implementation approach. This approach consists of five phases, namely:

- **Phase one:** Project preparation, where roles and procedures are explained; the project schedule, budget, and resources are defined; training for the project team is planned; technical requirements are defined; and meetings are organized.
- **Phase two:** Business blueprint, where customer requirements are obtained, training is provided for the project team, the development system is installed, and a review of the business blueprint is completed.
- **Phase three:** Realization, which involves customizing the "baseline" system so that it covers 100% of the organizational structure and 60% of all daily business operations. Then a check is made to see if this customizing covers (realizes) the business processes—the first integration test. The final integration test involves checking other business processes that may be indirectly affected by the implementation. In summary, phase three involves the design, development, and testing of interfaces, reports, and data conversions.
- **Phase four:** The final preparation phase, which is the planning for "go live" (full implementation). This phase involves training end users, testing for integration, volume of work, and any stress points that may appear. It also involves the establishment of a help desk.
- **Phase five:** The "go live" and start of operations. This involves setting up support, verifying the accuracy of the production system, measuring the business benefits, and optimizing performance.

Examples of the Positive Benefits of Global ERP Implementations

There are three advantages to global ERP systems, and they are related to the integration and automation of business processes, the sharing of data and the new business processes throughout the organization, and the generation of reports and other information in real time (Heizer & Render, 2003). ERPs are designed to overcome the fragmentation in data and business processes often found in large global organizations.

The literature has provided mixed assessments of ERP implementations, with both negative and positive aspects being reported. Some examples of the negative aspects have been outlined earlier in this chapter. However, many companies have had measurable and positive improvements to their bottom line through effective implementations. A case study at Texas Instruments provides an example.

Texas Instruments' ERP implementation (Sarkis & Sundarraj, 2003) has provided a model for other implementation projects. The implementation was a success because adequate resources were made available. The total cost of implementation was US$250 million over a three-year period. Sarkis and Sundarraj (2003) reported that the system response time was less than 3 seconds, and there were a total of 10,000 registered internal users and 3,000 registered external users. The system can handle 120,000 orders through 45,000 devices at any given time. According to Sarkis and Sundarraj, the lessons learned from this successful implementation are the same as those reported in the academic literature (outlined in this chapter); however, they are often ignored in practice for various reasons.

Issues to be Considered when Implementing Global ERPs

As mentioned earlier, global ERP systems are difficult to implement, and the examples shown above are indicative of many, although not all, implementations. There are many reasons for implementation failure; for example, Rockford Consulting (2006) has identified 12 major reasons why ERP implementations take longer than expected to be successful or sometimes fail.

They are:

- Lack of top management involvement
- Difficult or inadequate definition of requirements
- Poor ERP package selection
- Not enough resources being allocated to the implementation
- Employee resistance to change or their lack of ownership in the process
- Poor understanding of the time and effort required to finish the project
- Poor understanding of how well the software fits with the business processes
- Management's unrealistic expectations of the capabilities of the ERP
- Insufficient resources allocated to training staff in the use of the ERP
- Problems associated with managing the project
- Poor communication between management and staff
- Inappropriate cost savings

This section will look at these 12 problem areas in detail and provide examples from cases and the literature on how enterprises have addressed the problem.

Lack of Top Management Involvement

Lack of top management support has been identified as a major impediment to successful ERP implementations. Top management may believe that they have more important things to worry about than an ERP implementation, but the question should be asked: What could be more important than the future of the enterprise? Top managers need to continually explain the importance of the changes that are taking place in the organization during the implementation phase of the ERP. The changes could be very worrying to employees, many of whom could have concerns about their employment future after the ERP implementation. It is up to top management to give assurances to workers and, if downsizing is one of the aims of implementation, provide them with the necessary skills to ensure employment in other areas of the company or other sectors of the industry. Wang and Chen (2006) suggest that top management support can improve ERP implementations indirectly by providing conflict resolution between consultants and company employees. This is an example of how top management groups can enforce the necessary power to ensure that things get done.

King and Burgess (2006) cite Somers and Nelson (2001) as identifying top management support as the most important factor in relation to implementation success. Their research showed that this factor rated the highest of 10 components considered important to implementation success at 4.29 (1 being low and 5 being critical to success). According to King and Burgess, top management support can lead to "the appointment of a dynamic project champion who, in turn, encourages the project manager to introduce regular cross-departmental process redesign workshops involving a wide range of stakeholders." These workshops led to "greater inter-departmental communication and, consequently, to greater collaboration" (King & Burgess, 2006, pp. 61-62). These authors also suggest that a lessening of top management support may lead to less experienced staff being assigned to the project, and this could result in a reduction of team competence.

Other authors also consider that top management is important; for example, Motwani, Mirchandani, Madan, and Gunasekaran (2002, p. 83) suggest that "a cautious, evolutionary, bureaucratic implementation process backed with careful change management, network relationships, and cultural readiness can lead to a successful ERP project implementation." The same authors compare the ideal situation described above with the opposite state of affairs, which is often the case, namely, a mandated revolutionary approach that is implemented without the organization being

ready and without good change management processes (Motwani et al., 2002).

In summary, top management support is a critical success factor and an important precursor to effective implementation. Many authors cite support as being a major contributor to success, and both top management and vendor support are essential throughout the life of the implementation process.

Difficult or Inadequate Definition of Requirements

Requirements definition is a method used to identify a business need, write down the objectives of the project, negotiate and determine the client needs as separate from their wants, and document the results.

Verville and Halingten (2003) outlined requirements definition as being the team analysis of the existing technological environment of the organization, followed by the analysis of the requirements in relation to the following aspects:

- The functional requirements for the organization
- The technical requirements for the organization
- The organization's business, procedural, and policy requirements
- The different functions and locations of the users
- An analysis of the existing processes and how the new software will affect these processes
- Any other problems or opportunities considered

The points outlined by Verville and Halingten (2003) are also covered in other parts of this chapter. For example, the functional and technical requirements can impact on the resources required and managerial estimates of the time required to complete the project.

The development of requirement definitions and specifications is a laborious and time-consuming job. Many people try to take shortcuts with this process; however, this is false economy. For example, Dvira, Razb, and Shenharc (2003), in a study of 110 defense force projects conducted in Israel over a 20-year period, demonstrated a positive correlation between the time invested in requirements definition and the success of the project. The authors concluded that, although some claim that too much planning can curtail the creativity of the project workers or that milestone planning is all that is needed, it is still essential that at least a minimal level of planning should be done.

A common thread throughout the literature is that more time should be spent on defining the requirements for the ERP implementation. Correct and detailed requirements definition can make the other steps in the implementation process so much easier.

Poor ERP Package Selection

Poor selection of the right ERP is closely related to inadequate definition of requirements. It is also prevalent when employees do not spend the time to find out if the ERP is adequate for their requirements. Rockford Consulting (2006) suggest that this could also be related to executives who, having found the ERP adequate in their previous employment in other corporations, do not then consider the different circumstances in their new employment within another corporation.

Poor ERP selection has been the concern of many, with functional units within corporations often complaining that the selected ERP does not meet the requirements of their area. For example, Dery and Wailes (2005) describe a case with a company called FoodCo (a pseudonym) where the human resource unit of the company opted out of an SAP implementation because they felt that the SAP software was not the right selection for the human resource functions of the company. The

company had not consulted widely enough and, as far as the human resource section was concerned, the correct package was not selected.

Hecht (1997) provides an overview of ERP software selection. This author cites the Gartner Group as having identified four major problems associated with ERP selection, one being the time it takes to identify key criteria; for example, he reports cases where project teams can spend up to 14 months just identifying the key evaluation criteria and looking at alternatives. Another factor is cost, and the author reports cases where the cost of travel, vendor interviews, validating data given, and developing the requirements definition accounts for up to 30% of the total cost of the implementation. The third problem relates to finding objective data. In this case many companies have had to rely on vendor information because there is a lack of objective data on products and services.

Finally, Hecht (1997) outlines a lack of a structured process as being a fourth problem. He indicates a lack of a rigorous selection methodology, with many companies relying on limited data and "gut feelings." Hecht (1997, p. 58) recommended that a more in-depth evaluation and selection method was needed, based on the six major criteria of "functionality, technical architecture, cost, service and support, ability to execute and vision."

In an effort to overcome the deficiencies outlined by Hecht (1997), other researchers, notably Wei and Wang (2004), provided a comprehensive framework for ERP selection based on project, software system, and vendor factors. The project factors included the total cost of the implementation, the time it took to implement, and an assessment of the benefits and risks associated with implementation. Software system factors were based on the strategic fit to company goals and vision, and how well the software fitted local environmental requirements. The functions and technology assessments were based on reliability and quality, user friendliness, expansion and upgrades, and functional fit.

Vendor factors included the vendor's ability with respect to research and development technology, implementation and serviceability capabilities, and consulting services. The vendor's reputation was also considered in terms of financial conditions, their credentials, and overall reputation. The approach is mathematical in nature, being based on fuzzy set theory (Wei & Wang, 2004), and the model provided an approach to ERP selection that was objective in nature.

In another paper, Wei, Chien, and Wang (2005) discuss a seven-stage approach to ERP selection culminating in what they term as the analytic hierarchy process (AHP) method. According to the authors, the AHP method "directs how to determine the priority of a set of alternatives and the relative importance of attributes in a multiple criteria decision-making problem" (Wei et al., 2005, p. 48). The seven steps identified in this approach are:

- **Step 1:** Form a project team and collect all possible information about ERP vendors and systems.
- **Step 2:** Identify the ERP system characteristics.
- **Step 3:** Construct a structure of objectives in order to develop the fundamental-objective hierarchy and means-objective network.
- **Step 4:** Extract the attributes for evaluating ERP systems from the structure of objectives.
- **Step 5:** Filter out unqualified vendors by asking specific questions, which are formulated according to the system requirements.
- **Step 6:** Evaluate the ERP systems using the AHP method.
- **Step 7:** Discuss the results and make the final decision.

The AHP method is described by Wei et al. (2005, p. 51) as a "multi-attribute evaluation method that involves three phases: decomposition, comparative judgments, and synthesis of priori-

ties." This approach attaches a relative importance and global priority to alternatives explored and is claimed to help provide a consensus among decision makers.

These more analytical approaches can provide a basis for discussion founded on models developed from data and can assist in the negotiation and consultation processes by providing "hard" figures to complement and add to the "soft" discussions.

Not Enough Resources Being Allocated to the Implementation

According to Rockford Consulting (2006, p. 2), "the third greatest reason for ERP implementation failures is inadequate allocation of resources." Resources include time, money, and staff. Many companies try to save money with ERP implementations by increasing the workload of existing employees, and this often results in employee "burn out."

The lack of resources allocated to any information system project can have dire consequences in many cases, with perhaps the most drastic being termination of the project. Dilts and Pence (2006) have investigated the impact that a person's role in the organization has on project failure and even termination. These authors identify the resources gap and the expectation gap between initial expectations and final project results as being a problematic area. Interestingly, the authors have found that the scale of the project in terms of labor costs, time, or budget has little relation to the perception of failure. In other words, large amounts of effort and money spent on a project do not necessarily mean that the project will be considered successful. So throwing more money into the project in an undirected way or as an afterthought may not improve the situation.

Another area that has consistently been reported as being under-resourced is that of training and post-implementation help desks. The successful ERP implementation at Pratt and Whitney

(Tchokogue, Bareil, & Duguay, 2005) highlighted the importance of expending adequate resources in training. The company initiated a massive training program using its own employees as instructors, and this enabled a better transfer of knowledge because the employees were able to provide instruction in the context of the firm's existing culture.

Before committing to any ERP implementation project, the organization needs to have an understanding of the challenges and risks involved, and a firm commitment to ensure that all the resources needed for an implementation are available. It may be that there are more cost-effective ways of obtaining the same results as an ERP, for example improving existing processes, changing the structure of your organization, improving your supply chain, or implementing a performance management system (Kimberling, 2006).

Employee Resistance to Change or Their Lack of Ownership in the Process

Some ERP implementations suffer from employee resistance to change or employees feel that they lack ownership in the process, and this can be due to many reasons. In a lot of cases, resistance can be associated with poor communications and uncertainty about the future. As mentioned in the background section of this chapter, the lack of the presentation of a convincing case, lack of employee involvement, poor communications, lack of top management support, and fear of job losses are all critical factors associated with employee resistance.

Authors such as Bradford and Florin (2003) have applied the diffusion of innovation theory to understand implementation success of the ERP innovation. Diffusion theory directly relates to the acceptance of the ERP by employees as it looks at aspects of the innovation and how they are perceived by the people who have to use the system. These authors developed a research model for implementation success that involved the three

factors of innovation characteristics, organizational characteristics, and environmental characteristics. The innovation characteristics were divided into technical compatibility, perceived compatibility, and business process reengineering. The organizational characteristics were top management, organizational objective consensus, and training, while environmental characteristics were associated with competitive pressures. The authors suggest that these characteristics should be considered during the planning of any ERP implementation.

Many employees feel threatened by change, and ERP implementations inevitably result in very large changes. Employees may react in different ways depending on how open and understanding management is to employee concerns or how well they put forward the case for change. It may be that employee backlash to ERP implementations is directly proportional to their concerns about job security. Australian research within a government-owned corporation (sometimes called a Quango) with a policy of no job redundancies found that employee concerns about how the upcoming implementation impacted on their job security was minimal (Houghton & Kerr, 2006).

Poor Understanding of the Time and Effort Required to Finish the Project

Many projects are implemented with little understanding of the true time and effort required, and this is one of the major causes of cost overruns. For example, the timeframe for implementation of SAP R/3 at Rolls Royce was changed due to factors such as giving the organization more time to prepare, train, and clean up data; more time to pilot-test the system; and more time for prerequisite projects to be deployed and for the successful implementation of SAP at another company location (Yusufa, Gunasekaran, & Abthorpe, 2004). Revisions of timeframes such as those outlined above are common in most implementations, and in the Rolls Royce example little time was lost because these problems were addressed early enough in the program. A good understanding of the true cost in both time and hidden costs is important, and managers will not necessarily receive accurate information if the vendors and consultants associated with implementation are the only people consulted.

Time and cost overruns occur quite frequently with ERP implementations, and there are many examples of this occurring in the literature. Both cost and time overruns were identified as the top two factors associated with ERP implementation success or failure by Hong and Kim (2002). The four factors these authors associated with success or failure were:

- The cost of the ERP project was significantly higher then the expected budgets.
- The ERP project took significantly longer than expected.
- The systems performance was significantly below the expected level.
- The anticipated benefits of the ERP did not materialize.

Poor Understanding of How Well the Software Fits with the Business Processes

A poor understanding of how well the ERP fits the organization and its business processes can result in a reduction in the effectiveness of the ERP and can also result in cost blowouts. A software misfit is described by Soh, Klien, and Tay-Yap (2000) as the gaps between software functions and the requirements of the organization.

These authors demonstrate ERP/organizational misfits through a case study of a Singapore hospital. The authors describe three major misfit categories as being company specific, public sector specific, and country specific. Each of these categories has data, functional, and/or output misfits. Data misfits can be in the form of format and/or the relationships between data.

Soh et al. (2000) provide examples of data format misfits in relation to the ERP implemented in the Singaporean hospital case study. The example given was in terms of different names in Asian cultures—that is, the first name in the Asian adaptation of the ERP could capture the entire name in the first name field so as to avoid confusion in having to differentiate between first and last names (sometimes difficult with Indian, Malay, or Chinese names). The data relationship misfit can be exemplified through patient-unique identifiers (IDs). The ERP automatically generates a patient's ID, but in Asian societies all government systems use a predefined ID that is used in the ERP, therefore the built-in ERP function is overridden.

Functional misfits are categorized as access, control, or operational, and Soh et al. (2000) give examples of a functional access misfit in terms of the patient tracking system. Doctors had to use an independently developed add-on in the new ERP to track down patients, though it was a standard function in the old system. A functional control misfit is described by the authors as the ERP not allowing validation routines based on organizational business requirements, while a functional operational misfit example is the ERP not allowing a patient to pay his/her bill by a fixed amount every month (a common practice in the case study hospital).

Output misfits can be in the form of presentation format or information content. Examples quoted by Soh et al. (2000) include output presentation misfits where materials management information did not contain dates, timestamps, and page numbers, while examples of output information content misfits were where key parameters required by the organization were not available on the standard ERP.

Hong and Kim (2002) also describe the fit of the ERP within the organization as important, and these authors discuss the critical success factors for ERP implementations with respect to organizational fit. Their study found that the organizational fit of the ERP is critical with respect to implementation success, and that a major problem relates to the basic objectives of the organization and the ERP vendor. The organization is aiming for a business solution that fits its unique requirements, while the ERP vendors are trying to sell a generic solution that covers a broad market. This discrepancy in basic objectives is a major reason why many implementations are problematic or fail. It is therefore important that the organization selects an ERP that most closely fits its aims and objectives, or alternatively be prepared to make resources available for major adaptations of the selected ERP to fit its requirements.

Hong and Kim (2002) described organizational fit in terms of process fit, data fit, and user fit. With two alternatives to ERP fit, the first is the adaptation of the package to the needs of the organization, and the second is the adaptation of organizational processes to the package. Hong and Kim (2002) suggest that ERP vendors encourage the adaptation of organizational processes rather than changing the ERP because of a fear that these changes will adversely affect software performance, future upgrades, and maintenance.

Management's Unrealistic Expectations of the Capabilities of the ERP

Many ERP implementations have not provided the level of benefits or returns on investment that the software vendors stated they would prior to implementation. This is often because the total cost of implementation was not included. For example, planning, training, testing, and conversion of data are not included in the initial budget in many cases.

An unrealistic expectation of the capabilities of an ERP is another factor that affects managerial perceptions of the success or failure of an implementation. Expectations are usually created by the vendor's sales team, and the sales hype can sometimes exaggerate the return on investment estimates and underestimate the total cost of implementation.

In a field changing as rapidly as ERPs, it is difficult to obtain unbiased, objective advice, and even the white papers that are so freely available on the Internet may contain bias. Berinato (2002) suggests that white papers are sometimes written by technical journalists who have been offered money by vendors to ghost-write white papers that put a positive slant on their products.

Insufficient Resources Allocated to Training Staff in the Use of the ERP

According to Rockford Consulting (2006), the cost of training is almost always underestimated. Training in the ERP system is critical for success. Training must be relevant to the problem domain of the user in that it must relate to his or her area of work. Research by Archer-Lean, Clark, and Kerr (2006) indicates that training may be a purely mechanical process in some cases. These authors report a case study where employees were provided training that ended up being a mechanized process in that some employees quickly learned that continually pressing the enter key while working through the software enabled them to get through the required training modules very quickly. It appeared that most people were inclined to use this shortcut approach because the training modules were not providing a context for their everyday routine work requirements.

The recommended approach to training is to have key users who are company employees train other employees. This will ensure that the training is in context and fits the company culture. The Pratt and Whitney and Rolls Royce ERP implementation examples demonstrated the importance of adequate training.

Problems Associated with Managing the Project

A major problem in many implementation situations is the temptation to take shortcuts, and this has been reported as being problematic in many cases (Rockford Consulting, 2006). Just because schedules have blown out and critical project timelines have been extended does not mean that the implementation team should start taking shortcuts and bypass previously planned activities. It is usual for implementations to take longer than planned, and it is better to extend the project's timeframe than to take shortcuts in implementation. The ERP implementation should be treated like all other information systems implementations with respect to standard project management approaches.

As mentioned earlier, Hong and Kim (2002) outlined four factors that indicated success or failure of an implementation. The first two involved cost and time blowouts; however, the last two involved performance and benefits. These last two aspects will continue to be important factors for the long-term survival of the company, long after the cost and time blowouts have been forgotten.

Poor Communications between Management and Staff

Failure to inform staff of the progress and importance of the implementation is another common area of neglect. This usually starts with a failure of management to tell staff the reason for the change and to communicate to them the benefits of implementation. If the object of the implementation is to reduce head count, then it is advisable for the employer to provide assistance to redeploy displaced employees or help them in developing skills to find new jobs. Disgruntled employees can cause havoc to ERP implementations, as the FoxMeyer case demonstrated. Communications are very important to overcome the two sources of resistance employees have to innovations, namely, perceived risk and habit (Sheth, 1981). Perceived risk is the perception by employees of the risk associated with the decision to implement, while habit is concerned with the current practices that are part of the employee's routine. It is up to

management to point out the advantages of the change and to develop strategies to communicate these advantages to the workforce.

Australian research (Houghton & Kerr, 2006) has shown examples of the possible manipulation of the message by top management. For example, research conducted on an ERP implementation in a large transport corporation in Australia provided examples of the type of communication management may employ. In this example, intranet postings from management had biases in the reporting of the effectiveness of the ERP implementation. Employees were particularly suspicious of the motives of top-level management and the positive slant on the ERP implementation provided by management through these intranet postings. Other material appeared to reinforce some of the negative prejudgments among end user employees. It was perceived by lower to middle management that the information provided by top management was simply "spin" and that they felt pressured to say the implementation was a success because "they have spent millions on this and they have to justify the expense." This perception of management communications as being spin can also be an indicator of mistrust of the organizational intent with respect to the ERP implementation.

Inappropriate Cost Saving

Many implementation failures can be attributed to cost saving measures that could be considered high risk. For example, implementing over many sites rather than implementing and testing over one site to start with has resulted in setbacks or even failures in the past. Compression of the timeframe for implementation is another common mistake, and this is related to the shortcuts associated with managing the project. The successful implementations, such as Texas Instruments (Sarkis & Sundarraj, 2003), all ensured that adequate resources were available in the first place and that the temptation to take shortcuts was avoided.

Factors Leading to the Development of Systems Outside the ERP

The implementation of an ERP usually results in a major change in the working arrangements for employees. In many cases employees have a deep attachment to the way things were done before the change. For example, employee behavior associated with deeply entrenched beliefs and values from pre-implementation days have been reported.

Authors such as Al-Mashari and Al-Midimigh (2003) suggest that change management strategies associated with the implementation of an ERP system (in this case SAP) could be improved. These authors suggest that a lot of the factors concerning the implementation of such systems were of a social nature, for example, lack of communication, lack of ownership, lack of change management strategy, lack of social support, and other related issues. Kræmmergaard and Rose (2002) suggest managerial competencies are required and:

Managing the changeover to a new ERP system is exceptionally complex and requires a wide variety of knowledge (business, technical, human, organizational), skills (managerial, political, project management), and the ability to develop both of these in a practical way.

Kræmmergaard and Rose (2002) derived a list they considered to be skills required for managing ERP implementations. One skill mentioned was organizational competence. The authors argue that this is the ability to work with the organization, its culture, power distribution, and history in a successful manner. That is, any successful ERP implementation should take into account the history of the social environment and the distribution of power within the organization.

Investigations into supply chain management operations in a large government-owned corporation (GOC) showed that some employees misunderstood certain aspects of the distribution of power within the organization. This research found several instances of people ignoring the ERP implementation in favor of a kind of "skunk work" (Tushman & O'Reilly, 1999) activity that involved developing systems deemed by them to be relevant to their own area of work but not condoned by management. Such systems are referred to as "feral systems."

Feral Systems

Houghton and Kerr (2006) describe the phenomenon of feral systems in their study into supply chain management operations in a large GOC outlined above. A feral system is defined as "an information system [computerized] that is developed by individuals or groups of employees to help them with their work, but is not condoned by management nor is part of the corporation's accepted information technology infrastructure. Its development is designed to circumvent existing organizational information systems" (Houghton & Kerr, 2006, p. 137).

The development of feral system may be indicative of a general unease with the ERP implementation by employees, or it could be due to employees' attachment to existing legacy systems or a lack of training in the use of the ERP system. For example, this Australian research has shown that there appeared to be extensive use of feral systems in the case study organization (Houghton & Kerr, 2006), and these computer systems were developed by individuals outside the accepted ERP environment. This research suggests that there is a high level of internal information systems (feral systems) being developed and used to either supplement the ERP system or replace it. Evidence of the feral systems is demonstrated within this GOC with statements by middle management, for example:

We've got a diary that tracks all material usage on a daily basis so it will have on there how [much product] we unloaded today so Bruce [not his real name] will come and write in the diary in that section, how many items of [product] he does. That diary then goes into a database internally within here and onto a spreadsheet. (Engineer)

This indicates that a high level of internal information systems (feral systems) are developed and used to either supplement the SAP system or replace it.

The use of feral systems was further confirmed when the feral systems concept was mentioned during subsequent interviews, and respondents recorded statements such as:

Yes that's a very good point and the people that make these feral systems will have no end of argument about why they are needed and yes there may be justifications, but at the end of the day if everyone goes down their own little track with their own systems, we are going to be in the same position as we were before we implemented SAP R3. (Upper-Level Manager)

Other respondents indicated that feral systems may not be as much of a problem as indicated and that they could be confused with other reporting tools, for example:

Certainly we've pulled data out of SAP and put it into Access databases or Excel spreadsheets to do various manipulations, so to that extent yes we are doing that, but I don't see them as feral systems. I see those as different reporting tools. (Upper-Level Manager, Commodities)

On the other hand, the same respondent indicated that he could see problems with feral systems in certain cases where there was little or no visibility for the organization, for example:

At the other end of the equation there are a number of customers who are doing their planning outside of SAP so there is no visibility for the organization because their planning exists in Excel spreadsheets *or Access databases and isn't rolling up into any corporate plan, so that does create a problem.* (Upper-Level Manager, Commodities)

Studies are under way to attempt to analyze these factors and reward systems that drive the need to develop feral systems where end users develop their own systems, presumably because the ERP system does not provide the information they want, although it could equally be the case that these feral systems were developed some time ago (before the ERP implementation) and could be classed as legacy systems. Kwasi (2007) suggests that "users of these legacy systems typically have vested interests, valuable experience and know-how in those systems. Replacing legacy systems requires people to 'relearn' new skills and their unwillingness to do so might lead them to perceive the ERPs as being difficult to use." In some organizations, tolerance of feral systems can be reasonably high.

A Mistrust of the ERP

Mistrust of management with respect to ERP implementations is understandable when one of the main stated advantages of implementing an ERP is a reduction in staff numbers. Employees could naturally be mistrustful of the organization's intent. This mistrust can also extend to the data and reports generated by the ERP. For example, Australian research conducted at a large transport corporation indicated that employees were aware of the advantages that ERPs provided under ideal conditions with respect to integrated IT resources and better decision making through better access to data. However, in practice, these ideal situations did not always eventuate. This appeared to be due to social and other factors such as a lack of strategic and operational communication, a lack of alignment with other reporting systems, the use of feral systems instead of the ERP, and a general mistrust of the ERP itself. This could be due to low computer literacy levels, entrenched work and business process procedures, and poor training within the organization.

DISCUSSION

This chapter has covered the issues associated with ERP implementations and has provided some explanations as to the problems that have been encountered and possible solutions to the 12 implementation issues outlined earlier. It has not covered the possible reasons why a global enterprise may implement an ERP. Swanson and Ramiller (2004) discuss the concept of companies mindfully engaging in IT developments. The converse of this is a mindless implementation, and it could be considered that many enterprises implement ERPs for the wrong reasons. Swanson and Ramiller (2004) describe implementations that are done on a "me too" basis and go on the ERP "bandwagon" just because other similar companies have done so. It has become apparent that a mindless implementation has a direct influence on how employees perceive the benefits and usefulness of an ERP implementation, because it becomes apparent over time that the ERP does not link to organizational objectives. This is not to say that an ERP implementation undertaken because business partners have the same ERP is not a sensible thing to do; however, it is important that firms look at all aspects of an ERP implementation to ensure it fits their own requirements as well.

Another factor influencing ERP implementation decisions in global companies is the type of ERP used in different branch offices or head office. It may be company policy to use the same ERP across the whole enterprise. If this is the case, it could exacerbate the cultural problems outlined in earlier sections of this chapter, particularly in Asian cultures as suggested by Soh et al. (2000).

ERP implementations are never easy, and there is a great deal of literature outlining the problems. These problems are not insurmountable, but any organization must carefully weigh up the benefits and costs of such a massive undertaking. It may well be that a total ERP implementation is not necessary and that other approaches such as system-orientated architecture (SOA) or other methods of integrating legacy systems are more useful. Organizations must be wary of ERP implementation decisions based on "me too" or joining the ERP "bandwagon."

A natural place to look for information on ERP implementations is the Internet; however, readers should be wary of Internet white papers or other consultants' advice, as there is a lot of vendor "hype" in this area of business. Readers should make sure they have a thorough understanding of the information provided and not be unduly influenced by the information provided by vendors alone. This vendor hype has been attributed to many cases of unrealistic managerial expectations of the benefits of ERPs. These unrealistic expectations constitute one of the 12 stated reasons for ERP implementation failures as outlined by Rockford Consulting (2006). It is very much a case of "buyers beware," as even white papers on the Internet can have biased editorials, with assertions that some journalists may be unduly influenced by vendors.

The Australian research conducted by Houghton and Kerr (2006) indicated that employees in the case study corporation were aware of the advantages that ERPs provide under ideal conditions with respect to integrated IT resources and better decision making through better access to data. However, in practice these ideal situations did not eventuate, and this appears to be due to social and other factors such as a lack of strategic and operational communication, a lack of alignment with other reporting systems, the use of feral systems instead of the ERP, and a general mistrust of the ERP itself. These factors may be specific to the environment under which the research was conducted, namely a government-owned corporation with very different policies and procedures to a profit-maximizing company. However, it is contended that many of the factors, such as a lack of communication, the use of feral systems, and a mistrust of companies' intensions, could equally be associated with all companies.

FUTURE TRENDS

This section is designed to demonstrate the dynamic nature of the global ERP market and to identify future possible trends. Vendors and intermediary companies offer many alternatives to the established ERP software or to established approaches to implementation. Many Internet sites and white papers provide alternatives to established vendors, and products such as ERPII or XPR can be found. ERP II is a term used to describe a process that allows the extraction of business benefits from ERP software (Triniti, 2007). XPR is an enterprise application integration software approach working on the lines of enterprise applications integration (Document Sciences, 2007). These two examples are by no means an exhaustive list, but are illustrations of new products that are continually emerging.

These new products and/or services have the potential to either replace existing ERP systems or provide alternative approaches to implementing existing systems; however, the reader should always be wary of vendor hype, as mentioned in earlier sections in this chapter. In general, we can expect increased integration and more Web-based solutions in future versions of ERP. This will result in more global applications of ERP and will continue to favor global integration of information technology resources.

The author expects that further innovations in ERP development will revolve around wireless technology, allowing salespersons "on the road" to access the full corporate ERP system in a secure fashion. One major problem with wireless access is the lack of security, and this area of concern will have to be overcome before this technology takes

off. The author suggests that other innovations will be associated with improved data analysis and the development of predictive models for decision support from ERP data.

Many ERP companies are looking at expanding their market to small to medium enterprises (SMEs), and this general trend will continue. One method of making ERPs more affordable for SMEs is to reduce the number of functions available. This may mean that the ERP vendors provide well-tested functions that result in a much more stable product, but with more limitations than a fully functional ERP.

CONCLUSION

The 12 issues outlined earlier in this chapter are provided for consideration during implementation; however, it should be apparent that many implementation problems could be avoided if these factors were considered before any decision to implement was made. It is imperative that ERP implementations be well planned, and the 12 issues shown in this chapter can and should be considered during the planning process.

With regard to software misfits, the problem may be greater in Asian countries because of the inherent reflection of U.S. and European business practices associated with most ERP packages. These misfits could have major implications for ERP implementation strategies among global organizations. The seven misfit types as described earlier in this chapter need to be considered in the context of the country in which the implementation is sited.

Vendor selection is a vital component of any ERP implementation, and many approaches to this problem have been devised. There still appears to be a lack of objective information on the performance of ERPs, and this often leads to the company placing undue reliance on vendor information, which may be biased. In addition to this, the environment in which selection takes place is usually filled with internal politics and high expectations of an easy-to-implement, technical fix. It is important under these circumstances that a level-headed approach is undertaken, and this includes having realistic expectations of the software and a clear understanding of the changes that will have to occur within the organization.

Approaches to ERP implementations can either work on adapting the software to the organizational processes or adapting the organizational processes to the software. Both approaches can be problematic, but the vendor will always suggest the business reengineering approach because it is the easiest option and the least risky for the ERP company. The problem is then associated with change management and how well the organization can adapt.

Finally, it is up to the organization to decide if it is ready to implement an ERP. If the decision is made to implement, then the company must be fully committed in terms of managerial support and the provision of adequate resources, to ensure success. The implementation process is complex and can easily become problematic for many reasons. History has shown that in the majority of cases, half-hearted approaches to ERP implementations are doomed to failure.

FUTURE RESEARCH DIRECTIONS

This chapter has introduced the concept of feral systems. These systems are considered in both a positive and negative light, depending on the role the employee has in the organization. Future research should be undertaken to establish the usefulness of feral systems under a various ERP implementation environments. It may well be the case that employee reluctance to discontinue using feral systems may stem from their lack of understanding of the full functions of the ERP or it could be a training issue. On the other hand employees may have developed the feral (or legacy) system themselves over a long period of

time and do not wish to let go of a system that they developed and have a great deal of ownership in. These questions warrant further investigations into how effective ERP implementations are in both the private and public sectors.

Other research directions can be considered in light of the 12 factors that are considered problematic to successful implementations by ERP consultants; each of these factors can provide a fertile ground for future research into the problem area. In particular, little research has been conducted into the social and political factors associated with ERP implementations. An area of research that is of particular interest to the author is how companies can approach ERP implementations where the objective is to reduce employee numbers? This is potentially a very difficult area of change management, with employees expected to work with the company during implementation but with the final outcome being the loss of their jobs.

REFERENCES

Al-Mashari, M., & Al-Midimigh, A. (2003). ERP implementation: Lessons from a case study. *Information Technology and People, 16*(1).

Archer-Lean, C., Clark J.A., & Kerr, D.V. (2006). Evading technological determinism in ERP implementation: Towards a consultative social approach. *Australian Journal of Information Systems, 13*(2), 18-30.

Berinato, S. (2002). How to cut through vendor hype. *CIO Magazine.* Retrieved October 4, 2006, from http://www.cio.com/archive/010102/hype.html

Bradford, M., & Florin, J. (2003). Examining the role of innovation diffusion factors on the implementation success of enterprise resource planning systems. *International Journal of Accounting Information Systems, 4,* 205-225.

Davenport, T.H. (1998). Putting the enterprise into the enterprise system. *Harvard Business Review, 76*(4), 121-131.

Dery, K., & Wailes, N. (2005). Necessary but not sufficient: ERPs and strategic HRM. *Strategic Change, 14,* 265-272.

Dilts, D.M., & Pence, K.R. (2006). Impact of role in the decision to fail: An exploratory study of terminated projects. *Journal of Operations Management, 24,* 378-396.

Document Sciences. (2007). *xPressions 2.1.2 enterprise application integration strategies.* Retrieved February 14, 2007, from http://www.docscience.com/service/xpr_enterprise.htm

Dvira, D., Razb, T., & Shenharc, A.J. (2003). An empirical analysis of the relationship between project planning and project success. *International Journal of Project Management, 21,* 89-95.

Government Owned Corporations Act. (1993). Retrieved May 10, 2006, from http://www.legislation.qld.gov.au/LEGISLTN/CURRENT/G/GoOwnCorpA93_06C_030328.pdf

Gupta, M., & Kohli, A. (2006). Enterprise resource planning systems and its implications for operations function. *Technovation, 26,* 687-696.

Hecht, B. (1997). Choose the right ERP software. *Datamation, 43*(3), 56-58.

Heizer, J., & Render, B. (2003). *Operations management—international edition* (7th ed.). Upper Saddle River, NJ: Pearson Education.

Hong, K.K., & Kim, Y.G. (2002). The critical success factors for ERP implementation: An organizational fit perspective. *Information and Management, 40,* 25-40.

Houghton, L., & Kerr, D.V. (2006). A study into the creation of feral information systems as a response to an ERP implementation within the supply chain of a large government-owned corporation. *International Journal of Internet and Enterprise Management, 4*(2), 137-142.

Jones, M.C., Cline, M., & Ryan, S. (2006). Exploring knowledge sharing in ERP implementation: An organizational culture framework. *Decision Support Systems, 41*(2), 411-434.

Kimberling, E. (2006). *Best practices in ERP software selection.* Retrieved October 4, 2006, from http://blogs.ittoolbox.com/erp/roi/archives/best-practices-in-erp-software-selection-10867

King, S.F., & Burgess, T.F. (2006). Beyond critical success factors: A dynamic model of enterprise system innovation. *International Journal of Information Management, 26,* 59-69.

Kræmmergaard, P., & Rose, J. (2002). Managerial competences for ERP journeys. *Information Systems Frontiers, 4*(2).

Kwasi, A.G. (2007). Perceived usefulness, user involvement and behavioral intention: An empirical study of ERP implementation. *Computers in Human Behavior, 23,* 1232-1248.

Larsen, M.A., & Myers, M.D. (1999). When success turns into failure: A package-driven business process re-engineering project in the financial services industry. *Journal of Strategic Information Systems, 8,* 395-417.

Motwani, J., Mirchandani, D., Madan, A., & Gunasekaran, A. (2002). Successful implementation of ERP projects: Evidence from two case studies. *International Journal of Production Economics, 75,* 83-96.

Poon, P.P., & Wagner, C. (2001). Critical success factors revisited: Success and failure cases of information systems for senior executives. *Decision Support Systems, 30,* 393-418.

Rockford Consulting. (2006). Retrieved August 27, 2006, from http://www.rockfordconsulting.com/12sinart.htm

Sandoe, K., Corbitt, G., & Boykin, R. (2001). *Enterprise integration.* New York: John Wiley & Sons.

SAP. (2006). *End-to-end process integration with SAP NetWeaver.* Retrieved September 21, 2006, from http://www.sap.com/industries/highered/pdf/BWP_End_to_End_Proc_Int.pdf

Sarkis, J., & Sundarraj, R.P. (2003). Managing large-scale global enterprise resource planning systems: A case study at Texas Instruments. *International Journal of Information Management, 23,* 431-442.

Scott, J.E. (2006). *The FoxMeyer Drugs' bankruptcy: Was it a failure of ERP?* Retrieved August 26, 2006, from http://www.ndsu.nodak.edu/ndsu/bklamm/BPandTC%20references/BP%20TC%20Scott%201999%20Foxmeyer%20drugs%20bankruptcy%20was%20it%20a%20failure.pdf#search=%22The%20Delta%20III%20project%20at%20FoxMeyer%20Drugs%20%22

Sheth, J. (1981). Psychology of innovation resistance. *Research in Marketing, 4,* 273-282.

Soh, C., Klien, S.S., & Tay-Yap, J. (2000). Cultural fits and misfits: Is ERP a universal solution? *Communications of the ACM, 43*(4), 47-51.

Somers, T.M., & Nelson, K. (2001, January 3-6). The impact of critical success factors across the stages of enterprise resource planning implementation. In *Proceedings of the 34ᵗʰ Hawaii International Conference on Systems Sciences* (HICSS-34), Maui, HI.

Swanson, E.B., & Ramiller, N.C. (2004). Innovating mindfully with information technology. *MIS Quarterly, 28*(4), 553-583.

Tchokogue, A., Bareil, C., & Duguay, C.R. (2005). Key lessons from the implementation of an ERP at Pratt & Whitney Canada. *International Journal of Production Economics, 95,* 151-163.

Triniti. (2007). *Getting it right with ERP II. Business management.* Retrieved February 14, 2007, from http://www.triniti.com/downloads/articles/erpi.pdf

Tushman, M.L., & O'Reilly, C.A. III. (1999). Building ambidextrous organizations: Forming your own "skunk works." *Health Forum Journal, 42*(2).

Verville, J., & Halingten, A. (2003). A six-stage model of the buying process for ERP software. *Industrial Marketing Management, 32,* 585-594.

Wang, E.T.G., & Chen, J.H.F. (2006). Effects of internal support and consultant quality on the consulting process and ERP system quality. *Decision Support Systems, 42,* 1029-1041.

Wei, C.C., & Wang, M.J.J. (2004). A comprehensive framework for selecting an ERP system. *International Journal of Project Management, 22,* 161-169.

Wei, C.C., Chien, C.F., & Wang, M.J.J. (2005). An AHP-based approach to ERP system selection. *International Journal of Production Economics, 96,* 47-62.

Yusufa, Y., Gunasekaran, A., & Abthorpe, M.S. (2004). Enterprise information systems project implementation: A case study of ERP in Rolls-Royce. *International Journal of Production Economics, 87,* 251-266.

ADDITIONAL READING

Amoako-Gyampah, K. (2007). Perceived usefulness, user involvement and behavioral intention: An empirical study of ERP implementation. *Computers in Human Behavior, 23*(3), 1232-1248.

Campbell, S., & Mohun, V. (2006). *Mastering enterprise SOA with SAP NetWeaver and mySAP ERP.* Hoboken, NJ: John Wiley & Sons.

Choi, D.H., Kim, J., & Kim, S.H. (2007). ERP training with a Web-based electronic learning system: The flow theory perspective. *International Journal of Human-Computer Studies, 65*(3), 223-243.

Davenport, T.H. (2000). *Mission critical: Realizing the promise of enterprise systems.* Boston: Harvard Business School Press.

Forndron, F., Liebermann, T., Thurner, M., & Widmayer, P. (2007). *mySAP ERP roadmap.* Rockville, MD: SAP Press.

Grabski, S.V., & Leech, S.A. (2007). Complementary controls and ERP implementation success. *International Journal of Accounting Information Systems, 8*(1), 17-39.

Hamilton, S. (2006). *Maximizing your ERP system: A practical guide for managers.* New York: McGraw-Hill.

Hendricks, K.B., Singhal, V.R., & Stratman, J. K. (2007). The impact of enterprise systems on corporate performance: A study of ERP, SCM, and CRM system implementations. *Journal of Operations Management, 25*(1), 65-82.

Jacobs, F.R., & Whybark, D.C. (2000). *Why ERP? A primer on SAP implementation.* New York: McGraw-Hill.

Lozinsky, S., & Wahl, P. (1998). *Enterprise-wide software solutions: Integration strategies and practices.* Boston: Addison-Wesley.

Sheldon, D.H. (2006). *Class A ERP implementation: Integrating lean and Six Sigma.* Ft. Lauderdale, FL: J. Ross.

Srivardhana, T., & Pawlowski, S.D. (2007). ERP systems as an enabler of sustained business process innovation: A knowledge-based view. *Journal of Strategic Information Systems, 16*(1), 51-69.

Yusuf, G.A., & Canglin, W.C. (2006). Implementation of enterprise resource planning in China. *Technovation, 26*(12), 1324-1336.

Wang, E.T.G, Lin, C.C., Jiang, J.J., & Klein, G. (2007). Improving enterprise resource planning (ERP) fit to organizational process through knowledge transfer. *International Journal of Information Management, 27*(3), 200-212.

Wu, J.H., & Wang, Y.M. (2007). Measuring ERP success: The key-users' viewpoint of the ERP to produce a viable IS in the organization. *Computers in Human Behavior, 23*(3), 1582-1596.

Wallace, T.F., & Kremzar, M.H. (2001). *ERP: Making it happen: The implementers' guide to success with enterprise resource planning.* Hoboken, NJ: John Wiley & Sons.

ENDNOTE

[1]   A GOC is defined as "a corporatized commercial entity that is freed from the budget sector but that is managed by Governmental ministers" (Government Owned Corporations Act, 1993).

Section IV
Cultural Aspects

Chapter X
Experiences of Cultures in Global ERP Implementation

Esther Brainin
Ruppin Academic Center, Israel

ABSTRACT

The chapter considers the complexities of cultural differences for global enterprise resource planning (ERP) implementation. An extensive review of the literature related to societal and organizational culture is followed by a delineation of the stages of ERP implementation and the actors involved in each stage, reflecting the basic assumption that global ERP systems are not universally acceptable or effective, and that testing the cross-cultural generalizability of ERP systems in organizations will produce a managerial agenda that facilitates the implementation process. The recognition and discussion of these differences can provide a stimulus for identifying and modifying the limitations of technological implementation and use policies to improve the benefits generated by the technology. Topics of explicit concern to ERP implementation in global organizational economies related to organizational and societal culture are discussed, and suggestions for managerial mechanisms for overcoming major obstacles in this process are proposed.

INTRODUCTION

Enterprise resource planning (ERP) systems impose high demands on virtually all organizational members since these process-oriented technologies are designed to standardize business procedures across the enterprise. In addition to its potential benefits, the introduction of an ERP system into an enterprise becomes the means for achieving organizational standardization and integration. Hence, it can be viewed as an organizational "boundary crossing" channel, and as such, ERP integration processes are more than likely to face resistance to change. It is not surprising, then, that while companies worldwide have made substantial investments in the installation of ERP systems, difficulties in implementation and uncertain bottom-line benefits (Davenport, 1998; Kumar & Hillegersberg, 2000; Robey, Ross, & Boudreau, 2000) may be attributed to a failure in the implementation process (Brainin, Gilon, Meidan, & Mushkat, 2005; Klein, Conn, & Speer-Sorra, 2001) rather than a deficiency in the technology itself.

The complexity of ERP implementation is exacerbated when ERP systems are globally implemented since the integrative nature of this technology calls for the crossing of national or regional, in addition to organizational boundaries. Since countries, regions, and organizations differ in their absorptive capacity (Lane, Koka, & Pathak, 2006) and their societal and organizational culture (Hall & Hall, 1990; Hofstede, 1980; Javidan, House, & Dorfman, 2004a; Trompenaars, 1996), implementation of ERP systems in global enterprises requires a detailed examination of potential gaps or inconsistencies in the interaction between new technologies, end users, and organizations in different countries and/or regions (e.g., Boerma & Kingma, 2005; Dube & Robey, 1999; Krumbholz & Maiden, 2001; Leidner & Kayworth, 2006).

The approach taken here blends interpretive and positivist theories (Lee, 1991). The use of interpretive theories enables portrayal of technological systems as "cultural tools," ascribed with different interpretations. Utilizing positivist theories opens the way for mapping cultural differences between countries, scoring countries in accordance with their societal culture characteristics, and examining the relationship between societal culture and various outcomes such as leadership style, and economic and social indicators. The power of integrative examination is in producing helpful insights to poor global technology implementation antecedents. Technology does not constitute an entity per se, and despite its standard engineering components, its preferred pattern of use can differ as a result of what Orlikowski (2000) described as the diverse attributions of

meanings and power relation conceptions within and between organizations. The social construction of technological systems (Bijker, Hughes, & Pinche, 1987) as an interpretive theory maintains that different types of user groups differ in how they conceptualize, interpret, and exploit technologies and their potential. Accordingly, the effective utilization of a technology is the result of explicit and implicit "negotiations" between groups of users regarding the desired use of the technology and its organizational contribution and significance. "Technology should be treated as simultaneously social and physical and examine the interplay between the material characteristics of technology and the social context within which it is designed and deployed" (Grant, Hall, Wailes, & Wright, 2006, p. 4).

In the literature on culture, technology is viewed as a "cultural artifact" (Schein, 1992), thus constituting an integral and inseparable part of organizational culture, which is reproduced in everyday working routines. Consequently, global ERP systems must not be viewed only as large off-the-shelf software solutions that provide integrated business and software systems to a customer, but also as *cultural tools,* mostly designed and invented by the Western world but implemented in diverse local/regional settings, all having different cultural characteristics (Davison, 2002). In fact, cultural differences may impede ERP implementation even when its diffusion occurs within Western countries. Boerma and Kingma (2005) described Nestlé's ERP implementation as an example of a misfit between the decentralized organizational culture of Nestlé and the centralized culture imposed on the conglomerate by the adoption of the ERP system. Their example highlights differences in cultural attributes between a preexisting organizational culture and the new technological culture after ERP implementation.

The Nestlé study is an example of how ERP software packages, implemented in different organizational contexts, force local cultures to surrender to ERP mechanisms and logic that disregard local cultures and leadership styles. Such an implementation process may result in poor and delayed exploitation due to a misfit between the cultural characteristics that are embedded in and represented through the new technology, and the target organization's culture and its end user practices and perceptions.

Accordingly, transfer of technology from one region/country to another necessitates the addition of the cultural dimension to Bijker et al.'s (1987) theory of the social construction of technology among end users. Leidner and Kayworth (2006), who reviewed 86 studies on the cultural dimensions of ERP implementation, suggested the term "technology cultural conflict" to "…lend insights into the understanding of the linkages between IT and culture" (p. 357).

Cultural dimensions are entwined in technology implementation on different levels of analysis and operation (e.g., societal, organizational). This chapter outlines the various stages of ERP implementation, indicating the potential for cultural discordance or concordance at every stage. Managers and end users are defined as actors during this long process. They are likely to be involved in ERP implementation from the initial stage of strategic planning and decision making, and continue their involvement by leading and championing the implementation using goal setting, feedback, and reward techniques. Clearly, global ERP implementation positions managerial and leadership practices in a multicultural context. Past research relating societal culture to IT implementation was based on Hofstede's pioneering work (e.g., Ford, Connelly, & Meister, 2003). However, it would be unwise to assume any aspect of reality is quantifiable by a single measure. Consequently, the findings of the GLOBE project, an impressive research effort conducted by 170 investigators from 62 countries, will be presented. This project measured culture at different levels through both practices and values, and explored the relationship between culture

and societal, organizational, and leadership effectiveness (House, Hanges, Javidan, Dorfman, & Gupta, 2004).

The basic assumption here is that global ERP systems are not universally acceptable or effective, and that testing the cross-cultural generalizability of ERP systems in organizations will produce a managerial agenda that facilitates the implementation process. Topics of explicit concern to ERP implementation in global organizational economies related to organizational and societal culture, and proposal for managerial mechanisms for overcoming major obstacles in this process will be addressed. The first section of this discussion provides a brief overview of the dimensions of organizational and societal culture. This is followed by a description of the stages of ERP implementation and the actors involved in the process at every stage. Building upon this review, recommendations are proposed for the relationships between ERP implementation and cultural dimensions. The conclusion summarizes the key points drawn from the analysis.

"SOCIETAL CULTURE" AND ITS IMPACT ON ORGANIZATIONAL CULTURE

Cultural factors take center stage in the discussion of global ERP implementation. Implementation of the same technology in different countries produces various cultural encounters that may facilitate or inhibit its exploitation (Ford et al., 2003). Thus, the concept of organizational and societal culture should be addressed. Work organizations are distinguished by social experiences that can be called "cultures." Such experiences, however, do not necessarily represent the organization as a whole. In this sense, organizational culture is itself organized into various work settings (Frost, Moore, Louis, Lundberg, & Martin, 1985) and produces a form of locally recognized and common social knowledge, similar to the common knowledge that develops within a clan. The organizational culture is the glue holding a group of people together. It is produced over a period of time, and helps solve the group's problems of internal integration and survival in an external environment (Schein, 1992). At the same time, on a different level of analysis, employees working in the same local societal culture share the same societal meaning system (Hofstede, 2001), which supports their adaptation to their local organization. A shared meaning system can be formed at different levels, from the micro level of the group or team, the meso level of the organization, up to the macro level of nations and beyond (Shokef & Erez, 2006).

The question arises whether organizational culture is a reflection of societal culture, or organizations are culture-producers. The open system theory builds on the principle that organizations are 'open' to their environment, and devote a great deal of attention to understanding their immediate tasks or business environment, through direct interactions with their customers, competitors, suppliers, labor unions, and government agencies. All these stress the importance of being able to bridge and manage critical boundaries and areas of interdependence, and develop appropriate operational and strategic responses. Thus, the surrounding societal culture is an external source of influence on organizational culture through the behavior of organizational members who introduce their beliefs, norms, and values into the organization. Thus, consistent with the open systems theory, we expect to find systematic societal variations over and above within-societal differences. Yet individual organizations may also have their own unique culture: organizational culture can be examined as an independent entity that develops its own unique dimensions because of differences between tasks, expertise/occupations, and activities (Huang, Newell, Galliers, & Pan, 2003; Rousseau & Cooke, 1988; Sackmann, 1992; Trice, 1993). It is suggested that these different views be addressed as two perspectives that complement each other.

Methodological Issues Related to the Examination of Organizational and Societal Culture

Organizational culture has different layers of depth, ranging from the most visible layers of artifacts, practices, and behavior, to the less visible layers of values and basic assumptions (Schein, 1992). The multiplicity of organizational cultural layers and the range of areas that they cover make them difficult to study. Societal culture differences in various organizations are visible only if the same research methodology is used; but a study that examined how societal culture is reflected in an organization's culture encountered immense problems when researchers from many different countries were required to cooperate and use the same metrics, as was the case at the GLOBE research project (House et al., 2004).

Other researchers have argued that the description of organizational culture as a set of shared assumptions is rather oversimplified and misleading. Myers and Tan (2002) asserted that even the concept of a "national culture" is problematic since the nation-state is a relatively recent phenomenon, has continued to change in its form and makeup, and is composed of more than one cultural group. Martin (2002) proposed that the attribution of meaning (which is a central part of the cultural process) is complicated because of cognitive and normative diversity within an organization, and leads to integration as well as fragmentation, to unity as well as diversity. It is the actor's reality that forms the basis for further action—people produce and reproduce organizations by means of actions and interactions on a daily basis (routine).

Furthermore, culture research has been difficult to conduct (Straub, Loch, Evariso, Karahanna, & Srite, 2002) due to the lack of clear concepts or measures of culture. Another issue is what particular level of culture one should study (Pettigrew, 1990). Some researchers argue that culture cannot be objectively analyzed at a single level. Straub et al. (2002), for example, suggested a more real-istic view of culture. In these researchers' views, individuals are simultaneously influenced by an array of cultural values on the national, ethnic, organizational, or even sub-cultural levels.

A final difficulty in studying organizational culture relates to the content under investiga-tion, which is exceptionally large, since culture refers to the process of meaning construction and sense-making. Thus, any attempt to measure and describe culture in general, and organizational culture in particular, must focus on certain parts of the specific culture and disregard other ele-ments. Nonetheless, the necessity to improve research methodologies regarding cross-cul-tural differences does not reduce the impact that culture has on differences in work behaviors in general (Erez & Earley, 1993) and in information systems implementation in particular (Leidner & Kayworth, 2006).

Societal Culture and Globalization

Many firms struggle with the interpretation, implementation, and impact of globalization on their everyday operations. Adopting a *global mindset* challenges managers and companies to look beyond their own operations so that they may improve their practice of global manage-ment beyond the experience provided by their local businesses. The importance of international thinking lies in its "ability to serve as a bridge between the home country (i.e., the head office's country) and the local sites' environments, play-ing the role of *cultural interpreter* for both sides" (Jeannet, 2000, p. 37). The road map to strategic global competitiveness assumes that managers have an understanding of how attributes of so-cietal and organizational cultures affect selected organizational practices. This assumption is the key issue in global ERP implementation.

Researchers who have explored the link be-tween information technology and organizational culture claim that a firm-level study of culture's

influence on the use of information systems should not only examine organizational culture, but also its possible interaction with national or organizational sub-culture values and how these interactions potentially influence behaviors (Dube & Robey, 1999; Kaarst-Brown, 2004; Leidner & Kayworth, 2006). At the same time, they assert that in studying cross-cultural differences, research should address three types of methodological biases that have not been sufficiently taken into account (e.g., Hofstede, 1980): construct bias, method bias, and item bias. However, the GLOBE project's very adequate dataset was able to repli-cate and extend Hofstede's landmark study. It was able to test hypotheses relevant to relationships among societal-level variables, organizational practices of three different industries' sectors (financial, food, and telecommunications) in ev-ery country, and leader attributes and behavior. Furthermore, the data was sufficient to replicate middle-management perceptions and unobtrusive measures.

The project consisted of three phases related to three empirical studies: Phase One was de-voted to the development of scales that assess organizational and societal culture, and culturally shared implicit theories of leadership. Evidence for construct validity of the culture scales was provided from several sources such as Hofstede (1980) and Schwartz (1992) (for a detailed de-scription, see Hanges & Dickson, 2004). Phase Two was devoted to the assessment of nine core attributes of societal and organizational cultures. The nine cultural dimensions that served as independent variables in the GLOBE program are: uncertainty avoidance (Hofstede, 1980), power distance (Hofstede), institutional collec-tivism (Triandis, 1995), in-group collectivism (Triandis, 1995), gender egalitarianism (based on Hofstede's Masculinity index), assertiveness (based on Hofstede's Masculinity Index), future orientation (Kluckhohn & Strodtbeck, 1961), performance orientation (McClelland, 1961), and human orientation (Kluckhohn & Strodtbeck, 1961; Putnam, 1993).

When quantified, these attributes were referred to as cultural dimensions, and *62 societal cultures were ranked accordingly,* testing hypotheses about the relationship between these cultural dimensions and several important dependent variables such as economic prosperity, success in basic science, societal health, life expectancy, and so forth. Phase Two also investigated the interactive effect of societal-cultural dimensions and industry (finance, food processing, and telecommunication) on organizational practices and culturally endorsed implicit theories of leadership (House et al., 2004). By measuring these cultural dimensions across 62 countries, the GLOBE project liberated organizational behavior research from U.S. hegemony in theory and practice. It is a valuable database that can serve as an important tool for designing global project interventions.

In Phase Three, the impact and effectiveness of specific leadership behaviors and styles of CEOs on subordinates' attitudes and performance over three to five years were investigated. This phase also included testing of the moderating effects of culture on relationships between organizational practices and organizational effectiveness.

It seems clear that an ERP system that is developed in one specific region or state and implemented in another region (the regions may differ only in the language spoken) constitutes an inter-cultural encounter that generally ends in conflict on one level or another. These encounters must be managed and implementation processes must be planned to cope with the diverse gaps and expectations. The latter can create antagonism among end users at different levels, leading to partial or deficient implementation. Therefore, one of the most important challenges is acknowledging and appreciating cultural values, practices, and subtleties in different parts of the world. McDonald's is an illuminating example of cultural sensitivity. In France, McDonald's serves wine and salads with its burgers. In India, where beef products are taboo, it created a mutton burger named Maharaja Mac. To succeed in global business, managers need the flexibility to respond positively and effectively to practices and values that may be dramatically different to what they are accustomed. However, it is not easy for one to understand and accept practices and values that are different from one's personal experiences. The GLOBE research project has shown that the status and influence of leaders vary considerably as a result of the cultural force in the countries or regions in which the leaders function.

STAGES AND ACTORS IN TECHNOLOGICAL CHANGE

Technological change entails a long process involving different types of actors in each of several stages. Beyond having significant implications for the organization's form and function, the decision to purchase an ERP system for global implementation necessitates a heavy investment of resources. The uncertainty surrounding the decision and its implications, as well as the implementation itself, lengthens and complicates the process. In the developing body of academic literature related to ERP project implementation, researchers underline that it is important to divide ERP project implementation into several phases or levels, suggesting 'key activities' to be included in every phase (Al-Mudimigh, Zairi, & Al-Mashari, 2001; Markus & Tanis, 2000; Parr & Shanks, 2000) and using critical success factors (CSFs) for planning and monitoring ERP implementation. Dividing the process into stages and checking to see that the target is met at each stage may alleviate some degree of uncertainty and allow proper oversight, including clear definition of starting and ending points for every stage. Parr and Shanks (2000) related to the latter as "realistic milestones and end date…" (p. 293).

Although the purchase of the system can be viewed as the first stage in the implementation process, there is a consensus among researchers that organizational events and actions that precede the purchasing stage impact system selection and its eventual implementation. These stages are referred to by Al-Mudimigh et al. (2001) as "strategic levels," including current system evaluation, having a clear sense of vision and objectives, and implementation strategy. While Parr and Shanks (2000) relate to the first stage as the "Planning" stage, including clarification of the system rationale and determination of high-level project scope, Markus and Tanis (2000) call this stage the "Chartering Phase" and it includes the use of a sound business case for a sound assessment of business conditions and needs. The following proposed implementation stages can serve as a common denominator to the above models. They are proposed to address the implementation process as composed of five stages (most models pertain to four stages only)—three of them occur before the new technology is introduced into the organization, and the final two stages occur following the introduction of the system. Although several stages may overlap, it is correct to address each as a separate stage and manage the progress from one stage to the next based on achieving the targets in each stage.

Many organizational actors in the organization and its environment are involved in the implementation process, yet their level of involvement may vary from stage to stage. While the organization's senior managers are the dominant and central actors in the initial stages of the process, responsibility passes to project supervisors appointed by management, and to end users, as the implementation process proceeds. Stages that occur before the system is delivered to the organization include the following.

Initiative Stage

The need for a new global ERP system in an organization can emerge as a result of institutional isomorphism, a technology crisis or inadequacy, new technology boost, or global business development. In listing the reasons for adopting enterprise systems, Markus and Tanis (2000) differentiate between small companies' and large companies' reasons, and identify them as technical vs. business reasons (p. 180). In most cases, actors, within or from outside of the organization, identify a need or decide to promote technological change by initiating the implementation process. As a result of such actions, a careful review of the technological change should be conducted through strategic planning before any decision is made. ERP implementation calls for a major organizational transformation, which must be planned strategically and implemented thoroughly.

The process of strategic planning starts with identifying the impetus for changes in the company's business and IT systems, and their expected strategic and operational benefits. This process helps people understand the need for change; it sparks their interest in it and promotes their commitment to the process (Adams, Sarkis, & Liles, 1995; Al-Mashari, 2003). Strategic planning associated with ERP implementation relates to process design, process performance measurement, and continuous process improvement, also known as business process reengineering (Hammer & Champy, 1993). Additionally, it deals with critical success factors in early phases of ERP implementation (Nah, Zuckweiler, & Lau, 2003). In classical strategic planning, employees or representatives from all organizational ranks are commonly co-opted into the process. The case of ERP implementation at Texas Instruments (TI) described by Sarkis and Sundarraj (2003) illustrates how market forces compelled TI to make a radical shift in its business. TI's strategic response to these changes identified flexibility and time (speed) as the key strategic performance metrics that had to be stressed for them to be competitive in their business. As a result, this is what they focused on when designing and implementing a new ERP system for the company. Al-Mudimigh et al. (2001) suggested that a company's decision whether to engage in business process reengineering before, during, or after ERP implementation depends on the company's specific situation.

Decision Stage

This stage leads to a decision to invest resources in acquiring and assimilating a new system. When deciding to allocate resources for the purchase of a global ERP system, a cost assessment that includes cost estimations made by representatives of all operational departments (e.g., logistics, training) must be performed. In addition to the cost of the system, this must also include the costs of implementation processes. It is standard practice today to assume that 18% of an ERP implementation budget should be reserved for implementation and consulting (Gartner Group, 2006). The assured availability of resources for the entire implementation process is an important variable in predicting implementation quality (Klein et al., 2001).

Between the second and third stages, it is important to examine which system best answers the organizational needs defined in the strategic planning process. Organizational suitability is a compulsory condition, but it is not enough to ensure successful implementation. Transforming an off-the-shelf product into one that is appropriate for a specific organization requires customization. In this process it is essential that developers meet users, therefore potential end users of the new system should be involved in the selection process.

Selection and Leader Nomination Stage

A development or selection process leads to an order to produce a new technological system. Thus, at this stage, ensuring the involvement of users in system development is an important mechanism for improving system quality and utilization (Baroudi, Olson, & Ives, 1986). Sounder and Nashar (1995) referred to the matching process between new technology and end user needs as the "transfer of technology between a developer and a user" (p.225), and suggested that "failures

(of transfer) often occur as a consequence of many natural barriers within the transfer process (e.g., a developer's choice of an inappropriate technology or a user's risk aversion)." Leonard-Barton and Sinha (1993) stressed that effective internal technology transfer—the implementation of technical systems developed and disseminated to operational sub-units within a single organization—depends not only upon the cost, quality, and compatibilities of the technology, but also upon two processes of interaction between developers and users: user involvement in development, and adaptation by the developers and users of both the technical system itself and the workplace. A link between producers and users is needed to ensure a good fit of any global new ERP system to the organizations that must implement it.

Global ERP technology is based on "best practices" solutions, an ideal recipe for the most effective performance of business functions. Still, the organization must ask whether standard solutions fit its organizational requirements. Off-the-shelf ERP software packages are implemented in different organizational contexts, which often deviate considerably from the context in which these packages were originally designed and developed. Boersma and Kingma (2005) noted that the structure of ERPs typically requires the redefinition of work from the actor's point of view.

At this point it is important to nominate the project leader who will manage the fourth and fifth stages of the implementation process and achieve the organizational improvements that the new system was designed to accomplish. Hammer and Champy (1993) suggested that the implementation project leader establish a number of teams composed of potential end users, representing all the operational units where the new system will be implemented. The number of teams depends on the quantity and quality of operational processes that will be forced to undergo massive changes during system implementation. The teams should analyze the future changes and find solutions to problems that are likely to occur during the implementation stage. The leader operates as an advisor, assisted by a steering committee comprising the senior managers who are in charge of decision making during the process. Two of their most important tasks are to define priorities among the various change processes and to arbitrate the conflict of interest disputes that are almost certain to arise.

The final two stages occur after the new system is delivered to the organization. However, several activities must be performed between the third and fourth stages, in order to ensure a smooth transfer of responsibility for the implementation and the new system operation to the end users.

Basic Operational Stage

In this stage, the new system is installed in the workplace and employees "…ideally become increasingly skillful, consistent, and committed in their use of the innovation" (Klein & Speer-Sorra, 1996, p. 1057). Management attention should be directed to setting priorities for ERP implementation and influencing the implementation process and project duration (Sheu, Chae, & Yang, 2004). This is the stage for end user training, which—together with goal setting, feedback, and rewards—is a fundamental condition for system operation. The focus in this stage is on system customization; developers should interact with end users in fine-tuning the system. This is the stage that allows explicit and implicit 'negotiations' between groups of users regarding the desired use of the technology and its organizational contribution. Light and Wagner (2006) found in their study that "the use of customization to enable socio-technical integration allows for the recognition of existing forms of integration and the selective incorporation of existing socio-technical practices with new ones" (p. 225). Thus it is important to acknowledge that organizational actors can respond and influence ERP implementation.

Routine Operations Stage

In this final stage of ERP implementation, the new system becomes established and the employees who operate it adopt stable work patterns. At this stage, the organizational improvements resulting from system operation should be tested, and project leaders should conduct a post-project review of the entire process in order to achieve what Markus and Tanis (2000) called "technological and business flexibility for future developments."

Cultural dimensions impact the entire change process yet play varying roles in the different stages of the ERP implementation process. Since implementation methods are culturally dependent, they should be planned in advance after careful scrutiny of organizational and societal cultures.

THE INTERFACE BETWEEN CULTURE AND GLOBAL ERP IMPLEMENTATION

In global ERP implementation, the initiation, decision, and selection stages are usually dominated by the parent company and may reflect a desire for more control and standardization of work processes. Thus, the new system is imposed 'top-down' on most local managers and all end users, turning this process into a deterministic one, with no leeway for local impact related to structural and/or cultural adjustment. Indeed, corporations' different national and organizational cultures have been shown to be associated with problems during ERP implementation (Krumbholz & Maiden, 2001).

Using the contingency theory of organization, Donaldson (1987) presented a model wherein incompatibility between technology and organizational structure results in lowered performance. Donaldson believed that in such cases the organization will eventually make an adjustment to restore compatibility between the new technology and the organizational structure (SARFIT—structural adjustment to regain fit). Applying Donaldson's argument to global implementation, *cultural adjustment* must also be addressed to achieve adequate compatibility (Krumbholz & Maiden, 2001; Sheu et al., 2004). Implementation of global ERP systems implies that management must have an international perspective, or what Jeannet (2000) referred to as a "global mindset."

In the various stages of global ERP implementation, different encounters with cultural manifestations are to be expected. Thus, a cross-level analysis of cultural issues is indispensable. To understand the interface between culture and global ERP implementation, the difference between treating organizations as "culture producers" (Rousseau & Cooke, 1988) or as the reflections of the national-societal culture surrounding the organization must be examined. These two approaches can be seen as complementary. Although organizational culture is an internal attribute of an organization, Erez and Earley (1993) pointed out that studies that focus only on the internal dimensions of organizational culture, without considering the broad cultural context in which the organization operates, are deficient. The question of the impact of the broader culture when examining the culture of a specific organization has been considered in numerous studies (e.g., Hofstede, 1980; Schwartz, 1992; Trompenaar, 1996). These studies ranked approximately 60 countries according to cultural characteristics such as individualism/collectivism, power distance, uncertainty avoidance, universalism/particularism, affective/neutral culture, and specific/diffuse culture.

In line with this, the following analysis of the interface between culture and ERP implementation relates both to organizational and societal-national culture manifestations. It is important to stress that the analysis of the link between the implementation phases and cultural influences relates to *specific cultural manifestations,* since any attempt to measure and describe culture in

general, and organizational culture in particular, must be concerned with certain parts of the culture only.

In the context of information technology, an important point to be made is that information technologies are not culturally neutral and may come to symbolize a host of different values driven by underlying assumptions and their meaning, use, and consequences (Coombs, Knights, & Willmott, 1992; Robey & Markus, 1984; Scholz, 1990). Using a value-based approach reveals the types of 'cultural conflicts' that might arise from the development, adoption, use, and management of IT (Leidner & Kayworth, 2006). Thus, some implementation phases are influenced by the international, national, regional, and/or business-level culture, while other phases are influenced by the culture an organization produces. It should be emphasized that implementation of a global ERP system constitutes a force for cultural change, and new cultural dimensions may be expected to emerge in the assimilating organization at the end of the process. In this sense, organizational culture is conceptualized as both a dependent and independent variable. The purpose of portraying the cultural interface in global ERP implementation is to disclose the discrepancies and inconsistencies that must be addressed to restore fit or reduce culture conflict, with the end result being heightened global ERP implementation effectiveness.

Mapping the link between the societal and organizational culture and the global implementation of ERP systems requires us to relate separately to the three initial stages, as described before, which take place prior to the installation of the system, and to the last two stages, which occur after the organization has received the system. When a global organization decides to introduce an ERP system into its various worldwide branches, senior management is responsible for executing the first three phases, as outlined above. The decision to acquire a new system is one that is forced upon the organization's distant branches, which do not have the authority to make decisions of this type. In contrast, the fourth and fifth stages are within the range of authority and responsibility of the individual sites, and consequently, the latter must plan and implement these stages effectively. Only the local office (in which the organizational management resides) carries out all five of the stages. Assuming that the implementation is to be executed in a number of countries, the cultural implications of the global change involved in the first three phases need to be discussed by the central senior management. Stages four and five are assumed to be executed by the organization's local subsidiaries.

The Importance of Societal Culture in the First Three Stages of ERP Implementation

The product or end result of the first three stages is: (1) the decision to invest resources in acquiring a global information system, and (2) the selection of a suitable system. The central axis around which these decisions are made is the process of strategic thinking.

There are long-term implications of the strategic planning by firms' intent on becoming global enterprises. Such strategic planning requires a balanced choice between strategic decisions involving numerous variables such as values and problem-solving methods of owners, managers, and end users; formal recruitment procedures; reward systems; and regulation and control processes. As a company expands internationally, it needs to fit its corporate culture to the various societal cultures of its overseas operations to obtain the maximum benefits of the new implemented system.

Given that we are discussing a complex process of change, the cultural issues in this process take on critical significance since they may affect the sequence of countries in which the system is implemented.

The Initiating Stage

At this stage it is important to discover the degree of receptivity of companies in a particular culture (represented by a nation) to certain types of innovations, compared to companies in other cultures. This knowledge reflects the overall 'technological leap' that could be expected to occur as a result of global ERP implementation. This course of action is supported by empirical findings from several studies. Van Everdingen and Waarts (2003) compared ERP implementation in 10 European countries and found that "national culture has a significant influence on the country adoption rate" (p. 217). The extent of cultural openness (accommodation of another's culture) has a strong positive influence on the degree to which the technology transfer is successful (Hussain, 1998). IT is less readily adopted in *risk-averse* and high *power distance* cultures since technology is perceived as inherently risky (Hasan & Ditsa, 1999; Png, Tan, & Wee, 2001; Srite, 2000; Thatcher, Srite, Stephina, & Liu, 2003). Thus, the impetus for acquiring a global ERP system will most likely come from countries that have the cultural characteristics that allow them to cope with change and uncertainty. Findings from the project GLOBE related to future orientation can be used to assess a country's openness to change and flexibility. Societies that score higher on future orientation tend to achieve economic success, have organizations with a longer strategic orientation, have flexible and adaptive organizations and managers, and so forth. The two most future-oriented countries are Singapore and Switzerland, and the lowest are Argentina and Russia (Ashkanasy, Gupta, Mayfield, & Trevor-Roberts, 2004, p. 304). Studies on India and Southeast and East Asia showed a process of strategic planning quite distinct from the rational approach dominant in the West. Haley and Tan (1999) observed that "strategic planning in South and Southeast Asia has developed into a process which is ad-hoc and reactive, highly personalized, idiosyncratic to the leader and which uses relatively limited environmental scanning" (p. 96).

The Decision Stage

The decision to invest resources in a new system must be made only after a strategic process is undertaken by the parent company. This process will also help the parent company decide how and in what order the system is to be distributed to different countries. Such decisions are culturally endorsed. Moreover, target country selection has two important implications. The first relates to the examples given in our description of the first phase. The parent company must anticipate differences among the implementing countries in terms of their abilities to cope with change. The higher the implementing country is in *uncertainty avoidance* and *power distance,* the more resources should be allocated to them for the implementation process. Support by the parent company may greatly alleviate problems that such countries encounter in the implementation process.

Second, different countries may have different perspectives on the strategic goals of the new system based on differences in societal values. For instance: *Service quality* dimensions function differently across national cultures (Kettingen, Lee, & Lee, 1995). *Information privacy concerns* were found to vary across countries: countries high in *uncertainty avoidance* and *power distance* exhibited higher levels of government involvement in privacy regulation (Milberg, Burk, Smith, & Kallman, 1995).

Since agreement on strategic goals is an important condition for implementing and exploiting the new IT system, early mapping of the differences in the perception of these goals is imperative. Gaps will appear as a result of differences in national cultures, but knowing about them beforehand will allow the system's implementers to take appropriate action to sell the system to end users and convince them of its benefits.

The System Selection and Leader Nomination Stage

In the third global ERP implementation stage, two pivotal events must take place: system selection and nomination of a leader to oversee the project.

System Selection

At this stage, managers are shown a demonstration of the system under consideration. Differences in perceptions between developers of the system and managers of the purchasing organization constitute an important consideration in the strategic process of choosing a system. Leidner and Kayworth (2006) claimed that variations across cultural values may lead to differing perceptions and approaches in the manner in which information systems are developed. Thus managers should be aware that the system reflects the developers' view of the cultural organization, which might deviate considerably from that of their own organization or its strategic needs. These differences were conceptualized by Hazzan and Dubinsky (2005) in their discussion of the connections between a national culture and the culture inspired by software development methods. According to their proposed model of the tightness of Software Development Methods (SDM) and the tightness of a national culture, the fitness of a given SDM and a national culture can predict the degree to which a given SDM will be accepted by a specific national culture. Thus, the system developers and the organization's IT people must be involved in the ERP selection process.

Since IT developers are in charge of technical assistance during the implementation processes, it is important to understand that this assistance is also culturally dependent: Hassan and Ditsa (1999) found that IT staff are able to give advice to IT managers *in countries with low power distance.* This finding has implications for the fourth stage of implementation as well, in which end users operating the system require technical assistance in coping with problems that emerge. However, when cultural differences between the developer's support personnel and end users are significant, they may impede the implementation process.

Project Leaders for Global ERP Implementation

Global ERP implementation implies confronting work situations charged with dynamic cultural issues. Elaborating effective solutions for global implementation activities, influenced by nuances of culture, pose difficult challenges that may confound even the most skilled leader. Brake, Walker, and Walker (1995) portrayed the ideal global implementation leader as a strategic architect-coordinator who is able to recognize opportunities and risks *across national and functional boundaries*, and is sensitive and responsive to cultural differences. The implementation project leader should have a "global mindset" since global ERP system implementation requires fundamental changes in managerial practices in domestic as well as international organizations. The GLOBE project offers detailed examples of the cultural manifestation of countries and leadership attribution. The GLOBE's major empirical contribution to this stage in the implementation process was its identification of universally desirable and culturally contingent attributes of leadership. GLOBE's findings showed the relationships among cultural dimensions, organizational practices, and culturally endorsed leadership dimensions.

The Importance of Organizational Culture in the Fourth and Fifth Stages of ERP Implementation

Transfer of technology from the manufacturer to the end-user begins when the decision is made to implement the system in different branches of the organization worldwide. The products of these stages should include: the exploitation of the new system, final customization of the system to the needs of end users and to the special needs of specific organizations, a post-project review process, and a cultural change in the organization (if required).

The central axis around which these stages revolve relates to employee management, and it involves classic areas in organizational behavior and human resource management such as training, learning, and performance goal setting and reward.

In these stages of the process, the relevant cultural dimensions concern the differences *within the organizational culture*. An organizational culture is not uniform; it comprises horizontal as well as vertical sub-cultures. A horizontal sub-culture may be created on the basis of professional practices—a sub-culture of physicians, nurses, and managers (Trice, 1993). Similarly, a vertical sub-culture may emerge, based on the organizational structure—a sub-culture of the production department, the R&D department, or the HR department (Schein, 1996), or a sub-culture of technology-intensive departments as opposed to low-technology departments (Brainin et al., 2005). These sub-cultures imply that there will be differences in the implementation of the new IT system because each sub-culture perceives the role and function of the IT system in its work differently. This process of ascribing meaning to technology is labeled the "social construction of technology." Furthermore, different occupational sub-cultures have entirely different cultural interpretations of proposed technologies, and experience conflict and resistance to adopting certain technologies (Von Meier, 1999). Researchers found that clashing values among organizational sub-cultures hinder the information sharing and collaboration needed to effectively integrate technology.

In this stage it is important to appoint champions of technological change from within the organization (Howell & Higgins, 1990) to effectively lead the implementation process. Management style also influences the implementation approach and project duration. Management style relates to the attitude toward setting priorities for implementing an ERP system (Sheu et al., 2004). It must be stressed that societal culture also has an influence on the organization's activities, and therefore the techniques used in human resource management, as explained above, must be adapted to the local culture, for example, societal culture was found to influence instruction processes (Earley, 1994), goal setting (Erez, Earley, & Hullin, 1985), and many other areas.

There are organizational culture characteristics that facilitate technology implementation. Organizations with a high learning orientation are better able to adjust to changes on the whole (Lipshitz, Popper, & Oz, 1996), and to technological changes in particular (Brainin & Erez, 2002; DeLong & Fahey, 2003), because they have learning channels and can learn from experience. This is a very important condition for implementing new technology. Global ERP implementation can result in culture transformation over time.

CONCLUSION

A Managerial Agenda for a Positive Cultural Experience during Global ERP Implementation

The preceding discussion set forth to explain how variations in cultural aspects, which surface as a result of global ERP implementation, may be handled, based on the assumption that global ERP systems are not universally acceptable and effective. The increasing interrelations among countries and the globalization of corporations do not imply that cultural differences are disappearing or diminishing. On the contrary, as economic boundaries are eliminated, cultural barriers may present new challenges and opportunities in business. When different cultures come into contact, they may converge in some aspects, but their idiosyncrasies will likely amplify. As a means to

integrate work processes, ERP implementation becomes a method for organizational boundary crossing and requires special handling to overcome the resistance this change induces. The above discussion provides a detailed examination of the cultural discrepancies that arise at various stages of the implementation process. Cultural boundaries to be crossed as a result of global ERP implementation within the organization include: organizational sub-cultures as a result of organizational structure, and organizational sub-cultures as a result of different professions and roles. Further, between organizations this includes societal culture as a result of cultural differences between countries.

To overcome the problems arising from global ERP implementation, it was suggested that crossing the cultural boundary be treated as a process of *cultural exchange,* instead of as a *cultural conflict.* In order to restore fit and to prevent poor global ERP implementation and resistance to change, managers must harness the ERP systems to their needs by adapting it to their set of beliefs, thereby breaking the link between technology and Western logic. It requires them: to simultaneously examine their positions and behaviors and those of end users regarding ERP use, and analyze their reciprocal impact; to help formulate policy regarding utilization of ERP systems in different organizational settings across countries or regions; to coordinate expectations between themselves and end users in order to narrow the cultural gap; and to raise the consciousness of ERP engineers and designers regarding the impact of differences in the socio-cultural attributes of potential managers and end users, and hence increase their effective fit into different societies.

The following recommendations are proposed: Organizational leaders must be made aware of cultural differences and be prepared to cope with them. Financial resources must be available to allow investment in a complete mapping of the cultural gaps that may manifest themselves in the second implementation stage. Multicultural groups of project managers—glocal teams—and team leaders (see Appendix) can overcome the lack of communication between the host and subsidiaries that often results in mistrust, project delay, and budget overruns. Moreover, such groups will foster informal communication among representatives of different nationalities, which is critical for the success of global ERP projects, and will limit formal documentation channels that people tend to use in the absence of such groups. Solutions may include:

1. Multi-national teams for developing and implementing as a key to success
2. Local examination of the technological leap
3. Flexibility in implementation stages—even if the strategic stages were carried out in a deterministic fashion (were imposed on the organization), the later stages may allow participative actions and be culturally appropriate.
4. Involving users in the design of global ERP systems—although determining the key actors in user groups is especially challenging in international settings, their involvement may partially assuage subsequent perception conflicts since the greater the extent to which a user's group values are embedded in a system, the less vision conflict is expected.

The chapter addressed aspects of organizational and societal culture that are of explicit concern to ERP implementation in global organizational economies, and recommended managerial mechanisms for overcoming major obstacles in this process.

FUTURE RESEARCH DIRECTIONS

Cultural differences may impede global ERP implementation. Although the GLOBE project, used in this chapter to recognize and discuss differences in societal cultures, provides a profile of cultural dimensions for each society, it does not present a behavioral profile. Future research related to differences in societal culture is required to build up in-depth understanding of how people actually function and manifest different cultural attributes, to investigate how different cultural dimensions interact, and what the relative importance of each dimension in understanding each culture is (Javidan et al., 2004b). The suggested managerial mechanisms proposed for formulating policy regarding utilization of ERP systems in different organizational settings across countries or regions was the establishment of multicultural groups of project managers—glocal teams—and appointing team leaders. However, multicultural teams can face high levels of conflict and misunderstandings. Such teams need to develop a shared meaning system through socialization to the team, and through contacts and interactions among team members. Their ability to serve as 'mediators' and represent their countries is contingent upon collaboration dynamics that must overcome cultural differences. Research related to multicultural teams is scarce (Earley & Gibson, 2002; Earley & Mosakowski, 2000; Erez & Gati, 2004). Shokef and Erez (2006) suggested that a 'glocal' identity represents both the global identity and a strong local identity, and it seems to enable individuals to shift from one social context to another. Future research is needed to explore the coexistence of multiple identities and its contribution to glocal team work. Another research challenge relates to the issue of team leaders for multicultural teams—what are adequate selection and training processes? Current theories in management and psychology do not provide sufficient frameworks to explain the successes or failures of people working and managing in foreign cultures. It is suggested that the measure of one's 'cultural intelligence' (CQ) be used as a predictor of an outsider's natural ability to interpret and respond to unfamiliar signals in an appropriate manner (Earley, Ang, & Joo-Seng, 2006). Accordingly, a manager with high CQ can enter new cultural settings—national, professional, organizational, regional—and immediately understand what is happening and why, confidently interacting with people and engaging in the right actions. However, there is very little empirical research that explores this issue. The future research options presented in this chapter should serve to stimulate and challenge researchers to explore new research areas that will contribute to work experiences in a global economy.

REFERENCES

Adams, S., Sarkis, J., & Liles, D.H. (1995). The development of strategic performance metrics. *Engineering Management Journal, 1,* 24-32.

Al-Mashari, M. (2003). A process change-oriented model for ERP application. *International Journal of Human-Computer Interaction, 16*(1), 39-55.

Al-Mudimigh, A., Zairi, M., & Al-Mashari, M. (2001). ERP software implementation: An integrative framework. *European Journal of Information Systems, 10,* 216-226.

Ashkanasy, N., Gupta, V., Mayfield, M.S., & Trevor-Roberts, E. (2004). Future orientation. In R.J. House, P.J. Hanges, M. Javidan, P.W. Dorfman, & V. Gupta (Eds.), *Culture, leadership, and organizations* (pp. 282-342). London: Sage.

Baroudi, J.J., Olson, M.H., & Ives, B. (1986). Empirical study of the impact of user involvement on system usage and information satisfaction. *Communications of the ACM, 29*(3), 232-238.

Bijker, W.E., Hughes, T.P., & Pinch, T. (Eds.). (1987). *The social construction of technological systems. New directions in the sociology and history of technology.* Cambridge, MA: MIT Press.

Boerma, K., & Kingma, S. (2005). Developing a cultural perspective on ERP. *Business Process Management Journal, 11*(2), 123-136.

Brainin, E., & Erez, M. (2002, April). Technology and culture: Organizational learning orientation in the assimilation of new technology in organizations. In *Proceedings of the 3rd European Conference on Organizational Learning* (OKLC), Athens, Greece.

Brainin, E., Gilon, G., Meidan, N., & Mushkat, Y. (2005). *The impact of intranet integrated patient medical file (IIPMF) assimilation on the quality of medical care and organizational advancements.* Report # 2001/49 submitted to the Israel National Institute for Health Policy and Health Services.

Brake, T., Walker, M.D., & Walker, T. (1995). *Doing business internationally.* New York: McGraw-Hill.

Coombs, R., Knights, D., & Willmott, H.C. (1992). Culture, control, and competition: Towards a conceptual framework for the study of information technology in organizations. *Organization Science, 13*(1), 51-72.

Davenport, T.H. (1998). Putting the enterprise in the enterprise system. *Harvard Business Review, 76,* 121-131.

Davison, R. (2002). Cultural complications of ERP: Valuable lessons learned from implementation experience in parts of the world with different cultural heritage. *Communication of the ACM, 45*(7), 109-111.

DeLong, D.W., & Fahey, L. (2003). Diagnosing cultural barriers to knowledge management. *Academy of Management Executive, 14*(4), 113-127.

Doherty, N.F., & Doing, G. (2003). An analysis of the anticipated cultural impact of the implementation of data warehouse. *IEEE Transactions on Engineering Management, 50*(1), 78-88.

Donaldson, L. (1987). Strategy and structural adjustment to regain fit and performance: In defense of contingency theory. *Journal of Management Studies, 24,* 1-24.

Dube, L., & Robey, D. (1999). Software stories: Three cultural perspectives on the organizational context of software development practices. *Accounting Management and Information Technologies, 9*(4), 223-259.

Earley, P.C. (1994). Self or group? Cultural effects of training on self efficacy and performance. *Administrative Science Quarterly, 39,* 89-117.

Earley, C.P., Ang, S., & Joo-Seng, T. (2006). *CQ: Developing cultural intelligence at work.* New York: Oxford University Press.

Earley, C.P., & Gibson, C.B. (2002). *Multinational work teams: A new perspective.* Mahwah, NJ: Lawrence Erlbaum.

Earley, C.P., & Mosakowski, E. (2000) Creating hybrid team cultures: An empirical test of transnational team functioning. *Academy of Management Journal, 43*(1), 26-49.

Erez, M., & Earley, C.P. (1993). *Culture, self identity and work.* New York: Oxford University Press.

Erez, M., Earley, P.C., & Hullin, C.L. (1985). The impact of participation on goal acceptance and performance: A two-step model. *Academy of Management Journal, 28,* 50-66.

Erez, M., & Gati, E. (2004). A dynamic, multi-level model of culture: From the micro-level of the individual to the macro-level of a global culture. *Applied Psychology: An International Review, 35*(4), 583-598.

Ford, D.P., Connelly, C.E., & Meister, D.B. (2003). Information system research and Hofstede's culture's consequences: An uneasy and incomplete partnership. *IEEE Transaction on Engineering Management, 50*(1), 8-25.

Frost, J.F., Moore, L.F., Louis, M.R., Lundberg, C.C., & Martin, J. (Eds.). (1985). *Organizational culture.* Thousand Oaks, CA: Sage.

Grant, D., Hall, R., Wailes, N., & Wright, C. (2006). The false promise of technological determinism: The case of enterprise resource planning systems. *New Technology, Work and Employment, 21*(1), 2-15.

Gartner Group. (2006). *The Gartner scenario 2006: The current state and future direction of IT.* Retrieved from http://www.gartner.com

Green, S.G., Gavin, M.B., & Aiman-Smith, L. (1995). Assessing a multidimentional measure of radical technological innovation. *IEEE Transactions on Engineering Management, 42*(3), 203-214.

Haley, G., & Tan, C.T. (1999). East vs. west: Strategic marketing management meets the Asian networks. *Journal of Business and Industrial Marketing, 14*(2), 91-101.

Hall, E.T., & Hall, M.R. (1990). *Understanding cultural differences.* Yarmouth, ME: Intercultural Press.

Hammer, M., & Champy, J. (1993). *Reengineering the corporation.* New York: HarperCollins.

Hanges, P.J., & Dickson, M.W. (2004). The development and validation of the GLOBE culture and leadership scales. In R.J. House, P.J. Hanges, M. Javidan, P.W. Dorfman, & V. Gupta (Eds.), *Culture, leadership, and organizations* (pp. 122-151). London: Sage.

Hasan, H., & Ditsa, G. (1999). The impact of culture on the adoption of IT: An interpretive study. *Journal of Global Information Management, 7*(1), 5-15.

Hazzan, O., & Dubinksy, Y. (2005). Clashes between culture and software development methods: The case of the Israeli hi-tech industry and extreme programming. *Proceedings of the Agile 2005 Conference* (pp. 59-69), Denver, CO.

Hofmann, D.A., & Stetzer, A. (1996). A cross-level investigation of factors influencing unsafe behaviors and accidents. *Personnel Psychology, 49,* 307-339.

Hofstede, G. (1980). *Culture's consequences.* London: Sage.

Hofstede, G. (2001). *Culture's consequences: Comparative values, behaviors, institutions and organizations across nations.* Thousand Oaks, CA: Sage.

House, R.J., Hanges, P.J., Javidan, M., Dorfman, P.W., & Gupta, V. (2004). *Culture, leadership, and organizations.* London: Sage.

Howell, J.M., & Higgins, C. (1990). Champions of technological innovation. *Administrative Science Quarterly, 35,* 317-341.

Huang, J.C., Newell, S., Galliers, R.D., & Pan, S. (2003). Dangerous liaisons? Component-based development and organizational subcultures. *IEEE Transactions of Engineering Management, 50*(1), 89-99.

Hussain, S. (1998). Technology transfer model across culture: Brunei-Japan joint ventures. *International Journal of Social Economics, 25*(6-8), 1189-1198.

Javidan, M., House, R.J., & Dorfman, P.W. (2004a). A nontechnical summary of GLOBE findings. In R.J. House, P.J. Hanges, M. Javidan, P.W. Dorfman, & V. Gupta (Eds.), *Culture, leadership, and organizations* (pp. 29-48). London: Sage.

Javidan, M., House, R.J., Dorfman, P.W., Gupta, V., Hanges, P.L., & Sully de Leque, M. (2004b). Conclusions and future directions. In R. J. House, P. J. Hanges, M. Javidan, P. W. Dorfman, & V. Gupta (Eds.), *Culture, leadership, and organizations* (pp. 723-732). London: Sage.

Jeannet, J.P. (2000). *Managing with a global mindset.* London: Prentice Hall.

Kaarst-Brown, M.L. (2004). *How organizations keep information technology out: The interaction of tri-level influence on organizational and*

IT culture. Working Paper IST-MLKB: 2004-2, School of Information Studies, Syracuse University, USA.

Kettingen, W.J., Lee, C.C., & Lee, S. (1995). Global measures of information service quality: A cross-national study. *Decision Science, 26*(5), 569-588.

Klein, K.J., Conn, A.B., & Speer-Sorra, J.S. (2001). Implementing computerized technology: An organizational analysis. *Journal of Applied Psychology, 86*(5), 811-824.

Klein, K.J., & Speer-Sorra, J. (1996). The challenge of innovation implementation. *Academy of Management Review, 21*(4), 1055-1080.

Kluckhohn, F.R., & Strodtbeck, F.L. (1961). *Variations in value orientation.* New York: HarperCollins.

Krumbholz, M., & Maiden, N. (2001). The implementation of enterprise resource planning packages in different organizational and national cultures. *Information Systems, 26,* 185-204.

Kumar, L., & Hillegersberg, J. (2000). ERP experiences and evolution. *Communications of the ACM, 43*(3), 22-26.

Kunda, G. (1992). *Engineering culture: Control and commitment in a high-tech corporation.* Philadelphia: Temple University Press.

Lane, P.J., Koka, B.R., & Pathak, S. (2006). The reification of absorptive capacity: A critical review and rejuvenation of the construct. *Academy of Management Review, 31*(4), 833-863.

Lee, A.S. (1991). Integrating positivist and interpretive approaches to organizational research. *Organization Science, 2*(4), 342-365.

Leidner, D.E., & Kayworth, T. (2006). A review of culture in information systems research: Towards a theory of information technology culture conflict. *MIS Quarterly, 30*(2), 357-399.

Leonard-Barton, D., & Sinha, D.K. (1993). Developer-user interaction and user satisfaction in internal technology transfer. *Academy of Management Journal, 36*(5), 1125-1139.

Light, B., & Wagner, E. (2006). Integration in ERP environments: Rhetoric, realities and organizational possibilities. *New Technology, Work and Employment, 21*(3), 215-228.

Lipshitz, R., Popper, M., & Oz, S. (1996). Building learning organizations: The design and implementation of organizational learning mechanisms. *Journal of Applied Behavioral Sciences, 32,* 292-305.

Markus, L.M., & Tanis, C. (2000). The enterprise system experience—From adoption to success. In R.W. Zmude (Ed.), *Framing the domain of IT management* (pp. 173-207). Pinnaflex Education Resources.

Martin, J. (2002). *Organizational culture. Mapping the terrain.* London: Sage.

McClelland, D.C. (1961). *The achieving society.* Princeton, NJ: Van Nostrand.

Milberg, S.J., Burk, S.J., Smith, J.H., & Kallman, E.A. (1995). Rethinking copyright issues and ethics on the Net: Values, personal information privacy, and regulatory approaches. *Communications of the ACM, 38*(12), 65-73.

Myers, M.D., & Tan, F.B. (2002). Beyond models of national culture in information systems research. *Journal of Global Information Management, 10*(1), 24-33.

Nah, F.F., Zuckweiler, K.M., & Lau, J.L. (2003). ERP implementation: Chief information officers' perceptions of critical success factors. *International Journal of Human-Computer Interaction, 16*(1), 5-22.

Orlikowski, W.J. (2000). Using technology and constituting structures: A practical lens for studying technology in organizations. *Organization Science, 11*(4), 404-428.

Parr, A., & Shanks, G. (2000). A model of ERP project implementation. *Journal of Information Technology, 15*(4), 289-301.

Pettigrew, A.M. (1990). Organizational climate and culture: Two constructs in search of a role. In B. Schneider (Ed.), *Organizational climate and culture* (pp. 413-433). San Francisco: Jossey-Bass.

Png, I.P., Tan, B.C.Y., & Wee, K.L. (2001). Dimensions of national cultures and corporate adoption of IT infrastructure. *IEEE Transactions of Engineering Management, 48*(1), 36-45.

Putnam, R.D. (1993). *Making democracy work.* Princeton, NJ: Princeton University Press.

Robey, D., & Markus, M.L. (1984). Rituals in information systems design. *MIS Quarterly, 8*(1), 5-15.

Robey, D., Ross, J.W., & Boudreau, M. (2000). Learning to implement enterprise systems: An exploratory study of the dialectics of change. *Journal of Management Information Systems, 19*(1), 17-46.

Rousseau, D.M. (1990). Assessing organizational culture: The case of multiple methods. In B. Schneider (Ed.), *Organizational climate and culture* (pp. 153-192). San Francisco: Jossey-Bass.

Rousseau, D.M., & Cooke, A.R. (1988). Culture of high reliability: Behavioral norms aboard a U.S. aircraft carrier. In *Proceedings of the Academy of Management Meeting,* Anaheim, CA.

Sackmann, S. (1992). Cultures and subcultures: An analysis of organizational knowledge. *Administrative Science Quarterly, 37,* 140-161.

Sarkis, J., & Sundarraj, R.P. (2003). Managing large-scale global enterprise resource planning systems: A case study at Texas Instruments. *International Journal of Information Management, 23,* 431-442.

Schein, E.H. (1992). *Organizational culture and leadership.* San Francisco: Jossey-Bass.

Schein, E.H. (1996). Culture: The missing concept in organizational studies. *Administrative Science Quarterly, 41,* 229-240.

Scholz, C. (1990). The symbolic value of computerized information systems. In P. Galiardi (Ed.), *Symbols and artifacts: Views of the corporate landscape* (pp. 233-254). New York: Aldin De Gruyter.

Schwartz, S.H. (1992). Universals in the content and structure of values: Theoretical advances and empirical test in 20 countries. In M.P. Zanna (Ed.), *Advances in experimental social psychology* (vol. 25, pp. 1-65). San Diego: Academic Press.

Sheu, C., Chae, B., & Yang, C. (2004). National differences and ERP implementation: Issues and challenges. *Omega, 32*(5), 361-372.

Shokef, E., & Erez, M. (2006). Shared meaning systems in multiclutural teams. In B. Mannix, M. Neae, & Y.-R. Chen (Eds.), *National culture and groups. Research on managing groups and teams* (vol. 9, pp. 325-352). San Diego: Elsevier, JAI Press.

Sounder, W.E., & Nashar, A.S. (1995). A technology selection model for new products development and technology transfer. In L.R. Gomez-Mejia & M.W. Lawless (Eds.), *Advances in high-technology management* (vol. 5, pp. 225-244). Greenwich, CT: JAI Press.

Srite, M. (2000). *The influence of national culture on the acceptance and use of information technologies: An empirical study.* Unpublished Doctoral Dissertation, Florida State University, USA.

Straub, D., Loch, K., Evariso, R., Karahanna, E., & Srite, M. (2002). Towards a theory-based measurement of culture. *Journal of Global Information Management, 10*(1), 13-23.

Thatcher, J.B., Srite, M., Stephina, L.P., & Liu, Y. (2003). Culture overload and personal innovativeness with information technology: Extending the nomological net. *Journal of Computer Information Systems, 44*(1), 74-81.

Triandis, H.C. (1995). *Individualism and collectivism.* Boulder, CO: Westview.

Trice, H.M. (1993). *Occupational subcultures in the workplace.* Ithaca, NY: ILR Press.

Trompenaars, F. (1996). Resolving international conflict: Culture and business strategy. *Business Strategy Review, 7*(3), 51-68.

Van Everdingen, Y.M., & Waarts, E. (2003). The effect of national culture on the adoption of innovations. *Marketing Letters, 14*(3), 217-232.

Von Meier, A. (1999). Occupational cultures as challenge to technological innovation. *IEEE Transactions on Engineering Management, 46*(1), 101-114.

ADDITIONAL READING

Avgerou, C., & Madon, S. (2004). Framing IS studies: Understanding the social context of IS innovation. In C. Avgerou, C. Cibborra, & F. Land (Eds.), *The social study of information and communication technology* (pp. 162-182). New York: Oxford University Press.

Cao, J., Crews, J.M., Lin, M., Deokar, A., Burgoon, B.K., & Nunamaker, J.F. Jr. (2007). Interaction between system evaluation and theory testing: A demonstration of the power of a multifaceted approach to information system research. *Journal of Management Information Systems, 22*(4), 207-235.

Drori, G.S. (2006). *Global e-litism, digital technology, social inequality, and transnationality.* New York: Worth.

Erumban, A.A., & Jong, S.B. (2006). Cross-country differences in ICT adoption: A consequence of culture? *Journal of World Business, 41,* 302-314.

Gallivan, M., & Srite, M. (2005). Information technology and culture: Identifying fragmentary and holistic perspectives of culture. *Information and Organization, 15,* 295-338.

Gelfand, M.J., Nishii, L.H., & Raver, J.L. (2006). On the nature and importance of cultural tightness-looseness. *Journal of Applied Psychology, 91*(6), 1225-1245.

Gibson, C.B. (1997). Do You hear what I hear? A framework for reconciling intercultural communication difficulties arising from cognitive styles and cultural values. In C.P. Earley & M. Erez (Eds.), *New perspectives on international industrial/organizational psychology* (pp. 335-362). San Francisco: New Lexington Press.

Gregor, S. (2006). The nature of theory in information systems. *MIS Quarterly, 30*(3), 611-642.

Howcroft, D., & Light, B. (2006). Reflections on issues of power in packaged software selection. *Information System Journal, 16*(3), 215-235.

Iivari, N. (2006). 'Representing the user' in software development—A cultural analysis of usability work in the product development context. *Interacting with Computers, 18,* 635-664.

Iivari, J., & Huisman, M. (2007). The relationship between organizational culture and the deployment of systems development methodologies. *MIS Quarterly, 31*(1), 35-58.

Inglehart, R. (2000). Globalization and postmodern values. *The Washington Quarterly, 23*(1), 215-228.

Kallinikos, J. (2004). Farewell to constructivism: Technology and context-embedded action. In C. Avgerou, C. Cibborra, & F. Land (Eds.), *The social study of information and communication technology* (pp. 140-161). New York: Oxford University Press.

Karahanna, E., Evariso, R.J., & Srite, M. (2005). Levels of culture and individual behavior: An integrative perspective. *Journal of Global Information Management, 13*(2), 1-20.

Ko, D., Kirsch, L.J., & King, W.R. (2005) Antecedents of knowledge transfer from consultants to clients in enterprise system implementations. *MIS Quarterly, 29*(1), 59-85.

Kraemmergaard, P., & Rose, J. (2002). Managerial competences for ERP journeys. *Information Systems Frontiers, 4*(2), 199-211.

Lippert, S.K., & Volkmar, J.A. (2007). Cultural effects on technology performance and utilization: A comparison of U.S. and Canadian users. *Journal of Global Information Management, 15*(2), 56-90.

Martin, J. (1992). *Cultures in organizations.* New York: Oxford University Press.

Sassen, S. (2004). Towards a sociology of information technology. In C. Avgerou, C. Cibborra, & F. Land (Eds.), *The social study of information and communication technology* (pp. 77-99). New York: Oxford University Press.

Sawyer, S. (2001). A market-based perspective on information system development. *Communications of the ACM, 44*(11), 97-102.

Shepherd, C. (2006). Constructing enterprise resource planning: A thoroughgoing interpretivist perspective on technological change. *Journal of Occupational and Organizational Psychology, 79,* 357-376.

Srite, M., & Karahanna, E. (2006). The role of espoused national cultural values in technology acceptance. *MIS Quarterly, 30*(3), 679-704.

Tan, B.C.Y., Smith, J.H., Keil, M., & Montealegre, R. (2003). Reporting bad news about software projects: Impact of organizational climate and information asymmetry in an individualistic and a collectivistic culture. *IEEE Transactions on Engineering Management, 50*(1), 64-77.

Tolbert, A.S., McLean, G.N., & Myers, R.C. (2002). Creating the global learning organization (GLO). *International Journal of Intercultural Relations, 26*, 463-472.

Walsham, G. (2002). Cross-cultural software production and use: A structurational analysis. *MIS Quarterly, 26*(4), 359-382.

Weick, K.E. (2007). The generative properties of richness. *Academy of Management Journal, 50*(1), 14-19.

Weisinger, J.Y., & Trauth, E.M. (2003). The importance of situating culture in cross-cultural IT management. *IEEE Transactions on Engineering Management, 50*(1), 26-30.

APPENDIX

Stage No.	Stage Name	Experiences of Culture	Result	Solution
1	Initiation	Differences in societal cultures between initiating and implementing countries	Cultural gaps and a high level of technological leap	Glocal teams with representatives from all the countries
2	Decision 1. Strategic thinking 2. Resource allocation	1. Differences in perceptions of strategic goals 2. Differences in decision making	Need for promoting and persuading of the strategic goals and convincing the end users	Glocal teams with representatives from all the countries Local teams
3	System Selection	Language gaps, differences in developers' and owners' perceptions regarding critical performance factors	Misfit of the system to the societal culture	Glocal teams including developers and end user representatives of the countries
	Leader Nomination	Unique characteristics of a global approach–global mindset	Insensitive and unresponsive to cultural differences	Global selection processes
4	Basic Operation 1. Exploiting the system 2. Additional technical matching	Differences in sub-cultures	Inadequate training and goal setting processes	Local teams and representatives of the glocal team
5	Routine Operation and system exploitation: 1. Post-project analysis 2. Cultural change	Differences in management style and levels of learning orientation Culture	Lack of synergy	Local teams and representatives on the glocal team

Chapter XI
The Implementation of ERP Packages as a Mediation Process:
The Case of Five Brazilian Projects

Maira Petrini
FGV EAESP, Brazil

Marlei Pozzebon
HEC Montreal, Canada

ABSTRACT

This research has investigated the implementation of ERP as mediation process—that is, as an interactive process developed between the organization's members and external consultants. The adoption of a mediation lens helps identify how global and local skills have been combined in ERP projects, and how these different arrangements have affected the project results. Underlying our analysis were two main questions: (1) How do patterns of mediation emerge, and what kinds of elements influence their emergence? and (2) What kind of association can be established between patterns of mediation and project results? Our conclusions point towards certain drivers. The local firm's position regarding the head office and the meaning attached to each project have directly influenced the way external consultants are perceived by the local firm's members, and these perceptions influence team members' and consultants' roles. Team members' and consultants' roles, in turn, contribute to reinforcement or transformation of established mediation patterns.

INTRODUCTION

The globalization movement has pushed firms to seek increased competitiveness. Waves of managerial and technological imperatives strongly pressure organizations not only to survive, but to become more and more competitive. Therein lies one of the major challenges in information technology (IT) management: pointing to strategies and technologies that help drive this competitiveness. An increasing number of organizations are trying to achieve advantage from new "tools" available in the global market. Among technological "imperatives," enterprise resources planning (ERP) packages were widely adopted by firms during the 1990s. In addition to promoting internal process integration, one of the most promising and significant accomplishments of ERP projects has been to support exchange of information across organizational boundaries, a powerful instrument for global organizations.

Beyond the Y2K flap and other issues, the pervasiveness of ERP solutions can be explained through the myth, or belief, that an integrated and ready-to-use IT solution for replacing legacy systems and integrating all business processes was available (Alvarez, 2000). However, the countless ERP projects that experienced failure or severe difficulties in achieving full "integration" have shown that such a "tool" is neither a readily/easily implemented solution nor a complete answer for integration (Markus & Tanis, 2000). On the contrary, ERP was revealed to be a complex phenomenon requiring wider organizational perspectives rather than merely technical ones (Pozzebon & Pinsonneault, 2005).

There have been several initiatives in investigating implementation ERP systems from organizational perspectives. For example, Caldas and Wood (2000) criticize the "techno-reductionist" vision that has characterized most approaches to the subject, suggesting an alternative perspective that leads to the understanding of institutional and political elements involved in ERP projects.

Researchers identified with the social shaping perspective go further in approaching technology implementation as a social and political process, like Clausen and Koch's (1999) view of identification of occasions for negotiation, Koch's (2000) examination of internal political processes, and Swan et al.'s (2000) discussion of rhetorical mechanisms.

In this vein, a recent investigation, carried out in Canadian, Brazilian, and Portuguese firms, has proposed understanding ERP implementation projects as a complex "mediation" process (Pozzebon, 2003). In effect, the use of mediation as a theoretical lens has allowed the ERP phenomenon to be viewed in a new manner, outlining aspects not emphasized by existing literature, particularly the influence of the type of interaction developed by organizational members (the ERP clients) and external consultants (ERP vendors or third-party consulting firms) on the configuration process and the project results.

ERP packages can be seen as configurable technologies, meaning technologies that are highly parameterizable and that are built from a range of components to meet the very specific requirements of a particular organization. From a mediation lens, we can talk about local-global negotiations—that is, negotiations involving "local" knowledge (knowledge about the firm's local business practices and its contextual particularities) and "global" knowledge (knowledge about package functionalities and best practices that can be "designed" from these functionalities). The adoption of a mediation lens helps identify how global and local knowledge and skills have been combined in different ERP projects, and how these different arrangements have affected the project results.

The qualitative inquiry was guided by the present analyses of the process of ERP implementation and its interdependence with organizational context, the dynamics of interaction between three groups (global firm stakeholders, local subsidiary members, and third-party consultants) during the implementation, and the achieved results—all in an attempt to test and extend knowledge previously generated about mediation processes. Our analyses were underlain by two main questions: (1) How do patterns of mediation emerge, and what kinds of elements influence their emergence? (2) What kind of association can be established between patterns of mediation and project results? The chapter is structured as follows: The next section presents the literature review. We then describe research methods and present the data analysis and research results, before offering our final conclusions.

BACKGROUND

Notable among the pressures that characterize today's corporate context are integration of firms' internal processes and optimization of business processes through the use of IT, which explains the emergence of ERP packages. In practice, organizations that have implemented such systems have been confronted with their huge complexity. One of the elements contributing to this complexity is the fact that ERP software is an example of configurable IT, which typically provides hundreds or thousands of characteristics that can be combined in multiple ways. And the more sophisticated and flexible the configurable IT, the more complex and risky its configuration (Orlikowski, 2000). Configurable IT is an important trend in the information systems area, gaining popularity from the hope of benefits to be derived from the increase in economies of scale and from access to the accumulated knowledge of organizational practices that is "embedded" in the software. On one hand, a profusion of functionalities are offered; on the other, careful choices within this multiplicity are required to guarantee the resultant configuration's consistency with already existing or new organizational processes (Pozzebon & Pinsonneault, 2005).

Although ERP phenomena cannot be neglected, the scope of configurable tools goes beyond ERP solutions. Packages with varying degrees of parametrizability exist, are increasing in flexibility and sophistication, and have been pervasive in IS areas for some time (e.g., CAD/CAM, business intelligence systems, workflow management, groupware, CRM packages). Many organizations turn to packaged solutions in the first place because of their belief that the difficulties associated with software development have been overcome by the software vendor. The fit between software features and organizational needs is recurrently reported as the biggest challenge to package implementation success (Grudin, 1991). If the customer lacks knowledge of the functions supported by the package, it is advisable for the firm to hire or train individuals who do have this knowledge (Lucas et al., 1988; Wu, 1990; Montazemi et al., 1996; Fichman & Moses, 1999). As we discuss later, this choice between hiring external expertise or training internal users, or both, has a strong influence on the type of mediation that will characterize the process of implementation.

The implementation of configurable technologies is strongly influenced by users' understanding of their own needs and of the technology's characteristics (Fichman & Moses, 1999). Another influential element is the user's trust in consultants' knowledge of the technology and experience in prior projects. While ERP software defines a range of possible uses, it is the technology's effective configuration and use that determines its usefulness and value. All this is significantly influenced by the way people interpret and interact with technology (Orlikowski et al., 1995). Because configurable technologies cannot be viewed independently of their representations through external intermediaries—who "speak" for the technology by providing descriptions, demonstrations and, "solutions"—their implementation is always mediated, a process through which clients and consultants together influence the decisions that are made on how each configurable technology will work (Pozzebon, 2003). Briefly, the review of literature on several areas (configurable technologies, packaged software, ISD, ERP implementation) suggests the role of technology mediation to be worthy of investigation but poorly understood.

ERP Implementation as a Mediation Process

The configuration and implementation of an ERP package is neither unproblematically available nor easily implemented. To different degrees, it involves intense negotiation among a wide network of players, not only internal players from different departments and hierarchical levels, but also a network of external players like software vendors, external contractors or systems integrators, independent consultants, and vendors of ERP product extensions, supporting hardware, software, and telecommunication capabilities, and so forth (Markus & Tanis, 2000). Some of these players, especially consultants from software vendors or third-party consulting firms, act as mediators in the sense that they directly influence users' interpretations and decisions by providing them with images, descriptions, demonstrations, policies, and templates (Orlikowski et al., 1995). They "speak" for the technology, strongly influencing the users' understanding of it (Bloomfield & Danieli, 1995). On the other hand, the users' assumptions, expectations, knowledge, and experience also influence the mediators' strategies.

In the implementation of an ERP, neither the organization's requirements nor the software capabilities should be taken for granted because both are socially constructed and mediated (Bloomfield & Danieli, 1995). We suggest the concept of mediation as central, defining ERP mediation process as the process through which clients and consultants jointly construct a relationship and negotiate how the ERP will work. ERP mediation is composed of a set of activities (meetings,

training, prototyping, conversations, and product demonstrations) or vehicles (documents, manuals, consultancy reports, training material, and advertising) that influence the way people implement the packaged software. These activities take place in a scenario of intense negotiation, the result of which is an arrangement that not only reflects a given vision of organizing, but that also might please or empower some of the actors involved and disappoint or devalue others.

Past research on technology mediation has identified different types of interventions—such as champions (Beath, 1991; Howell & Higgins, 1990), chauffeurs (Culnan, 1983), expert users (Nardi & Miller, 1990), system staff (Bjorn-Andersen, Eason, & Robey, 1986), tailors (Trigg & Bodker, 1994), and facilitators (Kraemer & King, 1988)—which provide valuable insights. Yet, most of them are not directly related to technology-configuring mediation. For instance, champions, chauffeurs, expert users, and tailors intervene once technology is in place and in use. Intermediaries and surrogates (Keil & Carmel, 1995) help make the link between the design and the future user, although not focusing on implementation. Administrators, champions, and trainers influence adoption and use but do not directly mediate in the configuration of a technology. As previously discussed, the implementation of an ERP cannot be read independently of its representation through intermediaries that help to configure the components and parameters embedded in the technology. These intermediaries are often consultants. Consequently, when the focus is on interventions that mediate ERP implementation, the role of consultants and their relationship with clients become central.

Investigating ERP projects as a mediation process, Pozzebon (2003) identified patterns of mediation and perceived certain associations between the nature of the mediation process and the results obtained in the implementation. The patterns identified are:

- **Outsourcing control:** External consultants (from ERP vendor or consulting agencies) have total responsibility for parameterization and implementation.

- **In-house control:** Organizational team members, trained to be able to configure, lead the project. In such cases, the consultant's role is ad-hoc and/or secondary.

- **Mixed control:** Different combinations of the previous patterns occur, wherein both consultants and team members are responsible, to different degrees, for project planning, management, and results.

Mediation Processes and Project Results

Different perspectives can be adopted in examining the results of information systems projects. DeLone and McLean (1992) consolidate several success measures in six categories: system quality, information quality, use, user satisfaction, individual impact, and organizational impact. These six categories suggest that success in IS is a multidimensional concept and success measures in IS would probably represent an average, based on the comparative weight of different components.

Markus and Tanis (2000) add complexity to the concept of IS success. First, IS success depends on the perspective of whomever is being interviewed about it (high-level managers, end users, business analysts, IT consultants, etc.). Second, IS success is dynamic, may change from time to time, and depends on the exact period of time it is being evaluated (end of the project, two months or a year later, etc.). Third, because of its nature, success is multidimensional and relative to: (1) time, (2) the perspective from which it is being measured, and (3) the goals in terms of which it is being evaluated. Such a multidimensional character of project results was integrated into the way we present our results: *ERP fit* is viewed as the perception of the degree of adherence of the business processes to

the system, or vice-versa; and *ERP satisfaction* is considered the perception of overall satisfaction with the system (Gattiker & Goodhue, 2002; McGill, Hobbs, & Klobas, 2003).

All these assessments can vary from one group of users to another. For the purposes of this investigation, we have added a third dimension to the assessment of project results: *ERP "success"* is evaluated according to the project goals and objectives set from the beginning (Markus & Tanis, 2000).

ANALYZING FIVE ERP PROJECTS IN BRAZIL

A case-based, qualitative methodology is employed in order to capture the complexity of these processes (Stake, 1998). The case-based approach has been suggested as one of the most appropriate research strategies for conducting empirical work in process-oriented research, and the benefits of using case studies are likely to be strengthened when they are also comparative (Pettigrew, 1990). Indeed, the research design is multiple case studies.

In order to select firms to be empirically investigated, telephone interviews were carried out by one of the authors; this is a research strategy recently adopted by researchers seeking to identify ERP projects (Robey, Ross, & Boudreau, 2000). The target population of this research consisted of large Brazilian firms using ERP systems, all of whom were subsidiaries of global organizations. In the process of case selection, the most difficult barrier to overcome was the firms' lack of interest in participating in academic projects. After several refusals, four large firms—MINA, TELE, TEXT, and AUTO—whose ERP project implementations occurred between 1996 and 1999 agreed to participate.

A special situation was found regarding one of the selected firms, TELE. The implementation of different modules for TELE was not planned as a single ERP project. Actually, we can observe two different implementation processes, carried out with total autonomy, as they pertain to two different firms. Clear differences can be recognized regarding project structure and planning, creation of implementation teams, and choice of external consultants. Because both ERP projects were investigated, we can consider this an "embedded case study," that is, two cases embedded in one research site—TELE A and TELA B. Briefly, in the following paragraphs, we describe the analysis and results of five cases, located in four firms.

Over six months, we carried out a total of 18 interviews with people who directly participated in the ERP configuration process. They were business and IT analysts (the client-firm members) and external consultants. Each interview lasted an average of an hour and a half. While we had well-defined criteria for selecting interviewees, it was difficult to find and convince people to participate, especially among the external consultants. This explains the greater number of interviews involving organizational members as compared to those with representatives of external consultancy. Table 1 identifies project names and industries, some project characteristics, and information about who was interviewed. In addition to interviews, archival analysis was used to complement contextual information.

Data analysis was carried out based on the methodology of discourse analysis. Supported by linguistic and sociological theories, as well as by psychoanalysis, discourse analysis aims at going beyond the explicit content of interviews

Table 1. Profile of the five selected ERP projects

Project and Industry	Project Characteristics	Total of Interviews
MINA Mining	Project duration = 13 months Start = 1998; *Go-live* = 1999 Big bang. Little customization. Little client training.	1 Business analyst 2 IT analysts 1 Consultant Total: 4
TELE A Telecommunications	Project duration = 9 months Start = 1998; *Go-live* = 1999 Modular. Vanilla. Little client training.	1 Business analyst 1 IT analyst Total: 2
TELE B Telecommunications	Project duration = 10 months Start = 1999; *Go-live* = 2000 Modular. Little customization. Little client training.	1 Business analyst 1 IT analyst Total: 2
TEXT Textile	Project duration = 22 months Start = 1996; *Go-live* = 1998 Big bang. Vanilla. Little client training.	3 Business/IT analysts Total: 3
AUTO Automobile	Project duration = 30 months Start = 1997; *Go-live* = 2000 Modular. Customized. Little client training.	3 Business analysts 3 IT analysts 1 Consultant Total: 7

and attempting to evaluate the non-explicit or unspoken elements in the discourse. It encompasses everything that, despite not being expressed directly in the interviewee's speech, "escapes" through expressions, metaphors, ironies, and resistant and distant manners (Wood & Kroger, 2000). Publications using discourse analysis are emerging in organization studies (Grant et al. 2001; Phillips & Hardy, 2002) as well as in the information systems area (Alvarez, 2001, 2002; Heracleous & Barret, 2001). (Detailed description of the foundations and use of discourse analysis is available upon request.)

RESEARCH RESULTS

The data analysis aimed at identifying patterns of mediation, seeking to determine if the patterns previously identified—outsourcing, in-house and mixed control—were present in our five cases or, rather, if different patterns of mediation had emerged. For each case, we focused on the type of relationship constructed by consultants and clients, and its interdependence with the firm's organizational context, seeking elements in this context that might have influenced the process. Two main questions guided our analysis: (1) How did patterns of mediation emerge and what kinds of contextual elements influenced their emergence? and (2) What kind of association can be established between patterns of mediation and project results?

How Did Patterns of Mediation Emerge and What Kinds of Contextual Elements Influenced Their Emergence?

We identified six contextual elements that have influenced the emergence of patterns of mediation in a context where the global firm decides to implement an ERP in its subsidiary, a local firm. All the elements and their interdependence are illustrated in Figure 1 and are described above.

Element 1	Overall context

First, it should be noted that the political and economic context of our firms reveals great instability stemming from Brazil's experience with

Figure 1. Contextual elements and their interdependence

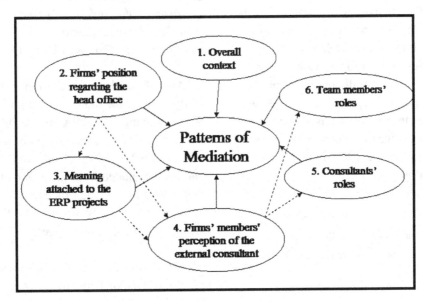

deregulation, privatization, market opening, and so forth, during the 1990s. During this period, the selected firms were facing intense processes of organizational change and were compelled to adapt themselves to "new times." Despite the assumption that ERP implementation, on its own, is supposed to produce considerable impact on organizational processes, we concluded that the ERP project represented a major source of instability for only one firm, AUTO:

We had two great fears. The first, regarding the culture of AUTO, strongly resistant to changes; for instance, they were not likely to accept to leave the mainframe for another platform…Second, they were leaving a "comfort zone" for hell! (Business Analysts, AUTO)

In the other firms, ERP implementation was just part of a broader process of organizational change within a turbulent external context:

Because it also coincided with the fact that the company was in that crazy rhythm for increasing its capacity…. (IT Analysts, TELE B)

We concluded that when global firms decide to implement complex systems that may entail deep organizational changes, a careful analysis of the local external environment is important. However, there is no recipe to tell us what impact the implementation will produce in local firms. In our study, even if the overall context is approximately the same in all five projects, the ways each group faced the turbulent and unstable environment differed significantly, and such differences strongly influenced the ERP implementation process that followed.

Element 2	Firms' position regarding the head office
Element 3	Meaning attached to the ERP projects
Element 4	Firms' members' perception of the external consultant

It is important to stress that all four firms are subsidiaries of large transnational organizations long established on Brazilian territory. From social theory literature, we have learned that a social group that feels constantly "threatened" by external elements—here represented by the head office (global firms)—might end up assuming a kind of "Manichean" stance in relation to such elements, that is, there is no middle term, but a contraposition between the group's participants vs. the group's enemy (Enriquez, 1992; Lapassade, 1977). Therefore, for each ERP project examined, it is important to understand the position taken by the local group (i.e., top management in Brazil) vis-à-vis the head office's top management (outside global firm), and consequently, the meaning assigned to the project and the firms' members' perception of the external consultant:

That was a guideline that already came 'ready'…At least this was what we felt: that the director, at that time, a [foreign] guy, he came with that mission of implanting ERP…. (IT Analyst, TELE B)

Because, unfortunately, at that moment of transition we had a new director that was 'unqualified': he put together the finance group in the auditorium, at that time 500 people, and he communicated that, with the ERP implementaiton, 60% of the group would be dismissed. (Key User, TELE A)

An additional element that emerged during the analysis was how the firm's members perceived the consultant. At MINA and AUTO, a process of *exclusion* of the local group vis-à-vis the head office (global firm) was clearly identified. MINA had been excluded from the group of companies that belong to the head office and was, therefore, going through identity crises and undergoing abrupt organizational changes:

Therefore, during the project, what happened was the definition that MINA would stop being part of the holding. (Consultant, MINA)

In turn, AUTO was excluded from the headquarters' decision-making process which ended by settling on ERP adoption:

The head office, in Europe, it had already made all the decisions. (IT Analyst, AUTO)

It was top-down. It was a determination from Germany. (IT Analyst, AUTO)

Although the feeling of exclusion was clear in these two firms, the way each firm dealt with exclusion was radically different, and this difference had clear consequences for the meaning attached to the ERP project and for the pattern of mediation developed. To MINA, the ERP project represented a possibility of showing the head office its capabilities, motivating the firm to assume control over the project. We clearly recognized *in-house control* in terms of its pattern of mediation:

We began to make proposals for the consulting group and even to dictate the norms we wanted for the consultants. (IT Analys, MINA)

In turn, AUTO perceived the ERP project as being imposed by the head office, and thus, nothing was its responsibility. They decided to delegate responsibility for the ERP project to the external consultancy. We clearly recognized an *outsourcing control* pattern of mediation:

The consultants had a strong influence...They showed the way and we followed like a robot, without knowing what we were doing, but we did.... (Business Analyst, AUTO)

In terms of the firm's perception, MINA and AUTO viewed the consultants as "enemies":

The consultants' methodology was ridiculous. (IT Analyst, AUTO)

Then the consultant explains, but he doesn't know your process, then you explain using language, and he explains technically, and you speak, and he explains, and it was a mess. (Business Analyst, MINA)

At MINA, because consultants landed on a firm trying to prove its own inherent capabilities, they were perceived as "intruders":

With the ERP imeplementation we have learned that external consulting is not always the the best solution for the company...I changed my position, where I was the IT analyst, with complete control of all the aspects of a project, and suddenly, I was undergoing consultants' norms, following their methodology, sometimes accepting, sometimes not, resisting. (IT Analyst, MINA)

At AUTO, because consultants had been neither chosen nor desired by the firm, they were perceived as omnipotent "dictators":

The consultant's role was always imposed, because in fact, he was the ambassador of a general law that was given for everybody: to accept the product as it was, without changes. This was like...a ghost that surrounded us. Then, because the consultant's voice was the product's voice, he could always impose his ideas. (Business Analyst, AUTO)

A different position can be recognized with regard to the other two firms, TELE and TEXT, and their head offices. We recognized a process of *inclusion,* to the extent that local groups see themselves as taking part in the overall decision-making process of their head offices. They perceive the ERP project as a useful tool for consolidating their position vis-à-vis the head office. TELE, originally a national public firm, was acquired by a large global organization which uses an ERP system and has a policy that all acquired firms must use the same technology. At the time of the ERP project, the firm saw the project as a way to show its aptitude for coping with change and with head office requirements, thereby proving themselves to be a mature and professional corporation:

The media 'sold' ideas like 'TELE's employees are slow'. When the consultants noticed that it was not like this, then our relationhsip with them became very good. (Business Anlayst, TELE B)

Specifically at the time of the ERP project at TELE B, several structural changes were being implemented, and these changes had a severe impact in the organization. Organizational identity was being reconstructed, instigating internal power conflicts. Thus, the ERP project was highlighted by a power dispute between functional and technological areas, both looking for the success of the ERP project to demonstrate their competency:

You are from the systems area, you think differently from the personnel of the functional area. (IT Analyst, TELE B)

We wanted to control the configuration, IT wanted to control the configuration. IT got it. Then we had a period of transition where we taught the analysts to configure our business processes. It was not a situation we enjoyed. (Business Analyst, TELE B)

TELE A and TELE B adopted a *mixed control* modality regarding the ERP implementation, building a partnership with consultants in which knowledge and experience were seen as important to the success of the project. Thus, the consultants were perceived as an "ally," with different aspects arising from the internal conflicts, as explained in the next section:

We had, from the part of the consultants, a coordination that was very good. They had enormous experience…they were also Brazilian, they had

a very big expertise, all this contributed…. (IT Analyst, TELE A)

The fourth firm, TEXT, is the result of a joint venture, and the ERP package was seen as a tool that would facilitate integration and enable the processes of consolidating a joint venture. They decided to follow a pattern of *in-house control,* leading to the emergence of a new driver, already discussed in the second section, to define the mediation process: global knowledge—meaning that the knowledge about package functionalities and best practices that can be "designed" from the functionalities presented by the consultants became the most influential element in the adopted pattern. At TEXT, the consultancy's legitimacy regarding its technical qualification was called into question at the very beginning of the project, leading the company to assume control of implementation. TEXT saw the consultant as an ally, or at least, not as an enemy.

Consultants didn't have ERP experience at that time, then it would be appropriate that we configure. Because they had to learn to teach us, it would be easier if we had be trained directly. (Business/IT Analyst, TEXT)

In short, all firms that perceived the ERP project as an opportunity sought to assume, to different degrees, control of the project. Our empirical inquiry corroborates the presence of the three patterns of mediation previously identified by Pozzebon (2003). In addition, we have analyzed a collection of contextual reasons for their emergence. In brief, in our cases, it appears to us that when a firm's position vis-à-vis the head office was one of exclusion, the consultant was perceived as an enemy. On the other hand, the consultant was perceived as an ally when the firm's relation to the head office was one of inclusion.

Element 5	Consultants' roles
Element 6	Team members' roles

Patterns of mediation reflect different types of relationships constructed by implementation team members (people from the client-firms) and external consultants (people from vendor or third-party consulting firms). In the section above, we introduced an important element: the way the firm's members perceive the consultant. In this section, we describe our understanding of how team members' and consultants' roles help to reinforce certain patterns of mediation and how such patterns influence the ERP configuration put in place. The *consultants' role* is partially a consequence of how they are perceived by the firm's members. In firms where external consultants are perceived as a kind of "enemy" (e.g., AUTO and MINA), their role ends up being limited to applying their knowledge without commitment. In our view, in their responses and actions, they unintentionally assume the role of external enemy in which they have been cast. With firms that perceive the external consultants as an "ally" (e.g., TELE and TEXT), consultants are likely to assume a more participative role, yet one that is marked by varying degrees of commitment. In fact, how consultants are perceived by the firm's members also influences the *team members' role,* and in turn, both roles (consultants' and team members') shape or reinforce the mediation pattern.

MINA perceived the consultants as "intruders" who could compromise their image with the head office by exposing their lack of "internal" capabilities or skills. Team members showed themselves to be very combative and assertive, always seeking their own solutions and reinforcing the pattern of mediation characterized by *in-house control*:

We had people attacking on one side, others defending themselves on another side, this is usual...Then, you make an effort in order to respect 'the change management', you make consessions, and it solved 90% of the cases. (Consultant, MINA)

At AUTO, consultants were perceived as omnipotent "dictators" (rather than intruders), who followed head office decisions and who needed to be defeated. This helps to explain the transition in the team members' role from passive victims at the beginning to components of a resistance movement as the project evolved. In this way, we identified a gradual change in the pattern of mediation from an *outsourcing control* pattern at the beginning of the project to *mixed control*:

Together with some business analysts, we start to work together with the consultants. We began to say 'this should be like this, this should go like like that!' The consultant proposed something and we tested—'no, it is not like this, no.' (IT Analyst, AUTO)

Firms that perceive the external consultant as an ally assumed a collaborative role. At TELE A and TELE B, two different kinds of participation were assumed by external consultants. Likewise, different degrees of internal conflict were recognized. In TELE A, we observed little internal conflict regarding the team project. Project team members truly integrated the external consultant into the team, resulting in the consultant being not only participative but actively engaged and co-responsible for the project's success:

The consultant, he was fantastic...he was a differentiated consultant. He was not just a partner, he bought the project for him. (Business Analyst, TELE A)

At TELE B, the ERP implementation occurred during a period of restructuring, when new areas were being created, others being eliminated, and most functions being redefined. Internal conflicts in the project were strong as business and IT areas sought to define their new positions in the firm. Team members intentionally sought a certain independence from the consultancy because they needed to prove their competence in order to gain or to strengthen better positions in the firm. This resulted in consultants being participative but less committed:

We had some conflicts, sometimes the consultants did want to impose...sometimes they leave the personnel [of the company] sideways...Perhaps even for orientation of their management, they try to maintain a certain distance, for not creating a link. (IT Analyst, TELE B)

At TEXT, because the consultants' technological knowledge was considered weak, the firm's members perceived themselves as more experienced during the project, thereby reinforcing the *in-house control* pattern of mediation as the project evolved. However, their collaborative team members' role seems to have led the consultancy to a stance that was participative but less committed:

Later we played: 'we didn't buy a consultoria, we bought a work hand.' (Business Analyst, TEXT)

Understanding the Dynamics of Patterns of Mediation

All the elements previously discussed and the pattern of mediation adopted in each project are summarized in Table 2.

What Kind of Association can be Established Between Patterns of Mediation and Project Results?

Regarding ERP implementation results, three dimensions of project results were investigated. First, *ERP success* was assessed, based on the perception of ERP's achievement of the proposed objectives. Second, *ERP fit* was evaluated, based on the perception of match between software features and organizational needs. Third, *user satisfaction* was evaluated, based on the perception

of overall satisfaction regarding the implemented ERP. Thus, assessment of project results was based on *perceptions,* but whose perceptions? As outlined earlier, the assessment of project results always depends on *who is being asked.*

Different stakeholders are likely to have different appraisals of IS success because, above all, they hold different interests and expectations regarding the project's outcomes. Different groups of actors can hold points of view that converge, diverge, conflict with, or complement each other. Briefly, each judgment of success or failure cannot be taken for granted but must be qualitatively considered and critically connected to its context. However, we believe that people from the same stakeholder group are more likely to share similar judgments than people from different stakeholder groups. The aggregation of individual perceptions in order to trace an overall perception by a stakeholder group or organizational level of analysis is a well-known practice, but it cannot be taken as an "objective measure" of such a higher level (Pozzebon, 2003).

Table 3 illustrates the project results from the perspectives of the people we interviewed (business analysts, IT analysts, and a few consultants), and we take their perceptions to be the predominant perceptions within their organizations. What is important is to be aware of the relativity of our assessments and to be transparent when reporting the results. Table 3 reports aggregate results that do not reveal internal divergences and conflicts, but reflect a perception of what element is perceived as dominant.

The first aspect we would like to outline is the multidimensionality of the project results. On the one hand, it is interesting to observe that a system may have been a success in terms of achieving its goals, but frustrating in terms of the users' satisfaction (for instance, TEXT). On the other hand, our analysis tends to identify user satisfaction as being associated with ERP fit. In the three projects that show at least a medium fit between ERP and business process, user satisfaction was

Table 2. Summary of contextual elements and pattern of mediation adopted

	MINA	TELE A	TELE B	TEXT	AUTO
Pattern of mediation	In-house control	Mixed control	Mixed control	In-house control	Outsourcing control moving to mixed control
Firm's position in relation to headquarters	Exclusion	Inclusion	Inclusion	Inclusion	Exclusion
Meaning attached to the project	Possibility of showing headquarters their qualities	Prove that the firm is receptive and apt to changes	Power dispute between functional and technological areas	Good tool that brings adaptation needs	Headquarters' imposition to be resisted
Firms' members' perception of the external consultant	As an enemy, an intruder	As an ally, part of the team	As a partial ally in the internal conflict	As an ally (or at least not an opponent)	As an enemy, an omnipotent "dictator"
Consultant's role	Uncommitted	Participative, strong commitment	Participative, limited commitment	Participative, limited commitment	Uncommitted
Team members' role	Combative, assertive, seeking own solutions	Collaborative, genuinely seeking to integrate the consultants	Collaborative, trying a certain degree of independence in relation to the consultancy	Collaborative, with more experience than consultants	Victim at first; later, resistant to the implementation

Table 3. Summary of project results

	MINA	TELE A	TELE B	TEXT	AUTO
Pattern of mediation	In-house control	Mixed control	Mixed control	In-house control	Outsourcing control moving to mixed control
ERP success regarding project goals	Yes, the objectives were accomplished	Yes, the objectives were accomplished	Yes, the objectives were accomplished	Yes, the objectives were accomplished	No, not all objectives were accomplished
ERP fit	Medium to high	Medium to high	Medium to low	Low	Low
User satisfaction with ERP	Completely satisfied	Partially satisfied	Partially satisfied	Unsatisfied	Unsatisfied

high or partial (MINA, TELE A, TELE B). In the two firms with a low fit (TEXT and AUTO), user satisfaction was very low.

Regarding patterns of mediation and their influence on project results, our insights are not conclusive. Our cases corroborated Pozzebon's results (2003) regarding an awareness resistant to *outsourcing control*: AUTO was the only firm which adopted this modality, and the results were not positive in all aspects investigated. The *mixed control* pattern seemed to be the one most favorable for establishment of balanced partnerships: it enabled a higher synergy level between global and local, which helped to increase the fit between business process and system features, as well as to raise user satisfaction. Finally, our insights regarding *in-house control* are mixed: in one case, MINA, it led to good levels of fit and satisfaction; in another case, TEXT, it led to low levels of fit and satisfaction. Pozzebon (2003) has found that user satisfaction may vary depending on the empowerment and scope of end user participation during the implementation. Findings at TEXT reinforce this insight and point to a new direction: it is not enough to train the end users in using the system, but it is also necessary that users develop knowledge of the processes on which they are working and of the impacts of their activities on other processes:

I would say that the ERP project was a pragmatic success, but it was a failure in terms of their audience. (Business/IT Analyst, TEXT)

Finally, according to Pozzebon (2003), in-house controls are likely to benefit the fit, because the client members who guide the implementation tend to know the internal contexts and user requirements very well. Our investigation shows MINA with a medium to high fit and TEXT with a low fit. This suggests that patterns of mediation represent different ways of understanding ERP projects, with further research being needed in order to establish more conclusive links.

CONCLUSION

The purpose of this study was to investigate ERP implementation in Brazilian firms from a perspective wherein ERP is seen as a configurable IT, and its implementation is seen as a mediation process. The main questions involve how the organizational context influences patterns of mediation, and how the patterns of mediation influence project results.

It can be observed that different historical and organizational elements might influence the mediation process, helping to shape projects' meanings and people's perceptions and roles. The understanding we have produced from five ERP projects is quite innovative in several aspects because we have tried to analyze how people's perceptions influence the process, which in turn influences people's perceptions, and so on. Using discourse analysis, we have developed some links between patterns, perceptions, and results which are very tentative but have helped us to make some sense of these projects. Among our main conclusions are:

- Surrounded by contextual elements, the meaning attached to the ERP project is an important driver for patterns of mediation, which in our cases was developed as a consequence of the firm's position in relation to the head office.

- The firm's position and the meaning attached to each project have directly influenced the way external consultants are perceived by the firm's members, and these perceptions influence team members' and consultants' roles. It is important to emphasize this fact because it defines the dynamic of the firm/consultant relationship where the consultant ends up having less power and adapts himself and his ways of acting to the firm's culture. This decision-making process does not occur rationally; it is shaped by the subjectivity inherent in the organizational culture.

- Team members' and consultants' roles contribute to reinforcing or transforming established mediation patterns. For example, *mixed control* is more easily sustained when a collaborative role is purposively assumed by team members, and vice-versa: established mixed control patterns create more conditions for collaborative roles.

Problems and solutions associated with the same technology tend to be recurrent, and certain patterns can be recognized, even though they do not present themselves in a deterministic manner (Orlikowski, 2000). In our investigation, we have tried to recognize patterns in the relationship between clients and consultants, in a context where global firms decide to implement ERP packages in their subsidiaries, located in different locations, and to relate these patterns to the project results. It is also important to stress that patterns of mediation are dynamic processes that can change over time. Therefore, understanding how patterns of mediation work and evolve is a route to the elaboration of better policies and methods for ERP implementation. Managers from both global and local firms should pay attention to the elements discussed in this chapter. We do not provide a precise recipe, but insightful concepts that can help them make better decisions.

FUTURE RESEARCH DIRECTIONS

Future research in this area may focus on expanding the study to other sectors and even to other countries than Brazil, in order to find out how different contexts influences the patterns of mediation, based on team members' and consultants' roles. Longitudinal study can also be one possible direction for future research, looking at how the same companies evaluate the ERP implementation success regarding project goals and the level of user satisfaction with the ERP project in further stages of implementation. Since

ERP implementation has huge impact all over the organization, and its success depends on the perspective of whomever is being interviewed, and considering that the research presented here is based only on business analysts, IT analysts, and consultants, other kinds of professionals can also be interviewed, such as those at the operational level, for instance, helping to build a broader understanding of the whole process involved in a configurable technology adoption.

REFERENCES

Alvarez, R. (2000). Examining an ERP implementation through myths: A case study of a large public organization. In *Proceedings of the 6th American Conference on Information Systems* (pp. 1655-1661), Long Beach, CA.

Alvarez, R. (2001). It was a great system. Face-work and the discursive construction of technology during information systems development. *Information Technology & People, 14*(4), 385-405.

Alvarez, R. (2002). Confessions of an information worker: A critical analysis of information requirements discourse. *Information and Organization, 12,* 85-107.

Beath, C.M. (1991). Supporting the information technology champion. *MIS Quarterly, 15*(3), 355-372.

Benbasat, I., Goldstein, D., & Mead, M. (1987). The case research strategy in studies of information systems. *MIS Quarterly, 11*(3), 369-387.

Bjorn-Andersen, N., Eason, K., & Robey, D. (1986). *Managing computer impact.* Norwood, NJ: Ablex.

Bloomfield, B.P., & Danieli, A. (1995). The role of management consultants in the development of information technology: The indissoluble nature of socio-political and technical skills. *Journal of Management Studies, 32*(1), 23-46.

Caldas, M., & Wood, T. Jr. (2000). Fads and fashions in management: The case of ERP. *RAE—Revista de Administração de Empresas, 40*(3), 8-17.

Clausen, C., & Koch, C. (1999). The role of space and occasions in the transformation of information technologies—Lessons from the social shaping of IT systems for manufacturing in a Danish context. *Technology Analysis and Strategic Management, 11*(3) 463-482.

Culnan, M.J. (1983). Chauffeured versus end user access to commercial databases: The effects of task and individual differences. *MIS Quarterly, 7*(1), 55-67.

Delone, W.H., & Mclean, E.R. (1992). Information system success: The quest for the dependent variable. *Information Systems Research, 3*(1), 60-95.

Enriquez, E. (1992). *L'organisation en analyse.* Paris: Press Universitaires de France.

Fichman, R.G., & Moses, S.A. (1999). An incremental process for software implementation. *Sloan Management Review, 40*(2), 39-52.

Gattiker, T.F., & Goodhue, D.L. (2002). Software-driven changes to business processes: An empirical study of impacts of enterprise resource planning (ERP) systems at the local level. *International Journal of Production Research, 40*(18), 99.

Grant, D., Kennoy, T., & Oswick, C. (2001). Organizational discourse—Key contributions and challenges. *International Studies of Management and Organization, 31*(3), 5-24.

Grudin, J. (1991). Interactive systems: Bridging the gaps between developers and users. *IEEE Computer, 24*(4), 59-69.

Heracleous, L., & Barret, M. (2001).Organizational change as discourse: Communicative actions and deep structures in the context of information technology implementation. *Academy of Management Journal, 44*(4), 755-778.

Howell, J.M., & Higgins, C.A. (1990). Champions of technological innovation. *Administrative Science Quarterly, 35,* 317-341.

Keil, M., & Carmel, E. (1995). Customer-developer links in software development. *Communications of the ACM, 38*(5), 33-44.

Koch, C. (2000). The ventriloquist's dummy? The role of technology in political processes. *Technology Analysis and Strategic Management, 12*(1), 119-138.

Kraemer, K.L., & King, J.L. (1988). Computer-based systems for cooperative work and group decision making. *ACM Computing Surveys, 20*(2), 115-146.

Lapassade, G. (1997). *Grupos, organizações e instituições.* Rio de Janeiro: Francisco Alves.

Lucas, H.C., Walton, E. J., & Ginzberg, M. J. (1988). Implementing packaged software. *MIS Quarterly,* 537-549.

Markus, M.L., & Tanis, C. (2000). The enterprise systems experience—From adoption to success In R.W. Zmud (Ed.), *Framing the domains of IT research: Glimpsing the future through the past.* Cincinnati, OH: Pinnaflex Educational Resources.

McGill, T., Hobbs, V., & Klobas, J. (2003). User-developed applications and information systems success: A test of Delone and Mclean's model. *Information Resource Management Journal, 16*(1), 24-45.

Montazemi, A. et al. (1996). An empirical study of factors affecting software package selection. *Journal of Management Information Systems, 13*(1), 89-105.

Nardi, B.A., & Miller J.R. (1990). An ethnographic study of distributed problem solving in spreadsheet development. In *Proceedings of the*

ACM Conference on CSCW (pp. 197-208), Los Angeles.

Orlikowski, W.J. (2000). Using technology and constituting structures: A practice lens for studying technology in organizations. *Organization Science, 11*(4), 404-428.

Orlikowski, W.J., Yates, J., Okamura, K., & Fujimoto, M. (1995). Shaping electronic communication: The metastructuring of technology in the context of use. *Organization Science, 6*(4), 423-444.

Pettigrew, A.M. (1990). Longitudinal field research on change: Theory and practice. *Organization Science, 1*(3), 267-292.

Phillips, N., & Hardy, C. (2002). *Discourse Analysis.* London: Sage.

Pozzebon, M. (2003). *The implementation of configurable technologies: Negotiations between global principles and local contexts.* Unpublished PhD Dissertation, McGill University, Canada.

Pozzebon, M., & Pinsonneault, A. (2005). Global-local negotiations for implementing configurable packages: The power of initial organizational decisions. *Journal of Strategic Information Systems, Special Issue Understanding the Contextual Influences on Enterprise System Implementation (Part II), 14*(2), 121-145.

Robey, D., Ross, J., & Boudreau, M. (2000). *Learning to implement enterprise systems: An exploratory study of the dialectics of change.* Center for Information Systems Research, MIT, USA.

Stake, R.E. (1998). Case studies. In N. K. Denzin & Y. Lincoln (Eds.), *Strategies of qualitative inquiry.* Thousand Oaks, CA: Sage.

Swan, J., Newell, S., & Robertson, M. (2000). The diffusion, design and social shaping of production management information systems in Europe. *Information Technology and People, 13*(1), 27-45.

Trigg, R.H., & Bodker, S. (1994). From implementation to design: Tailoring and the emergence of systematization. In *Proceedings of the ACM Conference on CSCW* (pp. 45-54), Chapel Hill, NC.

Wood, L.A., & Kroger, R.O. (2000). *Doing discourse analysis.* London: Sage.

Wu, M.S. (1990). Selecting the right software application package. *Journal of Systems Management, 41*(9), 28-32.

Yin, R. (1994). *Case study research: Design and methods* (2nd ed.). Thousand Oaks, CA: Sage.

ADDITIONAL READING

Abrahamson, E. (1991). Managerial fads and fashions: The diffusion and rejection of innovations. *Academy of Management Review, 16*(3), 586-612.

Brown, A. (1998). Narrative, politics and legitimacy in an IT implementation. *Journal of Management Studies, 35*(1), 35-59.

Brown, C., & Vessey, I. (1999). ERP implementation approaches: Toward a contingency framework. In *Proceedings of the 20th International Conference on Information Systems* (pp. 411-416), Charlotte, NC.

Butler, J. (1999). Risk management skills needed in a package software environment. *Information Systems Management, 16*(3), 15-20.

Gable, G.G., van Den Heever, R., Erlank, S., & Scott, J. (1997). Large packaged software: The need for research. In *Proceedings of the 3rd Pacific Asia Conference on Information Systems* (pp. 381-388), Brisbane, Australia.

Hislop, D., Newell, S., Scarbrough, H., & Swan, J. (2000). Networks, knowledge and power: Decision making, politics and the process of innovation.

Technology Analysis & Strategic Management, 12(3), 399-411.

Kelly, S., Holland, C., & Light, B. (1999). Enterprise resource planning: A business approach to systems development. In *Proceedings of the 5ᵗʰ AMCIS* (pp. 785-787), Milwaukee, WI.

Kumar, K., & Van Hillegersberg, J. (2000). ERP experiences and evolution. *Communications of the ACM, 43*(4), 23-26.

Markus, M.L., Axline, S., Petrie, D., & Tanis C. (2000). Learning from adopters' experiences with ERP: Problems encountered and success achieved. *Journal of Information Technology, 15,* 245-265.

Muscatello, J.R., Small, M. H., & Chen, I. J. (2003). Implementing enterprise resource planning (ERP) systems in small and midsize manufacturing firms. *International Journal of Operations & Production Management, 23*(7/8), 850-866.

Pereira, R.E. (1999). Resource view theory analysis of SAP as a source of competitive advantage for firms. *The Data Base for Advances in Information Systems, 30*(1), 38-46.

Section V
Auditing Aspects

Chapter XII
Sarbanes–Oxley Compliance, Internal Control, and ERP Systems:
The Case of mySAP ERP

Pall Rikhardsson
University of Aarhus, Denmark

Peter Best
University of Southern Queensland, Australia

Claus Juhl-Christensen
EDB Gruppen A/S, Denmark

ABSTRACT

The effort to comply with the Sarbanes-Oxley Act (SOX) has focused management attention in companies all over the world on the importance of assessing, developing, and maintaining an effective and efficient internal control system. Enterprise resource planning (ERP) systems are a crucial factor in developing such a system. Despite the attention this has attracted in practice, little academic research has focused on this area. This chapter addresses the question: How are ERP systems implicated in Sarbanes-Oxley compliance? It aims to show how SOX requirements regarding assessment and improvement of internal controls are related to the functionalities of an ERP system both in local and global implementations. It examines a solution (mySAP ERP) offered by one specific vendor (SAP) and what functionalities are relevant to global SOX compliance. Based on this, the chapter discusses likely developments regarding compliance functionalities in future releases of ERP systems.

INTRODUCTION

Corporate governance can be defined as the framework of rules, relationships, systems, and processes within and by which authority is exercised and controlled in corporations (Owen Report 2003 as cited in du Plessis, McConvill, & Bagaric, 2005, p. 2). Thus the concept embraces not only the models or systems themselves, but also the practices by which this exercise and control of authority are in fact effected. It should be clear that corporate governance is a complex concept encompassing values and ethics, systems and organizations, behavior and activities, and results and performance.

One aspect of corporate governance is complying with the rules and regulations of society. The term *compliance* has emerged as something of a buzzword in the past five years. Looking through various journals, it seems that compliance is yet another term that has different implications for different areas. In accounting and auditing, compliance has become almost synonymous with Sarbanes-Oxley and strengthening of internal controls and the quality of financial reporting. In production management, compliance can mean conformance with product specifications and quality standards as well as respecting environmental regulations. In human resource management, compliance means adhering to regulations and requirements related to employees including information privacy, health regulations, and codes of safety. Compliance seems to be a generic concept as well as focused on specific functions and processes.

The catalyst for the current focus on compliance in accounting and control is a series of high-profile financial frauds and bankruptcies including companies such as ENRON, WorldCom, Tyco, Parmalat, and Hollinger International Inc. These sent shock waves through the business world. How could well-renowned companies with assets worth billions of dollars disappear from the face of the earth in a matter of weeks, leaving thousands of employees without jobs and whole communities reeling from the aftershock? The answer was deemed to be lack of internal controls, management fraud, and fraudulent financial reporting.

The institutional reaction has been threefold (Baker, Bealing, Nelson, & Blair Staley, 2006). First, there was a government reaction where laws were enacted to strengthen internal control frameworks and increase the accountability of external auditors. This reaction mainly focused on reestablishing investor trust in financial reporting. Second, the monitoring of corporate accountability was strengthened with the emergence of new organizations such as the Public Company Accounting Oversight Board (PCAOB) in the United States. This reaction focused on strengthening the government control regime and possibilities of stepping in should the need arise. Third, there was a professional reaction in accounting and auditing institutions focusing on changing accounting and auditing practices and taking measures to ensure the independence of accounting firms. This reaction focused on reestablishing public trust in the accounting and auditing profession.

The legal reaction was spearheaded by the Public Company Accounting Reform and Investor Protection Act of 2002, more popularly known as the Sarbanes-Oxley Act (SOX) after its main architects, Senator Paul Sarbanes and Representative Michael Oxley. The Sarbanes-Oxley Act has brought about an extensive reform of the U.S. financial markets, with ripple effects spreading around the globe (PricewaterhouseCoopers, 2003) and into other areas of compliance (Atkinson & Leandri, 2005). As such it has changed the landscape for internal controls, auditing, and management accountability in thousands of companies all over the world—changes which will be visible for years to come.

One of the issues often mentioned regarding SOX compliance is the importance of information technology in the compliance effort (MacNally & Wagaman, 2005; Byington & Christensen, 2005; ACL, 2005; Cannon & Growe, 2004). This includes IT controls as well as the role of IT in making the SOX compliance more effective and efficient. Some of this discussion focuses on enterprise resource planning (ERP) systems. Hailed as one of the most significant IT innovations to affect companies, ERP systems are crucial in developing and maintaining an internal control system that enables companies to effectively and efficiently comply with Sarbanes-Oxley (ITGI, 2005; Fox, 2004; Cannon & Growe, 2004).

This chapter examines the question: How are ERP systems implicated in meeting the requirements of Sarbanes-Oxley? To answer this question the chapter first describes what SOX compliance means, shows the elements of a SOX compliance process, and based on that discusses internal control and ERP systems. It then examines a specific ERP solution (mySAP ERP) offered by one vendor (SAP) and describes what functionalities are relevant to SOX compliance when using that system. Following that, the chapter discusses likely developments regarding ERP systems and compliance, and presents several avenues for future research.

SARBANES-OXLEY COMPLIANCE

What are the Requirements of Sarbanes-Oxley?

The Sarbanes-Oxley Act is by no means the first of its kind. Historically it has been preceded by acts that were intended to improve corporate governance and increase accountability. These include, for example, the Securities Act of 1933 and the Foreign Corruption Act of 1977, both of which focused on internal controls, financial reporting, and the role of external auditors (Baker et al., 2006; Byington & Christensen, 2005).

In general terms, the Sarbanes-Oxley Act's provisions apply to four types of companies (PricewaterhouseCoopers, 2003):

1. Domestic U.S. registrants
2. Foreign private issuers, also referred to as 'foreign registrants'
3. Subsidiaries of U.S. registrants (only to the extent that some information applies to the consolidated financial statements)
4. Potentially, companies planning a U.S. registration in the future

In addition, the act appears to have set a benchmark for companies in Europe and Asia that have an interest in enhancing corporate governance, including risk management and internal controls. Regulations and guidelines for strengthening internal controls are being or have been developed at the European Union level and in countries such as Australia and Japan (PricewaterhouseCoopers, 2003; ITGI, 2004).

SOX is different from earlier legislation in that it makes the chief executive officers (CEOs) and chief financial officers (CFOs) legally responsible for (Kendal, 2004; PricewaterhouseCoopers, 2003):

1. Establishing, evaluating, and monitoring the effectiveness of internal control over financial reporting and disclosure
2. Designing, establishing, and maintaining 'disclosure controls and procedures' and reporting on the effectiveness of 'disclosure controls and procedures';
3. Disclosing to the audit committee and external auditor any significant deficiencies and material weaknesses in internal controls for financial reporting and any fraud (material or not) involving anyone having a significant role in those internal controls; and
4. Disclosing whether, after their most recent evaluation, significant changes occurred that affected internal controls for financial reporting and whether any corrective actions were taken with regard to significant deficiencies and material weaknesses.

Compliance with SOX is costly. Different sources estimate that companies around the world spend billions of dollars on SOX compliance projects (Charles River & Associates, 2005; IMJ, 2004). Companies are thus increasingly looking for ways to improve the efficiency of the compliance process through optimization of internal controls and IT integration (Waldman, 2005).

Complying with Sarbanes-Oxley: Internal Controls

SOX compliance involves various elements such as the role of managers, roles of external auditors, reporting to external stakeholders, and data quality. A key issue in SOX is the internal control system of the company. The Sarbanes-Oxley Act does not define internal controls as such. However, the PCAOB Auditing Standard No. 2, which interprets the act in the context of auditing, defines internal controls as (PCAOB, 2002, p. 147):

A process designed by, or under the supervision of, the company's principal executive and principal financial officers, or persons performing similar functions, and effected by the company's board of directors, management, and other personnel, to provide reasonable assurance regarding the reliability of financial reporting and the preparation of financial statements for external purposes in accordance with generally accepted accounting principles and includes those policies and procedures that:

1. *Pertain to the maintenance of records that, in reasonable detail, accurately and fairly reflect the transactions and dispositions of the assets of the company;*
2. *Provide reasonable assurance that transactions are recorded as necessary to permit preparation of financial statements in accordance with generally accepted accounting principles, and that receipts and expenditures of the company are being made only in accordance with authorizations of management and directors of the company; and*
3. *Provide reasonable assurance regarding prevention or timely detection of unauthorized acquisition, use or disposition of the company's assets that could have a material effect on the financial statements.*

Compliance with Sarbanes-Oxley thus requires establishing, improving, and monitoring certain control activities to ensure financial reporting data quality and system reliability (ITGI, 2004). The primary control-related requirements of SOX are shown in Table 1.

Regarding the baseline against which internal control systems have to be evaluated, the PCAOB requires companies to adopt an internal control framework by which its practices can be assessed. It mentions the Committee of Sponsoring Organizations (see COSO, 1992) as one framework, but other frameworks can be used as well. Most companies adopt the COSO framework, which seems to have become the de facto standard for the development of internal control systems in practice (Shue, 2004; COSO, 1992, 2004).

In the COSO framework, control is achieved through various internal control activities such as:

1. Authorization of transaction and activities
2. Segregation of duties (custodial, recording, and authorization functions)
3. Design and use of documents and records
4. Adequate safeguards of assets and records
5. Independent checks on performance

COSO also stresses that internal control is conducted in a control environment, influencing the control consciousness of organizational actors. It is the foundation for all other components of internal control, providing discipline and structure. Control environment factors include the

Table 1. Primary SOX compliance requirements related to internal control systems (based on PricewaterhouseCoopers, 2003)

Section of SOX	Requirements	Internal Control System Implications
301	Establish a process for anonymous complaints of employees to audit committee (SOX, 2002, p. 32)	An independent process for employees and managers for submitting communications to the audit committee
302	Establish the responsibility of the company signing officers (the CEO and the CFO) for setting up an internal control system, evaluating the effectiveness of this control system, and making public the results of the evaluation (SOX, 2002, p. 33)	Place unambiguous responsibility for the development, assessment, and documentation of the internal control system
401	Require financial reports to reflect all adjustments identified by auditors—all off-balance sheet transactions must be disclosed and pro forma figures must be reconciled with Generally Accepted Accounting Principles figures.	Require the internal controls to contain checks on inclusion of off-balance sheet transactions and pro forma reconciliations and whether auditor adjustments have been included
404	Require that the annual report contains an internal control report which must: • state the responsibility of management for establishing and maintaining an adequate internal control structure and procedures for financial reporting; and • contain an assessment, as of the end of the most recent fiscal year of the issuer, of the effectiveness of the internal control structure and procedures of the issuer for financial reporting The external auditing form is to attest to and report on this report (SOX, 2002, p. 45).	A process for establishing a baseline for internal control systems and assessing the internal control systems against this baseline has to be initiated. Also procedures for reporting on this assessment and the work of the external auditors must be established. Procedures to deal with weaknesses and deficiencies have to be in place, as well as procedures for 'controlling the controllers'.
409	Obligation to report on rapidly changing financial conditions to the public (SOX, 2002, p. 47)	The internal control system has to contain monitoring and evaluation mechanisms for changes in financial conditions.

integrity, ethical values, and competence of the organizational actors; management's philosophy and operating style; the way management assigns authority and responsibility, and organizes and develops its people; and the attention and direction provided by the board of directors. This is similar to what Chenhall (2003) calls control culture. Another central element in the COSO

guidelines is risk assessment and management. COSO recommends that companies initiate a risk assessment process with the aim of analyzing what threats the company faces and what control activities are needed to manage these risks. Risks include, for example, the risk of fraud and misappropriation of assets.

Implementing SOX Compliance

When SOX came into effect in 2002, companies scrambled to implement its requirements. In many cases companies approached SOX compliance in what has been called an "all hands on deck" approach (McNally & Wagaman, 2005) where companies threw employee hours, external consultants, and investments into the compliance effort without a full vision of what it should contain. Accordingly companies reported that the costs of SOX compliance were significant (Charles River & Associates, 2005). However, SOX compliance is a continuous effort that requires it to be integrated into business processes, policies, and information systems.

The implementation process of SOX has not been explored much in the literature. Some of the case studies that have looked at how companies have structured the implementation process show that it includes the following steps (Kendal, 2004; Matyjewicz & D'Arcangelo, 2004).

Preparation

1. Ensure management support: Given that SOX compliance in many cases is seen as a burden and non-value adding, ensuring management support and allocation of resources is crucial to the compliance effort. This includes top management as well as various involved functional managers.
2. Project planning involves planning the engagement, such as use of employee time, external consultants, roll-out plans, deadlines, milestones, accountability, and reporting obligations.

Identification and Documentation

1. Identify key accounts and controls: Includes identifying the key financial statement G/L accounts that should be examined.

2. Process identification and documentation focusing on those processes that affect the key G/L accounts: This could be, for example, revenue processes, payment of loans, and cost write-offs.
3. Control identification and documentation, where the controls that are in place are described and linked to processes and key accounts. This includes, for example, reconciliations, reviews, segregation of duties, and independent audits.

Assessment

1. Process assessment: This focuses on evaluating the processes identified regarding how they are described—that is, walkthroughs that compare the actual process flow to the description.
2. Control assessment: Both primary and secondary controls are tested, and/or third-party documentation or tests of these controls are reviewed.
3. Independent auditor assessment: SOX requires independent auditors to assess management reports regarding the reliability of internal controls.

Reporting

1. Internal reporting: The results of the compliance effort have to be reported to management in internal management reports. The experiences obtained through the compliance effort are disseminated among relevant employees.
2. External reporting: SOX required reports (404 reports and auditor assessments) that are to be included in annual reports.

Looking at the global company, SOX compliance has several implications:

1. SOX affects subsidiaries if the performance of these has a material impact on the consolidated financial statement. It does not matter where in the world these subsidiaries are located or what local accounting regulations are in place, SOX has to be complied with.

2. If the company has outsourced significant parts of its operations and these have a potential impact on the accounting systems, the control system, or on postings in the financial statements, the implementation process has to reflect this.

3. SOX compliance implies standardization of the internal control system regardless of business processes being addressed or where they are located—that is to say, standardization of descriptions, definitions, testing procedures, and evaluation criteria.

4. If the company is using a global ERP system, then SOX compliance will reflect this by drawing on common functionalities for supporting business process control.

Control involves checking, comparing, monitoring, and taking action when results do not match. Control systems also cost money. As this cost is a non-product-related overhead, there is an incitement to minimize it by making control systems as effective and non-disruptive as possible. Today information technology plays an increasingly important role in automating controls and thus increasing their effectiveness and efficiency (CFO, 2005). Lately compliance efforts in companies also have focused on making the compliance process more effective and efficient through the use of automated controls and IT controls (ACL, 2005). A survey by CFO (2005) show that after the first two years of SOX compliance, companies focus on making the Sarbanes-Oxley compliance process more effective and efficient. According to the respondents, remediation and optimization efforts will primarily focus on:

- Overall control structures and key controls
- Underlying business processes
- Monitoring
- Manual controls such as reconciliations and reviews
- Segregation of duties
- Risk assessment
- Application controls such as edit and validation checks
- Internal audit effectiveness
- Information and communication

In many companies first-year implementation focused on better documentation. However, the biggest gains in effectiveness and efficiency of controls are achieved by focusing on what financial control is all about—that is, testing, monitoring, and following up on control results and integrating these activities into business processes and workflows (Waldman, 2005).

SOX COMPLIANCE AND ERP SYSTEMS

It could be argued that at its core the Sarbanes-Oxley Act is about data quality. The act sets up mechanisms that aim to secure certain levels of financial data quality and minimize the risk of reported financial information being unintentionally or intentionally misleading. Most modern companies could not function without using information technology for capturing, processing, and reporting data. Therefore, IT is of crucial importance in complying with SOX, both as a part of the initial compliance project and as an integral part of the ongoing compliance process. The PCAOB Auditing Standard includes numerous references to information systems and states that "the nature and characteristics of a company's use of information technology in its information system affect the company's internal control over financial reporting" (PCAOB, 2002, p. 12).

Few IT innovations have had as much impact on business organizations in recent years as ERP systems (Davenport, Harris, & Cantrell, 2004). Such systems are comprehensive off-the-shelf application systems that offer integrated functionalities that support and integrate most business processes, such as accounting, sales, purchasing, and production. It is estimated that organizations worldwide spend approximately US$18.3 billion every year on ERP systems (Shanks, Seddon, & Willcocks, 2003). These systems have significant implications for internal control in general (Elmes, Strong, & Volkoff, 2004) and controls related to accounting and auditing in particular (Rikhardsson, Rohde, & Rom, 2006; CFO, 2005; Granlund & Mouritsen, 2003; ITGI, 2004; Bae & Ashcroft, 2004; Little & Best, 2003; Best, 2000).

All ERP systems have integrated modules. To illustrate, modules in mySAP such as financial accounting (FI) and management accounting (CO) are fully integrated in that postings of expenses in financial accounting also result in postings to cost centers in management accounting. Other modules in areas such as sales (SD–Sales & Distribution) or procurement (MM–Materials Management) automatically generate appropriate accounting postings to financial accounting and to management accounting, for instance in the case of procurement transactions. Integrated modules also share data. For example, the procurement module registers purchase orders involving vendors who have been assigned master records within financial accounting. In addition, within financial accounting, accounts payable and the general ledger share data structures that record vendor transactions and their corresponding postings to the accounts payable reconciliation (control) account in the general ledger. ERP systems provide extensive reporting facilities within each module and support integrated views of operational data through data warehouses and advanced reporting tools.

Information systems, including ERP integrated and non-integrated accounting information systems, face threats which can be grouped into four categories (Gelinas, Sutton, & Hunton, 2005; Romney & Steinbart, 2004):

1. Natural and man-made disasters including storms, earthquakes, and wars
2. Software errors and hardware malfunctions
3. Unintentional acts including errors caused by human carelessness, omissions, logic errors, and misplaced data
4. Intentional acts including fraud and sabotage

The Sarbanes-Oxley Act focuses mainly on the last two categories. Internal controls in ERP systems are focused on mitigating these threats. Apart from the control activities mentioned above in the context of the COSO framework, certain system reliability control objectives become relevant for information systems including ERPs (ITGI, 2005, 2004):

- Availability of the system when needed
- Security of the system against unauthorized physical and logical access
- Maintainability of the system as required without affecting its availability, security, and integrity
- Integrity of the system to ensure that data entry and processing are complete, accurate, timely, and authorized

Table 2 shows how the above system reliability control objectives can be related to SOX requirements.

To illustrate the above, the next section examines how the above ERP functionalities—data integrity, access security, and monitoring and testing of internal controls—are conducted in a specific ERP solution: mySAP ERP.

Table 2. ERP functionalities and SOX requirements

Section of SOX	Requirements	System Reliability Control Objectives
301	Establish a process for anonymous complaints of employees to audit committee (SOX, 2002, p. 32)	Maintainability: Monitoring internal controls
302	Establish the responsibility of the company signing officers (the CEO and the CFO) for setting up an internal control system, evaluating the effectiveness of this control system, and making public the results of the evaluation (SOX, 2002, p. 33)	Securing integrity of data Ensuring access security Maintainability: Monitoring internal controls
401	Require financial reports to reflect all adjustments identified by auditors. All off-balance sheet transactions must be disclosed and pro forma figures must be reconciled with Generally Accepted Accounting Principles figures.	Securing integrity of data Ensuring access security Maintainability: Monitoring internal controls
404	Require that the annual report contains an internal control report which must: • State the responsibility of management for establishing and maintaining an adequate internal control structure and procedures for financial reporting; and • Contain an assessment, as of the end of the most recent fiscal year of the issuer, of the effectiveness of the internal control structure and procedures of the issuer for financial reporting. The external auditing form is to attest to and report on this report (SOX, 2002, p. 45).	Securing integrity of data
409	Obligation to report on rapidly changing financial conditions to the public (SOX, 2002, p. 47)	Maintainability: Monitoring internal controls

SARBANES-OXLEY COMPLIANCE AND MYSAP ERP

mySAP ERP

SAP is one of the world's leading ERP vendors with approximately a 20% global market share and €9,400 million ($12,300 million) revenue in 2006. SAP employs more than 35,000 people in more than 50 countries and services over 32,000 customers worldwide (SAP, 2006).

The mySAP ERP solution combines complete and scalable software for enterprise resource planning with a flexible, open technology platform that can leverage and integrate SAP and non-SAP systems.

mySAP ERP builds on and extends functionalities in earlier SAP solutions, which have been on the market since the 1970s. SAP offers integrated modules for accounting, production planning, materials management, sales and distribution, quality management, project management, and more (SAP, 2005a). mySAP ERP is a complex system enabling companies to integrate most financial, human, asset, and data management tasks in one comprehensive IT infrastructure (SAP, 2005a). The mySAP ERP solution framework includes four individual solutions. These are mySAP ERP Financials, mySAP ERP Human Capital Management, mySAP ERP Operations, and mySAP ERP Corporate Services.

mySAP ERP Financials provides accounting-related functionalities, including legal financial reporting, segment reporting, international accounting standards compliance, parallel recording in multiple currencies, accounts receivable, accounts payable, fixed assets, cost center and profit center accounting, planning, and control. A supplementary module to mySAP ERP Financials is the SAP Strategic Enterprise Management or SAP-SEM (SAP, 2004). It includes consolidated financial reporting, planning, budgeting, and forecasting corporate performance management and scorecards.

In 2007 SAP located different compliance-related functionalities in SAP under a common heading: SAP Governance, Risk, and Compliance (GRC). The functionalities include[1]:

1. **SAP GRC repository:** This module centrally manages all GRC content, based on internal corporate policies and document.

2. **SAP GRC corporate sustainability management:** Functionalities for generating sustainability related key performance indicators by using generally applicable functionalities such as best practice templates.

3. **SAP GRC risk management:** Functionalities for identifying risk and conducting risk analysis, response, monitoring, and reporting.

4. **SAP GRC access control:** Functionalities for managing access and authorizations.

5. **SAP GRC process control:** Functionality for monitoring key controls for business processes and cross-enterprise IT systems.

6. **SAP GRC global trade services:** Functionalities for managing all foreign trade processes to ensure trade compliance, expedited cross-border transactions, and optimum utilization of trade agreements.

7. **SAP applications for environmental compliance:** Functionalities for managing environmental, occupational, and product safety regulations and compliance activities.

It is notable that a large part of the GRC functionalities are composed of functionalities that have been around for quite some time like the environmental health and safety module, the risk management module, as well as some of the access control functionalities. Furthermore, the corporate sustainability management functionalities to a large extent utilize generic functionalities that can be tailored to any number of issues.

The following focuses on how data integrity, access security, and internal controls monitoring is reflected in mySAP ERP. As the aim is to demonstrate how a specific ERP system could be used in SOX compliance, this only looks at the standard version of mySAP and presumes a "Greenfield" implementation. That is to say we do not take into account any specific company customization or implementation constellations. Furthermore, some of the modules and functionalities described have to be bought and activated separately from the main modules of mySAP.

Securing Integrity of Data

Data integrity controls are the basic internal controls aimed at securing data integrity (Gelinas et al., 2005). These controls have always been available in mySAP (and other ERP systems) but are receiving increasing attention because of corporate SOX compliance efforts (Pricewater-houseCoopers, 2003). Relevant and important to SOX compliance, these functionalities are not specific to the SOX compliance effort and are (or should be) a part of the overall internal control system. In mySAP ERP, these are divided into three major groups, which in mySAP terminology are called inherent controls, configurable controls, and reporting controls:

• Inherent controls are programmed controls that operate automatically, for example to check the validity of entered data. These controls refer to system configuration dynamically.
• Configurable controls are user-defined settings that tailor the way the system operates for the organization, including its organizational structure, chart of accounts, and tax rates.
• Reporting controls are present in mySAP ERP in the form of standard or ad hoc reports that show, for example, changes of account master data, customer master data, and so forth.

The inherent controls provided by mySAP ERP are extensive. Postings are restricted to general ledger accounts by the document type. Input fields are checked to verify that all required data is entered and validity checks are satisfied with reference to the data dictionary. Account numbers must exist in the chart of accounts used by the organization. Postings of transactions to sub-ledgers (accounts receivable and accounts payable) result in automatic postings to the corresponding general ledger reconciliation (control) accounts. Direct postings to these reconciliation accounts are prohibited.

mySAP ERP configurable controls are customizing settings that prescribe how the system should operate to meet the organization's needs. For example, the organization must define its 'fis-cal year' for reporting, such as July to June, and posting periods, in a 'fiscal year variant'. Every posting is assigned to a fiscal year and posting period with reference to this variant. This data is stored with each posting to permit reporting for ranges of posting periods (e.g., monthly or quarterly) and for the entire fiscal year. A 'posting period variant' controls into which fiscal years and posting periods transactions may be posted. Opening and closing posting periods are manual processes usually performed shortly after the beginning of a new month.

Validations are another example of configurable controls. Rules can be set up in the system that will enforce process logic from a SOX point of view. For example, a rule can be set up that stipulates that posting can only take place on certain revenue accounts if the business process in SAP is a system-generated invoice and the business area is in a predefined range. If a posting is made, the system will issue an error message telling the user that the posting is not allowed. Likewise, workflows can be used in order to provide automated routing and escalation of key information with alert capabilities. This helps ensure that the "right work is brought in the right sequence at the right time to the right people." Additionally, it allows process and control owners to monitor deadlines and provides statistics on the length of time to complete work processes, which can determine the workload with regard to individual employees.

Where transactions are entered involving foreign currencies, mySAP ERP refers to its table of exchange rates to convert amounts into local currency (the amounts are also stored in the foreign currency). Alternatively, the current exchange rate can be entered with the transaction. To detect data entry errors, a maximum exchange rate difference (tolerable percentage) can be set which will alert the user to intolerable differences between the rate entered and that stored in the exchange rate table. The system also accommodates the organizational requirement for recurring documents ('standing journal entries'). Routine transactions (e.g., rent payments) which are the same in each posting period may be defined and scheduled for posting.

Regarding reporting controls, in order to control changes in the system, predefined reports can be executed to monitor changes to master data in the system. Reports can show which changes have been made to G/L accounts, customer accounts, vendor accounts, and so forth in order to display changes to critical information. New capabilities for monitoring closing activities allow for managers to control the closing process more easily and provide timely accounting information. Furthermore, the system provides auditing capabilities with audit trails (more on this later) for every transaction, document flows that allow for easy control of the business process, and logging of changes to documents. A great number of reports delivered standard with the system allow for control of the above-mentioned issues, and ad hoc reports can easily be created for controlling changes.

Ensuring Access Security

Security controls allow the definition of authorizations for users in line with their organizational responsibilities and segregation of duties to reduce opportunities for fraud.

Security controls include authorizations as a critical ingredient for the maintenance of security in mySAP ERP. The system uses authorization objects to assign authorizations to users. An authorization object is a template for an authorization. For example, authorizations object *F_SKA1_BUK—G/L Account: Authorization for company codes* requires the specification of two field values: Company Code and Activity. To allow a general ledger supervisor to create a general ledger master record, he or she must be assigned an authorization to create accounts for a specific company code (e.g., Company Code, 2000). Such an authorization is created by assigning these field

values. Authorizations may be classified as general authorizations, organizational authorizations, or functional authorizations.

Profiles relating to an organizational role (e.g., general ledger supervisor) consist of a list of authorizations and links to other profiles. Such profiles are then assigned to users with that role and stored in their user master record along with other data (e.g., password).

A considerable investment in time and resources is required when implementing mySAP ERP. Configuring each module and establishing appropriate user roles and profiles must be performed in the development environment and then tested before transfer to the production system; only then can roles and profiles be assigned to the actual users. Correct configuration of the system is critical as it often proves extremely costly to change the setup at a later date (Bae & Ashcroft, 2004).

Determining whether authorizations have been properly assigned to users may be quite a challenge to those assessing the controls. There are more than 120,000 transaction codes in mySAP ERP, each requiring its own set of authorizations. Management may evaluate and compliance test the organization's security model (Institute of Internal Auditors, 1997; Ernst & Young, 1995). This approach is appropriate when authorizations have been implemented in a structured, well-documented manner. The security model is 'desk-checked' for completeness and proper segregation of duties, and then tested for proper implementation on a 'sample' basis by interrogating authorizations, profiles (or roles), and user master records. All users with the same responsibilities should be assigned the same authorizations and profiles (roles). Proper segregation of organizational responsibilities is a critical concern in this process.

mySAP ERP comes with an authorizations information system, which includes several standard reports that may also prove useful for reviewing authorizations. Examples of standard reports include:

- Users with 'critical' basis authorizations
- Users with 'critical' combinations of authorizations (transaction codes)
- Transaction codes that may be executed by a specified user, profile, authorization, or authorization object
- Comparisons of two user master records, profiles, or authorizations

SAP has recently launched an additional access control functionality under the name SAP access control. This basically incorporates the functionality of the Virsa system which was acquired by SAP in 2006 (SAP, 2005; Virsa Systems, 2005). The system can scan mySAP and match user rights with user activities in the system. This includes a database of segregation of duties rules that are grouped by business process with the possibility of customizing rules according to company needs. This involves a risk assessment and matching risks to transactions. Once rules are created, SAP access control automatically assigns the appropriate SAP authorization objects with suggested values. Finally, the functionality allows users to carry out custom code scanning, analysis of custom tables, and reference user violations alerts.

Maintainability: Monitoring and Testing Internal Controls

SOX compliance is an ongoing process. To ensure continuous compliance, internal controls need to be monitored and tested periodically.

SAP has recently released functionalities for internal controls management under the name of SAP process control for monitoring internal controls and supporting testing and assessments. It includes functionalities for documenting internal controls as well as control processes, control objectives, and the link between risks and controls. This was also originally a part of Virsa, which has been integrated into mySAP. SAP process control helps manage the assessment of the design and effectiveness of controls through identifica-

tion of issues and development, and tracking of remediation plans. It supports roll-up of control assessments and associated findings, and offers access for auditors to the final assessment. The module also includes executive dashboards for managing sign-offs, which gives senior managers better global visibility of the status of Sarbanes-Oxley projects throughout the organization. It includes centralized storage and online access to internal-control processes—which can improve the ability to catalog, distribute, and review internal controls.

An important element in process control can be developing, monitoring, and analyzing audit trails. Extensive audit trails are provided by mySAP ERP, including the security audit log, changes to master records, and accounting audit trails. These permit routine monitoring of controls and user activity. The security audit log facility provides a high-level overview of user activity at the transaction code level. A profile is created and filters are defined specifying which events are recorded in the log. Selected events are stored in a daily audit file on each application server. These audit files are retained until deleted. Filters specify which clients and users are to be monitored. Events may be selected for logging according to audit class (such as log-ons, transaction starts, and user master changes) or according to event class (critical events, important events, or all events). Alternatively, a set of individually selected events may be chosen as a detailed audit configuration. Once the filter(s) and profile are activated, the application server must be restarted and then logging commences.

Changes in master records are stored in two tables: *CDHDR Change Document Headers* and *CDPOS Change Document Items*. Changes include creation and deletion of master records and changes in fields. Each change document header record specifies: client, object class of the master record (e.g., category of vendor, customer, general ledger account, cost center, etc.), object value (i.e., vendor number, cost center code), change document number, user name that made the change, date, time, and transaction code (e.g., FK02 Change Vendor Master Record). For each change document number, there are corresponding change document items in the CDPOS table. Change document items have the following fields: client, object class of the master record (e.g., category of vendor, customer, general ledger account, cost center, etc.), object value (i.e., vendor number, cost center code), and change document number. Changes to users, profiles, and authorizations may also be reviewed using standard reports. The functions that may be performed by a user with a specified role may be listed and investigated. This user master record may then be compared with those of other users with the same role to highlight differences.

Another specific functionality that is related to internal controls monitoring and directly linked to Sarbanes-Oxley compliance is the whistleblower functionality (SAP, 2004, 2005). It enables employees to send anonymous complaints and messages to the audit committee of the company. The whistleblower functionality also offers limited possibilities for analyzing complaints by sorting and marking them.

Yet another element in monitoring of internal controls is the Auditing Information System (AIS). It is usually used by internal auditors and can play a role in the SOX compliance process. The AIS provides management or auditors with a structured menu containing standard control reports for performing system and business audits. The system audit monitors the more technical aspects of the system, for example, tables, authorizations, access statistics, critical combinations of transactions, system configurations, and so forth. The business audit concentrates on the business transactions and can be either account oriented or process oriented.

The structure is role based, providing only the relevant reports and transactions to each individual user based on the assigned role. A menu structure can therefore be generated for

monitoring different business processes and a different structure for monitoring the inherent and configurable controls. For example, users with incomplete address data or users who are dormant may be identified. System-wide security settings (e.g., password length or expiry) and passwords for 'super-users' may be reviewed. Likewise, data can be exported to external analysis software directly from the transaction data tables in mySAP ERP, thus enhancing the auditing capabilities. This applies to document line items, account balances, customer open items, vendor open items, and so on.

Another important set of functionalities in mySAP that could become relevant to auditing SOX compliance is consolidation (found in the strategic enterprise management or SEM module). Consolidating data from different subunits is subject to the basic controls mentioned above, but in addition SEM consolidation includes controlled consolidation from other systems, which becomes important for securing data quality when not all subunits use SAP. SEM consolidation also offers complete drill down audit trails to levels of both business units in the consolidation chains and individual documents.

The SEM consolidation module also enables identification of auditors' material adjustments as a separate document type and posting period, which is important in complying with SOX section 401. Likewise the SEM consolidation module enables the usage of alternative versions in order to support the calculation of effects of off-balance sheet transactions on the group financial statement. Comparison reporting and analysis of final financial statements and key figures can be performed.

FUTURE TRENDS

It is notable that ERP vendors have been relatively slow in responding to the need for compliance functionalities. SAP has only recently collected its compliance support functionalities under one heading, and other ERP vendors are following suit. As such SAPs functionalities are not new but a collection of old, existing functionalities and of third-party products that have been bought and integrated into mySAP. This development seems similar to the one in, for example, business analytics, where third-party products like Siebel and Cognos were strong in the market before the ERP vendors began to focus on data analysis and reporting as well as data registration.

Compliance support in ERP systems might evolve in the same manner as the business analytics, with many small vendors initially offering a variety of solutions. Currently there are a number of non-ERP vendors on the market who offer compliance systems for specific legislation or other compliance areas such as quality management or environmental management.[2] In the last two years, numerous products have also been marketed for SOX compliance (Markham & Hamerman, 2005). When the market grows, the established ERP vendors will become interested, and new compliance functionalities will emerge and new modules will be added to existing ERP suites.

Information technology in general and ERP systems in particular can affect performance-related issues such as coordination costs, span of control, decision times, and fragmentation of information. Compliance spans across business processes, organizational units, and geographical boundaries making these issues important. It is therefore likely that compliance practice and compliance performance will become more dependent upon information technology support in the future. Seeing how SOX compliance is reflected in the solutions offered by SAP, it is likely that future ERP development will include a broader compliance focus than just SOX compliance. It seems logical that ERP vendors will develop comprehensive and integrated compliance functionalities within the ERP solution framework, merging the variety of system functionalities currently supporting com-

pliance with, for example, environment, health and safety regulations, quality management, labor laws, and food safety regulations.

CONCLUSION

Compliance as such seems to be changing. The emergence of wide-reaching legislation such as SOX has spurred an interest in compliance management as a corporate function. Companies are hiring compliance managers and looking into how compliance management and processes can be standardized and harmonized across organizational and geographical boundaries. Compliance is seen as something that can even create competitive advantage if it is done more effectively and more efficiently than the competitor.

Sarbanes-Oxley is here to stay. Not only in the U.S., but also in other parts of the world, it seems to be having effects. For example, Germany and Australia have enacted similar changes in accounting regulations (Commonwealth of Australia, 2002; PricewaterhouseCoopers, 2003; Breandle & Noll, 2005). The 8th EU directive shows influences from the Sarbanes-Oxley legislation regarding auditor roles and independence. Developing and maintaining internal control systems are becoming something companies will focus on for years to come, even though they are not required to comply with SOX.

It goes without saying that internal controls are not the primary activity of business. The challenge is to reach a level of control that achieves the control objectives of the company without disrupting the primary objective of the company, which is to create value for its stakeholders. In creating and delivering value, modern companies are to a large extent dependent on information technology. The main conclusion of this chapter is that ERP systems provide the company with basic internal control functionalities as well as a framework for internal control management. As illustrated by mySAP, developing an effective and efficient internal control system is dependent on an intelligent integration of control activities and information technology.

FUTURE RESEARCH DIRECTIONS

Compliance is a broad concept including legal compliance such as SOX and environmental laws, compliance with internal policies, and compliance with voluntary standards such as ISO 9000 standards. The use of information technology in compliance and impacts on management practices and performance are interesting research areas. In this context, some interesting research questions could be:

- How are organizational accountability structures for global, regional, and local compliance evolving, and how are they managed?
- How does compliance affect corporate performance on local, regional, and global levels?
- Who are the various constituencies that have an interest in the performance of compliance and risk management, and how do companies address these concerns?
- What is the cost of compliance and how does IT affect these costs?
- How much do automation and integration in ERP systems affect the effectiveness and efficiency of internal control systems?

REFERENCES

Atkinson, J., & Leandri, S. (2005). Organizational structure that supports compliance. *Financial Executive,* (December), 36-40.

ACL Services Ltd. (2005). *Sarbanes-Oxley section 404 compliance survey release.* Retrieved May 11, 2006, from http://www.acl.com/solutions/sarbanes-oxley.aspx?bhcp=1

Bae, B., & Ashcroft, P. (2004). Implementation of ERP systems: Accounting and auditing implications. *Information System Control Journal, 5,* 43-48.

Baker, R., Bealing, W.E. Jr., Nelson, D.A., & Blair Staley, A. (2006). An institutional perspective of the Sarbanes-Oxley Act. *Managerial Auditing Journal, 21*(1), 23-33.

Best, P. (2000). Auditing SAP R/3—Control risk assessment. *Australian Accounting Review, 10*(3), 31-42.

Breandle, U., & Noll, J. (2005). A fig leaf for the naked corporation. *Journal of Management and Governance, 9,* 79-99.

Byington, J.R., & Christensen, J.A. (2005). SOX 404: How do you control your internal controls? *Journal of Corporate Accounting and Finance,* (May/June), 35-40.

Cannon, D.M., & Growe, G.A. (2004). SOA compliance: Will IT sabotage your efforts? *Journal of Corporate Accounting & Finance,* (July/August), 31-37.

CFO. (2005). *Compliance and technology: A special report on process improvement and automation in the age of Sarbanes-Oxley.* Retrieved March 20, 2006, from http://www.pwc.com

Chenhall, R. (2003). Management control systems design within its organizational context: Findings from contingency-based research and directions for the future. *Accounting, Organizations and Society, 28*(2-3), 127-168.

Commonwealth of Australia. (2002). *Corporate disclosures: Strengthening the financial reporting framework.* Retrieved March 20, 2006, from http://www.treasury.gov.au/contentitem.asp?NavId=&ContentID=403

COSO (Committee of Sponsoring Organizations). (1992). *Internal control—integrated framework.* Retrieved February 26, 2006, from http://www.coso.org

COSO. (2004). *Enterprise risk management.* Retrieved February 26, 2006, from http://www.coso.org

Charles River & Associates. (2005). *Sarbanes-Oxley section 404: Costs and remediation of deficiencies: Estimates from a sample of Fortune 1000 companies.* Retrieved March 1, 2006, from http://www.crai.com

du Plessis, J., McConvill, J., & Bagaric, M. (2005). *Principles of contemporary corporate governance.* Cambridge: Cambridge University Press.

Davenport, T.H., Harris, J.G., & Cantrell, S. (2004). Enterprise systems and ongoing process change. *Business Process Management Journal, 10*(1), 16-26.

Elmes, M., Strong, D., & Volkoff, O. (2005). Panoptic empowerment and reflective conformity in enterprise systems-enabled organizations. *Information and Organization, 15*(1), 1-37.

Ernst & Young. (1995). *Audit, control, and security features of SAP R/3.*

Fox, C. (2004). Sarbanes-Oxley—Considerations for a framework for IT financial reporting controls. *Information Systems Controls Journal, 1,* 1-3.

Gelinas, U.J., Sutton, S.G., & Hunton, J.E. (2005). *Accounting information systems* (6th ed.). Thomson, OH: South-Western.

Granlund, M., & Mouritsen, J. (2003). Introduction: Problematizing the relationship between management control and information technology. *European Accounting Review, 12*(1), 77-83.

IMJ. (2004). AMR research 2004: Compliance costs are rising. *Information Management Journal,* (November/December), 6.

Institute of Internal Auditors. (1997). *SAP R/3: Its use, control, and audit.* Altamonte Springs, FL: Institute of Internal Auditors Research Foundation.

ITGI (IT Governance Institute). (2004). *IT control objectives for Sarbanes-Oxley.* Rolling Meadows, IL. Retrieved March 1, 2006, from http://www.isaca.org

ITGI. (2005). *COBIT 4.0: Control objectives for information and related technology.* Rolling Meadows, IL. Retrieved March 1, 2006, from http://www.isaca.org

Kendal, K. (2004). A 10 step Sarbanes-Oxley solution. *Internal Auditor,* (December), 51-55.

Little, A., & Best, P. (2003). A framework for separation of duties in SAP R/3. *Managerial Auditing Journal, 18*(5), 419-430.

McNally, S., & Wagaman, D. (2005). *Hard climb is done, but trek continues: Sarbanes-Oxley compliance in year two and beyond.* Retrieved May 11, 2006, from http://www.ascpa.com/public/pressroom/azcpa.aspx?a=view&id=249

Markham, R., & Hamerman, P. (2005). *The Forrester Wave™: Sarbanes-Oxley compliance software. Evaluation of top SOX software vendors across 58 criteria.* Retrieved March 1, 2006, from http://www.forrester.com

Matyjewicz, G., & D'Arcangelo, J. (2004). Beyond Sarbanes Oxley. *Internal Auditor,* (October), 67-72.

PCAOB (Public Company Accounting Oversight Board). (2004). *Auditing standard no. 2—an audit of internal control over financial reporting performed in conjunction with an audit of financial statements.* Retrieved March 23, 2006, from http://www.pcaobus.org/Rules/Docket_008/index.aspx

PricewaterhouseCoopers. (2003). *Sarbanes Oxley—Internal control solutions framework.* Retrieved March 3, 2006, from http://www.pwc.com

Rikhardsson, P., Rohde, C., & Rom, A. (2006). Management control in enterprise system enabled organizations: A literature review. *Journal of Corporate Ownership and Control, 4*(2), 233-242.

Romney, M., & Steinbart, P. (2003). *Accounting information systems*. Upper Saddle River, NJ: Prentice Hall.

SAP. (2004a). *SAP service select Web seminar. SAP Sarbanes-Oxley*. Retrieved March 20, 2006, from http://www.sap.com

SAP. (2004b). *Strategic enterprise management—An overview*. Retrieved March 20, 2006, from http://www.sap.com

SAP. (2005a). *MySAP ERP functionalities—Overview*. Retrieved March 20, 2006, from http://www.sap.com

SAP. (2005b). *Enterprise governance and Sarbanes-Oxley compliance with mySAP ERP Financials*. Retrieved March 20, 2006, from http://www.sap.com

SAP. (2006). *Company information*. Retrieved April 3, 2006, from http://www.sap.com

Shanks, G., Seddon, P.B., & Willcocks, L.P. (Eds.). (2003). *Second-wave enterprise resource planning systems: Implementing for effectiveness*. Cambridge: Cambridge University Press.

Shue, L. (2004). Sarbanes Oxley and IT outsourcing. *Information System Audit and Control Association, 5*, 43-49.

Virsa Systems. (2005). *SAP compliance calibrator—White paper*. Retrieved March 20, 2006, from http://www.virsasystems.com

Waldman, M. (2005). *Operationalizing Sarbanes-Oxley: How to leverage Sarbanes-Oxley to add value to business operations*. Retrieved January 3, 2006, from http://www.percipiogroup.com

ADDITIONAL READING

Alles, M., Kogan, A., & Vasarhelyi, M.A. (2002). Feasibility and economics of continuous assurance. *Auditing, 21*(1), 126-138.

Bae, B., & Ashcroft, P. (2004). Implementation of ERP systems: Accounting and auditing implications. *Information System Control Journal, 5*, 43-56.

Bhimani, A. (Ed.). (2003). *Management accounting in the digital economy*. Oxford: Oxford University Press.

Caglio, A. (2003). Enterprise resource planning systems and accountants: Towards hybridization? *European Accounting Review, 12*(1), 123-153.

Chapman, C. (2005). Not because they are new. Developing the contribution of enterprise resource planning systems to management control research. *Accounting, Organizations and Society, 30*, 685-689.

Gerber, M., & Solms, R. (2005). Management of risk in the information age. *Computers & Security, 24*, 16-30.

Scapens, R., & Jazayeri, M. (2003). ERP systems and management accounting change: Opportunities or impacts? A research note. *European Accounting Review, 12*(1), 201-233.

Searcy, D., & Woodroof, J.B. (2003). Continuous auditing: Leveraging technology. *The CPA Journal*, (May), 46-48.

Spathis, C. (2006). Enterprise systems implementation and accounting benefits. *Journal of Enterprise Information Management, 19*(1), 67-82.

Spathis, C., & Constantinides, S. (2004). Enterprise resource planning systems' impact on accounting processes. *Business Process Management Journal, 10*(2), 234-247.

Sutton, S. (2000). The changing face of accounting in an information technology dominated world. *International Journal of Accounting Information Systems, 1,* 1-8.

Sutton, S. (2006). Extended-enterprise systems' impact on enterprise risk management. *Journal of Enterprise Information Management, 19*(1), 97-114.

Wieder, B., Booth, P., Matolcsy, Z., & Ossimitz, M. (2006). The impact of ERP systems on firm and business process performance. *Journal of Enterprise Information Management, 19*(1), 13-29.

ENDNOTES

1.   http://www.sap.com/solutions/grc/index.epx (accessed March 2007)

2.   See for example, www.ess-home.com, www.etq.com, www.openpages.com, www.businessplans.org (accessed March 20, 2007)

Chapter XIII
ERP Systems Effectiveness in Implementing Internal Controls in Global Organizations

Vinod Kumar
Carleton University, Canada

Raili Pollanen
Carleton University, Canada

Bharat Maheshwari
University of Windsor, Canada

ABSTRACT

This chapter examines the effectiveness of ERP systems in implementing internal controls in global organizations, particularly controls required by the Sarbanes-Oxley Act (U.S. Congress, 2002), or SOX. It aims to understand the extent to which ERP systems are able to meet these requirements and challenges organizations face in enhancing their ERP systems for this purpose. The chapter reports the results of interviews with ERP systems managers and directors in four organizations with significant global operations. It reveals a substantial degree of completion of SOX requirements by these organizations, often facilitated by consultants, and often accomplished as part of broader systems, processes, and strategic management improvement initiatives. It also highlights some significant technical and cultural implementation challenges, such as systems inflexibility and diversity, systems security weaknesses, and resistance to change, as well as some benefits upon completion, such as improved process efficiency and systems security, and potential intangible long-term benefits.

INTRODUCTION

The need for increased reliability and relevance of accounting and control information has long been recognized (Kaplan, 1984). The increasing popularity and adoption of both advanced information technology-based enterprise resource planning (ERP) systems, such as SAP R/3, and modern performance measurement and control systems, such as the balanced scorecard (Kaplan & Norton, 1996), have been considered as an organizational response to this need. During the past few years, this need has gained critical importance due to new internal control requirements imposed by the Sarbanes-Oxley Act (U.S. Congress, 2002), often called SOX. SOX imposed stringent internal control requirements over financial reporting following prominent business scandals, such as those involving Enron and WorldCom, in an effort to improve corporate governance and regain investor confidence. SOX stipulated management's and auditors' responsibilities for internal controls over financial reporting in public organizations. In addition to U.S.-owned public corporations, many multinational non-U.S. corporations that operate in the global business environment are also listed on U.S. stock exchanges and, as such, are also subject to SOX requirements.

ERP systems provide critical technical tools and solutions for collecting, analyzing, and reporting relevant financial and non-financial information for implementing SOX compliance. However, ERP systems, and regulations themselves, are dynamic and continuously evolving (Bititci, Turner, & Begemann, 2000). For example, new technological developments and organizational learning can provide needs and opportunities for redesign and continuous development of ERP systems. New knowledge and organizational learning can provide ways for organizations to respond to uncertainties in the global environment (Harrison & Leitch, 2000). In addition, regulatory requirements can vary in different environments

and evolve in multiple stages as experience grows (Bratton, 2003) and also require further systems modifications. Such dynamic environments can require innovative approaches and continuous monitoring, evaluation, and complex adjustments to controls, processes, and systems. Nonetheless, little guidance or models exist to help systems managers and researchers understand control implementation challenges and enhance ERP systems for control purposes in competitive global organizations.

This chapter addresses such a void by examining the effectiveness of ERP systems in implementing internal controls in global organizations. It aims to understand the extent to which ERP systems are able to meet control requirements imposed by SOX in global organizations and challenges organizations face in enhancing their ERP systems specifically for this purpose. In order to identify and understand these issues, interviews were conducted with ERP systems managers and directors in four organizations with significant global operations. This chapter reports qualitative exploratory findings of these interviews. As such, it provides systems managers some insight into successes and challenges in enhancing ERP systems for SOX compliance, which in turn can ultimately contribute to best practices and long-term organizational effectiveness. It can also serve as a basis for developing a comprehensive model of ERP systems effectiveness in implementing internal controls in future research.

The remainder of this chapter is organized into five main sections. The next section provides a background on internal controls, implementing internal controls using ERP systems, and implementation challenges in global organizations. In the following three sections, the method, results, and future trends are presented and discussed in turn. Finally, an overall summary of the chapter, concluding remarks, and future research directions are presented.

BACKGROUND

In order to comply with SOX requirements, ERP systems must be capable of handling new and evolving control and information needs. Effective control implementations may require significant enhancements to ERP systems (Colman, 2006; Damianides, 2004; Chan, 2004). However, technical systems enhancements can also be complicated by adjustments required to organizational structures, processes, norms, and employee skills. Such efforts can be further complicated in global organizations by differences in geographic distances, culture, language, existing technology and systems, and political and regulatory environments in different countries. Inadequate attention to any of these factors can pose serious challenges for successful control implementations. This section examines typical internal control requirements, implementing internal controls using ERP systems, and implementation challenges in global organizations.

Internal Control in Global Organizations

Internal controls consist of rules, procedures, and systems to ensure the efficiency and effectiveness of operations, reliability of financial reporting, safeguarding of assets, and compliance with laws and regulations (Simons, 2000). In addition to maintaining adequate records, they include segregation of duties, insuring and bonding employees, restricting access to data and assets, and conducting regular independent reviews. Internal controls are a part of a broader set of controls and measures in performance measurement systems (PMS), which provide performance measures and other control mechanisms for ensuring the achievement of strategic objectives in an efficient and effective manner. Simons (2000, p. 769) defines PMS as "information systems that managers use to track the implementation of business strategy by comparing actual results against strategic

goals and objectives." This chapter is limited to addressing only the internal control aspects of PMS as mandated by SOX. SOX regulations were enacted to improve investor confidence in corporate management and financial reporting following prominent business scandals, such as those involving Enron and WorldCom. As the main objective of SOX is to improve the quality, reliability, and transparency of financial reporting, effective internal controls over financial reporting have become crucial for all public U.S. organizations and many global non-U.S. organizations.

Although SOX is a legislation enacted in the United States, global organizations that trade on U.S. stock exchanges and foreign subsidiaries of U.S. organizations must also comply with it, bringing most large global organizations within the scope of SOX regulations. In addition, regulators in other countries—for example, Canadian provincial securities regulators and the European Union (EU)—are in the process of implementing similar regulations and guidelines. Although the proposed Canadian rules are somewhat weaker than the U.S. rules, they require equal managerial effort in implementing and certifying the effectiveness of internal controls (Canadian Securities Administrators, 2006). The EU also recently issued a directive enhancing collective management and board responsibility for annual reports and financial statements of public organizations (European Parliament & Council, 2006). Although the regulation and enforcement are responsibilities of member countries, the intent of the directive is similar to that of the North American regulations, as the EU also established the Committee of European Securities Regulators to improve coordination among European securities regulators and to advise the EU on securities measures. As a result, most Western global organizations and their subsidiaries around the world are subject to some regulations on internal controls over financial reporting.

The most extensive requirements of SOX, with the broadest implications for ERP systems, are those in Section 404, which requires senior management to establish and maintain adequate internal controls over financial reporting, assess the effectiveness of controls, and certify and report the conclusions of assessments. In addition, it requires independent auditors to certify and report on the adequacy of management's internal control assessments. An internal control framework developed by the Committee of Sponsoring Organizations of Treadway Commission (COSO, 1992, 2004) has been used almost exclusively as a conceptual foundation for implementing internal controls required by SOX (KPMG, 2003; Damianides, 2004; Brown & Nasuti, 2005).[1] It

is often combined with the COBIT framework for evaluating control over IT processes (IT Governance Institute, 2004, 2006), discussed in the next section. The COSO framework provides general principles for effective internal controls but does not prescribe what should be reported. It identifies five control components: control environment, risk assessment, control activities, information and communication, and monitoring. Some examples of control mechanisms for each component are provided in Table 1.

In order to comply with SOX requirements, the design and operating effectiveness of significant internal controls for each component need

Table 1. Control components and objectives (based on Committee of Sponsoring Organizations of Treadway Commission, 1992)

Control Component	Objective	Examples
Control Environment	To set structures and processes for organizational operations	• Organizational norms • Ethical values • Staff competencies • Management philosophy and style
Risk Assessment	To manage operational and environmental risks	• Environmental scanning • Risk management frameworks • Forecasting models
Control Activities	To ensure achievement of organizational objectives	• Approvals • Authorizations • Verifications • Reconciliations • Performance reviews • Systems and asset security • Segregation of duties
Information and Communication	To ensure individuals have information necessary to perform their responsibilities	• Collecting information • Analyzing information • Informal communication of information • Formal reports
Monitoring	To ensure the quality of internal controls over time	• Ongoing monitoring of systems performance • Supervision of employee activities • Monitoring of control compliance • Periodic effectiveness evaluations

to be evaluated, certified, reported, and audited. Successful implementation of SOX compliance follows a typical process-oriented approach, characteristic to managing any major project, including ERP/IT systems implementations (Chafee, 1985). A common process-oriented approach identifies a set of sequential processes, through which organizations pass when implementing such projects. SOX implementation guidance by KPMG (2003) outlines six major processes: plan and scope evaluation, document controls, evaluate design and operating effectiveness, identify and correct deficiencies, report on internal controls, and audit internal controls. These processes are based on

the COSO (1992) framework. A brief description of the six major SOX implementation processes is provided in Table 2. In global organizations, many of these processes are implemented using ERP systems.

Implementing Internal Controls in Global Organizations Using ERP Systems

ERP systems play a critical role in supporting effective implementation and operation of internal controls. ERP systems are comprehensive packaged software applications that automate

Table 2. SOX implementation processes (adapted from KPMG, 2003)

Process	Examples
Plan and Scope Evaluation	• Determines significant controls and business units to be included • Establishes control evaluation processes • Defines project approach, milestones, timetable, and resources • Assigns responsibilities • Provides training • Establishes policies, procedures, and communication channels
Document Controls	• Establishes company-wide documentation standards • Documents design of and processes for significant controls • Documents responsibilities and authorities for controls and processes
Evaluate Design and Operating Effectiveness	• Tests significant controls • Evaluates design and operating effectiveness of controls • Documents results of evaluations
Identify and Correct Deficiencies	• Identifies, accumulates, and evaluates design and operating control deficiencies • Provides sufficient evidence of control deficiencies • Documents reasons for control deficiencies • Communicates findings of evaluations • Corrects control deficiencies
Report on Internal Controls	• Prepares management's written certification on effectiveness of controls • Discloses significant control deficiencies and material weaknesses • Reports to the audit committee and independent auditors
Audit Internal Controls	• Allows independent external auditors to evaluate design effectiveness of controls • Tests operating effectiveness of controls • Certifies management's assertion about control effectiveness

and integrate organizational business processes across functional areas. Recognized as one of the most significant and widely adopted innovations in management information systems (Al-Mashari, 2002), ERP systems mark a major shift from proprietary made-to-order or homegrown legacy systems to generic off-the-shelf and vendor-developed applications (Davenport, 2000). ERP systems provide organizations with an environment for process remodeling and introducing best practices. Organizations, however, cannot just depend on advanced information technologies to produce competitive advantage and business benefits (Powell & Dent-Micallef, 1997). The implementation of information technology to support business processes in innovative ways, and the development of complementary business and human resources to exploit the new capabilities are critical for deriving sustainable long-term business benefits from ERP systems.

ERP systems are widely credited with providing organizations with abilities to process, track, analyze, and integrate large amounts of information from multiple functional areas, such as sales, marketing, production, and accounting, as well as from external sources (Rizzi & Zamboni, 1999; Davenport & Brooks, 2004; Shang & Seddon, 2002). As such, they effectively record accounting transactions, track key performance measures for evaluating internal controls, report them to individuals responsible, flag any violations for investigation, and provide a platform for benchmarking such information—for example, using balanced scorecards (Kaplan & Norton, 1996) or other similar control and reporting frameworks. ERP systems thus enable organizations to reduce data processing costs and to provide more frequent, timely, and integrated financial and non-financial reports to management, regulators, and auditors on control compliance (Matolcsy, Booth, & Wieder, 2005).

Complying with SOX regulations may require significant additional design, evaluation, and reporting features in ERP systems of most

organizations (Colman, 2006; Damianides, 2004; Chan, 2004). Although relatively little additional effort may be needed to meet SOX requirements in organizations with strong existing internal controls, Colman (2006) described experiences of several recent SOX implementers, who considered new software applications and technical support critical for successful implementation. Even in organizations with strong existing controls, the certification and audit requirements for control effectiveness are new and require significant additional design, evaluation, and reporting in all organizations subject to SOX. Damianides (2004) argued that advanced information technology provided by ERP systems is critical for feasible development and operation of internal controls required by SOX. Chan (2004) also recognized similar needs and the resultant enormous resource and redesign implications for ERP systems.

The key technical features of ERP systems, which rely heavily on advanced information technology (IT), include scalable client server software architecture, supported by a common relational database and a single development environment. Such features are capable of facilitating real-time integrated processing and management of information across all functional areas, as well as supply chain and customer relationships management (Kumar, Maheshwari, & Kumar, 2003; Davenport, 2000). Integrated real-time information, in turn, is necessary for developing strong controls (Markus & Tanis, 2000; Kumar et al., 2003). The understanding of business processes and policies, and how business processes are related to one another, is important for achieving integration (Kumar, Maheshwari, & Kumar, 2002).

The critical role of IT in SOX compliance in global organizations becomes evident through an example of key activities involved in implementing SOX requirements. For example, global organizations need a centralized and collaborative system to document their internal controls, processes, and control environment. Documentation on the development, implementation, maintenance, and effectiveness of internal controls should be accessible anytime to relevant employees and process owners across the organization through a secure and auditable system. Advanced IT solutions can help them collaboratively create and manage digital documentation, allowing worldwide access via corporate intranets with a single authentication and access security system. Similarly, monitoring the control environment requires IT features capable of verifying and evaluating systemic controls within the financial systems, flagging control violations, and documenting remedial actions. These objectives can be achieved by building internal control and data integrity checkpoints in the financial modules of ERP systems, or by integrating an external monitoring system with specific event-based controls within the financial modules.

In the IT-driven ERP systems, ensuring effective controls over the IT environment is critical for implementing SOX compliance. The IT Governance Institute (ITGI, 2004, 2006) has developed a framework for evaluating controls over IT processes, called control objectives for information technology (COBIT), which, among other control needs, specifically addresses internal controls required by SOX. The framework provides 34 control objectives grouped into four main domains—plan and organize, acquire and implement, deliver and support, and monitor and evaluate—and maps them against the five COSO (1992) control areas. The framework thus helps align the internal control requirements of SOX and IT features necessary for implementing them. Yet, implementing effective internal controls is not without major challenges in global organizations.

Implementation Challenges in Global Organizations

The characteristics of the global business environment have been subject to some debate in literature. Even before the advent of widespread advanced ERP systems and IT, Porter (1986, p. 12) commented that the term "global" has become "overused and perhaps under-understood," and defined global industries as those "in which the firm's competitive position in one country is significantly influenced by its position in other countries." As such, global industries were seen as linked industries that compete on a worldwide basis and require integration of their global activities. Gibbs, Kraemer, and Dedrick (2003) examined the diffusion of modern e-commence in the global environment and factors affecting successful diffusion. Although they noted different theoretical arguments as to what is meant by global environment, they concluded that: "Globalization is generally regarded as the increased interconnectedness of the world through flows of information, capital, and people facilitated by trade and political openness as well as information technology" (Gibbs et al., 2003, p. 5). Organizations that have operations in several countries are subject to forces of globalization and, for the purposes of this chapter, are considered to be global organizations operating in the global environment.

Several challenges can exist for effective control implementation in global organizations. ERP systems must be capable of accommodating various conditions and information requirements in different countries and environments. For example, Brown and Nasuti (2005) reported problems with data structures, difficulties in ensuring adequate security and business continuity, and variations in infrastructure between business units as the top four obstacles to SOX implementation. In particular, outsourcing programming and network security can impact SOX compliance and need to be carefully managed. Nonetheless, a survey by Deloitte and Touche (cited in Brown & Nasuti, 2005) indicated that "people problems" accounted for almost two-thirds of obstacles to successful ERP implementation. Sohal, Moss, and Ng (2001) found that economic factors, lack of top management support, and difficulty in justifying costs were the main impediments to IT implementation. However, there is some evidence that the most recent ERP applications are better able to accommodate some of these demands. For example, Robinson (2000) noted that the latest ERP systems are designed to address some global needs—for example, to comply with both international and U.S. reporting standards—and to provide real-time financial information to global investors.

Similar evidence is also available from experiences in implementing PMS. For example, Mills, Platts, and Gregory (1995) identified organizational culture as one of the key organizational constraints in implementing manufacturing strategy and processes. Beliefs, values, and expectations embedded in organizational culture evolve slowly and are difficult to change quickly, resulting in reluctance to change. Kennerley and Neely (2002) identified the most important barriers to facilitating PMS evolution to be the lack of effective processes, necessary skills, and human resources; inflexibility of ERP systems; and inappropriate culture. These barriers were manifest in *ad hoc* systems, resistance to change, and the lack of appropriate measures and rewards. Bourne, Neely, Platts, and Mills (2002) examined both drivers and barriers of successful PMS implementations. The two most important drivers of success were top management support and ultimate benefits that exceed costs. The four most important barriers, which successful implementers were able to overcome, were difficulties with data access and information technology; time and effort required to set up systems, collect data, analyze data, and report results; difficulties concerned with developing appropriate measures; and reluctance to implement measures and to report problems. Although these findings relate to PMS implementations in general, they apply equally well to implementing internal controls.

As to internal controls in particular, the global environment can significantly affect the applicability and implementation of regulatory internal controls. Different countries have different rules, accounting standards, and approaches to compliance. For example, the U.S. Securities and Exchange Commission (SEC) recognized, due to pressure from the European Union (EU), that different environments pose important factors that need to be considered in implementing SOX compliance, such as language, culture, organizational structure, and differences in accounting standards. As a result, the SEC postponed its initial implementation timetable for SOX compliance for non-U.S. organizations (U.S. SEC, 2005).

In a summary to the background section, internal controls required by SOX fall within more general control mechanisms embedded in PMS and are implemented through technology available in ERP systems, or enhancements to ERP systems, in most global organizations. However, global organizations need to overcome numerous challenges for successful control implementations. The research design and method are discussed next.

METHOD

This chapter examines the extent to which ERP systems are able to meet the internal control requirements imposed by SOX in global organizations and challenges organizations face in enhancing their ERP systems for SOX compliance. This topic is largely exploratory, as very little previous research exists. A qualitative case study approach is used, as it is valuable for exploring and understanding such complex phenomena in their organizational settings (Yin, 2003). Road maps provided by Eisenhardt (1989), Yin (2003), and Miles and Huberman (1994) can be used to enhance the validity of case study research.

Data were collected through semi-structured focus group and individual interviews with senior systems managers and directors of four multi-site ERP-adopting organizations. One of the organizations is listed on both the New York

Stock Exchange (NYSE) and the Toronto Stock Exchange (TSX), one on both the NYSE and Euronext, and two on the TSX. As such they are required to comply with SOX regulations and/or similar Canadian securities regulations. The effective compliance dates for control compliance in all organizations were for fiscal years ending in 2006 (after July 14, 2006, for SOX and after June 29, 2006, for Canadian regulations). As such, all four organizations must have already implemented significant controls at the time of this study in order to comply with these deadlines. However, none of the organizations were required to have implemented auditor certification requirements, which were subject to extended deadlines (fiscal years ending after July 14, 2007, for SOX only). All four organizations use ERP solutions provided by major vendors (SAP and Oracle), which were in place before beginning the regulatory control implementations. For confidentiality reasons, the organizations cannot be identified, but a brief profile of each organization, labeled A, B, C, and D, is provided in Table 3. The results of the interviews are presented and discussed in the next section.

RESULTS AND DISCUSSION

The results are presented and discussed in this section under four emerging themes: ERP systems characteristics, control implementation processes, control implementation challenges, and control implementation benefits. In order to facilitate the presentation and discussion, the four themes are also subdivided into several sub-themes raised by the respondents. Although the categorization is somewhat subjective, these themes represent the most important perceived issues raised by the respondents.

ERP Systems Characteristics

Technical features of ERP systems play a central role in implementing SOX and internal control compliance in all four organizations studied. In three organizations, the necessary technical enhancements to ERP systems were accomplished as part of broader change management and quality management initiatives. The participants identified three categories of technical characteristics as being particularly important: systems flexibility, systems security, and control adequacy. These characteristics are discussed in this section and some main examples summarized in Table 4.

Systems Flexibility

All four organizations used one of the two major ERP applications (SAP and Oracle), but some modifications were needed to the standard modules to implement some SOX control requirements.

Table 3. Characteristics of sample organizations

Characteristic	Organization A	Organization B	Organization C	Organization D
Operations	Canada and U.S. with some marketing in Europe and Asia	More than 130 countries	Canada and U.S.	Canada, U.S., Europe, and Asia
Industry	Forest Products	Communications	Professional Services	Telecommunications
No. of Employees	More than 10,000	More than 58,000	Approximately 2,200	Approximately 750
ERP Software	Oracle	SAP and Oracle	SAP	SAP
Approximate Sales (US$)	More than 3 billion	More than 10 billion	More than 150 million	More than 150 million

Table 4. ERP systems characteristics

Characteristic	Examples
Systems Flexibility	• ERP applications (SAP and Oracle) required some modifications for SOX. • For some SOX controls, ERP systems modifications would be too costly. • For some SOX controls, technical solutions outside ERP systems are needed. • Some differences exist in flexibility between ERP applications (SAP and Oracle). • Balancing of systems flexibility and adequate controls is needed.
Systems Security	• Process ownership and accountability needed to be established. • Data security needed to be enhanced. • Local "bolt-on" systems are problematic for establishing systems-wide controls.
Control Adequacy	• Many controls are already in place but needed to be formalized and documented. • Additional data input and output controls are needed, for example, security, inventory management, and segregation of duties. • Consultants and/or auditors are used in establishing and documenting controls.

For some control requirements, solutions outside the ERP system were also needed. In some cases, ERP systems were found to be somewhat inflexible, allowing only certain types of modifications. In other cases, the required ERP systems modifications would have been too costly. Some differences in the adaptability and flexibility between SAP and Oracle were also noted. One respondent indicated that once a commitment is made to a certain application, "we are stuck," as it is too complicated and expensive to change to other systems. Another respondent expressed the limitations of ERP systems as follows:

There are several things we can do within the system, which we are doing outside the system now. However, doing them within the system is not easy and straightforward; you cannot achieve it without a lot of customization and programming and workarounds.

Some differences between the ERP applications were expressed by one respondent as follows:

The main issue with [name of application] is…that there was a lot more control put in the users' hands in terms of not just access but also change management. [It] allows more 'open windows' in the access than [name of another application].

In other cases, changes to the ERP systems would have been too costly to warrant their implementation. In these cases, add-on applications were used, as demonstrated by the following comment by one respondent:

In some of the requests…it would have been cost prohibiting for us to make that change right and the benefits of making it didn't outweigh the costs, or the costs outweighed the benefits, so [we had to] get an [outside] solution…to comply with that control objective….

A reasonable degree of systems flexibility is desirable in effective systems in order to reduce excessive "red tape," but it has to be carefully balanced with loss of systems security and control. In other words, an effective balance needs to be struck between flexibility and control.

Systems Security

A particularly important technical issue to all organizations was systems security. Systems security can involve data security (e.g., password-protected data access), asset security (e.g., segregation of duties and inventory control procedures), and physical plant security (e.g., electronic surveillance and restricted entry to buildings). A particular concern for improving systems security was the existence of "bolt-on" systems, which are locally managed applications, not part of the centrally administered ERP systems. Different individuals could make changes to the systems, causing problems for establishing process responsibilities and data security. In one large global organization, "bolt-on" systems posed particular problems, as different ERP applications were used in the operations of some countries. The organization ultimately changed to one application for its SOX implementation in all operations, for the following reasons expressed by the respondent:

We were really surprised to see how much change management...an end user within a functional area outside of IT could do to a system...with the [name of ERP application] that we had in [name of country], there were a lot of 'bolt-on' systems that were also outside the management of your typical IT/IS area....

In another organization, the respondent expressed a similar frustration as follows:

...it was vulnerability of the 'bolt-on' systems into our ERP system. So we changed the access password and we have a compliance of xxx number of characters, and change had to occur 90 days after the first...What happened was that a couple of business communities had 'bolt-on' systems that were serviced outside the IS/IT system that had feeds into our ERP system that we didn't know about.

Any systems security problems would also have obvious negative implications for control adequacy.

Control Adequacy

The respondents from two of the four organizations indicated that adequate systems controls were already in place before beginning SOX implementation, and the major task was formalizing the control systems and documenting the controls and related processes. A respondent from one of these organizations reflected on control adequacy as follows:

A lot of it [control implementation] is formalizing what you already do, at least that is what we found especially in my group because a couple of people who worked for me were consultants, so they are used to documenting...So we always said that we believe what we are doing is right and now it is a matter of documenting it and getting approval....

On the other hand, significant new controls were needed in the other two organizations. In one organization, approximately 60 new control processes were needed, many related to inventory management. In the other, systems security and segregation of duties required attention. The respondent from this organization commented on a need for additional controls as follows:

We had a number of things that were implemented mostly around security. [An] easy way to identify segregation of duty activities was key; also 'sniffing' and monitoring of our systems and more stringent controls around where the data is going and what is coming into our systems, and how they are being accessed in terms of password control and [making] changes....

In a summary of ERP systems characteristics, systems flexibility, systems security, and control adequacy are important characteristics to all four organizations. Combined with appropriate control implementation processes, they contribute to successful control implementations.

Control Implementation Processes

All four organizations used a systematic approach to implementing internal controls. The respondents for the two larger organizations expressed a high degree of completion of SOX requirements, in the 80-95% range for systems and IT, but also recognized that some functional areas still have significant additional work to complete. However, it is notable that one organization suspended its registration with the NYSE for one year, reportedly to "buy another year" to comply with SOX. The degree of completion for the two smaller organizations is somewhat lower, approximately 70%, which is understandable given the extended compliance dates for smaller organizations and for non-U.S. organizations. In this section, examples

of implementation processes in the four organizations are provided, including process analysis, ongoing monitoring processes, and auditing processes. These processes and some examples of each are summarized in Table 5.

Process Analysis

In all four organizations, internal control implementations required the identification, analysis, and evaluation of business processes, and assigning process responsibilities and process ownership. All organizations involved auditors in these processes, and larger organizations also used consultants to analyze and document processes and to design appropriate controls. For evaluating IT controls, all organizations used the COBIT framework (IT Governance Institute, 2004, 2006). Although all organizations were not clear about the specific control requirements when beginning their implementations, the larger organizations appear to have been able to formalize existing

Table 5. Control implementation processes

Implementation	Examples
Process Analysis	• Thorough business process analysis needed first • Process ownership and responsibilities needed to be established • External consultants and/or auditors engaged by all organizations • Ambiguity about control requirements, particularly in early stages • Shifting compliance timelines for some requirements
Monitoring Processes	• Identifying users and their information needs • Monitoring data use patterns • Restricting access on need-to-know basis • Controlling remote access • Adjusting processes and controls based on monitoring
Auditing Processes	• Providing reliable process documentation • Providing transparent audit trail for tracking processes and transactions • Evaluating and reporting control effectiveness • Balancing control tightness, costs, and benefits • Promoting accountability for processes and results

controls and processes, and to implement new processes and controls reasonably quickly, with help from auditors and consultants. However, the smaller organizations still appear to be struggling with some aspects of implementation. The respondent from one of the smaller organizations expressed their difficulties as follows:

We found that even for [name of auditing firm] it was difficult because the rules were still changing...You are trying to get it implemented because there [are] deadlines, but the authorities still haven't...totally defined what they are looking for. The key to the change management system is that you have to make it scalable to your business. Obviously we are small; we couldn't have a big fancy system. So...we continue to use our help desk package...[to] track it, and we designed some [simple] forms...and we get that approval [for these process]...the key issue with any change within the system is getting somebody outside the group to take responsibility for that change.

A thorough analysis of all processes is an important first step in control implementation. After the initial implementation, the effectiveness of controls must also be monitored on a regular basis.

Monitoring Processes

An important component of SOX compliance is establishing ongoing systems monitoring and evaluation to ensure continuous compliance after controls and processes have been implemented. Based on monitoring feedback, some controls and related processes may need to be adjusted. Some areas of monitoring include: where the data is going, how and by whom they are accessed, and security of other applications and interfaces. For example, in one organization, managers need to sign off on who needs systems access, systems use patterns are continuously monitored, and systems access withdrawn for non-use. However,

the respondent from this organization encountered an implementation problem as follows:

[We have been] putting a lot of these 'sniffing things' on the servers, host intrusion protection systems and stuff like that [and] also had...managers sign off on people who had VPN remote access...[but when] I gave all...business process owners [a list of] the users and all the roles they have, I would get it back within an hour, so I really question how much they really are looking at it.

As another example of need for improved systems monitoring, in one large global organization, a new user account was often created by making a copy of an old account, rather than making a new account to reflect the roles and responsibilities of a new employee or position. For SOX compliance, ERP systems had to be updated to ensure that users were no longer able to access information that was not necessary for them to carry out their job responsibilities. The following comments by the respondent from this organization demonstrate this problem and a solution to it:

...[If] a new user comes on board, sometimes what they try to do is copy someone's account. So I am a new account AP clerk, give me the same [access] as Joanne...but Joanne used to work in manufacturing. Did we strip her of her production control transactions that would conflict with the [responsibilities of] AP clerk?

We actually created a new type of report on [name of ERP application]...at the database level, as well as at the transactional level, and we identified key transactions within the ERP system that would line up against [a] typical user account. So [for] an AP clerk or an ITBSA, you know what transactions would they hit, and which transactions would conflict...It is a [huge] report...like a tree mapping, so we can identify how many non-compliance issues we have with user access.

Monitoring and evaluating control effectiveness are ongoing management functions. In addition, control effectiveness under SOX needs to be audited and certified by the organization's internal and external auditors.

Auditing Processes

Documentation of internal controls and the related processes required by SOX enables an audit trail to be created, so that the same processes can be reliably repeated and any deviations from standard processes investigated and adjusted, as necessary. A transparent audit trail promotes the visibility of and accountability for processes and results. It is also necessary for granting a "clean audit opinion" on control effectiveness by external auditors. It is particularly important in large global organizations with diverse operations and environments. When establishing auditing procedures, it is important to consider the relative importance or materiality of each control or process in order to ensure that the benefits from investigations exceed the related costs. There is a need to strike a delicate balance between improved control and efficiency on one hand, and the risk of material errors, omissions, and misstatements in input data and output reports on the other. The respondents expressed the importance of these notions as follows:

If someone goes in and updates the number, we know through the authorization who is capable of doing it, and it might be easy to identify through an audit trail.

Different systems have different [materiality criteria], depending on how you configure it [sic]...Different limits could be by dollar value [or] by percent of invoice value...It was a matter of getting the process owner to define the rule.

They and we [regional teams for different countries] have one system that we put all our controls on, so it is visible worldwide, so the other countries can see how we are doing, and how we are doing against it [sic]...From a global perspective there is a lot of co-sharing. You know processes and challenges and so forth, similarly so [does] our global group audit service....

However, the redesign of operational, monitoring, and auditing processes can face significant implementation challenges in global organizations.

Control Implementation Challenges

In global organizations, the geographic distance and cultural differences can complicate effective communication and coordination, and hinder process and systems improvements. Different functions and systems need to work together in implementing effective controls across global operations. However, getting people to work together across functional and international boundaries can be challenging. The major challenges in implementing SOX compliance in the four organizations can be categorized as cultural, technical, and financial. These challenges are summarized in Table 6.

Cultural Challenges

A major cultural factor affecting SOX implementation in the four organizations was resistance to change. The loss of data access and authority seemed to cause significant problems to some users. With restructured and streamlined processes, some jobs and responsibilities changed and security procedures increased. Some users did not like the increased restrictions placed on their work activities and data access, and did not understand or appreciate the value of new processes and procedures. The resistance was more prominent by users in foreign countries, as they perceived SOX implementation as a centralized control activity, not necessarily affecting or ben-

Table 6. Control implementation challenges

Challenges	Examples
Cultural Challenges	• Resistance to change • Limiting systems access often problematic to existing users • Resistance to decreased individual controls and increased centralized controls • Lack of understanding of other cultures • Different accounting standards, rules, and terminology in different countries
Technical Challenges	• Systems inflexibility • Inadequate security and control features • Segregation of duties difficult, particularly in smaller organizations and units
Financial Challenges	• High costs of consultants in initial implementation • Increased ongoing monitoring and auditing costs • Lack of adequate vendor support, particularly in smaller organizations

efiting them. One respondent described the loss of data access resulting in:

...insecure feeling that maybe that person is not important anymore in the company, [as] you are taking away some of the authorization [and] you are segregating the duties, so they couldn't accept that.

Another important cultural factor was differences in rules and business conduct in different countries. Different countries have different accounting rules and different approaches to control. For example, some countries follow their own national accounting standards, which can vary from country to country, whereas some others have adopted international accounting standards. Different accounting rules may require different information or similar information reported in different ways. In addition, at least one large Asian country has restrictions on information that can be reported and accessed on the Internet, whereas other countries require reporting of corporate financial information in publicly accessible online databases. One respondent expressed a concern about the reliability of global financial information as follows:

I would say that the biggest challenge is where there are global applications serving multiple different countries...by their financial reporting system that everybody feeds into. Unless you have all the terminology all the same, it is not going to necessarily line up similarly with sharing of data, and the ability to change data....

In order to facilitate global coordination throughout its control implementation processes, one large organization established a cross-functional global team to ensure the visibility and co-sharing of local and global changes to business processes. Collaborative processes were required to create shared terminology and reporting rules. In order to manage these processes, the organization developed a tool, which involved defining top-level control objectives, sub-objectives, and steps within sub-objectives. The respondent from this organization expressed the basic structure of this initiative as follows:

We have structured ourselves for Sarbanes-Oxley. We have regional teams that are kind of compliance groups. Then within each of the regional teams, you have representatives from IT, finance, and operations...Then at the global level, we have a global representative that is from GAS or group audit services, which is an internal auditing team.

In other cases, compliance with regulations of a foreign country can also affect culture in the host country, by forcing local organizations to adopt different processes and ways of doing business, and vice versa. The following examples given by the respondents demonstrate this point:

European partners have different interpretations of user acceptance testing; how much we should share with clients and what level of access should we provide to customers. Our overseas partners had different opinions on such issues. In [the] U.S., all kinds of regulations exist around technology, while EU partners have [a] different level of technology sharing.

How our partners manage and record hours spent on R&D is different [than] the way we do. In [the] UK, for example, they tend to audit more diligently and detailed on [the] skill level, on approval processes related to inventory management, and how outsourcing decisions are taken.

Initially the corporate [staff] here had a hard time accepting the rules what were proposed by all the project managers in Europe, saying, no this is not how we want the accounting because we follow totally different rules.

Many cultural challenges (e.g., resistance to change) stem from attitudinal "people" problems or the lack of understanding, but some (e.g., segregation of duties) can also relate to technology.

Technical Challenges

An important technical challenge for all organizations was segregation of duties. Segregation of related duties in processing financial transactions is one of the key control requirements of SOX. Its purpose is to assign related tasks—for

example, handling cash deposits and recording cash transactions, or handling cash receipts and cash payments—to different individuals, in order to prevent one individual from stealing cash and falsifying the records to cover up. Leading ERP systems allow segregation of duties, but the process is not straightforward. As previously discussed, systems inflexibility and inadequate security and control features can pose significant technical challenges. Generally, it was relatively more difficult for organizations A, C, and D to segregate duties by making changes to ERP systems than for organization B, which can afford its own ERP competency center given its larger size. In addition, the finance function may not be large enough in smaller organizations to warrant several finance clerks, which is necessary for proper segregation of duties. However, organization B also provided examples of difficulties in segregating duties in its smaller operations, as expressed by this respondent:

So we have different divisions on our ERP system. We had smaller type units where they said [name of company]...[must] segregate an Accounts Payable clerk from an Accounts Receivable clerk, but we have one clerk and they're AP/AR and we need both accesses...It was a matter of then going through which [has] the higher potential risk.

Technical solutions are costly to implement and can lead to significant financial challenges for some organizations.

Financial Challenges

SOX implementation was costly and time consuming for all four organizations. They indicated using services of major auditing firms at least in the initial stages of implementation. The high compliance costs have also resulted in some organizations questioning: Have we gone too far with control legislations? Are there benefits of doing this? One organization is apparently spending approximately 3% of its revenues on control compliance projects. The respondent from this organization commented on the processes and costs as follows:

It [has] been four years now we are constantly going through control and process clean-up....It is the same people [management, auditors, and consultants] redefining it, redefining it, and...the internal auditors aren't even clear what has to happen. But one thing is that they are sure that their budget for the entire interim control process for [name of organization]...is just going up and up. Right now, if I remember it right, it is almost 3-4% of our revenue, which is really, really high.

The financial implications of SOX implementation in smaller organizations are intensified by the lack of adequate support from systems vendors. Although all organizations, except for organization A, use an ERP application from the same vendor, the smaller organizations found it more difficult to get information and support from the vendor. Smaller organizations were also not able to participate actively in user groups and forums through which vendors provide new information to customers.

Irrespective of several cultural, technical, and financial challenges, several actual and potential control implementation benefits were also identified by the respondents.

Control Implementation Benefits

Although it is still early in the SOX implementation process for most organizations to identify significant lessons learned, the respondents optimistically expressed some perceived benefits already realized, as well as some long-term potential benefits. Generally, the SOX implementation projects were perceived in a positive light, and often implemented as part of broader strategic change management initiatives. A number of benefits were expected to be realized over time.

However, the respondents also recognized that many long-term benefits are intangible and difficult to measure. Some examples of present and future benefits come from the areas of process efficiency, systems security, and other long-term intangible benefits. These benefits are summarized in Table 7.

Process Efficiency

One of the most immediate benefits was process efficiency improvements. SOX forced the organizations to review all their processes for compliance. Process review and control implementation exercises revealed several non-confirming processes for all organizations. The processes that were found to be outdated, redundant, inefficient, and risky were subsequently eliminated or improved. One respondent provided an example as follows:

Process maps and procedures have always existed, but they tend to get obsolete soon. Regulations such as SOX forces [sic] firms to keep them updated.

Some process efficiencies were also achieved through improved process documentation, as expressed by another respondent:

New people are coming into the company, and now the functional areas have documents that they can articulate to someone, and it says this is how we run our accounts payable process or our master scheduling process....

However, the implementers should be careful to ensure that process efficiency improvements are not achieved at the expense of systems security.

Systems Security

In addition, the process analysis in one organization led also to the identification of several local systems, which were interfaced with the ERP

Table 7. Control implementation benefits

Benefits	Examples
Process Efficiency	• Identification of redundant, inefficient, and non-compliant processes • Process elimination and improvement • Updated process maps and documentation
Systems Security	• Identification of local "bolt-on" systems with security hazards • Enhanced systems security features and processes • Improved systems-wide controls
Potential Long-Term Intangible Benefits	• Improved regulatory compliance • Improved strategic management practices • Enhanced public accountability and image • Improved investor confidence • Organizational learning

systems, creating systems security hazards. Interestingly, the IS teams were not even aware of the existence of some of these systems. Upon reflecting on the lessons learned, the respondent from this organization indicated that the critical systems security issues could have been, and should have been, addressed even earlier in the implementation process, expressing this concern as follows:

I would say in one area that we probably put off until later and probably should have brought it in earlier was around the security.

In summary, the respondents provided some examples of simultaneous process efficiency and systems security improvements as a result of their control implementations. They also suggested some possible, more intangible long-term benefits.

Potential Long-Term Intangible Benefits

In three of the four organizations, SOX implementation was part of a broader "quality management" or "change management" implementation initiatives. Functional needs, such as improved inven-

tory management and supply chain management, were specifically mentioned. Implementing SOX compliance, with its tight timelines, provided an impetus for beginning or fast-tracking such projects in these organizations. All these initiatives can ultimately lead to more transparent and accountable management practices and to improved investor confidence, which are major objectives of SOX. The following are two examples of potential intangible long-term benefits, as expressed by the respondents:

We had strategic objective to set up a change management process on the list for three years, now we have a deadline to complete it simply because of SOX.

So more secure systems…mean less vulnerability, maybe perhaps you can rate that in terms of [lower] number of lawsuits.

Ensuring ongoing effectiveness of internal controls is a dynamic and continuous process. Processes that are compliant this year can become non-compliant next year due to changes in the business environment or control requirements. Organizations need to establish processes for ensuring ongoing effectiveness of internal controls and learning from their experiences. One respondent expressed these notions as follows:

One of our objectives was not just do the process documentation [and] so forth, but actually test and provide artifacts that prove that step or that process was a good control. We definitely failed some processes and we passed some processes ...It seems that now we are going through the second audit, the ones that failed previously aren't failing, and other ones that may have passed have failed, because of ...the rigor in which we re-enforce the behaviors.

In conclusion, the exploratory results reported in this chapter provide some tentative evidence on desirable ERP systems characteristics for implementing controls, control implementation processes, and control implementation challenges and benefits in global organizations. They can also have significant implications for future managerial, regulatory, and research trends.

FUTURE TRENDS

The organizations in this study take compliance with SOX very seriously. They have substantially met the SOX requirements expected to be completed to date. They have also often accomplished these objectives as part of broader continuous process and strategic improvement initiatives. It is also obvious that the SOX regulations are here to stay. Similar control initiatives in other countries will further add to control demands for global organizations in the future. Although no internal controls can guarantee the prevention of future financial scandals, such as those involving Enron and WorldCom, they can reveal significant errors, omissions, and questionable activities early and thus allow timely corrective actions. Should other major financial scandals occur in the future, even tighter control legislation will

likely follow. Such threats can exert additional pressure on global organizations to continuously enhance their controls and ERP systems, resulting in a continuous cycle of control and systems adjustments.

CONCLUSION

This chapter examines the effectiveness of ERP systems in implementing regulatory internal controls required by SOX in global organizations. It aims to understand the extent to which ERP systems are able to meet control requirements imposed by SOX and challenges organizations face in enhancing their ERP systems for this purpose. The chapter reports the results of focus group and individual interviews with ERP systems managers and directors in four organizations with significant global operations. It indicates a substantial degree of completion of SOX implementations by these organizations, often facilitated by consultants and often accomplished as part of broader systems, process, and strategic management initiatives. It also highlights some significant technical and cultural challenges, such as systems inflexibility and diversity, systems security weaknesses, and resistance to change. On the optimistic side, it also reveals some actual and expected benefits, such as improved process efficiency and systems security, and potential intangible long-term benefits.

ERP systems provided a technological platform in all organizations for successful SOX implementation, but they were not able to meet all control requirements without significant modifications or add-on applications. All four organizations use one of the two major ERP applications (SAP and Oracle), but some modifications were needed to the standard modules in order to implement some SOX requirements. Some solutions outside the ERP systems were also needed due to the inflexibility of ERP systems or high costs associated with modifying ERP systems. As to functional uses, the respondents provided examples of using ERP systems for meeting various information needs, such as planning, monitoring, controlling, evaluating, reporting, inventory management, supply chain management, and change management.

SOX implementation in all four organizations has been a long, complicated, and costly process, which is not complete yet. The main challenges initially facing all organizations were the lack of proper implementation guidance and resistance to change. Audit firms and consultants were generally engaged early in these processes. In all cases, detailed analyses and documentation of existing systems, controls, and processes were completed. On the technical side, systems security and segregation of duties were seen as major challenges. These challenges were often associated with "bolt-on" systems, which were locally managed applications, not part of the centrally administered ERP systems. Some organizations also approached SOX implementation as part of major business improvement projects, for example, change management or quality management programs. It is evident that all organizations have been spending a great deal of effort and resources on their compliance projects.

Different systems, cultures, and financial reporting rules posed additional obstacles for global operations. For example, in one organization, two different ERP applications were used in different countries, complicating the standardization and documentation of some processes required by SOX. Resistance to change, although encountered in all operations, was more prominent by users in global operations, as SOX implementation was perceived as a centralized control activity, not necessarily affecting or benefiting them. Furthermore, different countries have different accounting rules and different approaches to control, complicating the implementation of controls and consistency of financial reporting. Nevertheless, most organizations have been able to address such challenges quite successfully and regard their own progress to date at least as satisfactory. Interestingly, lan-

guage was not perceived to be a major obstacle in these organizations, as all of them use English as their systems and business language.

Technical systems and operational process improvements were identified as the most visible and immediate benefits. SOX forced the organizations to review their processes and to improve or eliminate outdated, redundant, inefficient, and risky processes. In particular, the process analyses resulted in significant improvements to systems security in all organizations and inventory control practices at least in one organization. Other operational benefits included more consistent documentation, clearer roles and responsibilities, and improved training processes. Technical and process improvements can significantly improve the reliability of input data and hence the credibility of output reports—one of the key objectives of SOX. The respondents also identified some potential longer-term intangible benefits, such as improvements in strategic planning and management systems. It should also be noted that regulatory compliance in itself is an important benefit, which can improve credibility and reduce risk of potential lawsuits by investors. ERP systems that are well designed, implemented, and managed are critical enablers of such intangible long-term benefits and outcomes.

In conclusion, regardless of some early challenges and high costs associated with SOX implementations, exploratory evidence in this chapter indicates that organizations are well on track in completing their control implementations, with significant help from consultants and auditors in the early stages. In all organizations, ERP systems played a central role in implementing and monitoring SOX compliance, but required some enhancements or add-on applications. Interestingly, regardless of some early frustrations and high costs, the respondents generally described their implementation experiences in a positive light, citing SOX as a catalyst for other systems, process, and strategic improvement initiatives. Follow-up research with these organizations may be able to reveal more intangible long-term benefits after all control requirements will have been implemented and refined.

FUTURE RESEARCH DIRECTIONS

This chapter provides some exploratory evidence on how ERP systems facilitate the implementation of internal controls required by SOX. Further research opportunities exist in using a larger sample of organizations in different industries around the world and including managers with control implementation experience in different areas. Longer-term benefits and outcomes should also become more visible after organizations will have completed and evaluated all their control implementations. At that time, a more thorough evaluation of benefits and outcomes may be possible. In addition, the results provide an overview of some critical systems design features, processes, and challenges in global organizations and can serve as a basis for developing a comprehensive model of ERP systems effectiveness in implementing internal controls in future research.

REFERENCES

Al-Mashari, M. (2002). Enterprise resource planning (ERP) systems: A research agenda. *Industrial Management & Data Systems, 102*(3), 165-170.

Bititci, U.S., Turner, T., & Begemann, C. (2000). Dynamics of performance measurement systems. *International Journal of Operations & Production Management, 20*(6), 692-704.

Bourne, M., Neely, A., Platts, K., & Mills, J. (2002). The success and failure of performance measurement initiatives: Perceptions of participating managers. *International Journal of Operations & Production Management, 22*(11), 1288-1310.

Bratton, W.W. (2003). Enron, Sarbanes-Oxley and accounting: Rules versus principles versus rents. *Villanova Law Review, 48*(4), 1023.

Brown, W., & Nasuti, F. (2005). What ERP systems can tell about Sarbanes-Oxley. *Information Management & Computer Security, 13*(4), 311-327.

Canadian Securities Administrators. (2006). *CSA staff notice 52-316: Certification of design of internal control over financial reporting.* Retrieved October 29, 2006, from http://www.osc.gov.on.ca/Regulation/Rulemaking/Current/Part5/csa_20060922_52-316_certification-design.jsp

Chafee, E.E. (1985). Three models of strategy. *Academy of Management Review, 10*(1), 89-98.

Chan, S. (2004). Sarbanes-Oxley: The IT dimension. *Internal Auditor,* (February), 31-33.

Colman, R. (2006). Sarbanes-Oxley in review. *CMA Management,* (March), 20-25.

Committee of Sponsoring Organizations of Treadway Commission. (2004). *Enterprise risk management: Integrated framework (executive summary).* Retrieved October 28, 2006, from http://www.coso.org/Publications/ERM/COSO_ERM_ExecutiveSummary.pdf

Committee of Sponsoring Organizations of Treadway Commission. (1992). *Internal control: Integrated framework (executive summary).* Retrieved April 2, 2006, from http://www.coso.org/publications/executive_summary_integrated_framework.htm

Damianides, M. (2004). How does SOX change IT? *Journal of Corporate Accounting & Finance,* (September-October), 35-41.

Davenport, T.H. (2000). *Mission critical: Realizing the promise of enterprise systems.* Boston: Harvard Business School Press.

Davenport, T.H., & Brooks, J.D. (2004). Enterprise systems and the supply chain. *Journal of Enterprise Information Management, 17*(1), 8-19.

Eisenhardt, K.M. (1989). Building theories from case study research. *Academy of Management Review, 4*(4), 532-550.

European Parliament & Council. (2006). *Directive 2006/46/EC*. Retrieved October 28, 2006, from http://eur-lex.europa.eu/LexUriServ/LexUriServ. do?uri=CELEX:32006L0046:EN:NOT

Gibbs, J., Kraemer, K.L., & Dedrick, J. (2003). Environment and policy factors shaping global e-commerce diffusion: Cross-country comparison. *The Information Society, 19,* 5-18.

Harrison, R.T., & Leitch, C.M. (2000). Learning and organization in the knowledge-based information economy: Initial findings from a participatory action research case study. *British Journal of Management, 11,* 103-119.

ITGI (IT Governance Institute). (2004). *IT control objectives for Sarbanes-Oxley: The importance of IT in the design, implementation and sustainability of internal control over disclosure and financial reporting*. Retrieved October 17, 2006, from http://www.itgi.org/template_ITGI. cfm?template=/ContentManagement/Content-Display.cfm&ContentID=24235

ITGI. (2006). *COBIT mapping: Overview of international guidance* (2nd ed.). Retrieved October 17, 2006, from http://www.itgi.org/ AMTemplate.cfm?Section=Deliverables&Template=/ContentManagement/ContentDisplay. cfm&ContentID=24759

Kaplan, R.S. (1984).Yesterday's accounting undermines production. *Harvard Business Review, 62*(4), 95-101.

Kaplan, R.S., & Norton, D.P. (1996). *The balanced scorecard: Translating strategy into action*. Boston: Harvard Business School Press.

Kennerley, M., & Neely, A. (2002). A framework of factors affecting the evolution of performance measurement systems. *International Journal of Operations & Production Management, 22*(11), 1222-1245.

KPMG. (2003). *Sarbanes-Oxley section 404: Management assessment of internal control and the proposed auditing standards*. Retrieved April 4, 2006, from http://www.kpmg.ca/en/services/ audit/documents/SO404.pdf

Kumar, V., Maheshwari, B., & Kumar, U. (2002). ERP systems implementation: Best practices in Canadian government organizations. *Government Information Quarterly, 19*(2), 145-172.

Kumar, V., Maheshwari, B., & Kumar, U. (2003). An investigation of critical management issues in ERP implementation: Empirical evidence from Canadian organizations. *Technovation, 23*(9), 793-807.

Markus, M.L., & Tanis, C. (2000). The enterprise system experience: From adoption to success. In R.W. Zmud (Ed.), *Framing the domains of IT management: Projecting the future through the past* (pp. 173-207). Cincinnati, OH: Pinneflex Educational Resources.

Matolcsy, Z.P., Booth, P., & Wieder, B. (2005). Economic benefits of enterprise resource planning systems: Some empirical evidence. *Accounting and Finance, 45,* 439-456.

Miles, M.B., & Huberman, A.M. (1994). *Qualitative data analysis: An expanded sourcebook* (2nd ed.). Thousand Oaks, CA: Sage.

Mills, J., Platts, K., & Gregory, M. (1995). A framework for design of manufacturing strategy processes: A contingency approach. *International Journal of Operations & Production Management, 15*(4), 17-49.

Porter, M.E. (1986). Changing patterns of international competition. *California Management Review, XXVIII*(2), 9-40.

Powell, T.C., & Dent-Micallef, A. (1997). Information technology as competitive advantage: The role of human, business and technology resources. *Strategic Management Journal, 18*(5), 375-405.

Rizzi, A., & Zamboni, R. (1999). Efficiency improvement in manual warehouses through ERP systems implementation and redesign of the logistic processes. *Journal of Enterprise Information Management, 12*(5-6), 367-377.

Robinson, T.R. (2000). The global e-economy: Can your ERP handle it? *Journal of Corporate Accounting & Finance,* (September-October), 15-18.

Shang, S., & Seddon, P.B. (2002). Assessing and managing the benefits of enterprise systems: The business manager's perspective. *Information Systems Journal, 12,* 271-299.

Simons, R. (2000). *Performance measurement & control systems for implementing strategy.* Upper Saddle River, NJ: Prentice Hall.

Sohal, A.S., Moss, S., & Ng, L. (2001). Comparing IT success in manufacturing and service industries. *International Journal of Operations & Production Management, 21*(1/2), 30-45.

U.S. Congress. (2002). *Sarbanes-Oxley Act.* Retrieved October 29, 2006, from http://www.sec.gov/about/laws/soa2002.pdf

U.S. SEC (Securities & Exchange Commission). (2005). *Management's report on internal control over financial reporting and certification of disclosure in exchange act periodic reports of non-accelerated filers and foreign private issuers, release no. 33-8545.* Retrieved October 23, 2006, from http://www.sec.gov/rules/final/33-8545.htm

Yin, R.K. (2003). *Case study research: Design and methods* (3rd ed.). Beverly Hills, CA: Sage.

ADDITIONAL READING

Boudreau, M.-C., Loch, C.D., Robey, D., & Straud, D. (1998). Going global: Using information technology to advance the competitiveness of the virtual transnational organization. *Academy of Management Executive, 12*(4), 120-128.

Dechow, N., & Mouritsen, J. (2005). Enterprise resource planning systems, management control and the quest for integration. *Accounting, Organizations and Society, 30,* 691-733.

Goodfellow, J.L., & Willis, A.D. (2006a). *Internal control 2006: The next wave of certification—Guidance for management.* Retrieved April 27, 2007, from http://www.rmgb.ca/3/3/5/0/5/index1.shtml

Goodfellow, J.L., & Willis, A.D. (2006b). *Internal control 2006: The next wave of certification—Guidance for directors.* Retrieved April 27, 2007, from http://www.rmgb.ca/3/3/5/0/5/index1.shtml

McLeay, S., & Riccaboni, A. (Eds.). (2001). *Contemporary issues in accounting regulation.* Norwell, MA: Kluwer Academic.

Pritchard, A.C., & Puri, P. (2006). *The regulation of public auditing in Canada and the United States: Self-regulation vs. government regulation?* Retrieved May 7, 2007, from http://www.fraserinstitute.ca/admin/books/files/Public%20Auditing2.pdf

Quattrone, P., & Hopper, T. (2006). What is IT? SAP, accounting, and visibility in a multinational organization. *Information and Organization, 16,* 212-250.

Zeff, S.A. (1995). A perspective on the U.S. public/private-sector approach to regulating financial reporting. *Accounting Horizons, 9*(1), 52-70.

ENDNOTE

[1]   COSO is a voluntary organization dedicated to improving financial reporting quality. Although the US Securities and Exchange Commission (SEC) and the Public Company Accounting Oversight Board (PCAOB) have suggested the COSO (1992) framework for implementing SOX, they do not endorse it or any other framework. The updated COSO (2004) framework approaches internal controls within a more integrative risk management framework

Section VI
Success Evaluation Aspects

Chapter XIV
Implementing ERP Systems in Multinational Projects:
Implications for Cultural Aspects and the Implementation Process

Heinz D. Knoell
Leuphana University of Lüneburg, Germany

Lukas W. H. Kühl
Exsigno Consulting, Switzerland

Roland W.A. Kühl
Steria-Mummert Consulting AG, Germany

Robert Moreton
University of Wolverhampton, UK

ABSTRACT

In this chapter we present the factors for the success of ERP implementation projects. In the first section, we present the outcome of three surveys on the process and success factors for ERP projects. The first survey was undertaken in 2003 in Germany, the second in 2004 in the United States, and the third in 2006 in Turkey. The results are discussed in light of Hofstede's model of cultural factors. In the second section we evaluate common ERP lifecycle models. In spite of the great variety of potential advantages, it is also necessary to illuminate the real effects of standard ERP software in practice. Recent studies have revealed that 81% of German companies interviewed using SAP do not fully exploit the software's ability to optimize business processes, though 61% stated that SAP offers very good process optimization opportunities (Ploenzke, 2000). Therefore we evaluated popular lifecycle models with respect to their suitability to implement standard software in a process-driven way (Kuehl & Knoell, 2002). In the third section we present a semi-process-oriented approach lifecycle model for the implementation and release changeover of ERP systems. This lifecycle model was developed from the authors' experience in practice, and its practical relevance was evaluated in real-world projects. This approach is also assessed in light of the criteria presented in the second section.

INTRODUCTION

The widespread implementation of commercial standard ERP software has required considerable investment by industrial and service companies. However, research suggests that the claimed advantages of the systems' capabilities in terms of optimized processes have not been realized in many of the current implementations. Studies and interviews undertaken within companies confirm this finding. In Kontzer (2003), Joseph Langhauser, engineering group manager at General Motors, is quoted as saying: "We don't need more IT, we need to figure out the business processes we have."

Holland and Light (1999) note: "Successful ERP implementations are certainly publicized…but less successful projects have led to bankruptcy proceedings and litigation against IT suppliers. Approximately 90% of ERP implementations are late or over budget." Furthermore they write: "ERP implementation can reap enormous benefits for successful companies—or it can be disastrous for organizations that fail to manage the implementation process."

The problem starts with the selection of the ERP system supplier. Franch and Carvallo (2003) describe the dilemma of the selection process: "One of the biggest problems is the lack of standard terminology amongst a domain's software packages. Different vendors refer to the same concept by different names, or even worse, the same name might denote different concepts in different packages."

Further, in practice we find that the often-applied proprietary lifecycle models for implementation of ERP systems do not sufficiently support the optimization of a company's business processes, since they consider implementation as primarily a technical challenge. Although suppliers stress the necessity to improve the business processes by using the new software, there is a lack of clear instructions to guide the project team in analyzing and designing optimized business processes.

Daneva (2004) supports our earlier findings (Knoell, Kuehl, Kuehl, & Moreton, 2004) that the common lifecycle models for the implementation of ERP systems lack advice for project management on how to improve the company's specific business processes, how to form teams, and how to control these teams during the project.

This chapter is structured into six sections. In the second section we give an overview of ERP and previous research. Against this background we wanted to explore the implementation approaches organizations used for their ERP systems and how successful they considered these projects. The first survey was performed in Germany from 2003 to 2004. The outcome showed a surprisingly high rate in projects success and project satisfaction, which was inconsistent with the Chaos Reports of the Standish Group (1994, 1996) and other reports of failed software projects (Dorsey, 2003). From 2004 to 2005, a second survey was undertaken in the United States to determine if there were any differences in the software implementation approaches and their success rates. In 2006 we did a third survey in Turkey with the same questionnaire. In the third section we present the surveys outcomes and try to explain them in light of Hofstede's (1979) culture factors.

In the fourth section we draw attention to the business process optimization capability of standard ERP software implementation approaches and assess how they are used in practice. After that, we present the semi-process-oriented approach developed from our analysis and our experience; it is then evaluated with the criteria described earlier in the chapter. Finally, we give an outline of our future research and present our conclusions.

BACKGROUND AND PREVIOUS RESEARCH

Since the effects of ERP systems in business organizations is a relatively new research topic, there are limited sources available in the literature. An excellent overview of the research in this area can be found in an early paper by Holland and Light (1999).

The authors' consultancy experience in the implementation of *standard software* ERP systems suggests there are several drivers for the decision to replace the legacy software systems of an enterprise with a standard ERP software system. In Europe there have been two main drivers for moving to standard software ERP systems: first the Y2K problem and second the introduction of the monetary union of the EC, replacing the national currencies of many countries by the euro. These challenges often exceeded the capacity of the IT departments of companies so they moved to standard software systems, replacing their dependency on internal software developers with dependency on software companies.

The projects for the replacement of the individual software systems of the companies by the standard ERP systems required huge amounts of resources, staff, and money, considering that even the smallest budget for a SAP project for a medium-sized company is at least US$750,000. The vast majority of the projects have much higher budgets. It is no surprise that most of the CEOs and CIOs have been looking at the suitability of the software for their business domain, based on references, and on the total costs of implementation, covering software licenses, company staff, and consultants. The latter was the highest portion of the total costs. The software companies reacted to these market demands and developed

lifecycle implementation models for the rapid implementation of their software, and in addition reference models for the different business domains, for example, car manufacturing, civil engineering, banking, insurance, and so forth. The total cost of ownership (TCO)—that is, the costs of the software project plus the accumulated costs of maintenance plus the costs of staff—has been largely neglected.

It is not surprising that lifecycle models for business process engineering often neglect the systematic combination of process analysis/optimization, individualized software development, and standard software, despite the fact that the level of process organization is the main component of the TCO.

They often completely neglect the effects of the projects on the people involved. However, as stated in Franch and Carvallo (2003), the human factor is one of the most critical factors in IT projects.

The literature suggests that in many cases the implementation of a running system works very well, but in others the claimed advantages of the systems' capabilities in terms of optimized processes have not been realized. Studies and interviews undertaken by the authors with companies applying such software confirm this finding. In many cases more staff are required not only in the company's IT departments but also in their business departments, from bookkeeping to warehousing.

We find that the often-applied proprietary lifecycle models for implementation do not sufficiently support the optimization of a company's business processes, as they consider implementation projects as a technical challenge in the first place. Although suppliers stress the necessity to improve the business processes by using the new software, there is a lack of clear instructions that guide the project team in analyzing and designing optimized business processes.

The literature suggests that the success of a software project was mainly considered to be a result of the application of an appropriate lifecycle model (e.g., Fairley & Willshire, 2003; Stensrud & Myrtveit, 2003). This has not changed since Hofstede's first publication on the effects of national culture on work-related values (Hofstede, 1979). However, since that time many surveys have been published dealing with information systems and national culture. Whereas for a time information systems implementation success was considered as a purely technical challenge, it became evident that there is a further important factor to consider: the human being—in its psychological-based behavior (e.g., Knoell & Knoell, 1998), in its organizational context (e.g., Moreton & Chester, 1997; Kappos & Croteau, 2002), and in its national roots (e.g., Srite, 1999; Bagchi, Cerveny, Hart, & Peterson, 2003; Heales & Cockroft, 2003). Keil et al. (2000) found differences in the willingness to take risks in software projects depending on national culture.

OUTCOME OF ERP IMPLEMENTATION PROJECTS IN DIFFERENT CULTURAL ENVIRONMENTS

In order to evaluate the outcomes of ERP implementation projects in different cultural environments, the authors undertook surveys in three different countries. These surveys incorporated Hofstede's work on the cultural factors that influence people's behavior (Hofstede, 1979, 2000).

Hofstede, an ex-employee of IBM, in his surveys of 1968 and 1972 covering 116,000 respondents from 53 nations, defined four culture-related factors that influence the attitudes and the behavior of people. These factors are: masculinity/femininity, individualism/collectivism, power distance, and uncertainty avoidance. Following their first publication, the cultural factors have been further developed, for example the Confuzius Factor or Long-Term Orientation. However Heales and Cockcroft (2003) suggested

that all other factors—including the culture factors of the GLOBE project (House, Javidan, Hanges, & Dorfman, 2002)—are based on Hofstede's four original cultural factors (they are dependent variables of Hofstede's four independent ones). Hence, we restrict ourselves to these factors for the interpretation of the survey results.

The cultural factor "uncertainty avoidance" expresses the tendency of cultures to prefer a safe harbor rather than experimenting with new concepts. "Cultures with high levels of uncertainty avoidance will not nurture experimentation and as a consequence individuals from these cultures will be less innovative" (Srite, 1999).

The "individualism/collectivism" dimension expresses how much the people in a culture are willing to do things without consent of other members of the group. "People from individualistic cultures also tend to be more non-conformist than people from collectivistic cultures. Nonconformity can be defined as unwillingness to acquiesce or comply" (Srite, 1999).

The third dimension "power distance" expresses how much power the leaders or managers have over their subordinates. "In cultures where there is a less formal hierarchy in the office, individuals will be more willing to take a risk and experiment with a new technology" (Srite, 1999).

Finally, the masculinity/femininity factor concerns "the extent of emphasis on work goals (earnings, advancement) and assertiveness, as opposed to personal goals (friendly atmosphere, getting along with the boss and others) and nurturing" (Srite, 1999).

The Surveys

The first survey started in the summer of 2003 in Germany containing 22 questions on project goals, implementation process, and project satisfaction. When the pre-test with mailed questionnaires elicited nil response, the survey was conducted by telephone interviews. Of the 300 companies contacted, 88 valid responses were received. In total the interview process lasted one year.

The second survey was started in the United States in the winter of 2004/2005 with an expanded questionnaire containing 26 questions. In addition to the German questionnaire, questions on project budget and staffing pre and post the project were added. As in Germany, the pre-test with mailed questionnaires brought no responses, so again telephone interviews were conducted.

In contrast to German companies, not a single person of 50 contacted was willing to answer the questions. Most of them suspected a telephone marketing campaign, so the researchers switched to a Web-based questionnaire. A total of 9,386 U.S. companies received an e-mail with the link to the questionnaire's Web page. The outcome was 37 completed questionnaires, less than hoped for, but enough to undertake a comparison with the German survey.

In October 2006 a third survey was completed in Turkey covering all existing 76 SAP customers. Twelve companies returned the completed questionnaire; 10 of the respondents were Turkish companies, one with U.S. and one with Italian headquarters.

Results of the Surveys

As a prerequisite of the design of the surveys, 23 hypotheses have been postulated. These cover the process optimization as well as the satisfaction with the project outcomes. The full set of hypotheses and statistics can be obtained from the authors upon request. A summary of the results is presented in the next sections. Though not displayed, the results of the Turkish respondents were similar to the German ones in all aspects.

Project Priorities and Satisfaction

The first area of interest was the project objectives and the satisfaction of the enterprise with the fulfillment of these objectives. As can be seen in Figures 1 and 2, there is a considerable difference in the objective of improving the business processes as well as in the satisfaction with the outcome of the project with respect to this objective.

Table 1 shows two more objectives addressed in the questionnaires, which show the same trend: the German companies had a high focus on their goals and high achievement in these goals.

Figure 1. Project objective priority—improvement of business processes

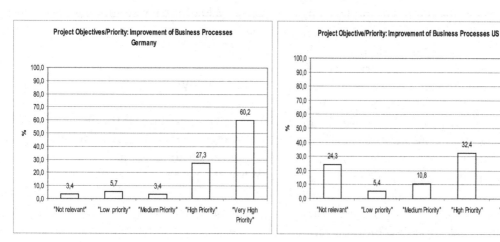

Table 1. Project priorities and satisfaction

Goal	Country		Very High Priority/ Goal Was Achieved	High Priority/ Goal Was Nearly Achieved	Medium Priority/ Medium Goal Fulfillment	Low Priority/ Goal Was Hardly Achieved	No Priority/ Goal Was Not Achieved
Improvement of Business Processes	G	Project Objective	60.2	27.3	3.4	5.7	3.4
	U.S.		27.0	32.4	10.8	5.4	24.3
	G	Project Satisfaction	43.2	34.1	4.5	6.7	11.4
	U.S.		8.1	32.4	27.0	8.1	24.3
Improvement of IT Systems	G	Project Objective	58.0	25.0	6.8	5.7	4.5
	U.S.		37.8	29.7	10.8	5.4	16.2
	G	Project Satisfaction	50.0	21.6	9.1	6.8	10.2
	U.S.		16.2	35.1	21.6	8.1	18.9
Consideration of Strategic Objectives	G	Project Objective	46.6	31.0	12.5	5.7	3.4
	U.S.		32.4	18.9	21.6	5.4	21.6
	G	Project Satisfaction	35.2	37.5	8.0	8.0	10.2
	U.S.		21.6	18.9	27.0	10.8	21.6

257

Figure 2. Project objective satisfaction—improvement of business processes

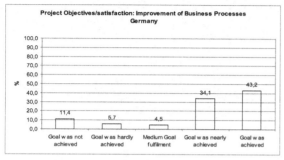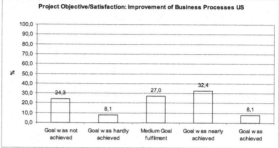

Figure 3. Project scope

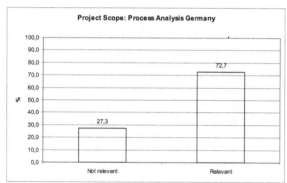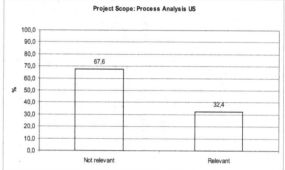

Figure 4. Analysis of as-is processes

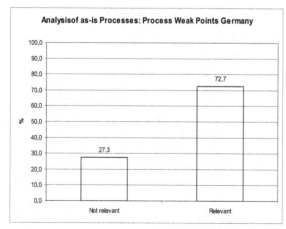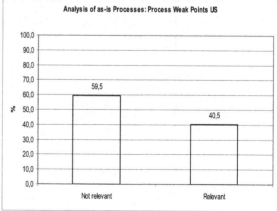

Table 2. Project scope

	Country	Relevant	Not Relevant
SSW Implementation	G	95.5	4.5
	U.S.	40.5	59.5
Process Analysis	G	72.7	27.3
	U.S.	32.4	67.6
Business Process Optimization	G	75.0	25.0
	U.S.	51.4	48.6
IT Strategy Development	G	35.2	64.8
	U.S.	32.4	67.6
Consideration of Strategic Objectives	G	46.6	31.0
	U.S.	32.4	18.9
Organizational Development/Change Management	G	44.3	55.7
	U.S.	32.4	67.6

Table 3. Analysis of as-is processes

	Country	Relevant	Not Relevant
Process Flow	G	75.0	25.0
	U.S.	67.6	59.5
Process Time	G	50.0	50.0
	U.S.	35.1	64.9
Process Costs	G	56.8	43.2
	U.S.	54.1	45.9
Organizational Responsibilities	G	60.2	39.8
	U.S.	32.4	67.6
Process Weak Points	G	72.7	27.3
	U.S.	40.5	59.5
Quality of IT Support	G	64.8	35.2
	U.S.	18.9	81.1

It seems that the sample of U.S. companies had a more "hands-on" approach—that is, they did not care so much about objectives other than the pure goal of making the software system run.

Project Scope

A look at the project scope (e.g., process analysis—see Figure 3) confirms the findings of the project objectives: the sample of U.S. companies shows less relevance in the project scope

Figure 5. Modeling of business processes

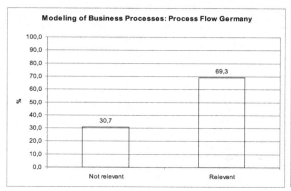
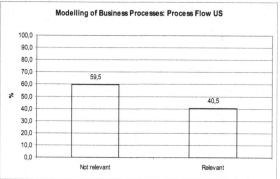

Table 4. Modeling of business processes

	Country	Relevant	Not Relevant
Sat Size	G	76.1	23.9
	U.S.	43.2	56.8
Process Flow	G	69.3	30.7
	U.S.	40.5	59.5
Pre/Post Conditions of Process Task	G	50.0	50.0
	U.S.	16.2	83.8
Organizational Responsibilities	G	59.1	40.9
	U.S.	24.3	75.7
Business Objects (e.g., lists)	G	54.5	45.5
	U.S.	16.2	83.8
Invoked IT Systems	G	58.0	42.0
	U.S.	18.9	81.1

Figure 6. Application of BPR tools

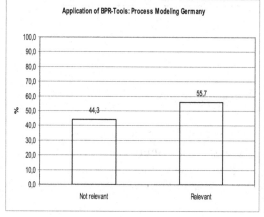
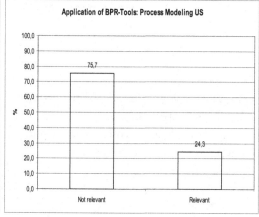

Table 5. Application of BPR tools

	Country	Relevant	Not Relevant
Process Modeling	G	55.7	44.3
	U.S.	24.3	75.7
Description of Business Tasks	G	45.5	54.5
	U.S.	27.0	73.0
Process Simulation	G	20.5	79.5
	U.S.	24.3	75.5
Activity-Based Accounting	G	38.6	61.4
	U.S.	13.5	86.5
Process Animation	G	9.1	90.9
	U.S.	8.1	91.9
Software Parameterization	G	25.0	75.0
	U.S.	16.2	83.8

compared to the sample of German companies. With regard to project scope, the sample of U.S. companies gives the highest scores of relevance to "business process optimization" (51.4%) and "standard software implementation" (40.5%). But these are still lower ratings compared to the sample of German companies, who rate these at 75% and 95.5%, respectively (see Table 2).

Analysis of As-Is Processes

The rating of the importance of the analysis of as-is processes is consistent with the rating of the projects objectives and the project scope. As Table 3 illustrates, the sample of German companies paid much more attention to the analysis of as-is processes. The process flow and the process weak points were important for 75% and 72.7 % respectively. For the majority of the sample of U.S. companies (67.6%), the analysis of the process flow was relevant, but only for 40.5% the analysis of the process weak points. For them the analysis of the process costs (54.1%) was more relevant and nearly as important as for the sample of German

companies (56.8%), who rated the relevance of the as-is analysis of the process costs.

Modeling of Business Processes

The relevance of the modeling of the different aspects of the business processes is also consistent with the findings above: the majority of the Germany companies rate all aspects of the business process modeling as important, whereas the minority of the U.S. companies think it is relevant. Figure 5 illustrates the outcomes for process flow, and Table 4 includes the broader range of factors.

Application of BPR Tools

Generally, the different aspects of the application of business process reengineering (BPR) tools were rated lower by the U.S. companies than they were by the German companies (see Table 5). However, in this context as Figure 6 indicates, only process modeling was rated as relevant by the majority of German companies (55.7%), followed by business task description (45.5%).

Figure 7. Structure of the implementation process

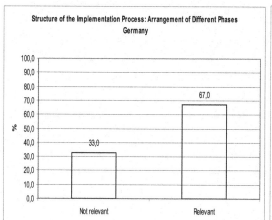
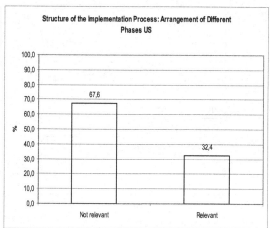

Table 6. Structure of the implementation process/structure of the project team

	Country	Relevant	Not Relevant
Arrangement of Different Phases	G	67.0	33.0
	U.S.	32.4	67.6
Derivation of All Projects Tasks from the Business Processes	G	62.5	37.5
	U.S.	24.3	75.7
Adaptability of the Project Method to Specific Objectives/Conditions	G	65.9	34.1
	U.S.	18.9	81.1
Availability of End Criteria for All Project Activities	G	64.8	35.2
	U.S.	16.2	83.8

Figure 8. Composition of the project team

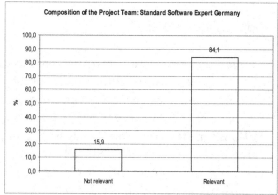
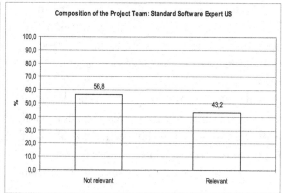

The authors, who have undertaken several research projects in the area of requirements engineering and especially in process animation in requirements engineering (Pahnke, Moreton, & Knoell 2004), found the low anticipated relevance of process animation to be surprising. Our research has demonstrated the positive impact of animation in combination with business process optimization on the quality of the software system. It might be, however, that these demonstrations are too recent to be utilized in practice and to be used on a broad scale.

It is also of interest that software parameterization has such a low relevance (16.2% U.S. sample, 25% German sample), as this is the main tool for the customization of the standard software system (like an ERP system) to the needs of the specific organization. This might be because more companies use the software vendor's reference models for implementing the system, rather than customization of the software for the company's needs after a thorough business process review. The implementation using a reference model saves costs in the implementation phase; the customization of the software after a business reengineering project saves costs in the post-implementation phase, which can yield savings over a longer period.

The fact that the relevance of business process modeling and application of BPR tools is much

Table 7. Composition of the project team

	Country	Relevant	Not Relevant
Functional Teams	G	38.6	61.4
	U.S.	51.4	48.6
Process Teams	G	63.6	36.4
	U.S.	24.3	75.7
Process Owner	G	72.7	27.3
	U.S.	54.1	45.9
Standard Software Expert	G	84.1	15.9
	U.S.	43.2	56.8
Domain/Business Expert	G	76.1	23.9
	U.S.	40.5	59.5
IT/Legacy System Expert	G	70.5	29.5
	U.S.	48.6	51.4

Figure 9. Project external communication

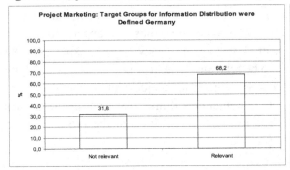 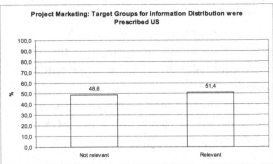

Table 8. Project internal communication

	Country	Relevant	Not Relevant
Network Communication	G	31.8	68.2
	U.S.	35.1	64.9
Star-Shaped Communication	G	55.7	44.3
	U.S.	21.6	78.4
Communication Structures Were Not Defined	G	15.9	84.1
	U.S.	21.6	78.4

Table 9. Project external communication

	Country	Relevant	Not Relevant
Communication Channels Were Prescribed	G	58.0	42.0
	U.S.	45.9	54.1
Communication Frequency/Rhythm Were Prescribed	G	54.5	45.5
	U.S.	32.4	67.6
Target Groups for Information Distribution Were Defined	G	68.2	31.8
	U.S.	51.4	48.6

lower for the U.S. companies might be an indicator of a more short-term management focus when compared with that of the German companies.

Structure of the Implementation Process

Even in the structure of the implementation process, there are significant differences between the estimated relevance of aspects like arrangement of different phases (see Figure 7). Again, Table 6 illustrates the significant differences in emphasis between the two national groups of companies. It would appear that U.S. companies have other aspects which they rate more highly or they have a more informal approach to the implementation process.

The structure of the project team is not as important for the U.S. companies as for the German ones, for example, the participation of a standard software expert in the project team is relevant for 84.1% of the German companies compared to 43.2% of the U.S. companies (see Figure 8).

For the majority of the sample of U.S. companies, it is relevant to have functional teams 51.5%, whereas for the majority of the sample of German companies (63.6%), process teams are more relevant (see Table 7). The majority of the sample of U.S. companies are not so concerned with the expertise of the team members. The majority of them think it is relevant to have a process owner (54.1%) as a member of the project team. However, a minority consider a standard software expert (43.2%), a domain or business expert (40.5%), or an IT systems or legacy systems expert (48.6%) to be relevant to the team.

The significant majority of the sample of German companies thinks that each of these roles are relevant, in addition to the process owner (72.7%).

Figure 10. Project success

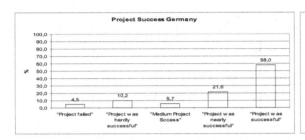
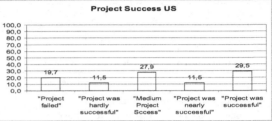

Figure 11. Project termination

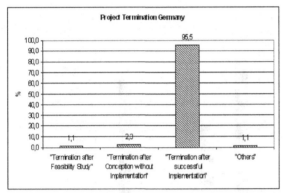
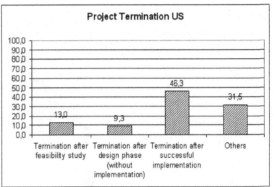

Table 11. Example of t-test group statistics, Germany

Germany	Analysis of As-Is Processes: Process Weak Points	N	Mean	Std. Deviation	Std. Error Mean
Project Objective/Priority: Improvement of Business Processes	Not relevant	24	4.00	1.216	.248
	Relevant	64	4.48	.926	.116
Project Objective/Satisfaction: Improvement of Business Processes	Not relevant	23	2.61	1.559	.325
	Relevant	64	4.41	.830	.104

Internal and External Project Communication

The aspects of the project internal communication were not relevant for the majority of the companies, both U.S. and German. The exception was the star-shaped communication (which means that all project members have to communicate via their supervisors). This aspect has been seen as relevant by 55.7% of the German companies, but by only 21.6% of U.S. companies.

The project external communication, also called project marketing, attracted much more attention (see Table 9). The most important aspect was the definition of target groups for the communication, which was considered relevant

Table 12. Example of t-test - group statistics, US

	Analysis of As-Is Processes: Process Weak Points	N	Mean	Std. Deviation	Std. Error Mean
Project Objective/Priority: Improvement of Business Processes	Not relevant	22	2.73	1.579	.337
	Relevant	15	4.20	1.014	.262
Project Objective/Satisfaction: Improvement of Business Processes	Not relevant	22	2.50	1.336	.285
	Relevant	15	3.53	1.060	.274

Figure 12. Test of Hypothesis 1

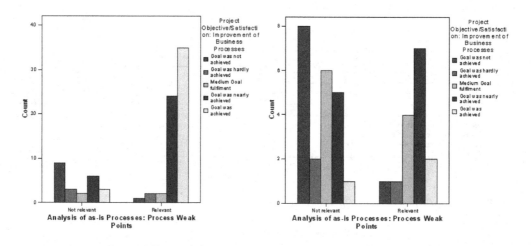

Figure 13. Test of Hypothesis 7

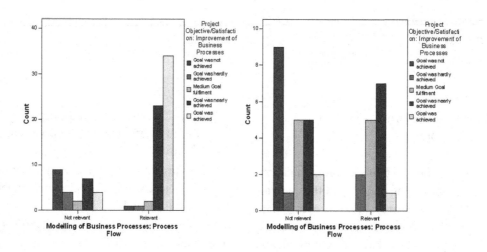

Figure 14. Test of Hypothesis 17

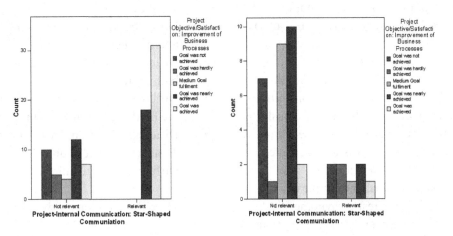

by 51.4% of the sample U.S. and 68.2% of the sample German companies (see Figure 9). Next in importance was the prescription of the communication channels, which was relevant for 45.9% of the U.S. companies and 58.0% of the German companies.

Project Success and Project Satisfaction

The results from the U.S. survey (Figure 10) indicate a project failure rate of 23%, and only 25% were considered successful. This is consistent with findings of other surveys, for example, a Deloitte survey suggesting a failure rate of 20% for ERP projects (Ke & Wei, 2005; Brown & Vessey, 2003).

The outcome of the German survey (Figure 10) was surprising: with 58% successful projects and only 4.5% failed projects, it clearly did not match previously published findings.

Project Termination

The project termination stage gives a consistent picture with project success: 62.1 % of the U.S. companies terminated their project after a successful implementation. Again, this is consistent with the findings of other surveys mentioned

above. The German companies report a success rate of 95.5%, which is far higher than expected from published results. However, this survey is the first in the public domain to focus on German companies.

Evaluation of the Results

The next step in the project was the test of the hypotheses (1 to 22).

Similarities and Differences in the Results

The authors performed a regression analysis of the answers using the SPSS package. Examples of the statistics are shown in Tables 11 and 12.

In the graphical representation (see Figure 12), one can clearly see the different distribution of degrees of satisfaction with improvement of business processes vs. the estimated relevance of the analysis of as-is processes, especially process weak points. Those who rated the analysis of as-is processes relevant reported a higher satisfaction with the improvement of business processes, which means that Hypothesis 1 (the analysis of a company's as-is processes helps to reveal the existing process-weak-points and thus provides a good starting point for improving the business process quality) was accepted.

Figure 13 presents another example of the cross-reference regression analysis: test of Hypothesis 7 (The creation of comprehensive business process models which show the entire process flow, business tasks, pre- and post conditions of process tasks, organizational responsibilities, etc. is a prerequisite for well-structured business processes and contribute thus to business process quality). This hypothesis was also accepted on the basis of the statistical evidence.

Figure 14 shows a further example of a cross-reference, which is the test of hypothesis 17 (A star-shaped communications structure contributes to better quality of business processes). Again, the hypothesis could be accepted.

The patterns illustrated for these three hypotheses were similar for all hypotheses.

Some Explanations for the Results

The main results of the research are: first, the 22 proposed hypotheses on the connection of an engineering-like approach with the satisfaction of the outcome of the ERP projects are to be accepted; second, there is a significant difference in the project success and in the project satisfaction of the national surveys.

As we have shown in the previous paragraphs, some of the U.S. companies gave a low priority to the objectives other than that of implementing the software itself. The results suggest those Americans were less concerned than the Germans with issues such as: consideration of strategic objectives, process analysis, business process optimization, IT strategy, integration of functions, and the staffing and communication structure of the project. It might suggest that Americans have a more informal approach to project management than Germans.

In discussions with academic colleagues, the authors identified several factors that could lead to the explanation of the differences in the results:

- Differences in the selection method of the samples
- Differences in the survey method (telephone and Internet)
- Differences in the answering attitudes of both groups
- Different management levels who decide the ERP implementation in each sample
- Different ERP implementation project approaches in each sample
- Different national cultures

Each of these options is discussed below.

Differences in the Selection Method of the Samples

As described in an earlier section, the sample selection was quite different: in Germany the researchers called CIOs of insurance companies, some CIOs of industrial companies, and SAP consulting firms, who reported on projects of their clients. The contact numbers were retrieved from individuals known to the researchers.

In the United States the data acquisition was much more difficult: because the first 50 phone calls brought nil response, e-mails were sent to nearly 10,000 e-mail addresses from a database purchased from a commercial address vendor.

Hence, the selection methods of the samples might have influenced the results of the surveys.

Differences in the Survey Method (Telephone and Internet)

In Germany the respondents were called by telephone. This was done by a research student. In total 88 valid questionnaires were completed.

In the United States a Web-based questionnaire was used, which was completed online by the anonymous participants. Of the 10,000 individuals who received the e-mail, 37 valid responses were received.

This leads to the conclusion that the survey methods might also have influenced the results of the surveys.

Differences in the Answering Attitudes of Both Groups

Discussions with academic colleagues raised the suspicion that there are different answering attitudes in the two national groups. For example it could be that Germans tend to exaggerate their success and Americans are more willing to confess a failure. This hypothesis was not investigated as part of the research.

Different Management Levels Who Decide the ERP Implementation in Each Sample

Again, discussions suggest that in U.S. companies, investment decisions are made at lower hierarchical levels than in Germany companies. Zurawski (2004) confirmed this fact based on his own experience. This may lead to a different scope of projects: middle management tends to see mainly the direct effect to its domain whereas top management thinks in strategic dimensions. This may be the reason why the German companies considered strategic objectives in the ERP implementation project and had a wider scope than the U.S. ones.

Different ERP Implementation Project Approaches in Each Sample

In many U.S. companies, teams of consultants are hired for the ERP implementation project and in many cases they even work offsite with only little connection to the target company (Zurawski, 2004). The reason for this procedure is that managers try to avoid disturbing daily business by such a project and to pass the responsibility over to the hired consultants. The consultants are in a competitive business environment and try to get the contract for a reasonable price and a reasonable profit. So, if they included a thorough as-is analysis plus a business process optimization in their offer, they would be unlikely to get the contract. This may be one reason why the U.S. companies did not care so much about strategic objectives and had a narrower scope compared to the Germans.

In Germany there is a different situation. The ERP implementation project is a top management decision because of the much tighter budget constraints. Companies try to avoid the hiring of consultants as they are considered too expensive compared to the core staff (Zurawski, 2004). In addition, managers try to be in line with their middle management and the clerical staff. This is due to the German business culture as well as to the power of the German trade unions, which have the legal right of one half of the seats on the supervising board.

Table 13. Hofstede's culture factors for selected nations (from Hofstede & Bond, 1988)

Nations	Uncertainty Avoidance	Individualism and Collectivism	Power Distance	Masculinity and Femininity
UK	35	89	35	66
U.S.	46	91	40	62
Germany	65	67	35	66
Turkey	85	37	66	45
France	86	71	68	43

One more factor that might influence the results is the nature of the German workforce. Hofstede (1993) states:

The highly skilled and responsible German workers ('Facharbeiter') do not necessarily need a manager, American-style, to 'motivate' them. They expect their boss or Meister to assign their tasks and to be the expert in resolving technical problems. Comparisons of similar German, British, and French organizations show the Germans as having the highest rate of personnel in productive roles and the lowest both in leadership and staff roles.

In Germany's industry, an IT–"Facharbeiter" profession has been established as one of the apprenticeship programs, called "Organisationsprogrammierer." These are the technical staff members for development and maintenance of IT systems, and they also know how to implement packaged software systems like ERP.

Different National Cultures

One further way to explain the differences in the project outcomes is to see them in light of Hofstede's (1979, 2000) four culture factors that influence the behavior of people, as described earlier. As shown in Table 13, the cultural factors that differ significantly between Germany and the United States are *uncertainty avoidance* and *individualism/collectivism,* which can mean that Americans are more likely to take the risk of a less formal approach in implementing an ERP system and are less likely to assure themselves of progress by reference to their 'social environment'.

From Table 13 one can recognize the factors in which U.S. citizens are different from the Germans: uncertainty avoidance and individualism/collectivism. The U.S. has a lower uncertainty avoidance (46) compared to Germany (65), which means Americans are more likely to take a risk. The second cultural factor that is significantly different is the individualism/collectivism factor. This is an expression of the high individualistic attitude (91) of U.S. citizens and a more collectivistic attitude (67) of the Germans.

These findings correspond with the consideration in the two previous sections on decision-making management levels and implementation approaches. The U.S. companies follow a more informal approach to ERP implementation due to their individualism and high willingness in

Figure 15. Functions and processes of a business environment

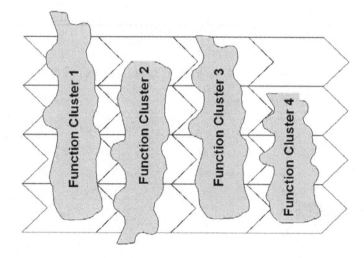

risk taking, while the German companies follow a more conservative approach as suggested by academics (e.g., Nah, Lau, & Kuang, 2001; Lau, 2003) and practitioners (e.g., Doane, 2004). They do so because they avoid risk and take advice from others to be concordant with the opinion of many members of the enterprise. By doing this they are rewarded by a higher success rate, but they have to pay the price by being involved in a slow decision process.

EVALUATION OF COMMON STANDARD ERP SOFTWARE IMPLEMENTATION APPROACHES

This section presents and evaluates several action models for implementing standard software systems. The purpose of this section is to provide and apply a framework of evaluation criteria for the capability of business process optimization. Based on this evaluation, and consideration of the survey outcomes presented above, the section presents a new approach to implementing standard software systems.

Figure 16. The ASAP procedure model

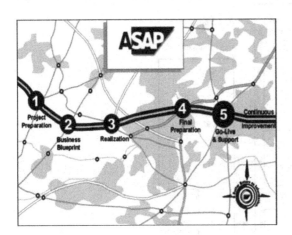

Overview of SSW Implementation Approaches

If we consider an enterprise, we have, depending on the internal organization, a set of business processes that are performed in different organizational units. According to Knoell, Slotos, and Suk (1996), processes are subdivided into several levels and finally into functions. These functions may occur in more than one business process. In small organizations the business processes are assigned to only a few people. But in large organizations the business functions are included in many business processes. Therefore the design of the functions, taking into account their reuse in different processes, becomes important.

As shown in Figure 15, there is a network of functions (vertical) and processes (horizontal) to consider in order to take not only the factual correctness of functions and processes into account, but also to design the functions in a manner so that the workflow in the processes runs smoothly.

On the other hand, the effectiveness and efficiency of the workflow of the processes cannot only be determined by their suitability to adapt to the pre-assembled functions, but is also driven by the demands of the customers and other organizational units. The organizational units, which have interfaces to a specific process, according to Deming (2000) and ISO 9000 (1990), should be treated as customers as well.

In spite of these issues there are still purely functionally driven approaches to software implementation in use (mainly by standard software vendors). There are also purely process-driven approaches (mainly by consulting firms who focus on business process optimization).

Example of a Function-Driven Approach: ASAP

The function-oriented approach is still very common in cases where the software implementation is only considered as the replacement of manually performed functions by computerized functions. This will include small to medium enterprises, where no elaborated workflows (or business processes) exist, or even in the larger ones with several thousand employees, where the management is not aware of the strategic importance of IT to the enterprise. This approach can work well and provide good results in minor software projects, where only a few functions have to be implemented, for example, the replacement of manual data entry of the incoming correspondence in an insurance company by digital scanners. In this case only one organizational unit of the enterprise is affected, so the effects to the other ones may be ignored (Schmidt, 1999). Such an approach requires a specific project management concept for the project phases as well as for the application developers and users in the enterprise (Knoell et al., 2001). One example of a well-documented function-oriented approach is ASAP.

ASAP stands for "Accelerated SAP." This approach from SAP AG aims to accelerate the implementation process of SAP R/3 systems.

Therefore, it is not surprising that the parallel meaning of ASAP is "as soon as possible." ASAP is a sophisticated approach derived from the original SAP procedure model. As with the original SAP procedure model, ASAP is phase oriented. All phases are arranged/depicted by means of a so-called roadmap (see Figure 16).

This roadmap is an essential part of ASAP, as it provides descriptions for each activity to be performed during the implementation. Each phase of the roadmap consists of work packages which include certain activities and tasks. In addition, ASAP provides support by means of specific tools and so-called accelerators, such as checklists, guidelines, documentation patterns, different kinds of templates for the creation of project plans, and examples.

SAP has also developed an ASAP approach which puts the focus on a release changeover. This specific procedure, denoted as "ASAP for Upgrade," provides work packages, tools, and accelerators which particularly address the upgrade of SAP R/3 systems (SAP, 2000). The

Figure 17. Kirchmer's strategy-based approach

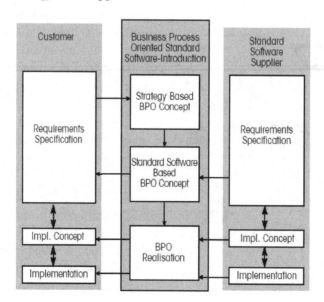

Figure 18. Overview Target Enterprise project phases (Baan, 1999)

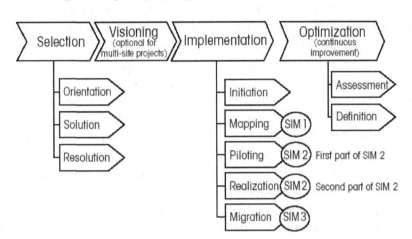

ASAP approach is widely used, as it gives the company's IT staff and the consultants clear guidelines for a fast and secure implementation of the SAP system.

Example of a Process-Driven Approach: Kirchmer's Strategy-Based Approach

Kirchmer (1996) has developed an implementation approach that focuses on the strategy-driven implementation of standard software. His experience indicated that too many standard software projects in practice are considered from a mainly technical point of view. For instance, developing interface programs and producing certain parameter settings are very often predominant project activities, instead of focusing on business targets. Therefore, his approach focuses on a company's strategic targets, which are to be followed throughout the entire implementation project.

The main components, as illustrated in Figure 17, are the strategy-based BPO (business process optimization) concept, the software-based BPO concept, the BPO realization, as well as measures for continuous business improvement. Scheer's (1996) purely process-driven ARIS architecture provides the basis for his lifecycle model. The requirements definition level of

the ARIS-architecture is subdivided into two phases. The strategy-based BPO concept deals with the company-specific business targets. The standard software-based BPO concept takes the system-oriented requirements specification into consideration. The design specification and implementation level of ARIS are reflected by Kirchmer's BPO realization. This phase utilizes the strategy-based and the software-based BPO concepts by implementing all process optimizations together with the standard software system (Kirchmer, 1996). Since it is mostly realized with Scheer's ARIS toolset, there is little opportunity to deviate from this approach.

Example of a Function-Oriented and Process-Driven Approach: Target Enterprise

Target Enterprise (TE) is a project management methodology that was developed by Baan to manage the selection, implementation, and optimization of Baan ERP systems (Baan, 1999). The main aims of TE (see Figure 18) are the acceleration and quality improvement of Baan implementations, reduction of implementation costs, and minimization of projects risks (Baan, 1999). The goal-directed project management (GDPM) approach, which was originally created by Coopers & Lybrand Consultancy, represents the underlying concept of TE (Hommes, Lichtenberg, Obers, & Roeleveld, 1998). Similar to Target, GDPM is a result-driven methodology that enables definition of project phases and milestones in a very flexible manner. In TE, milestones are a fundamental concept. TE enables a flexible mapping of milestones to project phases. However, the underlying character of the implementation project naturally determines the milestones to be selected (Hommes et al., 1998).

The flexible use of the dynamic enterprise modeler (DEM) is a particular characteristic of TE. It is function oriented and process driven, too. Due to the quasi-integration of DEM into TE, a company's business processes can be modeled during all project phases. For this reason, it is possible to integrate process adaptations into the Baan application in a dynamic way (Baan, 1999). TE provides further tools for defining, configuring, and managing implementation projects, such as project configuration tool, project cost planning, and controlling. In addition, there are numerous handbooks, forms, documents, presentation templates, and guidelines available which support the execution of Target's various project stages (Baan, 1999).

The authors' experience suggests very few projects use the capabilities of TE and DEM. The main reasons for not applying this method is, first, the lack of trained and experienced consultants who can apply this method, and second, the belief that money can be saved by applying the purely function-oriented approach. Consequently, in most of the Baan projects the purely function-oriented approach is applied. This is supported by the consulting experiences of Berger (2003) and Seibel (2003).

Quality Evaluation Framework with Respect to the Support of BPO

As indicated in the previous section, several action models for implementing standard software systems have been provided in the literature, by suppliers of ERP systems, and by consulting com-

Figure 19. Assessment of SSW-implementation approaches

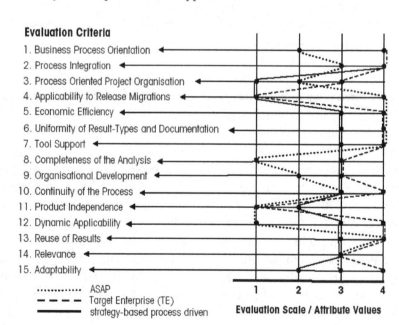

274

Figure 20. Principle of the semi-process-oriented approach

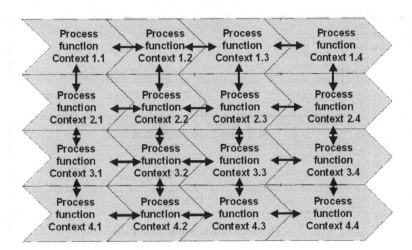

panies. Each action model may provide benefits in the context of a certain implementation scenario, for example, a function-driven implementation differs from a strategy-based approach. standard software projects do not necessarily succeed in optimizing the client's business processes and therefore do not fulfill the actual project objectives because the applied implementation approach often regards the implementation process as a technical challenge. Therefore it is essential to evaluate the available action models with respect to the underlying implementation scenario. Such an evaluation ensures selection of the appropriate action model that fits the project's implementation scenario and its scope. The purpose of this section is to provide and apply a framework of evaluation criteria for business process optimization.

ASSESSMENT OF SSW IMPLEMENTATION APPROACHES

This section considers the implementation methods capability for process improvement. It should be noted that the framework consciously neglects other criteria such as their capability for, for example, company-wide vs. site-specific implemen-

tations, legacy alignment vs. mass conversion, or phased vs. big bang implementations.

The criteria are taken from Kuehl and Knoell (2002), where they are explained in detail.

In Figure 19, each implementation approach is evaluated on a scale with four different attribute values:

1. The criterion is neither realized nor described or mentioned as a principle, objective, or characteristic.
2. The criterion is simply mentioned or described on an abstract level as a principle, objective, or characteristic. However, it is not realized or its realization is not sufficiently described in the form of precise project activities, guidelines, and so forth.
3. The criterion is realized within single project phases by means of defined project activities, guidelines, and so forth.
4. The criterion is realized throughout the implementation lifecycle—that is, all project phases meet this criterion by providing sufficient project activities, guidelines, and so forth.

Figure 18 summarizes the findings. For all implementation approaches (except the purely

Figure 21. The project phases of an ERP project (Kuehl & Knoell, 2002; Knoell et al., 2004)

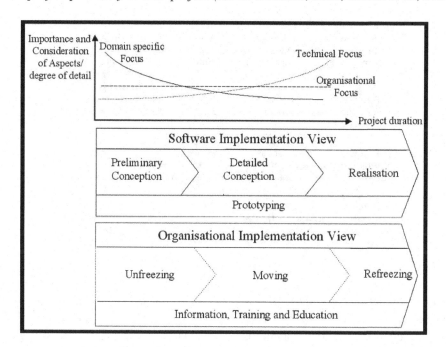

function driven), the implementation of the software is more or less business process-driven. Two approaches define appropriate project activities, and results that are able to realize process improvements. ASAP does not provide a sophisticated process optimization, as it primarily focuses on software functions. A process-oriented project organization is captured by only one of the assessed lifecycle models, namely Target Enterprise.

All lifecycle models aim for an efficient implementation of systems. The proprietary approaches have developed sophisticated toolkits to ensure an accelerated project execution and more uniform and consistent project results. These approaches also reuse existing solutions such as reference models, document patterns, or system templates.

Only TE provides a complete analysis in terms of actual processes, their weaknesses, and possible future improvements. ASAP disregards existing processes entirely. The dynamic applicability, which allows later requirements to be included

within the project lifecycle, is mainly considered by TE. ASAP does not offer opportunities for iterations as it is based on the sequential waterfall approach. Adaptability or tailoring of the lifecycle is consistently realized only by TE, as it provides predefined project scenarios with related phases, activities, results, and so forth.

SEMI-PROCESS-ORIENTED IMPLEMENTATION OF ERP SYSTEMS

Based on the results of the surveys and the investigations presented above, the authors developed a new approach to enhance the likelihood of a positive result of an ERP implementation project. It appears from the surveys that it is difficult for the company's top management to set appropriate goals for the project managers and to find enough skilled members of staff for the project teams.

Introduction

From the evaluation presented in Figure 18, Kirchmer's (1996) strategy-based approach proved to be the one that satisfies the strategic goals and leads to a system with optimized business processes. However, it is difficult to find enough members of staff who are capable of performing at the appropriate level for such a project. The other two approaches (ASAP and Target Enterprise) are proprietary or do not support business process optimization to a satisfactory degree.

Based on this background, the authors developed a new approach, which optimizes the business processes and does not require highly skilled staff to such an extent: the semi-process-oriented approach, which is explained in detail below.

Figure 20 shows the major goal of this new approach: the seamless interconnection of all business processes and all business functions in an enterprise.

The Project Phases

Figure 21 provides a general overview of the project phases and the importance of different aspects in each phase. The table compares technical, domain-specific, and organizational aspects with respect to their importance in the projects' progress.

Domain-specific aspects such as design decisions for business processes and requirements on the functional conception of the standard software are relevant for the early phases of the projects. A technical focus becomes more relevant as the project moves into the realization phase, in which parameterization concepts and program specifications have to be implemented and tested. However, even the conceptual phases must take into consideration fundamental technical aspects such as technical interfaces to collaborating systems, data migration, and the overall IT architecture, as they may have a significant influence on later implementation activities. For example,

the decision to link the system with middleware in order to organize the data interchange with collaborating systems may have substantial influence on the number and the complexity of interfaces to be developed. Such a decision must be carefully considered at an early stage of the project. Organizational development or change management measures relate to the entire project. Prototyping is an accompanying project activity for single business processes that might be realized by means of the standard software for demonstration purposes.

Each of the three phases covers in principle the same aspects of interest with a different level of detail. Generally the preliminary concept starts with a process analysis and optimization, which is the basis for the following IT function design and all further implementation activities. Functional requirements of a certain process are developed for each process-function context. They will be consolidated with the requirements of other business processes. All process-related dependencies will be regarded that way. This causes some sort of iteration of single activities within a project phase, but it does not lead to an iterative execution of all project phases. In contrast to a purely process-oriented approach, the entire system will not be developed incrementally. Yet, the main result types, such as the blueprint concept and the software specification, are based on business processes.

Although the realization phase is carried out once, each IT function will be parameterized repeatedly for every process. One function cluster is assigned to one responsible expert who does all system adjustments and parameterizations according to the specification. Such an expert only needs to know the assigned function cluster in detail. Figure 21 shows how the aspects of interest are addressed during the project's execution. All project activities are briefly denoted by a keyword in the table. Comprehensive explanations are provided in the sections that describe the respective phases.

Key Components of the Approach

An initial implementation project and a release changeover project are based on an evaluation of business processes in a slightly different way. We explain these differences by means of the process models that will be used for each of these project types. First, we have to introduce the different kinds of processes that are relevant for a standard software implementation.

A business process design as part of the implementation project generally uses four different kinds of model:

1. Model of actual business processes
2. Model of software-related reference processes
3. Model of optimized ideal business processes
4. Model of optimized target business processes

These four models are the conceptual core components of the entire software implementation.

Actual Processes

An actual model covers the present situation of the process flow. All processes have been selected by means of relevant criteria. The actual models capture the following essential processes' characteristics:

- All activities and IT functions in the form of parallel or sequentially executed process-steps
- The process-steps' pre- and post-conditions
- All performing organizational units
- The activities' important input and output information
- The involved IT systems, as well as their technical interfaces

- The actual models provide a solid basis for the evaluation of the processes' quality or possible optimizations that are not necessarily caused by the standard software.

Reference Processes

The actual processes will then be compared with the software's implied reference processes. By comparing these models, a reference model-based optimization of the actual processes becomes feasible.

Optimized Ideal Processes

An ideal model that depicts processes which have been optimized in every respect can then be produced. The techniques for process optimization are based on the ERP software reference processes and on standard process improvement techniques. Normally, many measures for a reference model-based process optimization are implied by the standard ERP software, through the flexible mechanisms provided by the software's parameterization capabilities. Hence, several ideal models can theoretically exist in parallel. The challenge for the analysis and optimization task is to build the ideal model that fits the company's requirements without any restrictions. The total range of possible optimization measures forms a so-called target space and the logical ideal models are located inside this target space.

Optimized Target Processes

In the last step, one has to decide on the target model which depicts the optimized business processes as they are intended for further implementation. A target model is located within the target space as well as the ideal model. It is based upon the ideal model, but both models are not necessarily congruent with another. This means that they are not located in the same position within the target space. A company may face

Figure 23. Functional release changeover

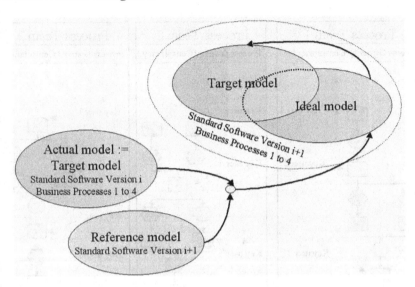

Figure 22. Key components in an initial implementation project

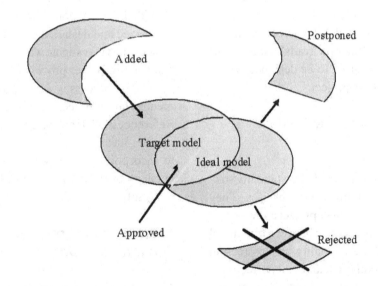

technical, organizational, and political restrictions that prevent it from realizing all measures. The difference between these two models is caused by the company's decisions around optimization measures/design aspects. As explained earlier, a lifecycle model should fulfill the criteria of a complete analysis, which means it should incor-

porate all future requirements and optimization possibilities (see Figure 22).

Project Type: Initial Implementation Project

In this case, the project objective is an initial implementation of the software. An optimizing

Figure 24. Rotational team member assignment

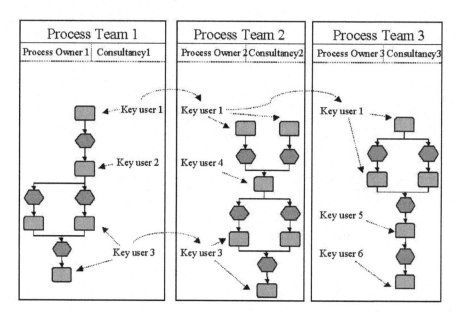

process design for all affected business processes is part of the project. Models for actual, ideal, and target processes will not be available before the project's start. They need to be designed within the early stages of the project.

Project Type: Functional Release Changeover

Permanent improvements of the standard software require further functional releases. They require a release changeover project as described earlier. One has to distinguish between functional releases with new functionality and correction releases, which merely provide error corrections. In the following, we assume a functional release changeover, as the implementation of a correction release has a limited technical character that is not within the scope of the semi-process-oriented approach. A functional release changeover may lead to two different types of projects.

One is illustrated in Figure 23. It is based on a process-oriented implementation project, on which software-based process optimizations have already been carried out. In that case, newly

provided IT functions need to be applied to the optimized and designed business processes. The project must investigate whether new IT functions can lead to further process optimizations.

Actual processes correspond to the implemented target processes of the previous project. Reference models are based on the new functional release. Ideal and target models must be revised to incorporate the new reference models. New versions of these models will be developed accordingly.

Project Team Composition and Communication

The project organization is an important ingredient of the semi-process-oriented approach; it incorporates well-recognized committees such as a steering committee, an advisory board, and so forth. It is not based on function cluster-oriented sub-project teams, but it utilizes process teams which are responsible for the optimization and implementation of entire business processes, for which specific roles have been defined. In this chapter, we briefly comment on the most impor-

Figure 25. Cooperation in centralized team structures

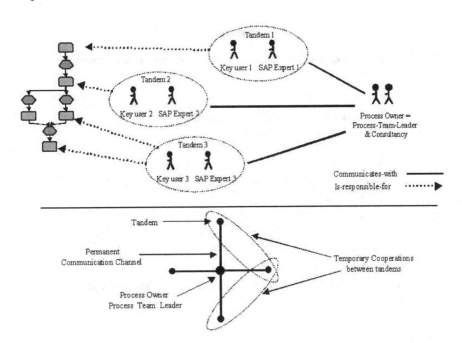

tant aspects of the project organization, namely the team composition and the communication between team members. As mentioned earlier, the project organization depends on the availability of appropriately skilled staff. This is influenced by the company's organizational structure. In the following sub-sections, we describe options for project team compositions and how they depend on a company's organizational structure.

Variant 1: A Process Organization Does Partly Exist

The company has partially implemented a process organization. This variant is likely for companies that have already attempted to migrate their organization. In practice, it is more realistic to find organizations in such an intermediate stage, which do not fulfill the ambitious claims for all-around processing.

Although the company strives for case-closing processing with "one face to the customer"-care, process organizations have not yet widely devel-

oped staff who are able to cope with all tasks. A process owner has general knowledge about the entire process, but detailed knowledge on a functional level may be contributed by individual staff members. For that reason, the project team needs to be composed of process owners and if necessary several key users. Each key user cooperates with one standard software expert for one IT function. Both are required to conceptualize and realize functions of the new system.

Practice shows that the key user's functional knowledge is often applicable to several processes. Thus it is sensible to assign key users to more than one team. Such a rotational assignment of team members is also applicable to standard software experts to implement an IT function in more than one process-function context (see Figure 24).

Again, such team structures are useful if the company has not sufficiently migrated to all-around processing teams. An historically evolved functional division of labor has yielded experts for single activities occurring in many processes. Implementation of standard software is an op-

Figure 26. Example of a process-driven project organization

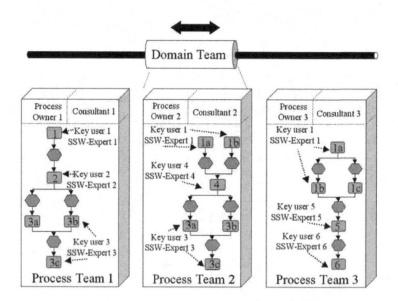

portunity to develop both process knowledge and system knowledge, so that process owners may become experts in the details of their processes and key users acquire important process knowledge.

For the purpose of goal-directed and efficient teamwork, rigorous communication structures are required. Coordination responsibilities are given to process owners as they have internalized the processes, their implications, and the mutual dependencies between activities. A process owner plays an important part in the overall process design, whereas key users and standard software experts are responsible for the later functional concept and parameterization of the system. As mentioned earlier, several key users may be assigned to the IT functions. Interfaces between IT functions and the side effects of parameterization require decisions to be made by several different team members. To do so, process owners coach their team members on the dependencies between functions and decide which team members need to cooperate to ensure integrated IT functions. Cooperation and coordi-

nation are based on a centralized team structure with a star-shaped communication model (see Figure 25). Information flows will be dynamically initiated by the process owner as required. Team members cooperate temporarily to solve the open functional integration and interface questions. A permanent communication channel is established only between tandems (i.e., key user and standard software expert) and the process owner. In contrast to a network communication model, which promotes equal knowledge acquisition of all team members, a star-shaped communication limits knowledge transfer to selected team members providing partial system information for system-induced tuning needs.

Variant 2: Process Organization is not Implemented

If the company takes the standard ERP software implementation as an occasion to migrate to a process organization, organizational development has to yield process teams for the company's organizational structure. In this stage, one must assume

Figure 27. Evaluation of the semi-process-oriented approach

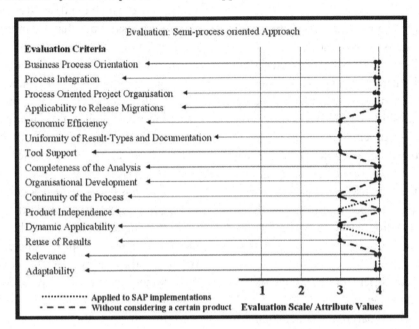

that process owners have not been identified, let alone well prepared, for the management of process teams within the new structure. The project team requires process teams and staff members who have a comprehensive process knowledge. An early identification of potential process owners ensures the involvement of qualified staff and their coaching for their future demanding role within the company. Experience shows that leaders of present work groups have often acquired a broad professional knowledge that exceeds their original sphere of responsibility; they may be familiar with the connections to previously execute and succeeding process activities and IT functions. Legacy system supervisors also represent the connecting link between the user department and the IT department, and have a good command of the IT systems and the underlying specialized knowledge. Both are probably suitable candidates for process team leaders (see Figure 26).

As already described, process owners cooperate with tandems composed of key users and standard software experts. Again, a rotational assignment of key users and standard software experts is useful, provided that similar IT functions occur in different processes. Unlike the previous organization, a broad process knowledge is not available and needs to be developed in advance. For that reason, process owners and accompanying external consultants (standard ERP software experts) must develop process designs as a basis for the further investigation and conception of IT functions. A so-called domain team composed of experienced professional experts with a broad view on the application domain must be established to provide information on dependencies and interfaces between process functions.

One or more domain teams may provide their services to several process teams, alternately. Cooperation between these teams needs to be well coordinated. Interview sessions should be scheduled and carefully prepared, as few domain experts are probably involved in many processes. Based on the outcomes, the process owner must initiate temporary cooperation between its team members if functional dependencies need clarification and consideration in several concepts.

Conclusions of this Section

Of the SSW implementation methods in the above analysis, Baan TE is the most sophisticated and flexible. It fulfills nearly all evaluation criteria, but unfortunately in many projects it is not used, as noted by the experiences of Berger (2003), Seibel (2003), and Zurawski (2003). This is in spite of the fact that it provides excellent tools for all phases of the ERP project including the DEM process modeler. Even projects implemented by Baan's own consultants do not use it in a sufficient way, if they use it at all. A second problem with TE is the fact that it is proprietary and generally not applicable to any software systems other than Baan.

ASAP seems to suffer from its pursuit of low costs and rapid implementation periods. Although a business blueprint is part of the conceptualization, it includes neither a sufficient process analysis and optimization, nor a complete specification of requirements which are possibly relevant to future implementation projects.

The strategy-based approach is very much focused on a process-driven implementation, which is regarded throughout all phases. It is also very much concerned with strategy development which may not be entirely relevant. Experience suggests that business strategies will not be incorporated within software implementation projects, but are relevant to higher-level strategy projects. Unfortunately, the strategy-based approach described here neglects the process-oriented project organization, which is an important ingredient of an applicable lifecycle model and needs high resources in staff quality and quantity.

A process-driven implementation of standard ERP software needs to be based on a suitable project organization. Team structures differ from conventional project organizations. Process orientation must meet the requirements of the dependencies between IT functions. Integration of functions within processes and between pro-cesses must be considered from the outset. For that purpose, suitable staff must be integrated into teams. Process owners have to initiate temporary cooperation between team members to provide coherent solutions, taking into account dependencies between process activities and IT functions. This is also important if the company does not intend to migrate their organizational structure towards a process organization. A centralized team structure should be applied for efficiency reasons.

Great challenges arise if a company intends to migrate its organizational structure together with the implementation of the new system. Organizational development and comprehensive training and coaching of staff needs to be carried out. Domain teams should provide professional support to process owners. Team members should start to integrate the process functions only when business processes have been redesigned and process owners have internalized the new process design.

A semi-process-oriented implementation of standard ERP software will lead to a complete analysis of system requirements and organizational requirements, and may therefore improve the technical integration and the organizational integration of the new standard software system. The probability of time-consuming change requests in the final stage of a project will be reduced.

On the other hand, the approach requires sound analysis and optimization methodologies and a rigorous project management approach to restrict the efforts for the process design activities, because the functional view (which is derived from processes in the form of process-function contexts) is also crucial for the implementation of the system. The approach described here has been used in various projects in German and Swiss insurance companies, which had previously used the process-oriented strategy-based approaches. Using the semi-process-oriented approach, not only was the project success better, but also the satisfaction in the user departments was improved.

CONCLUSION

In this chapter we have presented the results of surveys performed in three different countries on the outcome of ERP projects. The result is that there is a strong relationship between the structured implementation approach and positive project result. In our samples we found different attitudes to ERP implementation projects. The majority of the respondents from our U.S.-based sample had a more "hands-on" informal approach, whereas the respondents of the German- and Turkish-based samples used a more formal approach. These attitudes may result from different national cultures or from the way the samples were drawn. However it is a consistent result that the structured implementation approach gives a more likely successful project outcome.

The chapter also evaluated three common ERP implementation approaches and particularly their capability for business process improvement. Each of the three approaches has its advantages and drawbacks. ASAP does not strongly support business process optimization, Kirchemer's strategy-based approach requires high levels of skilled staff, while Baan's Target Enterprise provides excellent tools that are only useful in Baan implementations.

Instead, the chapter presents a new semi-process-oriented approach, which incorporates the advantages of the investigated approaches without such demands on highly skilled staff. The way this is achieved is by establishing process teams with experts from different areas who are responsible for the different aspects. The practicability of this approach has been proven in several ERP implementation and release changeover projects.

ACKNOWLEDGMENT

We thank Burt Swanson and Uday Karmarkar from UCLA Anderson School for their helpful suggestions and Ernst Leiss from the Department of Computer Science of the University of Houston for his comments. We gratefully acknowledge the financial support of the Volkswagen Foundation and the German Academic Exchange Service.

REFERENCES

Baan. (1999). *Target enterprise overview* (CD). Hannover, Germany: Baan-Invensys.

Baan. (2001). *Case study: Herman Miller implements extended process and knowledge management solution*. Hannover, Germany: Baan-Invensys.

Bagchi, K., Cerveny, R., Hart, P., & Peterson, M. (2003, August). The influence of national culture in information technology product adoption. In A. Hevner, D. Galletta, P. Cheney, & J. Ross (Eds.), *Proceedings of the 9th Americas Conference on Information Systems* (pp. 957-965), Tampa, FL.

Berger, M. (2003). *Personal communication*. Herne, Germany: EVU-IT.

Boehm, B.W., & Ross, R. (1989). Theory-W software project management: Principles and examples. *IEEE Transactions on Software Engineering, 7*(15), 902-916.

Boeing Corporation. (2003). *Define and control airplane configuration/manufacturing resource management*. Retrieved from http://www.boeing.com/commercial/initiatives/dcacmrm/dcac_summary.html

Brown, C., & Vessey, I. (2003, December). ERP implementation approaches: Toward a contingency framework. In P. De & J.I. DeGross (Eds.), *Proceedings of the 20th International Conference on Information Systems* (pp. 411-416), Charlotte, NC.

Daneva, M. (2004). ERP requirements engineering practice: Lessons learned. *IEEE Software, 21*(3), 26-33.

Deming, W.E. (2000). *Out of the crisis.* Cambridge: MIT Press.

Doane, M. (2004). *Ready, fire, aim: A failure of ERP readiness starts at the top.* Retrieved April 17, 2006, from http://techupdate.zdnet.com/techupdate/stories/main/Ready_Fire_Aim.html

Dorsey, P. (2003). *Why large IT projects fail.* Retrieved March 6, 2006, from http://www.datainformationservices.com/DIS/Forum/topic.asp?TOPIC_ID=21

Fairley, R.E., & Willshire, M.J. (2003). Why the Vasa sank: 10 problems and some antidotes for software projects. *IEEE Software, 3*(4), 18-25.

Franch, X., & Carvallo, J.P. (2003). Using quality models in software package selection. *IEEE Software, 20*(1), 34-41.

Heales, J., & Cockroft, S. (2003, August). The influence of national culture on the level and outcome of IS decision making in the IS evolution/redevelopment decision. In A. Hevner, D. Galletta, P. Cheney, & J. Ross (Eds.), *Proceedings of the 9th Americas Conference on Information Systems* (pp. 975-986), Tampa, FL.

Hofstede, G. (1979). Value systems in forty countries: Interpretation, validation, and consequences for theory. In L.H. Eckensberger, W.J. Lonner, & Y.H. Pootinga (Eds.), *Cross-cultural contributions to psychology.* Lisse, The Netherlands: Swets and Zeitlinger.

Hofstede, G. (1993). Cultural constraints in management theories. *Academy of Management Executive, 7*(1), 81-94.

Hofstede, G. (2000). *Culture's consequences.* Thousand Oaks, CA: Sage.

Hofstede, G., & Bond, M.H. (1984). Hofstede's culture dimensions—An independent validation using Rokeach's value survey. *Journal of Cross-Cultural Psychology, 15*(4), 417-433.

Hofstede, G., & Bond, M.H. (1988). The Confucius connection: From cultural roots to economic growth. *Organizational Dynamics, 16*(4), 4-21.

Holland, C.P., & Light, B. (1999). A critical success factors model for ERP implementation. *IEEE Software, 16*(3), 30-36.

Hommes, B.-J., Lichtenberg, L., Obers, G.-J., & Roeleveld, L. (1998). BaanWise. In P. Wenzel & H. Post (Eds.), *Business computing mit Baan.* Wiesbaden, Germany: Vieweg.

House, R., Javidan, M., Hanges, P., & Dorfman, P. (2002). Understanding cultures and implicit leadership theories across the globe: An introduction to project GLOBE. *Journal of World Business, 37*(1), 3-10.

ISO. (1990). *ISO 9000 standard series, guidelines for quality assurance.* Berlin: Beuth.

Kapp, K.M. (2003). *The USA principle—A framework for ERP implementation success.* Retrieved April 27, 2006, from http://facweb.cti.depaul.edu/rstarinsky/files/USAPrinciple.pdf

Kappos, A., & Croteau, A.-M. (2002, August). Organizational change and culture: Insight on BPR projects. In *Proceedings of the 8th Americas Conference on Information Systems* (pp. 2076-2084), Dallas, TX.

Ke, W., & Wei, K.K. (2005, May). Organizational culture and leadership in ERP implementation. In *Proceedings of the 2005 Pacific Asia Conference on Information Systems* (pp. 428-440), Taipei, Taiwan.

Keil, M., Tan, B.C.Y, Wei, K.K., Saarinen, T., Tuunainen, V., & Wassenaar, A. (2000). A cross-cultural study on escalation of commitment behavior in software projects. *MIS Quarterly, 24*(2), 299-325.

Kirchmer, M. (1996). *Geschäftsprozessorientierte einführung von standardsoftware.* Wiesbaden, Germany: Gabler.

Knoell, G., & Knoell, H.-D. (1998). Der mensch im IT projekt [The human in the IT project]. *IT Management, 9,* 28-32.

Knoell, H.D., Kuehl, L.W.H., Kuehl, R.W.A., & Moreton, R. (2001). *Optimising business performance with standard software systems.* Wiesbaden, Germany: Vieweg.

Knoell, H.D., Kuehl, L.W.H., Kuehl, R.W.A., & Moreton, R. (2004). Evaluation of standard ERP software implementation approaches in terms of their capability for business process optimization. *JCISE, 4,* 271- 277.

Knoell, H.D., Slotos, T., & Suk, W. (1996). Quality assurance of specifications—The user's point of view. In *Proceedings of the 8th SEKE* (pp. 450-456), Lake Tahoe.

Kontzer, T. (2003). Business guru queries benefits of IT—Peter Drucker claims corporate IT is not delivering what companies want. *Computing,* (February).

Kuehl, L.W.H., & Knoell, H.D. (2002). An improved approach to the semi-process-oriented implementation of standardized ERP systems. In *Proceedings of the Engineering Technology Conference on Energy* (ETCE 2002), Houston, TX.

Lau, L.K. (2003). Developing a successful implementation plan for ERP: Issues and challenges. *Proceedings of IACIS.*

Moreton, R., & Chester, M.F. (1997). *Transforming the business: The IT contribution.* London: McGraw-Hill.

Murray, M.G., & Coffin, G.W. (2001, August). A case study analysis of factors for success in ERP system implementations. In *Proceedings of the*

7th Americas Conference on Information Systems (pp. 1012-1018), Boston.

Nah, F.F.H., Lau, J.L.-S., & Kuang, J. (2001). Critical factors for successful implementation of enterprise systems. *Business Process Management Journal, 7*(3), 285-296.

Pahnke, C., Moreton, R., & Knoell, H.-D. (2004). Animated systems engineering (ASE)—Evaluation of a new approach to high quality groupware application specification and development. In *Proceedings of the 13th International Conference on Information Systems Development: Methods and Tools, Theory and Practice* (ISD 2004), Vilnius, Lithuania.

Ploenzke. (2002). *European SAP practice, umfrageergebnisse.* Wiesbaden, Germany.

Robey, D., Ross, J.W., & Boudreau, M.-C. (2000). *Learning to implement enterprise systems: An exploratory study of the dialectics of change.* Retrieved from http://www.cis.gsu.edu/~drobey/Cis8160/jmisvl8.PDF

SAP. (2000). *ASAP for upgrade, release 4.6C* (CD). Walldorf, Germany.

Scheer, A.W. (1996). *ARIS—House of business engineering.* Saarbruecken, Germany: Institut für Wirtschaftsinformatik an der Universität des Saarlandes.

Scheuss, R. (n.d.). *Wir kopieren zu viel.* Retrieved November 25, 2004, from http://www.manager-magazin.de/koepfe/artikel/0,2828,327331,00.html

Schmidt, W. (1999). *Personal communication.* Muenster, Germany: LVM Insurance Group.

Seibel, A. (2003). *Personal communication.* Frankfurt, Germany: CMG Group.

Srite, M. (1999, August). The influence of national culture on the acceptance and use of information technologies: An empirical study. In *Proceedings of the 5th Americas Conference on Information Systems* (pp. 1019-1021), Milwaukee, WI.

Standish Group. (1994). *The Chaos Report 1994.* Retrieved March 6, 2006, from http://www. standishgroup.com/sample_research/chaos_ 1994_1.php

Standish Group. (1996). *Unfinished voyages—A follow-up to the Chaos Report.* Retrieved March 6, 2006, from http://www.standishgroup.com/ sample_research/unfinished_voyages_1.php

Stensrud, E., & Myrtveit, I. (2003). Identifying high performance ERP projects. *IEEE Transactions on Software Engineering, 29*(5), 398-416.

Zurawski, M. (2003). *Personal communication.* Hannover, Germany: Deloitte Consulting.

Zurawski, M. (2004). *Personal communication.* Hannover, Germany: Deloitte Consulting.

Chapter XV
Success Factors for the Global Implementation of ERP/HRMS Software

Deanna House
University of Texas at Arlington, USA

Gert-Jan de Vreede
University of Nebraska at Omaha, USA
Delft University of Technology, The Netherlands

Peter Wolcott
University of Nebraska at Omaha, USA

Kenneth Dick
University of Nebraska at Omaha, USA

ABSTRACT

This research observes a global implementation of enterprise resource planning (ERP)/human resources management system (HRMS) software at an international company. The software was implemented in 16 countries. Variables such as cultural differences, communication-distance, management support, trust, and resistance to change were evaluated in the literature review. These variables have an impact on implementation success during global HRMS implementation. Further analyses on specific success factors faced with global implementations were evaluated using semi-structured interviews. The authors prepared a questionnaire to further explore the data. Respondents rated questions related to management support the highest overall. An interesting find was that the semi-structured interview results indicated that the software chosen was not a perfect fit for the global community. The mean for questions related to global HRMS success was higher for respondents located in the United States than those located in other locations.

INTRODUCTION

As companies expand globally, the challenge of integrating all parts of the business increases significantly. Many companies employ enterprise resource planning (ERP) systems to meet these challenges. However, ERP systems are difficult to implement successfully, and global ERP systems have additional challenges that compound the difficulties. This chapter summarizes research conducted to identify factors that influenced the success of a global implementation of enterprise resource planning/human resources management system (ERP/HRMS) software.

ERP software consists of a number of different information modules. Human resources management systems are a group of the modules of ERP software that typically house employee information such as payroll, compensation, training, and benefits. A majority of the research regarding ERP software does not specifically mention HRMS. However, because HRMS is one of the modules of ERP, HRMS and ERP are closely related.

Companies realize the value in storing global data using ERP software. Personal and work-related information about employees must be available for reporting and decision making. Typically human resources (HR) is the driving force behind the transformation to a global system. "If HR managers make it a top priority to link their systems on a global basis it will automatically elevate their role in expansion. HR departments must transform their operations in order to deal with the new global landscape" (Rothwell & Prescott, 1999, p. 7). Having access to global employee data gives companies the ability to get information quickly about the company as a whole.

The purpose of the research described in this chapter was to develop a better understanding of the factors that influence the success of a global ERP implementation. These factors included management support, resistance to change, communication-distance, trust, and cultural differences. We studied these factors in a case study of a global ERP implementation in a software company. Semi-structured interviews were conducted with key implementation team personnel. An evaluation was performed on the interview data and questionnaires were distributed to the entire global implementation team.

Global Software Inc. (the name has been changed to protect the identity of the company) is a software company that provides customer care and billing solutions for communications companies all over the world. Global Software Inc. provides services to more than 1,900 client sites—reaching over 40 million households worldwide. The publicly traded company employs approximately 2,600 employees. Global Software Inc. has offices throughout the United States, Canada, Mexico, Argentina, Brazil, France, the United Kingdom, Spain, Germany, Italy, Belgium, Singapore, Japan, Malaysia, Australia, India, and China. In 2002, Global Software Inc. nearly doubled its size by acquiring a global company. As a result, Global Software Inc. quickly went from a predominantly U.S.-based company to one with offices in multiple locations worldwide. The acquisition forced Global Software Inc. to evaluate its current business processes.

The HR tool in place before (and during) the acquisition was primarily a payroll tool that did not meet global business needs. The company needed a system that would store global data efficiently and be able to format that data to make strategic decisions. The executive management of the company knew that the current HRMS had to be reevaluated from a global perspective. The executive management was the main driving force behind the core global data requirements.

Global Software Inc. implemented a global HRMS so that all employee data could be located in the same system and be available to HR to make organizational decisions/evaluations. The company had one year to implement the ERP/HRMS system, and due to this time constraint it was necessary to focus on the components of the software that were necessary to house and process employee data—the primary requirement. Therefore, the global implementation consisted of the HRMS portion of the software. This included all HR functionality and processes such as payroll, employee self-service, benefits, compensation, and reporting. Additional software module implementations performed by Global Software Inc. are outside of the scope of this research. The literature research conducted includes ERP software as a whole. The Method section contains more detailed information about the project.

The next section discusses some of the key literature on global ERP implementation and the factors that influence success—cultural differences, communication-distance, resistance to change, management support, and trust. Subsequent sections discuss the research method and quantitative and qualitative results. Finally, we summarize key findings and identify limitations of the study and future research opportunities.

BACKGROUND

HRMS software is one of the modules within an ERP system. It is not surprising therefore that a substantial part of the literature on global HRMS implementations focuses on enterprise resource planning implementations as a whole. For the purpose of this research, ERP implementation research is considered to include HRMS implementations.

As companies increase business around the world and manage employees in many different global locations, they need to access organizational data not only to support strategic decision making, but also to have operational information about individual employees. Global systems assist in consolidating data, making the data consistent, accurate, more reliable, and faster to process (Loeb, Rai, Ramaprasad, & Sharma, 1998). When decisions need to be made, companies that have the ability to report on the entire employee population quickly and effectively are able to save both time and expense.

Global implementations face numerous challenges, including agreeing on common user requirements, introducing changes in business processes, coordinating applications development, coordinating software releases, and encouraging local users to support global systems (Laudon & Laudon, 2004). The subsequent implementation is further challenging as:

…global rollouts present unique issues with timing because dealing with multiple labor markets and economic conditions around the globe is much more challenging than planning around one labor market or one economy. (Wiechmann, Ryan, & Hemingway, 2003, p. 73)

A review of the literature reveals five key factors that appear to affect the global implementation of an HRMS: cultural differences, communication-distance, resistance to change, management support, and trust. Each is discussed below in detail.

Cultural Differences

It is important to keep culture in mind when implementing software globally. Cultural differences can cause noteworthy issues among global implementations. When several different cultures are working together in the same organization or on the same team, it is important to remain flexible and understanding of other cultures. Hofstede (1983) defines culture as "collective mental programming: it is that part of our conditioning that we share with other members of our nation, region, or group but not with members of other nations, regions, or groups" (p. 76). Mathis and Jackson (2000) state that "culture is composed of societal forces affecting the values, beliefs, and actions of a distinct group of people" (p. 116). "Our own culture conditions us, consciously and unconsciously, to the way things are done. In a thousand different situations every day, culture smoothes human performance—we know what is expected of us and what we can expect from others" (Elashmawi & Harris, 1993, p. 14). Elashmawi and Harris (1993) go on to state that our cultural values are based on experiences from childhood and beyond. The values that each individual has differ not only from country to country, but also within countries.

Hofstede conducted extensive research on culture. His seminal work describes four dimensions to characterize differences among countries: individualism vs. collectivism, large or small power distance, strong or weak uncertainty avoidance, masculinity vs. femininity (Hofstede, 1983). He later identified a fifth dimension, low vs. high long-term orientation. Global organizations can potentially use these dimensions to research differences among locations to help identify and avoid potential conflict.

Culture can affect a global implementation project in many ways. Cultural differences among team members can lead to conflict, misunderstandings, and poor team performance. Cultural differences among user communities can lead to differences in adoption of software implementations. But culture can also be a factor in successful implementations (Scott & Vessey, 2002). Open and honest communication engages employees in the system and creates loyalty for the product. Ives and Jarvenpaa (1991) found key issues involving the cultural environment and global IT. For instance, mangers should be sensitized to cultural, religious, and political differences and seek to agree on solutions that are the most mutually acceptable. Understanding and managing cultural differences is vital for successful implementation.

Gross and Wingerup (1999) suggest a strong global culture should be in place. A global corporate culture means "global planning, leadership, and governance that encourage multinational and cross-cultural collaboration. It means fostering global competencies and mobility of employees and managers. It means equipping people with a global mindset, social skills, and business skills" (Gross & Wingerup, 1999, p. 26). When values

are initially created, the organization founder can greatly influence these values. It is important not to devalue local cultures when this organizational culture is set. Hofstede found that even if an organizational founder is creating the culture, his or her national culture is typically reflected in the organizational culture and passed on internationally (Hofstede, 1985). It is important for the founder to ensure that values are in place for business reasons, not strictly because of his or her own beliefs.

Krumbholz, Galliers, Coulianos, and Maiden (2000) suggest that one way to prevent problems related to culture is to have the implementation team model business processes, the culture factors that influence these, and how these factors influence system solutions. Another suggestion for multi-cultural teams is to work on teambuilding activities. According to Fisher and Fisher (2001), teams that are separated by distance should participate in activities to get to know each other on a more personal level, keeping in mind that such activities should be appropriate for all cultures participating.

"Cultural and social changes should accompany and complement technological changes for sustained and effective organizational change" (Newell, Pan, Galliers, & Huang, 2001, p. 76). It is imperative that organizations evaluate and resolve any potential cultural issues before or during project implementations.

Communication-Distance

"Communication on a project involves the exchange of information, ideas and status between the core and extended project teams" (Purba & Shah, 2000, p. 9). When the team members are not in the same location or even the same country, communication can be difficult. Care must be taken to ensure that each team member feels that he or she is able to speak his or her mind.

Project teams must be able to communicate effectively when distributed around the world:

People in scattered locations must have reliable channels of communication and equal access to resources to avoid duplication of effort and redundant costs. Employees need to be able to collaborate with each other across great distances. And, to be competitive, companies need a technological infrastructure that helps them maximize productivity. (Solomon, 1998, p. 13)

Time zone differences can sometimes be an advantage. It may always be a workday at one of the locations.

Distance among team members may be beneficial for the team. According to Bagchi, Hart, and Peterson (2004):

ITs have provided a means for the complex, changing patterns of interdependence in individualistic societies to be managed. IT is commonly used to promote the strengths and overcome the limitations of these characteristics of individualistic societies. It does so by allowing people to work more independently from one another in the sense that they have the increased option to maintain greater physical distance and schedule their activities to meet the needs of the various groups to which they belong without concern for the location of others. (pp. 32-33)

As new technology emerges, employees may more easily collaborate globally.

However beneficial virtual collaboration may be, holding face-to-face meetings periodically may be necessary. Meeting face-to-face can cultivate trust among team members. Fisher and Fisher (2001) recommend periodic face-to-face meetings for milestones and items that are best addressed in person (such as training or social activities).

Language barriers can also cause miscommunications and misunderstandings during global implementations. If the shared language is a second language for some team members, they may need additional processing time for system setups and decisions. When different sites that do not speak the same language interact, communication can be very difficult (Sheu, Chae, & Yang, 2004).

Resistance to Change

According to a survey conducted to find challenges experienced during ERP implementations, "the main hurdle faced by all companies was resistance to change" (Gupta, 2000, p. 116). The implementation team must be considerate of the requirements and desires of global locations. Users must be involved throughout the entire lifecycle of the project. Zhang, Banerjee, Lee, & Zhang (2003) found that if users are involved early in the organization requirements gathering, resistance to the new system will be decreased. Early involvement in the project gives users a feeling of responsibility for the new system/processes.

Wellins and Rioux (2000) noted that differences between business practices and locations can cause resistance to change. Individual locations need to collaborate to evaluate acceptance of the new system and resolve any feelings of discontent with the changes. Additionally, communicating changes early on will help alleviate feelings of possessiveness.

Organizations must be careful when proposing changes so that the local staff understands the initiative. If the staff does not accept the changes, it can cause resistance. Keeping all global team members engaged is most important to prevent these issues from surfacing. Management support is a key factor in ensuring that the changes in current processes are accepted throughout the company. Management and executive management support are essential to preventing resistance to change. Additional information regarding management support is located in the next section.

Management Support

Management support for both the implementation efforts and the ongoing use of the system is important. Employees are willing to put more effort into an implementation if it is communicated that the software will be used for an extended period of time (Ross, 1999). Zhang et al. (2003) suggest that top management support can help make the implementation successful by "(1) providing leadership and (2) providing the necessary resources" (p. 5).

He (2004) mentions that management support "is important throughout the entire project life cycle" (p. 155). This is critical for the acceptance of the new system by the project team and any other personnel involved early on. Ghosh (2002) stresses the importance of management support for ERP implementations. He specifically states that corporate-level management support is necessary to keep everyone motivated. Communication from corporate-level management throughout the project will get the employees excited (and prepared) for the change. Key milestones should be broadcast and celebrated.

Have a steering committee in place for quick issue resolution and monitoring the direction of the project. Typically, upper-level or executive management should participate on the committee. Having upper-level management make final decisions for key issues throughout the implementation will allow management to remain visible. Aladwani (2001) states that involving key leaders in the decision-making process throughout the implementation process will make those individuals feel more committed to the system. This commitment will flow down from the leaders to other coworkers. In global implementations, representatives from each location or region should be present. Careful selection of the steering committee members can ensure that communication between the regions remains intact. Team project leaders should also be allowed to participate to give them insight to decisions being made.

Trust

In ERP implementations, "trust increases the positive assessment of IT usefulness" (Gefen, Pavlou, Rose, & Warkentin, 2005, p. 55). Trust

is an important variable for global implementations, because team members are from diverse cultural backgrounds and in distributed locations. According to Evaristo (2003), "higher levels of trust are supposed to result in more positive attitudes, superior levels of cooperation, and other forms of workplace behavior, as well as higher levels of performance" (p. 60). "Trust enables an environment where more cooperation, higher performance, and other attitudes and perceptions are more likely" (Evaristo, 2003, p. 60).

Trust can be developed using different methods. For example, Fisher and Fisher (2001) find that good communication is key. Interactions with team members should be predictable, honest, and consistent. This will help other team members learn to trust each other. Another recommendation is to remain visible and accessible. This can be a challenge when working across many time zones, but it is imperative to gain the trust of the team. Taking the initiative to check e-mail or take phone calls during off-hours can be an extremely effective means for building trust.

Evaristo (2003) states that a reason for mistrust among individuals is "lack of knowledge about rationale for past or present behaviors and intentions" (p. 62), which also influences risk taking of an unknown situation. Issues of trust can sometimes be resolved by having face-to-face meetings. If meeting face to face is not possible, having social time—even if over the phone—can give other team members a chance to get to know each other. This can improve relationships and help open up communication.

Model Presentation

Figure 1 depicts the research model, which consists of five success factors and their influence on the successful global implementation of ERP software. The success factors were chosen based on existing literature on global software implementations and (global) ERP implementations. These five factors were then used to evaluate the implementation of the HRMS module at Global

Figure 1. Research model

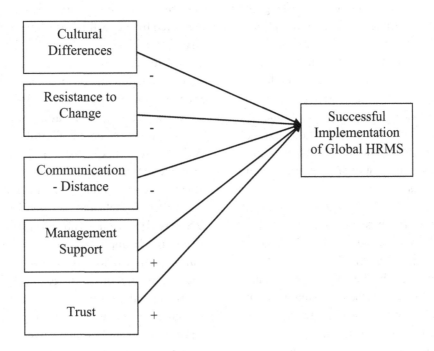

Software Inc. As mentioned previously, due to Global Software Inc.'s time constraints, the HRMS module was the scope of the "go-live" implementation and the focus of this study.

It is important for global implementation teams to include team members from different locations and different cultures. It is also important for all team members to have open and close communication channels throughout the project. Resistance to change must be mitigated through promoting understanding and goal alignment for all project stakeholders. Strong management support will facilitate motivation and alignment of efforts. Finally, trust appears to facilitate initial system adoption and further acceptance and use.

METHOD

The global HRMS implementation at Global Software Inc. was a field study that was conducted post-implementation. The research was conducted using a combination of semi-structured interviews

and a questionnaire. Both the interviews and questionnaire were grounded using existing literature and best practices to focus on how management support, cultural differences, communication-distance, resistance to change, and trust affect global ERP implementations. The interviews and questionnaire were administered to key global and U.S.-based personnel on the implementation team. The interviewees and survey respondents were chosen based on participation on the global project implementation team and availability. Individuals involved in the study were either global HR personnel or, if located in the United States, interacted extensively with global personnel and processes.

Global Software Inc. set up project teams for the United States, Europe, Asia, and South America (which included both Mexico and Canada). All HR functional areas had input to both the system requirements and the system setup. A support team, titled HRIS (Human Resources Information System), was already in place to assist with all areas of the implementation. The HRIS team was responsible for learning all aspects of the software, project management, and user guidance (including training for the international groups). HRIS was able to travel occasionally to the regions, but budget constraints prevented the team from traveling frequently. HRIS conducted meetings by conference calls and made the commitment to be on call during implementation and post-implementation. The combination of global travel and the commitment to support have helped HRIS build a strong relationship with the international locations.

Go-live, January 1, 2005, was on time and on budget. A few snags were encountered, and the international locations used e-mail and telephone to inform the support team of issues. Front-line support was provided by the HRIS support team. Any issues that needed to be escalated were forwarded on to the systems support team, named MIS. The MIS team was responsible for security, hardware support, and general HRIS administrative functions (backups, server issues, etc.).

Due to the fact that the HRIS team was located in the United States, the time change differences for training and support issues varied quite a bit. The HRIS team had conference calls early in the morning or late at night. It was important for the other locations to have input regarding the system. These calls were typically informal so that the international locations could feel comfortable with the new system.

The United States had one or more representatives from all functional areas (payroll, benefits, compensation, HR generalist, training, etc.). The international teams had representatives from each country with HR personnel in place. A total of 29 team members participated on the project team (17 U.S. based, 12 non-U.S. based).

The semi-structured interview questions were developed to gather background information about the project and find out additional information about the potential issues that were faced by project team members. The questions were written to gather data in regards to the five factors (cultural differences, trust, management support, communication-distance, and resistance to change) identified by the evaluation of existing literature on global implementations and ERP implementations. A total of seven semi-structured interviews were conducted at various locations—mostly outside of the place of business being studied. A few of the interviews were administered to global personnel over the phone. The interview data was evaluated to find key issues associated with the implementation. The interviewees were selected based on their availability and willingness to participate. We selected both non-U.S.-based and U.S.-based personnel who had participated on the global HRMS implementation team. Interviewees with a variation of job titles and departments were selected to get a broad range of experiences.

Additional data was gathered using a questionnaire. As no useful existing questionnaire was found that addressed the five success factors, we developed one specifically for this study. The questionnaire was administered online using Surveyz! software. A seven-point Likert scale was used. We selected the questionnaire respondents by viewing the project participation listing and identifying those individuals who had interaction with the global HRMS implementation. Seventeen individuals were contacted by e-mail and were informed that participation was completely voluntary and confidential. Of these 17, 14 completed the questionnaire. Seven of the 14 were U.S.-based team members and seven were non-U.S.-based team members.

The project role and location data are displayed in Tables 1 and 2. The location data is broken down by specific location. The project roles that responded as "Other" were: Interface and Report Specialist/IT PM, End User (2), Regional HR Head/Stakeholder, HR Personnel, and one blank "Other" response.

Using multiple instruments to collect data allowed for comparison and contrast of the information, which allowed the opportunity to collect richer data. Although both the semi-structured

Table 1. Respondent roles

Project Role	Number of Respondents
Project Manager	3
Subject Matter Expert	3
Executive Sponsor	1
Other	6
Left Response Blank	1

Table 2. Respondent location

Location	Number of Respondents
United States	7
Non-United States	7
(UK)	1
(Spain)	1
(Brazil)	1
(Argentina)	1
(Canada)	1
(Singapore)	2

interview questions and questionnaire were developed based on the five success factors, we were open to gathering any information that could lead to additional success factors. The semi-structured interview questions and survey instruments can be found in Appendices A and B.

RESULTS

Most team members felt that the implementation was a success, although some were neutral and some disagreed completely. Additionally, many team members defined success to be that the system was implemented on time and on budget. All of the data from the previous system was correctly converted into the new system and payroll processing was on time. However, when further analysis of the data was performed, it was evident that from a global perspective the implementation was not a success. Many respondents commented that the software was not a good fit for the global team and that the HRMS software was not being utilized as it was intended to be. The system was implemented to improve global data entry processes, yet some of the non-U.S. locations were still using spreadsheets to track data. The system was not an improvement for them.

Table 3 shows the quantitative results for global HRMS success.

The average mean and standard deviations for the different success factors are shown in Table 4. The mean calculations are based on a seven-point scale, meaning that all of the averages for the questionnaire answers are on the positive end of the scale. The number of respondents that participated in the research represented a majority of the global implementation team participants. Due to the small number of participants, some of the statistical analysis should be interpreted only as an indicator of problems with the implementation.

Table 5 shows Cronbach's alpha for each of the variables. The numbers for both global HRMS success and resistance to change are low, but at least over .6. This indicates that the internal consistency is fair. This is likely due to the small sample population. However, management support and communication-distance are both over .8, which is considered good reliability.

Communication-distance data collection took many aspects of communication into account. For instance, the distribution of the team across several different time zones affected the group's ability to meet as a whole. Time zone differences led to delays of half a day or longer in getting responses from the U.S.-based corporate location. The delay in response time was obviously

Table 3. Global HRMS success

Success Factors	U.S. Mean	Non-U.S. Mean
The implementation of the global HRMS was a success.	5.43	5.0
My region had a successful implementation.	6.14	5.14
The global Human Resources Management System (HRMS) implementation was completed on time.	6.0	5.29
The data in the HRMS contains valuable global information.	5.43	5.0
The HRMS implementation was completed with input from the global regions.	5.71	6.29
The HRMS improved the process for global data entry.	5.0	4.86
Overall Mean	5.62	5.26

Table 4. Overall averages for variables

Variable	Average Mean	Standard Deviation (Average)
Global HRMS Success	5.44	1.2
Management Support	5.73	1.06
Resistance to Change	5.63	1.33
Communication-Distance	5.63	1.21
Trust	5.34	1.53
Cultural Differences	5.34	1.44

Table 5. Cronbach's alpha for research variables

Variable	Cronbach's Alpha
Global HRMS Success	.629
Management Support	.854
Resistance to Change	.664
Communication-Distance	.884
Trust	.718
Cultural Differences	.772

frustrating to both parties. Some team members felt disconnected from the group, with limited ability to voice their opinions.

Geographic distance also limited face-to-face meetings. Travel to the different locations was costly, and only a few trips were made during the project. The entire team experienced frustration, since the regional teams and the U.S.-based team had difficulty communicating and making decisions effectively.

HR had personnel located in the United States, Brazil, Argentina, Canada, India, Singapore,

Spain, the United Kingdom, and France. The HRIS support team had difficulty managing communications with that magnitude of time difference. Both departments had job duties to perform besides the HRMS implementation and had to strike a fine balance to keep the project moving forward.

Language was also an issue for the global team. English was the second language for a majority of the global team members, creating some communications barriers. Additionally, the system itself created language barriers. For example, many countries do not use the same terminology for differentiating between employee job categories. However, because this was a requirement for corporate reporting, these terms had to be taught to the global HR employees.

Issues regarding trust did not show up in the respondent results. Although the team members were not able to communicate frequently as a whole, overall they felt that they were able to get to know their teammates and could be open about their feelings and opinions to other team members.

A key cultural difference between the U.S.-based and non-U.S.-based locations was the work environment. For example, the number of vacation days/legal holidays varied greatly among the different countries. Schedules had to be adjusted to allow for these differences. Most members of the respondent population felt that their needs were taken into consideration and that misunderstandings between team members were alleviated in a timely and appropriate manner.

The main theme associated with cultural differences was that payroll data entry processes did not improve for the global population. The system did not necessarily add value to the international HR team. The perception among respondents was that the system functionality did not match with the processes and needs of the locations outside of the United States.

Management support was present throughout the implementation project. The interview and questionnaire results both indicate that management support positively influenced the success of the global implementation. Notwithstanding their overall appreciation of management's support for the global implementation, respondents felt at times that issues were not easily resolved by the HR steering committee (which consisted of global executive HR management). The steering committee members were selected to provide management support both for system issues encountered during the implementation and to communicate the goals and expectations of the entire project.

Resistance to change did not clearly show up as an issue encountered by the Global Software Inc. implementation team. However, some respondents commented on the quality and amount of training for the software. Many of the hours spent showing the system to the non-U.S. population were performed over-the-phone using videoconferencing. Groups found this mode hindered their ability to learn. There was some initial resistance to the new tool, but primarily because the system did not follow the existing processes.

Many of the interviewees mentioned that there was a United States vs. non-United States mentality. The difference was partially due to the fact that the HRMS software was not needed to run payroll in locations outside of the United States. The system was chosen because 80% of the total requirements were met. However, many locations felt that the system did not meet their regional requirements. Team members felt that the non-U.S. locations should have been more involved earlier in the decision-making process for the selection of the HRMS tool. Both U.S. and non-U.S. team members commented that the system was not a true global system. This fact hindered acceptance of the system by the global team. The success of the implementation was affected because the system did not provide value for the HR team members outside of the United States.

In summary, the semi-structured interview/questionnaire results validated the issues related to global HRMS/ERP implementations that were identified in the literature. The issues identified in both the literature and the respondent data provide an excellent starting point for future research on how these issues affect the success of global HRMS implementations. Future research could also be expanded to include additional success factors not evaluated for this particular field study.

DISCUSSION

This field study examined one instance of a full-scale global ERP/HRMS implementation. Overall, the interviewees had a positive response to the system. That being said, a limiting factor of the responses was that many of the respondents commented that the system was successful based on an on-time, on-budget implementation. The factors contributing to implementation success confirmed many factors identified in the literature and introduced some additional ones.

Although the implementation experienced some problems, the semi-structured interview results indicate that overall it was a success. The software chosen met 80% of the requirements for all locations, but because the processes in different locations differed significantly, the software needed customization to work as users in the various regions envisioned. The respondents that indicated that the project was a success considered it so because the system was implemented on time and on budget. From the perspective of the locations outside of the United States, however, the implementation was not a success. Many of the team members outside of the United States experienced frustration because a majority of their customizations were not available at system go-live. Many customizations were pushed back due to time and budget constraints. Some of the core functionality necessary to improve day-to-day job function was not evident.

The questionnaire results support the interview results. Both show that the project overall was a success; however there were mixed feelings about the success of the system from the perspective of the non-U.S.-based locations. The questionnaire results indicate that while the project was seen as a success, data entry did not improve for the locations outside of the United States.

Responses of the U.S.-based participants and the internationally based participants differed in a few respects. For example, the questionnaire item "the implementation was the United States versus the rest of the world" had a higher mean for the international respondents than for the United States respondents. However, there appears to be no consistent pattern of disagreement.

The interview/questionnaire results validated the issues previously noted in the literature as related to global HRMS/ERP implementations. Table 6 shows which research results also appeared as factors in the literature review. The research indicates that the success of a global HRMS implementation is positively influenced when management support and trust exist, and resistance to change, communication-distance, and cultural issues are resolved.

CONCLUSION

The success of the global HRMS implementation in this case study was influenced by management support, communication-distance, alleviating resistance to change, and working out cultural differences. Of these factors, management support had by far the strongest influence as indicated by both questionnaire and interview results. Executive management was initially the driving factor behind the implementation, and this support and initiative continued from project inception through implementation.

The team experienced a few issues regarding communication, but overall the commitment to ensuring that the global team members were

Table 6. Comparison of research findings and literature review

Research Findings	Factor in Literature Review
Communication-Distance	
Time zone differences made it difficult to communicate	Yes
Response time issues between locations	Yes
Participants had support	No
Steering committee global members did not participate	Yes
Meeting times were not always convenient	Yes
Lack of face-to-face time	Yes
Cultural Differences	
Work ethic/work environment	No
Custom/regulation issues	Yes
Language–ESL	Yes
Communication barriers	Yes
Management Support	
Executive HR allowed team to make decisions	Yes
Globally, not a good fit	No
Steering committee formed with regional directors	Yes
Resistance to Change	
Resistance to training from global team members	Yes
Tool not meant to be used globally, which caused resistance	No
Global HRMS Success	
Was on time/on budget	No
Global data entry process did not improve	No
Software not intended to be used globally	No

included in the implementation process helped prevent the project from failing completely. The HRIS department provided support at all hours of the day, giving the global members the opportunity to work out problems and communicate issues. By incorporating weekly calls into team schedules, team members had time to build rapport and get to know one another personally. These personal relationships helped build trust and alleviate cultural issues as well. In fact, the global team member questionnaire respondents had a surprisingly positive response to the questions related to communication-distance, trust, and cultural differences. Time zones did create issues with the

ability to communicate, but the implementation team was able to work around these.

The factor that negatively influenced the implementation success was the choice of software for the company. Many team members mentioned problems of organizational fit and the software functionality. The software was not designed to be used in locations other than the United States and Canada, causing many frustrations among the regions outside of the United States and preventing the improvement of global data entry processes. The fact that the regions were still using spreadsheets to track employee data indicates that the software did not support their day-to-day functions. Research findings from both U.S.-based and global participants also validated this inhibitor. This factor was not included in the research because the executive management chose the software based on the fact that 80% of the software requirements were met. However, as was indicated above, there were problems related to software choice for the non-U.S.-based locations. Interview respondents indicated that many of the issues were not known until the implementation was well underway.

A few research limitations should be noted. The number of team members outside of the United States was small. With the sale of the global division of the company after the project completion in 2005, the number decreased further when global team members were no longer employed by the company. Fortunately, the researchers had built rapport with the global members. Nearly all of the team members contacted were willing to participate as respondents. The small team size likely affected some of the statistical analysis, but the numbers were helpful to look for further indication of positive or negative influence on the success of the implementation. The research was conducted post-implementation and after the non-U.S.-based team members were acquired by another company. This is an additional limitation and could have affected the opinions of the interview and survey respondents.

Not all of the questionnaire respondents participated in semi-structured interviews, so it is possible that the individuals interviewed did not perceive issues in areas of trust and cultural differences. With more background information, variance could be measured and conclusions could be drawn as to whether or not the respondents in the United States had different perceptions than those located outside of the United States. The short data collection period could have impacted the perceptions of the respondents. Further development and validation of the survey instrument used would be desirable. Testing a larger population of organizations would strengthen the statistical power of the survey.

FUTURE RESEARCH DIRECTIONS

This case study evaluated one company's experience with a global HRMS implementation. Many of the processes for the locations outside of the United States did not improve, which indicates that the implementation was not successful. The authors would like to continue to research similar topics, extending the research to other companies' experiences with implementing global HRMS/ERP software. Surveying multiple companies will identify additional issues, and the data collected can help predict and alleviate some of the problems that companies face when implementing HRMS software globally. The data collected for Global Software Inc. could also be expanded to include future implementations of other ERP modules.

Much remains to understand about global ERP implementations. The current research points to the fit between organizational structure and global ERP implementations as an important issue. A related area of interest is the perceived success or failure of global information system (IS) implementations for organizations of varying structures. Finding critical success factors for global IS implementations from the views of different roles in an organization (e.g., management, IT project managers, IT staff, or end users) will be key to alleviating future software implementation failures.

REFERENCES

Aladwani, A.M. (2001). Change management strategies for successful ERP implementations. *Business Process Management Journal, 7*(3), 266-275.

Bagchi, K., Hart, P., & Peterson, M.F. (2004). National culture and information technology product adoption. *Journal of Global Information Technology Management, 7*(4), 29-46.

Cronbach, L.J. (1951). Coefficient alpha and the internal structure of tests. *Psychometrika, 16,* 297-335.

Elashmawi, F., & Harris, P.R. (1993). *Multicultural management new skills for global success.* Houston, TX: Gulf.

Evaristo, R. (2003). The management of distributed projects across cultures. *Journal of Global Information Management, 11*(4), 58-70.

Fisher, K., & Fisher, M.D. (2001). *The distance manager.* New York: McGraw-Hill.

Gefen, D., Pavlou, P., Rose, G., & Warkentin, M. (2005). Cultural diversity and trust in IT adoption: A comparison of potential e-voters in the USA and South Africa. *Journal of Global Information Management, 13*(1), 54-78.

Ghosh, S. (2002). Challenges on a global implementation of ERP software. In *Proceedings of the 2002 IEEE International Engineering Management Conference* (pp. 101-106).

Gross, S., & Wingerup, P. (1999). Global pay? Maybe not yet! *Compensation and Benefits Review, 31*(4), 25-34.

Gupta, A. (2000). Enterprise resource planning: The emerging organizational value systems. *Industrial Management & Data Systems, 100*(3), 114-118.

He, X. (2004). The ERP challenge in China: A resource-based perspective. *Information Systems Journal, 14*(2), 153-167.

Hofstede, G. (1983). The cultural relativity of organizational practices and theories. *Journal of International Business Studies, 14*(2), 75-89.

Hofstede, G. (1985). The interaction between national and organizational value systems. *Journal of Management Studies, 22*(4), 347-358.

Ives, B., & Jarvenpaa, S.L. (1991). Applications of global information technology: Key issues for management. *MIS Quarterly, 15*(1), 33-49.

Krumbholz, M., Galliers, J.R., Coulianos, N., & Maiden, N.A.M. (2000). Implementing enterprise resource planning packages in different corporate and national cultures. *Journal of Information Technology, 15*(4), 267-279.

Laudon, K.C., & Laudon, J.P. (2004). *Management information systems: Managing the digital firm.* Upper Saddle River, NJ: Pearson Education.

Loeb, K.A., Rai, A., Ramaprasad, A., & Sharma, S. (1998). Design, development, & implementation of a global information warehouse: A case study at IBM. *Information Systems Journal, 8,* 291-311.

Mathis, R.L., & Jackson, J.H. (2000). *Human resource management.* Cincinnati, OH: Southwestern College.

Newell, S., Pan, S.L., Galliers, R.D., Huang, J.C. (2001). The myths of the boundaryless organization. *Communications of the ACM, 44*(12), 74-76.

Purba, S., & Shah, B. (2000). *How to manage a successful software project.* New York: John Wiley & Sons.

Ross, J. (1999). Dow Corning Corporation: Business processes and information technology. *Journal of Information Technology, 14*(3), 253-266.

Rothwell, W.J., & Prescott, R.K. (1999). Transforming HR into a global powerhouse. *HR Focus, 76*(3), 7-8.

Scott, J.E., & Vessey, I. (2002). Managing risks in enterprise systems implementations. *Communications of the ACM, 45*(4), 74-81.

Sheu, C., Chae, B., & Yang, C.-L. (2004). National differences and ERP implementation: Issues and challenges. *OMEGA: The International Journal of Management Science, 32*(5), 361-371.

Solomon, C.M. (1998). Sharing information. *Workforce, 77*(3), 12-16.

Wellins, R., & Rioux, S. (2000). The growing pains of globalizing HR. *Training & Development, 54*(5), 79-85.

Wiechmann, D., Ryan, A.M., & Hemingway, M. (2003). Designing and implementing global staffing systems: Part I—Leaders in global staffing. *Human Resource Management, 42*(1), 71-83.

Zhang, L., Banerjee, P., Lee, M., & Zhang, Z. (2003). Critical success factors of enterprise resource planning systems implementation success in China. In *Proceedings of the 36th Hawaii International Conference on System Sciences* (pp. 1-10).

ADDITIONAL READING

Arif, M., Kulonda, D.J., Proctor, M., & Williams, K. (2004). Before you invest: An illustrated framework to compare conceptual designs for an enterprise information system. *Information Systems Management, 4*(2), 119-135.

Barki, H., & Hartwick, J. (1994). Measuring user participation, user involvement, & user attitude. *MIS Quarterly, 18*(1), 59-82.

Bennett, K. (1995). Legacy systems: Coping with success. *IEEE Software, 12*(1), 19-23.

Brown, C., & Vessey, I. (1999, December 13-15). ERP implementation approaches: Toward a contingency framework. In *Proceedings of the 20th International Conference on Information Systems* (pp. 411-416), Charlotte, NC.

Donelly, M. (2005). Avaya's journey to global HR shared service. *Strategic HR Review, 4*(2), 20-23.

El Amry, R., Geffroy-Maronnat, B., & Rowe, F. (2006). The effects of enterprise resource planning implementation strategy on cross-functionality. *Information Systems Journal, 16*(1), 79-104.

Francalanci, C. (2001). Predicting the implementation effort of ERP projects: Empirical evidence on SAP/R3. *Journal of Information Technology, 16*(1), 33-48.

Greengard, S. (1995). When HRMS goes global: Managing the data highway. *Personnel Journal, 74*(6), 90-106.

Gwynne, P. (2001). Information systems go global. *MIT Sloan Management Review, 42*(4), 14.

Hossain, L., Patrick, J.D., & Rashid, A.R. (2002). *Enterprise resource planning: Global opportunities and challenges.* Hershey, PA: Idea Group.

Hustad, E. (2004). Knowledge networking in global organizations: The transfer of knowledge. In *Proceedings of the 2004 SIGMIS Conference on Computer Personnel Research: Careers, Culture, and Ethics in a Networked Environment* (pp. 55-64), Tucson, AZ.

Kremzar, M.H., & Wallace, T.F. (2001). *ERP: Making it happen—The implementers' guide to success with enterprise resource planning.* Hoboken, NJ: John Wiley & Sons.

Losey, M., Meisinger, S., & Ulrich, D. (2005). *The future of human resources management: 64 thought leaders explore the critical HR issues of today and tomorrow.* Hoboken, NJ: John Wiley & Sons.

Markus, M.L., Tanis, C., & van Fenema, P.C. (2000). Multisite ERP implementations. *Communications of the ACM, 43*(4), 42-46.

Miozzo, M., Vurdubakis, T., & Yeh, C. (2006). The importance of being local? Learning among Taiwan's enterprise solutions providers. *Journal of Enterprise Information Management, 19*(1), 30-49.

Nah, F.F., Zuckweiler, K.M., & Lau, J.L. (2003). ERP implementation: Chief information officers' perceptions of critical success factors. *International Journal of Human-Computer Interaction, 16*(1), 5-22.

Ocker, R.J., & Mudambi, S. (2003). Assessing the readiness of firms for CRM: A literature review and research model. In *Proceedings of the 36th Hawaii International Conference on System Sciences* (HICSS'03) (track 7, p. 181a).

Parr, A., & Shanks, G. (2000). A model of ERP project implementation. *Journal of Information Technology, 15*(4), 289-303.

Pollock, N., Proctor, R., & Williams, R. (2003). Fitting standard software packages to non-standard organizations: The 'biography' of an enterprise-wide system. *Technology Analysis & Strategic Management, 15*(3), 317-332.

Project Management Institute. (2004). *A guide to the project management body of knowledge.* Newton Square, PA.

Rioux, S., & Wellins, R. (2000). The growing pains of globalizing HR. *Training & Development, 54*(5), 79-85.

Tan, F.B. (2002). *Global perspective of information technology management.* Hershey, PA: IRM Press.

Tractinsky, N., & Jarvenpaa, S.L. (1995). Information systems design decisions in a global versus domestic context. *MIS Quarterly, 19*(4), 507-534.

Walker, A.J. (2001). *Web-based human resources.* New York: McGraw-Hill.

APPENDIX A: SEMI-STRUCTURED INTERVIEW QUESTIONS

1. Tell me a little about your background with Global Software Inc. (i.e., position, title, etc.).
2. How were you involved in the decision to implement a global HR system?
3. What was your role in the project?
4. What were some of the challenges that occurred during the implementation strictly because the software was being implemented globally? Do you think any of these could have been prevented?
5. What were the reactions from executive management throughout the implementation?
6. How do you think the regions felt regarding the fact that the United States was the main driving force behind the project?
7. Do you think the implementation was a success? Why or why not?
8. What influences did management have on the decision to implement a global HR tool?
9. What was the reaction to training from a global standpoint?
10. Looking back at the project inception until now, how would you say that the HR department has changed (because of the global implementation)?
11. What cultural issues (if any) were associated with the implementation?
12. What issues did you think the implementation team faced in regards to the globally distributed locations?
13. How do you think the implementation team (yourself included) accepted the changes associated with implementing a global ERP system?
14. What do you feel that your impact was to the success or failure of the implementation?

APPENDIX B: SURVEY INSTRUMENT

Variable Name	# of Items	Questionnaire Item #s
Background Data	2	1-2
Global HRMS Success	6	3-8
Management Support	6	9-14
Resistance to Change	5	15-19
Communication-Distance	6	20-25
Trust	6	26-31
Cultural Differences	6	32-37

Questionnaire—Implementing a Global HRMS

(1) What was your role in the global HRMS implementation project?
___ Project Manager
___ Developer/Programmer/Software Engineer
___ Business Analyst
___ Subject Matter Expert
___ Executive Sponsor
___ Other, please specify _____
(2) Where were you working during the HRMS implementation?
___ United States
___ Other, please specify _____

Strongly Disagree	Disagree	Somewhat Disagree	Neither Agree Nor Disagree	Somewhat Agree	Agree	Strongly Agree
1	2	3	4	5	6	7

Note: All questions from #3 on use the same seven-point scale (shown above).

(1) The implementation of the global HRMS was a success.
(2) My region had a successful implementation.
(3) The global Human Resources Management System (HRMS) implementation was completed on time.
(4) The data in the HRMS contains valuable global information.
(5) The HRMS implementation was completed with input from the global regions.
(6) The HRMS improved the process for global data entry.
(7) HR management was involved with making decisions related to the implementation.
(8) HR management was aware of the accomplishments of the global HRMS project.
(9) Issues that were unresolved during the global HRMS project could be escalated and resolved in a timely manner.
(10) My opinion was important, and my managers trusted me to make good decisions during the project.

(11) The steering committee was open to resolving issues related to the global HRMS implementation.

(12) Goals and milestones were adequately communicated from management to the implementation team.

(13) I feel comfortable learning new systems.

(14) Implementing a global tool will help the organization.

(15) The HRMS made my job easier.

(16) Improving the global data entry process is valuable to the company.

(17) I was able to easily fit processes that resulted from the HRMS implementation into my job duties.

(18) I was able to easily communicate with others on the implementation team.

(19) I had support available any time that I needed it.

(20) During global implementation team meetings, I was able to voice my opinions easily.

(21) It was comfortable to speak with many different team members on conference calls.

(22) My opinions were needed at meetings during the implementation.

(23) Meetings held throughout the implementation were at convenient times.

(24) When I was unable to participate in tasks, I trusted my teammates to communicate my opinions.

(25) During the implementation I got to know my other teammates well.

(26) If my other teammates volunteered to complete a task, I could rely on them to finish that task without follow-up.

(27) The implementation was United States vs. the rest of the world.

(28) I could be open and honest about my feelings during the implementation.

(29) I could relate to the other members on the implementation team.

(30) Everyone put a good effort into making the HRMS implementation a success.

(31) I was able to take part and share my opinions in the global implementation of the HRMS system.

(32) If I misunderstood something my teammate was trying to say, I had the opportunity to communicate until we both understood.

(33) My needs were taken into consideration during the global HRMS implementation.

(34) My teammates were able to reach consensus across the globe.

(35) Overall, the HRMS was a good value to my region.

Section VII
Trends

Chapter XVI
ERP Trends, Opportunities, and Challenges:
A Focus on the Gulf Region in the Middle East

Maha Shakir
Zayed University, United Arab Emirates

ABSTRACT

This chapter highlights the key trends in the ERP market, with a focus on the challenges related to the implementation of these systems in the Middle Eastern Gulf region. The key trends discussed here include consolidation of the ERP market, diversification of the ERP product, new modes for ERP application delivery, ERP and new technologies, changing ERP pricing structures, ERP support operations, growing demands for ERP vertical solutions, demanding ERP customers, inter-organizational ERP solutions, and regional adaptations for ERP products. The chapter further provides insight into emerging and future trends in the region. Awareness of these issues plus knowledge of the local environment gives us a richer understanding of key ERP issues and how they apply within the unique limitations and opportunities of this region.

INTRODUCTION

The economic slowdown in the developed world coupled with saturation of the high-end enterprise resource planning (ERP) market, post 2000, provides an opportunity to pause and reflect on the past, explore new avenues, and try to glimpse the future. The examination of ERP trends and the challenges they pose help us to seize this opportunity (Botta-Genoulaz, Millet, & Grabot, 2005). While many of these trends have similar global implications, some differ depending on regional context.

Contrary to the slowdown in economic growth experienced in the developed world at the start of the new millennium, the Middle East region[1] had and continues to experience continuous positive growth. Accounts of key ERP vendors in this region (Bowman, 2006; Branton, 2006e) confirm this trend, citing annual staff size increases of 50% to 100% over the last few years (e.g., SAP Arabia doubled its team from 2005-2006 and Epicor Scala tripled in size from 2003-2006). This economic growth was by no means limited to the IT industry, but was concurrent, and to a great extent, triggered by growth in unrelated industries. Real estate ranks high on the list of flourishing industries to the extent that "Dubai has been ranked a close second in the world in terms of office real estate construction activity" (Gulf News, 2006). Ports management, logistics, construction, and tourism are among other successful emergent industries in Dubai.

The objective of this chapter is to highlight the key trends in the ERP market, with a focus on the challenges related to the implementation of these systems in the Middle Eastern Gulf region.[2] This understanding of the regional context will give us a richer understanding of key ERP issues and how they apply within the unique limitations and opportunities of this region.

BACKGROUND

The ERP market has been an area of extensive study since the late 1990s (Esteves & Pastor, 2001; Moon, 2007). The surge in ERP implementations triggered by the need to replace legacy systems with Y2K-compliant ERP systems and the desire to explore integration opportunities has slowly plummeted. This slowdown is by no means an indication of lost interest, but is a chance to examine earlier achievements and explore new opportunities.

The Gulf region is at present experiencing exponential growth triggered by a combination of rising oil revenues and the diversification of local economies into non-oil-related industries. The new emergent industries range across the sectors of travel and tourism, manufacturing, construction, finance and banking, trading, media, logistics, and more recently, education, healthcare, and outsourcing. This growth is creating golden opportunities for both local businesses and multi-nationals due to the soaring demand for goods and services.

A summary of key regional features will assist in comprehension of the regional context (see Figure 1 for a map showing Gulf Cooperation Council (GCC) countries and Table 1 for basic regional statistical indicators).

- **Government structure:** Hereditary monarchies where the Head of State appoints ministers and advisory council members. Kuwait, having an elected council, is an exception.
- **Wealth generation:** While the discovery and exploitation of oil and natural gas are credited for the economic wealth these countries enjoy, recent streams of revenue are also considerable. Free-trade, duty-free economic zones and exemption of income and other taxes are prominent drivers of these new streams of revenue.
- **Business ownership:** Until recently, restrictions on foreign national business ownership were enforced to ensure that wealth generated was invested locally. However, these regulations are starting to be relaxed to convince foreign investors to set up businesses locally.
- **Workforce:** The region is sparsely populated and as a result there is a shortage of the manpower required to support economic growth. Consequently, these countries host a large population of expatriate workers. The workers fill positions in highly skilled, semi-skilled, and unskilled occupations. Their contribution to the overall workforce

Table 1. GCC countries: GDP and population over five years (adapted from ESCWA, 2006; Ghose, 2007)

Country	Nominal GDP (US$ in billions)					Population (Millions) *	
	2003	2004	2005	2006[a]	2007[b]	2003	2006
Bahrain	9,404	9,928	10,704	11,293	11,903	0.71	0.75
Kuwait	45,274	48,081	51,206	54,534	57,207	2.55	2.97
Oman	22,320	23,578	24,573	25,999	27,325	2.33	2.48
Qatar	21,091	22,884	24,967	26,714	28,691	0.72	0.84
Saudi Arabia	204,525	215,304	229,406	243,170	257,517	22.02	23.69
U.A.E.	82,040	89,990	97,360	103,981	110,220	4.04	5.04
GCC Total	**384,654**	**409,765**	**438,216**	**465,691**	**492,863**	**32.37**	**35.77**

* Including expatriates(a) ESCWA estimates, October 2006(b) ESCWA projections, October 2006

Figure 1. GCC countries map (adapted from The World Fact Book: Middle East, https://www.cia.gov/ cia/publications/factbook/reference_maps/middle_east.html). Note: GCC countries are Bahrain, Kuwait, Oman, Qatar, Saudi Arabia, and UAE.

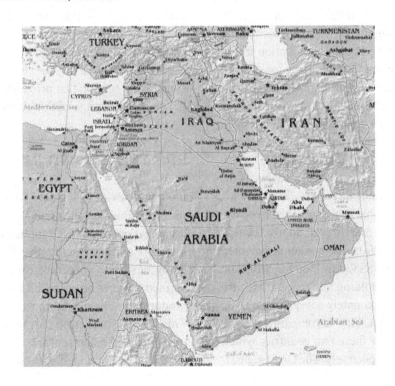

is substantial, ranging between 50-90% across the GCC member countries.

The flagship driving non-petroleum-related growth in the region is Dubai, one of the seven Emirates of the UAE. This emirate has shown remarkable success in creating world-class businesses that have seen it become the trading hub of the Middle Eastern region. Even more, trade names such as Emirates Airlines,[3] Dubai World,[4] and the Jumeirah five-star hotel chain[5] have become examples of business excellence worldwide. A recent *Harvard Business Review* article identified Dubai as one of the emerging candidates for offshoring; its strengths include a skilled multinational workforce, robust infrastructure, zero taxes, and five-star amenities (Farrell, 2006). With these resources, the country aims to specialize in IT disaster recovery and backup for the booming offshore IT operations in South East Asia (e.g., India, Bangladesh, and the Philippines).

The 7% growth rate enjoyed by GCC countries in recent years is also reflected by a flourishing information technology (IT) industry. Contrary to the slowdown in IT investment in western countries following the dot.com bust in the early 2000s, IT in this region is witnessing substantial growth. Considering that oil exploration in the region only started in the 1960s, the majority of business organizations in the region are relatively young. As a result, businesses are less mature in their use of IT when compared with their western counterparts. Hence, a considerable amount of IT investment is ERP-related. An IDC study (Nair & Rajan, 2006) forecasts that revenues for enterprise application software—ERP, CRM, and SCM—will double in size over the five-year period 2006-2010. Starting at approximately US$150 million in 2005, the market is expected to grow to around US$300 million by 2010. The two GCC countries holding the largest shares are Saudi Arabia (approximately 55%) and the UAE (approximately 30%). This is comparable to the GDP percentages for these two countries which are 52% and 22% respectively. The UAE is appar-

ently doing better because a significant part of its revenue comes from non-oil-related sources.

Holland et al. (2000) define ERP maturity using three implementation stages: (1) organizations are managing legacy systems and starting an ERP project; (2) implementation is complete and functionality of the ERP system is being exploited across the organization; and (3) ERP is embedded within work processes and organizations are developing strategic opportunities through linking their ERP systems to knowledge management, business intelligence, and supply chain management systems. The status of ERP maturity in this region will be examined using this model.

To fulfill the study objective, the next section identifies key trends in the ERP market through review of the practice[6] and academic literature as well as exploratory interviews with practitioners in the GCC region. Practitioners' opinions are sought to validate these trends and reflect on their application in the context investigated. The relationship between these trends and ERP maturity is then discussed to determine the status of ERP maturity in the region. The Discussion section is then followed by the Future Trends section, which provides insight into the future directions of ERP systems. Finally the chapter ends with the Conclusion section that provides a discussion of the overall coverage of this chapter.

ERP TRENDS AND IMPLICATIONS

It is clearly evident that the ERP market is slowly transforming over the course of time. For many organizations today, ERP applications are becoming more a requirement rather than an option of doing business. This transformation can be examined by looking at the ERP market, the ERP product, the client, and the local environment. This section focuses on current ERP trends and investigates their present and future implications for the aforementioned parties.

The Consolidation of the ERP Market

With the saturation of the high-end ERP market, post 2000, growth emerged as a major concern for ERP vendors, particularly large vendors. One way in which growth was stimulated was the acquisition of other vendors, capitalizing on the downturn in global economies following the dot. com bust of the early 2000s (Lohr, 2004). Through acquisitions and mergers, key ERP vendors added new functionalities and capabilities to extend their application portfolio. This eventually contributed to business growth and entry into new markets.

Consolidation enabled vendors to offer a broad set of functionalities. One obvious advantage is that customers are able to shop from one vendor for the portfolio of applications they need. On the other hand, users are becoming increasingly concerned with vendors who, in their aim for the one-size-fits-all ERP, are becoming less interested in supporting the specialized functionalities the customer demands.

Compounding this effect is the gradual elimination of many ERP brands, creating uncertainty among the user community with regard to future support for their exiting applications. There are several instances in the Gulf region where customers have switched vendors as a precautionary measure to decrease the risk of losing future support for their existing ERP applications. This was particularly evident for JD Edwards and PeopleSoft customers after the two ERP brands were acquired by Oracle (Edwards, 2006c). To overcome this, Oracle changed its limited support policy to one of lifetime support and promised new releases of these applications even after the anticipated launch of Oracle Fusion[7] in 2008 (Milne, 2006b).

The Diversification of the ERP Product

The boundary of what constitutes an ERP application is becoming increasingly blurred. While one of the widely accepted traditional definitions of an ERP considers such systems to be "commercial software packages [that] promise seamless integration of all information flowing through a company" (Davenport, 1998), this boundary is extending to include the integration of applications outside the company (Sammon & Adam, 2005). For example, customer relationship management (CRM) applications are gradually becoming a part of the ERP product portfolio. Vendors are utilizing this to their benefit by locking in customers and discouraging the use of best-of-breed solutions (James & Wolf, 2000).

Furthermore, ERP vendors are increasingly entering the markets of financials, retail, and/or adding business intelligence (BI) functionality to the standard ERP package. This form of diversification enables customers to benefit from lower costs and simplified integration. However, a comparison with best-of-breed offerings shows that these vendors disadvantage the customer by offering limited options and less powerful functionality. This is a trade-off that the customer must consider. The outcome of ERP market consolidation is that the balance is shifting towards a diversified package. In the Gulf region, evidence supporting ERP diversification is weak as a considerable number of ERP adopters prefer best-of-breed applications.

New Modes for ERP Application Delivery

A new delivery mechanism where the ERP application is both hosted and maintained by a third-party service provider is becoming progressively more popular. This software-as-a-service or the application service provider (ASP) model is being marketed as being more efficient (Ekanayaka, Currie, & Seltsikas, 2002). Efficiency is due to the service provider utilizing economies-of-scale in addition to expert product knowledge to drive costs down.

If implemented in-house, these applications would require substantial upfront investment as well as an initial year or more of effort before they would be fully operational. Therefore one of the key drivers for the ASP model is the short timeframe in which the system can be made operational. This is of particular importance for businesses operating in a dynamic environment. Other drivers are the accessibility to both mature application hosting technologies and a variety of functionalities covering ERP, CRM, and supply chain management (SCM) applications (Levinson, 2006; Wailgum, 2006).

The software-as-a-service model is very new to the Gulf region, hence adoption is still low. This is mainly due to: (1) businesses being uncomfortable with giving away the ownership of their systems, and (2) the fact that the information and communication technology (ICT) infrastructure needed to support this mode of delivery is still relatively immature. However, it is believed that this will soon change due to ongoing development in both public and private ICT platforms and when early adopters start to enjoy cost efficiencies. Just recently, one major GCC airline replaced its aircraft maintenance applications with a hosted ERP solution from SAP (Milne, 2006a). Both the hosted ERP and related IT support services are managed by a Swiss-based firm.

ERP and New Technologies

Two of the new technologies that are being integrated into the ERP suite of applications are radio frequency identification (RFID) technology and mobile applications. Some of the promising uses for RFID technology lie in logistics and retail management, both of which are industries that are flourishing in the Gulf region. Dubai, considered the trade hub of the region, is hosting the popular free zones[8] of Jebel Ali Port, Internet City, Media City, in addition to many others that currently are either in development or are near completion (e.g., Logistics City and Outsourcing City). Several other GCC countries are follow-

ing suit, with similar facilities in the process of development.

With logistic business flourishing in the Gulf region, RFID will create both efficiencies and effectiveness in business operations. One particular type of business where RFID is already proving to be very useful is the trading of precious metals, such as gold. The Jewelry Store, a Gulf group that brings together big names in the jewelry business, has recently implemented RFID to support a new model of financing gold (Stanton, 2006d; Swedberg, 2006).

Another new technology is mobile applications, particularly those supporting business collaboration. These technologies can extend the capabilities of ERP systems to mobile handsets (Lamba, 2006). This is an area where IT can add value to a business, especially where timely response significantly affects revenue. In addition, considering that mobile phone adoption in the Gulf region is one of the highest in the world (Gulf News, 2005), the integration of mobile technologies into ERP applications will play an important role in supporting business operations. Already several companies in the region are using mobile applications as an important component of their electronic procurement systems, such as the Jumeirah chain of hotels and Petroleum Development Oman (Beer, 2006a; Arabian Computer News, 2006).

ERP Pricing Structures

ERP vendors wanting to maintain continuous growth in the ERP market are targeting small and medium businesses (SMBs). A strategy vendors implement to appeal to SMBs involves making their software purchases more affordable. To achieve this, they altered their pricing structure from the conventional one of a single upfront payment for the software license to the increasingly popular format of multiple payments over the period of time the software is in use. The advantage to customers of the latter option lies in affordability and scalability. Organizations are able to beef up usage when needed and pay only for what they use.

In the Gulf region, Oracle has been very active in tailoring ERP pricing strategies to appeal to its diverse customer base. As a result, Oracle and not SAP, which is the market leader globally, claims to enjoy the position of ERP market leader in the Gulf region. Oracle now offers two separate pricing strategies: (1) by subscription, which is estimated at US$8 billion; and (2) by licensing, which is estimated to be worth around US$5 billion (Branton, 2006a, 2006c).

ERP Support Operations

One of the key limitations to IT operations in this region is the shortfall in disaster recovery practice. It is known that both a regional conglomerate with operations in 55 countries and a major airline company are only backing up their data and have no fully replicated disaster sites (Edwards, 2006a, 2006e). This is possibly due to the fact that the companies are still working on the standardization and consolidation of their systems, and once these issues are addressed, they will move to cater for high-risk situations through the addition of replicated site facilities. This issue has started to get attention recently, particularly from third-party providers. Several data centers in the region, which are designed to cater for the disaster recovery business, are either in development or near completion. Demand for these data centers is both regional and international (Stanton, 2006b). The GCC region, strengthened by its political stability and five-star amenities, is developing advanced ICT infrastructures to supply disaster recovery services to countries in South East Asia (Farrell, 2006).

Customers' Interest in Vertical Solutions Continue to Grow

ERP vendors are creating vertical solutions by tailoring their software functionality to different lines of business. For customers operating in a specific industry, a vertical solution is preferable to a generic ERP. The vertical solution provides a better fit to business operations in their line of business (i.e., vertical market). In a relatively stable ERP market, the ability of the vendor to offer a vertical solution becomes a key criterion for winning customers. For example, Epicor Scala's policy is to "target SAP and Oracle sites by supplying very specific and appropriate ERP products to end users with particular needs" (Beer, 2006b).

A recent study by IDC on ERP and related enterprise application software shows that five main industries account for approximately 75% of the market: (1) banking; (2) agriculture, construction, and mining; (3) retail; (4) government; and (5) manufacturing. Each accounts for approximately 10-15% of ERP sales. Wholesale, commercials, and utilities are the next three industries that together account for around 15% of the market, each with a market share of approximately 5%.

Vendors deliver vertical solutions either as part of their application offerings (e.g., SAP and Epicor-Scala) or in collaboration with partners (e.g., Microsoft Dynamics). Many growth plans for ERP vendors at present involve the acquisition of other vendor products to gain an in-depth expertise that enables them to satisfy these needs (for further details, refer to the "Consolidation of the ERP Market" section). Two key verticals that are predicted to be in high demand for this region are retail and banking.

Customers are More Demanding

Customers today are more knowledgeable in matters of ERP systems, owing largely to their experience with these systems and their ability to tap into a vast range of ERP-type expertise. As a consequence, it is more likely for user organizations to switch vendors when existing solutions either do not satisfy their needs or fail to accommodate business growth. Therefore, much of the expected growth in the ERP market in the Gulf region is driven by needs in these two areas. There are a number of cases, for example, that involve users switching vendors to support expected business growth; a considerable number of these involve an SAP win (Edwards, 2006d).

Customers' Integration Needs are not Fully Accomplished through ERP

Organizations are starting to realize that, although ERP satisfies internal integration needs, the external extension of the supply chain requires the employment of other technologies such as e-hubs, Web services, and e-portals (Daniel & White, 2005; Zeng & Pathak, 2003). Until recently, there has not been significant integration in the provision of these technologies to the customer. As a result, the customer is compelled to mix and match a portfolio of applications to support both internal and external integrations. This in essence makes the job daunting, more complex, and less efficient. When the software-as-a-service model for delivering ERP, CRM, and SCM applications gathers momentum, we may expect to see a simultaneous consolidation of both internal and external integration applications.

Many conglomerate type businesses in the Gulf region today are in the process of reexamining their IT solutions for both efficiency and effectiveness. As a result, they are following one of two paths. Either the conglomerates switch from one ERP vendor to another or they standardize implementations across regions to optimize internal integration. Once past this stage, the future will provide many opportunities for external integration (Sammon & Adam, 2005).

It is apparent then that the focus in this region remains on internal integration with the exception of a few external integration examples that support e-procurement. Most e-procurement providers in the region started operations in the early 2000s. These include a mix of local and international providers such as Tejari, Quadrem, Ariba, OTN, and EOS (Stanton, 2006a). With e-procurement

come new avenues for ERP vendors to become involved in creating another stream of revenue to generate continuous growth.

Regional Adaptations for ERP Products

In a study on company performance in developing countries, Khanna and Palepu (2006) reported that world-class global companies are less equipped to deal with institutional voids, and hence are more likely to lose business to local companies that can handle these better. This probably explains why SAP, despite being the global ERP market leader and credited with the largest ERP implementation in the region, still lags behind Oracle (Branton, 2006e). Oracle, the market leader in this region, has enjoyed a better understanding of the local market through its database business and has exploited this knowledge to tailor its ERP offerings. This proves that localization, particularly in developing countries, is a key issue vendors need to address when they contemplate entry and growth strategies (Liang & Xue, 2004; Martinsons, 2004; Rebstock & Selig, 2000).

Localization of IT applications is one of the challenges facing the effective use of ERP applications in non-western cultures (Liang & Xue, 2004; Liang, Xue, Boulton, & Byrd, 2004). Localization covers aspects such as language, regulations, and business context. Therefore, one successful strategy vendors can adopt to ensure sustained future growth is regional adaptation. Support for language, compliance with laws and regulations, and a sufficiently flexible product that easily adapts to changing business needs are among key criteria for success in these markets, particularly for western ERP vendors (Liang et al., 2004).

Language

Although English is considered the language of business and is widely spoken in the Gulf, Arabic remains the main language in member countries.

Hence, accommodation for both languages is needed. The two language-related issues in relation to ERP are: (1) the language that consultants use when talking to clients, and (2) Arabization of the ERP product.

Most GCC countries enjoy a healthy private sector involvement in business. The high reliance on expatriates[9] in business operations resulted in the adoption of English for the majority of commercial transactions. As a result, all white-collar employees in the private sector are expected to have a good command of both oral and written English. However, for the public sector, the Arabic language is still the language of communication. For example, there is a visible difference in workforce composition between the Abu Dhabi and Dubai Emirates of the UAE. The percentage of Arab speakers is much higher in Abu Dhabi because all federal government institutions are based in the capital. Having a team of Arabic-speaking ERP professionals can favorably position the vendor or the implementer. One SAP implementation services provider noted:

On a business level, Arabic language is very much in demand. We've had many requests from clients for consultants who speak Arabic[,] particularly governmental and public organizations. Speaking Arabic also helps to build trust between us and the client.

As for the Arabization of the ERP product, many ERP vendors in the region have started providing Arabic language enhancements, additions, or extensions to their products. Human resources (HR) module vendors such as Microsoft's Great Plains, Oracle, and Sage now come with Arabic language extensions (Edwards, 2006b; Howe, 2006; Sage Abra, 2006).

Compliance

Another aspect of localization is the need to respond to legal requirements at both country and regional levels. Our observations formed from discussions with IT professionals and by reviewing the practice literature in the region show that local compliance is not an issue of high importance. On the contrary, international compliance,[10] such as compliance with the Sarbanes-Oxley accounting legislation, Basel II[11] banking regulations, and IATA[12] electronic ticketing requirement, is a priority (Branton, 2006b, 2006d; Edwards, 2006a).

The reasons why local compliance is not being given attention is possibly because the region is growing at a comparatively fast pace. Furthermore, local regulations are either being developed or are lagging behind the pace of growth. Hence, there is no stability, and as a consequence, guidelines regarding local compliance continue to be flexible. To ERP vendors operating in this region, the issue of global compliance is considered more important, particularly for businesses that have global operations (Branton, 2006b, 2006e). However, once growth stabilizes, greater awareness of local compliance needs will develop and become an issue that international as well as local vendors will need to address.

Adaptation

The third aspect of localization entails adaptation to local business practices. The best example of this is Islamic banking. Islamic banking, which dates back to the mid-1960s, was developed in response to the guiding principles of Islamic law (i.e., Shariaa) that prohibits the payment of interest. A recent study by Gartner found that none of the international solution providers of core banking systems, currently occupying 50% market share, have an Islamic solution (Stanton, 2006c). Islamic banks are then left with no choice but to buy standard banking applications and try to customize them to deliver Islamic products. This however creates a problem of ERP and organizational misalignment (Soh & Sia, 2004). What complicates this process is the lack of standards, as there is no agreement between Muslim

Table 2. Types of Islamic financial institutions

Type	Description
Window	A conventional bank conducts Islamic banking separately from its conventional banking (e.g., in a separate unit with the banking entity).
Branch	A conventional bank sets up a branch that operates Islamic banking activities.
Subsidiary	The Islamic bank is a separate legal entity that is owned by a conventional bank.
Full Fledged	A bank dedicated to Islamic banking from its inception.

scholars on a unified set of banking requirements. Therefore, Islamic solutions differ from bank to bank and from country to country. One of the main challenges of Islamic banking is the lack of accounting and reporting standards

The Accounting & Auditing Organization for Islamic Financial Institutions (AAOIFI), which was established in Bahrain in 1991, has taken the job of developing Islamic banking standards as its mission (AAOIFI, 2006). AAOIFI classifies Islamic banking institutions into four types (see Table 2). Can any ERP vendor accommodate these four types with local and regional configuration options in a standard ERP banking module? The answer is yet to be known, but the task is challenging. With such challenges come many opportunities for ERP vendors and system integrators to get involved in this US$250 billion Islamic banking market that is operated by 280 financial services institutions worldwide, 35% of which are in the Middle East (Stanton, 2006c). In the UAE, for example, Islamic banking currently accounts for 15% of the market, but it is expected to grow to 35% by 2012 (Shouler, 2007).

Most ERP vendors now realize the importance of localization. For example, Microsoft recently awarded its customer-of-the-year award to a local system integrator in the UAE, ITQAN, for its successful implementation of Microsoft solutions (Edwards, 2006b). Part of the work ITQAN did was implementing eKawader, a localized version of both the human resources and payroll modules, in Microsoft's Great Plains ERP suite. This demonstrates that ERP vendors understand

the need to adapt their products to local business practices.

DISCUSSION

Despite the positive statistics for GCC countries that include a tripling in oil revenues over the last three years, a 7% growth rate, and a 10-fold increase in foreign direct investment over the last five years (Boer & Turner, 2007), not many organizations are now at the stage where their ERP system is highly mature (i.e., many are still in stage one of the ERP maturity model). Table 3 provides a brief analysis of the trends discussed in this chapter and indicates whether these trends have supporting evidence in both the practice literature and the exploratory interviews that were conducted for this study. The analysis shows that signs of stage two or three maturity are limited to a few cases, all of which are large organizations that operate in specific industries such as oil and gas, hospitality, airlines, or precious metals.

Growth in the enterprise application market is expected in both the SMB and large organizations. While the SMB market has not been addressed, the market for large organizations is expected to have CRM and SCM implementations, particularly for early ERP adopters. One interesting observation noted was that many companies, which were classified as SMBs according to the number of ERP users, were actually big when measured by the number of employees or organizational revenue. In western countries, it is common practice that

Table 3. ERP trends and supporting evidence

ERP Trends and Implications	Evidence in the Practice Literature	Evidence from Exploratory Interviews
The consolidation of the ERP market	Yes, but mainly in large organizations	Yes, but mainly in large organizations
The diversification of the ERP product	Yes, but weak	Yes, but weak
New modes for ERP application delivery	Yes, but very few cases are reported and are all in large organizations	No, as traditional modes of delivery are still favored
ERP and new technologies	Yes, but very few cases are reported, all are in large organizations and in specific industries	No
ERP pricing structures	Yes, however pricing is not advertised	Weak, maybe because pricing is not disclosed
ERP support operations	Yes, but many still have plans or are in the process of implementing plans to support uninterrupted operations	Weak, however some reported having plans or are in the process of implementing plans to support uninterrupted operations
Customers' interest in vertical solutions continue to grow	Yes	Yes, but mainly in large organizations with mature ERP implementations
Customers are more demanding	Yes	Yes, but weak as many customers are still deliberating what to do next
Customers' integration needs are not fully accomplished through ERP	Yes, but very few cases are reported, all are in large organizations and in specific industries	Yes, but weak
Vendors are offering regional adaptations for their ERP products		
—Language	Yes	Yes
—Compliance	Yes	No
—Adaptation	Yes	No

85% of employees use computers, while in the GCC the percentage is around 50%. International companies are often an exception as they have computer usage ratios that are comparable to their global operations. The low computer usage suggests that there is a substantial area of growth in the traditional ERP market once the business systems in these large organizations become fully developed.

The low level of ERP maturity is partly due to the fact that many organizations have immature IT systems. Despite the heavy promotional campaigns carried out by ERP vendors, many SMBs find the cost of an ERP system beyond their reach. These SMBs can continue to do business as usual, either in the region or internationally, as long as compliance issues are not enforced by law. Once local compliance becomes mandatory or when they choose to trade with countries that have stringent compliance regulations (e.g., SOX in the U.S.), SMBs will realize that an ERP-like solution is a must. The main advantages of an ERP system would be to make the extensive data collection and reporting, which are essential in documenting compliance, possible and manageable.

FUTURE TRENDS

The body of this chapter discussed ERP trends and implications with a focus on current trends. This section has a different purpose, which is to specify trends that will have a greater impact in the future. Understanding the future directions of ERP systems has implications for both research and practice as it provides a roadmap to show where efforts in these two areas can be efficiently and effectively exploited. A synthesis of the topics discussed in this chapter plus a re-examination of Table 3 shows the following:

1. SMBs are the future areas of growth for ERP vendors. Considering the low-to-medium level of maturity of the ERP market, this finding is in agreement with ERP studies in the developed world.
2. In a future mature ERP environment, two areas will provide substantial opportunities for ERP adopters. The first is the economies of scale attained by adopting third-party delivery mechanisms. The second is the integration of business intelligence tools with the ERP system. While the first will improve operational efficiency, the latter will improve operational effectiveness.
3. Regional adaptation will be key to implementation success, with the issues of language, compliance, and localization becoming both more challenging and more important.
4. The need for inter-organizational systems will gradually rise. An implementation mechanism such as Web services will come into play and either pose a serious threat to ERP-type solutions or create new integration opportunities. Developments in data exchange standard mechanisms such as

Extensible Markup Language[13] (XML) and Extensible Business Reporting Language[14] (XBRL) are other areas to consider. One area that would highly benefit from the development of these standards is Islamic banking.

5. Innovations that combine ERP with new technologies can provide endless opportunities for businesses that can exploit them. This chapter reported on innovative ways of integrating ERP with RFID to manage the precious metals supply chain and with mobile technologies to facilitate supply chain coordination in the hospitality industry. Both examples are believed to be the groundwork for future accomplishments.

CONCLUSION

This chapter explores the key trends in the ERP market, both globally and in the Gulf region. As the period of 1997-2001 was characterized by a surge of ERP implementations, exaggerated spending, lengthy implementations, and unstable technologies, it was only around 2005 that ERP applications came to maturity. Maturity is demonstrated by: (1) mature markets where demand is generated from SMBs as well as big companies; (2) mature technologies that are stable, have better integration capabilities across vendor products, and can be implemented in a variety of ways—in-house, outsourced, or hosted; (3) mature products that, despite being standard, are flexible enough to cater for both vertical markets and localization requirements; (4) mature vendors who survived the ups and downs of the dynamic IT market, consolidated their products, and extended ERP functionality to deliver better value and a higher return on investment for their customers; and finally (5) mature customers who are more knowledgeable, better understand implementation issues, and are less rushed to make quick and later regretted decisions.

The finding of this exploratory study indicates that a mature or advanced use of ERP applications in the region studied is limited to a few cases. These are mainly large organizations that operate in specific industries such as oil and gas, hospitality, airlines, and precious metals. The low level of ERP maturity is partly due to the fact that many organizations in the region have immature IT systems, immature business systems, or both. Hence, growth in this market is predicted in both SMBs and in large organizations. While demand from SMBs will be for standard ERP functionality, large organizations—particularly the early adopters—will be expected to acquire CRM and SCM functionalities.

The chapter discussed key trends in the ERP market and the challenges they pose with a focus on how these are manifested in the region studied. While many of these are important, the localization requirement is seen as essential, particularly for vendors and IT service providers that want to become well established in the Gulf. With the ERP products acquiring maturity, localization has become a key differentiator, particularly in a dynamic environment where business demands quick implementation and better responses to customer demands.

While the early 2000s saw the ERP application extended to include CRM and to a lesser extent SCM (Møller, 2005), the next phase will see an extension of ERP application outside the enterprise. To support e-commerce and collaboration activities, more SCM capabilities will be added to the standard ERP product. Two other technologies that are likely to play important roles in how the ERP product is shaped are RFID and mobile applications; both emphasize the supply chain capability of ERP applications.

FUTURE RESEARCH DIRECTIONS

This chapter provided an exploratory view of the enterprise application software market in the GCC countries. The chapter identified the main trends within this market, particularly those that are specific to the region. Future studies are suggested in the following areas:

1. A survey study of ERP adoption will provide a clear indication of the maturity of the ERP market in the region. The results reported here on ERP maturity are limited by the survey of the practice literature, the exploratory interviews conducted with key ERP players, and ERP sales data. Sales data may not be a reflection of ERP usage as vendors often package a whole set of ERP modules when making a sale. How many of these modules go into operation is still unknown.

2. Case studies of ERP implementations in the region will provide insight into both the organizational and technological challenges facing ERP stakeholders—vendors, consultants, implementation partners, and the organizations using these systems.

3. Both qualitative and qualitative studies that have tested some of the documented assumptions in mature markets can also be used to test if the same assumptions apply in this region. Comparative studies with developing countries in other parts of the world would also be interesting. These studies would have the potential to identify areas of similarities and differences that would add to the body of knowledge concerning global ERP implementations.

4. Studies of how ERP applications can cater for Islamic banking could both facilitate local implementation and serve as exemplars for implementations globally.

5. The integration of ERP applications with new technologies such as RFID, mobile devices, XBRL, and Web services has the potential to identify combinations that can deliver the most effective and efficient benefits.

REFERENCES

AAOIFI. (2006). *Certified Islamic professional accountant: CIPA.* Accounting & Auditing Organization for Islamic Financial Institutions.

Arabian Computer News. (2006). E-procurement buy-in. *Arabian Computer News,* (June 1). Retrieved June 4, 2006, from http://www.itp.net/features/print.php?id=4485&prodid=&category=

Beer, E. (2006a). Opening Oman. *Arabian Computer News,* (March 5). Retrieved April 29, 2006, from http://www.itp.net/features/print.php?id=3933&prodid=&category=

Beer, E. (2006b). Put IT together. *Arabian Computer News,* (March 26). Retrieved April 29, 2006, from http://www.itp.net/features/print.php?id=4055&prodid=&category=

Boer, K., & Turner, J.M. (2007). Beyond oil: Reappraising the gulf states. *McKinsey Quarterly, 2007 Special Edition,* (February), 7-17.

Botta-Genoulaz, V., Millet, P.A., & Grabot, B. (2005). A survey on the recent research literature on ERP systems. *Computers in Industry, 56*(6), 510-522.

Bowman, D. (2006). Scaling the ERP heights. *IT Weekly Middle East,* (April 16). Retrieved April 29, 2006, from http://www.itp.net/features/print.php?id=4173&prodid=&category=

Branton, P. (2006a). All eyes on future trends. *IT Weekly Middle East,* (July 16). Retrieved September 6, 2006, from http://www.itp.net/features/print.php?id=4736&prodid=&category=

Branton, P. (2006b). Banking on success. *IT Weekly Middle East,* (June 25). Retrieved July 8, 2006, from http://www.itp.net/features/print.php?id=4570&prodid=&category=

Branton, P. (2006c). Pay as you grow. *IT Weekly Middle East,* (May 21). Retrieved May 21, 2006, from http://www.itp.net/features/print.php?id=4385&prodid=&category=

Branton, P. (2006d). Roadmap to Basel. *IT Weekly Middle East,* (June 25). Retrieved July 8, 2006, from http://www.itp.net/features/print.php?id=4569&prodid=&category=

Branton, P. (2006e). The skyline's the limit. *IT Weekly Middle East,* (April 9). Retrieved April 29, 2006, from http://www.itp.net/features/print.php?id=4133&prodid=&category=

Cannon, J., & Byers, M. (2006). Compliance deconstructed. *ACM Queue, 4*(7), 30-37.

Daniel, E.M., & White, A. (2005). The future of inter-organisational system linkages: Findings of an international Delphi study. *European Journal of Information Systems, 14*(2), 188-203.

Davenport, T.H. (1998). Putting the enterprise into the enterprise system. *Harvard Business Review, 76*(4), 121-131.

Eccles, R.G., Watson, L., & Willis, M. (2007). The HBR list—Breakthrough ideas for 2007: Here comes XBRL. *Harvard Business Review, 85*(2), 32-34.

Edwards, C. (2006a). An airline in his hands. *Arabian Computer News,* (October 2). Retrieved October 17, 2006, from http://www.itp.net/features/print.php?id=5274&prodid=&category=

Edwards, C. (2006b). Itqan's awards. *Arabian Computer News,* (September 28). Retrieved October 17, 2006, from http://www.itp.net/features/print.php?id=5218&prodid=&category=

Edwards, C. (2006c). SAP attack. *Arabian Computer News,* (March 26). Retrieved April 29, 2006, from http://www.itp.net/features/print.php?id=4052&prodid=&category=

Edwards, C. (2006d). SAP migrations gather momentum. *Arabian Computer News,* (February 27). Retrieved April 4, 2006, from http://www.itp.net/news/print.php?id=19741&prodid=&category=

Edwards, C. (2006e). Ziic centralises IT. *Arabian Computer News,* (October 1). Retrieved October

17, 2006, from http://www.itp.net/features/print.php?id=5238&prodid=&category=

Ekanayaka, Y., Currie, W.L., & Seltsikas, P. (2002). Delivering enterprise resource planning systems through application service providers. *Logistics Information Management, 15*(3), 192-203.

ESCWA. (2006, October 26). *Economic situations and prospects for Western Asia: A note prepared for world economic situations and prospects 2007.* Retrieved February 2007, from http://www.escwa.org.lb/divisions/lib/Uploads/WESP2007WA_26Oct2006.pdf

Esteves, J., & Pastor, J. (2001). Enterprise resource planning systems research: An annotated bibliography. *Communications of the AIS, 7*(8), 1-52.

Farrell, D. (2006). Smarter offshoring. *Harvard Business Review, 84*(6), 84-92.

Ghose, G. (2007). Emerging from the mists of time. *Gulf News Quarterly Financial Review, 1*, 42-49.

Gulf News. (2005, August 6). *95% UAE residents own mobile phones.* Retrieved November 2, 2006, from http://archive.gulfnews.com/articles/05/06/08/168257.html

Gulf News. (2006, October 2). *Dubai is second worldwide in building offices.* Retrieved October 3, 2006, from http://archive.gulfnews.com/articles/06/10/02/10071646.html

Holland, C.P., Light, B., Beck, P., Berdugo, Y., Millar, R., Press, N., et al. (2000). An international analysis of the maturity of enterprise resource planning (ERP) systems use. In *Proceedings of the Americas Conference on Information Systems* (pp. 992-977), Long Beach, CA.

Howe, M. (2006). Oracle answers Etisalat's call for human resources. *IT Weekly Middle East,* (October 1). Retrieved October 3, 2006, from http://www.itp.net/news/print.php?id=22139&prodid=&category=

James, D., & Wolf, M.L. (2000). A second wind for ERP. *McKinsey Quarterly,* (2), 100-107.

Khanna, T., & Palepu, K.G. (2006). Emerging giants: Building world-class companies in developing countries. *Harvard Business Review, 84*(10), 60-69.

Lamba, A. (2006). M-enabling the enterprise. *Arabian Computer News,* (October 5). Retrieved October 17, 2006, from http://www.itp.net/features/print.php?id=5307&prodid=&category=

Levinson, M. (2006). Meet your new host. *CIO Magazine,* (September 1). Retrieved October 14, 2006, from http://www.cio.com/archive/090106/fea_midhosting.html?action=print

Liang, H., & Xue, Y. (2004). Coping with ERP-related contextual issues in SMEs: A vendor's perspective. *Journal of Strategic Information Systems, 13*(4), 399-415.

Liang, H., Xue, Y., Boulton, W.R., & Byrd, T.A. (2004). Why western vendors don't dominate China's ERP market. *Communications of the ACM, 47*(7), 69-72.

Lohr, S. (2004). Software sector enters an era of big mergers. *New York Times,* (December 15). Retrieved February 2005, from http://topics.nytimes.com/top/news/business/companies/oracle_corporation/index.html?offset=40&

Martinsons, M.G. (2004). ERP in China: One package, two profiles. *Communications of the ACM, 47*(7), 65-68.

Milne, D. (2006a). Gulf air swoops in for deal to outsource its IT support. *IT Weekly Middle East,* (April 23). Retrieved April 2006, from http://www.itp.net/news/print.php?id=20397&prodid=&category=

Milne, D. (2006b). Oracle promises lifetime support to its customers. *IT Weekly Middle East,* (May 7). Retrieved May 7, 2006, from http://www.itp.net/news/print.php?id=20556&prodid=&category=

Møller, C. (2005). ERP II: A conceptual framework for next-generation enterprise systems? *Journal of Enterprise Information Management, 18*(4), 483-497.

Moon, Y.B. (2007). Enterprise resource planning (ERP): A review of the literature. *International Journal of Management and Enterprise Development, 4*(3), 235-264.

Nair, V., & Rajan, B. (2006). *Arab Middle East and North Africa software solutions: 2006-2010 forecast and 2005 vendor shares.* Document #ZR03N, IDC.

Rebstock, M., & Selig, J.G. (2000). Development and implementation strategies for international ERP software projects. In *Proceedings of the European Conference on Information Systems (ECIS).*

Sage Abra. (2006). Sage Abra HR solutions learns to speak Arabic. *IT Weekly Middle East,* (May 13-19), 11.

Sammon, D., & Adam, F. (2005). Towards a model of organizational prerequisites for enterprise-wide systems integration: Examining ERP and data warehousing. *Journal of Enterprise Information Management, 18*(4), 458-470.

Sheikh Mohammed. (2005). *GCC countries.* Retrieved June 2006, from http://www.sheikhmohammed.co.ae/english/history/history_arabia.asp

Shouler, A. (2007). Gulf news financial review: Strong growth and reform to keep positive tone. *Gulf News Quarterly Financial Review, 1,* 14-16.

Soh, C., & Sia, S.K. (2004). An institutional perspective on sources of ERP package-organization misalignments. *Journal of Strategic Information Systems, 13*(4), 375-397.

Stanton, D. (2006a). Middle East buys into e-procurement at CIPS. *Arabian Computer News,* (May 9). Retrieved May 9, 2006, from http://www.itp.net/news/print.php?id=20618&prodid=&category=

Stanton, D. (2006b). Outside the box. *Arabian Computer News,* (September 4). Retrieved October 3, 2006, from http://www.itp.net/features/print.php?id=5083&prodid=&category=

Stanton, D. (2006c). Shariah support. *Arabian Computer News, Oct. 2.* Retrieved October 17, 2006, from http://www.itp.net/features/print.php?id=5269&prodid=&category=

Stanton, D. (2006d). Solid gold solution. *Arabian Computer News,* (October 5). Retrieved October 17, 2006, from https://www.itp.net/features/print.php?id=5305&prodid=&category=

Swedberg, C. (2006). RFID tracks jewelry sales: Inventory in Mideast. *RFID Journal,* (May 18). Retrieved November 2, 2006, from http://www.rfidjournal.com/article/articleview/2348/1/1/

Wailgum, T. (2006). Integration liberation. *CIO Magazine,* (October 15). Retrieved October 2006 from http://www.cio.com/archive/101506/integration.html?action=print

Zeng, A.Z., & Pathak, B.K. (2003). Achieving information integration in supply chain management through B2B e-hubs: Concepts and analyses. *Industrial Management & Data Systems, 103*(9), 657-665.

ADDITIONAL READING

Bennett, C., & Timbrell, G.T. (2000). Application service providers: Will they succeed? *Information Systems Frontiers, Special Issue on the Future of Enterprise Resource Planning Systems, 2*(2), 195-211.

Boersma, K., & Kingma, S. (2005). Developing a cultural perspective on ERP. *Business Process Management Journal, 11*(2), 123-136.

Boudreau, M.-C. (2006). A study in forms of organisational change induced by enterprise resource planning. *International Journal of Information Systems and Change Management, 1*(3), 285-300.

Brehm, L., Heinzl, A., & Markus, M.L. (2001). Tailoring ERP systems: A spectrum of choices and their implications. In *Proceedings of the Hawaii International Conference on Systems Sciences* (HICSS) (pp. 1-9).

Brown, C.V., Vessey, I., & Powell, A. (2000). The ERP purchase decision: Influential business and IT factors. *Proceedings of the Americas Conference on Information Systems* (pp. 1029-1032), Long Beach, CA.

Buonanno, G., Faverio, F.P., Ravarini, D.S., & Tagliavini, M. (2005). Factors affecting ERP system adoption: A comparative analysis between SMEs and large companies. *Journal of Enterprise Information Management, 18*(4), 384-426.

Búrca, S., Fynes, B., & Marshall, D. (2005). Strategic technology adoption: Extending ERP across the supply chain. *Journal of Enterprise Information Management, 18*(4), 427-440.

Cadili, S., & Whitley, E.A. (2005). On the interpretative flexibility of hosted ERP systems. *Journal of Strategic Information Systems, 14*(2), 167-195.

Chung, S.H., & Snyder, C.A. (2000). ERP adoption: A technological evolution approach. *International Journal of Agile Management Systems, 2*(1), 24-32.

Clemmons, S., & Simon, S.J. (2001). Control and coordination in global ERP configuration. *Business Process Management Journal, 7*(3), 205-215.

Davenport, T.H. (2000a). The future of enterprise system-enabled organizations. *Information Systems Frontiers, Special Issue on the Future of Enterprise Resource Planning Systems, 2*(2), 163-180.

Davenport, T.H. (2000b). *Mission critical: Realizing the promise of enterprise systems.* Boston: Harvard Business School Press.

Davenport, T.H., & Brooks, J.D. (2004). Enterprise systems and the supply chain. *Journal of Enterprise Information Management, 17*(1), 8-19.

Davison, R. (2002). Cultural complications of ERP. *Communications of the ACM, 45*(7), 109-111.

Everdingen, Y., Hillegersberg, J., & Waarts, E. (2000). ERP adoption by European midsize companies. *Communications of the ACM, 43*(4), 27-31.

Gupta, A. (2000). Enterprise resource planning: The emerging organizational value systems. *Industrial Management and Data Systems, 100*(3), 114-118.

Hayman, L. (2000). ERP in the Internet economy. *Information Systems Frontiers, Special Issue on the Future of Enterprise Resource Planning Systems, 2*(2), 137-139.

Holland, C.P., & Light, B. (1999). A critical success factors model for ERP implementation. *IEEE Software, 16*(3), 30-36.

Huang, Z., & Palvia, P. (2001). ERP implementation issues in advanced and developing countries. *Business Process Management Journal, 7*(3), 276-284.

Krumbholz, M., Galliers, J., Coulianos, N., & Maiden, N.A.M. (2000). Implementing enterprise resource planning packages in different corporate and national cultures. *Journal of Information Technology, 15,* 267-279.

Kumar, K., & Hillegersberg, J. (2000). ERP experience and evolution. *Communications of the ACM, 43*(4), 23-26.

Markus, M.L., Axline, S., Petrie, D., & Tanis, C. (2000). Learning from adopters' experiences with ERP-successes and problems. *Journal of Information Technology, 15*(4), 245-265.

Markus, M.L., & Tanis, C. (2000). The enterprise systems experience—From adoption to success. In R.W. Zmud (Ed.), *Framing the domains of IT research: Glimpsing the future through the past* (pp. 173-207). Cincinnati, OH: Pinnaflex Educational Resources.

Martinsons, M.G. (2004). ERP in China: One package, two profiles. *Communications of the ACM, 47*(7), 65-68.

Nandhakumar, J., Rossi, M., & Talvinen, J. (2005). The dynamics of contextual forces of ERP implementation. *Journal of Strategic Information Systems, 14*(2), 221-242.

Parr, A., & Shanks, G. (2000). A taxonomy of ERP implementation approaches. In *Proceedings of the 33rd Hawaii International Conference on System Sciences* (pp. 1-10).

Rashid, M.A., Hossain, L., & Patrick, J.D. (2002). The evolution of ERP systems: A historical perspective. In L. Hossain, J.D. Patrick, & M.A. Rashid (Eds.), *Enterprise resource planning: Global opportunities and challenges* (pp. 1-16). Hershey, PA: Idea Group.

Ross, J.W., & Vitale, M.R. (2000). The ERP revolution: Surviving vs. thriving. *Information Systems Frontiers, Special Issue on the Future of Enterprise Resource Planning Systems, 2*(2), 233-241.

Sandoe, K., Corbitt, G., & Boykin, R. (2001). *Enterprise integration.* New York: John Wiley & Sons.

Shakir, M., & Viehland, D. (2004). Business drivers in contemporary enterprise system implementations. In *Proceedings of the Americas Conference on Information Systems* (pp. 103-112), New York.

Shakir, M., & Viehland, D. (2005). The selection of the IT platform: Enterprise system implementation in the NZ health board. *Journal of Cases on Information Technology, 7*(1), 22-33.

Sledgianowski, D. (2006). Decisions concerning IT infrastructure integration: A case study of a global chemical company. *Journal of Information Technology Case and Application Research, 8*(1), 55.

Soh, C., Kien, S.S., & Tay-Yap, J. (2000). Cultural fits and misfits: Is ERP a universal solution? *Communications of the ACM, 43*(4), 47-51.

Souza, C.A., & Zwicker, R. (2001). Enterprise systems: A multiple-case study in eight Brazilian companies adopting ERP systems. In *Proceedings of the GITM World Conference* (pp. 1-18).

Sprott, D. (2000). Componentizing the enterprise application packages. *Communications of the ACM, 43*(4), 63-69.

ENDNOTES

[1] The Middle East region includes the countries in Southwest Asia between Iran and Egypt. These are: Bahrain, Egypt, Iran, Iraq, Israel, Jordan, Kuwait, Lebanon, Palestine, Oman, Qatar, Saudi Arabia, Sudan, Syrian Arab Republic, United Arab Emirates, and Yemen.

[2] The Gulf region, locally known as the GCC region, includes the countries of Bahrain, Kingdom of Saudi Arabia, Kuwait, Qatar, Sultanate of Oman, and United Arab Emirates (UAE); all are members of the Gulf Corporation Council (GCC), which was founded in 1981 with the aim of promoting coordination between these oil-rich neighbors (Sheikh Mohammed, 2005).

[3] Established in 1985, Emirates Airlines has evolved into a global travel and tourism conglomerate earning net profits of US$762 million at the end of 2005. The Emirates Group now includes a fleet of 92 aircraft, an international cargo division, a destination management and leisure division, an

international ground-handler division, and an airline IT developer (http://www.emir-ates.com).

4   DP World is one of the largest marine terminal operators in the world, with 51 terminals spanning 24 countries and five continents, a global capacity of 50 million TEU, and 34,000 employees (http://www.dpworld.com).

5   Jumeirah International, the world's most luxurious hospitality brand, operates a chain of hotels and resorts in the United States, United Kingdom, and Middle East (www.jumeirah.com).

6   The main local practice-oriented publications surveyed include *Arabian Computer News, IT Weekly Middle East, Logistics Middle East, Channel Middle East,* and GITEX reviews. Refer to http://www.itp.net for details on these publications.

7   Oracle is planning to move its own product line and the product lines it acquired (e.g., PeopleSoft, JD Edwards, Siebel, etc.) to a single product line called Fusion in 2008 (Branton, 2006e).

8   A free zone area is both a legal and administrative framework that governs companies operating in an assigned geographic area. Jebel Ali, the first free zone in the GCC region, was established in 1985 with the purpose of attracting overseas investments. Advantages to companies operating in a free zone include simple setup procedures, 100% foreign ownership, 100% repatriation of capital and profits, zero taxes, and a high level of administrative support from the Free Zone Authority.

9   Expatriates account for 80% of the workforce in the UAE.

10 For an overview on compliance, refer to Cannon and Byers (2006).

11 Basel II is an international accord for regulating capital requirements for large banks. Issued in 2004, it provides guidelines for managing risk in the banking industry. For further details refer to http://www.bis.org/publ/bcbsca.htm.

12 The International Air Transport Association (IATA) was established in 1945 with the mission to represent, lead, and serve the airline industry. Its members now comprise 260 airlines representing 94% of international scheduled air traffic. IATA's e-ticketing initiative dictates that member airlines should be able to issue electronic tickets by the 2007 deadline. For further details, refer to http://www.iata.org.

13 XML is a markup language for documents containing structured information. XML made it possible to share structure data over the Internet. For further information, refer to www.xml.com.

14 XBRL is a royalty-free, open specification to describe financial information for public and private companies and other organizations. XBRL was identified on HBR "List for Breakthrough Ideas for 2007" as an innovation in the means for improving the disclosure and sharing of information among organizations (Eccles, Watson, & Willis, 2007). For further information, refer to www.xbrl.org.

Chapter XVII
The Future of ERP and Enterprise Resource Management Systems

Carlos Ferran
The Pennsylvania State University, USA

Ricardo Salim
Universidad Autónoma de Barcelona, Spain
Cautus Networks Corp., Venezuela

ABSTRACT

Enterprise resource planning (ERP) systems integrate into one single system the control and account-ing of all the enterprise resources. Just like the previous systems (material requirements planning and accounting information systems among others) became ERPs, it is highly probable that ERPs will keep evolving towards a different and more comprehensive system. Logically, this evolution will be driven by the unsatisfied expectations of the current markets. One of these expectations is to lower the emphasis on the mid- and long-term planning functionality in favor of some kind of short-term, more dynamic plan-ning functionality. In this sense, the chapter glimpses at a system that could be called ERM, where the "M" stands for management instead of the "P" for planning. The chapter also discusses the potential effects of the Open Source Initiative on ERPs. Other outstanding expectations examined are: (1) lower cost and duration of the implementation process, (2) less dependency on external consultants for the implementation, and (3) improved and standardized interaction functionality—or middleware—between different ERPs.

INTRODUCTION

Enterprise resource planning (ERP) systems integrated in one single system the control and accounting of all the enterprise resources. However the markets seemed to expect much more out of them, and many organizations, especially small and medium-sized enterprises (SMEs), cannot afford the high costs and duration of the implementation process. They also expect a more dynamic and day-to-day management functionality instead of the rigid mid- and long-term planning functionality that characterizes the current wave of ERPs. Even the otherwise happy users are not satisfied with the way that ERPs have delivered in regards to two big promises: the transfer of best practices and the inter-organizational—suppliers, customers, subsidiaries, partners, and regulators—connectivity. The former resembles a long and traumatic reengineering process, while the latter still has the same problems that organizations used to have between departments before the advent of ERPs.

ERP developers are starting to offer more SME-oriented products. However, big software houses such as Microsoft, IBM, SAP, and Oracle do not show any clear trend towards the development of a "next-generation" ERP. No one is talking about a global standard for ERP comparable to, say, the Microsoft Office Suite. It is not even clear if there is an intrinsic impediment for the standardization of ERPs or at least of the middleware aimed to make different ERPs compatible and really serve as a vehicle to transfer the best practices. Some consulting firms see the Open Source Initiative (OSI) as a way of lowering the total costs by eliminating the licensing cost, but none of the attempts have produced an open source ERP propagation model like that of Linux.

The first and second sections of this chapter identify one of the needs the future ERP will have to satisfy in order to reach the global SME market and the global "extended organization": the need to emphasize managing and not planning. This includes the systematization of short-term management and thus proposes a system that responds to the name of enterprise resource management (ERM), emphasizing management instead of planning. The third section identifies a need that ERMs themselves would have to satisfy: a resource-centered data structure that would structurally strengthen and support the resource-oriented functionality already present in ERPs.

The next sections address the possible role of current large software houses—like Microsoft—in the standardization of ERPs, the possible incidence of the Open Source Initiative in that respect, and the possibilities of a substantial reduction of the consulting expenses in ERP implementations. Finally, the concept of the global ERP is revised in terms of the global ERM.

ERP FOR SMES: THE NEED FOR AN EMPHASIS ON MANAGING, NOT PLANNING

Most ERPs are designed and developed with the richest companies in mind—since those were the first to be able to pay the elevated prices. Today, they are developed mostly for the large and middle-size companies of the developed world, which is its primary target market. Thus, ERPs still have two critical characteristics:

1. Their prices are so high and their implementation times so long that only large and some medium-sized companies can handle them.
2. They emphasize a critical part of management for those organizations: planning. Moreover, an additional unconscious emphasis is given to planning because it is embedded in the name that marketing has given to these applications: enterprise resource planning systems.

Most SMEs cannot afford such large investments in time and financial resources (see a somehow "desperate" alternative in Olsen & Saetre, 2007) and the restrictive planning functionality does not allow them to timely react to the unexpected events that they tend to face in their day-to-day operations. Moreover, it is common that for reasons out of their control (that will be discussed later in this chapter), SMEs cannot develop medium-term plans even if they wanted to.

The major ERP packages currently in the market cannot operate optimally if the planning function is either ignored or sub-utilized. And they operate better as the plan extends for longer periods of time. Frequent changes to the plan are either difficult or next to impossible to accomplish. To be useful to an organization, this functionality requires the use of a budget, reliable and consistent historical data, or at a minimum a customer order flow that is stable or with very small fluctuations. However, these requirements are rarely satisfied by SMEs and by most organizations (no matter their size) that operate in environments hardly predictable. In fact, most organizations operating in developing countries cannot satisfy them. Budget, consistent historical data, and stable order flow are only available to a few select organizations of the developed world.

Maybe for this reason, the current wave of ERPs in the market has a reputation, particularly among SMEs and developing regions like Latin America, of requiring too much planning and therefore of being too rigid for the ever-changing needs. In fact, while we did not find current academic articles on the subject, the practitioners' press shows a clear perception that current ERPs are too rigid, particularly when it comes to changing the plans. A quick search of the Web on phrases like "flexibility of ERP" and "rigidity of ERP" returns more than 15 articles that discuss the topic. Results include phrases like: "ERP2 is characterized by truly open systems with a higher degree of flexibility"; "SAP has to transform its original strength of 'structure and rigidity' into one of "flexibility"; "But to disprove the so-called myths of its cost, complexity, and inflexibility, SAP will have to continue by documenting successful case studies"; "This was a clear conflict with Dell's overriding need for a flexible business model. The company ultimately decided not to deploy SAP"; and "This inflexibility is endemic today." In contrast, with these and similar Web searches we were not able to find any articles that would affirm or assert that any given ERP was considered to be flexible. This sample cannot confirm that current ERPs are quite rigid but does show that it is a generalized perception of practitioners.

It is interesting to ask to what extent the current development, marketing, and implementation of ERPs are adequate for those organizations for which the planning emphasis is of little use or even detrimental. However, it is better to first understand those organizations better in order to be able to answer that question properly.

Organizations with Low Planning Capacity and ERPs

Organizations with low or no capacity to plan are in general those that cannot rely on the environment being stable and cannot establish their planning variables on their own. These variables are mainly the cost of the raw materials, labor costs, financing terms, and acceptable estimations of the demand for their products. A quiet sea allows even small and fragile boats to establish their course and arrive on time, but the more agitated the sea, the heavier and larger the boats needed to navigate safely. SMEs can only do mid- or even long-term planning in a quiet, predictable economic environment. And only large monopolistic or at least market-dominant organizations can do it in an environment disturbed by political or social changes, non-clear regulations, frequent labor conflicts, out-of-control inflation rates, monetary instability, capital and brain runaway, and so forth.

Very few organizations, particularly businesses, can isolate themselves from their economic environment which in turn is strongly affected by social and political variables. There are very few (although they represent a considerable part of the world economy) economical environments predictable enough for businesses to appropriately plan their long-term raw materials, human resources, and financial requirements. These environments are circumscribed to the zones of high social, political, and economical development and to a few regions of the developing world that are highly influenced and protected by the developed nations (see Balassa, 1990; Outreville, 2005). Highly unpredictable business environments are characterized by one or more factors such as untrustworthy supply chain (Dobberstein, Neumann, & Zils, 2005), precarious financial system (Ghani, 1992; Shih, 2004), deficient or conflictive labor market (Cox, Al Arkoubi, & Estrada, 2006; Mellahi & Frynas, 2003; Robertson, 2003; Tessema & Soeters, 2006), and volatile demand (Naik, 2004).

Outside stable and mature markets, only companies that are considered of a "push" type can still plan ahead. Push organizations are those that have enough marketing power to push, canalize, or place its products regardless of existing demand; in other words, those that can create a demand for their products and, using their purchase power, control its costs. Thus, push organizations are quite large and generally operate in the mass market. Push organizations could also be those that have a monopoly in a market of basic products. However, the majority of the companies are not push organizations because they have no control over the market of their product or because they depend on a few clients or few orders that make up the bulk of their business.

Pull or demand-driven organizations are those that produce based on orders and not based on expected (or planned) demand. Depending on additional characteristics, their production could go from highly predictable to highly unpredict-able. The higher the atomization of their customer base, the higher their predictability. Those pull organizations that are not dependent on a few clients nor on a single order that represents more than, say, 20% of their total annual production are considered to be of low uncertainty.

Most organizations are neither push organizations nor pull organizations of low uncertainty. These are small and middle-size companies that operate in emerging or turbulent markets. They need to continuously alter their plans and adapt to the new conditions. We can call them pull organizations of high uncertainty, and they are structured to respond to unexpected orders and market fluctuations that represent a high percentage (say 20% or more) of their production capacity (e.g., Naik, 2004).

Finally, no business of any type and in any economic environment is exempt from falling into occasional periods of high uncertainty. For internal or external causes that are out of management control, organizations may become unable to plan some or all of their resource requirements even in the short range—for example, organizations under a deep restructuring process or whose financial environment suffers a crisis caused by a natural catastrophe or a terrorist attack (e.g., Klingebiel, Kroszner, & Laeven, 2002; Do & Levchenko, 2004).

Table 1 succinctly compares the organizations in terms of their capacity and willingness to plan.

The Need to Systematize Short-Term Management

Companies that cannot make medium and long-term plans may still be able to do it for the short term. But when the planning horizon becomes too short, it is not really planning but flexible, proactive short-term management. Some current ERPs are useful for flexible, proactive short-term management, but they are not really directed to meet their particular needs and in some cases they

Table 1. Organizations and planning

Planning-Oriented Organizations	SMEs/Organizations that Cannot Plan
• "Push" type organizations	• "Pull" type organizations
• Rule over the market	• Ruled by the market
• High predictability	• Low predictability
• The plan rules; management executes	• Management plans for the short term and executes
• Do not need to take unplanned orders	• Welcomes unplanned orders

in fact hamper their ability to be flexible since these systems are structured to enforce heavy planning. Even though there are many more organizations with low planning capacity than any other type of organization, they are not the ones that have the most money to spend in systems.

Flexible, proactive short-term management requires the capability to align and realign company resources in a monthly, weekly, and sometimes even daily frequency to respond to the changing and even contradictory signals of the unpredictable environment. Flexible, proactive short-term management should not be seen as a necessary evil or a transient state if the company expects to survive and even flourish in uncertain environments. By definition, flexible, proactive short-term management is the only and most appropriate option that such organizations have. Furthermore, they should cultivate and technify it. For this type of organization, planning can be an instrument for management; however, management must never be an instrument or an inflexible executer of planning (which unfortunately is often the case). Flexible, proactive short-term management requires a system whose emphasis is not in planning but in flexible and dynamic management. The short-term manager needs to both plan and execute instead of just executing a plan. This type of management would benefit from displacing the emphasis from planning into managing.

Many managers that currently operate in environments where mid- and long-term planning is realistic may have wondered how they could react if their environment became unpredictable. They would certainly welcome in their system a capability specially designed to support managing the short term when plans are not feasible.

ERM: ENTERPRISE RESOURCE MANAGEMENT SYSTEMS

Flexible, proactive short-term management requires a system whose emphasis is not in planning but in flexible and dynamic management. For this reason a better name for such a system would be enterprise resource management system (ERMS) instead of enterprise resource planning system. Following this idea, Baan promotes itself as "a fully integrated enterprise resource management system," and then argues: "It's a demand-driven world. Be a demand-driven enterprise. SSA Global extended ERP can help you make your customers' demands drive your entire enterprise" (Baan, 2005).

ERM as a Solution to Intermediate and Low Planning Capacity

An ERMS focuses on those problems that short-term managers face more often: diversity, volume, mobility, the space dispersion of the resources, and all those things that complicate tracking of resource requisitions and assignments. In such a system, the company is conceived as interconnected flows of physical, human, and financial resources that require each other to increase its net value. The system must allow the manager not only to see and plan the flow of resources, but more importantly, to affect and alter those flows through dynamic interactions with those processes (like purchase orders, transfer vouchers, production orders, delivery notices, etc.) that in fact cause the flows. It must allow managers to focus their attention on the resources. Therefore, the design of such systems must focus on resources.

The differences between ERP and ERM are not fundamental, but of emphasis. Some of them are:

- ERMSs have planning capabilities but they are not mandatory.
- ERMSs allow very short planning horizons.
- ERMSs have dynamic functionality that facilitates unplanned resource allocation.
- While incoming orders receive priority over the plan in ERMSs, the overall picture still includes both the plan and the new orders, allowing a consolidated procurement of all needed (and planned) resources.
- ERMSs include functionality that analyzes planned vs. ongoing reality.
- ERMSs do not reject changes in current plans and limit themselves to changes to future periods, but analyze the proposed changes and present the positive and negative consequences of both accepting and rejecting the changes.
- From a technical point of view, the development of an ERP system is much easier than that of an ERMS because ERMSs are far more dynamic and therefore much more complicated to systematize.

ERMs and Current ERPs

Current ERPs still have highly redundant databases that maintain the possibility of incon-

gruencies. ERPs incorporate most of the major information systems of the organization, and therefore they have the task of eliminating or at least minimizing the differences that usually occur between the balances of the same account across systems. These differences arise from the lack of appropriate synchronization or integration between systems, thus requiring data redundancy which in turn causes the inevitable inconsistencies. These inconsistencies are explained in detail in the early part of Ferran and Salim (2004), and we will call them inconsistencies due to redundancy. Current ERPs only synchronize or integrate the subsystems at a functional level without affecting the more profound level: the database. Their databases still maintain the traditionally redundant structures of a 500-year-old accounting system and add superficial relationships that mimic the 500-year-old manual processes (designed to update and maintain the redundancies), but still leave the redundancy and potential inconsistencies unresolved.

Table 2 provides a brief comparison between ERP and ERM.

The Need for a Resource-Centered Data Structure

Since a desirable characteristic of an ERP is the dynamic management of resources, it is therefore logical that these systems will benefit from a data structure oriented towards resources. However, the most current wave of enterprise-wide information systems has simply copied the paper ledgers described by Luca Pacioli during the renaissance into identical digital files and added some operative files.

Pacioli's model includes the use of "Balance Books," where the entries are totals or subtotals of entries contained in other books, or ledgers. These Balance Books were meant to avoid the need to recalculate the totals every time they are needed as long as there have been no changes to the primary data. An example of these Balance

Table 2. ERP-ERM

• **ERP**lanning	• **ERM**anagement
• Functional priority of the plan over the order	• Functional priority of the order over the plan
• Very strict planning	• Easy override of the plan
• Difficulties in assigning non-planned resources	• Functionality for assigning non-planned resources
• Awkward re-planning functionality	• Dynamic re-planning with live input
• Ex: SAP	• Tendency: Baan, Savannah

Books is the Account Trial Balance. Thus, after 50 years of developments in information technology, we still organize accounting data in a manner that is ideal for the paper-and-pencil limitations that Pacioli faced 500 years ago, but that is incongruent for today's computer-based world.

Of the three roots of ERPs—that is, the accounting information system (AIS), human resource management system, and manufacturing resource planning system (MRP II)—only the structure and functionality of the last two are focused on the resource and not on their accounting significance, as is the case of the first. On the other hand, AISs are the only ones with the structure and functionality to integrate all the resources (even if it is only from the accountant's perspective). Current ERPs, perhaps forced by time-to-market pressure, initially adopted the AIS structure and either lost the focus on resources or, in order to avoid such a loss, adopted the traditional redundant compartmentalized data structure. The results are functionally but not structurally integrated systems from the resource perspective. From this perspective, they are structurally compartmentalized and redundant.

When ERPs consolidate the many functional information systems (like sales, marketing, operations, logistics, procurement, and accounting), they also need to eliminate or at least minimize the differences between the balances of similar accounts. These systems integrate the lower-level functional system and synchronize their functionality, but do not go deeper and integrate

their data. They preserve the data structure from the traditional accounting information systems and add superficial rules and functionality that move the data back and forth without solving the inconsistencies.

Traditional Balance vs. Resource Balance

Resource assignment is reflected in the accounting ledger as a credit to a resource account and a debit to a provision/accrued account of a given resource. For example, we could assign $100 of raw materials to a requisition. To do that, we would credit the raw material inventory account by $100 and debit the provision/accrued account for the same amount. Once the assignment takes place, we credit the provision/accrued account for $100—instead of the inventory account as we would have done under normal conditions—and debit the appropriate account. In another example, we could assign $100 for a requisition of a raw material not currently available in inventory. We would credit the cash account (money) by $100 and debit the purchase provision/accrued account (item) for the same amount. Once the purchase takes place, let us say for $90 instead of the expected $100, we would debit the purchase provision/accrued account (item) for $100, credit Inventory (item) for $90 and cash (money) for $10. Therefore, when we assign resources that are not going to be used immediately, we move the resource amount from its own account to a provision/accrued account and then when we use the resource, we take it out of the provision/accrued account. Furthermore, when the resource is not even available but we need to first purchase it, we would move the funds (money) needed to the provision/accrued account. In conclusion, to assign—from an accounting point of view—a resource that will not be consumed/used immediately, we use a provision/accrued account to "reserve" or hold the resource. And provision/accrued accounts are always associated with a given resource.

The resource orientation does not contradict nor demerit the traditional accounting orientation. Each had its significance and place in time. In a paper-and-pencil world the traditional orientation is more appropriate, while in our current computer-based world the resource orientation is more fitting. To better understand the resource-based classification, Table 3 shows the concept and monetary value of each resource.

Therefore, from the analysis of the value of the financial resources, we derive the following as the basic resource balance equation:

Financial Resources = Physical Resources - Human Resources

The following business operations (Table 4) help further visualize and support the resource balance equation.

We can also rearrange the terms in the equation and present the resource balance as:

Physical Resources = Human Resources + Financial Resources

Now, the resource balance equation shown above is nothing more than a reformulation of the basic accounting equation:

Assets = Liabilities + Capital

The formal arithmetic and conceptual deduction of one equation from the other is beyond the scope of this chapter; however, such can be read in Ferran and Salim (2004). Nonetheless, as seen above, either side of the equation may be calculated independently of the other as required by the double-entry accounting practice. Therefore we can affirm that resource accounting is equivalent to traditional accounting—that using the resource balance instead of the traditional balance does not affect accounting orthodoxy. Furthermore, the resource balance can always be viewed (or presented) using the traditional balance format.

Table 3. PHF resources

Resource	Concept	Value in Terms of Money
Physical (Items)	All tangible and intangible assets that are used, consumed, applied, or depreciated in a production or value-added process	Sales revenue minus acquisition and production (or value-added) costs
Human (People)	People and agents that work in the organization (employees), provide resources (suppliers and stockholders), and purchase its products and services (customers)	What the company owes to employees (payroll), stockholders (capital), and suppliers and government (accounts payable) minus what clients owe it (account receivables)
Financial (Money)	Cash, bank deposits, and other liquid assets owned by the company that can be used to pay for other resources	The value of all physical assets (Items) minus the value of all human resources (People)

Table 4.

Description	Balance			
	FR	**MR**	**HR**	**FR-(HR-MR)**
Purchase two items (A and B) for $50 each. Pay $40 in cash and still owe $60 to the supplier.	-40	-100	-60	0
Add value to the item A (let us say by polishing it) using three hours of work from an employee at a total cost of $30.	-30	-30		0
Sell item A to a customer for $140. Obtain $40 in cash and $100 in account receivable.	40	140	100	0
Sell item B to another customer for $55 cash. No added value is given to the item (sold as purchased).	55	55		0
Total	**25**	**65**	**40**	**0**

We do not question (nor discuss) the value, strengths, and drawbacks of the traditional financial statements. The traditional balance sheet reflects resource ownership. It separates those resources that belong to the firm (assets) to those that the firm owes to third parties (liabilities) or to its stockholders (equity). The traditional balance sheet helps in determining the book value of a firm, and we are not trying to define a different way of valuing one. The statement of income and losses reflects the increase (or decrease) of firm equity as a result of the operation during a specific period of time. Furthermore, it details how those results came about from the sales of products and services minus cost of sales and other operating and financial expenses. Our proposal is not trying to provide a different way of analyzing the results of a firm. Furthermore, the concepts of assets, liability, equity, expenses, and revenues are commonplace and useful not only in accounting, but in management, economic science, social science, and general culture for several centuries. Therefore, we are not looking to eliminate them but to complement them.

There is ample literature in respect to the strengths and weaknesses of each of the traditional financial statements, but there is very little in respect to the usefulness of classifying resources based on ownership for the purpose of implement-

ing an ideal database for accounting, planning, or management information systems. Moreover, a classification criteria based on resource type instead of resource ownership (as described in the next section) facilitates data management while not impeding the use of the traditional financial statements and classifications.

In a review of the literature for non-traditional methods of classifying accounting (and administrative) data for the purpose of database structure, we were only able to find McCarthy's (1982) REA model. However, whereas his model is widely accepted as accurate and interesting, we found no practical implementations, and while the major elements of the model are found in most ERPs, they differ semantically in several critical areas because the model is too general (Weber, 1986).

The Item-Agent-Cash Database Model

In this section we describe a model with an alternate accounting data structure that radically eliminates the most pervasive and potentially inconsistent redundancies of the traditional administrative-accounting model. The model is called IAC and makes up the data structure of the SecureAccounting system (both property of

Cautus Network Corporation, Miami, FL). The system (and in consequence the underlying data structure—IAC) has been in place and under intensive use in more than 80 companies in the past three years. The name IAC comes from the initials of *items, agents,* and *cash.*

Items, Agents, and Cash

The traditional accounting model contains five types of entities: assets, liabilities, capital, revenues, and expenses. The three main entities of IAC, the model we propose, are items, agents, and cash. They reclassify and consolidate all the entities of the traditional model. While the IAC classification may be more or less intuitive than the traditional one, it is a more normalized data structure that in turn eliminates many of the redundancies present in the traditional model.

The traditional model subdivides the main accounts (entities) in sub-accounts. Many of the sub-accounts are kept in separate books because of their nature and structure. Furthermore, some sub-accounts that originate from different main accounts are also kept separate even though their structure is very similar if not the same. For example, accounts receivable is an asset and accounts payable is a liability; they are kept separate although their structure is almost the same. There probably is a third group of sub-accounts called *employees* (used for payroll purposes at a minimum), which is also kept separately. The IAC model consolidates customers, suppliers, employees, and stockholders into one entity: *agents.* In general, agents are all people and institutions that exchange cash, goods, and/or services with the company. They all have many attributes in common (like name, address, and balance), but what is even more important is that they all have the same type of database relationships with the other two main entities (items and cash).

The entity *item* consolidates fixed assets, inventory, and all the goods and services that the company buys or sells. They are kept in separate books although they have many attributes in com-

mon (like name, description, measurement unit, quantity, cost, and price). Furthermore, they all have the same type of database relationships with the other two main entities (agents and cash).

Finally the entity *cash* consolidates bank accounts, petty cash, and any other account that reflects the flow of money.

Administrative and accounting systems register the economic activity of a company. In general, this economic activity is made up of the exchange of goods or services for money (or in certain cases for other goods or services). The agent entity responds to the question of "who" (surrenders or receives the goods or services); item responds to the question of "what" (goods or services); and cash to the "how much" (money it is given or received in exchange for the goods or services). This way the three IAC entities cover all the entities involved in economic activity and therefore consolidate all the accounts of an administrative or accounting system.

However, consolidating all sub-accounts into three main entities is a necessary but not sufficient condition to eliminate the redundancies present in the traditional model. Further work and explanation is needed to eradicate them. Salim and Ferran (2004) explain in detail how IAC eliminates each of those redundancies

Advantages for the Application Programmer

As previously stated, the traditional accounting and administrative data structure responds to the need to optimize response times on paper-and-pencil (manual) systems; however, what is optimal for a manual system is not always such for a computerize system. Nonetheless, the traditional data structure has been kept and the ledgers are faithfully reflected in the database designs of most computerized accounting and administrative systems. In other words, the needed reengineering of the database structure never took place. Therefore, the reorganization task has been pushed to a different area: application programming, which was already overworked and is not the optimal area to solve this problem. Application programmers not only have to write the complex code for forms, reports, and data processing, but also must temporarily reorganize the database twice: once to take advantage of the computerized methods and a second time to display the information the traditional way. Under the IAC model this temporary database reorganization is unnecessary, freeing the application programmer to do the task that he or she was trained to do.

An example of how the IAC model simplifies the job of the application programmer is the existence of a simple (and quick) DBMS function that allows verification of the basic accounting equation from within a single administrative module. This way, any transaction that affects accounting may be validated directly from the application modules even if they are disconnected from the main accounting system. This validation is impossible to do under the traditional DB model for at least two reasons: First, the information is scattered through many different tables and therefore such testing would take a long time to process. Second, such a validation would never be definitive because the accounting transaction is not created immediately and requires a series of intermediate steps where inconsistencies may later appear.

Another example is the facility to develop summary and high-level reports. Under both the traditional model and the IAC model, it is fairly easy to develop detailed or low-level reports. Under IAC we scan the two major tables, applying filters to select the appropriate transactions and then applying sorting and presentation algorithms. In a similar way, under the traditional model, we do the same scanning of the tables (which would be of smaller size) and apply the same sorting and presentation algorithms. Summary reports under the IAC model are developed the same way as detailed ones; however, under the traditional model they are far more complicated. The programmer needs to scan several tables, each

with a different structure, and create a temporary table that includes all the selected transactions to then apply the necessary sorting and presentation algorithms.

In conclusion, under the IAC model, the application programmer concentrates on programming forms, reports, and processing data, and the DBMS takes care of most validations and search processes. Under the traditional model the application programmer needs to perform tasks that are not normally part of his or her responsibility, incurring the bad practice of using resources that are not meant nor optimal for such tasks.

The Fundamental Accounting Equation Under IAC

Assets are the resources that a company owns. When a company is started, the only assets it holds are those that stockholders provide as their initial investment. The company may also acquire additional assets by incurring debt. Therefore, total assets will be equal to the sum of the assets provided by the stockholders plus the sum of the assets provided by the creditors. This is what is called the fundamental accounting equation and it is written as follows:

Assets = Liabilities + Capital

The fundamental accounting equation must be held true at all times. Each side of the equation is calculated separately and compared to check that the equation holds. Therefore if we add all the assets, we will get the same number than if we add together all the debt provided by creditors and stockholders plus the equity.

As the accounting cycle develops, two more entities are used: revenues and expenses. At any time we may add all the revenues and subtract all the expenses and we would get the operating result which is part of the capital. Summarizing: the traditional accounting model contains five types of entities: assets, liabilities, capital, revenues, and expenses. Revenues and expenses are operating entities that show the results of the company's activity during a given period; they are cleared at the end of the period and the difference between them is added (or subtracted) from the capital account.

The traditional accounting model classifies information based on ownership (the company owns the assets, creditors own the liabilities, and stockholders own the capital). On the other hand the IAC accounting model classifies information based on data structure similarities which not only simplifies the use of information technology to process the data but also helps in eliminating redundancies. Moreover, although the classification is different, the model still allows easy testing of the fundamental accounting equation; in fact, it makes the process faster and easier.

We can apply the logic of the fundamental equation in different terms. For example, a company acquires assets in exchange for cash or debt from stockholders or third parties. It can also sell goods (or services) in exchange for cash or loans given to third parties. Therefore, following a similar method to the one applied earlier to obtain the fundamental accounting equation, we get:

Account of Goods (Items) = Accounts of People (Agents) + Accounts of Money (Cash)

where each side of the equation is calculated independently of the other as required by the double-entry bookkeeping method.

The process required under the IAC model to corroborate the fundamental equation is very simple, making it even more reliable than the traditional one. All we have to verify is that:

$$\sum \text{Items(Amount)} = \sum \text{Agents(Amount)} + \sum \text{Cash(Amount)}$$

and since all the data is in only three tables, very little programming is needed.

To guarantee that the fundamental equation holds for the whole, we need to assure that it holds for each part. In other words, every time we register an economic event (i.e., purchase, sale, etc.), we also need to check that the set of transactions recorded maintains the equation. However, this is quite easy and intuitive. Every merchandise or cash received or surrendered comes or goes to a person or institution (even if it is to the same company or unit or department). Therefore the amount of every transaction record in agents will be the same to the related transaction in cash and items. In more technical terms, let AgentTransID be the attribute in cash and/or items that contain the ID of the related transaction in agents (in other words, AgentTransID is the foreign key in cash and items that relates the records to agents whose primary key is ID). We then have:

$$\sum \text{Agent(ID, Amount)} = \sum \text{Item(AgentTransID=ID, Amount)} + \sum \text{Cash(AgentTransID=ID, Amount)}$$

STANDARDIZATION AND MODULARITY: WILL MICROSOFT SHOW UP?

The programs that have the largest market (in terms of units) are, without a doubt, the operating systems since each computer needs one. These are probably followed by games, Internet browsers, search engines, and office applications. Only after those comes the market for enterprise applications. However, if the market is measured in dollars spent instead of units then enterprise applications would take a much higher place.

The size of the enterprise application market has attracted a large number of developers. They have each competed to satisfy different niches by offering different products at very different prices. No one enterprise application has even tried to satisfy the needs of the entire market. Thus, we find applications that have minimal accounting functionality with a very low price tag (sometimes even zero) to very large applications that satisfy global needs and cost several millions of dollars. Some can be used right out of the box, but many require months, if not years of implementation time. For a few the total cost is just the licensing cost, but for most the licensing cost is just a small fraction of the total cost.

Even though the market is mature, it is still very fragmented and there is no single ERP whose popularity is comparable to that of MS Office. MS Office is a suite that satisfies the needs of individuals, small businesses, mid-sized businesses, and even the largest multinational corporation. It is the same package that is installed and used by both the individual and the corporation. There is nothing like that in the enterprise systems market.

Mass market software developers—like Microsoft—have not developed (from the ground up) an ERP, and those that have developed ERPs—like Software AG, the maker of SAP—have not gone into the mass market. Microsoft has acquired ERPs developed by third parties—like Solomon/Dynamics—but it has not been able to adapt them to the mass market. Software AG has launched versions of their ERP for SMEs—like MySAP.com—but it has not been able to tackle the mass market and still requires a considerable investment in its implementation (expressed in the form of high consulting fees). Oracle financed the development and later acquired NetLedger with the advertised purpose of satisfying the mass market, but NetLedger is still far from being a complete ERP and it has not received the expected acceptance by that market. QuickBooks (Intuit) has reached the masses but is even further of being a complete ERP, and Microsoft Money is massively distributed but is not even an integrated AIS. We could conclude that as the application gets closer to being an integrated ERP, it gets farther away from the mass market.

One has to wonder if there is a real dilemma between being a comprehensive and integrated system vs. being mass marketable or if the case is merely circumstantial. We believe that there is no dilemma and that a fully integrated and comprehensive ERP could be developed for the mass market. However, to do that we need to circumvent two problems: one technical and the other psychological.

From a technical point of view, we need to develop a two-layer system where one has the intrinsic ERP functionality and the other has the customized interface that presents the system the way the specific company operates. Let us elaborate these two layers.

All enterprises require some combination of human, material, and financial resources to satisfy their plans or orders. The plan or order of any enterprise requires that we: (1) determine which resources are needed and when, (2) verify if they are available internally or acquire them from a third party, (3) assign them if available in a timely manner or otherwise renegotiate the order or modify the plan, and (4) monitor this cycle, evaluate that it is being executed, and determine its profitability. From this point of view, all enterprises are alike and the only differences are based on quantities and times—in other words, the "when" and the "how much" of each resource. Therefore, all enterprises require an enterprise system that can: (1) "translate" any item of a plan or order into the needed resources—human, material, and financial—with the corresponding schedule; (2) generate the internal or external requisitions—with functionality for controlling, following, and renegotiating them; and (3) provide real-time information on the status and profitability of any cycle. This is the basic functionality that we described earlier for an ERMS.

The ERM functionality applies to any enterprise independently of how many resources it needs to process and for how long. A very small one would process a few daily items that would be satisfied with a few people, a few purchases or merchandise, and a few requests for cash or credit. A large enterprise would process thousands or hundreds of thousands of daily items, each of which would require some human resource, some materials, and some financing. The different enterprises (large or small) would not acquire specialized modules for each of their departments, as it is currently done, nor would it face the problem of connecting each of them with the corresponding redundancies and inconsistencies that such approach entitles. They would all acquire this one system oriented towards the resource, which is common to all enterprises, and not the departments, which are highly variable and particular for each organization. This system would be the lower layer that we mentioned earlier.

Then the organization would acquire a second system, the upper layer, which would provide the custom forms and reports. This system could be pre-designed for best practices in different industries and would be highly customizable. All customization would occur in this layer (not the lower one). This one would have the configuration for all the forms and reports. It would have the information on which events to reflect and which ones to ignore. Therefore the basic structure is kept intact no matter the industry or the organization.

These ERMSs would be sold in the mass market with the same powerful functionality to all customers (large or small) just like MS Office is currently sold. Users would use only the options that they need and they would develop (or contract) any customization of the interface as needed. This solves the technical hurdle for ERPs to become products of mass consumption.

However, there is yet another hurdle: a psychological one. Very few people accept the resource-oriented process described earlier because they deeply believe that their business must be different from that of others. Most managers will not accept that in essence what they do in their company is the same that others do in theirs and much less if the other company is in a different industry. This belief has also been transferred to programmers and analysts who, instead of trying to abstract and understand the entire business process, still try to develop systems that mimic the visible functionality of the organization.

Even though it may be simple to explain, these two hurdles will probably continue in the short and mid term. To overcome the first hurdle, a large investment is required and such investment is not made because of the second hurdle: no one believes that it is worthwhile to make such a large investment in a generic ERP that would satisfy all types of industries and enterprises and would be sold in the mass market just as MS Office is sold today since "each business must be different."

However, as has happened many times in the past, there will be a person with enough resources and long-term vision to realize that it is viable to develop such system and that there is a tremendous market for it. Bill Gates has had such vision in the past, certainly has the resources in the present, and no one is better positioned than Microsoft to bring it about; however, history could repeat itself. Just as IBM did not foresee the personal computers as the future of computing and relinquished their control over the market to Bill Gates (with the operating system), Intel, and the clones (by using standard components and no copyrights), Microsoft could be making the same mistake today by not developing the standard ERP (or ERM).

For a discussion on major ERP vendors as well as the industry consolidation that has recently occurred, see Jacobs and Weston (2007). For industry trends, see Saran (2005) and Møller (2005).

OPEN SOURCE SOFTWARE

Open source software (OSS) is not necessarily free, particularly when it comes to enterprise systems. The basic premise behind OSS is that the client has access to the source code. However, the current trend—based on the Open Source Initiative—is that the source code is freely distributed and nobody can claim ownership and charge royalties for a license to the system. On the other hand, even within the OSI, a consultant may charge for making the necessary adaptations to the ERP which customize it and make it useful to the specific client. Furthermore, it is not clear if it is ethical for that consultant to sell the same (or very similar) adaptations to a second client. The OSI specifies that the products cannot be sold but the analysts and programmers may charge for their services.

There are many different OSS licenses. Each one has its own limitations and permissions. Thus, for the purpose of this chapter, we define an open source ERP as a system that may be used, copied, and altered without legal or technical restrictions. And it does not imply that a developer cannot charge a client for making specific modification, for providing training, or for documentation. However, it does imply that there are no guarantees from the initial developer that the ERP does anything in particular nor that it does it properly. If you are using proprietary software, the vendor has an obligation to assist you in a timely manner; however, there are no obligations when you use an open source license and therefore have not paid any retribution to the vendor. Furthermore, even for simple questions, open source software is supported over forums and it is not unusual for questions to go unanswered. The open source community that developed the package does not have a legal obligation to answer your questions.

A common problem found with OSS is that there are many versions of the same system and not all versions are an evolution of the prior one. As an OSS comes into the market, many developers customize it and offer their improved version to the market, and each of these improved versions does not have to be compatible with the others. This proliferation of versions is also a cause for increased implementation costs for OSS. Furthermore, there are no assurances that any version will be supported and later improved as bugs are found or functions are added to the original package. However, in many cases the initial developer tries to keep what is called an

"official" version of the package and only he or she can improve it. Nonetheless, this limits the advance of the package and certainly disregards all the modifications that are made for a specific implementation.

Currently there is a discussion on the use of OSS licenses for ERP. Since the major cost component of implementing an ERP is not in the license but in the implementation, why not go the OSS route? However, to answer that question one must remember that often the consulting firm that implements the system may be different than the software house that developed it. Furthermore, to develop a comprehensive and integrated ERP is very costly and complex; thus why would someone make such investment and then give it away for free? There are many pieces of OSS in the market, but none is as complex as a comprehensive ERP, and its development cannot be easily modularized so that many OSS developers could share the burden. However, we cannot dismiss the possibility that a very good, comprehensive, and integrated OSS ERMS could be built (a large university, a rich philanthropic patron, or a socially oriented government initiative could make the investment).

Nonetheless, even a very good, comprehensive, and integrated OSS ERMS is not enough to lower the total cost of acquiring an ERP since the licensing costs are not a considerable part of the total cost of ownership. Moreover, while OSS reduces licensing costs, it also tends to increment the implementation costs in amounts sometimes similar but in others higher than those that were saved by eliminating the licensing costs. Commercial vendors are forced, by intense competition, to develop installation routines, functionality, and documentation that facilities the configuration, installation, and maintenance of their products. OSS tends to have much higher implementation costs because a greater degree of expertise is usually required for installation, configuration, operation, and maintenance. On considerations about OSS support and maintenance costs, see Kramer (2006).

CAN THE CONSULTING BE REDUCED?

To implement an ERP, internal personnel is never enough; there is always a need for external help. This external help comes in the form of consultants. These consultants are needed not just as additional man-hours because the existing ones are not sufficient, but as external and complementary knowledge that is needed for the implementation. An ERP implementation requires very specialized knowledge that is rarely found inside an organization. Furthermore, it would not be economical to have it inside since an ERP implementation is a non-recurrent event; therefore, once it occurred, these people are no longer needed and are even more valuable (thanks to the additional knowledge gained during the current implementation) in a future implementation elsewhere.

To reduce the amount of consulting one would need to (1) have the required knowledge in-house, (2) obtain the knowledge from a different source (like a manual, artificial intelligence system, or knowledge management system), or (3) simplify the implementation process.

To have the required knowledge in-house is not an economical solution. To exchange consultants for employees that still need to do the same tasks and need to know the same things is not only very expensive, but it is not a solution to the problem. Nothing would be gained by such exchange; the costs would remain the same (or probably even higher) and the process would not be shortened.

To obtain the knowledge from a different source would be a great solution if available. However, manuals are never enough and nobody has yet been able to develop a system that could provide all that knowledge efficiently. However, this is a potential avenue that combined with appropriate university training (during the formative years of all employees) could in the long-run reduce the consulting costs of ERP implementations.

The simplification of the implementation process would seem the only viable route left to reduce the consulting costs. However, such simplification is not easy to accomplish. Let us remember that during the implementation of an ERP, we need to adapt the ERP to the organization, adapt the organization to the ERP, or most commonly, both. See Saran (2007) for "acceleration" proposals on ERP implementation for SME.

If the acquisition of "best practices" was one of the goals of implementing the ERP, then we need to adapt the organization and not the ERP. On the "rigidity" at introducing best practices, see Volkoff (2003) and Clemmons and Simon (2001). Furthermore, since we did not have those best practices in-house, it is those consultants that will bring them in. On the other hand, if the organization was very efficient and we decide that it is the ERP that needs to be adapted, we will need a lot of specialized knowledge to first understand how the organization works and then be able to convert that knowledge into the required "parameters" that adapt the ERP to the organization (also a lengthy process that is not recurrent).

No matter which implementation route is used, a successful implementation will require the following processes:

Acquisition Processes

- Compile and analyze preliminary needs of the organization
- Select the appropriate ERP
- Purchase the ERP

Pre-Implementation Processes

- Compile and analyze detailed needs of the organization
- Design and/or reengineer organizational processes
- Conform working teams and define roles for all personnel
- Define all logistics and develop an implementation schedule

- Analyze previous systems
- Analyze installation, existing and needed platform, and architecture
- Analyze data migration

Implementation Processes

- Develop in detail each requirement (including necessary programming, testing, and documentation)
- Train users
- Test overall system
- Evaluate results of tests and make necessary corrections

Post-Implementation Processes

- Develop user-support procedures
- Initiate systems startup
- Develop maintenance and software support routines
- Analyze general overall business indicators
- Evaluate return on investment (ROI)
- Audit results
- Analyze the need for additional implementations and functionality

A better designed ERP or an ERM would still not be able to simplify the most costly and time consuming of the prior tasks. A standard ERP (like a standard operating system) could substantially reduce the acquisition processes since the choice would be obvious and the purchase contracts would be proforma. The pre-implementation processes are also susceptible to being reduced, although not as much. Each organization will require deep analysis, design, and/or reengineering, as well as complicated data migration operations, and so forth. The implementation processes can hardly be reduced at all, although the cost of the consultants could be reduced if there is not much variety in the ERP market. The detailed development of each requirement is an

irreducible activity and consequently so are all others activities that depend on them. Finally, since the post-implementation process depends, at least partially, on the previous one, it can only be partially reduced. For a more detailed discussion, see Quiescenti, Bruccoleri, La Commare, Noto La Diega, and Perrone (2006).

Will the Sets of Best Practices Come in Plug-In Packages?

Unless we overcome the two big hurdles (technical and psychological) mentioned earlier, the sets of best practices will never come as "plug-in" packages. A shrink-wrap standard ERM could accept best practices in the form of standard plug-ins; however, it would not be in the form of previous-client-to-new-client basis, but in a market-standard-version-to-a-market-new-standard-version basis, just like the versions of Windows, for example. No matter the complexity, the enterprise resources are always few and the same: human, material, and finance resources. Any enterprise practice is a process of combining or transforming those resources. For example, the minimum stock practice is a saving on financial and internal human resources—less material resources purchased and less people to handle them internally—in exchange for a better qualified internal human resource, capable of managing the supply chain, the internal processes, and the customer relationships more accurately and in a coordinated manner. It is expected that the financial resources invested in the training or hiring of more capable human resources, and even in better IT infrastructure—material resources—will later payoff by reducing costs. Therefore, the standardization of best practices by ways of a resource-oriented and structured standard resource management system (a mass-market shrink-wrap ERM) seems to be the real path to the transfer of best practices. Otherwise the best practices will not come in plug-in packages because there will not be a system in which to plug them in, nor will users accept that such standard package could satisfy the needs of their very special enterprise.

On ERP and best practices, see Dobbs (2006) and Dillard and Yuthas (2006), and for an industry point of view of ERP and best practices consulting, see Schiff (2003, 2006).

THE GLOBAL ERM

Microsoft Office is not a global office suite but an office suite that is used globally. A global enterprise-wide information system is not one that is used around the world, but one that would operate simultaneously over several regions. It is a system that simultaneously incorporates the needs of a diverse group of regions and is capable of moving the pertinent information from one region to another. A global enterprise-wide information system is becoming a necessity for many organizations.

The globalization process is not only for the large multinational corporations that operate in diverse cultures and countries. SMEs need to adapt themselves to the supply chains they are part of, and many of these supply chains are becoming global and following global practices. Otherwise these SMEs will have to depend on intermediaries and stay lagged in lower and lower levels of the distribution pyramid, and consequently have lower commercial margins. For example, a small local store that purchases its merchandise directly from one or more international suppliers can one day be required to place its orders in a new electronic format that needs, say, some kind of automatic currency conversion and transfer. Otherwise the store would have to make its purchases throughout a local dealer. Something similar can happen on the client side: not being able to satisfy the global practices adopted by one of them would imply the need to deal with intermediaries and thus suffer a reduction in their margin. Therefore a global ERM is becoming a need for organizations of all types and sizes.

It can hardly be expected that the next generations of ERM will incorporate and make compatible the innumerable administrative and commercial practices of the world's diverse regions and cultures. However, a single universally accepted enterprise-wide information system could facilitate this. Otherwise, the already enormous problem of making compatible the different national or cultural practices will at least double with the problem of making different systems compatible. As long as an ERM system establishes an internationally accepted standard, it will support—and thus facilitate—the construction of a global ERM.

In the long term we envision that the global ERP will also be used globally. Maybe the basic (or lower layer) ERM will become a Web service that every enterprise will use just like they use today's browsers (e.g., Coomber, 2000). Then, it will be customized by "downloading" the pertinent sets of regional or industry best practices (or upper-layer components). The costs of the related licensing and/or services (such as consulting or data maintenance) will be assumed by enterprises just like they assume today the cost of Internet connectivity. Maybe every regulator (government, multinational organizations, etc.) will publish in the Web their forms and procedure updates so that they can be "plugged-in" to "the" global ERM. And of course, the particular software makers would offer through the Web their improved or updated sets of best practices for every newfound deficiency or identified requirement.

CONCLUSION

This chapter narrows the uncertainty about the future of ERP by identifying its present market limits and glimpsing at one of the seemingly few ways for it to overcome them. Its market limits are the ones that separate today's big and mid/long-term-planning-capable organizations from the SME and more generally from the organizations that even though they may be big are still obligated by external or internal factors to dynamically manage themselves in the strict short term. The system capable of overcoming this limit should systematize and even facilitate short-term management, becoming what we called in this chapter an enterprise management system. This in turn requires the strengthening of the structure of the resource-oriented functionality. This functionality, although present in the current ERP, it is not currently supported by a solid resource-oriented database model. ERP database models are generally the same departmental and consequently inconsistent-by-redundancy models of the older integrated enterprise information systems. The structurally strengthened resource-oriented functionality in an ERM would permit it to capitalize the fact that the resources—human, material, and financial—are common to every organization, facilitating the possibility that it could become a commonly accepted system for every organization, no matter its size or industry.

This technological improvement will require without any doubt large investments in research and development, but it will be even more difficult to convince an investor that all this talk about resource-oriented systems could reach big and global markets. The conception that the administrative and managerial processes of an organization are very different to those of another organization prevails in the industry and in the markets. Maybe the open source ERP tendency is more open to the possibility of standardization, and instead of the Windows Operating System paradigm, the standard ERM will follow the Linux's paradigm. But since this paradigm does not expect to profit from licenses, maybe it will be aimed to increment, not to reduce, the need for consulting when implementing an ERP. The global ERP, whether that means the ERP for the global organizations or for every organization of the globe, depends more than the local ERPs on the viability of the ERM standardization.

REFERENCES

Baan. (2005). Retrieved from http://www.ssa-global.com/

Balassa, B. (1990). *Indicative planning in developing countries.* Policy Research Working Paper Series #439, The World Bank.

Clemmons, S., & Simon, S.J. (2001). Control and coordination in global ERP configuration. *Business Process Management Journal, 7*(3), 205-211.

Coomber, R. (2000). From ERP to XRP. *Telecommunications, 34*(12), 72-73.

Cox, J.B., Al Arkoubi, K., & Estrada, S.D. (2006). National human resource development in transitioning societies in the developing world: Morocco. *Advances in Developing Human Resources, 8*(1), 84-98.

Dillard, J.F., & Yuthas, K. (2006). Enterprise resource planning systems and communicative action. *Critical Perspectives on Accounting, 17*(2/3), 202.

Do, Q.-T., & Levchenko, A.A. (2004). *Trade and financial development.* Policy Research Working Paper Series # 3347, The World Bank.

Dobberstein, N., Neumann, C.-S., & Zils, M. (2005). Logistics in emerging markets. *The McKinsey Quarterly,* (1).

Dobbs, T. (2006). Changing assumptions in best practice. *EDUCAUSE Review, 41*(4), 76.

Ferran, C., & Salim, R. (2004). IAC accounting data model: A better data structure for computerized accounting systems. *The Review of Business Information Systems, 8*(4), 109-119.

Ghani, E. (1992). *How financial markets affect long run growth: A cross country study.* Policy Research Working Paper Series #843, The World Bank.

Jacobs, F.R., & Weston, F.C.J. (2007). Enterprise resource planning (ERP)—A brief history. *Journal of Operations Management, 25,* 357-363.

Klingebiel, D., Kroszner, R., & Laeven, L. (2002). *Financial crises, financial dependence, and industry growth.* Policy Research Working Paper Series #2855, The World Bank.

Kramer, L. (2006). The dark side of open source. *Wall Street & Technology,* (April), 42-43.

McCarthy, W.E. (1982). The REA accounting model: A generalized framework for accounting systems in a shared data environment. *The Accounting Review,* (July), 554-578.

Mellahi, K., & Frynas, J.G. (2003). An exploratory study into the applicability of western HRM practices in developing countries: An Algerian case study. *International Journal of Commerce & Management, 13*(1), 61.

Møller, C. (2005). ERP II: A conceptual framework for next-generation enterprise systems? *Enterprise Information Management, 18*(4), 483.

Naik, G. (2004). The structural qualitative method: A promising forecasting tool for developing country markets. *International Journal of Forecasting, 20*(3), 475.

Olsen, K.A., & Sætre, P. (2007). ERP for SMEs—Is proprietary software an alternative? *Business Process Management Journal, 13*(3), 379.

Outreville, J.-F. (2005). Financial development, human capital and political instability. *Finance-India,* 19(2), 481-492.

Quiescenti, M., Bruccoleri, M., La Commare, U., Noto La Diega, S., & Perrone, G. (2006). Business process-oriented design of enterprise resource planning (ERP) systems for small and medium enterprises. *International Journal of Production Research, 44*(18/19), 3797-3811.

Robertson, P.L. (2003). The role of training and skilled labour in the success of SMEs in develop- ing economies. *Education & Training, 45*(8/9), 461-473.

Saran, C. (2005, November). *Expense ahead with next-generation ERP.* Retrieved from http://www. ComputerWeekly.com

Saran, C. (2007). Oracle extends sector specific ERP for SMEs. *Computer Weekly,* (July 31), 16, 11.

Schiff, C. (2003). The implementation challenge: Key considerations in choosing a BPM consultant. *Business Performance Management,* (June), 20.

Schiff, C. (2006). BPM consulting 2006: More choices and more risk. *Business Performance Management,* (November), 9.

Shih, V. (2004). The politics of finance and development. *Political Science, 395*(Winter).

Tessema, M.T., & Soeters, J.L. (2006). Challenges and prospects of HRM in developing countries: Testing the HRM-performance link in the Eritrean civil service. *International Journal of Human Resource Management, 17*(1), 86.

Volkoff, O. (2003). Configuring an ERP system: Introducing best practices or hampering flexibil- ity? *Journal of Information Systems Education, 14*(3), 319.

Weber, R. (1986). Data models research in ac- counting: An evaluation of wholesale distribu- tion software. *The Accounting Review, 61*(3), 498-518.

ADDITIONAL READINGS

Basu, V., & Lederer, A.L. (2004). An agency theory model of ERP implementation. In *Proceedings of the ACM/SIGMIS Conference on Computer Personnel Research.*

Bond, B., Genovese, Y., Miklovic, D., Wood, N., Zrimsek, B., & Rayner, N. (2000). *ERP is dead—Long live ERP II.* New York: Gartner Group.

Brady, J.A., Monk, E., & Wagner, B.J. (2001). *Concepts in enterprise resource planning.* Boston: Thomson Learning.

Hitt, L.M., Wu, D.J., & Zhou, X. (2001). *ERP investment: Business impact and productivity measures.* Retrieved from http://grace.wharton. upenn.edu/~lhitt/erp.pdf#search='ERP%20inv estment'

Jacobs, F.R., & Whybark, D.C. (2000). *Why ERP? A primer on SAP implementation.* Boston: Irwin/McGraw-Hill.

Summer, M. (2005). *Enterprise resource planning.* Upper Saddle River, NJ: Pearson Prentice Hall.

Compilation of References

AAOIFI. (2006). *Certified Islamic professional accountant: CIPA.* Accounting & Auditing Organization for Islamic Financial Institutions.

Ackerman, L. (1986). Development, transition or transformation: The question of change in organizations. *OD Practitioner,* (December), 1-8.

ACL Services Ltd. (2005). *Sarbanes-Oxley section 404 compliance survey release.* Retrieved May 11, 2006, from http://www.acl.com/solutions/sarbanes-oxley.aspx?bhcp=1

Adams, L. (2000). Mapping yields manufacturing insights. *Quality Magazine, 39*(5), 62-66.

Adams, S., Sarkis, J., & Liles, D.H. (1995). The development of strategic performance metrics. *Engineering Management Journal, 1,* 24-32.

Adamson, C. (2004). *Java.net: The source for Java technology collaboration.* Retrieved November 4, 2006, from http://today.java.net/pub/a/today/2004/06/01/ofbiz.html

Adempiere. (2006). *Adempiere: It's just a community—Nothing personal.* Retrieved from http://adempiere.red1.org/

Akkermanns, H., & van Helden, K. (2003). Vicious and virtuous cycles in ERP implementation. *European Journal of Information Systems,* (11), 35-46.

Aladwani, A.M. (2001). Change management strategies for successful ERP implementations. *Business Process Management Journal, 7*(3), 266-275.

Alexander, J.R. (2002). *History of accounting.* Retrieved from http://www.acaus.org/acc_his.html

Allen, B.R., & Boynton, A. (1991). Information architecture: In search of efficient flexibility. *MIS Quarterly, 15*(4), 435-445.

Al-Mashari, M. (2002). Enterprise resource planning (ERP) systems: A research agenda. *Industrial Management & Data Systems, 102*(3), 165-170.

Al-Mashari, M. (2003). A process change-oriented model for ERP application. *International Journal of Human-Computer Interaction, 16*(1), 39-55.

Al-Mashari, M., & Al-Midimigh, A. (2003). ERP implementation: Lessons from a case study. *Information Technology and People, 16*(1).

Al-Mudimigh, A., Zairi, M., & Al-Mashari, M. (2001). ERP software implementation: An integrative framework. *European Journal of Information Systems, 10,* 216-226.

Alvarez, R. (2000). Examining an ERP implementation through myths: A case study of a large public organization. In *Proceedings of the 6th American Conference on Information Systems* (pp. 1655-1661), Long Beach, CA.

Alvarez, R. (2001). It was a great system. Face-work and the discursive construction of technology during information systems development. *Information Technology & People, 14*(4), 385-405.

Alvarez, R. (2002). Confessions of an information worker: A critical analysis of information requirements discourse. *Information and Organization, 12,* 85-107.

AMR Research. (2001). *Application spending and penetration report 2002-2003.*

AMR Research. (2002). *AMR Research predicts enterprise applications market will reach $70 billion in 2006.* Retrieved from http:www.amrresearch.com

Anthony, R.N. (1965). *Planning and control systems: A framework for analysis.* Graduate School of Business Administration, Harvard University, USA.

Anthony, T., & Turner, D. (2000). Measuring the Flexibility of Information Technology infrastructure: Exploratory analysis of a construct. *Journal of Management Information Systems, 17*(1).

Apache. (2007). *Apache license, version 2.0.* Retrieved March 8, 2007, from http://www.apache.org/licenses/LICENSE-2.0.html

Arabian Computer News. (2006). E-procurement buy-in. *Arabian Computer News,* (June 1). Retrieved June 4, 2006, from http://www.itp.net/features/print.php?id=4485&prodid=&category=

ARC Advisory Group. (2006). *ERP market to exceed $21 billion, says ARC advisory.* Retrieved October 2006 from http://www.tekrati.com/research/News.asp?id=6828

Archer-Lean, C., Clark J.A., & Kerr, D.V. (2006). Evading technological determinism in ERP implementation: Towards a consultative social approach. *Australian Journal of Information Systems, 13*(2), 18-30.

Ashkanasy, N., Gupta, V., Mayfield, M.S., & Trevor-Roberts, E. (2004). Future orientation. In R.J. House, P.J. Hanges, M. Javidan, P.W. Dorfman, & V. Gupta (Eds.), *Culture, leadership, and organizations* (pp. 282-342). London: Sage.

Aspray, W. (Ed.). (1990). *Computing before computers.* Ames: Iowa State University Press.

Atkinson, J., & Leandri, S. (2005). Organizational structure that supports compliance. *Financial Executive,* (December), 36-40.

Austrian, G. (1982). *Herman hollerith: Forgotten giant of information processing.* New York: Columbia University Press.

Baan. (1999). *Target enterprise overview* (CD). Hannover, Germany: Baan-Invensys.

Baan. (2001). *Case study: Herman Miller implements extended process and knowledge management solution.* Hannover, Germany: Baan-Invensys.

Baan. (2005). Retrieved from http://www.ssaglobal.com/

Bae, B., & Ashcroft, P. (2004). Implementation of ERP systems: Accounting and auditing implications. *Information System Control Journal, 5,* 43-48.

Bagchi, K., Cerveny, R., Hart, P., & Peterson, M. (2003, August). The influence of national culture in information technology product adoption. In A. Hevner, D. Galletta, P. Cheney, & J. Ross (Eds.), *Proceedings of the 9th Americas Conference on Information Systems* (pp. 957-965), Tampa, FL.

Bagchi, K., Hart, P., & Peterson, M.F. (2004). National culture and information technology product adoption. *Journal of Global Information Technology Management, 7*(4), 29-46.

Bagranoff, N., Simkin, M., & Strand, C. (2005). *Core concepts of accounting information systems* (9th ed.). New York: John Wiley & Sons.

Baker, R., Bealing, W.E. Jr., Nelson, D.A., & Blair Staley, A. (2006). An institutional perspective of the Sarbanes-Oxley Act. *Managerial Auditing Journal, 21*(1), 23-33.

Bakos, J.Y., & Treacy, M. (1986, June). Information technology and corporate strategy: A research perspective. *MIS Quarterly.*

Balassa, B. (1990). *Indicative planning in developing countries.* Policy Research Working Paper Series #439, The World Bank.

Bancroft, N., Sprengel, A., & Seip, H. (1996). *Implementing SAP R/3: How to introduce a large system into a large organization.* Englewood Cliffs, NJ: Prentice Hall.

Bandara, W., Gable, G., & Rosemann, M. (2005). Factors and measures of business process modeling: Model building through a multiple case study. *European Journal of Information Systems, 14*(4), 347-360.

Bandura, A. (1977). *Social learning theory.* Englewood Cliffs, NJ: Prentice Hall.

Bandura, A. (1986). *Social foundations of thought and action: A social cognitive theory.* Englewood Cliffs, NJ: Prentice Hall.

Bandura, A. (1991). Social cognitive theory of self-regulation. *Organizational Behavior and Human Decision Processes, 50,* 248-287.

Baroudi, J.J., Olson, M.H., & Ives, B. (1986). Empirical study of the impact of user involvement on system usage and information satisfaction. *Communications of the ACM, 29*(3), 232-238.

Barr, J. (2003). *The change curve.* Retrieved February 26, 2007, from http://trends.newsforge.com/article. pl?sid=03/10/18/1342204

Bartlett, C.A., & Ghoshal, S. (1998). *Managing across borders—The transnational solution.* Boston: Harvard Business School Press.

Bashe, C.J., Johnson, L.R., H., P.J., & Pugh, E.W. (1985). *IBM's early computers.* Cambridge, MA: MIT Press.

Bashein, B., Markus, M., & Riley, P. (1994). Preconditions for BPR success. *Information Systems Management, 11*(2), 7-13.

Beal, B. (2003, October 15). *The priority that persists.* Retrieved November 8, 2003, from http://searchcio.techtarget.com/originalContent/0,289142,sid19_gci932246,00.html

Beath, C.M. (1991). Supporting the information technology champion. *MIS Quarterly, 15*(3), 355-372.

Beer, E. (2006a). Opening Oman. *Arabian Computer News,* (March 5). Retrieved April 29, 2006, from http://www.itp.net/features/print.php?id=3933&prodid=&category=

Beer, E. (2006b). Put IT together. *Arabian Computer News,* (March 26). Retrieved April 29, 2006, from http://www.itp.net/features/print.php?id=4055&prodid=&category=

Benaroch, M. (2000). Justifying electronic banking network expansion using real options analysis. *MIS Quarterly, 24*(2), 197.

Benaroch, M. (2002). Managing information technology investment risk: A real options perspective. *Journal of Management Information Systems, 19*(2), 43-84.

Benaroch, M., & Kauffman, R. (1999). A case for using real options pricing analysis to evaluate information technology project investments. *Information Systems Research, 10*(1), 70-86.

Benbasat, I., Goldstein, D., & Mead, M. (1987). The case research strategy in studies of information systems. *MIS Quarterly, 11*(3), 369-387.

Benbasat, I., Goldstein, D., & Mead, M. (1987). The case research strategy in studies of information systems. *MIS Quarterly, 11*(3).

Berger, M. (2003). *Personal communication.* Herne, Germany: EVU-IT.

Berinato, S. (2002). How to cut through vendor hype. *CIO Magazine.* Retrieved October 4, 2006, from http://www.cio.com/archive/010102/hype.html

Berndt, E.R., & Morrison, C.J. (1992). *High-tech capital formation and economic performance in U.S. manufacturing: An exploratory analysis.* Economics, Finance and Accounting Working Paper #3419, Sloan School of Management, Massachusetts Institute of Technology, USA.

Best, P. (2000). Auditing SAP R/3—Control risk assessment. *Australian Accounting Review, 10*(3), 31-42.

Bijker, W.E., Hughes, T.P., & Pinch, T. (Eds.). (1987). *The social construction of technological systems. New directions in the sociology and history of technology.* Cambridge, MA: MIT Press.

Bingi, P., Sharma, M.K., & Godla, J.K. (1999). Critical issues affecting an ERP implementation. *Information Systems Management, 16*(3), 7-14.

Bititci, U.S., Turner, T., & Begemann, C. (2000). Dynamics of performance measurement systems. *International*

Journal of Operations & Production Management, 20(6), 692-704.

Bjorn-Andersen, N., Eason, K., & Robey, D. (1986). *Managing computer impact.* Norwood, NJ: Ablex.

Bloomfield, B.P., & Danieli, A. (1995). The role of management consultants in the development of information technology: The indissoluble nature of socio-political and technical skills. *Journal of Management Studies, 32*(1), 23-46.

Boehm, B.W., & Ross, R. (1989). Theory-W software project management: Principles and examples. *IEEE Transactions on Software Engineering, 7*(15), 902-916.

Boeing Corporation. (2003). *Define and control airplane configuration/manufacturing resource management.* Retrieved from http://www.boeing.com/commercial/initiatives/dcacmrm/dcac_summary.html

Boer, K., & Turner, J.M. (2007). Beyond oil: Reappraising the gulf states. *McKinsey Quarterly, 2007 Special Edition,* (February), 7-17.

Boerma, K., & Kingma, S. (2005). Developing a cultural perspective on ERP. *Business Process Management Journal, 11*(2), 123-136.

Bonaccorsi, A., Giannangeli, S., & Rossi, C. (2006). Entry strategies under competing standards: Hybrid business models in the open source software industry. *Management Science, 52*(7), 1085-1097.

Bond, B., Genovese, Y., Miklovic, D., Wood, N., Zrimsek, B., & Rayner, N. (2000). *ERP is dead—Long live ERP II.* New York: Gartner Group.

Botta-Genoulaz, V., Millet, P.A., & Grabot, B. (2005). A survey on the recent research literature on ERP systems. *Computers in Industry, 56*(6), 510-522.

Bourne, M., Neely, A., Platts, K., & Mills, J. (2002). The success and failure of performance measurement initiatives: Perceptions of participating managers. *International Journal of Operations & Production Management, 22*(11), 1288-1310.

Bowman, D. (2006). Scaling the ERP heights. *IT Weekly Middle East,* (April 16). Retrieved April 29, 2006, from http://www.itp.net/features/print.php?id=4173&prodid=&category=

Bradford, M., & Florin, J. (2003). Examining the role of innovation diffusion factors on the implementation success of enterprise resource planning systems. *International Journal of Accounting Information Systems, 4,* 205-225.

Bradford, M., Roberts, D., & Stroupe, G. (2001). Integrating process mapping into the AIS student toolset. *Review of Business Information Systems, 5*(4), 61-67.

Brady, J.A., Monk, E., & Wagner, B.J. (2001). *Concepts in enterprise resource planning.* Boston: Thomson Learning.

Brainin, E., & Erez, M. (2002, April). Technology and culture: Organizational learning orientation in the assimilation of new technology in organizations. In *Proceedings of the 3rd European Conference on Organizational Learning* (OKLC), Athens, Greece.

Brainin, E., Gilon, G., Meidan, N., & Mushkat, Y. (2005). *The impact of intranet integrated patient medical file (IIPMF) assimilation on the quality of medical care and organizational advancements.* Report # 2001/49 submitted to the Israel National Institute for Health Policy and Health Services.

Brake, T., Walker, M.D., & Walker, T. (1995). *Doing business internationally.* New York: McGraw-Hill.

Brancheau, J., Janz, B., & Wetherbe, J. (1996). Key issues in information management. *MIS Quarterly, 20.*

Branton, P. (2006). All eyes on future trends. *IT Weekly Middle East,* (July 16). Retrieved September 6, 2006, from http://www.itp.net/features/print.php?id=4736&prodid=&category=

Branton, P. (2006). Banking on success. *IT Weekly Middle East,* (June 25). Retrieved July 8, 2006, from http://www.itp.net/features/print.php?id=4570&prodid=&category=

Branton, P. (2006). Pay as you grow. *IT Weekly Middle East,* (May 21). Retrieved May 21, 2006, from http://www.itp.net/features/print.php?id=4385&prodid=&category=

Branton, P. (2006). Roadmap to Basel. *IT Weekly Middle East,* (June 25). Retrieved July 8, 2006, from http://www.itp.net/features/print.php?id=4569&prodid=&category=

Branton, P. (2006). The skyline's the limit. *IT Weekly Middle East,* (April 9). Retrieved April 29, 2006, from http://www.itp.net/features/print.php?id=4133&prodid=&category=

Bratton, W.W. (2003). Enron, Sarbanes-Oxley and accounting: Rules versus principles versus rents. *Villanova Law Review, 48*(4), 1023.

Breandle, U., & Noll, J. (2005). A fig leaf for the naked corporation. *Journal of Management and Governance, 9,* 79-99.

Broadbent, M., & Weill, P. (1993). Improving business and information strategy alignment: Learning from the banking industry. *IBM Systems Journal, 32*(1), 162-179.

Brown, C., & Vessey, I. (2001). Nibco's "big bang." *Communications of the AIS, 5*(1).

Brown, C., & Vessey, I. (2003, December). ERP implementation approaches: Toward a contingency framework. In P. De & J.I. DeGross (Eds.), *Proceedings of the 20th International Conference on Information Systems* (pp. 411-416), Charlotte, NC.

Brown, C.V., & Vessey, I. (2000). NIBCO'S "big bang." In *Proceedings of the International Conference on Information Systems.*

Brown, W., & Nasuti, F. (2005). What ERP systems can tell about Sarbanes-Oxley. *Information Management & Computer Security, 13*(4), 311-327.

Brynjolfsson, E. (1993). The productivity paradox of information technology. *Communications of the ACM, 36*(12), 67-77.

BSC. (2003). *Building the balanced scorecard—Practitioner's guidebook.* Sydney: Balanced Scorecard Collaborative.

Butler, T., & Pyke, A. (2003). Examining the influence of ERP systems on firm-specific knowledge and core capabilities: A case study of SAP implementation and use. In *Proceedings of the 11th European Conference on Information Systems.*

Byington, J.R., & Christensen, J.A. (2005). SOX 404: How do you control your internal controls? *Journal of Corporate Accounting and Finance,* (May/June), 35-40.

Caldas, M., & Wood, T. Jr. (2000). Fads and fashions in management: The case of ERP. *RAE—Revista de Administração de Empresas, 40*(3), 8-17.

Calegero, B. (2000). Who is to blame for ERP failure? *Sunsaver,* (June).

Campbell, S. (1998). Mining for profit in ERP software. *Computer Reseller News,* (October), 19.

Canadian Securities Administrators. (2006). *CSA staff notice 52-316: Certification of design of internal control over financial reporting.* Retrieved October 29, 2006, from http://www.osc.gov.on.ca/Regulation/Rulemaking/Current/Part5/csa_20060922_52-316_certification-design.jsp

Cannon, D.M., & Growe, G.A. (2004). SOA compliance: Will IT sabotage your efforts? *Journal of Corporate Accounting & Finance,* (July/August), 31-37.

Cannon, J., & Byers, M. (2006). Compliance deconstructed. *ACM Queue, 4*(7), 30-37.

Cap Gemini Ernst and Young. (2002). *Adaptive ERP.* Retrieved from http://www.capgemini.com

Carlino, J. (1999). *AMR research unveils report on enterprise application spending and penetration.* Retrieved July 2001 from http://www.amrresearch.com/press/files/99823.asp

Carlino, J., Nelson, S., & Smith, N. (2000). *AMR Research predicts enterprise applications market will reach $78 billion by 2004.* Retrieved from http://www.amrresearch.com/press/files/99518.asp

Carr, N. (2003). IT doesn't matter. *Harvard Business Review, 81*(5).

Carton, F., & Adam, F. (2003). Analyzing the impact of enterprise resource planning systems roll-outs in multinational companies. *Electronic Journal of Information Systems Evaluation, 6*(2).

Caton, M. (2006). OpenMFG: ERP basics and more. *eWeek, 23*, 44-45.

Cavaye, A. (1996). Case study research: a multi-faceted approach for IS. *Information Systems Journal, 63*.

CFO. (2005). *Compliance and technology: A special report on process improvement and automation in the age of Sarbanes-Oxley.* Retrieved March 20, 2006, from http://www.pwc.com

Chafee, E.E. (1985). Three models of strategy. *Academy of Management Review, 10*(1), 89-98.

Chan, R., & Roseman, M. (2001). Integrating knowledge into process models—A case study. In *Proceedings of the 12th Australasian Conference on Information Systems,* Southern Cross University, Australia.

Chan, S. (2004). Sarbanes-Oxley: The IT dimension. *Internal Auditor,* (February), 31-33.

Chan, Y., & Huff, S. (1993). Investigating information systems strategic alignment. In *Proceedings of the 14th International Conference of Information Systems,* Florida.

Charles River & Associates. (2005). *Sarbanes-Oxley section 404: Costs and remediation of deficiencies: Estimates from a sample of Fortune 1000 companies.* Retrieved March 1, 2006, from http://www.crai.com

Chenhall, R. (2003). Management control systems design within its organizational context: Findings from contingency-based research and directions for the future. *Accounting, Organizations and Society, 28*(2-3), 127-168.

Clausen, C., & Koch, C. (1999). The role of space and occasions in the transformation of information technologies—Lessons from the social shaping of IT systems for manufacturing in a Danish context. *Technology Analysis and Strategic Management, 11*(3) 463-482.

Clemmons, S., & Simon, J.S. (2001). Control and coordination in global ERP configuration. *Business Process Management Journal, 7*(3), 205-215.

Clemons, E.K. (1991). Evaluation of strategic investments in information technology. *Communications of the ACM, 34*, 22-36.

Clemons, E.K., & Gu, B. (2003). Justifying contingent information technology investments: Balancing the need for speed of action with certainty before action. *Journal of Management Information Systems, 20*(2), 11-48.

Cliff, S. (2003, 3/6/2003). Survey finds big variation in ERP costs. *Computer Weekly,* 8.

Colman, R. (2006). Sarbanes-Oxley in review. *CMA Management,* (March), 20-25.

Committee of Sponsoring Organizations of Treadway Commission. (1992). *Internal control: Integrated framework (executive summary).* Retrieved April 2, 2006, from http://www.coso.org/publications/executive_summary_integrated_framework.htm

Committee of Sponsoring Organizations of Treadway Commission. (2004). *Enterprise risk management: Integrated framework (executive summary).* Retrieved October 28, 2006, from http://www.coso.org/Publications/ERM/COSO_ERM_ExecutiveSummary.pdf

Commonwealth of Australia. (2002). *Corporate disclosures: Strengthening the financial reporting framework.* Retrieved March 20, 2006, from http://www.treasury.gov.au/contentitem.asp?NavId=&ContentID=403

Compiere. (2006). *Andre Boisvert joins Compiere team.* Retrieved from http://www.compiere.org/news/0522-andreboisvert.html

Compiere. (2006). *Compiere appoints open source thought leader to its board of directors: Larry Augustin will help drive continued growth of leading open source ERP and CRM provider.* Retrieved November 3, 2006, from http://www.compiere.org/news/0724-augustin.html

Cooke, D.P., & Peterson, W.J. (1998, July). *SAP implementation: Strategies and results.* R-1217-98-RR, The Conference Board, New York, USA.

Coomber, R. (2000). From ERP to XRP. *Telecommunications, 34*(12), 72-73.

Coombs, R., Knights, D., & Willmott, H.C. (1992). Culture, control, and competition: Towards a conceptual framework for the study of information technology in organizations. *Organization Science, 13*(1), 51-72.

Cooper, R., & Zmud, R. (1990). Information technology implementation research: A technological diffusion approach. *Management Science, 36*(2), 123-139.

COSO (Committee of Sponsoring Organizations). (1992). *Internal control—integrated framework.* Retrieved February 26, 2006, from http://www.coso.org

COSO. (2004). *Enterprise risk management.* Retrieved February 26, 2006, from http://www.coso.org

Cox, J.B., Al Arkoubi, K., & Estrada, S.D. (2006). National human resource development in transitioning societies in the developing world: Morocco. *Advances in Developing Human Resources, 8*(1), 84, 15.

Crom, S. (2007). *Ways to shorten the trip through the "Valley of Despair."* Retrieved February 27, 2007, from http://europe.isixsigma.com/library.content/c040825b.asp

Cronbach, L.J. (1951). Coefficient alpha and the internal structure of tests. *Psychometrika, 16,* 297-335.

Crosby, A.W. (1997). *The measure of reality: Quantification and western society, 1250-1600.* Cambridge: Cambridge University Press.

CSC. (2001). *Critical issues of information systems management.* Retrieved November 2002 from http://www.csc.com/aboutus/uploads/CI_Report.pdf

Culnan, M.J. (1983). Chauffeured versus end user access to commercial databases: The effects of task and individual differences. *MIS Quarterly, 7*(1), 55-67.

Damelio, R. (1996). *The basics of process mapping.* New York: Quality Resources.

Damianides, M. (2004). How does SOX change IT? *Journal of Corporate Accounting & Finance,* (September-October), 35-41.

Daneva, M. (2004). ERP requirements engineering practice: Lessons learned. *IEEE Software, 21*(3), 26-33.

Daniel, E.M., & White, A. (2005). The future of inter-organisational system linkages: Findings of an international Delphi study. *European Journal of Information Systems, 14*(2), 188-203.

Davenport, T. (2000). *Mission critical: Realizing the promise of enterprise systems.* Boston: Harvard Business School Press.

Davenport, T., Harris, J., & Cantrell, S. (2003). *Enterprise systems revisited: The director's cut.* Accenture.

Davenport, T., Harris, J., & Cantrell, S. (2004). Enterprise systems and ongoing change. *Business Process Management Journal, 10*(1).

Davenport, T.H. (1998). Putting the enterprise into the enterprise system. *Harvard Business Review, 76*(4), 121-131.

Davenport, T.H. (2000). *Mission critical: Realizing the promise of enterprise systems.* Boston: Harvard Business School Press.

Davenport, T.H., & Brooks, J.D. (2004). Enterprise systems and the supply chain. *Journal of Enterprise Information Management, 17*(1), 8-19.

Davenport, T.H., & Stoddard, D.B. (1994). Reengineering: Business change of mythic proportions? *MIS Quarterly, 18*(2), 121-127.

Davenport, T.H., Harris, J.G., & Cantrell, S. (2004). Enterprise systems and ongoing process change. *Business Process Management Journal, 10*(1), 16-26.

Davern, M.J., & Kauffman, R.J. (2000). Discovering potential and realizing value from information technology investments. *Journal of Information Management Information Systems, 16,* 121-143.

Davison, R. (2002). Cultural complications of ERP. *Communications of the ACM, 45*(7), 109-111.

Davison, R. (2002). Cultural complications of ERP: Valuable lessons learned from implementation experience in parts of the world with different cultural heritage. *Communication of the ACM, 45*(7), 109-111.

Deloitte Consulting. (1998). *ERP's second wave—Maximizing the value of ERP-enabled processes.* New York.

Delone, W.H., & Mclean, E.R. (1992). Information system success: The quest for the dependent variable. *Information Systems Research, 3*(1), 60-95.

DeLong, D.W., & Fahey, L. (2003). Diagnosing cultural barriers to knowledge management. *Academy of Management Executive, 14*(4), 113-127.

Deming, W.E. (2000). *Out of the crisis.* Cambridge: MIT Press.

Demmel, J., & Askin, R. (1992). A multiple-objective decision model for the evaluation of advanced manufacturing systems technology. *Journal of Manufacturing Systems, 11,* 179-194.

Dery, K., & Wailes, N. (2005). Necessary but not sufficient: ERPs and strategic HRM. *Strategic Change, 14,* 265-272.

Dillard, J.F., & Yuthas, K. (2006). Enterprise resource planning systems and communicative action. *Critical Perspectives on Accounting, 17*(2/3), 202.

Dilts, D.M., & Pence, K.R. (2006). Impact of role in the decision to fail: An exploratory study of terminated projects. *Journal of Operations Management, 24,* 378-396.

DiMaio, A. (2004). *Look beyond TCO to judge open source software in government.* Gartner (G00123983).

DiMaio, A. (2007). *When to use custom, proprietary, open-source or community source software.* Gartner (G00146202).

Do, Q.-T., & Levchenko, A.A. (2004). *Trade and financial development.* Policy Research Working Paper Series # 3347, The World Bank.

Doane, M. (2004). *Ready, fire, aim: A failure of ERP readiness starts at the top.* Retrieved April 17, 2006, from http://techupdate.zdnet.com/techupdate/stories/main/Ready_Fire_Aim.html

Dobberstein, N., Neumann, C.-S., & Zils, M. (2005). Logistics in emerging markets. *The McKinsey Quarterly,* (1).

Dobbs, T. (2006). Changing assumptions in best practice. *EDUCAUSE Review, 41*(4), 76.

Document Sciences. (2007). *xPressions 2.1.2 enterprise application integration strategies.* Retrieved February 14, 2007, from http://www.docscience.com/service/xpr_enterprise.htm

Doherty, N.F., & Doing, G. (2003). An analysis of the anticipated cultural impact of the implementation of data warehouse. *IEEE Transactions on Engineering Management, 50*(1), 78-88.

Donaldson, L. (1987). Strategy and structural adjustment to regain fit and performance: In defense of contingency theory. *Journal of Management Studies, 24,* 1-24.

Dorsey, P. (2003). *Why large IT projects fail.* Retrieved March 6, 2006, from http://www.datainformationservices.com/DIS/Forum/topic.asp?TOPIC_ID=21

du Plessis, J., McConvill, J., & Bagaric, M. (2005). *Principles of contemporary corporate governance.* Cambridge: Cambridge University Press.

Dube, L., & Robey, D. (1999). Software stories: Three cultural perspectives on the organizational context of software development practices. *Accounting Management and Information Technologies, 9*(4), 223-259.

Duncan, N.B. (1995). Capturing flexibility of IT infrastructure: A study of resource characteristics and their measure. *Journal of Management Information Systems, 12*(2), 37-57.

Dvira, D., Razb, T., & Shenharc, A.J. (2003). An empirical analysis of the relationship between project planning and project success. *International Journal of Project Management, 21,* 89-95.

Earl, M.J. (1993). Experience in strategic information systems planning. *MIS Quarterly, 17*(1), 1-24.

Earley, C.P., & Gibson, C.B. (2002). *Multinational work teams: A new perspective.* Mahwah, NJ: Lawrence Erlbaum.

Earley, C.P., & Mosakowski, E. (2000) Creating hybrid team cultures: An empirical test of transnational team functioning. *Academy of Management Journal, 43*(1), 26-49.

Earley, C.P., Ang, S., & Joo-Seng, T. (2006). *CQ: Developing cultural intelligence at work.* New York: Oxford University Press.

Earley, P.C. (1994). Self or group? Cultural effects of training on self efficacy and performance. *Administrative Science Quarterly, 39,* 89-117.

Eccles, R.G., Watson, L., & Willis, M. (2007). The HBR list—Breakthrough ideas for 2007: Here comes XBRL. *Harvard Business Review, 85*(2), 32-34.

Edwards, C. (2006). An airline in his hands. *Arabian Computer News,* (October 2). Retrieved October 17, 2006, from http://www.itp.net/features/print.php?id=5 274&prodid=&category=

Edwards, C. (2006). Itqan's awards. *Arabian Computer News,* (September 28). Retrieved October 17, 2006, from http://www.itp.net/features/print.php?id=5218&prodid= &category=

Edwards, C. (2006). SAP attack. *Arabian Computer News,* (March 26). Retrieved April 29, 2006, from http://www.itp.net/features/print.php?id=4052&prodid =&category=

Edwards, C. (2006). SAP migrations gather momentum. *Arabian Computer News,* (February 27). Retrieved April 4, 2006, from http://www.itp.net/news/print. php?id=19741&prodid=&category=

Edwards, C. (2006). Ziic centralises IT. *Arabian Computer News,* (October 1). Retrieved October 17, 2006, from http://www.itp.net/features/print.php?id=5238&p rodid=&category=

Eisenhardt, K. (1989). Building theories from case study research. *Academy of Management Review, 14*(4), 532-550.

Ekanayaka, Y., Currie, W.L., & Seltsikas, P. (2002). Delivering enterprise resource planning systems through application service providers. *Logistics Information Management, 15*(3), 192-203.

Elashmawi, F., & Harris, P.R. (1993). *Multicultural management new skills for global success.* Houston, TX: Gulf.

Elmes, M., Strong, D., & Volkoff, O. (2005). Panoptic empowerment and reflective conformity in enterprise systems-enabled organizations. *Information and Organization, 15*(1), 1-37.

Emigh, J. (1999). Net present value. *Computerworld, 33,* 52-53.

Enriquez, E. (1992). *L'organisation en analyse.* Paris: Press Universitaires de France.

Erez, M., & Earley, C.P. (1993). *Culture, self identity and work.* New York: Oxford University Press.

Erez, M., & Gati, E. (2004). A dynamic, multi-level model of culture: From the micro-level of the individual to the macro-level of a global culture. *Applied Psychology: An International Review, 35*(4), 583-598.

Erez, M., Earley, P.C., & Hullin, C.L. (1985). The impact of participation on goal acceptance and performance: A two-step model. *Academy of Management Journal, 28,* 50-66.

Erl, T. (2004). *Service-oriented architecture: A field guide to integrating XML and Web services.* Upper Saddle River, NJ: Prentice Hall.

Ernst & Young. (1995). *Audit, control, and security features of SAP R/3.*

ESCWA. (2006, October 26). *Economic situations and prospects for Western Asia: A note prepared for world economic situations and prospects 2007.* Retrieved February 2007, from http://www.escwa.org.lb/divisions/ lib/Uploads/WESP2007WA_26Oct2006.pdf

Esteves, J., & Pastor, J. (1999). An ERP lifecycle-based research agenda. *Proceedings of the International Workshop on Enterprise Management Resource Planning Systems* (EMRPS) (pp. 359-371), Venice, Italy.

Esteves, J., & Pastor, J. (2001). Enterprise resource planning systems research: An annotated bibliography. *Communications of the AIS, 7*(8), 1-52.

Esteves, J., Pastor, J., & Casanovas, J. (2002). *Monitoring business process redesign in ERP implementation projects.* Retrieved April 13, 2007, from http://coblitz.codeen.org:3125/citeseer.ist.psu.edu/cache/papers/cs/31804/http:zSzzSzwww.lsi.upc.eszSz~jesteveszSzBPR_amcis2002.PDF/esteves02monitoring.pdf

European Parliament & Council. (2006). *Directive 2006/46/EC.* Retrieved October 28, 2006, from http://eur-lex.europa.eu/LexUriServ/LexUriServ.do?uri=CELEX:32006L0046:EN:NOT

Evaristo, R. (2003). The management of distributed projects across cultures. *Journal of Global Information Management, 11*(4), 58-70.

Ezzamel, M. (1994). The emergence of the 'accountant 'in the institutions of ancient Egypt. *Management Accounting Research (Sarasota), 5*(3-4), 221-247.

Fairley, R.E., & Willshire, M.J. (2003). Why the Vasa sank: 10 problems and some antidotes for software projects. *IEEE Software, 3*(4), 18-25.

Fan, M., Stallaert, J., & Whinston, A. (2000). The adoption and design methodologies of component-based enterprise systems. *European Journal of Information Systems, 9,* 25-35.

Farrell, D. (2006). Smarter offshoring. *Harvard Business Review, 84*(6), 84-92.

Feller, J., & Fitzgerald, B. (2000). A framework analysis of the open source software development paradigm. In *Proceedings of the 21st International Conference in Information Systems* (ICIS 2000).

Fenn, J. (1995, January). *When to leap on the hype cycle.* White Paper, Gartner Group, USA. Retrieved February 27, 2007, from http://www.gartner.com

Ferguson, R.B. (2006). Open-source ERP grows up. *eWeek, 23*(27), 26-27.

Ferran, C., & Salim, R. (2004). IAC accounting data model: A better data structure for computerized accounting systems. *The Review of Business Information Systems, 8*(4), 109-119.

Fichman, R.G. (2004). Real options and IT platform adoption: Implications for theory and practice. *Information Systems Research, 15*(2), 132-154.

Fichman, R.G., & Moses, S.A. (1999). An incremental process for software implementation. *Sloan Management Review, 40*(2), 39-52.

Fichman, R.G., Keil, M., & Tiwana, A. (2005). Beyond valuation: "Options thinking" in IT project management. *California Management Review, 47*(2), 74-96.

Firestone, J.M. (2002). *Enterprise information portals and knowledge management.* Boston: Butterworth-Heinemann.

Fisher, K., & Fisher, M.D. (2001). *The distance manager.* New York: McGraw-Hill.

Fisterra (2007). *Fisterra.org: A short history.* Retrieved March 8, 2007, from http://community.igalia.com/twiki/bin/view/Fisterra/ProjectHistory

Fitzgerald, B. (2006). The transformation of open source software. *MIS Quarterly, 30*(3), 587-598.

Fitzgerald, B., Russo, N.L., & O'Kane, T. (2003). Software development method tailoring at Motorola. *Communications of the ACM, 46*(4), 65-70.

Fonterra. (2001). *Capital structure.*

Fonterra. (2004). *About Fonterra.* Retrieved October 2004 from http://www.fonterra.com

Fonterra. (2004). *An introduction to Jedi.*

Fonterra. (2004). *Jedi program: Key message guidelines.*

Ford, D.P., Connelly, C.E., & Meister, D.B. (2003). Information system research and Hofstede's culture's consequences: An uneasy and incomplete partnership. *IEEE Transaction on Engineering Management, 50*(1), 8-25.

Fox, C. (2004). Sarbanes-Oxley—Considerations for a framework for IT financial reporting controls. *Information Systems Controls Journal, 1,* 1-3.

Franch, X., & Carvallo, J.P. (2003). Using quality models in software package selection. *IEEE Software, 20*(1), 34-41.

Frost, J.F., Moore, L.F., Louis, M.R., Lundberg, C.C., & Martin, J. (Eds.). (1985). *Organizational culture.* Thousand Oaks, CA: Sage.

Gable, G. (1994). Integrating case study and survey research methods: An example in information systems. *European Journal of Information Systems, 3*(2).

Gartner Group. (1998). *1998 ERP and FMIS study—Executive summary.* Stamford, CT.

Gartner Group. (2006). *The Gartner scenario 2006: The current state and future direction of IT.* Retrieved from http://www.gartner.com

Gattiker and Goodhue. (2004). Understanding the local-level costs and benefits of ERP through organizational information processing theory. *Information & Management, 41,* 431-443.

Gattiker, T.F., & Goodhue, D.L. (2002). Software-driven changes to business processes: An empirical study of impacts of enterprise resource planning (ERP) systems at the local level. *International Journal of Production Research, 40*(18), 99.

Gefen, D., & Ragowsky, A. (2005). A multi-level approach to measuring the benefits of an ERP system in manufacturing firms. *Information System Management,* (Winter), 18-25.

Gefen, D., & Ridings, C. (2002). Implementation team responsiveness and user evaluation of CRM: A quasi-experimental design study of social exchange theory. *Journal of Management Information Systems, 19*(1), 47-63.

Gefen, D., Pavlou, P., Rose, G., & Warkentin, M. (2005). Cultural diversity and trust in IT adoption: A comparison of potential e-voters in the USA and South Africa. *Journal of Global Information Management, 13*(1), 54-78.

Gelinas, U.J., Sutton, S.G., & Hunton, J.E. (2005). *Accounting information systems* (6th ed.). Thomson, OH: South-Western.

Gerstein, M., & Resman, H. (1982). Creating competitive advantage with computer technology. *Journal of Business Strategy, 3*(1).

Ghani, E. (1992). *How financial markets affect long run growth: A cross country study.* Policy Research Working Paper Series #843, The World Bank.

Ghose, G. (2007). Emerging from the mists of time. *Gulf News Quarterly Financial Review,* 42-49.

Ghosh, S. (2002). Challenges on a global implementation of ERP software. In *Proceedings of the 2002 IEEE International Engineering Management Conference* (pp. 101-106).

Ghosh, S., & Ghosh, S. (2003). Global implementation of ERP software—Critical success factors on upgrading technical infrastructure. In *Proceedings of the International Engineering Management Conference—Managing Technologically Driven Organizations: The Human Side of Innovation and Change* (pp. 320-324).

Gibbs, J., Kraemer, K.L., & Dedrick, J. (2003). Environment and policy factors shaping global e-commerce diffusion: Cross-country comparison. *The Information Society, 19,* 5-18.

Giiford, A. (2004). JEDI has kicked out the boss at Fonterra. *New Zealand Herald,* (June 29).

GNU. (2007). *GNU general public license, version 2, June 1991.* Retrieved March 8, 2007, from http://www.gnu.org/licenses/gpl.txt

GNU. (2007). *GNU's not Unix! Free software, free society.* Retrieved March 8, 2007, from http://www.gnu.org/

Gorry, A., & Scott Morton, M.S. (1971). A framework for management information systems. *Sloan Management Review, 13,* 49-61.

Government Owned Corporations Act. (1993). Retrieved May 10, 2006, from http://www.legislation.qld.gov.au/LEGISLTN/CURRENT/G/GoOwnCorpA93_06C_030328.pdf

Graeser, V., Willcocks, L., & Pisanias, N. (1996). *Developing the IT scorecard*. London: Business Intelligence.

Graham, C., & Freely, M. (1990). Today, it's distributed MRP III. *Datamation, 36*(19), 117.

Granlund, M., & Mouritsen, J. (2003). Introduction: Problematizing the relationship between management control and information technology. *European Accounting Review, 12*(1), 77-83.

Grant, D. et al. (2001). Organizational discourse—Key contributions and challenges. *International Studies of Management and Organization, 31*(3), 5-24.

Grant, D., Hall, R., Wailes, N., & Wright, C. (2006). The false promise of technological determinism: The case of enterprise resource planning systems. *New Technology, Work and Employment, 21*(1), 2-15.

Green, S.G., Gavin, M.B., & Aiman-Smith, L. (1995). Assessing a multidimentional measure of radical technological innovation. *IEEE Transactions on Engineering Management, 42*(3), 203-214.

Gross and Ginzberg, M.J. (1984). Barriers to the adoption of application software packages. *SOS, 4*(4), 211-226.

Gross, S., & Wingerup, P. (1999). Global pay? Maybe not yet! *Compensation and Benefits Review, 31*(4), 25-34.

Grudin, J. (1991). Interactive systems: Bridging the gaps between developers and users. *IEEE Computer, 24*(4), 59-69.

Gulf News. (2005, August 6). *95% UAE residents own mobile phones*. Retrieved November 2, 2006, from http://archive.gulfnews.com/articles/05/06/08/168257.html

Gulf News. (2006, October 2). *Dubai is second worldwide in building offices*. Retrieved October 3, 2006, from http://archive.gulfnews.com/articles/06/10/02/10071646.html

Gunson, J., & de Blais, J.-P. (2002). *Implementing ERP in multinational companies: Their effects on the organization and individuals at work*. Retrieved April 13, 2007, from http://www.hec.unige.ch/recherches_publications/cahiers/2002/2002.07.pdf

Gupta, A. (2000). Enterprise resource planning: The emerging organizational value systems. *Industrial Management & Data Systems, 100*(3), 114-118.

Gupta, M., & Kohli, A. (2006). Enterprise resource planning systems and its implications for operations function. *Technovation, 26*, 687-696.

Guth, R., & Clark, D. (2005). Linux feels growing pains as users demand more features. *Wall Street Journal*, (August 8), B1.

Hackney, R., Burn, J., & Dhillon, G. (2000). Challenging assumptions for strategic information systems planning: Theoretical perspectives. *Communications of the AIS, 3*, article 9.

Haley, G., & Tan, C.T. (1999). East vs. west: Strategic marketing management meets the Asian networks. *Journal of Business and Industrial Marketing, 14*(2), 91-101.

Hall, E.T., & Hall, M.R. (1990). *Understanding cultural differences*. Yarmouth, ME: Intercultural Press.

Hammer, M. (1990). Reengineering work: Don't automate, obliterate. *Harvard Business Review, 68*(4), 104-112.

Hammer, M. (1997). Reengineering, SAP and business processes. In *Proceedings of SAPphire*, Orlando, FL.

Hammer, M. (1999). How process enterprises really work. *Harvard Business Review*, (November/December).

Hammer, M., & Champy. J. (1993). *Reengineering the corporation: A manifesto for business revolution*. New York: HarperCollins.

Hammer, M., & Stanton, S. (1995). *The reengineering revolution: The handbook*. London: HarperCollins.

Hanges, P.J., & Dickson, M.W. (2004). The development and validation of the GLOBE culture and leadership scales. In R.J. House, P.J. Hanges, M. Javidan, P.W. Dorfman, & V. Gupta (Eds.), *Culture, leadership, and organizations* (pp. 122-151). London: Sage.

Hares, J., & Royle, D. (1994). *Measuring the value of information technology, 7*, 109-122.

Harmon, R. (1996). *Reinventing the business—Preparing today's enterprise for tomorrow's technology.* New York: The Free Press.

Harrison, R.T., & Leitch, C.M. (2000). Learning and organization in the knowledge-based information economy: Initial findings from a participatory action research case study. *British Journal of Management, 11,* 103-119.

Hasan, H., & Ditsa, G. (1999). The impact of culture on the adoption of IT: An interpretive study. *Journal of Global Information Management, 7*(1), 5-15.

Hazzan, O., & Dubinksy, Y. (2005). Clashes between culture and software development methods: The case of the Israeli hi-tech industry and extreme programming. *Proceedings of the Agile 2005 Conference* (pp. 59-69), Denver, CO.

He, X. (2004). The ERP challenge in China: A resource-based perspective. *Information Systems Journal, 14*(2), 153-167.

Heales, J., & Cockroft, S. (2003, August). The influence of national culture on the level and outcome of IS decision making in the IS evolution/redevelopment decision. In A. Hevner, D. Galletta, P. Cheney, & J. Ross (Eds.), *Proceedings of the 9th Americas Conference on Information Systems* (pp. 975-986), Tampa, FL.

Hecht, B. (1997). Choose the right ERP software. *Datamation, 43*(3), 56-58.

Heizer, J., & Render, B. (2003). *Operations management—international edition* (7th ed.). Upper Saddle River, NJ: Pearson Education.

Heracleous, L., & Barret, M. (2001). Organizational change as discourse: Communicative actions and deep structures in the context of information technology implementation. *Academy of Management Journal, 44*(4), 755-778.

Hicks, J.O. (1997). *Management information systems: A user perspective.* Minneapolis/St. Paul: West.

Hitt, L.M., Wu, D.J., & Zhou, X. (2002). ERP investment: Business impact and productivity measures. *Journal of Management Information Systems, 19*(1), 71-98.

HK-Software. (2007). *HK-Software features and modules, reasons for using AvERP.* Retrieved March 8, 2007, from http://www.hk-software.net/h-k.de/content/doc_138099-3-5-1.php

Hochstrasser, B., & Griffiths, C. (1991). *Controlling IT investment: Strategy and management.* London: Chapman & Hall.

Hofmann, D.A., & Stetzer, A. (1996). A cross-level investigation of factors influencing unsafe behaviors and accidents. *Personnel Psychology, 49,* 307-339.

Hofstede, G. (1979). Value systems in forty countries: Interpretation, validation, and consequences for theory. In L.H. Eckensberger, W.J. Lonner, & Y.H. Pootinga (Eds.), *Cross-cultural contributions to psychology.* Lisse, The Netherlands: Swets and Zeitlinger.

Hofstede, G. (1980). *Culture's consequences.* London: Sage.

Hofstede, G. (1983). The cultural relativity of organizational practices and theories. *Journal of International Business Studies, 14*(2), 75-89.

Hofstede, G. (1985). The interaction between national and organizational value systems. *Journal of Management Studies, 22*(4), 347-358.

Hofstede, G. (1993). Cultural constraints in management theories. *Academy of Management Executive, 7*(1), 81-94.

Hofstede, G. (2000). *Culture's consequences.* Thousand Oaks, CA: Sage.

Hofstede, G. (2001). *Culture's consequences: Comparative values, behaviors, institutions and organizations across nations.* Thousand Oaks, CA: Sage.

Hofstede, G., & Bond, M.H. (1984). Hofstede's culture dimensions—An independent validation using Rokeach's value survey. *Journal of Cross-Cultural Psychology, 15*(4), 417-433.

Hofstede, G., & Bond, M.H. (1988). The Confucius connection: From cultural roots to economic growth. *Organizational Dynamics, 16*(4), 4-21.

Holland, C., & Light, B. (2001). A stage maturity model for enterprise resource planning systems use. *The Database for Advances in Information Systems, 32*(2).

Holland, C.P., & Light, B. (1999). A critical success factors model for ERP implementation. *IEEE Software, 16*(3), 30-36.

Holland, C.P., Light, B., & Gibson, N. (1998). Global enterprise resource planning implementation. In *Proceedings of the Americas Conference on Information Systems.*

Holland, C.P., Light, B., Beck, P., Berdugo, Y., Millar, R., Press, N. et al. (2000). An international analysis of the maturity of enterprise resource planning (ERP) systems use. In *Proceedings of the Americas Conference on Information Systems* (pp. 992-977), Long Beach, CA.

Hollander, A.S., Denna, E.L., & Cherrington, J.O. (1999). *Accounting, information technology, and business solutions.* Boston: Irwin/McGraw-Hill.

Holman, P. (2003). Unlocking the mystery of effective large-scale change. In T.D. Jick & M.A. Peiperl (Eds.), *Managing change: Cases and concepts* (pp. 509-515). New York: McGraw-Hill.

Hommes, B.-J., Lichtenberg, L., Obers, G.-J., & Roeleveld, L. (1998). BaanWise. In P. Wenzel & H. Post (Eds.), *Business computing mit Baan.* Wiesbaden, Germany: Vieweg.

Hong, K.-K., & Kim, Y.-G. (2002). The critical success factors for ERP implementation: An organizational fit perspective. *Information & Management, 40,* 25-40.

Hoover, L. (2006). Compiere is on the move—again. *NewsForge The Online Newspaper for Linux and Open Source.*

Houghton, L., & Kerr, D.V. (2006). A study into the creation of feral information systems as a response to an ERP implementation within the supply chain of a large government-owned corporation. *International Journal of Internet and Enterprise Management, 4*(2), 137-142.

House, R., Javidan, M., Hanges, P., & Dorfman, P. (2002). Understanding cultures and implicit leadership theories across the globe: An introduction to project GLOBE. *Journal of World Business, 37*(1), 3-10.

House, R.J., Hanges, P.J., Javidan, M., Dorfman, P.W., & Gupta, V. (2004). *Culture, leadership, and organizations.* London: Sage.

Hout, R., Porter, M.E., & Rudden, E. (1982). How global companies win out. *Harvard Business Review,* (September-October), 103.

Howe, M. (2006). Oracle answers Etisalat's call for human resources. *IT Weekly Middle East,* (October 1). Retrieved October 3, 2006, from http://www.itp.net/news/print.php?id=22139&prodid=&category=

Howell, J.M., & Higgins, C. (1990). Champions of technological innovation. *Administrative Science Quarterly, 35,* 317-341.

Howell, J.M., & Higgins, C.A. (1990). Champions of technological innovation. *Administrative Science Quarterly, 35,* 317-341.

Huang, J.C., Newell, S., Galliers, R.D., & Pan, S. (2003). Dangerous liaisons? Component-based development and organizational subcultures. *IEEE Transactions of Engineering Management, 50*(1), 89-99.

Huber, T., Alt, R., & Österle, H. (2000). Templates—Instruments for standardizing ERP systems. In *Proceedings of the 33rd Annual Hawaii International Conference on System Sciences.*

Hunt, D.V. (1996). *Process mapping: How to reengineer your business processes.* New York: John Wiley & Sons.

Hussain, S. (1998). Technology transfer model across culture: Brunei-Japan joint ventures. *International Journal of Social Economics, 25*(6-8), 1189-1198.

IBX Newsletter. (2003). Global e-procurement a winner for Ericsson. *IBX Newsletter,* (3).

Iggulden, T. (Ed.). (1999). Looking for payback. *MIS,* (June).

Ikavalko, H., & Aaltonen, P. (2001). Middle managers' role in strategy implementation—middle managers view. In *Proceedings of the 17ʰ EGOS Colloquium*, Lyon, France.

IMJ. (2004). AMR research 2004: Compliance costs are rising. *Information Management Journal*, (November/December), 6.

Institute of Internal Auditors. (1997). *SAP R/3: Its use, control, and audit*. Altamonte Springs, FL: Institute of Internal Auditors Research Foundation.

Irani, Z., & Love, P.E.D. (2001). The propagation of technology management taxonomies for evaluating investments in information systems. *Journal of Management Information Systems, 17*, 161-178.

Irani, Z., Sharif, A.M., & Love, P.E.D. (2001). Transforming failure into success through organisational learning: An analysis of a manufacturing information system. *European Journal of Information Systems, 10*, 55-66.

ISO. (1990). *ISO 9000 standard series, guidelines for quality assurance*. Berlin: Beuth.

ITGI (IT Governance Institute). (2004). *IT control objectives for Sarbanes-Oxley: The importance of IT in the design, implementation and sustainability of internal control over disclosure and financial reporting*. Retrieved October 17, 2006, from http://www.itgi.org/template_ITGI.cfm?template=/ContentManagement/ContentDisplay.cfm&ContentID=24235

ITGI (IT Governance Institute). (2004). *IT control objectives for Sarbanes-Oxley*. Rolling Meadows, IL. Retrieved March 1, 2006, from http://www.isaca.org

ITGI. (2005). *COBIT 4.0: Control objectives for information and related technology*. Rolling Meadows, IL. Retrieved March 1, 2006, from http://www.isaca.org

ITGI. (2006). *COBIT mapping: Overview of international guidance* (2ⁿᵈ ed.). Retrieved October 17, 2006, from http://www.itgi.org/AMTemplate.cfm?Section=Deliverables&Template=/ContentManagement/ContentDisplay.cfm&ContentID=24759

Ives, B., & Jarvenpaa, S.L. (1991). Applications of global information technology: Key issues for management. *MIS Quarterly, 15*(1), 33-49.

Jacobs, F.R., & Weston, F.C.J. (2007). Enterprise resource planning (ERP)—A brief history. *Journal of Operations Management, 25*, 357-363.

Jacobs, F.R., & Whybark, D.C. (2000). *Why ERP? A primer on SAP implementation*. Boston: Irwin/McGraw-Hill.

James, D., & Wolf, M.L. (2000). A second wind for ERP. *McKinsey Quarterly*, (2), 100-107.

Janke, J. (2006). *Compiere—Status & next steps*.

Jarrar, Y.F., & Aspinwall, E.M. (1999). Business process re-engineering: Learning from organizational experience. *Total Quality Management, 10*(2), 173-186.

Javidan, M., House, R.J., & Dorfman, P.W. (2004). A nontechnical summary of GLOBE findings. In R.J. House, P.J. Hanges, M. Javidan, P.W. Dorfman, & V. Gupta (Eds.), *Culture, leadership, and organizations* (pp. 29-48). London: Sage.

Javidan, M., House, R.J., Dorfman, P.W., Gupta, V., Hanges, P.L., & Sully de Leque, M. (2004). Conclusions and future directions. In R. J. House, P. J. Hanges, M. Javidan, P. W. Dorfman, & V. Gupta (Eds.), *Culture, leadership, and organizations* (pp. 723-732). London: Sage.

Jeannet, J.P. (2000). *Managing with a global mindset*. London: Prentice Hall.

Jones, M.C., Cline, M., & Ryan, S. (2006). Exploring knowledge sharing in ERP implementation: An organizational culture framework. *Decision Support Systems, 41*(2), 411-434.

Jones, S. (2005). Toward an acceptable definition of service. *IEEE Software, 22*(3), 87-93.

Jutras, C. (2007). *The role of ERP in globalization*. Retrieved from http://www.aberdeen.com/summary/report/benchmark/RA_ERPRoleinGlobalization_CJ_3906.asp

Kaarst-Brown, M.L. (2004). *How organizations keep information technology out: The interaction of tri-level influence on organizational and IT culture*. Working Paper IST-MLKB: 2004-2, School of Information Studies, Syracuse University, USA.

Kalling, T. (2003). ERP systems and the strategic management processes that lead to competitive advantage. *Information Resources Management Journal, 16*(4), 46-67.

Kaplan, R., & Norton, D. (1996). *The balanced scorecard: Translating strategy into action.* Boston: Harvard Business School Press.

Kaplan, R., & Norton, D.P. (1996). Using the balance scorecard as a strategic management system. *Harvard Business Review,* (January/February), 75-85.

Kaplan, R.S. (1984).Yesterday's accounting undermines production. *Harvard Business Review, 62*(4), 95-101.

Kaplan, R.S., & Norton, D.P. (1996). *The balanced scorecard: Translating strategy into action.* Boston: Harvard Business School Press.

Kapp, K.M. (2003). *The USA principle—A framework for ERP implementation success.* Retrieved April 27, 2006, from http://facweb.cti.depaul.edu/rstarinsky/files/USAPrinciple.pdf

Kappos, A., & Croteau, A.-M. (2002, August). Organizational change and culture: Insight on BPR projects. In *Proceedings of the 8th Americas Conference on Information Systems* (pp. 2076-2084), Dallas, TX.

Karimi, J., & Konsynski, B. (1991). Globalization and information management strategies. *Journal of Management Information Systems, 7*(4), 7-26.

Katz, A.I. (1993). Measuring technology's business value: Organizations seek to prove IT benefits. *Information Systems Management, 10,* 33-39.

Ke, W., & Wei, K.K. (2005, May). Organizational culture and leadership in ERP implementation. In *Proceedings of the 2005 Pacific Asia Conference on Information Systems* (pp. 428-440), Taipei, Taiwan.

Keil, M., & Carmel, E. (1995). Customer-developer links in software development. *Communications of the ACM, 38*(5), 33-44.

Keil, M., Tan, B.C.Y, Wei, K.K., Saarinen, T., Tuunainen, V., & Wassenaar, A. (2000). A cross-cultural study on escalation of commitment behavior in software projects. *MIS Quarterly, 24*(2), 299-325.

Kendal, K. (2004). A 10 step Sarbanes-Oxley solution. *Internal Auditor,* (December), 51-55.

Kennerley, M., & Neely, A. (2002). A framework of factors affecting the evolution of performance measurement systems. *International Journal of Operations & Production Management, 22*(11), 1222-1245.

Kettingen, W.J., Lee, C.C., & Lee, S. (1995). Global measures of information service quality: A cross-national study. *Decision Science, 26*(5), 569-588.

Khanna, T., & Palepu, K.G. (2006). Emerging giants: Building world-class companies in developing countries. *Harvard Business Review, 84*(10), 60-69.

Kimberling, E. (2006). *Best practices in ERP software selection.* Retrieved October 4, 2006, from http://blogs.ittoolbox.com/erp/roi/archives/best-practices-in-erp-software-selection-10867

King, S.F., & Burgess, T.F. (2006). Beyond critical success factors: A dynamic model of enterprise system innovation. *International Journal of Information Management, 26,* 59-69.

Kirchmer, M. (1996). *Geschäftsprozessorientierte einführung von standardsoftware.* Wiesbaden, Germany: Gabler.

Klaus, H., Rosemann, M., & Gable, G.G. (2000). What is ERP? *Information Systems Frontiers, 2*(2), 141-162.

Klaus, H., Rosemann, M., & Gable, G.G. (2000). What is ERP? *Information System Frontiers, 2,* 141-162.

Klein, K.J., & Speer-Sorra, J. (1996). The challenge of innovation implementation. *Academy of Management Review, 21*(4), 1055-1080.

Klein, K.J., Conn, A.B., & Speer-Sorra, J.S. (2001). Implementing computerized technology: An organizational analysis. *Journal of Applied Psychology, 86*(5), 811-824.

Klein, M. (1994). The most fatal reengineering mistakes. *Information Strategy: The Executive Journal, 10*(4), 21-26.

Kleiner, A. (2004). The world's most exciting accountant. *Culture & Change, 26.*

Klingebiel, D., Kroszner, R., & Laeven, L. (2002). *Financial crises, financial dependence, and industry growth.* Policy Research Working Paper Series #2855, The World Bank.

Kluckhohn, F.R., & Strodtbeck, F.L. (1961). *Variations in value orientation.* New York: HarperCollins.

Knoell, G., & Knoell, H.-D. (1998). Der mensch im IT projekt [The human in the IT project]. *IT Management, 9,* 28-32.

Knoell, H.D., Kuehl, L.W.H., Kuehl, R.W.A., & Moreton, R. (2001). *Optimising business performance with standard software systems.* Wiesbaden, Germany: Vieweg.

Knoell, H.D., Kuehl, L.W.H., Kuehl, R.W.A., & Moreton, R. (2004). Evaluation of standard ERP software implementation approaches in terms of their capability for business process optimization. *4,* 271- 277.

Knoell, H.D., Slotos, T., & Suk, W. (1996). Quality assurance of specifications—The user's point of view. In *Proceedings of the 8ᵗʰ SEKE* (pp. 450-456), Lake Tahoe.

Knoll, K., & Jarvenpaa, S.L. (1994). Information technology alignment or 'fit' in highly turbulent environments: The concept of flexibility. In *Proceedings of SIGCPR 1994,* Alexandria, VA.

Koch, C. (2000). The ventriloquist's dummy? The role of technology in political processes. *Technology Analysis and Strategic Management, 12*(1), 119-138.

Koch, C. (2001). BPR and ERP: Realizing a vision of process with IT. *Business Process Management Journal, 7*(3), 258-265.

Kontzer, T. (2003). Business guru queries benefits of IT—Peter Drucker claims corporate IT is not delivering what companies want. *Computing,* (February).

KPMG. (2003). *Sarbanes-Oxley section 404: Management assessment of internal control and the proposed auditing standards.* Retrieved April 4, 2006, from http://www.kpmg.ca/en/services/audit/documents/SO404.pdf

Kraemer, K.L., & King, J.L. (1988). Computer-based systems for cooperative work and group decision making. *ACM Computing Surveys, 20*(2), 115-146.

Kræmmergaard, P., & Rose, J. (2002). Managerial competences for ERP journeys. *Information Systems Frontiers, 4*(2).

Kramer, L. (2006). The dark side of open source. *Wall Street & Technology,* (April), 42-43.

Krishnamurthy, S. (2005). An analysis of open source business models. In J. Feller, B. Fitzgerald, S. Hissam, & K.R. Lakhani (Eds.), *Making sense of the bazaar: Perspectives on open source and free software.* Boston: MIT Press.

Krumbholz, M., & Maiden, N. (2001). The implementation of enterprise resource planning packages in different organizational and national cultures. *Information Systems, 26,* 185-204.

Krumbholz, M., Galliers, J., Coulianos, N., & Maiden, N.A.M. (2000). Implementing enterprise resource planning packages in different corporate and national cultures. *Journal of Information Technology, 15*(4), 267-279.

Kübler-Ross, E. (1969). *On death and dying.* New York: MacMillan.

Kuehl, L.W.H., & Knoell, H.D. (2002). An improved approach to the semi-process-oriented implementation of standardized ERP systems. In *Proceedings of the Engineering Technology Conference on Energy* (ETCE 2002), Houston, TX.

Kumar, L., & Hillegersberg, J. (2000). ERP experiences and evolution. *Communications of the ACM, 43*(3), 22-26.

Kumar, V., Maheshwari, B., & Kumar, U. (2002). ERP systems implementation: Best practices in Canadian government organizations. *Government Information Quarterly, 19*(2), 145-172.

Kumar, V., Maheshwari, B., & Kumar, U. (2003). An investigation of critical management issues in ERP implementation: Empirical evidence from Canadian organizations. *Technovation, 23*(9), 793-807.

Kunda, G. (1992). *Engineering culture: Control and commitment in a high-tech corporation.* Philadelphia: Temple University Press.

Kwasi, A.G. (2007). Perceived usefulness, user involvement and behavioral intention: An empirical study of ERP implementation. *Computers in Human Behavior, 23,* 1232-1248.

Lamba, A. (2006). M-enabling the enterprise. *Arabian Computer News,* (October 5). Retrieved October 17, 2006, from http://www.itp.net/features/print.php?id=5307&prodid=&category=

Lancashire, D. (2001). Code, culture and cash: The fading altruism of open source development. *First Monday, 6*(12).

Lane, P.J., Koka, B.R., & Pathak, S. (2006). The reification of absorptive capacity: A critical review and rejuvenation of the construct. *Academy of Management Review, 31*(4), 833-863.

Lapassade, G. (1997). *Grupos, organizações e instituições.* Rio de Janeiro: Francisco Alves.

Larsen, M.A., & Myers, M.D. (1999). When success turns into failure: A package-driven business process re-engineering project in the financial services industry. *Journal of Strategic Information Systems, 8,* 395-417.

Larson, V., & Carnell, M. (2007). *Developing black belt change agents: "Surviving pity city and the Valley of Despair."* Retrieved February 27, 2007, from http://isixsigma.com/library/content/c020812a.asp

Lau, L.K. (2003). Developing a successful implementation plan for ERP: Issues and challenges. *Proceedings of IACIS.*

Laudon, K.C., & Laudon, J.P. (2004). *Management information systems: Managing the digital firm.* Upper Saddle River, NJ: Pearson Education.

Lee, A. (1989). Case studies as natural experiments. *Human Relations, 422.*

Lee, A.S. (1991). Integrating positivist and interpretive approaches to organizational research. *Organization Science, 2*(4), 342-365.

Lee, T.A., Bishop, A.C., & Parker, R.H. (Eds.). (1996). *Accounting history from the Renaissance to the present: A remembrance of Luca Pacioli.* New York: Garland.

Lehm, L., Heinzl, A., & Markus, L.M. (2001). Tailoring ERP systems: A spectrum of choices and their implications. In *Proceedings of the 34th Hawaii International Conference on Systems Science.*

Leidner, D.E., & Kayworth, T. (2006). A review of culture in information systems research: Towards a theory of information technology culture conflict. *MIS Quarterly, 30*(2), 357-399.

Leonard-Barton, D., & Sinha, D.K. (1993). Developer-user interaction and user satisfaction in internal technology transfer. *Academy of Management Journal, 36*(5), 1125-1139.

Levin, R., Mateyaschuk, J., & Stein, T. (1998). Faster ERP rollouts. *Information Week.*

Levinson, M. (2006). Meet your new host. *CIO Magazine,* (September 1). Retrieved October 14, 2006, from http://www.cio.com/archive/090106/fea_midhosting.html?action=print

Liang, H., & Xue, Y. (2004). Coping with ERP-related contextual issues in SMEs: A vendor's perspective. *Journal of Strategic Information Systems, 13*(4), 399-415.

Liang, H., Xue, Y., Boulton, W.R., & Byrd, T.A. (2004). Why western vendors don't dominate China's ERP market. *Communications of the ACM, 47*(7), 69-72.

Light, B. (1999). Realizing the potential of ERP systems: The strategic implications of implementing an ERP strategy: The case of global petroleum. *Electronic Markets, 9*(4), 238-241.

Light, B. (2005). Potential pitfalls in packaged software adoption. *Communications of the ACM, 48*(5), 119-121.

Light, B., & Wagner, E. (2006). Integration in ERP environments: Rhetoric, realities and organizational possibilities. *New Technology, Work and Employment, 21*(3), 215-228.

Lipshitz, R., Popper, M., & Oz, S. (1996). Building learning organizations: The design and implementation of organizational learning mechanisms. *Journal of Applied Behavioral Sciences, 32,* 292-305.

Little, A., & Best, P. (2003). A framework for separation of duties in SAP R/3. *Managerial Auditing Journal, 18*(5), 419-430.

Liu, L., & Steenstrup, K. (2004). *ERP selection criteria for Chinese enterprises.* Gartner (COM-22-0114).

Loeb, K.A., Rai, A., Ramaprasad, A., & Sharma, S. (1998). Design, development, & implementation of a global information warehouse: A case study at IBM. *Information Systems Journal, 8,* 291-311.

Lohr, S. (2004). Software sector enters an era of big mergers. *New York Times,* (December 15). Retrieved February 2005, from http://topics.nytimes.com/top/news/business/companies/oracle_corporation/index.html?offset=40&

Lorenzo, O., & Díaz, A. (2005). Process gap analysis and modelling in enterprise systems. *International Journal of Simulation and Process Modelling, 1*(3/4).

Louis, R.S. (1991). MRP III: Material acquisition system. *Production & Inventory Management, 11*(7), 26-48.

Lucas, H.C. et al. (1988). Implementing packaged software. *MIS Quarterly,* 537-549.

Luo, W., & Strong, D.M. (2004). A framework for evaluating ERP implementation choices. *IEEE Transactions on Engineering Management, 51*(3), 322-333.

Mabert, V.A. (2007). The early road to material requirements. *Journal of Operations Management, 25,* 346.

Mabert, V.A., Soni, A., & Venkataramanan, M.A. (2001). Enterprise resource planning: Common myths versus evolving reality. *Business Horizons, 44*(3), 69-76.

Mabert, V.M., Soni, A., & Venkataraman, N. (2000). Enterprise resource planning survey of U.S. manufacturing firms. *Production and Inventory Management Journal, 41*(2), 52-58.

Macve, R.H. (1996). Pacioli's legacy. In T.A. Lee, A.C. Bishop, & R.H. Parker (Eds.), *Accounting history from the Renaissance to the present: A remembrance of Luca Pacioli.* New York: Garland.

Madapusi, A., & D'Souza, D. (2005). Aligning ERP systems with international strategies. *Information Systems Management, 22*(1), 7-17.

Magnusson, J., & Nilsson, A. (2004). A conceptual framework for forecasting ERP implementation success. In *Proceedings of the International Conference on Enterprise Information Systems* (pp. 447-453).

Marketwire. (2007). *Thinking global? Don't lose sight of profitable growth.* Retrieved from http://www.marketwire.com/mw/release_html_b1?release_id=224493

Markham, R., & Hamerman, P. (2005). *The Forrester Wave™: Sarbanes-Oxley compliance software. Evaluation of top SOX software vendors across 58 criteria.* Retrieved March 1, 2006, from http://www.forrester.com

Markus, L., Petrie, D., & Axline, S. (2001). Bucking the trends, what the future may hold for ERP packages. In Shanks, Seddon, & Willcocks (Eds.), *Enterprise systems: ERP, implementation and effectiveness.* Cambridge: Cambridge University Press.

Markus, L.M., & Tanis, C. (2000). The enterprise system experience—From adoption to success. In R.W. Zmude (Ed.), *Framing the domain of IT management* (pp. 173-207). Pinnaflex Education Resources.

Markus, L.M., Axline, S., Petrie, D., & Tanis, C. (2000). Learning from adopters' experiences with ERP: Problems encountered and success achieved. *Journal of Information Technology, 15*(4), 245-265.

Markus, L.M., Tanis, C., & van Fenema, P.C. (2000). Enterprise resource planning: Multisite ERP implementations. *Communications of the ACM, 43*(4).

Markus, M.L., & Tanis; C. (2000). The enterprise systems experience—From adoption to success. In R.W. Zmud (Ed.), *Framing the domains of IT research: Glimpsing the future through the past* (pp.173-207). Cincinnati, OH: Pinnaflex Educational Resources.

Markus, M.L., & Tanis, C. (2000). The enterprise system experience: From adoption to success. In R.W. Zmud (Ed.), *Framing the domains of IT management: Projecting the future through the past* (pp. 173-207). Cincinnati, OH: Pinneflex Educational Resources.

Martin, J. (2002). *Organizational culture. Mapping the terrain.* London: Sage.

Martin, T.C. (1891). Counting a nation by electricity. *The Electrical Engineer, 12,* 521-530.

Martinsons, M.G. (2004). ERP in China: One package, two profiles. *Communications of the ACM, 47*(7), 65-68.

Mathis, R.L., & Jackson, J.H. (2000). *Human resource management.* OH: Southwestern College.

Matolcsy, Z.P., Booth, P., & Wieder, B. (2005). Economic benefits of enterprise resource planning systems: Some empirical evidence. *Accounting and Finance, 45,* 439-456.

Matyjewicz, G., & D'Arcangelo, J. (2004). Beyond Sarbanes Oxley. *Internal Auditor,* (October), 67-72.

McAllister, N. (2005). You can't kill TCO. *Infoworld,* (August 29).

McCarthy, W.E. (1982). The REA accounting model: A generalized framework for accounting systems in a shared data environment. *The Accounting Review,* (July), 554-578.

McClelland, D.C. (1961). *The achieving society.* Princeton, NJ: Van Nostrand.

McFarlan, F.W. (1984). Information technology changes the way you compete. *Harvard Business Review,* (May/June), 98-103.

McGill, T., Hobbs, V., & Klobas, J. (2003). User-developed applications and information systems success: A test

of Delone and Mclean's model. *Information Resource Management Journal, 16*(1), 24-45.

McGrath, R.G. (1997). A real options logic for initiating technology positioning investments. *Academy of Management Review, 22*(4), 974-996.

McGrath, R.G., & MacMillan, I.C. (2000). Assessing technology projects using real options reasoning. *Research-Technology Management, 43*(4), 35-49.

McNally, S., & Wagaman, D. (2005). *Hard climb is done, but trek continues: Sarbanes-Oxley compliance in year two and beyond.* Retrieved May 11, 2006, from http://www.ascpa.com/public/pressroom/azcpa.aspx?a=view&id=249

Mellahi, K., & Frynas, J.G. (2003). An exploratory study into the applicability of western HRM practices in developing countries: An Algerian case study. *International Journal of Commerce & Management, 13*(1), 61.

Milberg, S.J., Burk, S.J., Smith, J.H., & Kallman, E.A. (1995). Rethinking copyright issues and ethics on the Net: Values, personal information privacy, and regulatory approaches. *Communications of the ACM, 38*(12), 65-73.

Miles, M.B., & Huberman, A.M. (1994). *Qualitative data analysis: An expanded sourcebook* (2nd ed.). Thousand Oaks, CA: Sage.

Mills, J., Platts, K., & Gregory, M. (1995). A framework for design of manufacturing strategy processes: A contingency approach. *International Journal of Operations & Production Management, 15*(4), 17-49.

Milne, D. (2006). Gulf air swoops in for deal to outsource its IT support. *IT Weekly Middle East,* (April 23). Retrieved April 2006, from http://www.itp.net/news/print.php?id=20397&prodid=&category=

Milne, D. (2006). Oracle promises lifetime support to its customers. *IT Weekly Middle East,* (May 7). Retrieved May 7, 2006, from http://www.itp.net/news/print.php?id=20556&prodid=&category=

Mintzberg, H. (1992). Five Ps for strategy. In H. Mintzberg & J.B. Quinn (Eds.), *The Strategy Process.* Englewood Cliffs, NJ: Prentice Hall.

Mintzberg, H. (1994). The fall and rise of strategic planning. *Harvard Business Review,* 107-114.

Mirani, R., & Lederer, A.L. (1998). An instrument for assessing the organizational benefits of IS project. *Decision Sciences, 29,* 803-838.

MIT. (n.d.). *Economic performance in U.S. manufacturing: An exploratory analysis.* Economics, Finance and Accounting Working Paper #3419, Sloan School of Management, Massachusetts Institute of Technology, USA.

Mohamed, M. (2002). Points of the triangle. Retrieved May 2004 from http://www.intelligententerprise.com/020903/514feat2_1.jhtml?/supply_chain%7Csupply

Møller, C. (2005). ERP II: A conceptual framework for next-generation enterprise systems? *Enterprise Information Management, 18*(4), 483.

Møller, C. (2005). ERP II: A conceptual framework for next-generation enterprise systems? *Journal of Enterprise Information Management, 18*(4), 483-497.

Montazemi, A. et al. (1996). An empirical study of factors affecting software package selection. *Journal of Management Information Systems, 13*(1), 89-105.

Moon, Y.B. (2007). Enterprise resource planning (ERP): A review of the literature. *International Journal of Management and Enterprise Development, 4*(3), 235-264.

Moore, G.A. (2005). *Dealing with Darwin: How great companies innovate at every phase of their evolution.* London: Penguin Books.

Moreton, R., & Chester, M.F. (1997). *Transforming the business: The IT contribution.* London: McGraw-Hill.

Motwani, J., Mirchandani, D., Madan, A., & Gunasekaran, A. (2002). Successful implementation of ERP projects: Evidence from two case studies. *International Journal of Production Economics, 75,* 83-96.

Mozilla. (2007). *Mozilla public license, version 1.1.* Retrieved March 8, 2007, from http://www.mozilla.org/MPL/MPL-1.1.html

Mullin, R. (1999). ERP users say payback is passé. *Chemical Week, 161,* 25-26.

Murphy, K.E., & Simon, S.J. (2002). Intangible benefits valuation in ERP projects. *Information Systems Journal, 12,* 301-320.

Murray, M.G., & Coffin, G.W. (2001, August). A case study analysis of factors for success in ERP system implementations. In *Proceedings of the 7th Americas Conference on Information Systems* (pp. 1012-1018), Boston.

Myers, M.D., & Tan, F.B. (2002). Beyond models of national culture in information systems research. *Journal of Global Information Management, 10*(1), 24-33.

MySAP ERP. (2007). *Globalization with localization.* Retrieved from www.sap.com/usa/solutions/grc/pdf/BWP_mySAP_ERP_Global_Local.pdf

MySQL. (2007). *The world's most popular open source database: About MySQL AB.* Retrieved March 8, 2007, from http://www.mysql.com/company/

Nah, F.F., Zuckweiler, K.M., & Lau, J.L. (2003). ERP implementation: Chief information officers' perceptions of critical success factors. *International Journal of Human-Computer Interaction, 16*(1), 5-22.

Nah, F.F.H., Lau, J.L.-S., & Kuang, J. (2001). Critical factors for successful implementation of enterprise systems. *Business Process Management Journal, 7*(3), 285-296.

Naik, G. (2004). The structural qualitative method: A promising forecasting tool for developing country markets. *International Journal of Forecasting, 20*(3), 475.

Nair, V., & Rajan, B. (2006). *Arab Middle East and North Africa software solutions: 2006-2010 forecast and 2005 vendor shares.* Document #ZR03N, IDC.

Nandish, V.P., & Irani, Z. (1999). Evaluating information technology in dynamic environments: A focus on tailorable information. *Logistics Information Management, 12,* 32.

369

Nardi, B.A., & Miller J.R. (1990). An ethnographic study of distributed problem solving in spreadsheet development. In *Proceedings of the ACM Conference on CSCW* (pp. 197-208), Los Angeles.

Newell, S., Pan, S.L., Galliers, R.D., Huang, J.C. (2001). The myths of the boundaryless organization. *Communications of the ACM, 44*(12), 74-76.

Ng, J.K.C., Ip, W.H., & Lee, T.C. (1999). A paradigm for ERP and BPR integration. *International Journal of Production Research, 37*(9), 2093-2108.

Nichols, D., & Twidale, M. (2003). The usability of open source software. *8*(1).

Nolan and Norton Institute. (2000). *SAP benchmarking report 2000*. Melbourne: KPMG Melbourne.

Nolan, S. (2005). Knowing when to embrace open source. *Baseline,* (48), 76.

O'Leary, D. (2000). *Enterprise resource planning systems*. New York: Cambridge University Press.

O'Leary, D.E. (2000). *Enterprise resource planning systems: Systems, life cycle, electronic commerce, and risk*. Cambridge: Cambridge University Press.

Oesterle H. (1991). Generating business ideas based on information technology. In R. Clarke & J. Cameron (Eds.), *Managing information technology's organisational impact II*. Amsterdam: Elsevier/North-Holland.

Olhager, J., & Selldin, E. (2003). Enterprise resource planning survey of Swedish manufacturing firms. *European Journal of Operational Research, 146*, 365-373.

Oliver, D., & Romm, C. (2002). Justifying enterprise resource planning adoption. *Journal of Information Technology, 17*(4), 199-213.

Olsen, K.A., & Sætre, P. (2007). ERP for SMEs—Is proprietary software an alternative? *Business Process Management Journal, 13*(3), 379.

Olson, D.L. (2004). *Managerial issues of enterprise resource planning systems*. McGraw-Hill International.

Open Source Initiative. (2005). *Open source definition*. Retrieved from http://www.opensource.org/

Open Source Initiative. (2006). *OSI Web site*. Retrieved October 24, 2006, from http://www.opensource.org/licenses/

OpenPro. (2007). *OpenPro: The open source ERP software solutions that give you more value and more features*. Retrieved March 8, 2007, from http://www.openpro.com

Orlikowski, W.J. (2000). Using technology and constituting structures: A practice lens for studying technology in organizations. *Organization Science, 11*(4), 404-428.

Orlikowski, W.J. et al. (1995). Shaping electronic communication: The metastructuring of technology in the context of use. *Organization Science, 6*(4), 423-444.

Outreville, J.-F. (2005). Financial development, human capital and political instability. *Finance-India,* 19(2), 481-492.

Pahnke, C., Moreton, R., & Knoell, H.-D. (2004). Animated systems engineering (ASE)—Evaluation of a new approach to high quality groupware application specification and development. In *Proceedings of the 13th International Conference on Information Systems Development: Methods and Tools, Theory and Practice* (ISD 2004), Vilnius, Lithuania.

Pant, S., & Hsu, C. (1995). Strategic information systems: A review. In *Proceedings of the 1995 IRMA Conference,* Atlanta, GA.

Parker, M., & Benson, R. (1988). *Information economics: Linking business performance to information technology*. London: Prentice Hall.

Parr, A., & Shanks, G. (2000). A model of ERP project implementation. *Journal of Information Technology, 15*(4), 289-301.

PCAOB (Public Company Accounting Oversight Board). (2004). *Auditing standard no. 2—an audit of internal control over financial reporting performed in conjunction with an audit of financial statements*. Retrieved March 23, 2006, from http://www.pcaobus.org/Rules/Docket_008/index.aspx

Peteraf, M.A. (1993). The cornerstones of competitive advantage: A Resource-based view. *Strategic Management Journal, 14,* 179-191.

Pettigrew, A. (1990). Longitudinal field research on change: Theory and practice. *Organization Science, 1*(3), 267-292.

Pettigrew, A. (1997). What is a processual analysis? *Scandinavian Journal of Management,* 13(4), 337-348.

Pettigrew, A.M. (1990). Longitudinal field research on change: Theory and practice. *Organization Science, 1*(3), 267-292.

Pettigrew, A.M. (1990). Organizational climate and culture: Two constructs in search of a role. In B. Schneider (Ed.), *Organizational climate and culture* (pp. 413-433). San Francisco: Jossey-Bass.

Phillips, N., & Hardy, C. (2002). *Discourse Analysis.* London: Sage.

Ploenzke. (2002). *European SAP practice, umfrageergebnisse.* Wiesbaden, Germany.

Png, I.P., Tan, B.C.Y., & Wee, K.L. (2001). Dimensions of national cultures and corporate adoption of IT infrastructure. *IEEE Transactions of Engineering Management, 48*(1), 36-45.

Poon, P.P., & Wagner, C. (2001). Critical success factors revisited: Success and failure cases of information systems for senior executives. *Decision Support Systems, 30,* 393-418.

Porter, M. (1985). *Competitive advantage: Creating and sustaining superior performance.* New York: The Free Press.

Porter, M. (1996). What is strategy? *Harvard Business Review, (November-December).*

Porter, M., & Millar, V. (1985). How information gives you competitive advantage. *Harvard Business Review, 63*(4).

Porter, M.E. (1986). Changing patterns of international competition. *California Management Review, XXVIII*(2), 9-40.

Porter, M.E., & Miller, V.E. (1985). How information gives you competitive advantage. *Harvard Business Review, 63,* 149-160.

Powell, T.C., & Dent-Micallef, A. (1997). Information technology as competitive advantage: The role of human, business and technology resources. *Strategic Management Journal, 18*(5), 375-405.

Pozzebon, M. (2003). *The implementation of configurable technologies: Negotiations between global principles and local contexts.* Unpublished PhD Dissertation, McGill University, Canada.

Pozzebon, M., & Pinsonneault, A. (2005). Global-local negotiations for implementing configurable packages: The power of initial organizational decisions. *Journal of Strategic Information Systems, Special Issue Understanding the Contextual Influences on Enterprise System Implementation (Part II), 14*(2), 121-145.

Prentice, B. (2006). *The advent of open-source business applications: Demand-side dynamics.* Gartner (G001412).

Price Waterhouse. (1996). *Information technology review 1995/96.* UK.

PricewaterhouseCoopers. (2003). *Sarbanes Oxley—Internal control solutions framework.* Retrieved March 3, 2006, from http://www.pwc.com

Purba, S., & Shah, B. (2000). *How to manage a successful software project.* New York: John Wiley & Sons.

Putnam, R.D. (1993). *Making democracy work.* Princeton, NJ: Princeton University Press.

Quiescenti, M., Bruccoleri, M., La Commare, U., Noto La Diega, S., & Perrone, G. (2006). Business process-oriented design of enterprise resource planning (ERP) systems for small and medium enterprises. *International Journal of Production Research, 44*(18/19), 3797.

Rackoff, N., Wiseman, C., & Ullrich, W.A. (1985). Information systems for competitive advantage: Implementation of a planning process. *MIS Quarterly, 9,* 285-294.

Raymond, E.S. (1999). *The cathedral and the bazaar: Musings on Linux and open source by an accidental revolutionary.* Sebastopol, CA: O'Reilly and Associates.

Rebstock, M., & Selig, J.G. (2000). Development and implementation strategies for international ERP software projects. In *Proceedings of the European Conference on Information Systems* (ECIS).

Reich, B., & Benbasat, I. (2000). Factors that influence the social dimension of alignment between business and information technology objectives. *MIS Quarterly, 24.*

Reimers, K. (1997). Managing information technology in the transnational organization: The potential of multifactor productivity. In *Proceedings of the 30th Annual Hawaii Conference on System Sciences.*

Remenyi, D., & Sherwood-Smith, M. (1999). Maximize information systems value by continuous participative evaluation. *Logistics Information Management, 12,* 14-25.

Reynolds, G.W. (1992). *Information systems for managers.* Minneapolis/St. Paul, MN: West.

Rikhardsson, P., Rohde, C., & Rom, A. (2006). Management control in enterprise system enabled organizations: A literature review. *Journal of Corporate Ownership and Control, 4*(2), 233-242.

Rist, O. (2005). Open source ERP. *InfoWorld, 27*(32), 43-47.

Rizzi, A., & Zamboni, R. (1999). Efficiency improvement in manual warehouses through ERP systems implementation and redesign of the logistic processes. *Journal of Enterprise Information Management, 12*(5-6), 367-377.

Robertson, P.L. (2003). The role of training and skilled labour in the success of SMEs in developing economies. *Education & Training, 45*(8/9), 461, 413.

Robey, D., & Markus, M.L. (1984). Rituals in information systems design. *MIS Quarterly, 8*(1), 5-15.

Robey, D., Ross, J.W., & Boudreau, M. (2000). Learning to implement enterprise systems: An exploratory study of the dialectics of change. *Journal of Management Information Systems, 19*(1), 17-46.

Robinson, T.R. (2000). The global e-economy: Can your ERP handle it? *Journal of Corporate Accounting & Finance,* (September-October), 15-18.

Rockford Consulting. (2006). Retrieved August 27, 2006, from http://www.rockfordconsulting.com/12sinart.htm

Rodrigues, C. (2001). *International management: A cultural approach* (2nd ed.). Cincinnati, OH: South-Western College.

Romney, M., & Steinbart, P. (2003). *Accounting information systems.* Upper Saddle River, NJ: Prentice Hall.

Ross, J. (1999). Dow Corning Corporation: Business processes and information technology. *Journal of Information Technology, 14*(3), 253-266.

Ross, J.W., & Vitale, M. (2000). The ERP revolution. Surviving versus thriving. *Information System Frontiers, 2*(2), 233-241.

Rothwell, W.J., & Prescott, R.K. (1999). Transforming HR into a global powerhouse. *HR Focus, 76*(3), 7-8.

Rousseau, D.M. (1990). Assessing organizational culture: The case of multiple methods. In B. Schneider (Ed.), *Organizational climate and culture* (pp. 153-192). San Francisco: Jossey-Bass.

Rousseau, D.M., & Cooke, A.R. (1988). Culture of high reliability: Behavioral norms aboard a U.S. aircraft carrier. In *Proceedings of the Academy of Management Meeting,* Anaheim, CA.

Sackmann, S. (1992). Cultures and subcultures: An analysis of organizational knowledge. *Administrative Science Quarterly, 37,* 140-161.

Sage Abra. (2006). Sage Abra HR solutions learns to speak Arabic. *IT Weekly Middle East,* (May 13-19), 11.

Sammon, D., & Adam, F. (2005). Towards a model of organizational prerequisites for enterprise-wide systems integration: Examining ERP and data warehousing. *Journal of Enterprise Information Management, 18*(4), 458-470.

Sandoe, K., Corbitt, G., & Boykin, R. (2001). *Enterprise integration.* New York: John Wiley & Sons.

Santos, B.L.D. (1991). Justifying investments in new information technologies. *Journal of Management Information Systems, 7*(4), 71.

SAP. (2000). *ASAP for upgrade, release 4.6C* (CD). Walldorf, Germany.

SAP. (2004). *SAP service select Web seminar. SAP Sarbanes-Oxley.* Retrieved March 20, 2006, from http://www.sap.com

SAP. (2004). *Strategic enterprise management—An overview.* Retrieved March 20, 2006, from http://www.sap.com

SAP. (2005). *MySAP ERP functionalities—Overview.* Retrieved March 20, 2006, from http://www.sap.com

SAP. (2005). *Enterprise governance and Sarbanes-Oxley compliance with mySAP ERP Financials.* Retrieved March 20, 2006, from http://www.sap.com

SAP. (2006). *Company information.* Retrieved April 3, 2006, from http://www.sap.com

SAP. (2006). *End-to-end process integration with SAP NetWeaver.* Retrieved September 21, 2006, from http://www.sap.com/industries/highered/pdf/BWP_End_to_End_Proc_Int.pdf

Saran, C. (2005, November). *Expense ahead with next-generation ERP.* Retrieved from http://www.ComputerWeekly.com

Saran, C. (2007). Oracle extends sector specific ERP for SMEs. *Computer Weekly,* (July 31), 16, 11.

Sarkis, J., & Sundarraj, R.P. (2003). Managing large scale global enterprise resource planning systems: A case study at Texas Instruments. *International Journal of Information Management, 23*(5), 431-442.

Scheer, A.W. (1996). *ARIS—House of business engineering.* Saarbruecken, Germany: Institut für Wirtschaftsinformatik an der Universität des Saarlandes.

Scheer, A.-W., & Habermann, F. (2000). Making ERP a success. *Communications of the ACM, 43*(4), 57-61.

Schein, E.H. (1992). *Organizational culture and leadership.* San Francisco: Jossey-Bass.

Schein, E.H. (1996). Culture: The missing concept in organizational studies. *Administrative Science Quarterly, 41,* 229-240.

Scheuss, R. (n.d.). *Wir kopieren zu viel.* Retrieved November 25, 2004, from http://www.manager-magazin.de/koepfe/artikel/0,2828,327331,00.html

Schiff, C. (2003). The implementation challenge: Key considerations in choosing a BPM consultant. *Business Performance Management,* (June), 20.

Schiff, C. (2006). BPM consulting 2006: More choices and more risk. *Business Performance Management,* (November), 9.

Schlack, M. (1992). IS has a new job in manufacturing. *Datamation,* (January 15), 38-40.

Schmidt, W. (1999). *Personal communication.* Muenster, Germany: LVM Insurance Group.

Scholz, C. (1990). The symbolic value of computerized information systems. In P. Galiardi (Ed.), *Symbols and artifacts: Views of the corporate landscape* (pp. 233-254). New York: Aldin De Gruyter.

Schultheis, R., & Sumner, M. (1989). *Management information systems: The manager's view.* Boston: Irwin.

Schwartz, S.H. (1992). Universals in the content and structure of values: Theoretical advances and empirical test in 20 countries. In M.P. Zanna (Ed.), *Advances in experimental social psychology* (vol. 25, pp. 1-65). San Diego: Academic Press.

Scott Morton, M.S. (1991). *The corporation of the 1990s: Information technology and organizational transformation.* New York: Oxford University Press.

Scott, J.E. (1999). The FoxMeyer Drug's bankruptcy: Was it a failure of ERP? In *Proceedings of the Association for Information Systems 5th Americas Conference on Information Systems.*

Scott, J.E. (2006). *The FoxMeyer Drugs' bankruptcy: Was it a failure of ERP?* Retrieved August 26, 2006, from http://www.ndsu.nodak.edu/ndsu/bklamm/ BPandTC%20references/BP%20TC%20Scott%201999 %20Foxmeyer%20drugs%20bankruptcy%20was%20it %20a%20failure.pdf#search=%22The%20Delta%20III %20project%20at%20FoxMeyer%20Drugs%20%22

Scott, J.E., & Vessey, I. (2002). Managing risks in enterprise systems implementations. *Communications of the ACM, 45*(4), 74-81.

Seddon, P.B., Graeser, V., & Willcocks, L. (2002). Measuring organizational IS effectiveness: An overview and update of senior management perspectives. *The Database for Advances in Information Systems, 33*, 11-28.

Seibel, A. (2003). *Personal communication*. Frankfurt, Germany: CMG Group.

Serrano, N., & Sarriegi, J. (2006). Open source software ERPs: A new alternative for an old need. *IEEE Software*, 94-97.

Shang, S., & Seddon, P.B. (2002). Assessing and managing the benefits of enterprise systems: The business manager's perspective. *Information Systems Journal, 12*, 271-299.

Shang, S., & Seddon, S. (2000). A comprehensive framework for classifying the benefits of ERP systems. *Proceedings of Americas Conference on Information Systems*.

Shanks, G., Seddon, P.B., & Willcocks, L.P. (Eds.). (2003). *Second-wave enterprise resource planning systems: Implementing for effectiveness*. Cambridge: Cambridge University Press.

Sheikh Mohammed. (2005). *GCC countries*. Retrieved June 2006, from http://www.sheikhmohammed.co.ae/ english/history/history_arabia.asp

Sheth, J. (1981). Psychology of innovation resistance. *Research in Marketing, 4*, 273-282.

Sheu, C., Chae, B., & Yang, C. (2004). National differences and ERP implementation: Issues and challenges. *Omega, 32*(5), 361-372.

Shih, V. (2004). The politics of finance and development. *Political Science, 395*(Winter).

Shokef, E., & Erez, M. (2006). Shared meaning systems in multiclutural teams. In B. Mannix, M. Neae, & Y.-R. Chen (Eds.), *National culture and groups. Research on managing groups and teams* (vol. 9, pp. 325-352). San Diego: Elsevier, JAI Press.

Shouler, A. (2007). Gulf news financial review: Strong growth and reform to keep positive tone. *Gulf News Quarterly Financial Review*, 14-16.

Shue, L. (2004). Sarbanes Oxley and IT outsourcing. *Information System Audit and Control Association, 5*, 43-49.

Silver, M. (1990). Decision support systems: Direct and non-directed changes. *Information Systems Research, 1*, 47-88.

Simons, R. (2000). *Performance measurement & control systems for implementing strategy*. Upper Saddle River, NJ: Prentice Hall.

SKAI Associates. (2004, September). *The change curve—A new lease on life or has it died with the source?* Retrieved February 26, 2007, from http://www.skai. co.uk/client_comm_200409.php

Soh, C., & Sia, S.K. (2004). An institutional perspective on sources of ERP package-organization misalignments. *Journal of Strategic Information Systems, 13*(4), 375-397.

Soh, C., & Sia, S.K. (2005). The challenges of implementing "vanilla" versions of enterprise systems. *MIS Quarterly Executive, 4*(3), 373-384.

Soh, C., Klien, S.S., & Tay-Yap, J. (2000). Cultural fits and misfits: Is ERP a universal solution? *Communications of the ACM, 43*(4), 47-51.

Sohal, A.S., Moss, S., & Ng, L. (2001). Comparing IT success in manufacturing and service industries. *International Journal of Operations & Production Management, 21*(1/2), 30-45.

Solomon, C.M. (1998). Sharing information. *Workforce, 77*(3), 12-16.

Somers, T.M., & Nelson, K. (2001, January 3-6). The impact of critical success factors across the stages of enterprise resource planning implementation. In *Proceedings of the 34ᵗʰ Hawaii International Conference on Systems Sciences* (HICSS-34), Maui, HI.

Somers, T.M., & Nelson, K.G. (2004). A taxonomy of players and activities across the ERP project life cycle. *Information & Management, 41*(3), 257-278.

Somogyi, E., & Galliers, R. (1987). *Towards strategic information systems.* Cambridge: Abacus Press.

Songini, M.C. (2004, August 23). *Ford abandons Oracle procurement systems, switches back to mainframe apps.* Retrieved from http://www.computerworld.com/softwaretopics/erp/story/0.10801,95404,00.html

Sounder, W.E., & Nashar, A.S. (1995). A technology selection model for new products development and technology transfer. In L.R. Gomez-Mejia & M.W. Lawless (Eds.), *Advances in high-technology management* (vol. 5, pp. 225-244). Greenwich, CT: JAI Press.

Spinellis, D. (2006). 10 tips for spotting low-quality open source code. *Enterprise Open Source Journal,* (September/October).

Srite, M. (1999, August). The influence of national culture on the acceptance and use of information technologies: An empirical study. In *Proceedings of the 5ᵗʰ Americas Conference on Information Systems* (pp. 1019-1021), Milwaukee, WI.

Srite, M. (2000). *The influence of national culture on the acceptance and use of information technologies: An empirical study.* Unpublished Doctoral Dissertation, Florida State University, USA.

Stake, R.E. (1998). Case studies. In Denzin & Lincoln (Eds.), *Strategies of qualitative inquiry.* Thousand Oaks, CA: Sage.

Standish Group. (1994). *The Chaos Report 1994.* Retrieved March 6, 2006, from http://www.standishgroup.com/sample_research/chaos_1994_1.php

Standish Group. (1996). *Unfinished voyages—A follow-up to the Chaos Report.* Retrieved March 6, 2006, from http://www.standishgroup.com/sample_research/unfinished_voyages_1.php

Stanton, D. (2006). Middle East buys into e-procurement at CIPS. *Arabian Computer News,* (May 9). Retrieved May 9, 2006, from http://www.itp.net/news/print.php?id=20618&prodid=&category=

Stanton, D. (2006). Outside the box. *Arabian Computer News,* (September 4). Retrieved October 3, 2006, from http://www.itp.net/features/print.php?id=5083&prodid=&category=

Stanton, D. (2006). Shariah support. *Arabian Computer News.* Retrieved October 17, 2006, from http://www.itp.net/features/print.php?id=5269&prodid=&category=

Stanton, D. (2006). Solid gold solution. *Arabian Computer News,* (October 5). Retrieved October 17, 2006, from https://www.itp.net/features/print.php?id=5305&prodid=&category=

Steadman, C. (1999). Calculating ROI. *Computerworld, 33,* 6.

Stedman, C. (1999). What's next for ERP? *Computerworld, 33*(August 16).

Stensrud, E., & Myrtveit, I. (2003). Identifying high performance ERP projects. *IEEE Transactions on Software Engineering, 29*(5), 398-416.

Stewart, G., Milford, M., Jewels, T., Hunter, T., & Hunter, B. (2000). Organizational readiness for ERP implementation. In *Proceedings of the Americas Conference on Information Systems* (pp. 966-971).

Strassmann, P. (1985). *Information payoff: The transformation of work in the electronic age.* London: Collier Macmillan.

Straub, D., Loch, K., Evariso, R., Karahanna, E., & Srite, M. (2002). Towards a theory-based measurement of culture. *Journal of Global Information Management, 10*(1), 13-23.

SugarCRM. (2007). *SugarCRM: Commercial open source.* Retrieved March 8, 2007, from http://www.sugarcrm.com/

Summer, M. (2005). *Enterprise resource planning.* Upper Saddle River, NJ: Pearson Prentice Hall.

Sumner, M. (2000). Risk factors in enterprise-wide/ ERP projects. *Journal of Information Technology, 15,* 317-327.

Swan, J. et al. (2000). The diffusion, design and social shaping of production management information systems in Europe. *Information Technology and People, 13*(1), 27-45.

Swanson, E.B., & Ramiller, N.C. (2004). Innovating mindfully with information technology. *MIS Quarterly, 28*(4), 553-583.

Swedberg, C. (2006). RFID tracks jewelry sales: Inventory in Mideast. *RFID Journal,* (May 18). Retrieved November 2, 2006, from http://www.rfidjournal.com/ article/articleview/2348/1/1/

Tallon, P., & Kraemer, K. (2003). *Investigating the relationship between strategic alignment and IT business value: The discovery of a paradox, relationship between strategic alignment and IT business value.* Hershey, PA: Idea Group.

Tallon, P., Kraemer, K., & Gurbaxni, V. (2000). Executives' perception of business value of information technology: A process-oriented approach. *Journal of Management Information Systems, 16*(4), 145-173.

Taudes, A. (1998). Software growth options. *Journal of Management Information Systems, 15*(1), 165-185.

Taudes, A. (2000). Options analysis of software platform decisions: A case study. *MIS Quarterly, 24,* 227.

Tchokogue, A., Bareil, C., & Duguay, C.R. (2005). Key lessons from the implementation of an ERP at Pratt & Whitney Canada. *International Journal of Production Economics, 95,* 151-163.

Teo, T., & King, W. (1997) Integration between business planning and information systems planning: An evolutionary contingency perspective. *Journal of Management Information Systems, 14.*

Tessema, M.T., & Soeters, J.L. (2006). Challenges and prospects of HRM in developing countries: Testing the HRM-performance link in the Eritrean civil service. *International Journal of Human Resource Management, 17*(1), 86.

Thatcher, J.B., Srite, M., Stephina, L.P., & Liu, Y. (2003). Culture overload and personal innovativeness with information technology: Extending the nomological net. *Journal of Computer Information Systems, 44*(1), 74-81.

Tonnessen, T. (2000). Process improvement and the human factor. *Total Quality Management, 11*(4/5/6), 773-778.

Triandis, H.C. (1995). *Individualism and collectivism.* Boulder, CO: Westview.

Trice, H.M. (1993). *Occupational subcultures in the workplace.* Ithaca, NY: ILR Press.

Trigg, R.H., & Bodker, S. (1994). From implementation to design: Tailoring and the emergence of systematization. In *Proceedings of the ACM Conference on CSCW* (pp. 45-54), Chapel Hill, NC.

Triniti. (2007). *Getting it right with ERP II. Business management.* Retrieved February 14, 2007, from http:// www.triniti.com/downloads/articles/erpi.pdf

Trompenaars, F. (1996). Resolving international conflict: Culture and business strategy. *Business Strategy Review, 7*(3), 51-68.

Tushman, M.L., & O'Reilly, C.A. III. (1999). Building ambidextrous organizations: Forming your own "skunk works." *Health Forum Journal, 42*(2).

U.S. Congress. (2002). *Sarbanes-Oxley Act.* Retrieved October 29, 2006, from http://www.sec.gov/about/laws/ soa2002.pdf

U.S. SEC (Securities & Exchange Commission). (2005). *Management's report on internal control over financial reporting and certification of disclosure in exchange act periodic reports of non-accelerated filers and foreign private issuers, release no. 33-8545.* Retrieved October 23, 2006, from http://www.sec.gov/rules/final/33-8545. htm

Umble, E.J., Haft, R.R., & Umble, M.M. (2003). Enterprise resource planning: Implementation procedures and critical success factors. *European Journal of Operational Research, 146*(2), 241-257.

Van Everdingen, Y.M., & Waarts, E. (2003). The effect of national culture on the adoption of innovations. *Marketing Letters, 14*(3), 217-232.

Venkataraman, N., Henderson, J., & Oldach, S.H. (1993). Continuous strategic alignment: Exploiting IT capabilities for competitive success. *European Management Journal, 11,* 139-149.

Verville, J., & Halingten, A. (2003). A six-stage model of the buying process for ERP software. *Industrial Marketing Management, 32,* 585-594.

Virsa Systems. (2005). *SAP compliance calibrator—White paper.* Retrieved March 20, 2006, from http://www.virsasystems.com

Vitale, M. (1986). The growing risks of information systems success. *MIS Quarterly, 10.*

Volkoff, O. (2003). Configuring an ERP system: Introducing best practices or hampering flexibility? *Journal of Information Systems Education, 14*(3), 319.

Von Meier, A. (1999). Occupational cultures as challenge to technological innovation. *IEEE Transactions on Engineering Management, 46*(1), 101-114.

Wailgum, T. (2006). Integration liberation. *CIO Magazine,* (October 15). Retrieved October 2006 from http://www.cio.com/archive/101506/integration.html?action=print

Waldman, M. (2005). *Operationalizing Sarbanes-Oxley: How to leverage Sarbanes-Oxley to add value to business operations.* Retrieved January 3, 2006, from http://www.percipiogroup.com

Walsham, G. (2000). *Globalization and IT: Agenda for research.* Boston: Kluwer Academic.

Wang, E.T.G., & Chen, J.H.F. (2006). Effects of internal support and consultant quality on the consulting process and ERP system quality. *Decision Support Systems, 42,* 1029-1041.

Ward, J., Griffiths, P., & Whithmore, P. (1990). *Strategic planning for information systems.* Chichester: John Wiley & Sons.

Watson, R., Wynn, D., & Boudreau, M.C. (2005). JBOSS: The evolution of professional open source software. *MIS Quarterly Executive, 4*(3), 329-341.

Watson, R.T., Boudreau, M.-C., York, P., Greiner, M., & Wynn, D. (2006). The business of open source. *Communications of ACM.*

Weber, R. (1986). Data models research in accounting: An evaluation of wholesale distribution software. *The Accounting Review, 61*(3), 498-518.

Wei, C.C., & Wang, M.J.J. (2004). A comprehensive framework for selecting an ERP system. *International Journal of Project Management, 22,* 161-169.

Wei, C.C., Chien, C.F., & Wang, M.J.J. (2005). An AHP-based approach to ERP system selection. *International Journal of Production Economics, 96,* 47-62.

Weil, M. (1999). Managing to win. *Manufacturing Systems, 17*(November), 14.

Wellins, R., & Rioux, S. (2000). The growing pains of globalizing HR. *Training & Development, 54*(5), 79-85.

Wernerfelt, B. (1984). A resource-based view of the firm. *Strategic Management Journal, 5,* 171-180.

Wernerfelt, B. (1995). The resource-based view of the firm: Ten years after. *Strategic Management Journal, 16,* 171-174.

Wexelblat, R.L. (Ed.). (1981). *History of programming languages.* New York: ACM Monograph Series.

Wiechmann, D., Ryan, A.M., & Hemingway, M. (2003). Designing and implementing global staffing systems: Part I—Leaders in global staffing. *Human Resource Management, 42*(1), 71. Retrieved February 17, 2005, from the ABI/INFORM Global Database.

Wight, O. (1982). *The executive's guide to successful MRP II (Oliver Wight Manufacturing).* New York: Simon & Schuster.

Wilderman, B. (1999). *Enterprise resource management solutions and their value.* Stanford, CT: MetaGroup.

Willcocks, L. (Ed.). (1994). *Information management: Evaluation of information systems investments.* London: Chapman & Hall.

Willcocks, L.P., & Lester, S. (Eds.). (1999). *Beyond the IT productivity paradox.* Chichester: John Wiley & Sons.

Wireless Newsfactor. (2001). Ericsson addresses globalization with sweeping restructuring plan. *Wireless Newsfactor.*

Wood, L.A., & Kroger, R.O. (2000). *Doing discourse analysis.* London: Sage.

Wu, M.S. (1990). Selecting the right software application package. *Journal of Systems Management, 41*(9), 28-32.

Wysocki, R., & DeMichiell, R.L. (1997). *Managing information across the enterprise.* New York: John Wiley & Sons.

Yin, R. (1994). *Case study research, design and methods* (2nd ed.). Newbury Park, CA: Sage.

Yin, R.K. (2003). *Case study research: Design and methods* (3rd ed.). Beverly Hills, CA: Sage.

Yusufa, Y., Gunasekaran, A., & Abthorpe, M.S. (2004). Enterprise information systems project implementation: A case study of ERP in Rolls-Royce. *International Journal of Production Economics, 87,* 251-266.

Zeng, A.Z., & Pathak, B.K. (2003). Achieving information integration in supply chain management through B2B e-hubs: Concepts and analyses. *Industrial Management & Data Systems, 103*(9), 657-665.

Zhang, L., Banerjee, P., Lee, M., & Zhang, Z. (2003). Critical success factors of enterprise resource planning systems implementation success in China. In *Proceedings of the 36th Hawaii International Conference on System Sciences* (pp. 1-10).

Zurawski, M. (2003). *Personal communication.* Hannover, Germany: Deloitte Consulting.

Zurawski, M. (2004). *Personal communication.* Hannover, Germany: Deloitte Consulting.

About the Contributors

Carlos Ferran is an assistant professor of management information systems at The Pennsylvania State University in Great Valley. He received his DBA in MIS from Boston University, a graduate degree in MIS from Universidad Central de Venezuela, a Cum Laude Master in Finance, and a licentiate in management sciences (BS) from Universidad Metropolitana. Dr. Ferran has been a visiting professor at IESA (Venezuela), INALDE (Colombia), and IAE (Argentina). He worked in the software industry for 10 years, acted as an IT/IS consultant for more than 10 years, and held the position of CIO for an important financial group in Venezuela. Dr. Ferran has written two books and many academic articles. His research interests span technology-mediated communication (particularly videoconferencing), accounting information systems, knowledge management, and the digital divide. He serves on the editorial board of several academic journals and is currently the editor of the AIS journal *Revista de la Asociación de Sistemas de Información para Latinoamérica y el Caribe*.

Ricardo Salim is the chief software architect for Cautus Network Corporation. He has more than 25 years of experience in developing and implementing enterprise software solutions for small and mid-size companies. He has worked as a consultant in IT/IS to over a hundred companies and government institution in developing countries. Dr. Salim is a successful entrepreneur who has founded several successful IT/IS companies in various developing and developed countries. He holds a BS in computer science from Universidad Central de Venezuela and is currently a PhD candidate at the Universidad Autónoma de Barcelona in Spain.

* * *

Peter Best is an associate professor in the School of Accountancy at Queensland University of Technology (QUT) in Brisbane. He has held positions at the University of Queensland, Newcastle University, Adelaide University, and Flinders University. He has qualifications in accounting, operations research, and information technology. His PhD examined the feasibility of machine-independent audit trail analysis in large computer systems. His teaching, research, and consulting experience include electronic business intelligence and data mining (SAS), enterprise systems (SAP R/3), IT governance processes and measurement, information systems security (SAP R/3), computer-assisted audit techniques (SAS, ACL), knowledge-based systems, fraud detection, and audit trail analysis. Best has performed projects for the South Australian Council of Social Services, the Institute of Chartered Accountants in Australia, CPA Australia, the Information Systems Audit & Control Association, Coopers & Lybrand, the SAS Institute, the Department of Primary Industries (Qld), Hall Chadwick, Education Queensland,

William Buck, the Health Insurance Commission, CS Energy, SAP Australia, Royal Dutch Shell, and the University of New South Wales ATAX program for the Australian Taxation Office.

Marianne Bradford is an associate professor of accounting at North Carolina State University, where she teaches enterprise systems and accounting information systems in the College of Management. She holds a PhD from the University of Tennessee in accounting and is a CPA. Bradford has been published in numerous journals such as *Journal of Information Systems, Journal of Cost Management, International Journal of Accounting Information Systems,* and *Strategic Finance.* Her research interests include systems documentation issues and SOX, enterprise systems implementation issues, and outsourcing of information systems. She has worked with KPMG as an auditor, and as an assistant controller for a school. Her more recent experience is with Ernst and Young's Technology and Security Risk Services group while on sabbatical from NC State.

Esther Brainin holds a PhD from the Technion–Israel Institute of Technology. She is an assistant professor in the Department of Behavioral Sciences at Ruppin Academic Center in Israel. Brainin focuses on the sociology of communication and information technology (CIT); her research interests include organizational change induced by information technologies, techniques for implementing IT successfully in organizations, and bridging the digital divide. She served as head of the Research Branch of the Department of Behavioral Sciences in the Israeli Defense Forces (IDF), and on the basis of her research, headed a forum for IT implementation in various IDF units. She is a member of the CIT section of the American Sociological Association and of the OCIS division of the Academy of Management.

Ashley R. Davis is a PhD candidate in the Terry College of Business at the University of Georgia. Her research interests include enterprise resource planning systems, open source business development, information technology impacts on agility, information technology infrastructure decisions, and service-oriented architecture. She is currently working on her dissertation focused on enterprise systems, information technology competence, and agility. Her work has been presented at an Academy of Management conference and published in the *Communications of the Association for Information Systems* journal. She has work experience in global ERP implementation, human resource configuration, EDI management, and small business management.

Gert-Jan de Vreede is Kayser distinguished professor in the Department of Information Systems & Quantitative Analysis at the University of Nebraska at Omaha, where he is director of the Institute for Collaboration Science. His research focuses on collaboration engineering, the theoretical foundations of (e)-collaboration, and the diffusion of collaboration technology. His articles have appeared in *Journal of Management Information Systems, Communications of the ACM, Communications of the AIS, Small Group Research, DataBase, Group Decision and Negotiation, Journal of Creativity and Innovation Management, International Journal of Technology and Management, Journal of Informatics Education and Research, Simulation & Gaming,* and *Simulation.*

Angel Díaz is currently a professor of operations and supply chain management and the director of the PhD program at the Instituto de Empresa Business School, Madrid. With extensive practical experience in operations, logistics and information technology as a consultant in industrial logistics, support manager for a metro system, and maintenance manager for a water supply system, he is the author of three books and more than 50 other publications. His research has appeared in the *European Journal of Operations Research, International Journal of Logistics, International Journal of Simulation and Process Modeling, Supply Chain Forum,* and the proceedings of POMS and EurOMA. He holds a master's degree form Cranfield University and a PhD from Maryland University.

Kenneth Dick is a senior research fellow at the University of Nebraska at Omaha. His interests include telecommunications, the systems needed to support heterogeneous networks, and regulations/standards. He has presented work at various classified and non-classified venues. His current research areas are network/protocol optimization and network security. He earned his PhD from the University of Nebraska–Lincoln.

Robert S. Gingras was most recently the CIO and VP of information technology for Muzak LLC, where he was responsible for enterprise information management, business systems, and infrastructure. His achievements in process innovation and technology enablement have been documented and presented in various industry forums and publications, and have generated numerous benefits to the companies he has worked with. Prior to Muzak, he was the CIO and director of process design for Cequent, a Trimas Company responsible for business system consolidation and process alignment; and director of e-commerce, architecture and technology in General Motors Corporation's Global Customer Experience Group. In addition, he has held leadership positions for Snap-On Tools Incorporated, Allendale Insurance, Citizen's Bank, and Payco American Corporation. He currently lives with his family in Charlotte, North Carolina.

Paul Hawking is a senior lecturer in the School of Information Systems in the Faculty of Business and Law at Victoria University, Melbourne, Australia. He is past chairperson of the SAP Australian User Group and is coordinator of Victoria University's ERP Research Group. His research is primarily in the area of ERP systems and business intelligence, and the use of these systems by Australian companies. He has very strong links with industry which is reflected in his research and commissioned reports. He also has a very strong research history with numerous publications and presented to industry and academia on many occasions. He is one of Australia's best-selling IT authors.

Jonathan Hornby is a director in worldwide marketing for performance management at SAS. He is a visionary and thought leader in the field of performance management and currently leads global marketing direction. His experience comes from a hands-on background within the UK banking sector, followed by extensive travel, dialogue, and collaboration with customers, management consultants, and respected thought leaders around the globe. He led the design and introduction of SAS's solutions for strategy, cost, profitability, and risk management. Joining SAS in 1996, he brought 15 years of business experience from the banking sector, including activity-based management, process reengineering, performance analysis, and marketing.

Deanna House is currently working on her PhD in Information Systems at the University of Texas at Arlington. She holds a master's degree in Management of Information Systems from the University of Nebraska at Omaha, where she completed her thesis on Global Enterprise Resources Planning/Human Resources Management Systems (ERP/HRMS) success factors. A few of her research interests include global software implementations, ERP/HRMS implementation success factors, and human resources information systems-related topics.

Claus Juhl-Christensen is a managing consultant at the EDB Group, an international consulting firm based in Denmark. He has extensive experience in managing large-scale SAP projects, mostly focusing on accounting processes.

Kai Kelzenberg is a research fellow in the Research Group on Electronic Business at RWTH Aachen University. He studied business administration at RWTH and majored in electronic business and international management. He is currently working on his PhD project; his main fields of research are implementation of ERP systems and project management.

Don Kerr is a senior lecturer of information systems at Griffith University. His research areas include factors influencing ERP implementations and intelligent decision support systems development, implementation, and evaluation. He has extensive industry experience and has been commissioned to do consultancies for industries such as dairying, cotton, and railways. Kerr has written 60 peer-reviewed publications and has obtained competitive research grants from the Australian Research Council and Dairy Australia. His PhD was multidisciplinary in nature in that it incorporated statistical and heuristics modeling with decision support development for the dairy industry. Kerr worked as a principal research scientist for the Queensland Department of Primary Industries prior to coming to Griffith in 2000.

Heinz D. Knoell is currently professor of IS in the German Department of IS, Marmara-University, Istanbul, Turkey. In 2004/2005, he was a visiting scholar at the UCLA Anderson Graduate School of Management. He is professor in information systems at the University of Lüneburg, Germany, and visiting professor at the School of Computing and Information Technology University of Wolverhampton, UK. He received his BSc, MSc, and PhD from the University of Muenster, Germany. He is a member of the AIS and the German Chapter of the ACM.

Lukas W.H. Kühl is a senior consultant at Exsigno Consulting, Dübendorf, Switzerland. He received his BSc from the University of Lueneburg and his MSc from the University of Wolverhampton, UK.

Roland W.A. Kühl is a senior consultant at the Steria-Mummert Consulting AG, Hamburg, Germany. He received is BSc from the University of Lueneburg and his MSc from the University of Wolverhampton, UK.

Vinod Kumar is a professor of technology, innovation, and operations management and a former director of the Sprott School of Business (1995-2005). He has published more than 150 articles in refereed journals and has been awarded Carleton University's Scholarly Achievement Award twice and the Research Achievement Award three times. He has led several research projects funded by the Social Sciences and Humanities Research Council, the Natural Sciences and Engineering Research Council, Industry Canada, the Ontario Research and Development Challenge Fund, and several industry partners. He has won 12 best paper awards at prestigious conferences. He is on the editorial boards of two international journals. In addition, Kumar has also served on the board of governors and the senate for Carleton University, and on the board of the Ontario Research Network of E-Commerce.

Oswaldo Lorenzo is currently a professor of operations management and enterprise systems at Instituto de Empresa Business School, Madrid. He has participated in consulting projects related to enterprise systems implementation and business process redesign. His research has been published in *Communications of the Association for Information Systems, International Journal of Simulation and Process Modeling, Revista Latinoamericana de Administración, Supply Chain Forum: An International Journal,* and the proceedings of EurOMA, AMCIS, POMS, and BALAS. He holds a PhD in industrial and business studies from Warwick Business School.

Bharat Maheshwari is a PhD candidate at the Sprott School of Business and author/coauthor of several peer-reviewed articles. He has more than 10 years of experience in the areas of information systems and operations management. He has led small engineering teams in industry and has been coordinating e-business research activities at the Sprott School of Business. He is currently the chair of the Operations Management Division of the 2007 ASAC Conference and is a key member of the Ontario Research Network of E-Commerce research team at Carleton University. With Dr. Vinod Kumar, he has completed numerous studies on issues and challenges facing organizations in adopting, implementing, and institutionalizing enterprise systems.

Alok Mishra is an associate professor of computer and software engineering at Atilim University, Ankara, Turkey. He holds a PhD in computer science (software engineering), in addition to dual masters in computer science & applications and human resource management. His areas of interest and research are software engineering, information system, information and knowledge management, and object-oriented analysis and design. He has extensive experience in distance and online education related to computers and management courses. He has published articles, book chapters, and book reviews related to software engineering and information system in refereed journals, books, and conferences including the *International Journal of Information Management, Government Information Quarterly, IET-Software, Behaviour and Information Technology, Public Personnel Management, European Journal of Engineering Education,* and the *International Journal of Information Technology and Management.*

Robert Moreton is a professor of computer science and dean of the School of Computing and Information Technology at the University of Wolverhampton, UK. He received his BA (Hons) from Exeter University and his Mtech in Computer Science from Brunel University. He is a member and fellow of the British Computer Society.

Bruce Olshan is global supply chain manager for E.I. du Pont de Nemours and Company. He has worked with DuPont for 20 years in many areas including operations, manufacturing, sales, and marketing. Olshan is a recognized expert in integrated business management, establishing and optimizing global supply chains, implementing ERP systems, and inventory management. Prior to becoming global supply manager, he was a global ERP champion and successfully led a global implementation for a multi-billion-dollar business. Olshan received a BS in mechanical engineering from The Pennsylvania State University.

Maira Petrini is a professor at the FGV-EAESP as of June 2000. Her research interests are business intelligence and corporate strategic planning. She has also worked as an IT consultant since 2001 and has published in major Brazilian journals.

Raili Pollanen is an assistant professor of accounting and a former accounting area coordinator (2001-2006) at the Sprott School of Business. She brings to the research team expertise in accounting, management control, and performance measurement systems in both private and public sectors. Her recent research has been funded by the Canadian Academic Accounting Association, the Canadian Institute of Chartered Accountants, and the Association of Canadian Financial Officers (formerly, APSFA). Her research has been published in several academic and professional journals, books, and conference proceedings. She is also an author or a coauthor of numerous professional reports and a textbook, *Management Accounting* (Canadian 6th edition, Thomson/Nelson, 2004). She served on the Public Sector Accounting Board task force that developed a statement of recommended performance reporting practices published in the *PSA Handbook* in 2006.

Denise Potosky is an associate professor of management and organization at Penn State Great Valley. She earned her PhD in industrial relations and human resources from Rutgers University. She teaches graduate courses in human resources management, leadership communication, and organizational behavior. Her research focuses on personnel staffing and the use of valid assessments to predict job performance, and she is a recognized expert regarding computerized and Web-based assessments. Her research also examines the interplay between individual characteristics and contextual factors that facilitate the emergence of leadership and performance outcomes in organizations. Potosky's work has been published in leading academic journals, and she has worked as a consultant to several organizations.

Marlei Pozzebon is an associate professor at the HEC Montréal as of June 2002. Her research interests are the political and socio-cultural aspects of information technology implementation, the use of structuration theory and critical discourse analysis in the information systems field, business intelligence and the role of information technology in local development, and corporate social responsibility. Before joining HEC, she worked at three Brazilian universities. She has also worked as an IT consultant since 1995. Previously, professor Pozzebon worked as a systems analyst. She has published in the *Journal of Management Studies, Organization Studies, Journal of Strategic Information Systems,* and the *Journal of Information Technology.*

Kai Reimers is a professor of information systems at RWTH Aachen University, Germany. He earned a doctorate in economics from Wuppertal University and a *venia legendi* at Bremen University. He has published in the *European Journal of Information Systems, Electronic Markets, Electronic Commerce Journal, Journal of Information Technology, Communications of the AIS, International Journal of IT Standards & Standardization Research,* and the *International Journal of Production Economics,* among others. He authored or co-authored five books in the field of information systems. His main fields of research are inter-organizational systems, IT standardization, and implementation of large-scale information systems.

Pall Rikhardsson holds a masters degree and a PhD from the Aarhus School of Business in Denmark. He joined the Aarhus School of Business in 2000 after working seven years as a consultant for PricewaterhouseCoopers in its Global Risk Management Solutions Department. His teaching and main research interests lie within management accounting and management controlling, with a specific focus on the use, impacts, and benefits of information technology applications in those fields. Current research projects include: (1) Impact of Information Technology on Accounting, (2) Impact of Sarbanes-Oxley on Internal Control in Danish Companies, and (3) Identifying the Corporate Cost of Occupational Accidents: An Activity-Based Analysis. Rikhardsson has published in international and national scientific journals and trade magazines, presented at conferences and workshops around the world, and is used as a consultant in various contexts. In 2006 he spent six months at the Queensland University of Technology researching corporate compliance and internal control. In 2007 he was teaching management accounting and accounting information systems at the undergraduate and graduate levels.

Maha Shakir is an assistant professor of information systems at Zayed University, UAE. Her primary research areas are information system strategy, strategic management of information systems, and the implementation of enterprise system applications (e.g., ERP, SCM, and CRM). Her current work involves studies of enterprise systems in the Arab Gulf Countries and e-procurement in the petroleum industry in the Middle East. Her publications appeared in the *University of Auckland Business Review, Journal of Cases on Information Technology, International Journal of Information Systems and Change Management, Journal of Decision Systems,* ERP edited books, a Laudon & Laudon MIS textbook, and several international IS conferences.

Thomas Wagner is currently a PhD candidate and research fellow in the Group on Electronic Business at RWTH Aachen University. He studied business administration and majored in electronic business, and technology and innovation management. His main fields of research are inter-organizational information systems and information management.

Peter Wolcott is an associate professor of management information systems at the University of Nebraska at Omaha. He has long-standing interests in the international dimensions of information technologies. His current research projects are in the areas of IT for development, municipal e-government, and the global diffusion of the Internet. His work has been published in *Communications of the ACM, IEEE Computer, Journal of the AIS, Communications of the AIS, The Information Society, The Journal of Data Warehousing,* and other journals and proceedings. He earned his PhD at the University of Arizona in business administration (management information systems) in 1993.

Index

A

access security, ensuring 219
adaptations for ERP products 316
analytic hierarchy process (AHP) method 153
anticipating the valley of despair 97
Apache License Version 2.0 58

B

B2B procurement implementation process 129
business benefits from ERP systems 78
business benefits from ERP systems, achieving
       77–93
business orientation 40
business process reengineering 108–125
business process reengineering tenets 112

C

change curve, understanding 97
clay tablets to the double-entry 2
clay tablets to the tabulating machine 2
control adequacy 237
control implementation benefits 243
control implementation challenges 240
control implementation processes 238
cost accounting 3
cultural differences 291
customer relationship management (CRM) 28

D

different national cultures 270

E

empower 32
enterprise resource management systems
       (ERM) 332
enterprise resource planning (ERP) systems 2
enterprise resource planning, under open source
       software 56–76
enterprise resource planning systems 27
enterprise resource planning systems in a global
       environment 23–36
enterprise system benefit framework 84
enterprise systems, as an enabler of fast-paced
       change 126–146
Ericsson case study, lessons learned 137
Ericsson case study, phase one (dealing with
       growth) 128
Ericsson case study, phase three (coping with
       market turndown) 134
Ericsson case study, phase two (preparing for
       market deceleration) 132
Ericsson España (EE) 129
ERP's resource 11
ERP and new technologies 314
ERP application delivery, new modes 313
ERP benefits framework 81
ERP for small and medium-sized enterprises
       (SMEs) 329
ERP implementation as a mediation process
       192
ERP implementation procedure 45
ERP implementation process 47
ERP implementation projects, outcome 255
ERP implementation strategies 43